Sidney Hillman: STATESMAN OF AMERICAN LABOR

Books by Matthew Josephson

GALIMATHIAS (poems)

ZOLA AND HIS TIME

PORTRAIT OF THE ARTIST AS AMERICAN

JEAN-JACQUES ROUSSEAU

THE ROBBER BARONS

THE POLITICOS

THE PRESIDENT MAKERS

VICTOR HUGO

EMPIRE OF THE AIR

STENDHAL: OR THE PURSUIT OF HAPPINESS

SIDNEY HILLMAN: STATESMAN OF AMERICAN LABOR

by Matthew Josephson

SIDNEY
HILLMAN

Statesman of

American Labor

DOUBLEDAY & COMPANY, INC., 1952

GARDEN CITY, NEW YORK

Library of Congress Catalog Card Number 52-11080

Copyright 1952 by Matthew Josephson
All Rights Reserved
Printed in the United States at H. Wolff Book Mfg. Co., Inc.

Contents

BOOK ONE

FOREWORD AND ACKNOWLEDGMENTS   9

1. Boyhood and Youth   17

2. The Chicago Years: 1907–1911   38

3. Arbitrating   59

4. Founding of the Amalgamated   86

5. The Heroic Age: 1914–1919   111

6. Expansion: 1916–1917   133

7. The First World War   160

8. "The New Unionism"   194

9. Depression and Counterattack: 1920–1921   213

10. New Fields for Labor: 1921–1924   242

11. The "New Era": The Trade-Union Doldrums   268

12. Consolidation: The Middle Years   282

13. An American "Fabian"   311

BOOK TWO

14. *The Struggle with the Racketeers*   327

15. *The Great Slump; Leadership in Crisis: 1929–1933*   340

16. *The New Deal: Hillman in Washington*   359

17. *The Rise of the CIO: 1935–1937*   381

18. *The TWOC; Labor's Civil War: 1937–1938*   416

19. *Lobbying: 1938*   431

20. *"The Blind Giant"*   461

21. *National Defense Commissioner*   503

22. *The OPM*   529

23. *The War Manpower Commission*   566

24. *Labor in Political Action: 1944*   587

25. *"Clear It with Sidney"*   613

26. *The Last Crusade*   636

SOURCE REFERENCE NOTES   671

INDEX   687

FOREWORD AND
ACKNOWLEDGMENTS

Sidney Hillman has become a sort of legend for the multitudes of American workers whom he led and whom he served. They have not forgotten him. Pictures of him and bronze plaques engraved with his characteristic words of counsel or prophecy are hung up in hundreds of those plain branch offices and meeting halls throughout the country where union people regularly forgather. Hospitals, health clinics, and low-cost housing developments have been named for him, monuments of the useful sort such as he doubtless would have preferred—if during his hurried life he ever thought of monuments. These, at any rate, are the testimonials given by thousands of persons of small means, showing not only reverence but also the sense that he was very human and close to them always.

Informed persons have held Hillman to have been perhaps the most creative of modern American labor leaders. Yet he was more than a labor leader; and I say this knowing that the role of a good trade unionist may be, in many ways, more constructive, more deeply satisfying than that of men in almost any other calling. For at the end he may measure his achievements in the values of what

Hillman used to call "a better life," or "a larger life," for thousands or even millions of fellow human beings. In the later phase of his career, however, during the epoch of the New Deal and World War II, Hillman clearly transcended his own role as head of a strong labor group and became a great force in national politics.

The endless controversies that raged over him, the frequent mention of his name in the sensational press as the ally and friend of President Roosevelt, or even as one of the mythical "thirty" or "one hundred" men who "rule" America, all attest to an influence on our public life like that enjoyed in past times by some of our great money magnates. It was an influence denied to his famous forerunners in the labor movement, such as John Mitchell and Samuel Gompers.

That an immigrant clothing worker risen from the ranks of organized labor should come to fill such a large place in the highest councils of the land and at times help to write the nation's laws is in itself a significant phenomenon of recent change in America. It speaks, of course, not only for Sidney Hillman's qualities but also for the rising power of modern labor to which he himself contributed so much. The story of Hillman is bound up with labor's coming of age.

Hillman's ideas for effective political action by organized labor and liberal groups—as exemplified chiefly by his tactics—seem to me of immense significance and yield us rich lessons about our present problems. Yet only a few who stood close to him knew Hillman's thoughts. For during the Rooseveltian era perhaps no man, save F.D.R. himself, was more slandered and libeled than was Hillman. Part of my task is that of just reparation: to set the record right by the presentation of the pertinent facts.

Our political institutions, as is well known, are endowed with such ingenious "checks and balances" that in their operation there often results more check than anything else. In his later years Hillman gave the closest study to this whole problem and showed great patience and resourcefulness in encouraging the democratic process to work—where others used all their skill and power to win delay or frustration. It was, for example, in the face of a minority resistance sustained in Congress for years on end that Hillman, more than any other man—as President Roosevelt declared—helped to win passage of the minimum-wage law of 1938, which now stands as one of the basic reforms introduced under the New Deal. He thereby displayed what Sidney and Beatrice Webb have defined, in the instance of another and British public figure, as the highest of all political talents, namely the "thorough understanding of the art of getting things done." It was precisely his mastery of great obstacles in the way of popular democratic action—as instanced by the launching of the CIO-PAC movement of 1944—that earned him the warm attentions of habitual adversaries. But as he used to say cheerfully, the torrents of abuse were, after all, the opponent's involuntary tribute to one's effectiveness.

This biography, like Hillman's career, is divided into two parts: the first treats of his work as a union officer and of the rise of his union, the Amalgamated Clothing Workers of America; the second deals with his activities, after the depression of 1929, as the political leader *par excellence* of labor.

The Amalgamated, some thirty-five years ago, was widely accepted as "the most advanced" of American trade unions. It bore the stamp of the young Hillman's inventive spirit; its officers and members alike were imbued with his philosophy of labor: a blend of social idealism and practical common sense about the hard facts of this world. It was "militant" for industrial democracy, but also pioneered in the field of social security and arbitration, which pointed the way to stability and peace. With its varied and large cooperative enterprises, its housing projects and its banks, this great union became a veritable storehouse of new social techniques, the knowledge of which would one day help chart the course of reform under a Roosevelt. The colorful earlier history of the Amalgamated has therefore been treated as a pilot case illuminating the problems and aspirations of American labor as a whole.

Hillman's lifework had thus prepared him to serve, with John L. Lewis and Philip Murray, after 1933, as one of the leading spirits of our "labor renaissance." His knowledge of industry and labor problems also fitted him to become, as John L. Lewis said, "the driving force behind many of the measures attributed to the New Deal."

His role in national affairs and his friendship with Roosevelt (not always smooth in its course) have been underestimated by some of the New Deal personalities who have already published their memoirs. On the other hand, they have also been grossly misrepresented by his political opponents, who in 1944 made the country resound with the slogan: "Clear it with Sidney." Now, after some lapse of time, it is more possible to estimate, for example, Hillman's distinctive contribution to the government's defense program in setting up democratic labor policies for World War II. For the first time in our history, at any rate, as war was declared upon us, a man of labor sat beside the representative of industry (Mr. Knudsen) as equal and co-director of our national defense-production board.

Something like a religion of humanity had determined his early choice of career and showed itself in him to the last, for all his famous "realism" and his "dynamic" temper. For him the main question would always be: "Have we helped the constructive forces that are making for a better future?"

The years since his death in 1946 seem to have witnessed a series of retreats by what may be called the party of progress in this country. Intolerance has spread itself wide again, and attempts are made to impose control even over people's ideas and inward beliefs, while many who might resist such trends shrink from the disagreeable controversy resistance might provoke. One could wish that Hillman were with us at this hour. When things sometimes went badly for his friends in labor or public office, he would say with emphasis that it was vain to lament at hard times. The thing to do was to work, prepare, and "organize" so that two or four years hence the whole picture might be changed for the better.

After the end of the war, to the very last, he was aflame with new projects to help "the constructive forces" making for peace and social progress at home and abroad. But there was too little time. Some of the grand designs of his last days have been abandoned or changed out of all recognition since his passing, though they were bound up with the hope of preserving human civilization itself. The blueprints remain, however. Other men who come after him may have to take them up again and go on from the point where he fell.

He lived among us strenuously and swiftly. No thought was ever given by him to the preservation of any coherent record of his public career. Hence it has been necessary to sift and piece together whatever one could of the great mass of public papers, speeches, and correspondence he has left, the scraps of memoranda, notations of ideas—conceived as if on the wing—and also the recollections of his intimate talks by old friends and associates. Fortunately the Amalgamated Clothing Workers Union has preserved voluminous records both of its proceedings and of Hillman's activities as its leader during thirty-two years. A collection of many thousands of contemporary newspaper clippings, pamphlets, and magazine articles was available for study. Indeed, I have been given free access to all material bearing on Hillman's life by the general officers of the union and by the members of its Executive Board who head its regional branches throughout the country. I am under deep obligations to all of them. I may add also that my debt to Hillman's old friends and union colleagues, many of them life-long associates of his, is all the greater since they have not only given me of their knowledge, their recollections, and of their time (in numerous interviews), but have done so under conditions allowing the fullest freedom to the biographer. What was more, they proved usually to be walking repositories of much contemporary history and labor lore, which has made acquaintance with them all the more memorable.

Many others among Hillman's old friends or associates outside of his labor organization were also solicited for such knowledge or documentary material as they might have. Among those whose kindness to me I must acknowledge here were: Mr. Justice Felix Frankfurter; Philip Murray; John L. Lewis; Professor Earl Dean Howard; Dr. Isador Lubin; William Hammatt Davis; Max Lowenthal; David Drechsler (of the New York Clothing Manufacturers' Exchange); Herbert J. Emmerich; John Lord O'Brian; Mrs. Eleanor Roosevelt; the late Robert P. Patterson; Dr. William M. Leiserson; J. B. S. Hardman; Heber Blankenhorn; and Ann Washington Craton. George Soule, author of an earlier biography of Hillman (published in 1939), was also most helpful. And there were many others.

These good persons reflect points of view often at variance with each other and certainly differing on many grounds with my own views and conclusions. Any reproaches merited by the opinions or interpretations set forth in this book should accrue to me and not to those who, in their different ways, and out of attachment to the memory of Sidney Hillman, have helped me in this undertaking.

The Office of the Chief of Military History, Department of the Army, Washington, was of assistance in ascertaining the facts about Sidney Hillman's wartime contributions. My grateful acknowledgments are also owing to the Franklin D. Roosevelt Memorial Library,

Hyde Park, New York, and to its director, Dr. Herman Kahn, for extending its facilities to me and for permission to quote from the Roosevelt Papers.

From beginning to end of this task of three years I have benefited from the unfailing encouragement and co-operation of Mrs. Sidney Hillman. Charles W. Ervin, the veteran labor editor, possessing both exact records and an uncanny memory of public events witnessed during nearly nine decades, also helped most generously. Similar aid in obtaining precise information was furnished by Elias Rabkin of the Amalgamated's newspaper staff. The union's excellent Research Department gave its constant assistance in the hunt for facts. One member of its staff in particular, Miss Catherine K. Williams, having specialized for several years in gathering and collating Hillman material, was able to render me signal services indeed. Her devoted aid in the initial work of research, and later of correction, has been of incalculable value. I am also indebted to my wife, Hannah Josephson, for extensive editorial assistance.

Matthew Josephson

SHERMAN, CONNECTICUT

Sidney Hillman: STATESMAN OF AMERICAN LABOR

BOOK ONE

Chapter One

BOYHOOD
AND YOUTH

The tidal wave of immigration from Europe to America at the turn of the century, upon which millions of people, literally whole nations, were transported to these shores, appeals to us as one of the most colorful pages of the history of recent times. Such movements of population had not been seen perhaps since the days of Ferdinand and Isabella of Spain and the religious wars of Europe four hundred years ago. But where our earlier immigrants had been mainly English, Irish, and German, in the decade of 1900–10 nearly half of them were of Italian and East European origin. And of those who migrated here from the territories of the Russian Empire, about half were Jews.

In those days many Americans who considered themselves prophets of some sort made predictions that our native stock would be sadly "corrupted" by the more recent influx of Italians, Slavs, and Jews, whose folkways and religions were so different from those of the earlier comers. There was blood-thinking then too. The findings of latter-day sociologists that brains, talent, and courage are the exclusive possessions of no one race of men, least of all of a favored class, were then but dimly understood. That the new immigrants brought immense and fresh energies to the upbuilding of the American continent, that they were to create wealth beyond dreams through their labor and fertility, was also ignored. Nor was it generally foreseen that the later comers were to contribute rich spiritual resources to our culture, and that unknown genius and talent among them were to play their part in the advancement of our industries and techniques, our arts and public life.

In the two years 1906–07, following a period of extreme revolutionary disorder and repression in Russia, the crest of the Jewish immigration to the United States was reached when a total of about 100,000 came annually to seek new fortune here. Whereas earlier Jewish immigrants from Germany had been typically small merchants or middlemen, these later and more numerous arrivals were now, in great part, manual workers (often tailors); for even in backward Eastern Europe there had been a rapid upswing of industry in late decades. Among these later Jewish immigrants, also, there were many thousands who came not merely to better their material conditions but in quest of freedom. Many of these young Russian workers had run the risk of death or banishment to Siberia to organize trade unions, then banned by law; others had fought both to liberate their fellow Jews and to aid their brother workers who were Poles or Russians in the recent struggle for political freedom. In this respect, in their longing for equality and civil rights, they differed but little from the earlier Americans who had risen against England.

Among the 100,000 Eastern Jewish immigrants who arrived here in 1907, driven into exile by their lost struggle for liberty in Russia, was Sidney Hillman, then a youth of twenty. He was one of the ill-nourished, shabby crowd in the steerage decks of a British steamer from Liverpool entering New York Harbor on an August day of that year. In appearance, however, he was distinctly the Jewish intellectual, with his pale face, his curly brown hair, dark gray eyes, straight nose, and high, square forehead. Though thin and slight of figure, he carried himself with a natural dignity. This former rabbinical student from Lithuania was, in a sense, already old in experience. He had resolutely left the closed circle of the seminary and the synagogue when he was little more than a boy to join in the broader, more arduous movement that aimed at liberating Jew and Christian alike in old Russia. And now all that was in the past. As part of the human torrent that flowed here from Europe, he had come to the gateway of America and set his foot upon the dock at Ellis Island, ready to begin his life anew. For the first time he breathed the air of the new country of freedom, almost in the shadow of the colossal statue bearing its torch.

The great harbor, already ringed with cliff-like buildings, was a beautiful and animated scene, prefiguring that "golden America" of which the poor immigrants had long heard so many glowing tales. Of course the immigration officials were "no better than Cossacks," as the Jews used to say. But once out of their hands, in the noisy, crowded streets of lower Manhattan, one could see that plain people were dressed "like barons in Russia." It was true, then, that the common man might win to independence and prosperity here; that there were opportunities on every hand; that one would be immune at last to the cruel disabilities and persecutions suffered in the ghettos of the Russian Pale.

Had not a Jewish poet told his people that in the American "wonderland" there was

> *Chicken soup served on weekdays,*
> *And white bread eaten every day. . . .*

The young Hillman had known danger and privation; he had suffered hunger; he had been forced to leave friends and family and flee into exile across the border. Despairing of early liberation for Russia after 1906, he had chosen finally to come to the United States and make his life here, though he might have found means of living elsewhere in Europe.

Here, at least, no one asked him for his passport or identity papers. Nobody cared who he was. He was a human being like any other, with the rights of a free man. It was a heady experience to which one must become inured gradually, as to the effect of a sudden strong light after darkness.

In later years he would say: "After all, I like our American system best. I have seen something of the other systems in the Old World. Here at least a man can say what he thinks." For who would cherish our democratic liberties or fight to defend them more strongly than those who had journeyed thousands of miles from their native land to enjoy them?

The process of being uprooted, of transplantation to a new soil, is a profound experience. To be sure, the immigrant type coming to

America is likely to be one of the more energetic or aggressive figures in his native community, one willing to break with the past. Then in submitting himself afterward to the social mold of America he is all the more eager in his acceptance of the new folkways, the new standards of life. He may retain his foreign accent all his life, or the faith of his fathers, whether Orthodox Greek or Orthodox Hebrew, but should he revisit his homeland, his former compatriots would perceive at once that he was no longer one of them, but hopelessly American, with all the rude strength and the democratic equality of the type.

Young Hillman, like many immigrants arriving in worn clothes from the Old World, was to throw away all his old baggage. His Americanism, his love of America, was a determined and ardent courtship.

On one occasion, almost thirty years after he had come here, Hillman took up the challenge of a native American who ventured to speak disparagingly, almost in insulting tones, of persons of foreign birth. Hillman, with much spirit, remarked that it appeared absurd to praise or blame a man for the place where his parents had chosen he should be born, but that he, for his part, felt that being an American was no mere accident of birth for him but a matter of deliberate choice.

Sometimes the first days in America are not amusing. Hillman made his way to the address of a person living in the East Side of Manhattan, to whom he bore a letter of introduction from relatives. Bewildered by all the unfamiliar sights and sounds, unable to speak with any but his own compatriots, the poor Jewish immigrant, like young Hillman, often went straight to the "ghetto" and found his livelihood, at first as a common laborer in the needle trades, to which he had easiest access through ties of race and language.

Passing through the grimy streets of the East Side where he lodged with the family to whom he had been directed, Hillman could see what Jacob Riis described of the ghetto and "sweatshop district" (in *How the Other Half Lives*) as glimpsed from the Second Avenue Elevated:

> Every open window of the big tenements that stand like a continuous brick wall on both sides of the way gives you a glimpse of one of those shops as the train speeds by. Men and women bending over their machines or ironing boards at the windows, half naked . . . The road is like

a big gangway through an endless workroom where vast multitudes are
forever working. Morning, noon and night, it makes no difference; the
scene is always the same.

In his early days here Sidney Hillman knew loneliness and hunger.
Yet he was never heard to complain or to regret those difficult times.
There was a business depression when he came to this country, the
Panic of 1907. For several weeks, almost destitute, he took what odd
jobs he could find, working by the hour; he lived literally from hand
to mouth in a squalid tenement in New York's ghetto. It was impossible for him, try as he might, to find decent work, even the lowest-
paid manual labor, for which he had no experience. For all their
freedom, the people here were not free of anxiety, of unemployment,
of hunger even. This freedom-endowed society, the American "paradise," had its own problems, which would bear looking into.

The first long-lingering impressions upon the perceptive immigrant
are of a land of incredible contrasts: evidences of fabulous wealth
side by side with those of hopeless poverty; manifestations of callous
indifference and imposing institutions for the dispensation of charity.
There were new skyscrapers and handsome residential quarters all of
marble, and then hideous slums for workers or recent immigrants.
There were restless masses of people who now worked for cruelly
long hours, or now languished in idleness, and no one seemed concerned at how this happened. It was a society run as if by a series of
invisible escalators, in which part of the crowd trampled over each
other to be borne upward to the heights, while the others, unhappily,
reluctantly, were carried downward. In short, there was food for a
lifetime of reflection and room for all sorts of improvements by those
who might be of a mind to make them.

In a passage of one of his earliest letters written in English, Hillman
alluded to this first period of hardship in New York: "It would have
been the same old story—to live without knowing what will happen
the next day. I am tired of it . . . and therefore I left for Chicago." [1]

In response to a letter from a friend he had known at home, Sidney
Hillman took train and rode a thousand miles into the Western hinter-
land, to seek his bread in a great metropolis of whose existence he
had scarcely known.

II

The shabby young immigrant was of respectable, middle-class Jewish stock. He was born on March 23, 1887, in Zagare, a village in Lithuania, the second of seven children of Samuel Hillman, a grain and flour merchant, and Judith Paiken Hillman. It is noteworthy that the Hillman side of his family had for generations produced rabbis known for their piety and good works in the towns and villages of the Jewish Pale. This meant that the most extensive educational training possible for Jews in the old Orthodox communities during the past century was traditional with the Hillmans, and that they stood forth as worthies and dignitaries among their people. Such was Sidney Hillman's grandfather, Rabbi Mordecai Hillman, who served his flock at the nearby village of Parlich for thirty-eight years with an old-time fervor and devotion. Likewise, a great-uncle, in the same office at another Lithuanian town. And there was a cousin, Samuel Isaac Hillman, who was to become a noted rabbi in London; while still another relative was to be Grand Rabbi of Jerusalem.

A rabbi, such as Hillman's grandfather Mordecai, was in effect a local magistrate as well as a priest. Since the Russian Government took little interest in the day-by-day activities of the Jewish ghettos, the congregations, headed by their rabbis, governed themselves in somewhat theocratic form. The rabbi helped to adjust civil disputes, to keep law and order in some measure, and to succor the poor; as a consequence, he might levy small taxes on salt, candles, and such things in his little congregation and, though living modestly enough, enjoy some security of life. Rabbi Mordecai Hillman, who was Sidney's great model in childhood, was credited with possessing much religious learning, as well as a deeply spiritual nature which made him somewhat indifferent to the temporal duties and even the meager emoluments of his office. An exalted soul, he would preach constantly, in the tradition of the mystical Jews, that "all is vanity—we must live only for God and forget the world." One day a delegation of the members of his flock called on the saintly man to present him with a sum of money which had been collected to pay for the installation of a wooden floor in his cottage.

Rabbi Mordecai thanked them, but protested: "Why should I care to have a floor of wood when I have the canopy of God over my head?"

Sidney Hillman's father, Samuel, was not unlike his own enraptured parent in character. A man of good height and figure, wearing an imposing beard as befitted an Orthodox Jew, he turned out to be no great success in business. From the peasants around Zagare he would buy grain, have it milled into flour, and would sell it in the neighborhood or for export. His reputation was for stiff-necked honesty in trade; but his earnings were slim. It was said of him that he was a "dreamer." Very devout and given to much fervent prayer, he went about chanting hymns all day while his family waxed in size and his wife, a woman of quite different mold, worked harder and harder to manage for her children.

From his mother's line Sidney Hillman inherited the resourceful and energetic spirit of generations of small merchants. His maternal grandfather was a dealer in buttons and sundries who lived in Riga, the provincial capital of neighboring Latvia. He was keen in a trade, and his frugality was proverbial. But he was also a merry and affectionate old man. On Jewish holidays when he would arrive for a visit with his daughter, his pockets would be filled with presents for the children, sweets and even oranges (a rare delicacy) from the shops of Riga.

His daughter, Sidney's mother, showed herself a woman of enterprise. All day long her hands would be flying at a hundred different tasks necessary to provide for her brood. The Hillmans owned their own small house in Zagare, which had four rooms and, unlike most of the other humble cottages around it, boasted a wooden instead of an earthen floor, and a veranda. When Mr. Hillman's flour business declined, Sidney's mother opened a small grocery shop in the front room of their house; she kept a cow, sold milk, and also managed a small bakery. In hard times the Hillman children, though they were fed on the simple, coarse fare of the Lithuanian Jews, were at least well nourished.

Mrs. Hillman was small and had a pleasant and lively face. Sidney resembled his father in physique, but his dark gray or hazel-colored eyes were his mother's, and he had her firm, rounded chin and expressive mouth.

Of her second son Judith Hillman used to say that he was a most beautiful child at birth. He was named Simcha (which means in

Hebrew "the joyful one"), later anglicized as Sidney. The circumcision ceremony for a Jewish boy could be, in the old Russian Pale, an occasion for extended festivities, washed down with much sacramental wine and schnapps. Mrs. Hillman used to recall: "We celebrated Sidney's birthday for a *whole week!*"

Dogged by poverty, the family managed to keep afloat only through Mrs. Hillman's untiring exertions. From earliest childhood Sidney learned to measure carefully the value of each kopeck. And yet their lot was not hard in comparison with that of the great mass who dwelt, as Sholem Aleichem has written, ". . . In that blessed Pale into which the Jews have been packed as closely as herring in a barrel and told to increase and multiply." In the ghettos or ghetto-villages of Poland and the Western Provinces, the overwhelming majority of Jews had no opportunities to better themselves, no right to common schooling or higher education leading to the learned professions, but were doomed to be peddlers, small traders, or poor artisans.* And yet village life in Poland and Lithuania had its charms. Zagare offered the color and gaiety of its two market days a week, when the peasants of the countryside gathered together to hawk their varied wares, an animated scene for Sidney and the other Hillman infants playing among the carts. And there were the cheerful festivities of the Jewish holy days.

Mrs. Hillman would slave and stint all through the week, but on Friday their home would be all shining, and at dusk the candles would be ceremoniously lit, prayers said, and the feast of goose or chicken would begin; or if there were no fowl, then meat or fish and fresh-baked bread.

On Saturday, Mrs. Hillman rested from her labors. The children remembered long afterward how, on Saturday afternoons, she would gather them together and read to them from the Bible or simply from Jewish storybooks. Then as dusk fell early in winter in that Baltic land, and candles were very precious, she would cease her reading but continue to sit with them in the twilight for a long time—thus postponing the lighting of candles—and tell them tales from memory, until it was time for their supper and bed.

* The Jews had not been badly off in Poland and Western Russia in the nineteenth century, until 1881, when, following the assassination of Czar Alexander II, restrictions and disabilities, previously enacted, were rigorously carried out and pogroms directed openly by the police against the Jewish communities.

Freedom was soon curbed for Sidney, as for his brothers, by the severe routine of *chaider,* or Bible class, every day under the local rabbi, which began when he was no more than five. The children were made to read and memorize the Scriptures in Hebrew, and later the Targum. For the thoughtful and imaginative Sidney, the study of the Old Testament, though done by rote, was not irksome, but held great appeal. He would become forgetful of everything else as he read and re-read and memorized his text.

One day, as he sat thus lost in his studies, the other boys in his class stole up on him and slyly snipped off all the buttons on his coat. He returned home all unaware of what had been done to him by his schoolmates.

"Oh, Simcha!" his mother exclaimed. "Where are your buttons? What have you done now!" He looked at his coat in complete surprise.[2]

As in childhood, so in later life his habit of intense concentration and of introspection would render him absent-minded, unaware of what he was eating, or that the familiar furnishings of his home had been removed or changed. At home he would often sit in his room, continuing his reading and recitations, while his mother stood listening outside the door, hesitating to interrupt him and call him to his meals.

In the Hillman family it was a tradition that Sidney was his mother's Benjamin; and he in turn was deeply attached to her, who was so plainly the real head of the family and gave it all her protective strength. As the family grew more numerous—there were two younger sisters, and then two brothers and a baby sister also—it was he who looked after the smaller children when his mother was too occupied. By the age of ten he also helped her in the grocery shop.

As a child, Sidney Hillman responded to the strength and tenderness of his mother. He witnessed her endless exertions, shared her fears, heard with compassion the complaints that escaped her or her involuntary expressions of disappointment. By contrast his father assumed habitually the figure of insuccess, of failure.

Since the elder brother seemed indifferent as a Hebrew scholar, it was the apt Sidney, his parents resolved, who would carry on the family tradition and study to be a rabbi. His religious mentor sang his praises, calling him a "deep one"; at twelve he had mastered all that local instruction could afford, but was still too young to be sent to the seminary. Therefore a woman teacher was engaged to tutor him in the Russian language. She too expressed much satisfaction with him, declaring that he was a youth of promise. "You ought to have Sidney study to be a doctor," she advised his mother.

"Oh no," Mrs. Hillman replied firmly, "he is to be a rabbi."

The other woman said: "It is a pity to waste his brains as a rabbi. You have other boys. Take them. They will be good enough for rabbis!" But Mrs. Hillman would not hear of it.[3]

In 1901, when he was fourteen, he was sent to the Yeshiva, the Jewish seminary, at Kovno, a school then famous among Europe's Jewry as a center of theological learning.

III

A noted Hebrew writer of the nineteenth century, Peretz Smolenskin, describing the life of the Jewish seminary students in Lithuania and White Russia, relates: "They would suffer privation and want, would sleep on the bare benches of the synagogues, or at the homes of charitable members of the congregation." Sidney Hillman received six rubles a month ($3.00) for his food allowance, barely enough, even in those days, to buy a loaf of bread, some pickled cucumbers, and a slice of herring and tea each day. His days began with prayers at sunrise and ended with prayers at sunset; the long hours between were filled with the laborious interpretation of the Scriptures and the higher studies of the Talmud, all the legal-religious lore of the Jews. After four years of such devotion and self-denial, and after meeting all the exacting requirements of the rabbinate, he might be assigned to some small congregation and then, perhaps, with good fortune, win the hand of some rich man's daughter. Such were the fond hopes of his parents for him; such were the dreams of many of the seminary students who were desperately poor like himself. Thus his path seemed clearly marked for him by ancient puritanical traditions, regulating his every act according to the Jewish Law, imposing abstinence from the pleasures of the world and the flesh, and fixing his thoughts only upon the unitary God of the Israelites. It must be noted that the way of religion appealed strongly to Sidney Hillman's imaginative nature in his boyhood. When he turned from it later, his religious faith, instilled in childhood, may be said to have assumed merely a different, more temporal form.

He was, when he came to Kovno in 1901, a shy, skinny village youth, bred by pious and conservative folk. Now in this big town of 70,000, bustling with trade, its people seeming by contrast educated and well clad, his eyes were opened to the greater world beyond Zagare, his mind exposed to new ideas he heard discussed covertly even among the Yeshiva students.

There had been for a generation a strong intellectual current among the rabbinical students opposing the medieval forms of the Jewish religion and its spirit of social resignation; new voices urged positive action against racial-religious persecution, arm in arm with the rising democratic movement of the Russians. There were others who championed the Zionist party and its call to the homeland in Palestine. After his first bewilderment at finding himself alone in a large city, the boy of fourteen began to think for himself.

When he had passed a year in Kovno he became aware that the walls of the seminary were narrow for him. What he longed for was to continue the study of the Russian language and its literature, and after that something of mathematics and modern science, "impious" subjects excluded from the curriculum of the rabbinical college.

At this stage Sidney made the acquaintance of a boy named Michael Zacharias, who was about a year older than himself. This youth, who had had a Russian education, gave lessons in the Russian language, sometimes teaching without fee those who were too poor to pay him. When young Hillman appealed to him for aid, Zacharias undertook to instruct him free of charge, since Sidney had no funds for such purposes. During his second year at the seminary in Kovno, Hillman came to Zacharias for Russian lessons twice a week, and later every day.

As the seminary was situated actually in Slobodka, a suburb of Kovno, on the other side of the Velikaya River, he was obliged to walk a distance of about three miles each way in order to reach Zacharias' home for an hour's lesson. Yet he never missed those appointments. Indeed one day, during the time of the spring thaws, when the ice had suddenly melted and swept away the pontoon bridge across the river, the boy of fifteen arrived at Zacharias', breathless, pale, and drenched to the bone. "I was nearly drowned," he exclaimed. He had made his way across the river with a man on a raft, fighting the swift current, and several times had narrowly escaped being swept into the stream. After a change of clothing he went on with his lesson.

In his first talks with Hillman, Zacharias found that he held Orthodox religious views, and was disposed, after thinking upon the Jewish problem, to join in the recently launched Zionist movement. Now Zacharias dwelt with his uncle and aunt, Dr. and Mrs. Matis, whose home for some years had been a secret headquarters for political and trade-union activity. Dr. Matis, a chemist, believed that in order to end the special disabilities and persecutions suffered by the Jewish population, efforts must be made to gain justice and democracy for all the Russian people; hence he was active in the larger Russian revolutionary movement as well as in the illegal trade-union organization of Russian Jews known as the Bund. At considerable risk to himself, Dr. Matis had made his home a center for committee meetings of the Bund, and for the distribution of political pamphlets and translations of foreign books on socialism and democracy, which were of course forbidden circulation in Russia.

Sidney now heard the talk of these enlightened people at the house of Dr. Matis and began to read this forbidden literature. His old ideas began to dissolve. Soon he and young Zacharias were fast friends, devoted heart and soul to the common cause.

One day in the autumn of 1902, Sidney came to Michael Zacharias in a state of great mental distress. The chief rabbi of the Yeshiva, he said, had learned that he had been secretly taking lessons in Russian and had given him a terrible calling down. Sidney had tried to reason with the great man, but had been told that he was a sinner and must mend his ways or leave the school. The chief rabbi had also determined to report the affair to his father, for rabbinical students were then sternly forbidden to study Russian and other lay subjects. Shortly afterward, Sidney had received a letter from his father admonishing him to be a good and obedient boy and heed the orders of the Yeshiva authorities, lest his food allowance, meager as it was, be cut off. To this Sidney wrote in reply, though in respectful terms, that he was determined to continue learning Russian and mathematics, and that if his allowance were stopped he would have to manage somehow for himself in Kovno. He was then but fifteen and a half years old.

The rebel thus showed itself early in the deceptively gentle nature of young Hillman. When it was discovered that he persisted in his error, he was called again before the chief rabbi. One sees the stern dignitary cloaked in all his long-bearded religious authority confronting the small thin boy, who, once so obedient to his elders, now shows a surprising fund of stubborn will. His father arrived also and added his pleadings to the admonitions of the rabbi. But Sidney was resolved to leave the rabbinical college and pursue his non-religious studies at all costs. He assured his father that he would try to support himself while doing this.

Young indeed, almost without friends in this strange city, he had rebelled against his father and rejected the opportunity for a relatively safe and respectable career as a rabbi. It was an emotional storm through which he passed early in life and which marked him deeply.

He now asked young Zacharias if he knew of any work he might find or of cheap lodgings. When the other boy appealed to his relatives, the Matis couple, it turned out that the chemist had a job for Sidney. Their hired man had left them, and Sidney was engaged to clean the laboratory and run errands for Dr. Matis. Soon he was busy washing bottles and cleaning retorts and separators every morning. A cot was set up for him in the laboratory of the Matis house. Though his wages amounted to not much more than his previous allowance, the work was light, his master was a very kindly man, and he had time to continue with his self-education.

In later years Dr. Matis described Sidney Hillman as a well-behaved and intelligent boy who was extremely fond of reading. The doctor had an excellent library of general literature lining the walls of his study, which adjoined the laboratory. At every free moment young Hillman would go into the study when the doctor was out and take down some book in which he would lose himself for hours at a time. Dr. Matis, coming in to give the boy some errand to do, would find him with his nose deep in a book, and so absorbed that he had not even heard the doctor enter. Smiling, the older man would say: "Excuse me, would it interfere very much with your reading if I asked you to do some work for me?"

At first Sidney lived chiefly on bread or rolls and tea. But Mrs. Matis (like her husband a person of education, who conducted a school for girls in Kovno), on noticing how little he ate, saw to it that he partook of the family's supper. Evenings, Sidney continued his lessons regularly with Michael Zacharias. He was in a fever of reading, of studying, questioning, and learning. The elder pair grew quite fond of the homeless boy, who was treated almost as a member of the family. Dr. Matis, a generous and idealistic soul, was like an older brother and mentor at once, whose influence quickened the boy's mind.

The Matises belonged to the group among the Jews known as "assimilationists"; at their home leaders of the Jewish underground labor movement in Kovno forgathered regularly. For at this time the belated industrial revolution was already changing the old order in Russia. Instead of working in little shops or acting as middlemen, most Russian Jews were now employed as artisans or laborers in textile mills, tanneries, or lumberyards, at wretched wages. More and more they were joining in the common struggle of Russians of all races and religions for freedom. Since the 1890's, and especially in the period from 1900 to 1905, this country without constitution or civil rights seethed with secret revolutionary activity which aimed at supplanting the imperial regime with a democratic government like those of Western Europe and America.

In this atmosphere Hillman lived during the impressionable years of his youth. His days were filled with excited discussions with Zacharias and other young intellectuals who came to the Matis place. These young men had formed a club which held meetings every two weeks. Each one would read certain books, usually of a scientific character, and then prepare a paper or a talk on what he had read. It was a sort of home university for those who were denied formal schooling and, in an organized manner, pursued the study of modern evolutionary science, sociology, and economics. They read Morgan on heredity, then Darwin, Herbert Spencer, John Stuart Mill, Karl Marx, and various Russian popularizers of science and economics.

When Sidney was thought competent enough in Russian he was invited to be a member of the club, and rather haltingly or timidly at first—for he was a poor linguist and keenly aware of the gaps in his knowledge—took part in its discussions and debates on every subject under the sun, from the nebular hypothesis to the problems of conducting labor unions. Here for the first time he learned to stand up and express his thoughts before a group of people, and with increasing self-confidence. He loved the give-and-take of those discussion meetings, and in later years said they represented the beginning of his real education.

Dr. Matis related afterward that Hillman did not have much to do in his laboratory; in any case, he had no intention of becoming a chemist.

. . . His free time was spent at the secret meetings [of the Bund]. He was often called upon for revolutionary assignments. In this way he became involved in the revolutionary movement, to which he devoted himself with heart and soul.[4]

The Jewish labor movement in the Western Provinces had been all but crushed out in 1902 by the severe measures of the czarist police. By 1903 and 1904 it was rising again, especially after the Russo-Japanese War had begun. Hillman was only sixteen when he first volunteered to work under the orders of the outlawed trade-union leaders, thereby risking imprisonment or banishment to Siberia. He carried messages from the directing committee to groups of workers who were being organized by the thousands in more or less secret unions. Despite the police, these unions managed to hold meetings, conduct strikes, and negotiate settlements with employers. According to an eyewitness, Zacharias, young Hillman helped to organize the typesetters of Kovno and took an active part in one of their strikes. One of his tasks was to take charge of his group's hectograph, on which leaflets or small newspapers were crudely printed, and to keep it moving from one hiding place to another.

IV

On May 1, 1904, the good citizens of Kovno rubbed their eyes at the sight of a little procession of about a hundred workingmen marching down the main street of the town, bearing banners and singing. It was perhaps the first time such a thing had been done openly in Kovno, although there were public demonstrations now in many Russian towns. At the head of the little column was Sidney Hillman, the former rabbinical student, then a stripling of seventeen, pale but determined enough, and carrying one of their banners.

It was an act of sheer bravado, according to one of his friends of that time, who did not take part in the parade. Kovno, a fortified city of the western border, held a garrison of thirty thousand troops. In a few minutes police and military officers, recovering from their astonishment, bore down upon the marchers. Sidney was seized, hustled into a carriage, and driven by his guards to the Kovno prison. There he was held without trial for long months.

He received the routine treatment given to political prisoners in Russia. After he had been beaten sufficiently, cold water was poured over him until he revived, then the beating was resumed. This was by way of encouraging him to inform the police about the other members of his organization, which he refused to do. He was also placed in solitary confinement for a time. Afterward he remembered how the prisoners used to converse with each other by tapping on the walls of their cells, also that one of his guards was quite friendly and talked with him for hours.

At first nothing was known of his fate, and his parents were distraught with grief. His father came to Kovno and saw Dr. Matis.

"What a scandal, what a disgrace!" he said. "Nothing of this kind has ever happened in our family."

"You ought to be proud of your son," he was told.

The elder Hillman, with the help of Dr. Matis and a lawyer they had engaged, made earnest petitions to have his son released. After about five months, perhaps because of his extreme youth, he was set free, returning to Zagare in November 1904 as something of a hero. Soon he was back again in the service of the popular revolution, carrying out secret missions among the workers and peasants of the Baltic provinces.

In Russia tremendous events were taking place one after the other. By the beginning of 1905 it was known that the war in the Far East had turned into a great military disaster. The people were rising everywhere, everybody was shouting for reform, and the government showed mortal fear. In June 1905, the Czar issued his promise of a constitution and a representative parliament. But a few weeks later, when the disappointing terms of the proposed reforms were made public, a wave of great strikes swept over European Russia, beginning in July and continuing through the summer.

Sidney Hillman, one of the thousands of unknown workers in that popular uprising, had been at work early that summer near the town of Reshitza, at the Latvian border, as an organizer for the Social Democratic Party. At that time, when he was eighteen, he considered himself a follower of Martov, a leader of the Menshevik (right-wing

Socialist) faction. During the turmoil of that summer he was arrested again and brought back to Kovno Prison.*

Now the old prison was jammed with more than five hundred political prisoners, men who came from every walk of life, among them persons of much talent and education. At this period, when the imperial throne seemed to be tottering, political prisoners were apparently treated with greater mildness than before. Sidney Hillman, in recollection, spoke of those months of confinement in 1905 as almost festive. Up to six in the evening the prisoners visited one another's cells or strolled about freely in the corridors or prison yard, talking, exchanging books, and reading newspapers that were smuggled in. Sidney had never enjoyed so much leisure, had never read so many books or met so many brilliant persons, among them authors and university professors. Regular lecture hours and meetings were organized, the announcements of them being posted on the walls by the prisoners without fear of their guards. It was like being at a wonderful "university," he used to say, for here were the "best people" of Russia, many of them young, some doomed to suffer exile or death, others destined to enjoy brilliant public careers.[5]

On November 3, 1905, after about four months had passed, the Czar's proclamation of amnesty, at the height of the insurrectionary movement, set Hillman and thousands of other political prisoners free once more. He returned to Zagare again, this time somewhat tired and ill, only to find that the unrest had spread to his native village. In the Baltic provinces, including Lithuania, there was now the threat of an agrarian revolt. The peasants were rising and taking things into their

---

* The uprisings of 1905, which Sir Bernard Pares, in a *History of Russia*, has called the "Movement of Liberation," has been described as a confused action, carried on sporadically under no central direction. Several reformist, upper-class parties, including the Liberals and the Constitutional Democrats, participated in the earlier stages of the movement together with the Social Revolutionaries (the party of the peasants), who were the largest opposition party, and the Social Democrats. The latter were divided into the moderate or Menshevik faction—to which young Hillman gave his adherence—and the rival Bolshevik faction led by Lenin, who played but an obscure part in the 1905 movement. (Pares: *A History of Russia*, pp. 401 ff., and pp. 429 ff., 4th edition, 1946, New York.)

It is interesting to note that Sidney Hillman, even in those days of his youth, amid scenes reminiscent of the French Revolution, was not a member of the extremist faction. Moreover, in his youth he was an admirer of La Salle, the leader of the right-wing German Socialists.

own hands. In Zagare, one day in December, crowds of people assembled in the street, as his mother afterward recalled, and Hillman was called out to address them from the porch of his home. He was already a young man of consequence. For a few days a Committee of Public Safety was set up in the village, at the time when Moscow and St. Petersburg were all but captured by the revolutionists.

He had changed greatly during those years when experience crowded upon experience. When he was but a boy of sixteen or seventeen he showed at first some pride in his exploits, as in enduring the beatings of the police in the Kovno prison rather than betraying his associates. In those days he made rather a cult of exhibiting his courage and firmness of will. Tenderhearted by disposition, he strove to overcome his instinctive revulsion against violence. On a night when there was a little insurrectionary rioting in Zagare, in December 1905, his parents had barred the doors and windows of the house in fear for their lives. He had insisted on walking out to see what was going on.

His father protested: "You cannot go, you will be killed."

He insisted angrily: "I must go," and took his two little sisters with him. The peasants were destroying the government-monopoly liquor shops in the village. But their leaders treated Sidney with respect and permitted him to pass through their lines unmolested.

By the age of nineteen he had already lived through a great deal. He had learned to submerge his own personality in the interests of the great movement of liberation. Nowadays he said little or nothing of what he was doing, or what adventures he passed through. Burning with zeal for the cause which it was hoped would soon triumph, he thought nothing of his personal fate. "He was an ardent idealist for the democratic revolution in Russia, and showed much courage," his friend Zacharias said, "but even then, I think, he had a quite realistic or practical side." [6] He seemed less interested in theory than in how to work with people, how to organize them and to lead them. At nineteen it was apparent that he had dedicated himself to the hazardous life of a labor organizer and a political leader.

Knowledge of this filled his parents with forebodings. "Ah, what will become of our Sidney?" his mother would exclaim, weeping. "He will be sentenced to death or exiled to Siberia." His father also attempted to reason with him, urging that he give up the outlawed Bund and forget about being a "politician." Sidney would avoid altercations and say nothing. In the house of his father he would put on his

phylacteries and recite his prayers morning and evening like a pious
son of Israel.

The drive of the revolutionary leaders was broken early in the
following year by the pitiless repressive measures of the czarist government. Sidney Hillman was denounced. Police agents, once more
in charge of Zagare, came often to his home to inquire for him. He
would usually be off somewhere, making only rare and unexpected
visits to his family. But soon there was literally no place where he
could hide.

His mother begged him to flee the country and go to Manchester,
England, where his uncle, Charles Paiken, was established in business, and where his elder brother, Joseph, and his next younger
brother, Harry, had already preceded him.

He said: "No, I will leave only when there is no more hope of
doing anything here." But by the summer of 1906 those who had
opposed the government were leaving en masse. The first Duma, or
parliament, had been dissolved; the Czar's promises of political reform
were broken again.

In October 1906, Sidney Hillman, arming himself with a false passport, at last made his sad farewells to his family and took the train
to the nearby German border. Thence he proceeded to Bremen and
by ship to England, where he was kindly received by his uncle in
Manchester, and by his younger brother, Harry, a skilled jewelry
worker, who shared his lodgings with him.

v

It is doubtful that Sidney Hillman got much out of his stay of nine
months in England. In the first place, he knew nothing of the language
and always found difficulty in mastering a strange tongue. Then he
frequented chiefly the circles of the Russian exiles; 200,000 a year
had been leaving Russia, and numerous members of the Jewish Bund
and the Russian Socialist Party whom he had known well had turned
up in London and Manchester.

For a time the exiles hoped that the movement of reform would be
resumed and they would be able to return and help remake the unhappy land of their birth. Hillman took part for a while in the activities of the Russian refugees, acting on one occasion in a play they

gave at St. James Hall, Manchester, in order to raise money. He also attended several British trade-union meetings in that same hall, a working-class forum, with a friend who interpreted for him.

The world's most advanced labor movement was in full swing here, and the common man lived well and with a sense of personal dignity and worth unknown to Russian workers. Yet Sidney Hillman felt that, despite her democratic laws, he did not want to establish himself in England; there was much grinding poverty, and the class lines in society were still sharply drawn. If there was to be no returning to Russia, then he would go farther on, to America, where some of his comrades had already preceded him.

His uncle, Charles Paiken, who ran a furniture and small loan business in Manchester, was well off and often received the young exile at his home. He had been something of an idealist and intellectual himself in his youth in Russia, and was attracted by his nephew who, he perceived, possessed brains and character. Seeing that Sidney was idle and penniless, his uncle offered him a place in his concern, one that would give him ample opportunity to rise in the world. Though he often went hungry these days, he politely refused. His uncle, then, in vigorous argument, demonstrated that his absorption in "politics" and other such "dreams" would lead him to no good end, and he was strongly urged to be sensible. But the younger man insisted that he had his plans, his heart was in the labor movement, he was determined to remain a worker, and had no slightest wish to become a man of business like his uncle. Though Mr. Paiken was a clever fellow, Hillman could not abide his ideas, which were now narrowly middle-class or conservative. Yet he parted from his uncle on the friendliest terms.

In England he subsisted for long months in penury. The poor young Russian exiles helped one another as a matter of principle. If Sidney came into a few shillings he would share them at once, without further thought, with a friend who was hungrier still. In the main, however, it was his younger brother who kept him alive, and Sidney later richly repaid all such help from his family or friends. On the other hand, he was proud and reserved; if he had eaten nothing but a crust of bread since morning he would tell no one, nor ask for help, but would sit in his room reading all day long.

On August 1, 1907, he boarded the Cunard liner *Cedric* at Liverpool and sailed for New York, arriving there ten days later.

Some years passed and he was able to write his wealthy uncle in polite terms that he was established in the field he had chosen for himself, and in a useful and important post.

Needless to tell you, as far as the work is concerned, I like it—or rather enjoy it. You know that these were always my desires to be affiliated [with] the labor movement. I do not know what your views are on the subject at this time after all the labor troubles in your country. . . . It may be that you feel rather inconvenienced about it. . . . Our relations will be just as friendly, nevertheless.

What he did not tell of were the years of hardship, of struggle with himself and with those around him, the difficult, stony path he had traversed to gain even that first, modest post of command.

Chapter Two

THE CHICAGO
YEARS: 1907-1911

He had gone to Chicago at the end of August 1907, after his brief stay in New York, in response to a letter from his good friend Michael Zacharias, who held out hope of finding a good job there. The bustling, thriving metropolis of the Middle West was only less a melting pot of immigrant populations than New York. Zacharias had met him on his arrival and helped him to find lodgings on Fairfield Avenue, near Douglas Park, on the north side of the city. On his second day in Chicago, Hillman found work in a warehouse at $6.00 a week; but a fortnight later he shifted to a better-paying job at the huge mail-order shop of Sears, Roebuck and Company, as a stock clerk in their infants' wear department.

In a letter of this period to his uncle in England, he wrote:

I am working for one of the biggest houses in the United States. There are more than 8,000 employees. I am getting $8.00 a week and the work is not hard. It is a fine place. And I am much surprised the management is satisfied with my work. I expect a raise in the near future.[1]

He was also studying English, he reported, at the Hebrew Institute of Chicago, and announced the intention of entering night college later on in order to prepare for some profession such as the law.

Up to May 1909, for twenty months, he worked at Sears, Roebuck, an industrious young immigrant who was trying to better his position and learn the ways and the speech of his new country.

In those early years in Chicago he kept to himself a good deal. When business was slack and he was laid off temporarily he would haunt the public library. Or, according to the people with whom he lodged, Russian émigrés like himself, he would stay in his room all day long, living on tea and bread, smoking an endless chain of cigarettes and reading. For a time he devoured all sorts of modern literature: Tolstoy, Dostoevski, Ibsen. The only way to lure the seemingly unsocial young man out of his room was for his hosts to invite him to hear their new talking machine playing records of classical music or opera, which he was passionately fond of. On Sunday mornings he would walk all the way to the Loop district to hear the lectures of a famous Socialist speaker, Arthur Morrow Lewis, at the Garrick Theater.

He had few acquaintances; he dressed carelessly, almost shabbily, as if indifferent to his appearance. In manner he was reserved; but when people broached subjects that interested him and drew him out they were struck by the air of independence with which he spoke his mind.

Plainly he was not happy in those first years in America. The émigrés of the 1905 revolution in Russia often experienced an emotional letdown after coming here. While his life over there had been perilous, at least he had worked and fought for something more than his own daily bread, together with other courageous souls. Here he was free and, materially speaking, better off. Yet to the idealistic type of immigrant the folkways of his new country, at first acquaintance, reflected only the harshest materialism.

Michael Zacharias thought that even then young Hillman "believed in his star." He had ambitions, and a program for himself that was different from that of most of the other foreign workers around him. He had some awareness of his own potentialities or talents, but as an immigrant laborer, speaking English poorly, he scarcely knew what to do about them. From his table in the stockroom of Sears, Roebuck, where he packed clothing in parcels sixty hours a week, the prospect seemed cheerless and difficult enough.

Some years later, in writing to a younger friend in Chicago, he spoke of himself "as one who met all kinds of disappointments";

these, he remembered, were bound up with a deep sense of humiliation at being deprived of "the opportunity of doing things that I consider more important than anything else." He had his own standards of "our values of life," he added, by which he strove to measure himself. When the realization of them seemed impossible, when he felt frustrated, then "it merely means that gray is the color." But he also believed that obstacles were things you had to overcome.[2]

One day at Sears, Roebuck, the foreman came by, stopped at the table of a man working beside Hillman, gave him a little envelope, and passed on. The man opened it, turned pale, and looked as if he were going to faint away. He told Sidney that he had just been given his notice of dismissal, though he had a wife and two children and needed his job badly. The other people near them, who had guessed at the meaning of the incident, bent silently to their tasks, their faces showing their fear.

Sidney Hillman felt a great sorrow for the man working beside him. Why should they have fired a man who supported a family, and not himself? Did no one care about justice in managing the everyday work of human beings? Or was this man let go because he had been working there for years and earned more wages than a beginner?

Hillman thought of going to the foreman and offering to resign if he would keep the older man. As he later recollected the incident, which made a profound impression upon him, he thought of saying, "I am alone, and I can manage with little." But his fellow workers explained to him that he would only be replaced by a boy receiving even less than he. Many years later he remembered the atmosphere of fear under which the people at the great Sears, Roebuck plant worked. There were 7,000 girls working at the place ten hours a day and in addition to that three nights a week (in return for their suppers in the company restaurant), making some 70 hours a week all told; and all lived in fear of sudden dismissal, in fear of hunger for their families.[3]

"There is something terribly wrong with this system!" he would exclaim. Why should people live in such fear in this rich country? It was then, in 1908 or 1909, according to his later recollection, that he decided to devote himself to the labor movement in America, as he had done in Russia.[4]

The records of Sears, Roebuck show that Hillman was rated as a good worker and that he was given raises in pay until he earned $11.

Then he too was suddenly sacked during a seasonal slump in business. There he was in the spring of 1909, back in his room, smoking his chain of cigarettes, drinking strong tea, and reading, reading.

Through his friendly host, a clothing worker, he was recommended for a job at the men's clothing factory of Hart, Schaffner and Marx. He was to work for six weeks without pay while learning his task, that of an apprentice cutter; thereafter he would receive $6.00 weekly, but might hope for advancement, as he acquired skill, to $15 or $20 eventually. Thus, at least, he might save money and educate himself for something better. But after a year's hard work he was earning only $8.00 a week, just enough to exist.

Tailoring used to be an art. But this was America. Sidney Hillman worked in the world's largest clothing factory, producing ready-made or hand-me-down men's suits, which had come into great vogue in the last third of the nineteenth century.

Every day from 7 A.M. to 5:30 P.M. he stood at a long table in one of the factory's cutting rooms, wielding a pair of big shears to cut through several thicknesses of cloth. The bundles of cut cloth would then be wheeled off to the other departments or shops where whole battalions of pants makers, coat makers, pocket makers, seamers, finishers, and pressers contributed their labor, stage by stage, to the completion of the garment. For the machine age had arrived in the clothing trade. Power-driven sewing machines were being speeded up, and operations were being broken down constantly into ever simpler movements which an inexperienced laborer could master in a few weeks. The tailor in an "efficiency shop" like Hart, Schaffner and Marx was more properly a "clothing worker"; he was the human adjunct of a machine or of a whole battery of machines.

At this period the trend toward efficiency of manufacturing had led to the establishment of quite a number of these large clothing factories or "inside shops," where all the work was combined and completed in one location instead of being divided up among numerous small contractors or "outside shops." This tendency toward big, self-contained units was more marked in Chicago than in New York. The greatest and most successful of these modern producers of ready-made men's clothing was Hart, Schaffner and Marx, which alone accounted for about a fourth of the entire Chicago output and employed from 8,000 to 10,000 workers.

Those were prosperous years for this pioneering firm, which was in advance of the others in volume, in the use of labor-saving machinery, and in maintenance of good standards of design, quality, and fit. A campaign of nationwide advertising, unusual and costly for the early 1900's, had won for its product wide acceptance among the country's prosperous middle classes. But while the men's clothing industry expanded, growing to a billion-dollar business toward 1920, its workers ranked low in the scale of American labor.

Sidney Hillman was one of an army of about 45,000 clothing workers in Chicago, half of whom were women and girls; three fourths were recent immigrants, chiefly Italian, Russian-Jewish, Polish, Bohemian, and Lithuanian. Ignorant of our language, ill-educated, unfamiliar with American customs, these immigrants, who had been arriving lately in larger numbers than ever, herded together with their compatriots in the slums of Chicago, as they had done earlier in New York and the Eastern cities. Since the women knew how to sew a little, and the needle trades and clothing shops required only modest skills, great numbers of these "greenhorns" flooded the clothing market with their labor. Its wages were notoriously low, and the work was seasonal, but these people had nowhere else to go.

The wage levels of the efficient manufacturers were scaled down toward the standards set by the small, intensely competitive contractors or sub-contractors who were still numerous then in Chicago as well as in the larger New York market. These small undertakers, with a few light machines and a capital of as little as $50 or $100, would begin by employing members of their families or relatives. Later, even when they prospered, they would deliberately recruit uneducated recent immigrants. One of these in Chicago was reported as saying to his forewoman: "I want no experienced girls. They know the pay to get. I got to pay them good wages and they make me less work, but these 'greenhorns,' Italian people, Jewish people, all nationalities, they cannot speak English and . . . just come from the old country, and I let them work hard, like the devil, and these I get for less wages." [5]

The raw immigrants were crowded together in whole "foreign quarters" of their own—Italian, Slav, Jewish, Greek—along far-spreading Halsted Street in Chicago. In this region were centered the many "sweatshops" installed in shabby framehouses or tenements, such as Jane Addams of Hull House described in 1910:

An unscrupulous contractor regards no basement as too dark, no stable loft too foul, no rear shanty too provisional, no tenement room too small for his workroom, as these conditions imply low rental. Hence these shops abound in the worst of the foreign districts.[6]

Since great numbers of the clothing workers were employed in such sweatshops, at wages as low as $2.50 and $3.00 per week for unskilled girls, and there was always a surplus of cheap immigrant labor, the large, efficient manufacturers, though paying better rates, were able to keep a very tight rein on their labor. The sweatshop blighted the lives even of the more fortunate workers.

The whole industry, furthermore, was fiercely competitive and speculative. The big wholesalers squeezed the small contractors. These would wait until they received orders from the wholesalers before hiring help and "making up." There would then be a rush season in the summer months or late winter, after which a third or more of their people would be dropped. On the other hand, there was no union worth speaking of in this trade. The unhappy clothing workers had risen in bitter strikes in 1895 and 1904, but each time they had been thoroughly defeated. Only a fraction of the workers, some 10 per cent, mainly skilled cutters, were organized along craft lines, and this had little effect.

II

"Sidney Hillman was a cutter," one of his colleagues said later, "but, if I may say so, he was a damn poor cutter." He lacked the physical co-ordination of one who might become a skilled worker. He made mistakes and showed a quick temper when he was corrected. If the reprimands of the overseers or foremen seemed to him unjust, he would make open complaint. But in a dispute his word, as a laborer, counted for nothing against the word of a foreman. At Hart, Schaffner and Marx the fastest workers would be made "pacemakers," and their speed would be increased until they reached the highest possible output. This quota would then be required of the other people, and then piece rates would gradually be reduced.[7]

In the cutting rooms at Hart, Schaffner and Marx, the foremen were petty tyrants who drove the workers hard, and behind them, driving them too, was the burly figure of H. R. Peth, a sort of "Prussian drillmaster," superintendent and production manager of the whole plant. Peth set the standard of quality and style that made his firm's merchandise celebrated. "But he knew only the old autocratic ways of ruling his shop." [8]

Hillman, testifying on conditions in this great factory, said:

I especially recall the feeling of fear, besides the wages. I believe I started in with $7.00 a week, and during three years I worked up to $11 or $12; but what I consider more important is . . . the constant fear of the employees of being discharged without cause at all. There really was no cause at all sometimes. The floor boss, as we called him, did not like a particular girl or man, and out they went. I remember especially the panic of 1907 when the employees were in constant fear of "Who will be thrown out?" I remember, we tried all of us to get into the good graces of the floor boss. . . . I remember when I made the first complaint I packed up my tools and went out.[9]

Hillman had flared up in anger and quit his job that time, as he related, but in a few weeks, having found nothing else to do, he was back again in the same shop.

Others were less fortunate. There was, for instance, a girl worker, a Miss Bessie Abramowitz, employed at first by another large firm in Chicago, who sewed buttons from dawn to dark at 2½ cents per coat. Sometimes she would take her work home at night when she had not finished her quota. But when her foreman deliberately scratched out the figures on her work sheet and lowered her piece rate by a fraction of a penny, she had the spirit to form a committee of girls and protest to the management. She was fired at once, and found herself blacklisted. All the other clothing shops that were members of the Chicago Wholesale Clothiers' Association, by agreement, refused her employment. She was forced to leave town and seek other, lower-paid work. After many months she returned to Chicago and, by concealing her real name, was able to obtain a job as a button sewer at Hart, Schaffner and Marx. But the pace was even swifter here; the atmosphere was depressing; the foremen here, too, were always finding pretexts for grasping at minute advantages in labor costs, which meant large profits to management when carried out in terms of many thousands of units.[10]

In Russia, Hillman had known the tyranny of the Czar. Now, transplanted to America, he saw that he and thousands or millions of workers lived in insecurity and fear. Was the American freedom enough? Was it enough to have equal rights for rich and poor alike "to sleep under the bridges"? From his earliest days here the contrast between the promise of American life and its hard realities was borne in upon the young Hillman, who saw our society with the perspective of a recent arrival from the Old World. We had freedom, but also "slavery"; that is, "industrial slavery," he would say. Had not President Lincoln (whom he greatly admired) said long ago that a nation could not exist "half slave and half free"? Neither could an individual live half slave and half free, "free politically and slave industrially." [11]

One evening in 1910, after he had been working at his job for about half a year, Hillman quietly slipped off to attend a small union-organizing meeting for the clothing workers of Chicago, announced by a leaflet stealthily circulated in his factory. There was, after all, some sort of union in the field, though weak and ill-led even by the standards of forty years ago. It was called the United Garment Workers of America and was affiliated with the American Federation of Labor. After having met with heavy reverses in Chicago in 1904, its business agents were cautiously at work again to fill the ranks of its four small locals there.

The labor movement as a whole was then experiencing a vigorous upswing, marked by rapid membership increase in the still youthful AFL. In New York, for example, the shirtwaist girls had begun a spectacular fight and won a partial victory for their union by 1910. News of this began to stir the Chicago men's clothing workers as well as those in New York. But on the whole the foreign-born garment workers were considered poor timber for trade unions in those days. The UGWA, the small union in their field, was interested mainly in organizing the cutters and other skilled craftsmen, in accordance with the craft-union principles of President Samuel Gompers of the AFL. That was how the apprentice cutter Sidney Hillman one day came upon a union leaflet in his shop.

It was not as simple to join a union then as it is now. To be seen at a meeting with union folks meant almost certainly the loss of one's job. The employers in the Wholesale Clothiers' Association were themselves closely organized in order to deny the benefits of similar organization to their employees. Undercover agents spied on the activities of the unionists and denounced those who came under suspicion, their names, as earlier noted, being entered in a blacklist maintained by the Association at its headquarters in the Medinah Temple building.

To be sure, the giant Hart, Schaffner and Marx firm, for competitive reasons of its own, remained independent of the Wholesale Clothiers' Association; but its managers also took a dim view of trade unionists.[12]

When Sidney Hillman first came to a small meeting with union organizers at Hod Carriers' Hall, Chicago, he sat in a corner of the room, looking at no one, averting his face, and listened. The others who glanced covertly at the young stranger with curly hair wondered if he was a "stool" for the bosses. If so, they would know it soon, because they would surely be fired at the end of that week.

Around that time a young cutter named Frank Rosenblum, employed by the same firm, was spotted at a union meeting and the next day was ordered to take his tools and go to the front office. There Mr. Harry Hart greeted him with the question: "Well, Rosenblum, what do you think of unions?"

Rosenblum answered with much spirit: "Well, if I told you I'm in favor of them you would only fire me, and if I say I'm against them you won't believe me, so I'm not saying anything."

The employer laughed and sent him back to work with a warning. In those days the manufacturers played the game of tolerating, to some extent, the unionization of the small group of skilled cutters, less than 10 per cent of their employees, "in order to prevent the great mass of [unskilled or semi-skilled] tailors from organizing themselves." [13]

At that first meeting Sidney Hillman gained from the others present a more precise notion of what had been going on in his industry. The cutters, "aristocrats" among the workers, organized as local No. 61, UGWA, had actually gained recognition in Chicago in 1901; but after the defeat of their strike in 1904, their condition had deteriorated again. Yet the past five or six years had been a period of great prosperity, of rapid growth in the ready-made-clothing industry. By 1910, "the new people," as well as "those who still remembered the better times of 1901–04," were restless and bitter toward their employers.[14]

Nothing hardens the resentment of workers more than the feeling that improvements gained by great effort on their part are being taken from them. And besides, there was the awareness that the standards of other sections of the labor army in America were rising noticeably, as shown in a remark of Sidney Hillman's made at about this same period. While the girls in his clothing factory worked ten hours every day, he said, "around the corner there were the printers, big strong healthy men, working only eight hours a day."

Week by week the grievances of the workers accumulated, especially at the efficient, harshly disciplined shops of Hart, Schaffner and Marx. Many of their grievances were of a petty character, as Joseph Schaffner, the head of the firm, rightly said. The worst of it was that the workers, as he himself admitted, felt that there was no one to hear them; the foreman's word against theirs was always enough. In short, they had no *rights*.

Hillman's own oral testimony in 1914 touches upon the deepest grievance of the workers that they were "not treated . . . like human beings." They toiled for a huge, coldly impersonal corporate machine. "As a matter of fact," Hillman said in a revealing statement, "the working people do not know who is the real head of the firm, only the people directly above them." [15]

III

Toward 1910 the noticeably restless and "rebellious" mood of the clothing workers was connected broadly with the rise of large-scale manufacture in the needle trades at this period and the numerous changes of machinery and method being introduced. At the Hart, Schaffner and Marx shops it needed but little provocation to arouse the smoldering anger of the labor force.

Trouble began on September 22, 1910, when a small group of girl workers protested a reduction of the piece rate for seaming pants from 4 cents to 3¾ cents per piece. When their petitions went unheard, fourteen of them, including Miss Bessie Abramowitz, walked out of Shop No. 5. Some of the workers in the other shops now refused to handle the work finished by those who remained in that department, and more workers, day by day, began to straggle out.

Sidney Hillman recalled later that the affair seemed like a joke at first: a few girls had flown into a temper and walked out. "I remember we made fun of it," he said. But the action spread, though apparently without anybody's orders. In Hillman's department the cutters who were in the union discussed the affair heatedly for several days. Then some of their bolder spirits, such as Frank Rosenblum and Sidney Rissman, walked out and yelled to the others to follow them. A foreman tried to stop them, but they pushed him aside. Hillman packed his tools and went out with the first cutters. This was about three weeks after the girls had started their walkout. By mid-October most of the 8,000 Hart, Schaffner workers were out on strike and thousands in other plants were joining them.

The movement swelled: headquarters of the impromptu strike organization were set up at Hod Carriers' Hall, the AFL center. As one of the rank-and-file leaders, Marimpietri, relates:

In sixteen halls in various parts of the city, the tailors met every day from early morning until late at night, listening to speakers and discussing among themselves the numerous complaints that had brought them together.

In some of the halls the workers met in national or language groups: the Poles, the Bohemians, the Lithuanians, the Italians, the Jews. Such separate meetings were necessary, for most of them did not understand the English language. When that was possible, workers met by branches of the trade: cutters, coat makers, vest makers, pants makers.[16]

Hillman, also present at these meetings, described the unorganized character of the movement:

There really were no definite demands. The demands were that conditions must be changed; nobody knew really exactly what they wanted; they wanted something better of course, or something different. . . . And from the start our people thought that the "closed shop" was the remedy for everything.[17]

The trouble was that the only union in the field was so weak. The small United Garment Workers of America (AFL), though organized in 1891, had, in the ranks of its Chicago locals, only some 2,000 members, mostly special-order (custom) tailors and cutters; that is, the craftsmen. Its main strength then lay in the Eastern cities, especially New York. But for some reason the relations of the union's national officers were not sympathetic with the mass of foreign-language-speaking immigrants, the recently arrived Jewish, Italian, and Slavic workers—an undisciplined rabble of sweated workers who looked like poor union men. The UGWA's veteran president, Thomas Rickert, and Secretary B. A. Larger belonged to the earlier generation of Irish, Swedish, and German craftsmen who had formerly manned the trade, and they followed the policy of developing the union along stable craft lines. Yet the unorganized Chicago strikers turned at once to the union's local business agents and appealed for their guidance and help.

Rickert, at his New York office, hesitated for weeks; the problem of handling a great mob of angry strikers, mostly "greenhorns," and outnumbering the whole union, seemed too much for him. Appeals by letter and telegram brought no sign of action. And yet it was a magnificent opportunity to take over the second largest clothing market in America. By the end of October, 18,000 were on strike, and there was tremendous pressure from below. More and more people were coming out. Meanwhile several firms in Chicago that maintained union-label agreements with the UGWA were actually completing work diverted to them by the strike-bound factories.

At this point a small weekly newspaper, the *Chicago Socialist,* edited by one Robert Dvorak, began coming out daily with reports of the developments in the clothing strike. Now that the movement had been spreading for four weeks, Dvorak threatened to publish a general strike call to all the city's clothing workers. This forced the hand of the UGWA's local officers, who urged Rickert to come to Chicago. He arrived there late in October. On the twenty-fifth of that month the Hart, Schaffner and Marx executives met with a delegation of their workers and made an offer to take all their employees back; they also promised to consider grievances, though with the understanding that there was to be no recognition of any union.

Later that same day Rickert addressed a mass meeting of the strikers and presented these proposals to the Hart, Schaffner workers. "We want the union! Closed shop!" they all yelled madly. Rickert was now persuaded to issue a general strike call for all Chicago, beginning October 27. About 35,000 to 40,000 came out, and the strike was solid.

With high spirits the workers manned picket lines in all the clothing centers of the city and withstood the battering given them by police and armed detectives. Suddenly, on November 5, Thomas Rickert announced that he had signed an agreement with Hart, Schaffner and Marx on behalf of their 8,000 workers, which he would shortly submit to them for approval. This provided for arbitration of the dispute between the company and its employees, but for no union recognition.

The first thing the strikers knew about the proposed settlement was when they read reports of it in the Chicago newspapers on a Saturday morning. Their rank-and-file leaders, however, went into action at once and hurried out with announcements to the afternoon newspapers that the settlement reported as approved by the UGWA president would undoubtedly be rejected.

At a mass meeting held the following Monday at Hod Carriers' Hall, Rickert presented his proposals. "To my surprise," Rickert related, "the people voted it down—they gave it practically no consideration." [18]

This was a remarkable understatement. In reality Rickert and his Chicago lieutenant were given such a warm reception that they found it advisable to leave the hall by a rear exit.[19]

Sidney Hillman, meanwhile, had shown himself staunch on the picket line and had commended himself, by his zeal, to the rank-and-file committee. They now appointed him one of a delegation of four men who were to call on John Fitzpatrick, president of the Chicago Federation of Labor, and appeal for his aid. The strikers had been made extremely suspicious by Rickert's maneuvers. Fitzpatrick, noted for his integrity as a leader in Chicago's turbulent industrial disputes, learned from Hillman and his comrades that the strike action was disorganized, that relief was needed, and that the people, suspicious of the union officers in charge, were getting out of hand. Fitzpatrick and the excellent Edward Nockels, secretary of the Chicago AFL body, both promised all possible aid and advised setting up a Joint Strike Conference Committee in whose leadership the clothing workers would feel confidence.

Help also came at about this time from the Women's Trade Union League, headed by Mrs. Raymond Robins. In accordance with Fitzpatrick's suggestions, a joint committee was now formed which included representatives of the United Garment Workers' Union, of the ready-made tailors (not yet unionized), as well as Fitzpatrick and Nockels and two persons representing the Women's Trade Union League, which donated funds and supplies of food and clothing.

The regular UGWA officers, under Rickert, now announced that strike benefits would be given in return for vouchers distributed among the strikers at their meeting halls. But on the morning of November 11, the day appointed, when a great crowd of about ten thousand congregated before the doors of the small UGWA headquarters on La Salle Street, there were riotous scenes. The police and firemen prevented the crowd from entering the building and drove them away. The hungry strikers, most of whom knew no English, felt they were being tricked. In their rage they fought back, attempting to lay siege to the building, only to be beaten off with clubs, women and girls as well as men. In despair many of them tore up their vouchers. Others, learning that they were to repair to their union halls for relief, found, on going there, that there were not enough funds or supplies for all.[20]

Hillman, observing for the first time a large-scale American strike, involving about 10 per cent of all Chicago's laboring population, never forgot the confusion, the heartbreak of that day. The clothing workers also long remembered the incompetence of their official trade-union leaders. Impressive also to Hillman was the extreme violence attending an industrial dispute in democratic America. Mounted police rode down the lines of workers; clubs swung; revolvers went off.

Chicago was a "raw town" in those days, with a free-swinging police force. But there were also great numbers of humane and charitable citizens who showed compassion for the hungry army of clothing workers. The city's leading newspapers expressed the sympathy felt by Chicagoans in all walks of life. Jane Addams, director of Hull House in the immigrants' quarter, with her associate, Ellen Gates Starr, and Grace Abbot and Mrs. Raymond Robins of the WTUL, joined with Dr. James Mullenbach, superintendent of the United Charities of Chicago, to gather funds for coal and food. Various Jewish organizations also brought assistance. Thus some $20,000 was raised in November and December. John Fitzpatrick also exerted himself to bring donations from Chicago's trade-union coffers. Four commissary stores were opened up; milk was provided for children; doctors treated wounded strikers free of charge.

This demonstration of generous emotion on the part of the good citizens of Chicago, including a number of society women, was touching enough. However, the contribution of the union involved (which then had a sizeable treasury) was, by comparison, downright stingy. Sidney Hillman felt it was humiliating, as he said afterward, that the workers in this struggle "for the recognition of human rights in the shop" should have been forced "to beg for charity outside the labor movement."

Winter came early that season, but the ill-clad men and the women pickets in their long skirts continued to trudge up and down the snow-covered streets before the walls of the clothing factories. As strike-breakers showed themselves in increasing numbers, there were more and more violent episodes, until a climax was reached on December 3, 1910, when a picket named Charles Lazinskas was shot and killed.

Public opinion was aroused at this. Three days later Chicago saw a macabre procession of 10,000 ragged workers, extending for nine blocks, silently marching through the main streets of the city as they carried their dead brother to his grave. They bore banners announcing their grievances and demands, but "preserved a strange and frightening silence. No dirge sounded and not an outcry was heard." [21]

The tone of the newspaper editorials now grew more urgent in their appeals for some decent settlement of the dispute. Clarence Darrow, the celebrated trial lawyer, came forward to act as counsel for 400 strikers under arrest. A liberal young attorney named Harold Ickes also volunteered his help. Church leaders made vigorous public protests at the employers' conduct.

At about the same time, Professor Charles E. Merriam of the University of Chicago, then a member of the City Council, introduced a resolution which was passed on November 29, 1910, calling for arbitration and settlement of the strike through the agency of the mayor. The manufacturers, banded together in the Chicago Wholesale Clothiers' Association, as before, responded to this with an absolute refusal to treat with union representatives. Alderman Merriam thereupon issued a strong statement condemning the manufacturers' group, a statement which was given great prominence in the leading Chicago dailies. At length the Illinois State Legislature moved to investigate the long-drawn-out strike—for clothing was then Chicago's second largest industry—and its hearings were set to begin on January 10, 1911, with striking workers as well as employers invited to testify.[22]

IV

As if in response to the growing pressure of public opinion, and specifically to Merriam's statement, Hart, Schaffner and Marx, biggest of the clothing firms, now came forward with an offer to meet the proposed mayor's arbitration committee and the strikers' leaders in an effort to find a basis of agreement. This firm acted independently, not being a member of the Association. Thus, at the beginning of December 1910, a breach was suddenly opened in the ranks of the employers. The impulse to this action came at last from the troubled conscience of the wealthy Joseph Schaffner, head of the firm bearing his name.

Joseph Schaffner was the founder and guiding genius of his concern, a self-made business magnate of wide repute and a philanthropist in private life. Having gone into men's clothing when it was a fly-by-night business, he had built up a giant firm for those days, one admired for its credit rating as well as for its efficiency and the quality of its merchandise. As for its labor standards, Mr. Schaffner had thought they were in a most "satisfactory state" on the eve of the great walkout. The truth was that he concentrated on the financial management of the business, leaving the production end to his associates. For years he had not even looked into his factories.

He was therefore greatly shocked when the strike broke out in his own plant. At first he had determined to keep his hands off the labor problem, in accordance with a long-standing agreement with his partners. But as the reports came to him of violent collisions, of shooting and stabbing, he grew more and more tormented. He was a kindly soul who loved books (especially the works of Emerson) and, ironically enough, at this very time was busy with a project to endow night classes at Northwestern University for workers who could not afford higher education. Meanwhile he was being denounced as a labor-crusher by ministers and rabbis. Now he wondered, citing Emerson, whether he had not been a "moral failure" rather than a success in life.[23]

To a younger friend, Earl Dean Howard, professor of economics at Northwestern University (who helped establish the night classes), Schaffner had said after Thanksgiving Day, "This strike is killing me!" At length he made up his mind to take over the labor problem from his associates, asking Howard to make an independent investigation and report to him.

Howard looked into conditions in the Hart, Schaffner and Marx plants for several days. He also called on Jane Addams, who with the Women's Trade Union League, was struggling to feed thousands of clothing workers' families. Miss Addams, a woman who was no mere visionary reformer, but one who knew the world and its troubles, rather frightened Howard when she declared that this was no ordinary union-managed strike but "a spontaneous revolutionary movement," an uprising of the crowd, embittered by long-gathering resentments and hates. These people, she said, had no faith in their official leaders, and no one knew what violent explosions might be expected.

When Howard reported to Mr. Schaffner that the situation seemed to be getting out of control, the head of the firm determined to act promptly. The fatal shooting of a picket, coming at this point, hardened his determination to overrule his associates. He now conveyed to President Thomas Rickert of the UGWA his proposal for a settlement, the so-called "City Hall agreement," which was submitted to a vote at a mass meeting of 3,500 of Schaffner's employees at Hod Carriers' Hall on December 8, 1910.

It looked like the first real break for at least 25 per cent of the strikers after a struggle of ten weeks. The strike committee recommended acceptance; the cutters' local voted acceptance subject to the approval of the other strikers. Honest John Fitzpatrick addressed the mass meeting and urged that the "City Hall agreement" be accepted. It provided for an arbitration committee to deal with the workers' claims and for rehiring of all strikers save those held guilty of violence.

But this crowd was in an ugly mood by now. One speaker after another shouted from the floor that the rank and file would never abandon the rest of their fellow workers (who had been offered no agreement so far), nor would they allow their more militant comrades, who were under charge of violence, to be deprived of their jobs. The meeting became chaotic; Fitzpatrick, unable to make himself heard, left without even taking a vote. The strike went on.

There were several other mass meetings held at this period, during which the strike leaders argued that Schaffner's proposal offered the basis for substantial union recognition. At one of these gatherings an opposing faction came in to stir up the strikers against their leaders, and the report reached strike headquarters that a fair-sized riot was on. Several reliable men were hurriedly sent over to calm the crowd, one of them being Sidney Hillman. The chairman, a tailor named A. D. Marimpietri, stood on the platform helplessly, unable to make himself heard, while most of the strikers mounted their chairs to hurl threats and insults at one another.

Hillman kept asking for the floor in vain, then made his way to the platform. As he began to speak almost everyone there seemed to be shouting more angrily still: "Get off the platform! Throw him out!" Almost none of the workers present knew him. He was a slender young man, then twenty-three, and with his pale face and high fore-head looked more like a divinity student than a labor leader. Men-acingly the crowd kept pressing forward toward the platform. Some friendly voices now warned both the chairman and the new speaker to leave by the rear exit, lest they be manhandled. Two of the regular UGWA officers had already left by the back door. But Hillman faced the crowd. He said to Marimpietri that he was going to "hold onto the chair" and that these people would take it from him "only over my dead body." Marimpietri also remembered his saying: "If I have to die, this is as good a place as any." [24]

Hillman had something that good labor leaders usually need, a voice unusually deep, harsh, and resonant, that carried over the din. He spoke in English that was then poor enough, yet "a remarkable thing happened. He seemed to get the attention of the crowd. Soon those standing on chairs began to slide down. Within a few minutes quiet was restored." [25] His analysis of the Schaffner offer, done with great logic and persuasive power, showed that it constituted an en-tering wedge for the union. From that step they might proceed further and perhaps work out a victory for the other people. When he had finished he seemed to have that stormy crowd well in hand and re-ceived a long round of applause.

He had caught the eye of everyone there, including the courageous leader of the women workers, Miss Bessie Abramowitz.

She recalled afterward:

It was the first time I ever saw him. He spoke very well at that meet-ing, but my first impression, I must say, was *unfavorable* [laughing]. He was too prudent, too nice, and I felt suspicious of him then.[26]

The clothing workers had so often been deluded and misled that they scarcely knew whom to trust. But when Bessie Abramowitz soon afterward had occasion to meet and talk with Sidney Hillman she became convinced that he was a young man of the utmost integrity.

He had known how to master the crowd at that first meeting he addressed. But the majority of the strikers, voting by secret ballot at other halls, defeated the proposed agreement. The strike continued through December. Then another picket, Frank Nagrekis, was shot and killed, this time, as it happened, before the gates of the Hart, Schaffner and Marx plant. Again there was a great funeral procession; but this time the mourners were brutally attacked by the police.

Mr. Schaffner's conscience now permitted him to wait no longer. Over the protests of his associates, he brought forth, early in January 1911, a third and more palatable offer to the strikers, which eliminated the provisions for the dismissal of those who might have opened themselves to charges of violence. A committee of three, one member for the employers, one for the strikers, and a third to be chosen by both, was to arbitrate all grievances and wage demands. All were to return to work, without discrimination, within ten days of the signing of the agreement.

The Joint Strike Committee gave full approval to this third proposal, which was far more concrete than the earlier ones. After sixteen weeks the weary rank and file of 8,000 Hart, Schaffner and Marx workers seemed ready for peace. To have refused the offer would have meant sheer catastrophe. Yet the strike committee heard of more trouble at one of the mass meetings, and Hillman, who had emerged from the ranks as a young leader, was sent down again to help win ratification of the agreement.

Against him there was a bitter-end faction, including representatives of the Industrial Workers of the World (then showing strength in the Middle West), who opposed any plan of arbitration or collective bargaining that did not grant the closed shop. "A surging and excited throng of eleven nationalities shouted approval and dissent in many languages. Some of them had been misled by a fanatical religionist to take their oath on the crucifix never to accept the agreement which had been fairly and squarely negotiated by the chosen representatives of both sides." Then Hillman spoke, with an air of dedication, and declared: " . . . You shall not repudiate this agreement while I live." [27] The opposition speakers were given time to speak; Hillman and other union leaders answered them fairly. This time the majority were persuaded to ratify the terms of the proposed settlement, which went into effect as of January 14, 1911.

The rest of the clothing workers, more than 25,000 in number, to whom nothing had been offered, were for continuing the strike when the UGWA president, Rickert, decided to wind up the affair. On February 3, 1911, at a meeting of a small group of his own associates among the strike committee members, he suddenly called off the general strike, and this without consulting the representatives of any of the other organizations that had taken part in it or shared its costs. The great majority of the clothing workers, as Hillman related

. . . were forced to return to their old miserable conditions, through the back door; and happy were those who were taken back. Many who had participated in the 1910 strike were victimized for months afterward. They were forced to look for other employment and to wait until their record in the strike was forgotten.

As for the Hart, Schaffner workers, who trooped back in more hopeful mood, what had they won, after all? he asked himself. An uncertain agreement "not granting the workers recognition of their organization, but merely giving them an opportunity to have their complaints considered." [28] Everything would depend on the good faith of both parties and upon how the agreement was carried out.

It is significant that Sidney Hillman's initial role in the labor movement in America (in contrast with his action in Russia) was as an advocate of moderation. He stood against the "fanatics" and apart from the compromised UGWA officers, in the camp of the new, provisory leaders who had risen from the ranks: Sam Levin, Frank Rosenblum, Anzuino Marimpietri, and Bessie Abramowitz.

Marimpietri, a tall young fellow from northern Italy, and the idealistic Russian Jew, Sam Levin, both had taken a fancy to young Hillman. During the ten days of grace following the signing of the agreement, he helped shepherd the Hart, Schaffner employees back to their former jobs. On the last day he said to Marimpietri: "What now? Tomorrow you and I must go back to work or lose our jobs. What will become of these people? Who will be there to give them encouragement to build our union? If one of us can do it, this is our opportunity." He would gladly work for a bare subsistence, he said, if he could devote himself to organizing their new local. Marimpietri asked him how much he would need. "Ten dollars a week," said Hillman. The other man then vowed that he would see to it that Hillman had that if it came from his own pocket. A skilled craftsman, Marimpietri went back to his bench, while Hillman stayed out and was elected the first business agent of Local 39, the coat makers' local of the UGWA, at $10 a week and $1.00 for expenses.[29]

The terms of the agreement under which the Hart, Schaffner and Marx people returned to work were vague and incomplete. The small phalanx of unionists among them were alone in a great market of non-union shops. Yet partial or incomplete as was that 1911 arbitration agreement, it was the acorn out of which a mighty oak of a trade-union structure would grow. With his quick, analytical mind, the former rabbinical student of Kovno had seen the opportunities opening before them.

From his first experience of a large American labor conflict he had absorbed many lessons. The ineptitude of the "professional" AFL officials who had been unable to manage that great crowd had been carefully noted. The role of newspapers, of public opinion, of the more liberal or charitable citizens of Chicago had impressed itself on his mind. The psychology of a capitalist like Mr. Schaffner had also played its part in the affair. Finally, the courage of the ill-organized, ill-led clothing workers, poor immigrants that they were, had made the deepest impression of all. Could not these people go far someday under strong and honest guidance?

He and the other young leaders bent themselves to the task of building their little union out of almost nothing. A warm fellowship had arisen between the workers who had fought together. The group of new union members met in the evening twice a week, and this without being urged to do so by their national officers in New York. "The tailors are studying," one of them reported, "and when another strike comes another story will be written." [30]

Chapter Three

ARBITRATING

In January 1911, Sidney Hillman began to work as a trade-union officer; he was the full-time business agent of the newly formed Chicago local, No. 39, UGWA, having but a few hundred members to start with, and it was his job to strengthen his little organization by canvassing for members, educating them, gathering in their dues. In addition he was to be their representative or spokesman whenever any complaint or grievance arose, under the arbitration plan that Mr. Schaffner, in good faith, was establishing in his shops. It was the kind of work he had dreamed of for himself when he had refused an opportunity to enter the business of his uncle in England. His life, his "mission," was to be bound up with that of the workers among whom he had determinedly cast his lot. Of course nobody knew whether the union would last. His salary was wretched, yet he saw a future here. Full of eagerness and zeal, the young man hung about the gates of the Hart, Schaffner and Marx factory in the dead of winter, always carrying his union books and his little tin box with him, in order to buttonhole the workers and collect the dues of 15 cents weekly that would enable their local and its officers to survive.

Under the new system of arbitration put in force, the workers, or the "workers' representatives," were allowed to air grievances before the management. But when Hillman, in the company of a tailor who had some complaint, first entered the shop, the superintendent, Peth, bawled: "What the hell are you doing around here? Get out!" Hillman quietly left.

Arbitration, the practice of union-management co-operation and of peaceful collective bargaining, does not spring up by itself or by decree. It grows out of "the mutual will to understand, respect, and possibly even support the specific interests of the other side. . . ." It requires a deep change in the ingrained habits or traditions of thinking of two classes, almost a "revolutionary break with the past." [1]

The first agreement between Hart, Schaffner and Marx and its employees, dated March 13, 1911, was worked out by an arbitration committee of two men: Carl Meyer, the firm's attorney, and Clarence Darrow, lawyer for the union. (The neutral third man, chosen by both sides as chairman, had been unable to serve because of illness, and no replacement for him was agreed upon for more than a year.)

The essential terms of the agreement, which was to run for two years, provided: (1) for improvement of sanitary conditions in the shops and a regular dinner hour; (2) efforts to spread the work in the slack seasons; (3) an arbitration or adjustment machinery with a Board of Arbitration as the final court of appeal; (4) wage increases of 10 per cent for the tailors and 5 per cent for the cutters, and a minimum wage of five dollars a week for women and seven dollars for men; (5) a 54-hour week with time and a half for overtime.

Shortly after this agreement was approved, Joseph Schaffner appointed Professor Howard as full-time manager of the company's labor department, with authorization to investigate and rule on all complaints and abuses by foremen or workers, to represent the company before the Board of Arbitration, and negotiate for the company with the union.

However, all this was only on paper. The strikers, still bitter and suspicious, had come back to work in an "open shop" side by side with non-union people who had stayed at their jobs during the strike. The same managers and foremen who earlier would have no truck with any union proceeded to fire workers (especially union members) in the old way, for the slightest delinquencies. These old-time "autocrats" were furious at all the fussing over the grievances of common laborers and at the intrusion of "the professor." Howard's task, according to the head of the firm, was to act in a "disinterested way" to win the good will of the employees, to "prevent further strikes, and to translate ethical ideals of justice into practicable policies and programs." [2]

Very soon, however, Professor Howard found that he could not possibly manage such an assignment in a factory of 8,000 workers. In the early weeks trouble surged up on every hand. As Hillman recalled: "Those were hard days. Many a union member lost his job; and to lose a job in Hart, Schaffner and Marx, in the only place where union people worked, was tantamount to being barred from employment by all the other concerns in the city."

The domineering superintendent, Peth, and his foremen found many ways to show their dislike of the newfangled arbitration scheme. Groups of workers, in sections or shops, would retaliate by walking out in "flash strikes," for which the men's clothing industry had long been noted. Howard, beset by these troubles, went to the officers of the four union locals that had been organized at Hart, Schaffner's and appealed to them for their co-operation. That was how he first met young Hillman, who impressed him as "a fine young man, calm and clear-headed, very honest and responsible." [3]

Hillman had been driven to post himself about a block away from the entrance to the factory. Now, under the protective wing of Earl Howard, he worked his way back to the vestibule and even inside the shops, though Mr. Peth might glare at him murderously. For behind Howard stood Mr. Schaffner, who, on meeting the young union officer, also took a great liking to him. He had "a spirit of sweet reasonableness," it was said. On the one hand, he could show endless patience and ingenuity in explaining to his fellow workers the right and wrong of each situation. On the other hand, he could be most tenacious or aggressive in argument when convinced that justice lay on the side of an aggrieved employee. In his fledgling years as a union officer he exhibited the greatest devotion and pride in shepherding his little flock of needleworkers. Both Howard and Schaffner thought him "a unique and highly original character." [4] Soon the labor manager and the local agent were working together every day all over the shop, handling complaints of employees or the foremen's charges of incompetence.

Marimpietri relates that Hillman's visits "kept up the morale of the few members of the union—and in the beginning they were very few indeed." At least they felt themselves represented, if not by a shop chairman, which was forbidden, then by "an individual fellowworker," who communicated something of his hope and courage to the others.[5]

Howard was by no means a compliant agent of the unionists. But as Hillman worked with the labor manager and felt his way along, they gradually evolved the practical techniques of industrial arbitration— a phenomenon then relatively new in this country, certainly in its application to large-scale factory production.

Industrial arbitration was in the air around 1910–15, a time of fresh thinking on the great labor struggles. The idea of voluntary arbitration of industrial disputes dated back to the 1820s in England; the typographers' union in America had used a sort of court of arbitration in 1898. More recently a big strike of the International Ladies' Garment Workers in New York, beginning only two months before the uprising of the men's clothing workers in Chicago, had been settled on September 1, 1910, by an agreement incorporating an elaborate machinery of conciliation. Two noted lawyers, Louis D. Brandeis and Louis Marshall, had volunteered their services as peacemakers in the New York strike, working out the plan which was to be known as "The Protocol of Peace." (Mr. Marshall, it is said, had concocted this phrase on observing that the union men hated the very word "arbitration.") News of this remarkable arrangement for the continuous adjustment of labor disputes in the much-disrupted women's garment trade of New York stimulated the Chicago clothing workers and Mr. Schaffner to try the same scheme, though under quite different provisions. But in New York, after several years of experimentation, the whole plan was to break down eventually. In Chicago the system of arbitration, or "industrial self-government," as Hillman called it, was made to work. This pioneering experiment, with its great promise of industrial peace, was to win nationwide fame as the "Hart, Schaffner and Marx Plan"; its lessons and its gains were to be passed on to all the industry and to the American labor movement as a whole. By all accounts it was the young Hillman who made the largest contribution to the practical success of the plan.

At first the difficulties had seemed insuperable. For about a year little progress was made in eliminating those brief, unauthorized "stoppages" in different departments that seemed to come about once a week. Earl Howard relates:

I used to go about in the shops whenever there was a strike and make a speech to them and describe the agreement. Mr. Hillman used to do so too, and we had to instruct the people that this really meant a new way of adjusting grievances. The old way was the only way they knew.[6]

The headaches of arbitration after a while proved too much for the busy Clarence Darrow; his partner, William O. Thompson, who took his place, had to stop practicing law in order to handle all the complaints that came up every day.[7]

Many disputes arose over the lack of uniformity in piece-rate payments. The company, in changing its methods of operation or introducing new machinery, would draw up specifications for new piece rates which sometimes lowered workers' earnings. Though this would be met with an immediate challenge, the workers were forced to wait for arbitration to decide the issue. Their discontent grew again, until in March 1912, following long and tense conferences between representatives of both sides—during which it was feared the whole plan might collapse—the rules laid down a year before were revised, and a Trade Board was set up as a sort of lower council to adjust disputes and fix prices in the shops with greater promptness, for the Board of Arbitration, still having only two men, was swamped with 800 cases of complaint in its first year.

The distinguished social worker and churchman, Dr. James Mullenbach, who had come to the defense of the strikers in 1910, acted as chairman of the Trade Board, which was composed of ten persons of "practical experience," the membership being divided evenly between management and labor. In effect, Hillman and Earl Howard, who served as chief deputies for either side on the Board, constituted themselves as a "commission form of government"; instead of waiting for the ten to sit and argue everything out, these two went into the shops to settle all difficulties on the spot whenever possible. Mahomet, as Hillman said, went to the mountain. He added: "For arbitration to be effective it must be a speedy arbitration." Only when agreement could not be reached quickly, which happened infrequently, was the case sent up to the Trade Board. Only in about one out of a hundred cases was it necessary to appeal thereafter to the final Board of Arbitration. As Hillman explained in the testimony he gave on this plan before the United States Industrial Commission at Washington in 1914:

This Trade Board . . . was really a new method of adjusting complaints—and that is an adjustment by the workers themselves. *It introduces really what I call the new principle . . . that if the workers are to be disciplined for any violation of the agreement, they themselves should partly be the judges.*[8]

It was for the most part questions of rates, prices, delinquency, or abuse that were handled on the spot by Hillman and Howard. The two men, after negotiating with each other every day, tended to follow those procedures for reaching agreement which had worked previously. Thus out of their experience and the precedents they established, as Howard has related, there was "an organic growth of a body of law," a sort of living constitution providing for representative government in the factories where thousands of men and women spent the best part of their lives. It was a long step toward the "recognition of human rights in the shops," as Hillman felt. "Industrial democracy" was no mere phrase but a matter of supreme importance for the everyday life, the food and shelter of the workers.

After the original agreement of March 1911 had been revised, the arbitration plan operated with great fairness. The company's able lawyer, Carl Meyer, turned out to be a man of very broad views whom Sidney Hillman greatly esteemed. William O. Thompson, now counsel for the union, held strongly pro-labor views. He too became deeply attached to the young Hillman and, a man of independent fortune, served the Chicago union without fee for long years. Earl Howard could be very stubborn at times, especially when the management side, which he represented, pressed him to be so. Yet he too came to see what Hillman urged, that the growing responsibility of the union in the shop, its increasing strength, was the key to the success of the whole plan for peace in industry. And behind these people there stood always Joseph Schaffner, who seemed determined to make arbitration work, whatever the cost, and however bitterly his managers complained of the great bother it caused them. These, together with the gentle and wise Dr. Mullenbach, made up a remarkable group of Chicago characters of the old liberal school.

But in the autumn of 1912 the two-man Board of Arbitration at the top of the system, which had managed skillfully thus far, ran into difficulties when there was a prolonged deadlock over the dismissal of a worker, which the union group held was an affair of anti-union discrimination. It was now seen that a third or neutral member of the

Board of Arbitration was needed in order to have the top, policy-making Board function better. A man acceptable to both sides was sought; and the name of John E. Williams of Streator, Illinois, was favorably mentioned. Williams was a former coal miner who had won a reputation as the editor of a country newspaper and as an industrial arbitrator, since 1910, for the United Mine Workers and the Illinois coal operators' association.

Sidney Hillman went down to Streator to investigate him before the union would approve of his appointment, for Williams was to be the salaried member of the Board, and both sides were to share his modest fees. He turned out to be a man of "Lincolnesque character," then in his early sixties, living with his wife in a small two-room workingman's cottage in Streator, where he hoped he would always reside. He was self-educated and widely read, a sort of provincial philosopher of the Midwestern mining region who was ardently devoted to the labor movement which he had served well in his youth. He was, moreover, profoundly religious, a leader of the Unitarian Church in Illinois, and described by his townspeople as "incorruptible." Three years earlier, at the time of the great Cherry Mine disaster, he had undertaken, at his own cost, a long and difficult legal suit in behalf of 500 women and children left destitute by that catastrophe and eventually won a large settlement for the dead miners' people. Sidney Hillman liked what he saw and heard of the man and returned to urge his acceptance by his union colleagues and by Mr. Shaffner. Neither side ever had occasion to regret their decision.

John E. Williams, a well-spoken man, was the theorist and philosopher of labor arbitration in its early years and proved to be the most remarkable of the group that made the Hart, Schaffner and Marx Plan an effective instrument. As he worked closely with Sidney Hillman for years, the two men became warm friends. The older man, with his experience, his generosity, and his Christian idealism, may be said to have had a large influence in forming the young labor leader's mind and also in giving it, early in his career, a distinctly American direction.[9]

With the addition of Mr. Williams in the role of Impartial Chairman (as he was called) of the Board of Arbitration, the Plan was more or less complete, and stood, with the exception of minor changes, essentially as it stands today, forty years later. Williams, it must be noted, was not expected to be an aloof judge between the contesting parties, but a sort of professional adjuster, working constantly to make the system effective, gathering knowledge of details and of rates or prices as he went along, and helping both groups to serve each other's real interests. He became in effect the pivotal man in the higher Board, since the pro-union and pro-employer men who sat beside him tended to cancel each other off. With his naturally judicial and measured spirit, he was the model of the successful Impartial Chairman, whose work was to be imitated, in future years, in many other industries.

Sidney Hillman never wrote, as many hoped he would, of his share in the pioneering of the arbitration scheme. But he told Mr. George Soule, an earlier biographer, that he regarded the device of the Impartial Chairmanship as the "focal point" of an arrangement for permanent collective bargaining. He would insist on adopting this device in every subsequent agreement he reached as a labor leader. Only enforcement by a continuous adjustment machinery could make an agreement workable; without it, all the hard-won provisions might be gradually whittled away.

On the other hand, as the Hart, Schaffner and Marx Plan continued to operate successfully, it proved highly advantageous for the manufacturers; it eliminated stoppages and strikes and helped to raise efficiency. This development aroused nationwide interest, and the Plan was made famous by hundreds of newspaper and magazine articles during the decade after 1914.[10]

Hillman showed himself a tireless negotiator. According to Howard, he had one disarming approach: "Isn't there some way we could work things out so that it would be good for both parties?" With Professor Howard and Mr. Schaffner, Hillman took the line that, in the first place, it would "pay" them to deal with the union, and secondly that he could assure them that the union would be *responsible* in carrying out its agreements. Nonetheless, to the company representatives he seemed always the shrewd and tenacious negotiator, while to his more militant union brothers, who disliked the idea of arbitration and held that nothing could be gained without the closed shop, he seemed all too yielding and too much the "compromiser."

Hillman has made it plain that he and the other union officers had a great deal to learn about the business of Hart, Schaffner and Marx —"We had to learn the details of management within our own ranks," he said—in order to understand the real problems the employer faced. This was, in Marxian parlance, "class collaboration."

"Of course we *collaborated*," Earl Howard says; but the labor manager for the firm also notes that this "collaboration" was "a very deliberate, calculated thing with Hillman, who never deceived himself about the capitalist ideology." [11] Events soon showed that Sidney Hillman, no mere opportunist, could take the offensive whenever the situation required, with a pugnacity that none would have suspected in such a well-mannered young man.

II

Their union in Chicago, "like all great things started small," as their staunch friend, John Fitzpatrick, said in recollection of its early days. Hillman, Sam Levin, Frank Rosenblum, Anzuino Marimpietri, and their companions "worked and dreamed of the organization of the clothing workers." [12] Their first three locals at Hart, Schaffner and Marx had such a small membership that the numbers were kept a dark secret. Jacob Potofsky, then a young pants maker, recalls that his own local, whose business agent was Bessie Abramowitz, had for its office a room on the top floor of an old house on Blue Island Avenue, at Twelfth Street, with one broken chair, a battered desk, and no funds for equipment.

The lack of numbers was offset by their youth and ardor. Hillman worked indefatigably all day long adjusting grievances; at night he conducted organizing meetings, often speaking at three or more meeting places each night. These tireless exertions steadily swelled the membership.[13]

"We were poor, romantic young dreamers," Mrs. Bessie Hillman recalls. "When we borrowed $250 for our locals from Mr. John E. Williams, who was not rich, it took us five years to pay it off." [14]

Yet, thanks to Hillman, the coat makers' local, No. 39, developed into the largest local. The cutters of Local 61 also formed a core of strength, since they were the key men in the production line. It is significant that this group of craftsmen, though enjoying a large advantage in wages over the other workers, now devoted themselves to bringing the unskilled and poorly paid groups in their industry into a broad mass organization. The sweating of the unskilled workers, they realized, kept the whole industry in a state of chaos. Even at Hart, Schaffner's, though some departments were largely unionized, most of the others were non-union, which added to their problems.

Marimpietri explains also the difficulties of race and language they encountered. He would be at his bench during the dinner hour, talking about the organization plans with fourteen workers around him

. . . comprising ten different nationalities. There were two Italians, a girl by the name of Angelina and myself, two Jewish boys, Bennie and Gordon, two Croatians, Mike and Frank, two Swedish girls, Ella and Lillie, one Slavic boy, Martin, one Bohemian girl, Maggie, one French widow . . . one Lithuanian man . . . one Russian fellow . . . and a Polish girl. . . . We developed friendship of a sort. . . . We used to sing together, each of us a song in his own tongue, but every now and then a sentiment, not very complimentary, was expressed showing plainly that the national feeling was ever present and needed only a spark to make it flame.

This confusion of races the management now exploited; but perhaps, Marimpietri reflected, their union would be the "melting pot" that would someday fuse them all together.[15]

Hillman was entirely wrapped up in his plans for developing the organization. Like many persons of an analytical temperament, he would be absent-minded about small things. Lost in thought, he would go out in the rain without an overcoat, or forget that he had taken nothing but some bread and a cup of tea all day. He would even forget to cash his small salary check at times, as young "Jack" Potofsky, who became the secretary of his local, would discover when the difference appeared in their bank account. And when the exalted young man found himself with a little cash he might give it away to the firstcomer who seemed poorer than himself.

"We all worked terribly hard over our Hart, Schaffner locals," Potofsky relates. "Evenings I would walk about Chicago with Hillman, talking over our plans and hopes. We would pass the great factories near Halsted Street . . . saying to ourselves: 'Ah, if we could only organize Kuppenheimer, or Alfred, Decker and Cohn!' Their walls loomed over us, terribly high, seeming impregnable to attack." [16]

Hillman constantly, in those days, stressed the need for idealism and sacrifice on the part of the union's founders. The best organizers, he would say, were those who brought in hundreds of new members without being paid for it. "I am convinced," he wrote to a friend in 1914, "that the people who make these sacrifices are the only people who should remain in the business." But the sort who "look for jobs and politics" should be kept out.

Of his exhausting struggles at this period he wrote: ". . . The more I go through these things the more I feel that it is the only thing worth while."

When he spoke before his union members, "his people," many of them ardent Socialists, he sounded quite different from the polite character who sat at conferences with the manufacturers' lawyers. As his English improved, he displayed natural powers as a speaker. Though he did not care to use "high-sounding phrases," he would talk with a close-gripping logic that always absorbed his hearers. In his thinking he showed an ability to "distinguish quickly between the important and the unimportant, the essential and the unessential."

He had a "deep feeling" for the labor movement, his associates recall. He would say again and again that the workers' goal, which they must never lose sight of, was "labor power." His convictions about the rights of labor had a crusading fervor:

After all the toilers are always right. Even when they are wrong they are right. The capitalists have everything and they have nothing but the power of labor.

The capitalists make thousands or millions, as profit and surplus—why should not the workers be entitled to a few pennies? [17]

And yet how bitterly some of those wealthy employers fought to avoid paying five cents more a day—"five cents more a day to a poor button sewer!" he would exclaim derisively. And Hillman would fight like a lion to win that five cents from them.

But when he treated with an employer, he believed, like a famous politico of that era, that "one should speak softly and carry a big stick." Some labor leaders liked to talk tough. The young Hillman was soft-spoken, had a warm and pleasing manner, but gave a sense of inward strength and self-command. Modest, unimpressive at first glance, he "grew on people," it was said.

It was Hillman's good fortune, after but a short period in Chicago, to fall in amongst a remarkable circle of native Americans who were liberal churchmen, social workers, and progressives, constituting the Better Element in the industrial "jungle" that Upton Sinclair had called Chicago. To such persons Hillman, as the "idealistic young Jew," made great appeal, for in his young manhood he was very sensitive and ascetic-looking. Indeed, it has sometimes been a matter for jesting comment that he became somewhat "the darling of the social workers."

Legends were circulated that touched upon his uncommon integrity. Early in their association, Professor Howard, desiring to talk with Hillman in confidence, invited him to lunch at the elegant Blackstone Hotel. Hillman, on grounds of principle, politely declined, but led Howard to a cheap eating place on some side street where he paid for his own frugal meal.

Jane Addams saw him as a zealous, yet long-headed labor leader, and judged that he would go far someday. For many years Miss Addams held a considerable sway over his mind.

She was then fond of citing John Stuart Mill on the distinction between those who, being dissatisfied with things as they are, think only of radical change or "ultimate aims," and those others who, though equally discontented, work mainly in the region of the "immediately useful and practically attainable." The latter were *trade unionists*. She defended and succored the workers who were embroiled in strikes. But Hillman often heard her express her deep regret at "the cruelty and waste of the strike as an implement for securing the reasonable demands of the workers"—words he himself often repeated. Men spoke much nowadays of the scientific management of industry, of "Taylorization"—must they continue to fight like beasts of prey? Was there not some better method, the way of arbitration, the Hart, Schaffner and Marx Plan, in short?

Among Miss Addams' associates were Ellen Gates Starr, a young society woman who often joined the needleworkers' picket lines; also Mrs. Margaret D. Robins, wife of Colonel Raymond Robins and head of the Women's Trade Union League, who was a staunch ally of Sidney Hillman, Bessie Abramowitz, and the other clothing workers. From association with these accomplished ladies, who were often consulted on the workings of the Hart, Schaffner and Marx Plan, Hillman acquired some polish.

In Miss Addams' circle Hillman came under influences that were "conservative" in the best sense; namely, that the intention was to conserve—instead of waste—human lives and man-made wealth and labor, so that the present order of things might, with improvements, function all the better.

On the other hand, the idea of industrial unionism, as will be seen presently, representing a radical reform of the existing craft-union structure, was much to the fore in the period from 1910 to 1919. It held a powerful attraction for Hillman as for his young associates in the Chicago union, and fired all their hopes. Thus, it would be fair to say that he came under the influence of both radical and conservative ideas at this time.

Other friends whom he frequented at this period were Clarence Darrow, the unpredictable "philosophical anarchist," who was the hero of so many spectacular court battles for justice for the underdog; William Thompson; and Joseph Schaffner himself, who said that he learned much from his talks with the young man. These older men were, in a sense, his teachers. "Each day under their tutelage the quick-witted Hillman made noticeable progress in his English speech. New words or expressions heard at an arbitration conference or private conversation were quickly adopted by him and always well placed." He was not, by nature, a linguist, and his Russian-Jewish accent, as he was sadly aware, clung to him persistently. But he became adept at "putting over an idea"; his talk was pungent and reflected the originality of his mind. "Often, on hearing him, one would come across phrases that had unconscious beauty and balance." [18]

He loved people and had a gift for friendship. But the "older brother" whom he most admired at this time and who (like Dr. Matis in Kovno, years before) had the strongest influence over him was John E. Williams.

This former coal miner, whom they called "The Great Mediator" at Hart, Schaffner's, had rare gifts of wisdom, tact, and psychological finesse; also a real eloquence in speaking and writing. He was an inspiration to Sidney Hillman and his union brothers, communicating to them his own convictions of the high moral values implicit in the labor movement. With deep pride he would describe his earlier years among the coal miners and his work in their great union, the United Mine Workers. His real education, which he held to have been "finer than any college career," had begun in the eager, high-spirited discussions of the miners down in their underground rooms, dimly lit by miners' lamps. The labor movement was his religion. He would say:

Trade unionism is the greatest educational force that we have. It is through their unions that men become intelligent in the things they need to know most. It is the best school of ethics that we have. Even at its worst, it compels one man to subordinate his individual greed to the interests of the group.[19]

A keen student of trade-union tactics, he knew that "the first thing a labor union seeks is power, which is never 'bestowed' but must be 'taken.'" But after power came responsibility, he insisted. As to systems of mediation, he held frankly that they could not be made successful or permanent unless there was a responsible union in the picture; and no union could be responsible unless it was strong.

When expounding his own philosophy of arbitration, he would maintain that an arbitrator

has to be a thorough believer in unionism. In that sense he is not at all disinterested or impartial. He must see to it that his decisions and the measures he takes are calculated to strengthen the organization, and make it, as such, more efficient. . . . Because we need a strong union to enforce the decisions. A weak union, or a man who is at the head of a lot of guerrillas, is unable to make the undisciplined workers do what they do not want to do.[20]

These views Williams candidly explained to the employers before accepting his appointment.

Hillman thought he was a rare soul of "mature views," with a "deep faith in the mass of people, a belief in democracy." He wanted labor to wield greater power "constructively and unselfishly." For "labor too must be educated," he said. Working every day as a professional adjuster—for he believed that mediation must be prompt and constant, rather than intermittent, in order to be most effective—Williams became the key figure in the Hart, Schaffner and Marx labor situation. His contributions to the lore of labor-management relations were of the highest importance. They were never forgotten by those who worked beside him.

In the winter of 1912–13, as Williams arrived on the scene, the company and the union people had reached an absolute deadlock over two issues in dispute. A new material for binding buttonholes (gimp-cord) had been introduced and the workers claimed it made for more work and lower earnings. Hillman firmly demanded a higher piece rate, which the company as firmly refused. Williams now showed his mettle by appealing to "the will to agree" in both parties and persuading them to set up a joint price-adjusting machinery, which was in itself a unique device, later widely adopted in the trade. The result was that the buttonhole sewers earned as much or more than before, and the company was also satisfied.

The other case in dispute was much more difficult of solution. It arose from the discharge of a man named Greenspan, very popular among the workers, who had been accused of some wrongdoing by his foreman. The Trade Board, or "lower council," had approved of his dismissal after hearing the evidence; but Hillman, who had been "reasonable" in other such cases, this time demanded the reinstatement of Greenspan and back pay. He explained:

. . . Behind the discharge of Greenspan the union saw an attack on its prestige and an attempt to demoralize its ranks. The power of organization itself was at stake and . . . no compromise could meet such a situation. The firm, on the other hand, felt that to back down and not give its unlimited support to the foreman who had discharged Greenspan, against whom, the union claimed, evidence had been framed, would destroy discipline in the shops and would make proper management impossible.

Williams' strategy was to interpret to each side where its real interest lay and so find a common ground upon which they could terminate the dispute. The case had been fought for long months and the threat of a costly strike was always present. At length the man was reinstated and given back pay. Abstract justice might have ruled the other way; Williams persuaded Mr. Schaffner that this would have weakened the union seriously. Either no union at all, he advised, or a real union. The favorable settlement of this case made a deep impression on those workers in the shops who had hitherto avoided union membership.[21]

The breadth of vision shown by the Impartial Chairman gave new heart to the young union leaders. Their arbitration scheme was working, despite friction and despite the ill-concealed hostility of the plant managers. Hillman now came and told Williams that the spirit of the rank-and-file members was rising strongly. The "actual work of unionism," day by day, was having a surprisingly "educational effect," he said now, just as Mr. Williams had predicted. Even the meetings of the shop chairmen were becoming "inspiring." These people had formerly thought of nothing but their pay; now they were beginning to believe that they had "a cause that enthuses them like a religion. . . . They make sacrifices for it, they will not only fight for it, but will work for it—which is a severer test."

Williams, for his part, had never before known many of the recent immigrants from Eastern Europe, Russia, and Italy. Having read much adverse opinion of these recent arrivals, he was surprised by the combination of character they suggested: a fusion of ardent idealism, mental alertness, and self-discipline. With endless patience they worked over the regulation of all sorts of wearisome details; questions of shop standards, of quality, of piecework prices, of workers' discipline were their daily fare. And Williams himself had seen how the attractive young brunette, Miss Bessie Abramowitz, as a local officer, "quietly sacrificed her two-dollar opera ticket one Saturday afternoon to attend an unexpected arbitration meeting." Doubtless she would sacrifice her life too, if need be, for their union, he reflected. And no less ardent and self-denying were men like Sam Levin, also a refugee from revolution-ridden Russia, the chief deputy of the cutters, who was then Sidney Hillman's closest friend. Here one had, as Williams wrote, "a living demonstration of the fact that there are people who believe in things that are better than money-making, and are devoting their lives to them." [22]

III

The agreement of 1911 approached its term on April 1, 1913, when it would be brought up for renewal. Everyone involved wondered what would happen next. The leaders of the small band of organized clothing workers in Chicago felt that they must advance, must win new advantages. Arbitration was not enough, the radicals in the union were shouting. Some of them were saying that unless the closed shop was won even this friendly firm of Hart, Schaffner and Marx, where they were still in a minority, could not be held for the union in the long run. But if their demand for the closed shop brought on a strike, could they win?

Hillman relates that early in 1913

. . . We met in the little office at Hod Carriers' Hall or at 317 Quincy Street, the headquarters of the cutters' local 61, and it appeared as if the organization would not be able to weather the storms which arose from time to time. Was it possible for a small group of organized workers surrounded by open shops to work out its own destiny? The answer to that was definitely: no. The organization could survive only if it could make headway, To stand still would be merely to await patiently our annihilation.[23]

A secret vote was taken on the proposition that an exclusively union shop, the closed shop, be established at Hart, Schaffner's in the name of the Chicago District Council of the UGWA—as a result of which Hillman was authorized to call a strike if this was denied.

At a conference with the heads of the firm Hillman then presented the workers' demands, including a reduction of hours and increased wages. But this was only preliminary to the principal demand, which read: "All workers must be members in good standing of the United Garment Workers' Union, and new employees must join the union within two weeks after employment." In making this demand he was impassive and gravely pointed to his pocket, saying that he carried there the "loaded gun" of a strike vote. All but a few hundred of the 8,000 workers, he warned his hearers, favored a strike unless the closed shop was granted. He spoke with the secret knowledge that the Chicago union had actually a membership of only 2,592 regular dues-paying members at this stage, and that 30,000 non-union people could be drawn upon by the firm elsewhere in Chicago if a strike was called. In short, it would need a miracle, at least a huge bluff, to win out.

Thus they came to the verge of war. No explicit mention had been made up to now of there being a *union* in the picture, though in fact the working of the adjustment machinery had already allowed for the activity of shop chairmen as regular representatives of the workers. Mr. Schaffner and Earl Howard were disappointed in and even much vexed at the formerly "moderate" Hillman, who now seemed to set his face like flint against all compromise of the principal point at issue. With great effort John E. Williams persuaded both parties to postpone action temporarily and work under the old agreement for two months longer.

Meanwhile Hillman had informed himself about an alternate plan for the closed shop, the so-called "preferential union shop," which had been introduced in New York in 1910 by Louis D. Brandeis when he had helped in the settlement of the Ladies' Garment Workers' strike. By this system the employer would give *preference* to union men in the hiring or discharge of workers, while reserving also the right to hire non-union men in addition during a busy season when there weren't enough union men available.

Hillman discussed such a proposal at a meeting with the leaders of the union's Joint Board, urging that the alternate plan would result, in a brief period of time, in more or less complete union control of the job. After gaining their provisory assent he decided to put out some feelers for the new compromise plan and spoke privately to Williams about it. The Impartial Chairman, in his correct and judicious way, although refraining from any decisive statement, intimated that the alternative plan might have merits. But Hillman sensed that he liked it and when the occasion arose would recommend it to Schaffner and Howard.

Soon thereafter, during the interval when they were preparing to resume their conference on renewing the old contract, Howard asked Hillman to meet him privately. As Howard recalled later, Hillman began by saying that the men wanted "a real union" and would take nothing less. Summarizing the position, Howard admitted that the plant manager, Peth, was spoiling for a fight in order to get rid of the union; and that Mr. Schaffner, for his part, would never accept a contract for the closed shop. Howard ended by appealing to Hillman to help him "settle this thing by working out some new rules that would avoid another terrible strike." He now brought out a memorandum outlining the plan for a "preferential" shop. Hillman studied it with a straight face, knowing that Williams had communicated his original suggestion, and finally said he might consider it if the union members could be made to accept the idea. In the meantime they both agreed "to support each other" and, if they could settle things in no other way, leave the final decision to Williams.[24]

The final conference was called by Williams in May, with about twenty persons, representing both sides, participating. His own written account of the affair gives the full flavor of his thinking as an Impartial Chairman:

I found the "closed shop" to be practically the sole issue, and on this both sides seemed to be adamant. To the employers the phrase seemed like a red rag; to the workers it looked like a star-spangled banner of liberty. . . .

My first effort was to divest this "closed shop" of its emotional and oratorical content and bring it down to earth.

"Why do you object to the 'closed shop'?" I asked the employers, and I found that . . . they thought it un-American. But pressing further, I found a more concrete objection, namely, that the union was not strong enough in Chicago to furnish them with the needed help.

Turning to the union leaders, I asked the question: "Aside from union sentiment, what practical advantage will the 'closed shop' give you that you cannot get without it?"

Without exception each answered that he wanted it to prevent the company from discriminating against the union men. Although the company had been working with the union for two years, the leaders still seemed to feel that the company was against the union and would destroy it if it could.

Williams again called on the heads of the company and asked them to give full assurance that they "harbored no secret designs against the union." Now, since Williams had shown that no real difference existed between the two parties, it was up to them to find a way of avoiding warfare for the sake of "a mere sentiment, a flag, a battle-cry, and not a real grievance." He then proposed the alternative plan of the preferential shop, which overcame the objections both parties had raised, ending discrimination on the one hand and safeguarding the employer against a shortage of help in busy seasons on the other. After lengthy discussion this plan was accepted, and both sides eventually seemed well pleased with the solution.[25]

Hillman had guessed all along that Williams would throw his influence toward the preferential shop. ("Hillman often got the better of us in a bargain," Howard said in later years.) Now he had only to win over his union membership at a mass meeting held to discuss the plan.

In the debate on that occasion tempers ran high. Very much present were the union's radicals, who assailed Hillman for his apparent compromise on the closed-shop issue. Some of the union's rank-and-file leaders sincerely believed that arbitration itself would never work. One of the ablest of these used to say: "I for one will always register myself against arbitration on principle." *

In a word battle that ran far into the night, their young leader pleaded that his brother workers should grasp at the substance of labor power and forget the form. With all his customary earnestness

---

* The president of the Brotherhood of Railroad Trainmen at this time publicly expressed the objections of his union members to plans of arbitration provided under the Newlands Act—though good results were noticed several years after the Hart, Schaffner and Marx Plan was inaugurated in 1911.

of speech he entreated them to believe that this new agreement for a preferential shop would also bring that which they desired above all, real union control of the job. But there were people who kept crying for the closed shop. Mere words, words, to Hillman. He said in effect that the closed shop, like the rose, "By any other name would smell as sweet."

They would have their closed shop too, he predicted. In the end his logic prevailed.

"We radicals learned a lot from him," one of his followers said not long after this. "When we tried to prevent Hillman from speaking he always won our respect, so that we had to hear and agree with him. When we were hotheaded, he always kept us back; when we were asleep, he waked us up." [26]

The all-important agreement which signalized the success of the two-year-old Hart, Schaffner and Marx Plan was approved by the union and adopted as of March 29, 1913, to run for three years. *

Overnight, remarkable things happened in consequence. Shortly after the announcement that union members would receive preference as to employment, the overwhelming majority of the workers at Hart, Schaffner's were induced to sign union pledges, and the organization more than tripled in size, reaching a membership of 8,900 in Chicago by the end of the year. For those early days of trade unionism it was a brilliant coup, the more so as it was executed without fighting and starving, and without bloodshed.

Joseph Schaffner, no fool, had foreseen that the new agreement might bring complete unionization of his shops. It meant also the nuisance of dealing with the system of "workers' self-government." But he trusted Sidney Hillman. During a period of recurrent labor disorders in the men's clothing market, Hart, Schaffner and Marx worked their 8,000 to 9,000 employees full blast. Their people, now all good union men, were virtually "locked in" at this one pro-union house by the blacklist system used against union men elsewhere. They worked all the harder, and even took pride in being employed by a company whose benevolent labor plan won it fame throughout the country.

* The plan, not always successful elsewhere, worked under severe restrictions at first, with many non-union men still being hired from the open market. But as the union saw to it that its men were always available and given "preference," the shops became "closed" in effect.

Hillman said that the establishment of a painstaking system of arbitration and true collective bargaining filled a great void in the life of industrial America:

I believe there is such a change that really it cannot be explained. *The people really felt themselves a little more like men and women. Before there was not a feeling like that in any non-union shop. Contrary to any statement by people who defend the open shop, I do not believe it is possible to have the full feeling of manhood.* [Italics added.] [27]

IV

These innovations in a small sector of the great labor market of Chicago were, to the outside view, unspectacular on the whole. Peace wins no headlines, though its problems take more thought than war. Shop chairmen and "price committees" toiled away at the routine tasks of adjusting rates and wages, constantly changing, in this very intricate industry.

Gradually the legend of Chief Deputy Hillman—aged twenty-six, still an underpaid, threadbare union officer—as one destined to be a sort of "statesman of labor," grew up in Chicago.

Mr. Schaffner would have liked to put him in charge of his entire business. He once said to Williams:

That man Hillman is a wonderful genius. If he only had been educated in the English language, what a speaker, what a writer he would have made! There's no height he wouldn't have reached. Even at that he's a wonder, and beyond his supreme talent in leading men he has a quality that is even more remarkable. That is his absolute integrity. He is the squarest labor leader I have ever known.[28]

As Impartial Chairman, Williams had seen Hillman pitting himself against shrewd men of business who were two or three times his age, and yet taking them into camp regularly. Earl Howard describes him as a "good listener," who always spoke slowly and deliberately, always courteous, never in heat.

He had a profound sense of realities. Big employers confronting him seemed shortsighted by comparison. They would see only the immediate "profit-picture" rather than the long-run advantage. Hillman would guess quickly enough what these men would be willing to pay in return for the responsible pledge of uninterrupted production for the present moment, and so would wring the best price he could get.[29]

But later on, he would come back and ask for more. The preferential shop proved to be a Trojan horse quietly introducing union job control in the factory. The employers heard from him no threats or bombastic speeches about the "downtrodden toilers," but only the quiet assurance that he could make a proposed union agreement *pay* for them. He spoke in the language they understood, the American language of practical business.

It was strange how the former agitator for a popular revolution in Russia had, in a few short years in Chicago, become wholly *Americanized,* and in a most admirable way. The ideas, plans, ambitions that formed themselves in his mind were shaped by a close observation of purely American conditions, under the special environment of a typically mid-American industrial city. Here, among Wilsonian liberals and philanthropic capitalists, his concept of industrial democracy, his ideas of the trade-union movement, his opportunistic strategy were molded. Yet his union associates saw how persistently, how imaginatively he pursued his *Fabian* tactics step by step, until their little union rabble, of which he had naturally assumed command, had grown to be a sturdy labor bloc, about a fourth of the membership of the old United Garment Workers' Union. Now the unfolding pattern of his immense ambitions for their union or for himself as strategist of labor advance could be glimpsed a little.

At about this period one of his young assistants, who preserved notes of conversations with Hillman, wrote: "It is remarkable how little the early influences affected his future life. Only the Talmudic habit of mind, of looking at all angles of a question, remained." The "Talmudic mind" was, of course, much like the "Socratic" mind of J. E. Williams, for example, and sought always, through the analysis and comparison of surface appearances, to penetrate to the underlying realities of a situation.

The diarist continues:

A gifted leader is one who is capable of touching your heart. Hillman is such a leader. He is capable of understanding and seeing through you and quickly grasping a problem in all its contingencies.[30]

Around Sidney Hillman there was a group of quite remarkable, high-willed young union leaders. "They tended at first to speak to the plant managers at the top of their voices when they had some complaint. Hillman taught them to listen and speak quietly." [31] They were to blend "aggressiveness and militancy with responsibility," he urged. He was the indefatigable teacher of the older men as of the very young, such as the nineteen-year-old Potofsky, whom he counseled to stay and "grow up" with the labor movement rather than seek another path, saying: "After all, this is the most interesting." [32]

After the successful negotiation of the agreement of March 1913 he looked ahead to new fields and gave notice of this. In April the Chicago union gave a little banquet in honor of their lawyer, William O. Thompson, who was leaving for Washington to assume the newly created post of Commissioner of Industrial Relations, under the Wilson Administration. (It was before his commission that Hillman, Williams, and Howard and others were invited to give their valuable testimony on labor conditions of that time.) Among the guests were Louis F. Post, Assistant Secretary of Labor, Mrs. Raymond Robins, the union officers Hillman, Marimpietri, Sam Levin, and others.

Only two years before they had been starving; now they could afford not only a meal ticket, but a banquet. It was all symptomatic of the change that had come over them since those days of mad struggle in 1910, as one of those present reflected. "As we talked to one another at the table and as we listened to the speakers that night, it was not only among the leaders . . . but among the rank and file that there was a new spirit at work."

Hillman struck the keynote of the evening when he reminded his listeners who had gained so much through organization "that neither their work nor their duty ends there. In justice to themselves and to their fellow workers in other factories . . . they must devote their efforts to extending the benefits of organization to *all* the garment workers of America." [33]

Scarcely 20 per cent of the needle-trade workers in the country were organized at the time he spoke.

At a period of widespread labor unrest, in 1913–14—when the "red peril" in the form of the IWW was rising—a great number of articles by liberal journalists such as George Creel, Ray Stannard Baker, and others appeared in the press on the Hart, Schaffner and Marx Plan for industrial peace. John E. Williams also wrote an article on the same subject for his local newspaper, the Streator *Independent-Times,* in June 1913, which was soon after reprinted in *The Survey,* published in New York. Because of his unusual experience in Chicago with recent foreign immigrants (at a time when there was much agitation for closing the door on them) he chose to make his article also a plea for understanding the Jews and entitled it: "The Russian Jew in American Industry."

Like many liberal Americans of that era, Williams, one might have said, was "philo-Semitic." He had met every day in the flesh the heroes of Israel Zangwill's *The Melting Pot* and Mary Antin's *The Promised Land,* and declared himself "profoundly impressed." The Russian Jew, though "dreaded in some quarters," he predicted "will make the richest intellectual contribution to American life of any of the incoming tribes, and especially . . . in the world of labor." Of the people he had met in the Chicago clothing trade, he said:

It is really amazing to see the adaptability of these people, their genius in all problems of human relations, their largeness of grasp, their keenness of intellect, and above all, their responsiveness to ethical ideals.

Here are people who until six or seven years ago lived in a country . . . in which trades organizations were unheard of. They come here, enter an enormously complicated industry, and in a short time rise to the top as leaders in an organization which their enterprise and genius has in large measure created. Perhaps two thirds of the people in the industry are of other nationalities, and they are loyal members of the union; but the initiative, the enterprise, the leadership is largely in the hands of those whom the Christian world has despised and persecuted for these 2,000 years—the Russian Jews.

Williams' article concluded with some warm pen portraits of Sam Levin as an idealistic young labor leader; of Miss Bessie Abramowitz, who alone had organized whole battalions of workers at Hart, Schaffner and Marx; and finally of Sidney Hillman as the young "statesman" and "master mind" of the group.

The chief deputy is as yet only twenty [six] years old, and the most remarkable characteristic in one so young is his power of restraint. We expect youth to be fiery, enthusiastic, daring; but we rarely find it coupled with that poise, repose, selfmastery so necessary to great achievement of any sort. I have known him when he had a strike vote in his pocket, and when a wave of his hand would have summoned his comrades to battle, refuse the temptation to make himself an idolized leader . . . and see his name in three deck heads in the daily papers, and choose the harder, less spectacular role of a practical constructive builder of an organization that would get results for his people. And that to me is the highest test of . . . leadership.[34]

The article was soon afterward translated and published in the largest Jewish-language daily in America, the *Jewish Daily Forward* of New York, and made a strong impression on various persons facing serious problems of labor mediation in that city.

One day in January 1914, a telegram from New York reached Hillman, inviting him to take over the post of "chief clerk" for the International Ladies' Garment Workers' Union, whose occupant was about to resign. This meant that he would be the chief representative of 50,000 New York women's garment workers before the board of conciliation set up for the trade under Brandeis' "Protocol of Peace." The offer carried with it the princely salary of $50 a week—he was drawing then, as a matter of principle, but $15 from the Chicago union.

It was a brilliant opportunity for a young man still in his twenties who was resolved to make his career in the American labor movement, for it brought him to the larger stage of New York. For several days he kept the offer a secret while he pondered over it. The Hart, Schaffner and Marx Plan was running smoothly; he was almost bored with it. But to leave Chicago and his strong friends and followers there after seven years would be quite a wrench.

During a heart-to-heart talk he had with Williams, the older man tried to dissuade him from leaving, though saying it was up to Hillman. After a quick reconnaissance trip to New York, Hillman wrote to him:

I have made my decision wisely or unwisely, and the only thing for me to do is to go ahead and make good. I know I will have your warmest sympathies with me in this matter.[35]

His union comrades were greatly moved when he imparted the news to them. Saddest of all was the girl organizer, Bessie Abramowitz. Sidney was not only leaving his old fellow warriors—though he promised to keep close to their affairs in his new post—he was leaving (temporarily) the young lady to whom he had already pledged more than friendship.

Mr. Schaffner one day in 1913 had said to Hillman: "You ought to get married, you work too hard, you have no life of your own." He then offered to introduce Sidney to a small dark girl, with fine features and brown eyes, who was in his office; she was Bessie Abramowitz. Sidney Hillman was reserved always about his personal life, but he had as a matter of fact been a close friend of Bessie's since 1910, and they were secretly engaged a short time before his departure from Chicago.

Before leaving he helped arrange the affairs of his organization. His friends, A. D. Marimpietri and Sam Levin, were to take charge of his own Local 39. He himself would write them every day from New York and make as frequent visits as possible.

In a note written from New York (January 28, 1914), Hillman told John E. Williams:

I would like very much that the work I left in Chicago should not be interrupted on account of my absence. I would like to do away with the impression that matters depend on me entirely. You will find Mr. Marimpietri quite intelligent and willing to co-operate . . . in the coat shops. Mr. Levin and Miss Abramowitz can be trusted to take care of their own matters entirely.

His departure was the occasion for another dinner gathering, for labor unionists are exceedingly fond of pomp and ceremony—if only that of a modest banquet in a side-street restaurant. The shop chairmen of Hart, Schaffner and Marx were on hand to give him a watch as a "token of their esteem"; members of the firm and its arbitration officers and several Chicago social leaders were also present and vied with each other in singing the young man's praises. At twenty-six Sidney Hillman had become accustomed to hearing himself named "one of the leading labor statesmen of this generation" in Chicago's trade-union circles. His special reputation preceded him to New York.* J. E. Williams was the main speaker of the evening before this earnest little group and declared that in his wide experience he had "never met a man in the labor movement who embodies so many of the qualities demanded by modern economic conditions." The clothing workers had a right to be proud of him but were exhorted to let him depart "without regrets and misgivings, and give him

* To a person active in social welfare work in New York, Mrs. Raymond Robins wrote on February 4, 1914: "We do not know here in Chicago whether to rejoice with you or to grieve for ourselves because of Sidney Hillman's election as chief deputy for your garment workers. He is a very remarkable young man. . . . Please see him and meet him and have him for dinner or something where you can have a long quiet talk together. He has wonderful power over his people. . . ." (M. E. Dreier: *Margaret D. Robins,* p. 108, New York, 1950.)

courage to face the tremendous problems that confront him in New York." He continued:

> . . . The . . . workers of his union . . . grieve over his loss; and yet they cannot deny him to their more needy brethren in New York.
> Is Hillman rich? Perhaps he had to borrow his fare to New York. And yet who would not rather have his wealth than the billions of all the steel magnates and oil kings in the world? [36]

The guest of honor, whose head might well have been turned by all this well-intentioned flattery, made a gracious response in words that reflected well his personal intellectual idiom:

> There seems to be a certain Mr. Hillman referred to, but he isn't myself. It is not I. It is the personification of the new idealism of our organization which you have referred to.
> If I had done the work [alone], it would have been wasted because it would not have endured. It is the result of a movement bigger than any man or any locality. Out of this movement for industrial peace and democracy, you and I are getting more than we give. . . .
> This new spirit of men and women is infinitely more important than any money or material thing contributed to the movement. . . .

Hillman was always very taut when he spoke; his voice, deep and resonant, conveyed the intensity, the sincerity of his feeling when he spoke thus among his old comrades.

Marimpietri, who sat next to Bessie Abramowitz, said to her in a voice full of emotion: "I feel so sad that Sidney is leaving us."

Bessie turned to him and exploded: "But how do you think *I* feel? I *love him!*" And with this she burst into tears.[37]

Chapter Four

FOUNDING OF
THE AMALGAMATED

When Hillman came to New York in February 1914 to help establish "industrial democracy" and "law and order" in the women's garment trade, there was no government authority that might intervene in the disputes of labor and management. Factory inspection was still in its infancy, and the sweatshops were everywhere in New York. Yet public opinion had been strongly aroused in recent years by incidents like the terrible Triangle Waist Company fire, in which 146 girl workers were trapped and burned alive, and by the powerful strike movement of the cloakmakers in 1910. Some of the nation's "best minds," as President Wilson called them, now devoted themselves to the problem of eliminating the conditions that led to these episodes of violence and tragedy. Outstanding among these reformers was Louis D. Brandeis, often called "the People's Lawyer," who was soon to be appointed a Justice of the United States Supreme Court.

It was at this time that Sidney Hillman first met the brilliant jurist with whose ideas for industrial conciliation he felt a profound sympathy; it was the beginning of a friendship lasting more than twenty years. The guiding spirit and architect of the Protocol of

Peace, Brandeis urged that industrial war was "unscientific" and in fact obsolete. He believed in reason, in social peace, in the partnership of capital and labor. Employers and employees *must try to agree,* he held, for they were naturally partners. "Nine tenths" of the serious controversies between them arose largely from "misunderstandings." To eliminate these it would require "hundreds of conferences" between both parties, conducted with infinite patience, careful argument, and full "willingness to listen and to consider." But there had been so much strife in the past that he foresaw that the process of conciliation would be long and would need great "industrial ingenuity." [1] In essence, he looked upon his plan for the dressmaking trade as a process of education.

Yet high-minded though Brandeis' policies were, Hillman soon perceived that they were being carried out in a rather artificial and unrealistic fashion. After more than three years of operation, the Cloakmakers' Protocol was threatened with complete breakdown by 1914. A momentous conference had been held in January of that year between the representatives of the International Ladies' Garment Workers' Union and those of the manufacturers in the trade, with Brandeis, Morris Hillquit, Samuel Gompers, John Mitchell (former president of the United Mine Workers), and William O. Thompson, U. S. Industrial Relations Commissioner, participating. The previous chief clerk had been induced to resign a few weeks earlier, and at the recommendation of Mr. Thompson and of Abraham Cahan, the New York Socialist leader and editor of the *Jewish Daily Forward,* Hillman had been brought in to apply his experience here. He was the fourth person to occupy the key post of chief clerk for the women's garment workers.

Hillman, as a high executive officer for the ILGWU, was supposed to administer the "industrial charter of peace" on behalf of the cloakmakers, in co-operation with the chief clerk for the employers' association, who was his opposite number. But the picture here was entirely different from that of the arbitration plan in Chicago imposed by one big unionized concern and its well-disciplined labor force.

"The work ahead of us here is tremendous—the problems are very difficult," Hillman had written to J. E. Williams on February 4, 1914. Before he would proceed any further, he had insisted that Mr. Williams be engaged to act as Impartial Chairman and handle shop troubles on the spot, together with himself and the employers' chief clerk, who was reputed to be a tough customer. Williams was borrowed from Chicago for an interval, and they set to work.

The women's garment industry was even more chaotic, competitive, and "unpredictable" than that of men's clothing, and the task of bringing order into it seemed baffling beyond description. Following the strike of 1910, the employers had pledged themselves to a benevolent partnership with the union, which had imposed the closed shop, after a fashion. But the fixing of standards and wages, where there were still so many different style factors and qualities, so many small contractors, and "scab" shops, was plainly going to take a long time. The trade in New York, it used to be said, was run by some 2,000 "Potash and Perlmutters." Each of these small employers set different prices for piece work, sometimes more than a thousand different rates in a season. The union shops also allowed for wage differentials, as Williams reported:

On one side of the street a cloak may be made for $5.00; on the other side it may be made for $4.00 by an equally good union man. It is a system of legalized "scabbing," and of course the factories that make goods cheapest get the lion's share of the business.[2]

In slack seasons the cloak-and-suit manufacturers often dismissed active union men in their employ and insisted on the right to reorganize, or "rationalize" their shops with other, more tractable personnel. Adjustment of grievances proceeded slowly under the Protocol, and the discontent of the workers rose with each delay.[3]

Under the cloakmakers' arbitration scheme, the burden of judgment fell chiefly on an eleven-man Board of Grievances, made up of five members for each side and a neutral chairman. These people were much more disputatious than those Hillman had dealt with in Chicago, and were often deadlocked. Their rulings, then, usually waited on the final "court of appeals," or Board of Arbitration, made up of three members who served without pay and met together only at intervals of several weeks. This board passed judgment on questions of policy or interpretation rather than on the details of individual cases. It was all very neat and logical, but it did not work.

As chief clerk for the union, Hillman managed to get on smoothly enough with the man who was the manufacturers' chief clerk, and avoided having cases under adjustment go to the slow-moving Board.

of Arbitration. He might have made much headway in removing the causes of friction, if not for the fierce dissension raging in the union itself.

The International Ladies' Garment Workers' Union, affiliated with the AFL, was then the very heart of the Jewish labor movement in New York; it boasted 85,000 members and was one of the largest and most progressive trade unions in the country. These immigrant workers were closely wedded to the Socialist Party. Their militant leaders and organizers were strong on the oratory of the "to-hell-with-the-capitalists" school. At the time when Sidney Hillman came to work for the ILGWU its New York Joint Board, controlling the bulk of the union memberships, was split by the rivalry of the Socialist bloc, led by Abraham Bisno—a colorful figure of those days —and the moderate faction of practical craft unionists who held the top union offices.

Behind the scenes, also, Abraham Cahan, reputed "boss of the East Side Socialists," moved with a view to the interests of his local political organization, with which the ILGWU was closely linked. The union's lawyer, Morris Hillquit, the intellectual leader of the Socialist Party, was also a powerful figure in the background, serving with Brandeis and Hamilton Holt as a member of the Board of Arbitration for the Protocol. Men like these and also the rising militant leaders, Benjamin Schlesinger and Morris Sigman, had long volleyed and thundered before their turbulent followers at the evils of the cloak-and-suit market. They were, to be sure, making notable contributions to the reform of one of the most backward sections of American industry. But as personalities they seemed to Hillman too often swayed by their own belligerent rhetoric and jealous passions; some of the cleverest among them were too much given, he felt, to the vice of intellectual pride. They might be Socialists, yet in their contests with each other for some local or petty political advantage, some of them, as he said, showed they were "lacking in principles." [4] In this union "the killing off of leaders seems to have been a favorite practice," John E. Williams wrote in an article published in May 1915.

At first Hillman greatly enjoyed the work he was doing. But by the end of the summer he reported that he was overwhelmed by troubles of all sorts: "With the strain I am under, and I am facing now the most terrific situation—I am afraid a hopeless one—I need all the inner strength possible." [5]

At this time the radical faction in the ILGWU's New York Joint Board was up in arms over cases of anti-union discrimination. The "radicals" soon brought about an overturn of the union control, replacing the old president with Benjamin Schlesinger, and demanding the freedom of strike action. The cloak-and-suit "charter of peace" was on its way out. The surprising thing was that it had lasted so long.

Hillman, by the autumn of 1914, was shifting his attention to another growing labor crisis, that of his union comrades in Chicago. For during his nine months' service with the ILGWU his heart was always far off in Chicago.

II

He had kept up a constant correspondence with his friends at the Hart, Schaffner and Marx locals, writing them at least twice a week and asking eagerly for news. On two or three occasions during the spring and summer of 1914 he made the long train journey to Chicago in order to advise them in person on various difficulties that had arisen. By the autumn of that year Hillman's union brothers were increasingly absorbed in the internal conflict developing within the United Garment Workers' Union on the eve of its biennial convention in October.

The Chicago section of the UGWA was run with considerable local autonomy. "We paid our per capita dues into the union treasury, and then just tried not to think of the national officers in New York," Frank Rosenblum recalls. The ideas of Hillman and his friends on new methods of organization and on the need for a big, close-knit industrial union suited to the modern large-scale clothing factories were completely out of tune with the policies of President Rickert and his supporters.

Much sharper opposition had arisen, meanwhile, in the large New York market. In 1911 a dissident faction (mainly of New York and Baltimore workers), styling themselves the "Brotherhood of Tailors," had held a conference in Philadelphia at which resolutions were passed severely censuring the UGWA's national officers for neglecting the underpaid tailors and for expending large treasury funds mainly on advertising and promoting the union's label. The opposition group insisted, moreover, that the tailors' locals were being treated as "stepchildren" by the national organization, which advanced the interests chiefly of its overall makers through the union-label campaign. The label, of course, was effective in helping the sale of work clothing and was being sold, sometimes, as it happened, even to non-union firms.

The national officers, however, had continued to charter new small locals consisting mainly of overall workers in out-of-town manufacturing centers, whose delegates seemed more favorably disposed to the administrative machine than those of the much larger locals in New York and Chicago. Hillman, appearing as a delegate at the 1912 convention in Indianapolis, had protested vigorously at President Rickert's moves to unseat two tailors' delegates without a hearing. He had seen Rickert and Secretary B. A. Larger, despite strenuous opposition, gain passage of amended bylaws extending the power of the national executives to suspend locals which disobeyed their orders.[6] Then, as for years past, the presiding officers had proceeded to have themselves re-elected by "acclamation" of the delegates at the convention instead of by referendum to the entire membership. Resolutions demanding an increase in organizing activity, such as Hillman introduced, were passed, placed in the minutes—and forgotten.

The New York men's tailors were now very eager to emulate the strikes of their sister union, the Ladies' Garment Workers. The successes of the Hart, Schaffner and Marx locals also stimulated them. In 1912, working as an autonomous body within the UGWA, and raising funds themselves, the New York faction, under the leadership of Isaac Goldstein, carried on a most vigorous organizing drive which brought many union recruits. With growing strength their opposition to the union's national officers hardened. The cry was on for the closed shop in New York, a 48-hour week, and reform of their union's "rotten-borough" rule. In December 1912, the men's clothing workers' locals of New York took a strike vote on their own, and then, demanding wage increases and shorter hours, began a city-wide walkout in which about 40,000 workers left their jobs.

This action had the apparent approval of the UGWA's executive board, which, in any event, could do little to stop it. But after the strike had run for two months the union's executive board, without consulting the striking members, suddenly announced that a settlement had been arranged with the manufacturers' association, providing for an increase of only $1.00 a week and no reduction in hours. When these disappointing terms were made public and the strike declared at an end by the *Jewish Daily Forward,* which advised that the agreement be accepted, the tailors saw red. In a large and by no means peaceful procession they marched down to Seward Square and smashed in the windows of the Socialist newspaper's offices. The lapidation of Mr. Abraham Cahan's windows was an episode long remembered in the needle trades of New York.

Raising fresh funds, the rank-and-file leaders now pressed on with the strike. The *Forward,* which had many Jewish tailors among its readers, felt obliged to reverse itself and come to their support again. On March 13, 1913, the contest came to a close when an agreement with the employers' group offering a 52-hour week and other important concessions was approved, this time by a referendum vote.

The New York tailors would never forget the highhanded behavior of their president, Mr. Rickert, and his lieutenants in this strike. There had previously been a democratic clause in the union's constitution providing for a popular referendum, in certain cases, by which a decision of the convention delegates might be set aside. Rickert had managed to have this clause eliminated in order to increase the authority of the union's executive group, calling the referendum vote "a bar to progress and advancement." Officially the president and the other national officers of the United Garment Workers continued to direct the organization, but they had lost control of the majority of its membership, the tailors. What was happening here was perhaps not unusual in the AFL craft unions of those days, often run by rigid bureaucrats. But a majority of the union's members were now convinced that they suffered from taxation without representation. Resentment was spreading in Baltimore, in Boston, in Chicago, as well as in New York, where the membership had been roused to new confidence by their recent victory. It was inevitable that the insurgent groups should make a supreme effort, at the approaching union convention, to wrest control of it from the Old Guard.

On arriving in New York, Sidney Hillman had gone to live at first in a room of the East Side settlement house directed by Miss Lillian Wald, the counterpart of Jane Addams in Chicago. Here he came to know Miss Wald and also Paul Kellog, editor of *The Survey,* who was to be one of his lifelong friends. Besides such eminent social workers he also met leaders of the great city's trade-union movement, including those active in the insurgent faction of the New York tailors. There was J. B. S. Hardman, a labor journalist; there was Joseph Schlossberg, a former garment worker, and also a labor journalist for the Jewish press since the 1890's, who had become secretary of the Brotherhood of Tailors and helped lead the 1913 strike action; there was August Bellanca, an Italian-American journalist and, like his brother Frank Bellanca, a leader of the Italian tailors; and with him, usually, a stocky young lawyer with a big round head, named Fiorello La Guardia, who had helped bail out many of the pickets arrested in the 1913 tailors' strike.

To this group the young man from Chicago seemed to bubble with an inner enthusiasm and fire, yet was surprisingly moderate in speech. Isaac Goldstein, the firebrand of the New York tailors, thought him "too conservative." They talked much of labor and social questions. In fact, Socialism was intellectually fashionable at that period, when most college professors and even some society leaders were said to have been converted to its doctrines, and Eugene Debs gathered in nearly a million votes as candidate for President of the United States. Yet Hillman, even then, expressed misgivings about the current crop of Socialists he met in New York, who, he felt, were "forever talking, talking, talking." Very much the realist, he declared he was for action, continuous action in an ever-expanding labor movement—and then one would see, after having recorded some achievements, what social improvements would follow.

Meanwhile his heart was set upon uniting the different insurgent groups in the UGWA for common action against the union's discredited administration. He hoped fervently that the opposition would come out into the open at the forthcoming convention. His companions of that season recall that he suggested no ambitions for himself, no idea of taking power, but only of helping the popular movement on its way.[7]

Thus while Hillman familiarized himself with conditions in the Eastern sector of his own industry, on his trips to Chicago he communicated something of the hopes and emotions that were stirring the New York rank and file to his old associates. On one visit to Chicago he conferred for a long time with Sam Levin, A. D. Marimpietri, Frank Rosenblum, and Bessie Abramowitz, and a plan of procedure was tentatively mapped out. It was agreed that the Chicago delegates, headed by Sam Levin, representing 10,000 members, were to come to the union's convention as staunch allies of the insurgent New York faction.[8] Letters were exchanged between the Chicago delegates and union groups in various cities, such as the following, dated Chicago, September 1, 1914:

> We in Chicago recognize that there is something radically wrong in the management of our international organization, and we desire to co-operate with delegates of New York and other cities who are of the same opinion.
>
> We would like to be informed of all movements along those lines so that when we meet in Nashville . . . we will be able to work together much better. . . .
>
> Fraternally yours,
Frank Rosenblum
A. D. Marimpietri
H. Schneid

Mr. Rickert, a well-spoken man, veteran of many a trade-union storm, was under no illusions about what the insurgent groups intended to do, and took his own measures. The site deliberately chosen for the approaching convention was Nashville, Tennessee, which was no clothing center and was then served by rather awkward train connections from New York. The place was considered quite convenient for the (generally native-born) delegates from the shirt and overall "label shops" in upstate New York and the Middle Western cities.

At this time union members of more recent immigrant stock, Jewish, Italian, and Slavic, were of the opinion that the Rickert administration played upon racial divisions among the workers.*

Then another shrewd blow was struck at the opposition party when the UGWA's general secretary, Larger, announced by letter to

---

* Later on, on the eve of the Nashville convention, spokesmen for the ruling "hierarchy" were said to have attempted to prejudice the delegates against the "progressive" opposition in every manner. One woman member of the Executive Board was overheard, in the hotel lobbies, appealing to the native-born delegates to save their union from the "anarchists and Jews," who were accused of plotting to replace the present slate of officers. Yet some of the conservative officers associated with Mr. Rickert were also of Jewish descent. (Proceedings, ACWA Convention, 1914, p. 24.)

all the local officers the harsh rulings that were to be enforced in passing on the credentials of delegates.

As in most unions, a per capita share of the dues collected by the local agents, based on the number of members in good standing, was paid at stated intervals into the union's national (or international) treasury, and the convention delegates apportioned in ratio to per capita payments. Exceptions could be made by the executives in periods of costly strikes or unemployment; or the time limit could be extended for clearing of such intra-union debts. But at this late hour it was suddenly announced that locals which had not paid up in full would be refused credentials at the approaching convention. The group of New York locals alone, after a hurried auditing of their books, were ordered to pay in $75,000 at once or be deprived of representatives at Nashville. Thus the delegates for the most populous locals were to be unseated, since their treasuries had been drained by a long strike and a season of widespread unemployment. It was adding insult to injury. But for this measure, cooler heads among the opposition leaders might have prevented a trade-union "revolution" born of despair.

The United Garment Workers' delegates, 305 in number, arrived in Nashville from all over the United States and from several Canadian cities by various routes—some borrowing money for their train fare—and gathered together on the eve of the convention. The atmosphere was bad. The "progressives" from New York, Chicago, Baltimore, and Boston noticed with interest the careful preparations made to receive them: a large body of Nashville police and detectives were on hand to keep order.

On the Sunday evening before the convention began, the Chicago group met with some of the other "progressives" at their hotel, the Duncan, and prepared their own measures. They had learned that the union's executives were adamant in their resolve to unseat the opposition delegates. Yet this bloc, including the Chicago contingent, represented almost two thirds of the UGWA's 60,000 membership. Before the group broke up that evening it was agreed that the Chicago delegates, whose seats were not challenged, were to lead the fight on the floor for their "betrayed" brothers.

Marimpietri, in a letter posted that night, gives something of the tense feeling of the first conferences among the insurgent leaders:

Nashville, Tenn.
Oct. 11, 1914 (10:30)

Dear Jake:

. . . Whatever the result may be, it will be for the best of the industry in the long run. Our boys are all doing their duty and showing the rest of the delegates that Chicago is no second to anyone. Myself, Levin, Schneid, Rosenblum, are holding important places among the progressives. I forgot to say about Bessie [Abramowitz], for she is not a boy, but she is working very nicely, in fact she [has become] one of our very important delegates.[9]

III

A Protestant minister opened the convention next morning with an invocation to the spirit of the Good Samaritan and the brotherhood of man. His timely prayer, alas, had little effect on either camp. As soon as the preliminaries were done with, Brother Frank Rosenblum of Chicago, the parliamentary leader of the "progressives," went into action and asked the chairman if the report of the Credentials Committee was complete. President Rickert replied that it was not, but that 198 of the 305 delegates, representing approved locals, had been recommended for seating. At this point the first session was adjourned.

When the meeting convened the next morning, all delegates whose status had not yet been reported as approved were refused admittance and physically barred from the floor. There were 107 of these, representing cutters' and tailors' locals from New York, Boston, Rochester, Philadelphia, Baltimore, and Cincinnati, who were now told that they could only sit in the visitors' gallery and watch the convention as passive spectators.

At this, Rosenblum raised a point of order, declaring that the convention was not legally organized, inasmuch as all the delegates' credentials were not granted or disposed of. President Rickert ruled that Rosenblum's point of order was not well taken, and was sustained by a vote in which over a third of the delegates could not participate. Rosenblum then jumped up and, addressing himself to the galleries in stentorian tones, called for a true vote on his motion—which was delivered with a mighty shout from the excluded delegates up above. He thereupon declared that a majority had opposed the chair's ruling.

The proceedings went on in this unorthodox fashion, with Rosenblum, Miss Abramowitz, and Marimpietri in turn addressing the convention and fighting to have the suspended delegates up in the gallery included in roll calls. In the face of threats of violence, Rosenblum cried out as he gestured toward the galleries: "These people are here to express the rights and aspirations of the workers who have elected them." He charged that the treatment of the New York locals had been illegal according to the union's constitution; that the required two months' notice in such cases had not been given in good time; that the executive officers were using unlawful and dishonest tactics to ensure their retention in office. His tirade brought tremendous cheers from the visitors' section and mad howls from the floor, at which Rickert shouted that he would clear the gallery unless the "visitors" kept order.

Repeatedly motions made by Rosenblum and his associates were put to a vote before the people in the gallery as well as the seated delegates and then declared "passed." One bluntly demanded the removal of President Rickert as chairman. A last defiant motion urged that, whereas a minority of the delegates had evidently captured "physical possession" of the convention hall, the "lawful" delegates (meaning those suspended and their allies) should leave this convention to its usurpers and reconvene immediately afterward in a "regular" convention at the nearby Duncan Hotel. This motion was also declared "passed," with accompanying cheers from the gallery, whereupon the excluded delegates with their Chicago allies, numbering 130 in all, marched out of the hall.

The "bolters," swept by moral indignation, met at noon of that same day, October 13, 1914, in a rump session and declared that their union's legislative body was now properly convened. Jacob Panken, a New York lawyer associated with the Brotherhood of Tailors, exhorted the delegates to begin the "real work" of the United Garment Workers' Union The rump convention found that its members actually spoke for almost 75 per cent of the union's population, who had been deprived of their democratic rights.

This meeting of the "progressives," which foreshadowed the drastic step of secession, then took up the problems that lay ahead in a serious and dedicated mood. Unionization had only scratched the surface of their industry thus far; the delegates at the Hotel Duncan meeting pledged themselves to organize a quarter of a million workers. One ruling idea that came out of this earnest gathering was that the old petty divisions over crafts or "departments" in their trade must be eliminated in favor of a closely knit industrial-union structure, similar to that of the United Mine Workers. The delegates then considered the election of permanent officers as their next business, but held this over until the session of the following day.

That night the secessionists' leading spirits, meeting in informal caucus groups, eagerly debated the question of who was to be elected as their leader. There had been much sentiment in favor of Joseph Schlossberg, the high-minded leader of the New York delegation, which was the largest among them and, by its militant action in 1913, had precipitated the final break with Rickerts' "machine." The smaller Chicago contingent was, however, much more united, and enjoyed high credit both for its progressive record and for its generous action at Nashville in taking up the cause of the New York locals. Frank Rosenblum, in particular, had won glory at the Nashville convention because of the spirited fight he had led on the floor. But the thoughts of most of the Chicago group turned at once toward their old comrade, who had been the soul of their organization at Hart, Schaffner and Marx.

Sidney Hillman was in New York eagerly awaiting news from his friends at Nashville. There, in the night-long conferences of the Chicago delegates, as one of those present has said, "we discussed and discussed who should be head of the union until three in the morning, and always came back to Sidney Hillman." [10] One point in his favor was that he happened to have remained outside the immediate struggle at Nashville. Joseph Schlossberg, for example, had at first refused to consider any office in the new organization, lest he open himself to charges of having instigated the insurgents for this purpose. Hillman, as his friends knew, could make an inspiring leader; but what was more to the point was that he was regarded everywhere as a "moderate" or conciliatory figure, noted for his peacemaking labors in courts of arbitration.

The business of president-making, in this case, was not without its romantic side. Bessie Abramowitz, a power among the Chicago group, fought for the nomination of the young man who was to her something more than a good trade-union officer. Jacob Panken of the New York delegation (later a judge of the Domestic Relations Court in his city) long afterward reminded her of the part she played in this affair:

I remember that night in Nashville, Tennessee, thirty-two years ago, when you walked me up and down the streets of the city arguing that Sidney was the only logical person to be president of the Amalgamated. I did not know him as well as you did, but I deferred to your judgement. I am glad that I did.[11]

Several telegrams had been dispatched to Hillman earlier that same evening—for his friends had to know whether he would leave his present post and accept this hazardous assignment. It was soberly foreseen, of course, that the formidable power of the AFL would be thrown at once against the secessionists. The devoted Sam Levin wired Hillman:

YOU MUST ACCEPT PRESIDENCY. WE ARE THE MAJORITY SO DECIDE AND WIRE AT ONCE.

Hillman replied by reminding Levin of his present obligations to the ILGWU and pleading for time to consider the proposal, which, he said, offered the prospects of "martyrdom" rather than the pleasures of office.

That very evening Hillman was at a late dinner with a few friends, including J. B. S. Hardman and John E. Williams, at a small restaurant near his office at Twenty-third Street. Casually he mentioned the proposals he had just received and, as was his habit—though his mind might be made up—invited their counsel, if only to compare notes.

Williams warned him seriously against the risks he was running. Though he had a low opinion of Rickert, he urged that the unity of labor was paramount, and "secession never pays."

Hardman added to this: "Sidney, surely you're aware that you are staking your head and reputation on a hazardous gamble?"

Hillman's answer was: "Quite so. It means taking chances. But I owe my present standing to the tailors. . . . The tailors, it seems, need me now and they should have me." [12]

He had made up his mind. A second telegram had come from Levin:

SIDNEY YOUR TELEGRAM RECEIVED. PANKEN WILL GIVE YOU ALL PARTICULARS ABOUT THE SITUATION. DO NOT HESITATE TO TAKE IT. IT MUST BE DONE AT ANY COST . . . WE NEED YOU IN THIS SITUATION. WE HAD TO ACT IN A HURRY.

SAM LEVIN

And finally one from the irrepressible Miss Abramowitz:

UNDERSTAND THAT PERSONAL PLEDGES MUST CEASE WHEN SISTER ORGANI-
ZATION AT STAKE. TO BECOME A MARTYR I URGE YOU TO ACCEPT OFFICE.[13]

He had been deeply moved at the call from his old friends and the opportunities and dangers it offered—though, as Hardman relates, he had spoken of the matter in a quiet, offhand way. But his response to a 3 A.M. telephone call from Levin was "positive and heart-warming." He would be with the tailors in their new departure, with all his soul.

Later that morning in Nashville he was nominated unanimously as the provisory president of the insurgent organization. To cement the bond with the New York tailors, Schlossberg, then thirty-eight years of age, was persuaded to accept the post of general secretary of the new organization. A committee of the seceding delegates was also appointed to present their case before the next convention of the American Federation of Labor. Sidney Hillman resigned from his post in the cloakmakers' union, quickly installed himself in small offices at 32 Union Square, New York, and set to work.

IV

Our path, as you know, was not strewn with roses when we returned from the convention at Nashville to New York to take hold of the business of our union. We had to enter upon our duties without a cent in the treasury, without even an office or stationery.

Thus runs the first report of the secessionists' General Executive Board, written by Hillman and Joseph Schlossberg in 1914. "There are about 50,000 members on the books of our local unions," Secretary Schlossberg reported at this period. But, he added, trade was very dull and only about 25,000 members were paying dues.[14] Later estimates have shown that the number of President Hillman's constituents in his first year of office ranged from 35,000 to 38,000, while something under 20,000 remained in the "old" UGWA.

The "New" United Garment Workers' Union—for both groups at first fought to keep the old name—was off to a shaky start in mid-October 1914. Hillman and Schlossberg headed a union whose very existence and right to a name was disputed. A small two-room office was their international headquarters. Hillman was paid a salary of

$50 a week, with $10 weekly for expenses. But there were many weeks when he and Schlossberg and other officers failed to receive any salary at all, for Mr. Rickert proceeded at once to start lawsuits, tying up the treasuries of the insurgent locals. Hillman's organization countered by laying claim to the union's label, its treasury, and its comfortable headquarters and furniture at Bible House, on Astor Place. There was prodigious confusion, subpoenas being fired off by both sides.

No conflict between capital and labor can be more bitter than a battle of rival labor factions. At the end of October, Secretary Larger of the UGWA sent out a circular letter warning all local officers that the secessionists who had taken the name of the "New United Garment Workers" were an unlawful organization. Local officers were warned to refuse requests of the insurgents for funds, and heed only orders of the UGWA's secretary, written under the old union's letterhead.

Meanwhile strikes broke forth, even in this season of depression that greeted the new organization, for the opening of World War I in Europe had disrupted American finances. What was worse, the old UGWA, formerly so lethargic in industrial disputes, threw itself into these 1914–15 conflicts with all its resources. While claiming that they fought to preserve law and order in their union, the old officers, as will be seen, acted on numerous occasions as strike-breaking agents.

But even as harrying strikes began in those first weeks of litigation and civil war among the tailors, Hillman directed his principal efforts to winning recognition for the majority of the union's membership from the American Federation of Labor.

He could have had no illusions about receiving any mercy from Samuel Gompers, the powerful president and founder of the Federation, which then constituted America's official labor movement. Gompers' fixed abhorrence of the sin of "dual unionism" was well known. He stood close to Tom Rickert, one of his political supporters in the AFL. Yet Hillman was determined to force the issue out in the open.

In late October his followers organized numerous mass meetings, such as that of the Chicago District Council, at which thousands of workers were given an account of the old union officers' alleged illegal actions at Nashville. Numerous resolutions were then voted to support the new officers; and these Hillman presented to the executives of the AFL at their national convention in Philadelphia in November 1914. In addition, the Hillman faction circulated a leaflet among the delegates at this same convention, setting forth their grievances and urging that the delegates appearing for the dissident majority had the strongest claims to be seated. Their petition warned:

Hundreds of thousands of workers in the trade have been brought within labor organizations affiliated with the AFL. Many more are still outside of the ranks of the labor movement and must be won over to our cause. . . . These workers, men and women, are very largely of foreign birth, and it has been a difficult task to inculcate in them ideals of trade unionism. The tricky tactics and high-handed methods of Messrs. Rickert and Larger have had a very depressing effect upon them. If sustained by the AFL convention it is bound to have a demoralizing effect upon the entire labor movement.[15]

But when Hillman, at the head of his alternate delegation, appeared before the Credentials Committee of the AFL, he was informed that "no one knew" him or the delegates accompanying him; that only the "regular" representatives of the UGWA would be admitted to the floor of the convention. He then induced President Schlesinger of the International Ladies' Garment Workers to offer a motion from the floor calling for an investigation into the affairs of the men's clothing workers' union and of charges of illegal acts and corrupt practices. But Gompers would have none of this, and on November 16, 1914, addressed a stern letter to all the locals of the UGWA, admonishing them to disregard "misrepresentations . . . by persons claiming to be officers of their union."

Those were hurried, breathless weeks for Hillman, who rushed from New York (where a lockout was threatened) to Chicago and thence to Philadelphia, via Baltimore (where a large strike was also being fought). He wrote:

No doubt you heard by this time that the Rickert delegation was seated at the convention. While that was expected, we did find out that there is very little to expect from the AFL, and as a matter of fact *most of the International [Unions] are in the position where Rickert is today;* and the more reasonable our argument would be the more opposition it would arouse.

We are introducing a resolution for a committee to investigate. We are not quite sure if this is the best way. . . . It isn't our intention to have this matter patched up by the AFL. The further things go the more

FOUNDING OF THE AMALGAMATED

obvious that the matter will have to be fought to the finish. I don't know
how many of you have seen this before. As far as I am concerned it
was my intention to fight it out.[16]

For six or seven years now the fight for reform of the AFL's craft-
union structure had been going on. The movement for industrial or
"vertical" unionism had touched more than one AFL union, such as
that of the mine workers and the ILGWU, and now the men's clothing
workers. But to Gompers, then at the height of his power, only the
craft union and established union authority were legitimate; industrial
unionism, which would eliminate or diminish those craft jurisdictions
that, in his belief, gave basic strength and stability to the modern
labor movement, appeared as an intolerable threat. Dual unionists,
therefore, must be crushed out at all costs. As Hillman shrewdly observed, most of the long-established AFL unions were in the same
condition as Mr. Rickert's; their leaders had grown old in office; they
divided local unions according to crafts, so that it became easy to
set up little made-to-order locals of their own device and thus pack
conventions and override the will of the membership.

The prospects were dark. The new union group was to be outlawed.
Hillman had foreseen what perils must be faced; had his people realized as much? He wrote to his friend Levin in Chicago:

There is no question that there is a whole lot of trouble before us.
We have in New York a strike involving 800 people which is instigated
by the crowd [at Bible House]. You will have to be on guard now all
the time. . . .
Our expense is increasing from day to day, having several strikes on
hand, and being forced to put more and more organizers in the field.
Trusting that we will not find you people lacking in courage, and
that you will *see the thing through,* I am
Very sincerely yours,[17]

Against such opposition Hillman sought what allies he could find.
Friendly parties appealed to Gompers, urging that he judge the case of
the secessionists upon its merits. He was said to have replied: "Right
or wrong—no act of secession will be tolerated." [18]

Shortly after the new organization of the ready-made tailors was
launched, the Journeymen Tailors' Union, AFL, made up of some
12,000 custom tailors, surprisingly enough, took steps to join forces
with it. Eugene Brais (chief officer of this distinguished craft union

founded in 1847), who had been instrumental in furthering the proposed alliance, was elected a member of the new clothing union's Executive Board, and worked for several months with Hillman over problems of jurisdiction that arose between the two groups. Then Gompers brought all sorts of pressures to bear here, and the Journeymen Tailors, though reluctantly, were induced to withdraw from the proposed alliance.

When the new union was involved in a serious strike in Chicago not long afterward, the American Federation of Labor again took hostile action, its central labor council in that city being prevented from giving direct aid to the strikers.

At this one of the loyal friends of Sidney Hillman and the Chicago clothing workers, Miss Ellen Gates Starr, assailed Gompers in a public letter charging that

the hand which should have been the strongest and readiest to aid those brave and oppressed people was the one which shut off from them the most powerful sources of aid. . . . Because a spirited body of people had dared to secede and form a new and clean organization under honest leadership.[19]

One phrase in Miss Starr's letter stung Sam Gompers to write a public reply: *"Heavy lies the hand of Gompers on the trade-union world of Chicago."* In effect, the great antagonist of Hillman and of the unorganized clothing workers, or other mass-industry laborers, was the man who headed the AFL, himself a former immigrant from England, and of Jewish descent.

The hardheaded Gompers now set forth his own views on labor policy. The power of the labor movement, he argued, rested on solidarity and united action; yet it was a "voluntary association . . . and subject to all the shortcomings of democracy," he admitted candidly. The government structure of trade unions was no more perfect than the wisdom and understanding of the members. But experience had taught that "they must stand together and fight out their differences within the organization. . . . Secession or any other disruptionary movement is fatal." The action of Hillman and his associates was likened to that of the Southern states in 1861, when they had been unwilling to abide by the decision of the majority. When the clothing workers chose to secede, they brought all the evil consequences of such a movement upon themselves.[20]

In truth, Gompers' statements may not be dismissed as insincere or dishonest, in the light of his own long experience and remarkable achievements. He himself had been a "radical," or Marxian, in his youth; he had lived through the vicissitudes of the old Knights of Labor, who represented an earlier form of industrial unionism, and had seen how much trouble beset them because they were not an "economic" federation, pursuing purely economic ends. The lack of class-consciousness or cohesiveness in American workers, the baffling mobility of our social classes, with laborers turning into merchants or industrialists overnight, had convinced Gompers finally of the utter rightness of his vision in the early 1880's: that a new national labor movement must be built up of strictly craft unions, binding together only the most skilled, the steadiest of union men, who were "job-conscious" and would stay unionized in boom or slump.

"The overshadowing problem of the American labor movement has always been the problem of staying organized," he said. And only with the coming of Gompers and the American Federation of Labor had we learned in this country to hold a labor movement together on a national scale. For this reason very stern controls "from above," by national officers of unions, had been instituted, and a tradition of pitiless reprisals against "outlaws" or "dual unionists" had been developed in America, as in no other country.[21]

Any notion that the seceders at Nashville might have represented a majority of their union members, he said, was a "mere opinion," contradicted by the facts and figures in the possession of authorized officials. Miss Starr, or anyone else who questioned the rulings of the AFL, need only apply to Mr. Thomas A. Rickert for the "true facts of the situation." [22] Meanwhile the "New" United Garment Workers must be placed beyond the pale of all good trade-union folk. In effect this meant that they were to fight the employers on their front and the resolute agents of the AFL on their rear.

Up to this time, as an American labor leader, Hillman had been a man of moderate opinions, leaning to Fabian or gradualist tactics. On resigning from his recent post in the cloakmaking industry, he had been given flattering testimonials for his fairness of judgment by manufacturers in the trade as well as by the union members. Joseph Schlossberg, a leader of the small Socialist Labor Party (the "Daniel De Leon Marxists"), was a rigid doctrinaire compared with Sidney Hillman. Still farther to the "left" stood the rising IWW movement, whose advocates preached incessant class war on the labor front. But events were forcing Hillman's hand. Thus we see, again, that it is not ambitious or scheming individuals (so-called "subversives") who create radical or insurgent movements, but the force of realitics, especially economic realities, which call forth such individuals to play their part. Hillman did not push the members of his union toward extreme or perilous positions; his people, aroused by intolerable conditions, like a tide carried him along. Nor were they alone.

The American Federation of Labor, under its aging bureaucrats, having reached a position of great strength and record membership by 1914, had tended to slow down its advancing movement and come under the attack of many reformers within its family. This growing criticism was "part of the general expansion of social ideas and programs" which had produced the Progressive Party "bolt" in 1912, swept Woodrow Wilson into power, gave the Socialist Party nearly a million votes, and "made the IWW a name to conjure with." [23]

The insecure, underpaid clothing workers who had gathered themselves behind Hillman were but part of a great mass of workers who were unorganized or were waiting to be truly organized for collective bargaining, as had been done for many of the older unions in the AFL. Gompers, Rickert, the AFL offered them nothing. In these people a strong vein of idealism was manifest, and they were not ashamed to give expression to their social aspirations or to dream of "ultimate aims," of something better than the conditions they endured, as they worked all day at their benches and sewing machines.

They were asking themselves how long they would suffer from "discrimination" while the conflicts of different national groups among them were viciously exploited. How long would the unskilled workers among them be neglected? How long would they remain divided into separate crafts?

v

From Chicago, Bessie Abramowitz, head of the vest makers' local at Hart, Schaffner's wrote to her oft-distant fiancé on November 20, 1914:

Dear Hillman

I am bombarded with questions about what we are going to do next, and to my sorrow I do not know what answer to give them. Some say,

"Are we going independent?" and others say: "Are we going to join the Journeymen Tailors' Union?" I really do not know . . . which name we are going to name ourselves, but I know one thing, that we must act at once in order to be able to do more effective work.

At this very time the court struggle between the two union organizations appeared on the road to settlement through a composition of their claims against each other. Rickert's faction, through an injunction, held possession of the New York headquarters, the union's label and name, and its treasury. Hillman's group, on the other hand, with the aid of Clarence Darrow, managed to retain the property of the UGWA's District Council in Chicago, and locals and local funds there as in Boston, Cincinnati, and elsewhere. It was therefore agreed that by an "exchange of releases" the old officers were to be left with what they retained, while they in turn were to waive all legal claims against the seceding locals. The "New" United Garment Workers' group also agreed to change its name, and was now free to press on with the job of organizing and reconstruction that lay ahead.

At the beginning of December the Executive Board of the new union issued a call for a constituent convention to be held at Webster Hall, New York, on December 26, 1914. It was to be the true founding convention of the seceding workers, whose leaders announced that they intended the new constitution to offer the fullest scope for the "truly progressive spirit of our membership." The constitution, moreover, was to be thoroughly democratic, with the general officers elected by the entire membership and the convention decisions, even the choice of a site for the convention, subject to the referendum. Hillman and his fellow executives, in their report to the first convention, urged that the principles of *industrial unionism* be proclaimed openly in the new union's charter, despite the public abuse which then attached itself to those words.

Their industry suffered greatly, Hillman's report declared, from the division of the tailors into thirteen different groupings, such as the cutters, coat makers, children's clothing tailors, pants makers— each functioning in relative independence of the other. These time-worn craft divisions, and the local autonomy they provided for small groups or weak locals, had to be eliminated, so that their loosely connected organization might become one massive "vertical" union and so gain unison in action capable of challenging the power of the great mass-production factories rising in the clothing field.[24]

"We need real education for our members," the report stressed. "We need a new type of organizer ... a new type of labor leader." They were to be leaders not in "business-union" affairs, but men and women dedicated to "social service."

The constitution was adopted at Webster Hall by delegates from 68 locals in the United States and Canada, representing about 40,000 people—the heart of America's clothing trade. As its first business this convention chose a name for the union clearly reflecting its "industrial" character. "Article 1: This body shall be known as the *Amalgamated Clothing Workers of America.*" The name symbolized the ruling idea of the founders that different crafts, different local groups, and national and language groups were to be combined as one mass organization. It was a concept that was somewhat advanced for the times and, as Hillman knew, would expose the new union to the abuse of all the bigots. He knew also that it would exert a powerful attraction for all workers who were aware of the abuses they suffered under the "business-union" leaders.

A student of the labor movement, writing in 1916, has described the Jewish labor organizations of that time in America as having "traditionally Socialist aspirations"; and though fundamentally united with the official working-class group in the AFL, feeling repelled by the "destructive tactics of the craft-union leadership [and] its petty squabbles and corruption." The émigré Jewish workers from Europe and the compatriots of Garibaldi, also, tended to look at unionism from the standpoint of social service and not as a "business investment." They placed "ultimate aims above immediate gains." [25] *

* In contrast, Professor Selig Perlman pictures the typical American trade unionist of thirty or forty years ago as one who had really "despaired of the 'American Dream.'" Like the guildsman of earlier times, he sought "a secure, though modest, return for his labor, that is a mere livelihood ... in a world of unlimited opportunity." In the bewildering maze of markets and risks, in which the individualistic enterpriser flourished, the typical manual worker turned to collective action, chiefly in order to protect himself. At most he aspired to reinforce his "proprietary right to the job." (*A Theory of the Labor Movement,* pp. 246 ff.)

And yet unless the worker cared about social justice and "ultimate things," or unless an ethical content were infused in his movement, so that he had the sense of participating in the collective labor action as a "mission" imposing ethical concepts upon society, he might not be useful even in the struggle to win the mere right to the job.

It was to these insurgent tailors that the new name "Amalgamated" and the new constitution made their appeal. It was to them also that the famous "revolutionary" preamble of the original Amalgamated's constitution was addressed:

The economic organization of Labor has been called into existence by the capitalist system of production. . . . A constant and unceasing struggle is being waged between those two classes. . . .

But in order to be efficient, and effectively serve its purpose, the Union must in its structure correspond to the prevailing system of the organization of industry. Modern industrial methods are wiping out the old craft demarcations.

The working class must accept the principles of Industrial Unionism, or it is doomed to impotence.

The same forces that are making for Industrial Unionism are making for a close inter-industrial alliance of the working class. . . .

Every oppressed class in history achieved its emancipation only upon having attained economic supremacy.

These phrases of the preamble were, of course, but expressions of pious hopes, Hillman was fond of pointing out, not *facts*. The constitution of the American Federation of Labor also had a "class-struggle" preamble. Yet a glance beneath the surface would have revealed that even in the beginning there was a marked infusion of the practical and realistic that contrasted strangely with the tone of moral fervor or idealism habitually used by the Amalgamated people. This realistic temper was largely the contribution of Sidney Hillman. He would say that it was "good to have our dreams"; it was good for the workers' morale to share a great faith, to believe that they were struggling for more than "pork chops," toward some heavenly city of justice and brotherhood. For men's will to believe could be a mighty force in itself. But it was good also to be coolheaded in planning and action, and to base one's tactics upon the patient study of realities rather than appearances.

What was more important, therefore, than the economic abstractions in the preamble was that the embattled tailors now had their industrial-union charter. And it was this that they celebrated in the tarnished old ballroom of Webster Hall, usually frequented by bohemians from Greenwich Village, as they shouted and sang at the birth of the Amalgamated Clothing Workers of America.

The founding of the Amalgamated Clothing Workers' Union won scarcely any notice in the metropolitan press—it seemed but one more squabble among the union brethren. President Hillman, in the public interviews he gave at the time, described its plans as being constructive and peaceful. He was for extending the Hart, Schaffner and Marx Plan everywhere. The clothiers had nothing to fear, but, on the contrary, he said, would later "heap blessings on this instrument [of the Protocol agreement] after they have once experienced the advantages it confers." [26]

But the infant years of the Amalgamated were to be in no sense peaceful. Its members were greeted with lockouts or were embroiled in violent strikes before the ink was dry on their new constitution. As Hillman observed, no great organization was ever built without struggle and sacrifice. Long years afterward he could say truthfully: "In every city our dead are buried, and I bow to them."

Chapter Five

THE HEROIC

AGE: 1914-1919

Hillman and his few assistants were furiously busy from the start trying to organize the scattered pieces of the old union in many different cities. Strikes and lockouts burst upon them, in Baltimore, New York, and Boston, at the worst possible moment, before they could gather their breath, before their union was even legally constituted. This was industrial war in all its violence and trickery, with the rival labor faction repeatedly intervening. Up to 1914 Sidney Hillman had never been the leader of a strike action; he was to receive some rude lessons from the start.

The trouble in Baltimore centered at the big manufacturing plant of Henry L. Sonneborn and Company, which had recently begun to introduce the Taylor System into its shops. In the slack season of early October its managers planned to close the place, dismiss the workers, change the machinery, and then rehire the labor force on a reduced scale. Operations were to be stepped up to meet the "efficiency" quotas fixed by time-and-motion studies; then the strongest specimens among the workers, as proven by physical examination, would be offered re-employment and enrolled in a company union.

But the 3,000 workers at Sonneborn's, many of them members of the United Garment Workers, on hearing of these new arrangements, walked out spontaneously on October 1–3, 1914, declaring they were really "locked out." It was at this very moment that the split in the union had developed at Nashville. Two big Baltimore locals of tailors and operators, a majority of the force, voted to join the secessionists, while the cutters' local (about 10 per cent of the workers) elected to follow their old officers of the UGWA. Thus the craftsmen were on one side, and the semi-skilled, production-line people in overwhelming majority were in the new industrial union. The strike continued, awkwardly enough, under two rival sets of leaders, the secessionists being headed by the young pocket maker, Hyman Blumberg, as well as the Bellanca brothers and a girl worker named Dorothy Jacobs.

The established AFL officers began to exert pressure against their rivals by subtle measures at first, though the affair soon developed into a brawl. Generous strike-relief payments of as much as $6.00 a week were sent at once from Bible House, New York headquarters of the UGWA, to the 250 "loyal" cutters, while no aid of any kind was offered the larger mass of secessionist tailors and operators. Hillman, though his treasury was bare, made strenuous efforts to raise funds among the New York and Chicago locals and was able to pay out $1.50 or so each week to the neediest among the more than 2,000 tailors on strike. The cutters, however, with their larger relief checks, taunted the other workers for joining the "outlaws"—this was even before the schism had become complete—thus attempting to wean away the other clothing workers from their new leaders. But Hillman sent several of the union's first organizers—among them Isaac Goldstein and Louis Hollander—to address daily meetings of the Baltimore strikers and keep up their courage. For eight weeks they held their picket lines stubbornly.

At this point, late in November, it was learned on good authority, through a friendly Maryland state welfare officer, that the UGWA had reached a secret agreement with the company to call off the strike and have the cutters go back to their jobs at an early date with some increase in pay. The cutters were, of course, the key men, standing at the head of the production line. As for the poor tailors, the UGWA, it was reported, intended to have them return as non-union people.[1] To the new leadership this seemed nothing less than "scabbing" by the rival faction.

Hillman, meanwhile, had been taking measures of his own and

managed to contact the employers at the Sonneborn company, to whom he offered a peaceful compromise in accordance with methods he had used with success in Chicago. An advisory committee of three was to be appointed by both sides, headed by an impartial figure, Professor George E. Barnett of Johns Hopkins University, and the committee was to fix the final terms of an agreement. In a tentative outline of such an agreement Hillman proposed that the employees still on strike were to return "without discrimination"; dismissals under the Taylor System were to be restricted to no more than 240 workers; and those discharged were to be kept on a "preferential list" for rehiring, as members of the new union group. The scheme thus involved tacit recognition of the new union as representing all but the cutters.

A mass meeting was called for November 23, 1914, and Hillman hurried down to Baltimore to appeal to the strikers for approval of the preliminary agreement he had worked out. The young president made a strong speech in which he argued that the present was a very dangerous moment for their still poorly organized union to fight a long strike; that the rival labor group was prepared to call off the strike and help the employer resume output; that his compromise proposals, which the company would "probably" accept, would result in a "preferential union shop"; and that it was important, above all, to begin to "deal with the employers *as a union.*"

But feeling ran high among those Baltimore workers. They were bitter at the proposal that they abandon 240 of their brother workers, and protested that they knew nothing about "Chicago methods" and cared nothing for arbitration schemes. They were for continuing the strike without any compromise, and their local leaders, including Blumberg and August Bellanca, loudly disagreed with their president.[2]

Hillman, while continuing to urge the plan he had laid before them, now made it clear that he was presenting the strikers not with a settlement, but with a "proposed settlement which they could accept or reject as they willed." If they rejected it, he "would never use the authority of his office to force an agreement on them," as had been repeatedly done by their old union's officers, but would stand by them to the bitter end. At length he called for a vote. The hands went up, and the meeting seemed divided by only a narrow margin, as those who were present recall. Hillman took in the situation at a glance and, smiling, announced that his motion had been defeated.[3]

The local officer, Blumberg, remembered the vote as having been more or less even. And Hillman, a resourceful man on the platform, could have pressed for acceptance of his proposals. He himself said later that he thought he could have had his way in the end but had sensed the sharp division among the strikers and did not want approval of his settlement "at the price of splitting the Baltimore membership."

Instead he declared himself fully satisfied that the strike must go on. The magnanimity of his attitude drew a tremendous outburst of cheers from the 1,500 persons in the meeting hall, while one speaker after another exclaimed that it was the first time in twenty years that a general officer of their union had not "rammed a settlement down the throats of the strikers."

At this stage Hillman made still another dramatic flourish; he drew a check from his pocket which he said was being donated by the union's national office for strike relief, adding that he was returning to New York at once to raise more funds. More thunderous acclamations greeted this fine gesture, while Hillman whispered to Blumberg, who was on the platform: "See that you don't deposit that check for two days, till I can raise enough to cover it at the bank in New York." The amount was only $200.[4]

Hillman had "lost" his motion for a settlement, but won the hearts of all the union members and made quite an impression on their local leaders. The next day rumors were spread by the UGWA local officers that the president of the seceding union group had attempted a "sellout," only to be repudiated by his own followers, and that there was hopeless dissension among the strikers. In the confusion of the moment the UGWA officers suddenly marched their 250 loyal cutters, according to their prearranged plan, back into the Sonneborn factory.

News of this aroused the tailors to fever pitch. Blumberg and the Bellanca brothers that morning quickly gathered together an army of 1,200 as a mass picket committee and closed in to besiege the factory. The police of Baltimore repeatedly drove them off, making numerous arrests, yet they held their line.

Inside were 250 cutters, locked in, fearing for their lives, for the crowd outside was tumultuous. Dinner was brought to them, and cots were provided for the night. Amid the din made by the strikers down below, the cutters inside the plant tried to go on cutting cloth, though there were no sewing-machine operators to sew them up. Finally, at three o'clock in the afternoon, the manager of Sonneborn's told them they might as well go home. Shame-faced, the "loyal" AFL cutters marched out in a body, to the great and uproarious delight of the crowd of pickets outside.

The Sonneborn company now hauled down its flag and offered better terms to the striking tailors, including a promise to take back the 240 workers who were to have been dismissed. Blumberg and his colleague, Sam Silverman, as heads of the Baltimore locals, were to select a committee of "workers' representatives" to negotiate and implement the settlement. It was a first taste of victory: the new union had broken through the doors of one of the four largest clothing firms in the country.

Hillman was feeling his way and learning to work with all sorts of different people. The strikers in Baltimore had been fighting mad at the idea of having 240 of their tailors dismissed. The settlement turned out to be better than Hillman had hoped for, and he was glad to go along with the workers. As for the local leader, Blumberg, who had stubbornly clashed with Hillman on the terms of settlement, his fighting spirit was duly noted and he was marked for advancement in the organization. Here once again we see the young Hillman, though strongly disposed to the way of conciliation, swept along by his own union members toward a more militant policy.

II

After the first weeks of confusion Hillman and his fellow executives began to take stock of their situation and map out large-scale plans for their union's development. At the start of 1915, the Amalgamated, in membership, stood at a ratio of about 2 to 1 to the United Garment workers. Both organizations together controlled less than 25 per cent of the 250,000 workers in men's clothing. The Amalgamated membership included chiefly ready-made clothing workers in the large cities, while the UGWA consisted mainly of producers of work clothing and overalls in "label houses." This division of the industry continued in the same status under an oft-interrupted truce, though gradually the Hillman-led union was to increase its advantage in size until it stood as four or five times larger than the stagnant AFL organization.

In New York the Amalgamated held a commanding position,

thanks to the 1913 uprising of the New York locals. Efforts of the UGWA to win back the New York cutters, sometimes by devious arrangements between the older union's executives and groups of employers, were easily blocked. By February 1915, most of the principal manufacturers in New York signed agreements with the officers of the Amalgamated, and the UGWA was never again a serious factor in the clothing industry of the metropolitan market, though it frequently raised its head in other markets.

New York was the nation's biggest clothing center, "unionized," but very loosely unionized then; nobody knew how many thousands of small contractors' shops there were in the sprawling area of the city's five boroughs and its suburbs. Here was concentrated about half the total ACWA membership. Yet for a decade the Amalgamated controlled only about 40 per cent of the New York market.[5] Its administrative setup here was also weakened by the fact that there were five different "joint boards," one each for cutters, coat makers, pants makers, vest makers, and children's clothing workers, a hang-over of the old craft-division system. Underlying these were strong local bosses who had been running things in their own way for twenty years. Some of them were honest and high-minded, like Abraham Miller, chief of five pants makers' locals, who, with his 7,000 members, gave staunch support to the Hillman administration from the start. Others reflected the low moral standards prevailing in this much-sweated industry.

Hillman thought that the New York district of the Amalgamated could stand a great deal of reorganizing and improvement, but he was forced to bide his time.

In this growing union he represented the "Chicago school," but his powerful New York lieutenants knew the tricks of the trade in their market much better than he. Some of them he had no use for, yet he approached them with the utmost diplomacy.

"How could you bear to smile and shake hands with that low scoundrel? How could you even touch his dirty hand?" one of his intimates of that period asked him.

Hillman laughed: "Well, I shake hands with him, and then I go to the washroom and wash my hands, and I'm clean again!" But in good time he forced the resignation of those persons he regarded as dishonest. The habits of a generation of union members and their numerous petty officers could not be changed overnight. Moreover, the union's problems in other large cities were much more pressing.

The Amalgamated had a good foothold in Boston; it had weaker local groups in Philadelphia, Cincinnati, Cleveland, St. Louis, and other Midwestern cities; a very strong position in Baltimore (then an important clothing market) under courageous young leaders. In Rochester, a rising center of large-scale modern clothing factories, the Amalgamated was frozen out. In Toronto and Montreal there were only a few weak locals. In Chicago, second only to New York as a market, there were only a fourth of the 35,000 to 40,000 clothing workers organized, nearly all of these in the Hart, Schaffner and Marx locals. Chicago was the worst spot on the map so far as the Amalgamated was concerned. At the same time it offered the greatest opportunities for rapid unionization of the whole market because of the solid nucleus of the Hart, Schaffner and Marx employees, whom Hillman regarded as the most advanced unionists in his organization. This small army would serve as the vanguard for all the other workers. Since the New York market was largely organized after 1913, the Amalgamated could not stand still in Chicago, or it would continue to offer the most destructive competition to the New York manufacturers who were under union agreements.

In February 1915, Hillman assigned to Frank Rosenblum the task of studying the ground in Chicago and making a detailed report on plans for organizing the entire men's clothing trade there.[6] Preparations along the lines marked by Rosenblum then went forward for long months, with a view to calling a general city-wide strike.

The different union shops were "felt out" secretly; men were contacted who were willing to join the union and quietly given their assignments. In each section of the industry the union's leaders tried to measure how much unrest there was and how much union sentiment could be aroused.[7]

It was all hard, uphill work. Some 150 manufacturing firms, including large ones like Kuppenheimer, Alfred, Decker and Cohn and Royal Tailoring, with from 1,500 to 2,500 employees each, were combined in a tight anti-union defense association which used the blacklist with effect.

In addition to the sub-soil operations, big, open mass meetings of the clothing workers were also held in the late winter and spring of 1915, at which Hillman, Schlossberg, and other national officers addressed crowds of clothing workers. A large demonstration was also planned for May Day, 1915. "We are not talking strike here, but we are simply talking organization," Hillman reported.[8] Organizers were now carefully selected: one, Stephen Skala, would speak in Bohemian; another would appeal to the Italians; a third would address himself mainly to the Polish workers. Weekly dues were raised now from 15 cents to 25 cents, and the per capita tax was increased slightly in order to accumulate a "war chest."

Enthusiasm mounted among the clothing workers in Chicago, long held back by their old UGWA leaders. Soon reports came in that several fair-sized firms had been infiltrated by Amalgamated people and were "more or less under the influence and control of our organization." The May Day parade, swelled by the thousands of Hart, Schaffner workers, was "the biggest thing of its kind" in Chicago.[9]

The manufacturers were not slow to hit back. Several of the Amalgamated's earnest missionaries who had taken jobs in certain non-union shops suddenly found themselves out in the street. The other clothing workers became wrathful. In a small strike that took place in July, they came out in force, using their muscles freely against the "scabs" who were staying in, and at the end of a serious scuffle laid out twenty of their opponents on the ground. Although union men were arrested by the police, the employer found it difficult to keep going, and accepted a union-shop agreement.

The Chicago leaders now pressed Hillman to take action and inaugurate strikes on a large scale. But he determinedly held them back, while careful preparations went on for months longer.

All that year, 1915, he had to rush from one troubled sector to another. There was not only the overshadowing problem of Chicago, but in Boston also a costly strike of 600 employees at the manufacturing firm of Leopold Morse. The company, after having signed an agreement with the Amalgamated local (formerly a long-established UGWA unit,) had violated its contract only a month later and served notice on its tailors that they must go back to membership in the UGWA or be dismissed. The rival faction, it was reported, had come forward with "bargain terms" for a union agreement. In indignation the workers walked out, and Hillman supported them to the uttermost, feeling that an employer who broke his agreement must be taught a lesson. But police and court action bore hard on the pickets; as many as 200 were arrested, and fines of $2,000 were imposed.[10]

"The situation in Boston looks very bad. It looks like a losing fight and is eating up our finances," Hillman wrote on April 15. The union's national office needed $100,000 a year now to keep going and had not a third of that sum. "You have no idea of how pressed we are for money, and it would be shameful to lose that fight [in Boston] for lack of funds." [11] Yet he kept this strike going for three long months— until he was forced to abandon the position. The calls for help in bailing out union men under arrest came to him from many points. Hillman, at such tight moments, would borrow a few hundred dollars on his personal note and live on half pay or less. He urged his associates to practice the most stringent economy and engage volunteers whenever possible to do organizing work.

One of his letters of this difficult season runs:

I made a personal loan of $250 . . . to pay you people off, but within the time that I sent out the checks to you I received the above news from Boston and I had to send this money to them. . . . The General Office owes me over $400 and I owe about $500 over the country. I shall send you money as soon as the National Office is in a position to pay me something. Explain this to Marimpietri and Bessie.

Then he adds encouragingly:

We all must carry the burden. I am hopeful as to the outcome. As a matter of fact conditions are improving.[12]

The problem of keeping order among the different local leaders of the union also gave him concern. They were warm-blooded, strong-willed individuals, each fighting stubbornly for his own idea of the best way to help his fellow workers. The young president, as peace-maker, saw to it that internal dissensions among his assistants were kept in the family and out of the newspapers. This became an Amalgamated tradition from the very beginning.

There were times also when Hillman had to impose discipline on members of his own staff, as when a union group or local leader had violated an agreement with an employer. Thus in one case where a "flash" strike broke out over the firing of a single man, Hillman hurried down to restore order, then wrote a biting letter to the business agent who was responsible:

. . . A few more victories of such a nature and our organization will be confronted with real danger. I realize more and more that the system where the discharge of one man might cause a strike of thousands is very dangerous. . . .[13]

Hillman's thoughts in 1915 were largely centered on the Chicago sector. But in many instances some of the New York manufacturers had begun to break away from their union agreements; these must first be forced into line before any large attack could be made in Chicago. Therefore an elaborate demonstration of union strength was arranged for New York in the summer of 1915 to show the employers there that the Amalgamated was on its mettle.

Its members were bitter because wages in several departments had dropped below the levels of 1913. They were ready, as often before, to come storming out as a mob. But Hillman's strategy called for military precision in the arrangement for this walkout.

On July 12, 1915, as the General Executive Board's report relates:

Ten thousand pants makers were the first division in the field. The unanimity and enthusiasm of the walkout made a marked impression on the labor movement, the employers and the general public. Five thousand vest makers and 6,000 knee-pants makers followed.

On the third day of the strike our largest division, the coat makers, were called to the colors. They were instructed to work in their shops until noon and report at meetings at one o'clock. Over 25,000 coat makers crowded all the halls prepared for them. . . .

Six meeting halls in different parts of the city had been designated as gathering places for the strikers. Hillman tore about the city during the day, addressing legions of his members; at night he talked settlement with the employers. "We desire peace, but are ready for war," he said. They were apparently impressed by the martial spirit with which the tailors arrayed themselves for battle and broadened their walkout day by day under the new leadership. On the third day of the "stoppage"—before those 25,000 coat makers were to come out —the manufacturers' associations asked for a peace conference. Within the week an agreement providing for restoration of most of the recent wage reductions was completed and signed by representatives of the two manufacturers' associations then separately covering men's and boy's clothing in New York.[14] Meanwhile small but vigorous strikes were directed against those firms which did not participate in the agreement.

Formerly different agreements had covered the separate crafts and provided for different dates of expiration. In this way it was possible, as Hillman's report to his members later pointed out, for the employers to use one group of workers against the other, as if they were "mutual strikebreakers." But now a common term was set for the contracts covering the Amalgamated cutters, coat makers, and pants makers, fixing the collective-bargaining pattern "on the basis of the entire industry as one indivisible unit. The agreement begins and ends alike for all workers." Such was the plan of industrial unionism.

III

At the beginning of August 1915, Hillman met privately with the six other members of his Executive Board, and the decision was taken to begin the long-planned attack on the non-union manufacturers in Chicago. Frank Rosenblum had completed his preparations. The president then moved on to Chicago and set up strike headquarters at the La Salle Hotel. According to a procedure which became habitual with him, he first drew up a proposal for a clear-cut collective-bargaining agreement which he presented to the Chicago Wholesale Clothiers' Association, together with a letter (soon issued to the press) in which he made a strong appeal for a peaceful conference. He also made every effort to approach the large manufacturers in person, but met with no response. The truth was that he was still uneasy about the steadfastness of the people in the non-union shops. A series of union mass meetings was held in late August and early September at which Hillman did all he could to raise the morale of the tailors. "The fear of the workers for a strike is passing and everybody is more courageous," he reported on August 13, 1915. But a few weeks later, as preparations went forward, he wrote:

> The situation here is such that we will be forced to call a strike within two weeks if nothing happens. There seems to be very little possibility of getting the manufacturers to a conference. They are arrogant and stubborn. They think they can defeat the union the way they have done in the past.
>
> Our organization committee has decided to draft a letter today to the manufacturers giving them ten days' notice. Our own strength is not clear as yet . . . but it is doubtful whether we will ever have it in better shape. The outcome would be doubtful under all circumstances.[15]

In public he exuded good cheer and confidence but felt the deepest apprehensions inwardly. There were many and grave reasons to doubt the outcome of this struggle which, up to the last hour, he would have preferred to avoid. He was a man of peace and foresaw that violence would be unloosed once the industrial struggle began in earnest. It was his conviction, even at this period of militancy, that the strike, "the weapon of the jungle," was destined to become obsolete; that it represented "a tremendous waste . . . and the greatest indictment of the present system [was] that it was necessary to strike to secure a betterment of conditions."

Moreover, he knew at this time, as he wrote to an associate, that though the Amalgamated union claimed 50,000 members, "the average dues-paying membership in the last six months was a little over 20,000." Money was lacking for a protracted struggle. The wealth of the biggest "inside shops" in Chicago, save for Hart, Schaffner and Marx, would be thrown against the weak union. The rival UGWA officers were now making public statements predicting that the Amalgamated would not last out the year, and denouncing its leaders as "outlaws" and "anarchists." In Hillman's report to his New York office at this moment one may read his profound uncertainty on the eve of battle, his calculation of the risk involved.

The danger of backing out at this time is that we may lose our opportunity in the future. It is a tremendous responsibility to decide.[16]

To test the strength of their following the union issued a call for a great mass meeting in Hod Carriers' Hall on September 24. A crowd of 5,000 assembled and responded with such enthusiasm to the proposals of their leader that Hillman called it a clear commitment to action. That night his supporters saw a Sidney Hillman they hadn't known before, a "generalissimo," as old John E. Williams called him.

He was by now an orator of no mean ability; he knew how to hold the crowd and make them share his anger. He told of how he had conferred for hours on end with Mr. Jacob Abt, head of the manufacturers' organization, offering to submit all demands of the union to impartial arbitration. He said:

We want peace so badly that we are willing to fight for it. We do not want the peace of the graveyard, nor the peace of the slave. We do not want welfare work. . . . We do not want charity, we want justice.

The answer from the other side had been that the workers were "contented," that there was "nothing to arbitrate." But if the workers were so happy, Hillman observed ironically, why were their employers unwilling to appear before an impartial committee? He ended on a note of passionate protest that his hearers long remembered:

All we want is to be recognized as human beings and not machines. Open shops mean open for those who work for less; open for the least price. Closed shops mean freedom of the heart. We do not want foremen to become czars in this land of liberty. . . . If the strike is called, *strike hard,* so that victory comes quickly.

In his strike call Hillman had promised the clothing workers that for the first time their action would be thoroughly organized. Only five picked leaders in Chicago knew what the plan of action was, or how or when the signal would be given. The city had been divided up into four separate districts, each with its own headquarters, meeting halls, and relief organization, under the command of Frank Rosenblum, Sam Levin, Marimpietri, and Bessie Abramowitz. The Clothiers' Association had posted police and armed detectives before the factory gates, but inside the shop, chairmen knew their orders and were ready.

Hillman's demands (which he indicated were maximal and subject to negotiation) were for the 48-hour week, a 25 per cent average wage increase, union recognition, and the establishment of collective bargaining and adjustment machinery. Nearly all the Chicago newspapers had commented favorably on the union president's earnest appeals for an arbitration conference that would spare the city a prolonged strike. (Incidentally, Hillman had taken the precaution, rather novel then, of engaging an experienced newspaper man to handle the union's publicity.) The final reply of the Association, through its attorney, was contemptuous; he would not "dignify" the request for arbitration by admitting there was anything to arbitrate.

On September 27, when the waiting period fixed by Hillman was over, shop chairmen inside the heavily guarded plants jumped up at varying "zero hours" set the night before and blew their whistles to stop work. At several of the larger factories that were first struck thousands of men and women fought their way past their guards and out into the street. There were 15,000 out on the first day, and 25,000 on the second. Hillman had given strict orders prohibiting any violence by the strikers and declaring that picketing would be unnecessary. But after a few days of quiet, trouble flared up when crowds of workers surrounded plants in which non-union personnel had stayed on the job. Bricks flew, windows were shattered, and police on horseback charged the crowds or laid about them with their clubs.

The autumn weeks passed, while the union kept a sharp watch on New York and other cities to see to it that orders for Chicago's clothing factories were not shifted elsewhere.

John E. Williams, a friendly observer of the strike front, related:

Strikes there have been before in the garment industry, and they have been fierce, violent, and hotly contested; but there has been none like this in organization, management, and in the thoroughly planned and scientific efficiency of the campaign. . . . The present strike was planned with a coolness and thoroughness comparable to that of the general staff in Germany. Although the hand of the general was forced rather prematurely, yet the war . . . had long been regarded as inevitable. . . . Organization had been perfected with each factory as a unit, and in charge of each factory was placed a chairman who was made responsible for his people. Over the chairmen were placed district leaders, over these department commanders, and above all the chief generalissimo, President Sidney Hillman.

When the strike was called the general . . . could give a command from his headquarters in the La Salle Hotel, and instantly the general staff at Hod Carriers' Hall would transmit it to the eager and expectant chairman on the north, south, and west sides, who would put the order into execution on the second.[17]

The eighth week of the contest was reached, and despite many violent collisions and arrests, "General Hillman" assured Williams that his lines were intact and munitions were flowing in steadily.

The employers, on their side of the trenches, though production was paralyzed, maintained a stony silence. Williams, who was well known to them, approached some of them to learn if they would consider terms of peace. But the reply given by one member of the Association was:

We regard Sidney Hillman very highly. We believe him honest, high-minded, and capable. But we don't believe he can control his people. It is notorious that union leaders in the garment trade are short-lived. They kill each other off. With Hillman dead or dethroned we would be back in the hands of the old grafting pirates, who would not enforce an agreement, who would foment shop strikes for the purpose of extorting money from us . . . who would destroy the quality of our work, which has cost us so much to build up.

Williams repeated this to the union leader, who said laconically: "Why don't they give Hillman a chance?"

Had not he and his associates introduced a plan for responsible self-government in the greatest of the Chicago clothing factories? And now, while the rest of the industry was in turmoil, its 8,000 employees worked more busily than ever and in a spirit of peace and good will. Indeed the Hart, Schaffner and Marx shops were swamped with orders, and each week most of their workers paid a 10 per cent assessment on their wages into the union's strike-relief fund so that their brothers might carry on. Sooner or later the Association's employers would have to come to the union, as Mr. Schaffner was saying. Why not now? But instead they called for ever-sterner measures by the Chicago police, who now exerted themselves to escort strikebreakers through the picket lines.

Hillman made strong protests through the press:

I issued instructions to our people to observe the law . . . and they have kept within their rights as law-abiding citizens. In spite of that mounted policemen have run their horses on the sidewalks among our women and girls, motorcycle policemen have clubbed our girls and have committed acts of brutality that are a disgrace. One of our men was shot by an employer, and, from the statements of eyewitnesses, the attack was entirely unprovoked and uncalled for.[18]

His telegrams reporting developments to the New York headquarters of the union started out in cheerful vein. On September 28 he wired:

OVER 20,000 PEOPLE OUT TODAY—PRESS FILLED WITH NEWS—CITY FILLED WITH SLUGGERS

Another dispatch, dated October 5, 1915, ran:

SITUATION UNCHANGED—SOCIETY WOMEN WILL HELP PICKETING.[19]

The next day persons like Mrs. Medill McCormick, Miss Ellen Gates Starr, and assorted ministers and social workers moved into the trenches. Several among them were subjected to abuse and arrested.

The arrest of a former debutante, Miss Starr, made good newspaper publicity.

Hillman continued to pursue this trail with a keen nose for public opinion. Another of his telegrams reads:

HAVE DISCUSSED STRIKE SITUATION TODAY WITH 700 METHODIST MINISTERS.

The newspapers reflected a friendly spirit by giving unbiased accounts of parades of the strikers being broken up by the police, while publishing headlines to the effect that

STRIKE LEADER HILLMAN URGES MEN TO SHUN VIOLENCE [20]

Hillman related afterward that the publicized brutality of the employers and the police definitely inspired much popular sympathy for the strikers.

Early in October, at the head of a delegation of prominent local citizens and trade unionists, and accompanied by a flock of 5,000 clothing workers, Hillman paid a call on Mayor William H. ("Big Bill") Thompson and petitioned for mediation of the strike by the city government. His delegation was refused an audience by the mayor, and the workers outside were driven off with clubs by the police. News of this affair made a painful impression on decent citizens. As a consequence, an Aldermanic Committee was soon prompted to begin an investigation of alleged unsanitary and immoral conditions in the Chicago clothing sweatshops where, as Hillman charged, poor working girls were sometimes forced into white slavery:

> Sixty per cent of these workers are young women and they are absolutely dependent on the whims of the shop foremen who . . . force them to endure all manner of indignities in order to retain their places. The conditions are degrading, and I can only say that the majority of the girls have remained clean morally by a narrow margin.[21]

The girls themselves were excellent witnesses for the union. One girl testified that in the rush season she worked as long as twenty hours in a day to earn as little as $1.25. To charges that the union was "outlawed" by the AFL a stouthearted Polish girl said: "I'll tell you what it is, they [the UGWA] have got the charter and we have got the membership and that's all there is to it!" Another high-spirited girl picket, after being arrested for slapping a non-union worker, was asked whether Mr. Hillman had ordered her to do such things.

She replied proudly: "Nobody *told* me anything—I knew enough to do it myself!"

The Chicago strikers held their heads high, though the weather turned cold and strike relief amounted to a meager two dollars a week, and at that was granted only in hardship cases. Hillman seemed to be everywhere at once in this contest. If a besieged factory provided beds and meals for its non-union help, he quickly brought the Illinois State Factory Inspector to begin suits and close up such places. He was in touch with union agents at points ranging from New York to St. Louis to check the shifting of orders from Chicago firms to other towns. Above all, he left no stone unturned to win help for some 8,000 of the unionists who he feared would soon be starving. Once more Jane Addams came to his aid by raising $22,000 for relief from non-labor sources. But in the main the cost of the strike was borne by the union members themselves, $90,000 being provided over a period of three months by the Hart, Schaffner and Marx workers in Chicago and by donations through the general office of the Amalgamated in New York.

To Secretary Schlossberg and other colleagues Hillman sent heart-rending cries for cash: the struggle, he said, was becoming a test of endurance, and $15,000 weekly was needed to support the strike. The members who had jobs in Chicago were raising among themselves from $9,000 to $10,000 of this sum, but, he wired—his temper fairly snapping—"New York is getting on my nerves. . . . I have asked for money and all you sent was $3,000." At this rate, he warned, the strike would soon be broken.

When Schlossberg indicated that he was offended at Hillman's scolding, Hillman promptly apologized, saying that his feelings had been overwrought by the strain he labored under, and so "all I can do is talk to the people, chide them, and give them hell." [22]

Chicago then seemed much farther from New York than it does today. Despite Schlossberg's earnest efforts, the New York members, though three times more numerous than the Chicago section, raised but half as much money. [23]

Hillman never forgot the lessons he learned in the Chicago strike of 1915. The first was that you need money to win a strike. This poor, makeshift union in its first months had done wonders, actually raising $112,000 in twelve weeks. But it was not enough. "We were a burden to all sorts of charitable organizations in those days," Hillman said afterward. Yet the help of the social workers and philanthropists had counted for little in the balance, less than 20 per cent of the total. If only the employed members had contributed a little more, the battle could have been won with ease. Hillman resolved that his union must be self-sustaining. If the members wanted the benefits of collective bargaining, they must be induced to pay for them.

The economic weakness of the union also showed itself in its inability to stop orders for clothing from being shifted to other centers, especially New York. A third problem was the political one personified by Mayor Thompson, who showed extreme hostility to the clothing workers, reflected in the systematic brutality of his police officials. During the investigation of the strike by members of the Chicago City Council, the acting police commissioner had been asked whether he had worked in collusion with the employers, as evidenced by reports of police spies infesting the union meetings. With the approval of the city's attorney, he had refused to answer, saying: "It would be unfair for the police to tell their source of information if perchance they had secret agents at the meetings of the strikers." This defiance of the City Council again made an unfavorable impression on public opinion, yet with the approval of the mayor, the police of Chicago continued their methodical violence, as in the strike of 1910.[24]

The strike went on through October, though hundreds of hungry men and women began to drift back to their jobs now. Every two or three days a picket would be shot and wounded, or a girl worker might be slugged and carried off to the hospital, in one instance with a fractured breastbone. When citizens attempted to remonstrate with the mayor, he refused to intervene, saying that the strikers were guilty of violence on their own part. Hillman conceded that young workers who were "terribly in earnest" and made desperate by the behavior of the police could not be restrained from fighting back in self-defense.[25]

On October 27, 1915, events took an even uglier turn. There had been a crowd gathered near a factory at Harrison and Halsted streets, a short distance from the union's headquarters, when a sudden charge by police and plain-clothes men struck them. Everybody turned and ran, save a deaf-mute tailor named Samuel Kapper, who moved too late. Several shots were heard, and there lay poor Kapper, a good worker and a loyal union man, with a bullet through his back. The police and workers alike looked on in a stupor. Young Jacob Potofsky, then a local secretary, had seen the whole drama and wired to New York:

SEVERAL MEN SHOT BY STRIKE BREAKERS AT HARRISON AND HALSTED AT SIX O'CLOCK TODAY KAPPER 2147 CRYSTAL STREET KILLED OTHERS WOUNDED I SAW STRIKER'S BLOOD STREAMING LIKE WATER ON THE SIDE-WALK CORONER'S INQUEST TOMORROW 10 A.M. FUNERAL THURSDAY.[26]

The police claimed that they had fired in self-defense. But once again there was the sight of a long funeral procession, of 10,000 ragged men and careworn women carrying babies, that slowly wound through the city, all grimly silent as they paid their last respects to their dead comrade.

After the shooting of Kapper, Hillman suddenly felt sick and in great pain took to his bed, being confined to his hotel room for a week. He wrote to New York: "I am laid up for a few days by order of the doctor. There is nothing serious. I cannot walk but expect to be all right within a few days." [27] It was the first manifestation of an arthritic condition that often showed itself thereafter when Hillman was under great stress.

His venerable friend, John Williams, who knew and loved him well, came to sit by his bedside. With keen insight Williams noted that the illness masked an emotional crisis. The spirit of compassion was strong in Hillman; he was by nature a very gentle, even a senti-mental, soul. Now, after having for years expounded labor mediation and peace, he saw that a labor union could survive and grow strong in the jungle of modern society only by hard and bloody combat. Nineteen-fifteen was his baptism of fire; after that one sensed in the soft-spoken union leader a vein of iron. Williams related:

. . . The thing that burned into Hillman's soul and made him a hun-dred years older was the killing and slugging. Each murder sent him to bed for a couple of days; his overwrought nerves could not stand it. He told me once that the police of Chicago were more brutal than those of Russia; that its prisons were more loathsome; that the treatment of prisoners was more barbarous. And he knows whereof he speaks, for he has been inside of both. He says his people have been thrown into prison, given third degree, and come out with bruised and bleeding faces and with heads beaten to a pulp. When once a man passes the police line, he says, all civilization, all human rights come to an end. You are back in savagery with nothing to protect you from the cruelty of the men clothed with the power of the law. . . .

I asked:

"But is not their twentieth-century training . . . sufficient to make them use their power justly?"

"It makes it all the worse," he replied. . . . "A Russian officer . . . might beat a prisoner because he was in a rage himself; but your American police beat or torture a man with a cool, calculating fiendishness, and a smile while they are doing it. You think you have got rid of the rack and torture chamber, but in the third degree you have a more devilish engine than anything the Inquisition could boast." [28]

From his sickbed Hillman reviewed the results of the struggle thus far in a report to the New York office, which, by its cheerful tone, sought to conceal his anxiety:

. . . In the sixth week of the strike, everything seems to be in fine shape. I never thought that a fight of this nature would ever occur. I feel that it is good for another six weeks. That is the good side of it. The other side is that work is being made in large quantities in New York, also in other places, leaving a depressing effect on the morale of the strikers . . . [who feel] that the manufacturers can find some way of making some of the work.

Exhausting as the struggle was for the union, it was likewise costing the manufacturers many millions. Eighty-six small employers had ended by signing union-shop agreements by now; and one of the large ones, Lamm and Company, had broken from the ranks of the Clothiers' Association, offering to take back its 500 workers without discrimination. Thus about 5,000 were returning to their jobs as union men. "Things may turn for good or otherwise any minute," he judged. There were still chances to win the whole market, he continued:

. . . The strike is becoming a war, with so many actually wounded every day, but the spirit seems to be there, a real fighting spirit to be admired by everybody. . . .

Try to do something so that we do not blame ourselves no matter what the outcome. I want you to understand that I am far from being pessimistic. Things look better than at any time during the strike.[29]

But for all this air of confidence, one feels that his thoughts had already turned to the possibilities of a strategic withdrawal. In early December, after a conference with his colleagues of the Chicago Joint Board, the decision to call off the strike was taken. The painful thing was to break the news to the plucky men and women on the picket lines.

"We have begun our retreat," he said to Williams one night. "Like the armies of the Allies we are retiring . . . to better positions." No general recognition for the union had been won in Chicago, but that could wait, he said. Unionism was creeping in through the back door. The arrogant Association employers would be a long time recovering from their losses. Would they be willing to face the same thing again every two or three years?

Had the struggle been worth while? Hillman was asked. There were two dead and more than 800 wounded, or injured enough to require medical attention, by his count. Yet it was only by great sacrifices that powerful loyalties could be generated in such a movement as theirs. This was war, too, but for nobler ends, he believed, than the great slaughter in Europe:

> We have done something better than punish the enemy. We have infused a new solidarity among our people. . . .
>
> It is fine for people to give their heart's blood for something better than killing their fellow men as they are doing in the Old World. If you could have seen our people, as I have day by day, suffering, denying themselves for a cause—if you could see men refusing to draw on the relief fund, even though in want, that there might be more for weaker ones—if you could see with what enthusiasm they have responded to a call to meet at 5 A.M. to go out on the picket line—if you could see not only men, but weak women and girls volunteer to . . . expose themselves to the clubs . . . of brutal sluggers and policemen—if you could see the splendid qualities of leadership developed among our hastily improvised captains and generals, working day and night . . . under the most nerve-racking strain, with a terrible sense of responsibility for the safety and the lives of those they lead—you would not ask if it was worth while.[30]

There were 16,000 who had stayed out to the end. The decision to call off the strike was submitted to the approval of a union mass meeting on December 12, 1915, when Hillman, in a long speech (not preserved, but well remembered for its unusual warmth of feeling), "courageously faced his comrades with the unpleasant facts," as Williams said. Frank Rosenblum, who was present, recalls: "It was one of Hillman's finest traits that he had the courage always to tell the painful truth"—in this case, that the union was simply at the end of its rope and must make whatever settlement it could.

These long-abused clothing workers had never known real union leadership in the past, nor organized action, nor regular strike relief; nor were they accustomed to being consulted about the settlement of a strike. In defeat the stature of young Hillman grew greater for them. They saw how worn he looked; they had seen also how he had expended himself in the fight. The simple, straightforward words he spoke moved their hearts. Bessie Abramowitz remembers that final strike meeting in Chicago as "the saddest day of my life," and how she and the other 3,000 persons shed tears as Hillman spoke,[31] They wept when he dwelt upon the sacrifices they had borne, but voted for the termination of the strike, as he recommended. They cheered when he spoke of the serious penetration they had made into this non-union market and the growing power the union had shown. The stubborn enemy had been hurt, Hillman declared; the union had "lost a battle" but not the war; "the war" would go on, again and again, next year, and the next. The members raised the roof with their deep roar at Hillman's determined, parting words: *"We will come back!"*

Chapter Six

EXPANSION: 1916-1917

In its first two years the Amalgamated fought through a series of losing strikes, but, in the manner of George Washington, retreated only to return in stronger force. The manufacturers of men's clothing who had paid but little heed to the sentiments of their labor force in the past now felt the organizing hand of young Mr. Hillman almost everywhere in the trade. In Chicago the employers claimed that they had "beaten the Amalgamated people to their knees." The truth was that both sides licked their wounds—yet the union emerged with 12,000 members in that city where it had had but 8,000 at the end of 1914. The Association houses showed fear of the union by "voluntarily" granting improvements in hours and wages that approached or equaled the union's standard. This "lost strike" had brought important gains, as often happened in our industrial struggles. Indeed, after a quick trip to New York and Baltimore, Hillman, his health restored, speedily returned to Chicago in January 1916 to help reconstruct the organization there "in view of the large number of new members, and the entrance of the union into new fields, whereas before it had been confined to one firm." [1]

No sooner was the Chicago strike over than the union was faced with a greater threat in New York. Without pause to take breath Hillman returned to deal with an impending city-wide strike, and at a time when the Amalgamated treasury boasted mainly evidences of debt. Schlossberg wrote: "The Chicago strike has drained this office so dry that we remain absolutely penniless." [2]

There had been some progress toward a union agreement for the New York market in the summer of 1915. But many of the manufacturers deliberately delayed carrying out their agreements to set up union shops, especially in children's clothing. In addition, one of the country's largest clothiers, Cohen and Goldman, refused to join with other members of the New York Clothing Manufacturers' Association in collective bargaining with the union. The workers, in consequence, began walking out in groups or sections. The situation was "full of fire," Hillman said, adding in a letter to his Chicago colleagues:

I imagine you people may think I have lost my senses in advising more strikes after what we went through. Unfortunately, or perhaps fortunately, the people do not wait for our orders. [3]

The Amalgamated leaders in New York, where union enthusiasm had been rising ever since 1913, now swiftly organized a series of twelve large mass meetings at numerous halls throughout the city. There was once more a show of furious activity. [4] But in reality Hillman had no stomach for a large-scale conflict now, when there was no "ammunition" left. This was but feinting at a general walkout to impress the opposition.

"The power of decision for peace or war and chaos," Hillman proclaimed, "rests with the employers now." Within a week, however, he was able to bring about conferences with their representatives leading to a peaceful compromise of opposing demands. Now that business was beginning to improve, as the war raged on in Europe, the clothing manufacturers were disposed to avoid stoppages. Hillman had asked for a $2.00 average wage increase but was content to settle for $1.00, with the proviso that true union recognition and a scheme of arbitration (patterned roughly after that at Hart, Schaffner and Marx) were to be accorded by the employers. A three-man Board of Moderators, which was to handle disputes in the men's clothing trades, was now established by mutual agreement. However, it began its work in a market in which some 2,000 small contractors or sub-contractors defied union supervision.

"Why did you settle for a $1.00 raise when you could have got $2.00?" one of his colleagues asked him at this time.

Hillman laughed: "I knew I could have forced $2.00 out of them, but we wouldn't really have held it. And so I grabbed at that $1.00 raise. But we will go back to them for more, in six months or a year." [5]

To unionize the men's clothing trade, now the tenth largest manufacturing industry in the country, seemed a task that would have daunted the boldest of labor leaders. This was predominantly a city industry. As late as 1927, out of 4,118 clothing firms listed by the Census of Manufacturers, only 14 employed a thousand workers or more, and only 110 employed 300 or more. The business was in the throes of rapid change and expansion; large "inside shops" were becoming more numerous; new methods for the division of labor into more simplified and efficient operations, new machines, not only for sewing, but for rapid pressing, buttonhole making, button sewing, cloth examining and sponging, were being constantly introduced into the ready-made garment trade. Yet as late as 1923 approximately 60 per cent of the establishments were small contract shops employing, on an average, only 19 workers per shop.

The seasonal character of the industry also made it more difficult, in those years, to hold a union following together. In 1919, in the four states having the bulk of the clothing workers (New York, Pennsylvania, Illinois, and Maryland), unemployment ranged from 32 to 38 per cent during the two slack months of the year.[6] In the rush seasons, beginning in May and November, people would be hired quickly in accordance with the "sell-then-make-up" system, after which about a third of them would be dismissed. Changing styles, as well as changing methods of production, introduced further elements of confusion. And wages were low in comparison with other industries. The effort to unionize such an industry involved a struggle with endless details, an immense day-by-day drudgery, which the predecessor union had frankly abandoned, contenting itself with organizing only a small fraction of the field.

On the other hand, among the factors highly favorable to the unionizing movement, we must reckon with the "revolutionary" morale of the needle-trades rank and file of those days. They served the most sweated industry in America; they were often desperately poor, but engendered among themselves a tremendous enthusiasm for action through their union which promised, so to speak, their salvation. About half of the men and women in the union, toward 1914, were Jewish, and many of these had been indoctrinated either in Russia or in New York and Chicago with the ideals of the Social Democratic movement. To the revolutionists from Russia a union was a "sacred institution" and not a mere business device. As one historian has related, their leaders sometimes "issued calls to union meetings in the terms of proclamations exhorting the Russian masses to rise against the tyranny of the Czar. . . ." [7] And for at least the first six years of its life the Amalgamated tended

to interpret all its principal activities in the terms of the class struggle, and to look at ultimate objectives as motivating all current work. The writings of its leaders . . . addresses and discussions at the conventions breathed more of idealism than of business. Even the biennial reports of the Executive Board read a future workers' paradise into the defeats and victories of the present.[8]

More than Hillman, Joseph Schlossberg, in his fervent orations, embodied the longings of the foreign-born (mainly Jewish and Italian) workers of forty years ago.

At the outset of their nationwide organizing campaign, Hillman and his colleagues pointed their efforts toward building labor power in several of the largest cities, and in these, at first, singled out some of the big "inside shops" for attack. The large factories were more vulnerable to the union drive; a walkout in one section could tie up the whole line.

Another favorable factor appears to have been the strongly individualistic and competitive character of the clothing manufacturers themselves, mainly small or middle-sized capitalists centered in the large Eastern and Middle Western cities, whose trade associations proved to be none too firmly defended against the tactics of Sidney Hillman, now those of peaceful diplomacy, now those of fierce aggression.

No concept of "grand strategy" seemed feasible at the start. Rather, it was an opportunistic approach that was followed: able and devoted organizers were hired and sent out to win recruits. Despite the union's poverty, Hillman expended about $30,000 for this purpose in the first year. Different clothing centers were felt out for weak places; testing strikes would be called and broken off if no results were obtained quickly. Yet the pressure of the new labor organization grew more intense from season to season. Though strikes were limited in scale, many of them were stubbornly fought against individual firms, as the union attacked its opponents "piecemeal." The ill-paid foreign-born garment workers, as in Chicago in 1915, proved themselves to be rich in courage and in the spirit of sacrifice and loyalty. The actions in which they were led show that careful planning on the part of the leaders and the gathering of precise intelligence about each market situation usually preceded each "drive." This creeping advance went on, despite many checks. By the end of 1916, after two years, the dues-paying membership had been doubled and stood at a little under 50,000; not long after that the Amalgamated Clothing Workers were in a position to take advantage of immense opportunities that were suddenly opened by the entrance of the United States into war.

II

In charting the first unionizing drives Hillman chose organizers for the national staff with an eye toward assigning them to different racial or language groups. Thus the brothers August and Frank Bellanca and Paul Arnone, ardent young Socialists and leaders in the Italian-American labor movement, were sent forth to work among their compatriots in Baltimore, Rochester, and Boston. Leo Krzycki, later the Socialist under-sheriff of Milwaukee, was assigned to educate the numerous Poles of Chicago and other Midwestern cities. Krzycki, a torrential orator, had long been affiliated with the AFL central trades council of Milwaukee. For him to join forces with the "secessionists" of the Amalgamated meant a break with his old union associates. Yet Hillman, who had appealed to him for help during the 1915 Chicago strike, had been so eloquent, "so magnetic," that Krzycki had found himself unable to refuse the call.

Another young Socialist leader of those days, who served as a paid speaker for the Amalgamated, was B. Charney Vladeck, later a New York City alderman. Vladeck, who was an accomplished speaker in Yiddish and also a poet, was a great drawing card for the

Jewish immigrants. He would picture the work of their union as a holy crusade, saying:

The most beautiful within us, the noblest within us is brought forth not in contentment, but in discontent, not in truce, but in fight! [9]

And no less inspiring was the famous journalist and lecturer, Dr. Max Goldfarb, a benevolent-looking, bespectacled gentleman, who often traveled about from city to city rallying the Jewish clothing workers. Goldfarb on occasion sounded eloquently those notes of Socialist idealism that gave the new union so much "religious" fervor. One of his memorable phrases that Hillman liked to recall was:

Let us make of this new union a structure that is a temple within and a fortress without. That is, let us keep the *religion of labor* within it and let it be to our enemies without as an impregnable fortress! [10] *

The Amalgamated was one of the first unions to engage paid speakers such as Dr. Goldfarb (at $25 to $30 a week) to travel about the country educating and lecturing to its members.

It was General Secretary Schlossberg, however, who led all the rest in preaching those "ultimate aims" of democratic Socialism, toward which the day-by-day union action seemed to be directed. The petty officers or organizers shared this faith and often gave themselves to a life of arduous toil and sacrifice. Thus in Montreal, during a long winter strike of the Amalgamated local members in 1916, one of the leaders was a frail, undersized Russian immigrant named Elias Rabkin, who refused to accept any compensation for his services, until the union's New York office, learning that he was in danger of starving and freezing to death, allotted him $10 a week —over his protests that he might "lose honor" thereby among his fellow workers. [11]

In Baltimore during 1916 and 1917, Hyman Blumberg and August Bellanca lived in constant danger of their lives: both received wounds whose scars they bear to this day. Beside them worked a slender girl button-sewer of eighteen, with fine dark eyes, who had risen to be

---

* In 1908–12 the Socialist Party reached its zenith, with almost 900,000 votes. "We figured that at this rate of growth a Socialist candidate would certainly be elected as President of the United States by 1924." (Abraham Miller to M. J.)

a leader of the women garment workers. She was Dorothy Jacobs, who was soon afterward to marry her co-worker, August Bellanca. Having been forced to work in sweatshops since she was thirteen, her health had already been impaired; the rest of her strength she was to sacrifice thereafter to the union. Hillman, on Blumberg's recommendation, soon marked this young girl, whose courage and intelligence all admired, for promotion to the union's national staff. In 1918, despite masculine prejudice still ruling in labor circles, she was elected a member of the General Executive Board. Such were the young people, some of them Socialist intellectuals, most of them rank-and-file workers, but all of them long on idealism, whom Hillman gradually gathered together as the organizing corps of the new union.

He was all for educating the workers in his industry to know their opportunities, their rights, and their responsibilities as well. They were to be deluged with printed literature, pamphlets, and union newspapers as soon as money could be found for this purpose. Meanwhile their "crusade" toward democratic self-rule was to be no somber struggle, but as far as possible a happy and festive movement. "Nothing is too good for labor," he would say. A communal life must be built up around the workers' local with the purpose of maintaining or raising the morale of the members. After laboring for ten hours a day with a hot pressing iron or at a sewing machine, the worker must not only hear talk of grievances or shop reports but must have regular social recreation, with singing, dancing, and impromptu dramatic entertainments. "These social features have worked wonders to break down the national and religious lines that heretofore divided the workers in the shop," wrote one of the organizers from a Middle Western city. During a long strike in Baltimore, another wrote: "Here in Baltimore, the office has a continuous picnic. Our members are dancing and laughing . . . one encourages the other." [12] In Chicago a sudden walkout of the cutters was opened in the most festive spirit on a day in spring, the workers parading jubilantly about the garment-trade district on West Van Buren Avenue, waving yardsticks and long shears and singing lustily.[13] Similarly, the spirits of the people involved in a strike of many months' duration at Louisville, Kentucky, under the leadership of Frank Rosenblum, were maintained by frequent picnics and dances.

Meanwhile Hillman made restless journeys back and forth across the country, constantly studying the different city markets, strengthening the local organizations, and devising ways of penetrating the various clothing centers. "He fairly lived in trains in those days," it was said by his associates. Though others in his union might pray for the eventual triumph of Marxism, shrewd young Hillman put his faith in the gospel according to Hart, Schaffner and Marx.

He would stop at Rochester, now a rising clothing center, made up of large new integrated factories, and also a non-union stronghold. Here there was a close-knit combination of manufacturers called the Rochester Clothiers' Exchange, which presented a sort of Chinese Wall to the labor union. But here, too, there was one "independent" manufacturer who seemed to be at odds with the rest of the group; and Hillman learned that there were chances of moving in. The man turned him away, but Hillman would be back soon, trying other, less polite measures where moral suasion had failed. He wrote:

I found Rochester in the same situation as before [anti-union]. I visited Michaels, Stern's place and had quite a long conference with Mr. Stern. . . . Rochester needs a whole lot of attention. If we can create a situation by the end of May there are all kinds of possibilities. My advice is to send Arnone as soon as possible over there with the proper instructions. I may send Elbaum from Chicago. He speaks German, Polish, and English well. . . .[14]

Whenever he spies a chance of "creating a situation," the union's organizers soon arrive on the scene. The different shops are studied; the names and addresses of workers are gathered patiently. Within two weeks Rosenblum and Paul Arnone, called by Hillman to take charge of this job, organize a meeting of 150 people employed by this firm; in May a small strike is called but is quickly defeated by the employers' strong-arm measures. Rochester looks like a hard nut to crack. But every town is like that at first.

In Montreal, Canada's chief clothing center, a vigorous organizing movement was undertaken in 1915 and 1916. Here a score of clothing manufacturers employed some 5,000 sweated workers, mostly French-Canadian, but including some English and Jewish immigrants. Not a few of these employees were French girls of no more than twelve years of age. Yet when a strike that had been deliberately provoked by the employers gripped the entire garment trade in the

winter of 1915, the manufacturers banded themselves together and—
with the country at war—invoked every possible weapon of the law
to crush the alleged "alien agitators." Pickets arrested and sentenced
by a local magistrate heard him denounce the union's local leaders
in terms reflecting the most violent prejudice:

They draw fat salaries which should never go to men of such deficient
moral and mental capacity as exemplified in the secretary before me who,
with the three Jewish defendants, stands up and gives evidence directly
contrary to that of five constables who . . . are at least Christians.[15]

Hillman went to Montreal to see what he could do to help. He
witnessed scenes of uncommon hardship even for a labor union of
those earlier days. In temperatures of twenty below zero the picket
lines were filled mostly by young girls who came out at six in
the morning, only to be ridden down by the Royal Mounted Police.

He always felt much optimism about what he, personally, might
accomplish by a face-to-face meeting with the employer in any labor
dispute. But in this case none would see him, or even the union's
lawyer, who was a member of the Provincial Parliament. Rebuffed,
Hillman would say to himself: "I did not manage things well enough
that first time. I must try and find some new 'angle' to the situation,
some way in which I can, somehow, open the door—just a little
bit!" [16]

After much probing, and after having dispatched many telegrams
to friendly business leaders in New York, he did at last get his foot
through the door at Montreal. Through the intercession of a certain
New York philanthropist who admired Hillman, one of Montreal's
largest clothiers, at length, agreed to receive him. Here again, after
much talk of the Hart, Schaffner and Marx Plan, Hillman ended by
gaining the entire confidence of the manufacturer, a leader in the
local clothiers' association, who accepted a limited agreement with
the union. Afterward others were induced to do likewise.

At the end of that first Montreal campaign, the union had little
to show but a meager increase in wages and partial union recognition. Yet, as Hillman said: "We must first let the employers know
there is a union." Its Montreal membership had actually been on the
verge of utter rout; it would have disappeared as an organization if
not for the compromise agreements Hillman alone had managed to
negotiate.

Indeed, he was back again in Montreal in 1917, directing a larger union action. Mr. Mederic Martin, the mayor of Montreal, and Mr. Mackenzie King, future Prime Minister, were now helping the Amalgamated, while an impartial Committee of Inquiry, in typical Hillman style, sat in judgment of the union's new demands. He wrote:

We had quite a time up here for a while . . . some of our people lost courage, but all is well so far. . . . I feel quite happy about the situation, as I consider it about the best outcome under the circumstances.[17]

And not long afterward he could report, surprisingly enough, that the leading clothiers of Montreal, who had shunned him a year before, had ended by giving a luncheon in his honor at the Canadian Club. He made a speech on the labor problem and was heard with great respect. And he added hopefully: *"We may come to an agreement."* [18]

Thus he worked indefatigably to enhance the power of his union by using alternately the diplomacy of Fabius or the tactics of power. He would offer to show the employers how "they might make money" by dealing with a responsible union. But where they would not listen to reason, or showed bad faith, then his mood would turn to cold fury. "The strike is the weapon of the industrial jungle," he would say. "If the employers force us down to that level, we'll fight as they do, like beasts of prey." Then he would become, it was said, "utterly ruthless." [19]

In meeting deception with ruse, or violence with more violence, labor merely invoked the law of self-defense, he held. At this stage, the genteel Mr. Hillman grew "tough," as much so as employers who turned the guns of a purchasable police squad or of armed detectives against the union members.

III

In May 1916, the Kuppenheimer Company, one of the largest firms in Chicago, after an interval of uneasy truce with the Amalgamated, resumed the tactics of firing men active in the union's organizing campaigns. Hillman, on receiving urgent calls, came back to lead a struggle which the stubbornness of the employer made unavoidable.

Quite different tactics from those of 1915 were used now; instead of the general or city-wide strike, 1,000 cutters and trimmers, the key workers, suddenly walked out at Kuppenheimer's and various other factories, effectively paralyzing production in the anti-union shops. When the Chicago manufacturers took steps to divert orders to New York and have their cloth cut there, to be sewn up later in Chicago, the Amalgamated union's prompt intelligence of such moves now barred the way. Returning to New York, Hillman used the increased power of the union there to cut down work for the Chicago employers, reporting to Frank Rosenblum:

> The New York factory, of which I wrote you some time ago where work was being made for Kuppenheimer's, employing 23 cutters, has now been given up completely. The people that ran it realized that they could not make any headway.[20]

On May 12, 1916, Judge F. A. Smith of Cook County Circuit Court issued a sweeping injunction against the officers and members of the Amalgamated, restraining them from picketing or from strike activity of any kind. The scope of the injunction reduced the efforts of the union to a furtive guerrilla warfare. Amalgamated cutters would walk out in "flash strikes," then return after a time. In instances where the union men were locked out and "scabs" imported from other cities, loyal Amalgamated members, posing as "strikebreakers," managed to slip in and spread considerable confusion.

Hillman, in New York, would find out that Kuppenheimer of Chicago was hiring New York workers to come out there. He would wire Rosenblum:

IF YOU THINK IT WOULD BE WISE FOR ONE OF OUR MEN TO GO TO CHICAGO AND FIND OUT WHAT IS INSIDE WE WILL SEND HIM. WIRE ANSWER.[21]

This harrying action went on for seven weeks—despite court injunction—then it was called off in late June 1916. The non-union clothiers in Chicago had suffered serious loss and inconvenience. Hillman said: "We must make it *expensive* for the employers to run non-union shops."

The going was often rough in the union's early campaigns in Chicago, but by all odds the most spectacular and violent struggle was fought in Baltimore in 1916. Here the Amalgamated battled for its very existence on fairly even terms, not with the employers, but with a unit of the rival United Garment Workers under a determined local leader, John W. Ferguson, who was also head of the AFL's central trades council in Baltimore.

This city then was the country's fifth largest clothing center. On the outcome of the contest here depended the new union's destiny in other large markets such as Philadelphia and Rochester, or even New York. More than half of the city's clothing workers were employed in three large, modern "inside shops," those of Sonneborn and Company, Strouse and Brothers, and L. Greif and Company, with the rest scattered among almost two hundred small firms or contract shops. Hyman Blumberg, the aggressive leader of the Amalgamated's Baltimore district council, or "Joint Board," therefore concentrated the union's efforts upon winning over the employees of those three big firms.* A union-shop agreement had been won by the beginning of 1915 at Sonneborn and Company, covering the majority of 3,000 tailors there; a similar agreement had been reached with Strouse and Brothers, which had 1,000 employees. But little progress was made in unionizing the 500 workers of the Greif company, which maintained the lowest wage scale of the "big three" in Baltimore and thus enjoyed a competitive advantage over the others. This weakened the force of the ACWA's union-shop agreements in Baltimore.

The situation was still further complicated by the fact that the Amalgamated controlled only the tailors at Sonneborn and Strouse; the jurisdiction over the cutters in those firms, about 10 per cent of the working force, was still held by a loyal local of the UGWA. Hostilities between the two unions were suspended for a while in 1915, with a majority of the clothing workers enrolled in the Amalgamated and the minority of skilled craftsmen in the United.

This condition of a divided house for labor could not last long in Baltimore. In January 1916, a strong Amalgamated push to organize the Greif firm's tailors caused a brief strike, followed by a quick settlement allowing partial recognition of the union as bargaining agent. But within a short time the company suddenly announced that it proposed to repudiate its agreement with the Amalgamated since it had reached an understanding with the rival union, by which cutters and trimmers of the UGWA were to be employed exclusively. What was more surprising was that the Greif company also indicated, at

* In the Amalgamated union the term Joint Board came into usage to designate city-wide groups of locals forming a regional branch (or district council).

the same time, that for its numerous tailors and other semi-skilled operatives it had reached—with the help of John Ferguson of the AFL—a union-shop agreement with representatives of the IWW in Baltimore. This was a wholly new and unexpected development in the affairs of this clothing firm.

The period 1914–19 was the heyday of the Industrial Workers of the World, who, far more than independent or reformist unions like the Amalgamated, constituted a growing threat to the AFL. The IWW was then making serious inroads among the underpaid, foreign-born textile workers in the East, as at Lawrence, Massachusetts. Their leaders proclaimed the unceasing class war and scorned all forms of agreement or arbitration arrangements as "treason." The sudden emergence of the IWW at Greif and Company, an anti-union house, side by side with the conservative AFL cutters, was not only astonishing, but indicated to Hyman Blumberg that Ferguson of the AFL was using the IWW to drive the Amalgamated out of Baltimore.

War began at once between the Amalgamated people and the two other rival union groups. The Greif plant was struck and soon besieged by a human wall of Amalgamated pickets. The "Wobblies'" strong-arm squads attacked these pickets, and there was a spate of fighting and rioting along Baltimore's Milton Avenue. On occasion the Amalgamated local headquarters was invaded by the IWW people. "Hy" Blumberg and August Bellanca both were waylaid and blackjacked.

Hillman brought down what union funds could be spared, and conducted large mass meetings at which he and the young labor lawyer Fiorello La Guardia rallied the spirits of the ACWA followers. Production at Greif's was now demoralized by a prolonged strike, while its two big rivals enjoyed a booming trade. Hillman made earnest offers to the Greif company to have the dispute settled peacefully by recognition of the Amalgamated and the elimination of the IWW element. But Greif firmly rejected all such proposals.[22]

The next move came from John Ferguson, acting presumably for the United Garment Workers, when he opened a counterattack on the two rival employers operating under union agreements with Hillman's organization. One hundred and twenty-five cutters, who were still in the AFL union, were suddenly called out on strike at Strouse and Brothers, though they had no grievance at the time. With the cutters out, the mass of ready-made tailors were left without cloth to sew up into suits. Mr. Strouse was now in a box and called on Hillman for help. It was up to Hillman and Blumberg to see to it that Strouse, who had loyally observed his agreement with their union, was kept going. Thus the Amalgamated leaders entered upon the business, so very unusual for them, of playing off one manufacturer against another, and helping to break the "sympathetic" strike called by the UGWA cutters by bringing in skilled cutters from Philadelphia, New York, and Chicago.

The reports to Hillman in New York from August Bellanca ran:

This morning three cutters arrived in Baltimore from St. Louis. . . . This evening three more arrived from New York. Our boys from New York are working like little devils on the cutting floor.[23]

This confused struggle between the Amalgamated and a tenacious manufacturer, accompanied by a jurisdictional fight between the three rival clothing workers' unions, raged on for months. Ferguson of the AFL camp, it was reported, was resolved to drive the Amalgamated union out of Baltimore and present the trophy of this victory to the approaching AFL national convention scheduled to open soon in that city. Using his considerable political influence and also the aid of the "Wobblies," he managed to defeat the Amalgamated strike at Greif and Company and then moved to break their hold upon the firms of Strouse and Sonneborn. As a part of the campaign, the AFL declared a boycott against the merchandise of the Strouse firm, which received many embarrassing inquiries on the score of its labor troubles. A general strike was also threatened by the AFL-IWW contingent against both the big firms employing Amalgamated people.

Hillman, though hard pressed by labor disputes elsewhere, was obliged to return repeatedly to the explosive Baltimore scene, not only to support his union members, but also to defend the employers who were their allies. His aid, August Bellanca, reported from the field:

Our Hillman has done splendid work and the matter of Strouse is 99 per cent better. . . . Hillman informed me this afternoon that tomorrow Mr. Sonneborn is going to give an ultimatum to the cutters to join our organization.[24]

He managed to hold the two big Baltimore firms to their agreement with his union, and carried union-management co-operation to the length of offering to write letters to retailers throughout the country defending the boycotted Strouse firm against charges of unfair labor practices. In short, he was ready even to act as a salesman in the interests of the Amalgamated. A letter of his to one of the leading department stores ran:

New York, October 6, 1916

Messrs Kaufman & Baer Co.,
Pittsburgh, Pa.
Dear Sirs:

Our attention has been drawn to the fact that an organization calling itself the United Garment Workers of America has endeavored to persuade some retailers not to buy the "High Art Clothing" manufactured by Strouse & Bros. of Baltimore, Md. . . .

. . . The United Garment Workers invited the trouble they speak of by bringing about a "sympathetic strike" in support of a small group of Industrial Workers of the World, who tried to force upon Strouse & Bros. demands that were disapproved of by at least 90% of the workers. . . . The overwhelming majority of the workers of Strouse & Bros. have always been members of the Amalgamated Clothing Workers of America, an international organization with branches in the United States and Canada. As a matter of fact the United Garment Workers . . . are trying to force Strouse & Bros. to discriminate against our members, so that they may . . . revive their dying union. . . . We feel that a great injustice is being done to Strouse & Bros., who are fair employers and have been employing organized labor for years. . . .[25]

The great objective was always held in view: to win supremacy in the clothing labor market of Baltimore. The Strouse firm was kept in operation. Having themselves been driven from the Greif factory, Blumberg and Bellanca now maneuvered to drive the UGWA cutters out of their own stronghold in the great Sonneborn factory. Some progress was made by approaching the cutters singly or in small groups and appealing to them to come over to the Amalgamated. Then late in August 1916, three Amalgamated men were deliberately introduced into the cutting department of the Sonneborn factory, whose 250 cutters had been hitherto under the jurisdiction of the United Garment Workers. This could make for serious trouble, which Blumberg expected and was prepared for.

On the morning of August 26, 1916, the shop chairman of the UGWA cutters suddenly blew a whistle, at which his 250 union brothers rose as one man from their tables and fell upon the three Amalgamated union cutters in their midst. But a watcher gave the alarm at once and the far more numerous Amalgamated people who worked on the floors above and below the cutting room came rushing to the rescue. The brawling tailors and cutters in a confused mass fought and rolled over each other down the long steel stairs of the factory. "At each floor," according to an eyewitness, "the fighters were reinforced by men of both factions, until fully 2,000 were engaged." When the milling crowd came out of the factory the fight was continued in the streets. A riot call brought the police, who found men girding at each other with huge shears. Scores of people were injured and hospitalized; many more were arrested. Such was the "Battle of the Scissors" at Baltimore, as the event was recorded in the Amalgamated annals.[26]

Hillman, on hearing the news of this riot, hurried to Baltimore that evening. But Blumberg met him at the train and strongly urged him to leave town at once, before his presence was known. This was a perfect "mess," and it would be better if Hillman kept out of it until the situation was clarified, when he could return in the role of peacemaker.

A strike call was being issued now by the UGWA to the key mechanics at Sonneborn's. But Blumberg assured Hillman that, according to confidential information he had received, the opposing faction was filled with dissension, low in spirits, and ready to give up the fight. Hillman left for New York feeling confident of the outcome and knowing that the whole affair had been provoked by his aggressive lieutenant, Blumberg.

A few weeks later the inter-union strife at Sonneborn's was ended when all the UGWA cutters there came over in a body to join the Amalgamated union and returned to work. Blumberg's persistent overtures to them had brought them around. They were weary of all the jurisdictional fighting, and now were promised good jobs.

This was the last serious jurisdictional battle offered by the old UGWA element in Baltimore, except at the factory of Greif and Company. But leaving aside this firm for the present, Blumberg could report that the Amalgamated's Baltimore union at the end of 1916 controlled almost 75 per cent of the men's clothing labor in that city. "I work for 6,000 bosses now," jested the hard-driving Blumberg. This was brilliant progress.

IV

Some months before the sanguinary Battle of the Scissors in Baltimore, Hillman had been greatly occupied with the far more peaceful
business of negotiating a renewal of the union's three-year contract
with Hart, Schaffner and Marx of Chicago, which terminated in May
1916. For the Amalgamated the framing of this third agreement,
affecting the livelihood of about 8,000 union members, was a vital
step at the time.

Rumors were circulated in Chicago that friction had developed
under the famous Plan, and that the whole arbitration system might
end, after five years, in a violent strike.

The real picture was strikingly different. Hillman had held preliminary talks with Professor Howard and Mr. Schaffner regarding
the terms of a new agreement. Then in March and April there had
been numerous day-long conferences between both sides, attended
by a score of the union's Chicago officers and almost as many
attorneys and managerial persons in behalf of the firm. Where there
had been some threat of force in 1913, now, as J. E. Williams said,
"there was not the faintest suggestion of militancy." [27] The experience
of five years had shown, as a later head of the firm wrote, that a
capitalist and a strong union could work together. For the new union
it was a source of satisfaction that the world's largest clothing manufacturer was its friendly partner, while the firm itself benefited richly
from the fame and good will it won through its experiment in enlightened labor relations.[28]

Hillman was in his element in the conference room. Though still
in his twenties, the former apprentice cutter bore himself with dignity
as he undertook discussions involving millions of dollars in wage
payments for the years ahead. He was tactful, deliberate of speech,
and unostentatious. The employers' representatives and experts, for
their part, treated him with great deference—which was always a matter of pride to his followers.

Both parties talked like "statesmen" of their "responsibility to the
future" and their willingness to subordinate selfish interests to ultimate progress. To be sure, there were decided increases of wages in
order, in view of the current prosperity in American industry; and
further improvements in working conditions were also expected on

the union side. Schaffner and Howard recognized these facts and did
no haggling. But how much would the union ask for?

Hillman and Sam Levin, the Chicago leader, asked for a good deal:
a reduction of hours from 52 to 48 per week, a 20 per cent raise
in wages, and the closed shop. In the end Hillman settled for a 49-hour
week, a 10 per cent wage increase, and (a tacit agreement for) the
closed shop by grant of added authority to the shop chairmen and
joint "price committees." These last would allow for continuous adjustment of wages and prices as business and technical changes
warranted.

Some of the union men felt that more could have been wrung from
this peaceable corporation. But Hillman argued stoutly: "We have
got to *live* with our industry." His colleagues must be "realistic" and
see to it that a firm working in friendly agreement with a labor union
was not penalized for this policy.

It was, as a matter of fact, a magnificent contract for the union
and brought some groups, especially apprentices, increases of 100
per cent above the scale of five years earlier. One remarkable feature
of the agreement was the provision that the 10 per cent increase in
average pay, involving a total of $1,500,000 over a period of three
years, was not to be applied horizontally to all workers, but was to
be allotted in inverse proportion to their standing in the wage scale;
that is, the lowest-paid were to receive the largest increases, ranging
up to, say, 20 per cent, while the highest-paid categories, such as
cutters, were to gain smaller increases, ranging down to 5 or 6 per
cent. This allotment, following long discussions between the employers
and the union's officers, was left entirely to the decision of the union.

Reports of the successful conclusion of the negotiations were published on the front pages of the Chicago newspapers and aroused
nationwide interest among businessmen and trade unionists. Hillman,
in an interview, declared: "I may be somewhat prejudiced, but it is
my opinion that no trade agreement is in force which is more just
and democratic than this." For him this was the *civilized way* of industrial relations which must be made the rule in the entire clothing
trade.

At the April 14 mass meeting of 3,000 workers at Hod Carriers'
Hall, Hillman, for two hours, patiently explained all the clauses of
the agreement with Hart, Schaffner and Marx, which the members
were now asked to ratify. They responded in the affirmative with tre-

mendous ovations for their president. In concluding his talk, he said to them:

Remember that it was organization that made it possible to get what we have. You workers are leading the way, not by yourselves but through your union.[29]

The 1916 agreement with Hart, Schaffner and Marx, running three years, firmly anchored the Chicago section of the union in its industry and gave it the reputation of a "school" for enlightened labor relations. Hillman had all his life a passion for experiment and innovations when applied in a practical spirit; it gave him deep satisfaction that his union of foreign-born workers should stand in the forefront of progress. The special apportionment of the over-all wage increase, as J. E. Williams said, was unheard of, for it meant that "the stronger and more skilled workers voluntarily denied themselves an equal share in order that justice might be done their more needy brethren."

What was no less significant was that the non-union houses in Chicago (whose workers were secretly joining the Amalgamated union) were forced to make wage adjustments in the form of "bonuses," so-called, to meet the increases granted by the largest firm in the market. The union now exercised strategic control over the wage level in the Chicago field: it was only a question of time before the other 20,000 workers would be included in its membership rolls.[30]

Hillman stayed on in Chicago to work out the final details of the agreement. Some of the workers were human—all too human— on the subject of the allotment of wage increases, and "while the high-paid people voted for it," as Hillman wrote, "they may change their minds." He saw to it that they did not.[31]

v

Spring came to Chicago, and May Day approached; it was a time for festivities and parades. At the end of April, in great secrecy, the Chicago union officers prepared an elaborate banquet in honor of Hillman's signal services in the recent trade conference. There was also another reason for celebration. Their young leader, it was rumored, was soon to be married.

He had worked long and late at the union office on April 27, 1916, and at length turned to Marimpietri beside him and said: "Well, we've done a good day's work. Let's go to the banquet and eat something."

Marimpietri, astonished, said: "You're a sly fellow. How did you know?" Hillman laughed. "Oh, I have ways of finding things out." His associates had tried to keep their preparations secret because it was known that he usually tended to avoid such ceremonies.

The occasion marked the announcement of Sidney Hillman's approaching marriage to his old union comrade, Bessie Abramowitz, to whom he had been engaged for more than two years. This alliance of the president with the Chicago union's courageous woman leader gave great joy to the Amalgamated rank and file, who had long admired and loved the attractive Bessie. They had literally found no time to be married up to now. Hillman scarcely ever stayed anywhere two days on end; he had "lived in trains" during those first months of the union's organizing campaigns. Such money as he had left after his barest needs were paid for he would send to his parents in Russia, and Bessie did likewise. "We never had a spare dollar between us," she recalled.[32] But now the union gave the feeling of a solidly growing economic movement; Hillman was no longer forced to wait for months to collect his small salary. As Jacob Potofsky, who now functioned as assistant secretary of the union, reported, it had doubled in membership in 1916.[33] It was time for Sidney Hillman to take a wife and have a home of his own, something he had not enjoyed since his childhood in Russia.

On May Day a parade of thousands of clothing workers from Hart, Schaffner and Marx was held in Chicago, with Sidney Hillman and his future bride marching at the head of the procession. Afterward, at the union's headquarters at the Hotel La Salle, delegations from the different national groups, Jewish, Italian, Polish, and Bohemian, came to offer their compliments to the young couple. The girl vest makers and buttonhole sewers were also on hand to present Miss Bessie with a gigantic bouquet of roses.

In the metropolitan press much was made of the romance of the labor leader and his young lieutenant, which was said to have "bloomed amid fierce and bloody industrial conflicts." One of the headlines of that day ran:

8,000 IN BIG PARADE OF WORKERS AT PEACE WAS
THE WEDDING MARCH OF SIDNEY HILLMAN
AND HIS BRIDE TO BE [34]

They were married on May 3, 1916, at Chicago; and together they proceeded to Rochester to attend the second biennial convention of their union. After her marriage Bessie Hillman resigned from her salaried post as business agent of Local No. 152 and resided in a three-room apartment in the Washington Heights section of New York. She continued, nonetheless, to devote herself to the affairs of the union which she had helped to found.

There were deep bonds between Sidney Hillman and Bessie, bonds of common experience and suffering and of years of comradeship. The diary of an intimate friend of those days records, not long after their marriage: "Hillman was fortunate in having married one who knew and understood him and his mission to a degree that made it possible for him to do his work unhampered by any restrictions." [35] She knew that the largest part of his life would be given to the union; she knew that this would be her life too.

Bessie Hillman, a "character" in her own right, was born in a village near Grodno, in White Russia, one of a family of ten children. At fourteen she left home to seek work; and at fifteen, during the upheavals of the 1905 revolution, journeyed with relatives to America and found a job in a Chicago sweatshop. It was later, when she was employed at Hart, Schaffner and Marx, that she rose to leadership of the clothing workers in their strike of 1910. Jane Addams befriended her, and Mrs. Robins of the Women's Trade Union League appointed her an organizer of women at $18 a week. To John E. Williams she was the embodiment of Russian-Jewish idealism in contact with the American labor movement, "a power among the women workers and a friend and counselor to the young girls in the industry." She had also a strong vein of common sense and the will to get things done. "Let us stop all this talking and draw up terms for a proposed agreement," she would exclaim amid the turbulence of a strike meeting.

The friendship she formed with Sidney Hillman during the 1910 strike soon grew very warm. Hillman always shrank from talk of his intimate feelings or attachments, but it was common knowledge that he had the highest regard for Bessie's abilities and relied on her support.

Bessie's attachment to him was founded on her growing admiration for his mind and character, on the tremendous potentialities, the boundless ambition and will she had glimpsed in him. There were some in their union circle who thought Hillman was too much the opportunist or compromiser. But at an early stage of their friendship Bessie grasped that no matter how much men of wealth and power might tempt or flatter him, Sidney would remain unbought. She knew that many bribes and splendid business opportunities were tendered him, but knew also how great were his pride and sense of honor. "I had an implicit faith that he would accomplish whatever he set out to do, *and in his own way,"* she said.

In Bessie, Hillman had found a mate of tremendous loyalty and sympathy—though by no means docile, or wanting in friendly criticism. He had lived a dog's life for years, scarcely conscious of where he was or what he ate, or whether he ever slept. He was to continue at the same terrible pace, often lost to his family, during weeks or months of nightmare strikes in the critical years ahead, yet Bessie Hillman bore this uncomplainingly. They were wedded also to a life of semi-poverty in the early years, for Sidney Hillman, as a matter of principle, was austere in his ideas of personal economy. His union might grow rich, expending millions for strikes, yet his private office remained plainly furnished, while in the early days his small apartment, usually far uptown in Manhattan or the Bronx, cost only $30 a month. The standard of living of a cutter was good enough for him, he insisted.

But he was rich in his affections and sentiments, a busy, absent-minded, but tender and even sentimental husband and father. "He had a feeling of responsibility in everything he did," Bessie Hillman said. His lifelong assistant, Potofsky, recalls his surprise at the contrast between Sidney's practical spirit in running the business of his union and his extreme "sentimentalism" in private life and in personal friendships.

His sympathy for all who were poor or ill-fortuned was "subconscious" and powerful. One winter night he was returning home very late, accompanied by two friends, in a taxicab which became mired suddenly in a bad road far uptown in New York. Hillman got out and did his best to help the driver pull the car out of the hole. His friends wanted to call for another car, but Hillman refused to leave the man and angrily berated the others for not going to his help. It was a bitter-cold night. Only when they had been able to arrange for emergency aid would he leave in another taxicab, after giving the unlucky driver a large tip.

He would become similarly agitated when Mrs. Hillman showed

some slight indisposition or illness. Once he was absent from his office when Bessie, as a result of an accidental fall, fractured her leg. When the news reached him, only after some unavoidable delay, he flew into a rage that alarmed his associates. All the next day he was irritable and depressed and could do no work.

Yet, though his moods were changeable and he lived under constant tension, he was too well adjusted or well balanced to be regarded as in any sense neurotic. In moments of adversity he would be collected, even hopeful, communicating his optimism to his gloomier colleagues. He enjoyed people; he enjoyed life on simple terms.

When his first child, a daughter, was born on November 18, 1917, his associates still recall his great joy. Although he seldom had time for personal letters in those days, or later, he now dashed off a fairly long and good-humored one to his old friend John Williams:

December 26, 1917

My dear Mr. Williams:

I thought many times of writing to you, but organization matters as well as personal matters have always interfered with my good intentions. . . .

I suppose you know by this time that I am the father of a little girl. It just happens to be the wisest, best, etc. . . . I am very modest in my views about my own daughter. Whether she will live up to her name time will tell.

The child had been named Philoine, a derivation from the Greek word for "love."

Hillman had some years before borrowed money from Mr. Williams to help tide the union over an emergency. And now, in this hour of good fortune, he repaid the old debt:

In going over my accounts I find that I am $250 ahead. This reminded me of my indebtedness to you. I enclose herewith a check for that amount with my appreciation. . . .

When Philoine was an infant, her father greatly enjoyed having her brought by Mrs. Hillman to his office for a visit and would interrupt his business conferences to present her proudly to his colleagues or callers.

His temperament was happy and sanguine, but the extreme nervous tension under which he generally worked took its toll. His mind would be plunged in calculation, in the endless labyrinth of analysis, while he strove to know fully or anticipate events. Though considerate by nature, he would, at such moments, forget home, family, and everything but the problem on hand. At such times he would never rest while

lying awake all night or walking by himself, thinking through a situation. . . . But when the job was done a reaction set in. He would become nervous . . . impatient. When this happened the best thing was for him to go away for a week's rest. . . . However, shipping him off was quite an ordeal . . . he would regard any vacation in the nature of a forced rest for the sake of being able to carry on.[36]

One day toward 1924, when they were living in a small house at Lynbrook, Long Island, Mrs. Hillman bought an old grand piano. There were now two daughters, including Selma, born in 1921, and Mrs. Hillman intended that they should study music. Months passed, Sidney came and went, and never noticed the large new object of furniture. Then suddenly he awoke and looked about him in surprise, asking "What is this piano doing here?"

"But we have had it here for six months and you never saw it before!" his wife and elder daughter exclaimed, laughing.

"Oh no," he protested, "you're joking. It was never here before."

Bessie Hillman, vivacious and attractive in youth, had been accustomed to gallantries from young men before she was married. One friend often used to bring her flowers, which she loved. "But Sidney was a man who never thought of such things," she relates. "Then one day of heavy rain—we were living in the Bronx at the time—he came in with an enormous bunch of flowers, some three or four dozen of them, which he presented to me. I had longed so much for him to remember to bring me flowers. How had he happened to think of it? And such a quantity! It wasn't anyone's birthday. He said: 'I was coming out of the subway station, when I saw a ragged old man standing there in the rain offering his flowers and nobody buying. "Here, give me your flowers," I said. "How much are they? And now go on home!" ' His present to me was the old man's whole stock in trade." [37] He was full of surprises like that. Bessie Hillman remained absorbed and amused to the very end.

May 8, 1916, the day when Sidney Hillman opened the second convention of the Amalgamated Clothing Workers at Rochester, New

York, was a happy occasion. The president joined the three hundred assembled delegates from twelve states and two provinces in Canada wearing the fresh laurels of his diplomatic triumph in the recent Hart, Schaffner and Marx agreement. Bessie Hillman sat on the dais by his side amid masses of flowers that had been presented to the newly-weds.

To Hillman the convention, occurring every two years, embodied the national (or international) representative system of the union. His administration must give an account of its stewardship during the past term in office, and the delegates must "legislate for hundreds of thousands of men and women." Such meetings in other trade unions often became an affair of dull parliamentary routine, accompanied by much swilling of beer. But this was not Hillman's idea of a union convention. A complete and detailed report of the Amalgamated activities during 1914 to 1916, almost a hundred pages in length, had been prepared by Hillman and Secretary Schlossberg. The facts themselves made quite an impact: there had been more action in these sixteen months than in ten years under the old UGWA. The union was making itself felt in its industry as a fighting organization, though a majority of the workers were still unorganized. Wages had risen 10 to 15 per cent. Hours were being shortened throughout the country, these improvements often being granted "voluntarily" by non-union employers to forestall the union's action.

Hillman opened the sessions with a brief and highly optimistic keynote talk:

Only 16 months ago we gathered in New York with the hope and determination to organize the industry. . . . There is no other national organization in this country that can boast of a record such as ours. Only 16 months have passed and what wonderful progress! You will hear in the report of your officers in detail the main struggles we passed through. . . .

. . . You were told at the beginning: How can the Amalgamated hope for success, having no treasury? We have illustrated to the Labor Movement that the loyal spirit of the membership, the spirit of brotherhood, goes further than millions in the treasury.

Whatever the employers may think of our organization, they know that it is honest and incorruptible. They also know that while we . . . do not want to rush into strikes, when a strike becomes necessary the Amalgamated is ready to fight, fight all the time and is not to be discouraged by a temporary defeat. . . .

Knowing the tailors as I do, I feel confident that they will never be satisfied until their rights as men and women to be organized and to deal collectively will be recognized by the employers of the country. [Applause.]

Habitually he spoke in modest terms of the part played by leadership:

I could go on talking all through the convention about the achievements of the organization. . . . Those achievements were not made by your officers, they were achievements of the rank and file. And that is why I am proud of the tailors.

This meeting was notable mainly for its extremely democratic procedure and the wide range of labor problems the delegates discussed. The questions of improving the union's structure by establishing different types of District Councils or Joint Boards; of basing wages on weekly payments instead of piece rates; or whether Executive Board members should be allowed salaries as organizers were all fully and frankly ventilated. Ambitious plans for working-class education were explored, and decisions made to issue newspapers printed in several foreign languages, Polish, Italian, Yiddish, as well as English. To organize and improve the material lot of the workers was not enough, this convention resolved,

that when the body of the worker is more rested and better fed his intellect should likewise be taken care of. . . . We can give the "wealth-producers" that which will make [them] a higher species of human beings, and enable them to understand society and themselves. It will make their lives worth living. . . .

The recorded proceedings show the tailors' delegates making many fresh and penetrating observations on life and labor. A very clear conception was set forth of collective bargaining as a permanent, continuing machinery—instead of a series of temporary strike settlements whose terms could be quickly forgotten or evaded afterward. The present program of the workers, it was declared, paralleled that of men in earlier ages who had struggled against absolute rulers for the rights of political democracy. The "divine right" of the employers of today to determine wages, hours, and working conditions must be abolished, and the organized workers must participate in a system of joint government which would constitute "the beginning of industrial democracy." [38]

The debates at times touched notes of high social idealism, but these flights, oddly enough, were interlarded with numerous expressions of strong common sense and logic. This combination truly reflected the "Amalgamated philosophy of labor." The chairman in amiable humor gave time to those who opposed policies favored by himself. For a while the issue of "week work" versus "piecework" threatened to arouse strong tempers. Though Hillman favored the piecework system under union-shop committee surveillance, he skillfully compromised this issue by leaving the question for the present to the local option of the different districts. The meeting ended in a spirit of harmony, with President Hillman and Secretary Schlossberg being renominated amid enthusiastic ovations, and without opposition. Their actual election by mass referendum vote was to take place in July.

Those were the crusading days of the Amalgamated Clothing Workers. Their second convention was already refreshingly different, especially in the level of debate, from those of most trade unions of that day and gave a foretaste of the larger Amalgamated "labor parliaments" to come. Its spirit was that of ardent social idealists who not only entertained utopian visions but devoted themselves to patient, daily, inch-by-inch action, designed to advance the present status of workers in industry. The members were to think always in terms of "this world," the realistic Hillman constantly admonished them, and not in the terms of "a book." [39]

Chapter Seven

THE FIRST
WORLD WAR

The war in Europe since 1914 touched deeply the sentiments and emotional ties of the clothing workers, a majority of whom were of Eastern European and Italian origin. Many
were concerned for their families and compatriots. On the other hand,
since many of the Amalgamated members, at least during the union's
first six years, tended to interpret its activities in terms of Socialist
ideas, the war was also regarded by them as a catastrophe wrought by
the "imperialist" conflict between capitalist states. Their fervent
hope was that the United States would remain neutral in this most
destructive of military conflicts. Nor were they alone in this view, up
to 1917, since not only President Wilson but large groups among our
native American labor in the AFL, such as the United Mine Workers
and the International Brotherhood of Teamsters, also made firm declarations in favor of neutrality.

When, nonetheless, war was finally declared against Germany in
April 1917, the Amalgamated had just launched the first issue of its
long-planned newspaper, the fortnightly *Advance,* published in English (which had been preceded two years before by smaller periodi-
cals printed in Italian and Yiddish). The editorial expressions of *The*

Advance, under its first editor, Schlossberg, an earnest pacifist, invited the attentions of Postmaster General Burleson once the war began; and Hillman feared that the union's newspaper would be censored or suppressed, as happened to many another Socialist and labor publication. While granting that Brother Schlossberg had a perfect right to his own convictions, Hillman, with the support of the union's Executive Board, now ruled that editorial criticisms of the government in time of war should be avoided. "There were enough forces in and out of the labor movement seeking to destroy the Amalgamated without getting the U. S. Government to assist them." [1]

Hillman now advocated full support of the war effort by organized labor. The triumph of autocratic Germany, he held, would mean a heavy defeat for labor; it would be "a victory of industrial autocracy also." To be sure he had no liking for those who had unleashed the dogs of war, for, as he said when speaking at the union's convention of 1918 in Baltimore:

My friends, the war was started overnight. The peoples of the world knew nothing about it. It was done by individuals with tremendous power over the lives of the people. It was in their secret sessions that war was declared. Labor has a responsibility to see to it that peace should not be made in the same fashion.

The Socialists had split into patriotic and pacifist factions; Eugene Debs, of the latter group, was sentenced to a Federal penitentiary. But to Hillman the immediate question was: How could the position of organized labor be defended, or even improved, in this dark hour?

Radical laborites came under prosecution; freedom of speech was being restricted. The coal miners, for example, were given to understand by government authorities that they would be "frozen" to their jobs for the duration. Efforts were to be made to ban strikes in vital war industries, while millions of young men were being conscripted into the Army. In the clothing trade a slump had begun in the summer of 1917, when many persons postponed buying civilian suits in expectation of being given free uniforms at an early date. To the indignation of the Amalgamated members it was learned that the first large orders of the Quartermaster General for hundreds of thousands of uniforms had been awarded to non-union concerns in Philadelphia on the ground that these had proffered the lowest bids. The Quartermaster Corps, at that period, took the position that the government was not concerned with the advancement of organized labor.[2] Prospects for the new clothing workers' union looked black. Yet from the outset of the war Hillman was hard at work to extricate the union from its menacing situation. He was one of the first important union officers to appear in Washington and appeal to the Administration of President Wilson in behalf of the rights of union labor. He "wore out the railroad ties between New York and Washington," it was said by his associates, during the summer of 1917, and at the capital city pounded at the doors of all the various cabinet secretaries and government departments he could approach.

Unscrupulous employers, he argued, were using this emergency of war to crush labor organizations:

They were ready, under the cloak of patriotism, to crush democracy at home, no matter what happens abroad. . . . We found at a time when tens of thousands of skilled workers were out on the streets that the uniforms went to the tenements—to be made under the most unsanitary conditions. . . . These employers saw their opportunity to bring in child labor, to replace men by women, all, understand me, under the cloak of patriotism. . . . One firm, conspicuous in this market for the brutal conditions prevailing in its shops, appealed to the women to "enlist." Enlist for what? To help this particular manufacturer profiteer on the government! [3]

Hillman literally went on the warpath to stop the awarding of Army contracts to sweatshop operators. He had his numerous admirers among the merchant princes of clothing whom he had converted to his ideas of labor relations, such as Hart, Schaffner and Marx, and Louis Kirstein, head of Filene's department store in Boston. He now appealed to them to bring pressure upon the government at Washington. At the same time he particularly urged the New York clothing manufacturers who were under union-shop agreements and the Fusionist Mayor John P. Mitchell to help fight the movement of war orders to out-of-town contractors.

Finally Hillman roused his old friends, the social workers. One of these was Mrs. Florence Kelley, former Inspector of Factories in Illinois, an old champion of underprivileged women and children, who was now president of the National Consumers' League, with headquarters in New York. To engage her sympathetic aid he caused investigations to be made of the new sweatshops being set up in the outskirts of Philadelphia and in northern New Jersey. We find his assistant, Jacob Potofsky, writing to one of the local officers at this period:

Dear Brother —— :
    . . . Try to snap boys and girls under 16 years of age and send us the photos immediately. You can take the 11-year-old boy with a couple of young strikers in one picture, and a few girls from the —— plant as they quit work.[4]

These photographs from the field and other evidence Hillman showed to Mrs. Kelley. She, in turn, indignant at the reversion to child labor, went to protest before Secretary of War Newton D. Baker. Baker asked that Hillman come to Washington and see his assistant, Walter Lippmann, a former editor of the *New Republic*. Washington, then in the heyday of the New Freedom, was full of liberal journalists and college professors who composed President Wilson's circle of "best minds," the forerunners of the Brain Trusts of 1933–45. Newton D. Baker was, himself, a former protégé of the radical congressman, Tom L. Johnson of Cleveland. His assistant, Lippmann, had learned from Florence Kelley that Mr. Sidney Hillman had "the most accurate and far-reaching knowledge of the needle trades in the possession of any man," and that the situation there was growing worse every day.[5]

Hillman's first meeting with Walter Lippmann was on June 28, 1917. The youthful political scientist impressed him as "a very interesting man" and giving evidence even then of being "a profound thinker." [6] With Lippmann there was Secretary Baker's young legal aid and adviser, Felix Frankfurter, whom Hillman also met for the first time. The future Supreme Court Justice in those days of young manhood, after a series of investigations of industrial conditions, showed himself a strong friend of organized labor and, from the outset, an admirer of Hillman.

At this first conference, and at a second in early July, at which he was accompanied by Louis Kirstein, Hillman harped on the glaring contradictions between the government's stated foreign policy of waging a "war for democracy" and its domestic actions which encouraged sweatshops and child labor. Army clothing, he insisted, was being made under extremely unsanitary conditions, in places where contagious disease was rampant. Thus our soldiers and sailors, he suggested (perhaps without scientific authority), were being exposed to tuberculosis germs, while garment workers producing their uniforms, were being driven back to homework, child labor, long hours, and small wages.[7]

Hillman reported at the time of his conference of July 3, 1917, with Lippmann:

I was very frank in my criticism and at the same time submitted constructive suggestions. Whatever the outcome I feel satisfied that I have done my duty to the government as well as to the organization.[8]

He also sent word to his chief lieutenants in Chicago and Baltimore that they must keep a sharp eye on the handling of Army uniforms:

Confidentially I may inform you that I am taking up the question of uniforms with the government and I am very hopeful about results. Nothing about this should be mentioned to anybody. . . .[9]

Despite its liberal professions, the Wilson Administration in wartime moved slowly to accept the counsels and representations of American labor. Mr. Gompers, who had urged that two union men be included in a war labor board set up to fix labor policy for government contracts, was disregarded. What was needed, as Hillman saw, was vigilance and pressure on the part of labor. The coal miners' union, after threatening trouble, scored a first victory in mid-June by having union representatives included in a government-sponsored Coal Committee. Hillman, one of the early birds in wartime Washington, worked busily to have a similar commission set up for the manufacture of Army clothing. Meanwhile he stimulated liberal journalists to publish articles on the dreadful conditions that had suddenly returned to this trade; and at the same time addressed letters, such as the following, to Secretary Baker:

We feel that we have a right to ask of our government not to permit conditions which make for the breaking down of the standard of labor established in our industry through many sacrifices and bitter struggles in the past. . . .

Some of the employers are trying to make this war an opportunity to enrich themselves and to enslave labor. Our organization had the power to stop it by using the weapon of the strike. But we felt, and we still feel, that we should not do anything that might hinder our government. We felt certain that when these matters [would] be brought to the attention of your department all the evils complained of would be promptly remedied.

At the numerous meetings of our members we have pleaded with them to be patient. . . .[10]

By mid-August, Hillman informed the General Executive Board at a conference in Boston that he was making good progress in his efforts to have a commission of control established in their industry. If things worked out favorably the proposed system of wartime control of labor standards might be one of the happiest developments in all the history of American labor.

Later that month he was back in Washington, flanked by Louis Kirstein and W. O. Thompson, and pressed matters to a conclusion. His jubilance at the outcome was scarcely restrained in the report sent to his associates:

Mr. W. O. Thompson was with me in Washington. All the people involved in any manner . . . were seen, and the position of our organization was once more placed before them [the War Department officials] in as forcible a manner as was possible under the circumstances.

I had a long conference with Mr. Felix Frankfurter, the Assistant Secretary of War, and Walter Lippmann, and as a result of all these conferences, the Board of Control was appointed with full powers.

If these powers will be properly used by the Board of Control our organization has a right to expect a great deal of improvement in the situation. . . . The agreement that is being drawn at this time will, according to my information, *contain a clause for collective bargaining. It will also include the eight-hour day, a standard wage, sanitary conditions, and practically everything the organization asked for outside of representation on the Board.* . . .[11]

Secretary Baker's directive of August 1917 governing the award of Army contracts for uniforms was for that era a remarkably enlightened declaration of labor policy. (It was said to have been written, at Baker's request, by Felix Frankfurter.) Under its terms the Quartermaster General was authorized to enforce the maintenance of sound industrial and sanitary conditions in the manufacture of Army clothing, to inspect factories, and to pass on the industrial standards of bidders. It was declared also that

The government cannot permit its work to be done under sweatshop conditions and cannot allow the evils complained of to go uncorrected. Only through the establishment of such a body as the Board of Control now created will the government be assured that Army clothing is manufactured under recognized industrial standards and in an atmosphere of good will between manufacturers and operatives.[12]

As Secretary Baker himself said in a speech of November 1917, the government in this industry of Army clothing "for once, at least, assumed the character of a model employer." Drawing the lesson of the affair, he added:

It will do us no good whatever to send our sons to France . . . if while they are waging the battle we surrender our industrial and social rights here at home. . . . Let them find that, as they were fighting at one end of the frontier and winning one corner of freedom's fields, we at home were enlarging the boundaries of industrial liberty . . . here among ourselves. . . .[13]

This was nobly said, but perhaps could never have been said had it not been for the patient sub-soil work of Sidney Hillman.

The choice of members for the Board of Control and Labor Standards for Army Clothing proved to be most fortunate, since it included Florence Kelley and Louis Kirstein as well as Captain Walter Kreusi of the Quartermaster Corps.

Mr. Kirstein was one of the country's largest buyers of men's and women's garments and represented industry on the Board. He had met Sidney Hillman three years before when he first came to New York as chief clerk under the Cloakmakers' Protocol of Peace. At the time Mr. Kirstein had received a report from some manufacturer that Hillman was a "racketeer" or extortionist of some sort and came to confront him with this accusation. Hillman, on learning who his accuser was, offered to prove to Mr. Kirstein's entire satisfaction that it was his accuser who was dishonest and had attempted to bribe him to betray the union. The man had then been lured into meeting Hillman and repeating his corrupt offer, involving a sum of several thousand dollars, while Mr. Kirstein, by previous arrangement, was posted behind the door of an adjacent room as a witness. From that day on, Sidney Hillman was in Mr. Kirstein's eyes a sort of saint of the labor movement and the rich, hard-boiled merchant from Boston was his apostle.

Hillman took Mr. Kirstein on personally conducted tours of the lower East Side and pointed out the grimy sweatshops, some of which were in tenements marked by the city health authorities then as places of contagion. All this had a good effect on the Control Board's rulings.[14] Thus the very confusing and difficult situation in the clothing trade at the outbreak of war was turned almost overnight to the account of the organized workers and the "better element" among the employers. During World War I, the Amalgamated experienced a spectacular growth, and within two years emerged as one of the giant unions of that time.

II

Hillman had seen what a benevolent government, with a stroke of the pen, might do to assure just dealing between capital and organized labor, and he never forgot this. One might say that from that day in August 1917, when Baker's directive was issued, he was all for the "welfare state," so-called.

To be sure, the Federal Government could not be everywhere or see everything that was going on in a thousand different places or industries. With much discernment he wrote words that apply as well three decades later:

I have been in Washington a number of times and it is always with a feeling of discouragement that I leave the capital. . . . It is unfortunate that so few people who would do the most good are connected with the government activities. What they need is ten times as many people and that they should be ten times as *big*.[15]

The government's labor policy evolved slowly, until the spring of 1918, when the War Labor Board, headed by ex-President Taft and Frank P. Walsh, was appointed to mediate industrial disputes, as a "court of appeals" for various subordinate adjustment agencies. Soon afterward the War Labor Policies Board, with Felix Frankfurter as chairman, was also set up to co-ordinate labor policies and standards for the different government departments. Strikes and lockouts were forbidden, though no penalties for strikes were fixed, and "coercion" in organizing unions was also banned; but collective bargaining and union wage standards, on the other hand, were recognized by the Taft-Walsh Board and anti-union "discrimination" was ruled out, which alone was immensely stimulating to union activity.

In the spring of 1918, Mr. Kirstein returned to his private business, and the Control Board he had headed was reorganized as a one-man agency under Professor William Z. Ripley of Harvard University. Like

Kirstein, Ripley, who was a man of much good will, became greatly attached to Sidney Hillman; the two of them together, in effect, ruled the Army-uniform industry for the remaining months of the war, though in a highly judicious and even-handed manner.

Meanwhile, Hillman had called together the leaders of the Amalgamated before the ink was dry on the directive of Secretary Baker, and urged that simultaneous organization drives be launched at once in the principal clothing markets of the country. The mass production of uniforms had begun. Some shops, by speed-up methods, were already turning out 10,000 standardized uniforms each day. In New York and Chicago alone about 35,000 workers were employed in filling Army and Navy contracts. Outside of Philadelphia, at Vineland, New Jersey, a number of sizable plants had been set up which were hiring boys of fourteen to make uniforms and working them 57 hours a week, for $7.00 to $14. These non-union points had to be eliminated.[16]

As the Amalgamated organizers hit the highroad in 1917 and 1918, new members began to pour into the union. A similar boom in unions was going on in most other war industries now. Hillman himself quickly negotiated a settlement with the Vineland sweat shops, with the government's board (then under Kirstein) acting as an umpire or Impartial Chairman. The anti-union employers in New York and Chicago were in a panic, sensing that the Amalgamated now held the upper hand. They promptly resorted to the newspapers to publish numerous attacks on the union as one "outlawed" by the AFL and associated with the radical People's Councils, a pacifist organization. Hillman replied to these slanders in a long letter to the New York *Times:*

The Amalgamated Clothing Workers is not affiliated with the People's Councils or any similar organization. It is not a pacifist organization. . . .

Since the declaration of war we have co-operated with the government in every way by suspending our union rules whenever the needs of the government so required. . . . We have permitted overtime work, as well as work on Sundays, to speed up production. . . . We have naturally met the opposition of unscrupulous employers and their agents. Let us say here that not a single strike has been called by our organization in any of the uniform factories working under a collective agreement.[17]

The government's wartime labor policy did not, by any means, guarantee union-shop control or collective bargaining agreements, where the workers were shown to be opposed or indifferent to union-ization. In fact, the War Labor Board rulings "froze" the status quo of union and open-shop plants. Where labor organizers were found to have used "coercive" methods to force workers into their organization, Professor Ripley, as Administrator of Control and Labor Standards for Army Clothing, was authorized to eject the union men. Yet the Amalgamated people found it wonderfully easy now to organize practically their whole industry. This was how it worked.

In Philadelphia there was a non-union concern named Wanamaker and Brown which employed 700 workers on Army contracts. Louis Hollander, one of the leaders of the New York organization, was sent down at once to bring those Philadelphia workers into the fold. Soon after he had made his presence felt the firm locked out its employees and brought charges before the War Department against the Amalgamated of obstructive action, designed to halt production. Professor Ripley at once wired the employers and union representatives to meet him in New York for a hearing. As Hollander related: "Through the influence of Brother Hillman we had, in Philadelphia on the next day, Dr. N. I. Stone [assistant to Ripley]"—who investigated the affair. The next day the dispute was settled at Ripley's office in New York.[18]

Administrator Ripley's settlement required the employer to bring wages and hours to union standards, under pain of having his Army contract canceled. When the company, a few weeks later, in June 1918, sought to evade these requirements, Hillman learned of this and promptly reported it to the War Department in Washington. Difficulties of production were now encountered, as often happened when the workers felt aggrieved; in consequence of which a pending agreement for renewal of contracts was held up by Professor Ripley until the firm of Wanamaker and Brown yielded. Thereafter production went forward smoothly again and the Amalgamated union members in the shop saw to it that standards of quality were scrupulously maintained.[19]

There were, nevertheless, stubbornly anti-union manufacturers, such as the big Scotch Woolen Mills in Chicago, who, faced with a strike, obtained injunctions from the Illinois courts restraining the Amalgamated from all picketing or strike activity. This was not the only firm to take advantage of every possible loophole provided them by divergences between recent Federal wartime regulations and state law.

Professor Ripley thereupon recommended that all War Department contracts with this firm be withdrawn, and this was done. But most other firms having war contracts did not care to incur such losses of business. Hence the Amalgamated organizers swept on with their missionary work in the atmosphere of a great labor boom.

The wartime situation which made the government the country's largest consumer of clothing, as of many other articles, had changed the whole labor picture. Working smoothly first with Mr. Kirstein, then with Professor Ripley, Hillman, at times during the war emergency, had what appeared to be an enlarged Hart, Schaffner and Marx Plan in operation. W. Z. Ripley, in discussing later his own role in this remarkable partnership, explained that what he desired at all costs was to maintain production of Army goods at the maximum by avoidance of strikes or protracted litigation. Thus he and his assistants held swift hearings and made decisions promptly, which was to the advantage of the union side. Moreover, Hillman's willingness to settle disputes at the conference table, often by making very reasonable concessions, was exceedingly helpful to the War Department's representatives in this field. His co-operation struck Ripley as patriotic and constructive in a time of growing labor scarcity. To help speed production and settle disputes the Amalgamated president was constantly on the road during those war years. His associates repeatedly called on him to come to Baltimore, or St. Louis, or back to Boston for some emergency, until Potofsky, in despair, wrote one of them: "It is a physical impossibility for Hillman to keep on traveling without even a chance to rest for a day and without a chance to see his family." [20]

In return for the benevolent attitude of the government Hillman, in effect, pledged that his union would refrain from strikes and assume responsibility for uninterrupted output. He proved to be strict in keeping to the very letter of his agreements and in holding some of his ambitious lieutenants in line also. During the boom of 1918 it was often hard to keep workers on the job, with manufacturers now bidding against each other by offering wages far above the union scale.

The power of the Amalgamated was growing, but Hillman often used to say on the subject of labor leadership: "It must be remembered that there is a fine line between the use of power and its abuse, and a transgression over this line will not infrequently turn victory and power into defeat and weakness." [21]

The problem now was to preserve discipline in a time when American labor was taking to silk shirts. One of his lieutenants, in charge of the Philadelphia organizing campaign, proved to be overzealous, and trouble arose there. Professor Ripley telegraphed a friendly warning to Hillman in June 1918:

STRONGLY ADVISE YOUR PEOPLE NOT TO CARRY LONKER & STEVENS STRIKE OVER UNION SHOP ARBITRATION THINK BOUND TO LOSE. ADVISE MORE MODERATE POLICY THERE IN PROSECUTING ORGANIZATION IN WARTIME OR GRAVE SETBACK FROM WASHINGTON WILL FOLLOW. . . . WAGES ALSO TOO HIGH TO ENCOURAGE CONVERTS WITHOUT MANIFEST COERCION. ADVISE FRIENDLY COUNCIL WITH YOU AND YOUR PHILADELPHIA PEOPLE TO AVERT THIS DANGER.[22]

Hillman then administered a reproof, which eliminated the trouble:

I have seen the memorandum submitted by Dr. Keir [Ripley's assistant]. He mentions that you have threatened to take away the best people from Lonker & Stevens and also threatened to make trouble for the firm. I trust you understand that this kind of attitude only tends to prejudice the Washington administration against us.[23]

Those were great days for the Amalgamated. A leading member of the clothing-trade association in Chicago has related that during the war "the representative of the War Department, Professor Ripley, just came here and told us we had to deal with the union." [24] It was not as simple as that. The manufacturer in question had the gates of his factory still guarded in 1918 and 1919 against Hillman's organizers. But workers could no longer be blacklisted or dismissed for being members of the union. Some of the most resourceful Chicago union men were planted inside those last big factories which still held out against the Amalgamated. At the convention of May 1918, Hillman could report: "We represent an army of over 100,000 organized clothing workers!"

III

The drive toward labor power over the principal men's clothing markets really began moving in the last year of the war. Here and there strong points were met which the union men could not overcome at the first or second assault. The vanguard of the unionized clothing workers then pushed forward elsewhere, leaving small groups to watch over the non-union centers in their rear and trusting that they could be reckoned with later. Such a point of resistance was Rochester, New York.

In any plan for unionizing the clothing industry as a whole, the rising market of Rochester—third largest in the country toward 1918 —loomed as all-important. From the start Sidney Hillman's overtures had been met with rebuffs in this rich "company town" of the garment industry. Rochester's clothing factories were predominantly large, modern, "inside" plants, several having 700 to 1,500 workers, and in no sense sweatshops. A widely used "welfare" system provided incentives for workers of a type not easily swayed by old-time union or "class-conscious" slogans. At the ACWA's 1916 convention held in Rochester itself, one resolution had exhorted the clothing workers there

to respond to our organization with all the manhood and womanhood that is left in them to overthrow the accursed "Welfare System" that the Rochester manufacturers have inflicted upon the 12,000 men and women of that city.

Hillman had sent some excellent organizers here, but a first strike in 1917, previously mentioned, had wound up badly. Later a "steady set of organizers" was posted in Rochester, headed by Aldo Cursi and Emilio Grandinetti, who made strong appeal to a large Italian group. By the spring of 1918, the union was already being "felt" in this city.

The Amalgamated's leader studied the situation incessantly, but waited and held back zealots who were for calling a city-wide strike each time there was some small disturbance. On one such occasion Hillman wrote:

Whatever situation is created in Rochester, it has to be on its own merits. In order to win a strike in Rochester, the issue must be absolutely clear and no camouflage will serve the purpose. . . .

In a letter of instruction written by Potofsky, closely reflecting Hillman's tactics, it was urged that the will to unionize must be strong in the local workers themselves:

This must be done first from the inside. . . . The active people have to pass the word of unity around to all the workers in the shops and then when the situation is ripe, make an effort at a large mass meeting at which our organizers will complete the work.[25]

Then suddenly, in early July 1918, Hillman had a clear-cut issue. A small strike broke forth in one of the larger concerns, where a shop chairwoman had been discharged on some minor pretext in violation of the Taft-Walsh Board rulings against "discrimination." An apparently spontaneous walkout of other departments soon forced the employer to reinstate the discharged girl. The Amalgamated local leaders had been working in this instance behind the scenes, and the sudden display of union power spread fear among Rochester's clothiers. Instead of dying down, as before, the mood of unrest spread quickly to another big shop where people walked out "spontaneously" on July 16, 1918, demanding an increase of wages. Two days later there was panic among the manufacturers when news came that Sidney Hillman himself had arrived in town and was taking personal charge of things. At this stage the Rochester manufacturers were busy with Army and Navy orders, but also, in anticipation of an early end of the war, had accumulated a tremendous backlog of orders for civilian clothing and were "tooling up" for this. (In the past two years clothing prices had risen approximately 120 per cent.)

The manufacturers who were members of the Rochester Clothiers' Exchange had never before considered meeting Hillman face to face. There was an odd legend circulating then that "if you got into a room with Sidney Hillman he could persuade you to do anything he wanted." But this was wartime; the complaints of the manufacturers and the complaints of the union must now be heard before the Administrator for Army Clothing or his assistants. Ripley arrived in Rochester, flanked by Dr. N. I. Stone, and found that Messrs. Max Holtz and Samuel Weill of the Fashion Park Company, heads of the Clothiers' Exchange, and Jeremiah Hickey of the old-line firm of Hickey-Freeman would not even stay in the same room with Hillman. During the conference that began now Ripley and Stone were forced to run back and forth between the rooms in which the union leader and the manufacturers sat separately.

The Amalgamated had made a first show of power in Rochester. "But instead of further demonstrations of strength, Hillman gambled on the peaceful route." To the surprise of the manufacturers, who believed that he was a "cutthroat" deliberately making havoc in their happy families, Hillman sent the tailors back to their jobs at once. While the people were to go back to work pending negotiations, it was agreed, on the other hand, that the whole case was to be left to arbitration by William Z. Ripley and Louis E. Kirstein, a large buyer of Rochester clothing.[26] Thus the organized clothiers of Rochester found themselves at last bargaining directly with the leader of the clothing workers.

They had felt the threat of a general strike overhanging them, and here they saw Hillman, a man of peaceful mien, who ordered thousands of workers back to their jobs. To their surprise, he seemed to have his followers under full control. Discussing the whole affair in highly civilized fashion, he spoke of "partnership," of law and order in industry, of the responsibility of his union to its pledges, and of the success of Hart, Schaffner and Marx.

Mr. Samuel Weill and Mr. Hickey had been in fear that Hillman intended to "take over their affairs." But at long last Kirstein—a nationally known business leader—acting as go-between, managed to bring Hillman together with both of these men for long talks. Mr. Weill, a man of excellent character and education, though previously very suspicious of union people, ended by shedding all his anxieties. Hillman, it was said, "talked him into playing the Joe Schaffner of Rochester." [27] Mr. Hickey, a man of very decided opinions, had also sworn that he would have no dealings at any time with this Hillman fellow. Dr. N. I. Stone, then a young economist and government official with a pro-labor reputation, remonstrated with Mr. Hickey, saying: "All right, if you refuse to take the proffered hand when it is offered to you don't be surprised when you are stabbed in the back." But a few weeks later, after Armistice Day in 1918, Mr. Hickey came to Stone and said: "The thing I told you we would never do, and that you told me we should do—we have done! We have signed with the union." [28]

The Rochester story has the full flavor of Hillman's personality and strategy. He had first developed some tactical labor power in Rochester—how much was a closely guarded secret. The manufacturers were under the impression that about 40 per cent of the workers were in the union then, or about 5,000 in all.[29] But the per capita records show what has not been generally known up to now, that Hillman had only a "Light Brigade" of 600 behind him, about

5 per cent of the clothing workers in that city. Nevertheless, they were picked men and could be counted on to bring serious pressure "from below." [30]

While the arbitration proceedings prolonged themselves the Amalgamated now exerted its full power to organize the Rochester workers. Hillman, at numerous mass meetings, expressed great confidence in the government's mediation efforts. He was even more pleased at the fact that thousands of workers were joining the union en masse. One of his speeches (of August 2, 1918) is highly characteristic of his "educational" methods:

A great change has come over this city. . . . For the first time in the history of the Rochester clothing industry the employers and the employees are meeting on an equal basis to discuss the grievances of the employees. . . . Not so long ago the rule was autocracy, benevolent autocracy, to be sure, but it was autocracy just the same.

The message we bring to you is of the [entrance] of democracy into your shops. I am happy that I can bring this message of peace to you instead of a message of war.

The ACWA desires nothing but peace in the industry. But we want a peace that will be an honorable peace. We don't want a Prussian peace in our shops. . . .

At this time, when the whole world is bleeding so that freedom and right may prevail, the employer who fights to prevent the organization of workers is stabbing his country in the back. He is betraying those who are fighting across the seas for freedom.

No man can claim to be free unless he has a wage that permits him and his family to live in comfort. There has been a tremendous increase in the cost of living in the last two years. . . . We have asked for a 20 per cent increase of wages and a living wage for those to whom a 20 per cent increase will not bring such a wage.

While praising the employers for their apparent conversion to democratic methods in industry, Hillman also felt he must allay the fears of many workers who seemed suspicious of arbitration:

The arbitration hearing was a remarkable example of the new method of settling disputes. The representatives of the shops came there and courageously told their stories. It was a wonderful sight to see a young girl come before the board, and, without the least fear of the employers who were there, tell her reasons in support of the demand for a wage increase. The worker and the employer both represented their sides. . . .

Instead of the old method of "We won't do it" there is the new method of "Let's get together and do what's right."

Labor has nothing to fear when it submits its case to arbitration. . . . All I ask is that you be patient and await a decision.

The Amalgamated's missionaries in the hall were meanwhile busily collecting union pledges and initiation fees; and, to speed this good work, the president remarked shrewdly that his hearers would see that it paid well to be a union member.

Dr. Ripley's message to you is that all will be done to bring a favorable decision and that whatever is awarded to you will be *retroactive* to July 15. Those who think they are paying a lot of money to the organization will find in their back pay enough to pay their dues to the union for the next ten years.

Members were urged to report any grievances they felt to the Amalgamated headquarters in Rochester, where four new locals were being organized for about 7,000 workers. But with an eye to conciliating the employers also, Hillman made the good-humored observation that: "Your officers are going to protect you—but if you think they are going to protect you from work you are very much mistaken." Labor, he would say, "must never try to defeat its industry—for then it only defeats itself."

On August 21, 1918, the government arbitrators, in handsome fashion, awarded a wage increase ranging from 10 to 20 per cent; also the 48-hour week and time and a half for overtime work. Both sides accepted these terms, and collective bargaining, though at first in limited form, was off to a peaceful start in Rochester.

IV

"To an extraordinary degree the Amalgamated union in its early years was stamped with the mind and personality of Sidney Hillman," a keen student of the labor history of that period has said.[31] Surrounding him were strong lieutenants in charge of the big-city organizations, some of them older and more experienced than he, persons who would have been reckoned as outstanding labor men in any union. They instinctively deferred to Sidney Hillman. At thirty he seemed at the height of his intellectual capacities.

The end of the war in Europe approached in October 1918, as all men with eyes could see. The effort of the Amalgamated to strengthen its organization in time of war had been pushed to the farthest limits under Hillman's leadership—there were by now but a few non-union positions left to be mopped up. But with peace, the end of government mediation in industrial disputes (which business regarded then as "pro-labor") was foreseen; millions of soldiers would be returning to look for jobs; a shift from war goods to peacetime production and a possible slump in business and employment were also anticipated by the economic soothsayers. The clothing manufacturers who were fed up with paying high wages were already, as Hillman learned, sharpening their knives for battle with the powerful union.

In October 1918, Hillman called a meeting of the General Executive Board and unfolded to his associates plans for a "grand counteroffensive" to be timed with the coming of peace. The last convention at Baltimore in May of that year had passed a resolution calling on the union's executive officers "to start an agitation throughout the country for the establishment of the 44-hour week." Hillman had said then that, while passing resolutions might seem to some an idle sport, this proposal concerned "what we must and can have." This campaign was to follow the cessation of Army clothing manufacturing. Instead of awaiting these unhappy events passively, he proposed that the union now turn to the offensive. A large "war chest" of roundly $1,000,000 was to be raised for possible general strikes in various cities, and this by assessments on the members' wages.

At that period the American Federation of Labor was still fighting for the 48-hour week and 8-hour day. The Amalgamated was to be the first union in the United States to call for the 44-hour week. This was pioneering for the higher standard of living on the part of the formerly downtrodden foreign-born tailors whom the AFL leaders had long regarded as poor timber for trade unions.

Hillman's proposals for resuming the offensive, for an "expanding program," were given enthusiastic approval by his associates. Numerous rallies and mass meetings were held as November came. The union's publications, newspapers and pamphlets, which were of excellent quality, were now disseminated more widely than ever and printed in six languages. Efforts were made to prepare the minds of the members, as in an article of October 25, 1918, in *The Advance*:

A large number of clothing workers are now in the American Army. . . . It requires no high flights of the imagination to see the employers "most patriotically" offer to give the returned soldier "preference" provided he is willing to work for less wages than the other workers, and not to belong to the union. . . . The employers . . . are eagerly looking forward to the time when those who are now fighting for democracy will be made to fight for autocracy in industry by creating a large oversupply in the labor market. *A reduction in the working time will mean . . . not only more humane working conditions . . . but will make room for our own flesh and blood, who will otherwise either have to "kill or be killed" . . . throw somebody out of a job, or starve because of unemployment.*

Hillman continued to speak softly to the little tycoons of the clothing industry concerning the virtues of labor-management co-operation, but kept in readiness the "big stick" of labor power.

Trouble soon arose in the great New York market, where the union had, by now, upward of 50,000 members. The two clothing-trade associations there had lately been merged as the American Men's and Boys' Clothing Manufacturers' Association. A demand of the union, made in August 1918, for an advance in the wage scale for children's clothing workers was met by a firm refusal. On November 9, when the end of the war was expected at any hour, the New York men's clothing manufacturers took action by "locking out" all the cutters working in their shops. Hillman responded with a call for a general strike in New York City beginning two days later, amid the jubilation of Armistice Day, November 11.

The New York market, still featured by the chaotic contract system, had been relatively quiet since 1916, when the Amalgamated, after a brief seventeen-day strike, had gained sharp increases of wages. During the war the big metropolitan garment center had been busy turning out approximately 75 per cent of all military uniforms produced in the country. Now the strike of 1918 proceeded quietly for about two months, and with considerable discipline on the part of the union members, 50,000 of whom were made idle.

This was the slack season of the year and coincided, as it happened, with a drastic change-over from the production of Army clothing to civilian goods. Hillman sensed that when the period of readjustment was over the clothiers of New York would have to decide whether they were to lose all the profits of a boom season that faced them in 1919 as a result of pent-up demand. He saw to it also that the New York trade heard much of the remarkably favorable agreements which the Amalgamated was negotiating at this very time in Chicago and Rochester, and that there was to be no stoppage of production in those large clothing centers.

The New York Men's and Boys' Clothing Association looked determined enough. But the strike remained solid; the union seemed possessed of ample funds for the relief of its needy members. Silence hung over the immense garment center along lower Fifth Avenue and the adjacent districts.

Meanwhile Hillman was away in Chicago, deeply absorbed in secret negotiations with the heads of the largest clothing concern in the country, Hart, Schaffner and Marx. Some "feelers" that were put out between the strike-bound New York employers and the union spokesmen indicated that the former were not yet ready to talk business on points which the union held of paramount importance: the regulation of the small contract shops, and establishment of union standards for orders going from the large wholesale concerns to such contract shops.

On January 7, 1919, Hillman telegraphed big news from Chicago. A new agreement with Hart, Schaffner and Marx, providing for the 44-hour week and granting an average increase of 8¾ per cent, had just been consummated. Coming after three substantial wage increases over the past four years, this was another "glorious victory" for Hillman, as his union associates in New York wired back. It foreshadowed a break in the Eastern market's deadlock.[32]

He was back in New York in the second week of January, and now managed to meet with some of the leaders of the Association. His friends, at this period, were convinced that Sidney Hillman could sense just the right psychological moment when his adversaries were fed up with the cost of a prolonged fight. When he now proposed that all questions between the two parties be turned over to an advisory board whose rulings would "guide" (without binding) them to a peaceful solution, the offer was accepted with alacrity. Agreement was also reached regarding the three persons who were to serve on this neutral body. They were the lawyer, Louis Marshall, Professor W. Z. Ripley (still Federal Administrator for

Army Clothing for several months in 1919), and Felix Frankfurter, chairman of the War Labor Policies Board.*

Hearings before this committee, which Frankfurter presided over, now went on for a whole week, with spokesmen for both parties presenting their cases. The record of its proceedings gives us a "close-up" of Sidney Hillman as negotiator, friendly, patient, and shrewd throughout these day-long arguments, his reasoning often very fine-spun.

On the manufacturers' side, serious complaints were made of bad morale in the shops, of the excessively high costs in New York, of the need to establish an efficient piecework scale (as in Chicago), and of the restrictions imposed by the union or its officers.

To which Hillman replied that industry must learn that "it will have to work with labor wholeheartedly" despite the undeniable difficulties met. He continued in reasonable tones:

The test will be if the proper spirit comes in the shop, not in this room. . . .
What impresses me most . . . is that in these conferences we present . . . the eternal struggle that is going on between capital and labor, and which I would call more the struggle for power. All these measures that the employers would like to have would simply be giving more power to their side, to take away power from the union. . . . Our position is that we are entitled to the power that we possess, but we are willing that every provision should be made so that this power should not be abused.

Labor, he maintained, had certain "inherent" rights, and capital must learn that these rights must be accorded without the need of resort to economic force by labor. He continued:

You say you are for collective bargaining, you are dealing with labor, you are negotiating with labor, and at the same time you can't say at each door, "No union officer is admitted." . . . We are, as I say, a *government*. We have to take care of tens of thousands of people. And if you are going to take away the power of the union official, then you may as well not deal with the organization.[33]

* An "advisory board" or "committee of inquiry" is one of the mediative processes frequently used to take the heat out of a strike situation and, through its weight on public opinion, bring pressure toward peaceful compromise.

In the other big clothing centers the union was winning the conditions it demanded—wage increases, the 44-hour week, and permanent adjustment machinery—and the New York employers were weary of the contest. It helped also that Felix Frankfurter conducted the hearings in the spirit of that enlightened labor philosophy he had voiced during the recent arbitration of the Packing House strike in Chicago. There the decision favored shortened hours for labor, and was made on the ground that it was as vital to preserve workers from "depreciation" as machines.

Yet it is not by reasonable arguments before a just tribunal of philosopher-statesmen that such issues are usually decided. William Z. Ripley, in reminiscences published some years afterward, told the "inside story" of how agreement was reached:

Hillman called me up and said, "We are now ready to talk business. The Amalgamated is all in. All its war bonds are used up. But . . . the employers have also about reached the end of their rope. Why not start something?"

Upon sounding out the other side, things looked equally gloomy— that is to say, bright; so that I proceeded at once to . . . find out what would "go down" with both sides. Hillman and I drove around and around Central Park in a cab for two or three hours, talking things over. He insisted upon 44 hours a week, but was ready to concede the need of re-establishment of morale and discipline. Then the manufacturers' association was taken in hand. And I discovered that they in turn, if they could be guaranteed the right to manage their shops in the interests of production, would come across in the matter of hours. Thus everything being fixed up in the back of our heads, arbitration was solemnly proposed and as solemnly accepted. Each side was to nominate a representative and I was immediately agreed upon as chairman. No one but the chairman, mind you, knew the state of mind of the principals. The subsequent proceedings are a high spot in my existence. Seldom is one privileged to stage such an affair, knowing precisely what the outcome is to be and yet solemnly putting everybody through the motions of reaching an agreement. It was no end of fun.

Each contestant took his day in court. Everybody blustered and threatened to ride through blood up to the stirrups. Then suddenly the lawyer for the employers had an inspiration. . . . Suppose they granted a 44-hour week? I caught the inspiration on the fly and besought Hillman to aid me in the restoration of discipline and production. New thought to him! . . . And after a solemn interval (except for the three of us, who were already laughing up our sleeves) Hillman imperiously granted the right to restore morale. That ended the strike except for the slight matter of detail of enduring several thousand pages of an official record, fixing up the minutes. But it taught me the advantages attendant upon a careful prearrangement of one's program.[34]

During these protracted conferences of January 1919, Hillman had been rushing back and forth by the night train between New York and Rochester, a pivotal position in his industry. With the Hart, Schaffner and Marx agreement and then the New York agreement for 44 hours in his pocket, he was back almost in a nod to continue his talks with the magnates of the Rochester Clothiers' Exchange, Messrs. Holtz, Weill, and Hickey.

"Well, gentlemen, what are you going to do now?" he is reported to have said. He wanted the 44-hour week here too, a contract for collective bargaining, and a continuous adjustment machinery. Let economists or labor managers be appointed to represent the manufacturers, he advised, and let an Impartial Chairman be chosen for the whole Rochester clothing trade—in short, they were to set up all the paraphernalia which had been worked out at Hart, Schaffner and Marx eight years ago to make arbitration a going thing.

The Rochester clothiers admitted now that they were tired of those strikes that came every five years or so, and Mr. Weill urged that they "give Hillman a chance." On January 23, 1919 (a day after the New York agreement), the newspapers reported that the Rochester Clothiers' Exchange had agreed to accord the 44-hour week.

In the final stages of the deal at Rochester, Hillman had found that when he spoke of the "closed" or union shop, the manufacturers grew emotional and cried that they would rather see everything they had built up through long years destroyed than "permit outsiders to run their affairs." Never would they yield on the issue of the closed shop. Hillman, then, suddenly seemed to yield and agreed, on behalf of the union, to include as the first clause in their agreement a guarantee of the manufacturers' right to "operate their plants on the so-called 'open-shop' principle."

He was to have quite a job squaring this "open-shop" declaration with the flock of new Amalgamated members, whose anticipations had been raised so high by the exciting union drive of recent months. At this period of labor unrest the American Federation of Labor, in one of its great upswings, was fighting everywhere under the slogan of the closed shop. What Hillman had settled for was, in effect, the "preferential union shop"; for, as he explained at mass meetings of the union members, the second clause of the Rochester agreement nullified the open-shop declaration. It read: "The employers recognize the right of their employees to bargain collectively." The whole contract had only four clauses and was only twelve lines in length. Mr. Jeremiah Hickey had said that any contract which had "too many words in it" could be broken by a smart lawyer. This one would depend actually upon the good will and the good faith established between Hillman and the Rochester clothiers.[35]

The Fabian methods of Hillman were applied here once more. The manufacturers had conceded the "preferential" shop with much apprehension, because they had feared labor scarcity. But when they found later that the union helped supply them with good mechanics, their resistance gradually weakened. At Hillman's suggestion Dr. William M. Leiserson of Toledo University had been chosen Impartial Chairman for the Rochester clothing trade. The union was now entrenched in this vital market. The Rochester agreement began to work, despite many difficulties and still persisting mutual suspicions. It was to become, as a working model of union-management co-operation—during three decades of industrial peace—only less celebrated than the historic Chicago arbitration plan of which Hillman had been one of the principal architects.

In the New York men's clothing trade, meanwhile, a permanent system of bargaining and adjustment was also being set up, actually for the first time. The manufacturers' association, after having decided (for the time being) to go along with Sidney Hillman, had agreed to the establishment of an arbitration board whose Impartial Chairman was George H. Bell, formerly an official of the War Labor Board. In behalf of the Association, Major B. H. Gitchell had been appointed labor manager; he was regarded by the Amalgamated as friendly to labor.

The first sessions before the New York Impartial Chairman resulted in an award of a 10 per cent wage increase, which put the union members in good humor. Thus as 1919 began, the broad structure of union-management co-operation, having the stamp of the "Amalgamated school," was being extended rapidly over the principal clothing markets of all America. Of these only Chicago remained a house divided, with great non-union factories looming up side by side with those in which union men and women worked as self-respecting "citizens of industry."

v

In the late winter of 1919, Hillman made frequent trips to Chicago to confer with his old comrades there on plans for the completion of the job in that city.

During the war there had been few strikes of any size in Chicago. But in the case of one firm, the Scotch Woolen Mills, which, under protection of local court decisions, continued its anti-union discrimination, the union fought hard to drive the company out of Chicago. Its managers had actually given up Army-uniform contracts rather than deal with the union. Were these people, then, not as "disloyal" as it was alleged were the IWW men now in jail? [36] Now it was the turn of the Amalgamated union members to give such employers lessons in real patriotism as, one of them, Jack Kroll, related:

> On November 11, 1918, Armistice Day, the cutters and trimmers of Hart, Schaffner and Marx, celebrating the cessation of the war in Europe, paraded the clothing district of Chicago with a large American flag and the banner of Local 61 at their head. When they attempted to pass the Scotch Woolen Mills they found police drawn clear across the street forbidding them to pass, but the men pressed on. In the scuffle the flag dropped low and an officer stepped on it; and when his attention was called to what he had done, said: "To hell with the flag."
>
> When that was heard the men could no longer be held back; they swept the police lines aside and charged on the doors of the factory. It was these men, who would not be denied, who carried the fight . . . in Chicago.[37]

The non-union houses by now had lost control of their working force. When Hart, Schaffner and Marx announced the 44-hour week at the beginning of the year, the large firms of Kuppenheimer and Alfred, Decker and Cohn promised the same reduction of hours— to begin, however, three months later, in April 1919. Angered at the delay, the workers instituted the 44-hour week themselves by leaving their jobs en masse at 4:30 P.M. instead of at 5:15 as hitherto. The foremen were thrown into a panic, thinking a strike was on; but the workers were only fixing union hours.[38]

Sidney Hillman came and went mysteriously, while turmoil spread in Chicago's garment trade. Despite the guards at the factory gates, the union's agents flitted in and out of the Association shops. There were "flash strikes" in sections or departments. If the pocket makers were out, how could you make coats? Shop committees held open meetings during their lunch hours, before the factory gates. Kroll used to recall how some of the employers, in order to keep their skilled cutters away from the infection of the Amalgamated missionaries, would send them home in automobiles.

A man seen talking to a union man would be fired the next day. Sluggers and police were . . . in front of the factories even before the strikes were on. Banquets were given, profit-sharing and bonuses "à la Rockefeller Foundation" were proposed.

Yet the Amalgamated organizers managed to distribute 25,000 union leaflets in an hour throughout the clothing district, and the unionizing job went forward relentlessly. Some of its cost was unwittingly borne by the employers through the use of "floating cutters" by the union:

The "floating cutters" were . . . union men who secured jobs in non-union shops, talked unionism at noon and received a full week's wage and a discharge in the evening; they secured another job the next day and went through the same performance.[39]

On March 20, 1919, when this "guerrilla warfare" was at its height, Hillman was on hand in Chicago to address a mass meeting of 5,000 clothing workers at Carmen's Hall. The newspapers of that day noted the rare excitement of this meeting, at which resolutions were adopted that carried the threat of a city-wide strike against all the non-union clothing houses:

A rush of crowds, a clamor and surge of seat hunting . . . Middle-aged men and women listening with passionate intentness [to] sentences you could put your teeth into, like: "While the World War was fought to make the world safe for democracy, we are fighting, we are organizing, and shall continue to fight and organize until . . . we can make the world a fit place and a decent place for working people to work in. . . ." Lavish literature everywhere, lavish in quantity and style. . . . The gustiness of it caught you up. They did not ask things or plead for them. They crisply formulated demands.[40]

The cutters walked out first at Kuppenheimer's, tying up production, while the other workers remained on the payroll for the time being. Their demand was for a wage increase of $10 a week but their spokesman, Sidney Rissman, said: "Five dollars a week will be enough if you recognize our union." [41]

The strike was settled momentarily by partial recognition of the cutters' local, but a few weeks later the ready-made tailors, some 1,500 strong, all walked out at Kuppenheimer's. Next a strike was called at the plant of Alfred, Decker and Cohn, involving 3,000 people. Up to the last days of April the tactics had been to have the employers pay for strike relief since production was effectively stopped by calling out only strategic groups of workers.

The manager of Kuppenheimer's now called up the president of the Chicago Wholesale Clothiers' Association, Jacob Abt, and said: "We are through; we are going to sign an agreement with the union." Mr. Abt, an old foe of Sidney Hillman, said finally that in that case they might as well make it a general agreement for the other members of the Association, as had been done at Rochester. Besides, Sidney Hillman was in Chicago to frame the treaty of peace and keep the clothing workers under control.[42]

It was May 13, 1919, a day of splendid spring weather when, as one of the union's Chicago veterans wrote, "the world never seemed so bright and the sky so blue," that news came that the Amalgamated and the Association were to sign a full-fledged union-shop agreement. It was the end of almost a decade of fierce struggle. The victory had been gained without bloodshed.

The chairman of the Board of Arbitration for the Chicago clothing trade, appointed by agreement of both sides, was Professor Harry A. Millis of the University of Chicago. He was to become, like Dr. Leiserson, who was stationed at Rochester, one of America's famous labor mediators, originally trained in the "Amalgamated school."

Their "wildest dreams" of long years ago, as Potofsky said, the full unionization of the Chicago market, had been realized. How happy they would have been if John E. Williams, their philosopher and guide, could have lived to see this. He had become ill and died soon afterward in January 1919. Hillman, though involved in the strike in New York, had turned up in Chicago and hastened to the old man's bedside in his last hours. He mourned the loss of Williams with all his heart, and wrote to the widow in commiseration:

In the struggle that was just successfully concluded, time and again I took courage in his philosophy of life and in his great love of humanity. I trust that you will find consolation in the knowledge that he is today living through many of us.[43]

In the short space of four and a half years the secessionist group which had broken away from the old United Garment Workers' Union, with only about 25,000 bona fide members, had become one of the country's greatest trade unions. New York, Chicago, Rochester, Baltimore, Boston, and many other centers were organized now; the Amalgamated reports claimed approximately 85 per cent unionization of the entire men's clothing industry by 1920. At the convention of that year in Boston, Hillman reported the membership at a peak of over 175,000, adding:

We come to you to report that the mandate of the Baltimore Convention of 1918 for the 44-hour week has been carried out. [Tremendous applause.] That the shorter week is here not only for our industry, but for every industry! . . .

Organized labor in America in general made striking gains in membership during the war and the post-war boom of 1919–20; the total increase for all unions was approximately 90 per cent in the period 1914–20. The growth of the Amalgamated Clothing Workers in those years had been almost threefold greater than that of the American labor movement as a whole. Although the union had a record of preserving lasting agreements with many firms, it had a wide reputation for militancy also. The ACWA, it was said, "in proportion to its membership has waged a greater number of strikes than any other militant union in the field. This applies to the years since the consolidation of the industry in 1919, as well as to the early years of organization." [44] At the 1920 convention of the union it was recorded that clothing workers' wages, on the average, had advanced 75 per cent in the recent five-year period, with much higher gains applied to the category of the unskilled workers in the trade.

By now one could easily perceive the striking change that had been wrought, in a few short years, in the condition of the once-degraded garment workers. Hillman said that he, for his part, was "tired of being applauded for every $5.00 raise" that the union won. The improved wage scale was to be regarded as but a symbol of the advancement in human dignity that labor aspired to, of the added opportunities given to "better workers and better citizens" to enjoy life.[45]

"Jack" Potofsky, who had been stationed at the union's general office in New York since 1916, on returning to his home city of Chicago, wrote:

. . . The wearing apparel of the women clearly indicated the financial and social success of the clothing workers. . . . The higher wage rates . . . the shorter hours certainly have had an effect upon the people. It seems to me that one could read in their countenance some joy of life, a testimonial to the usefulness and progressiveness of your organization.[46]

While another union spokesman, commenting at this time on the changed atmosphere of his own district in Brooklyn, a center of foreign-born garment workers, said:

There are more lectures now, more social and musical clubs, there is a greater reaction to everything that is going on in the world. I want you to understand, you tailors . . . that your work is not only the work for the union, it is work which lifts the whole standard of living from the bottom.[47]

What was most remarkable of all, as a leading liberal weekly of this period said in commenting on the 44-hour week, was that these "despised immigrants," whom the AFL had tried to exclude from the official labor movement, out of fear that they would tend to debase the American standard of living, had now taken a position of leadership among our unions and had ended by establishing a new high standard in one of the most important of American industries.[48]

VI

The fight for organization, which meant for existence itself, seemed all but won in those first "heroic years" of the men's clothing workers' union. The Amalgamated already wielded a great power in its industry. How would this be used? Where would labor go in America after the war? Such were the questions that Hillman and his associates asked themselves now and often discussed with the union members.

Labor was on the march in 1919, a record year in which 4,160,000 workers were involved in strikes. President Wilson himself had observed that when the soldiers returned from the war they would not be content any longer with "economic serfdom." In Russia the old regime had fallen and the Bolshevists were in power; in England the rise of the British Labor Party, offering its inspiring post-war program, seemed also to foreshadow sweeping social changes. In the United States in the hitherto prudent circles of the AFL plans were made at last for organizing the nation's half million steel workers, and a great steel strike began in September 1919. In October Acting President John L. Lewis of the United Mine Workers also called out 411,000 coal miners in defiance of President Wilson— who denounced this action as "an attack upon the rights of society and the welfare of the country." Was it to be revolution in America too? many now wondered.* Moreover, the powerful railway Brotherhoods now urged that Congress enact a law providing for the government's retaining ownership of the railroads, which had been taken over during the war. The miners' union also called for the nationalization of the coal mines. It seemed that we were truly "on the threshold of a new system," that the "post-war world would be different," as one enthusiastic speaker at the Amalgamated Convention of May 1918 exclaimed.[49]

To Sidney Hillman too—wary and realistic though he was—the thought came now that organized labor might come into its own, not in some distant future, but much sooner than most men believed. His ideas and hopes, the outlines of his own plans and dreams also, were given expression in very characteristic form in two speeches he made early in 1918 in Montreal, one before a gathering of businessmen, the other at a meeting of his own union members. The two talks, as noted by the newspapers, were naturally different in tone, yet consistent enough.

His union had made progress in Canada during the war. In Mon-

* The question was seriously raised at this time, in the autumn of 1919, by Herbert Croly, writing in the *New Republic,* Thorstein Veblen in *The Dial,* and Harold J. Laski in *The Nation.*

treal, the manufacturers had formed a high opinion of the Amalgamated's leader, and during his visit of January 1918 tendered him a luncheon and invited him to speak at their club. With candor he talked of the effects of the current war and labor's future role:

The world is in the midst of a new social era—the establishment in industry of the principles of social democracy. . . .

I am not going to argue with you gentlemen whether my views are right or not. The change is coming—what are you going to do about it?

What labor is demanding all over the world today is not a few material things like more dollars and fewer hours of work, but the right to a voice in the conduct of industry.

Labor, he said, had learned the one great lesson in this war; it had learned that it had power. It was determined that its power should be recognized, and the only real question was how this should be brought about.

Hillman thought that there were two possible ways: the Russian way of revolution, and the parliamentary way. In Russia everything had been done by the old ruling class to block the movement of the workers and the progress of society, and the result had been the Russian Revolution. In England, on the other hand, labor was accorded a voice in the conduct of the war; there were co-operation and mutual understanding, and the prospects pointed to a peaceful reconstruction of society.

Drawing the lesson of these events, he now warned his hearers to guide themselves by what had happened in Russia, where the working people and peasants had come to believe that revolution was the only way out. Thus democracy had been crushed there. Yet Hillman refused to believe that men should go back to autocracy and dictatorship. Without democracy, he urged,

even under the most efficient autocracy that would provide everyone with all the necessities of life . . . life would be meaningless if one could not find a mode of self-expression. . . . All men wanted to live their own life, make their own mistakes and correct themselves.

Mr. Hillman [as reported in a Montreal newspaper] said that a friend of his had lauded the German thoroughness in doing everything and looking after the German people. He had replied that in a hospital there was splendid organization, meals were given in the right quantities and at the proper times. . . . Then he had asked the admirer of Germany: "Would you like to go and live in a hospital?" [Laughter and applause.]

No one wanted an autocracy, even if it were a benevolent one. Labor wanted to carry the same principles into the shop. . . . Children could not be taught to love liberty and freedom and democracy, and then be put at fourteen into a shop where all these principles were denied, where the foreman was an autocrat, even if sometimes a "benevolent autocrat." [50]

At the speech he gave in the evening of that same day before the Amalgamated members at Prince Arthur's Hall, the same thoughts were presented, yet in an entirely different spirit. Using as his text a recent statement in a newspaper interview by Charles M. Schwab, head of the Bethlehem Steel Company, that labor was "destined to rule the world," Hillman affirmed that labor was coming into its own. The Czar of Russia was gone; in England the Labor Party was a rising force.

The war, he said, had brought about a breakdown of private management; the mining of coal, the operation of railroads had had to be taken over by governments—and yet if, instead of permitting millions to be unemployed, there had been a full use of labor in the past, there would have been enough of everything to meet the greatest needs of the present emergency. The managers of private business had got their millions, but they had not done the work, and so the workers were thinking: "If you cannot run it efficiently in spite of all we have done for you, we will come in and run it ourselves. We cannot possibly make a worse job of it." He went on to say that

labor would never be satisfied until it had won power. . . . President Lincoln had once said that a nation could not exist half slave and half free. Neither could an individual live half slave and half free, free politically and a slave industrially.

On the other hand, Hillman also propounded his now familiar belief that only by inuring itself to hard work and responsibility could labor hope to lead in the regeneration of society:

Labor had before it the task of building up, not of tearing down. It could not be done in an irresponsible way. When workers had a say in the shop they would also have responsibilities. The change taking place was to make all the people work, not to make all the people not work. [Laughter.] The world's work had to be done. The aim of labor was not the loafer's aim. It hoped for the time when everybody would do constructive labor and enjoy it, not for the time when the workers would do nothing.

Without work life would be worthless and aimless, and work should still be the principal aim of the worker, but they would make an effort all their own, not under compulsion.

The old order, especially in Europe, appeared bankrupt as the war drew to its end. It would be "labor's duty to reorganize society in a constructive way," he urged at the end.

Thus Hillman at thirty expressed the same convictions that he would repeat two or three decades later. Not by prating of some "inevitable" Socialism, but only by its efficiency, its intelligence, its discipline, could organized labor in day-by-day action prepare to assume the leadership of society.

The 3,000 Montreal members of the Amalgamated (unlike their employers earlier) responded with great emotional warmth to this speech.[51] Hillman himself was stirred by the very hopes and longings he had aroused in his hearers. Returning to his hotel room, as if too tired to sleep, he sat up and wrote letters about the incident.

One was to his wife—actually it was addressed to his daughter Philoine, then only six weeks old, as if he wished the thoughts of that night to be preserved for her. Here, in the intimate outpourings of this letter, one feels the realist or the skeptic in Hillman contending with the prophet of social regeneration; one feels the antithetical tendencies within him, as in all complex natures; but there is also a tone of deep compassion and love of the workers which seems to prevail in the end. It is one of Sidney Hillman's rare ventures into autobiography or self-confession:

> 1918, January
> The Windsor Hotel, Montreal
>
> Dear Philoine,
>
> I am just coming from a mass meeting. I have discussed the issues of the day. The hall was crowded with men and women who toil. They came to hear the message I may have for them—in their looks I saw the plea for a word of hope, because, my dear, that is the only thing that gives color to their life. Their present is so colorless that their only joy lies in the future. I have told them the same things I said yesterday at the Canadian Club. (I have sent you the clippings about that meeting.) But what a different reception. There at the Windsor Hotel were the Masters of today; here in Prince Arthur Hall—perhaps the masters of

tomorrow—still the Slaves of today. There they were listening with apprehension to the challenge that a new champion—Labor—is contesting for their place of power, and that the new champion is irresistible—his power absolute—that he knows no defeat—and while even admiring the beauty of his majesty they were fearful lest he will invade their territory and establish justice in their land—justice that will deprive them of their position of privilege. They are perfectly willing to let justice rule elsewhere. Here were those who are now waiting for ages for this new Messiah—messenger of love, freedom and plenty to all; those who struck, starved and sacrificed themselves to make their hopes possible. There were the well fed, the rested, the rulers of the world, whose word is law for the great masses of the people—here were the slaves of those rulers, looking for a message of deliverance. As I was looking in their eyes, and some of those eyes belonged to young and pretty girls—I could not resist, I told them what they wanted to hear—that their Day is at hand, Messiah is arriving. He may be with us any minute—one can hear the footsteps of the Deliverer—if he only listens intently. Labor will rule and the World will be free. And as I was telling them these words, a new fire kindled in their eyes—the fire of hope, will and determination. A thrill went through me at this time—I was watching them and behold, a wonderful change took place. At first I only felt his presence and then I actually saw him in all his wonderful majesty—strong—determined, full of love. The Champion was with us in the Hall, ready to do battle. The people —an awakened people——

Dear do you think this could be true—or perhaps it is a vision of a tired and inflamed brain. Good night Dear.

Love to your mother.

P. S. Do not tell anybody the contents of [this] letter—they may not understand.

Chapter Eight

"THE NEW
UNIONISM"

*You are the pacemakers of the
American Labor movement.*
—Felix Frankfurter
(May 11, 1920)

"What next?" the restless Hillman was saying after the
summer of 1919. Rather optimistically he observed that
his union had "successfully passed through its time of storm and
struggle." The problem now was: "What shall we ask for next? How
shall we use the power we have obtained?" [1]

The Amalgamated had gone far in a few short years. In 1919 and
1920 its officers could scarcely handle the work of signing up new
members and organizing new locals. Laborers in other clothing fields,
such as the shirt industry, were clamoring to be admitted into the
Amalgamated union. Now in many cities arbitration boards for men's
clothing sat together peacefully, presided over by a "judge" or Impartial Chairman, and debated all the difficult and tedious questions of
production schedules and piece rates. It was a pleasing and civilized
picture. A liberal journalist visiting Rochester at a time when building workers were engaged in strikes throughout the Eastern states
noted that the officers of the ACWA, headed by Hillman, met with the
leaders of the city's garment trade in a ballroom of a local hotel.
Economists, engineering experts, and statisticians for both sides, together with shop chairmen and "labor managers," sat at a long table,

surrounded by gilt mirrors and potted plants. This was the "class struggle in a ballroom." [2] Would strikes become obsolete? Would wage bargaining become, as Hillman predicted, "a thing of the past," with the workers' share of industrial rewards apportioned "scientifically"?

In reality much routine work still remained for the union people in the way of strengthening their organization and cleaning up non-union strong points in their rear. To Hillman's mind it was imperative to stabilize the entire American men's clothing trade, whose evils of competition, chiseling, and inefficiency were still to be reckoned with. The logic of the situation drove him constantly to the position of union-management co-operation. As he said in later years:

There were definite limits upon our ability to improve and maintain wage and hour standards of workers employed by a single manufacturer or in a single industry, unless we succeeded in raising the standards of all competing manufacturers and markets up to the same level.[3]

The industry itself must establish uniform wage scales and standardized methods of operation or "equalized labor costs." In New York men were paid by the week, and in Chicago at piece rates. No one seemed to know what a "fair" standard or "normal" work day was; how many pockets should be sewn in a day; or how many coat shoulders could be basted in a given time. Hillman himself was going to look into such questions.

At the end of the war, he called together the General Executive Board of his union and laid before them his scheme for trade agreements, not of local scope but of nationwide scale, to be worked out with the combined clothing associations of the different city markets. The idea, at first, rather dismayed his associates; it seemed almost too "Napoleonic."

"But, Sidney, you are strengthening our enemies," Potofsky recalls having protested at the time, early in 1919. "Look what you are doing—why, you are building up a *trust,* a National Association of Manufacturers in our trade!"

Hillman replied: "At all costs we must take the laboring man out of competition. You will see that I am right." Their union was now strong enough, he believed, to "control the job," despite any combination of manufacturers. But it could never deal even partially with the rigors of cutthroat competition and seasonal unemployment unless progress were made in stabilizing the industry. For this reason he did not fear the danger of the cartel system in 1918–19, nor in the emergencies of 1933–35, when his own farsighted schemes for industrial planning were tried anew under the NRA codes.[4]

In June 1919, representatives of the four largest men's clothing centers in America met in conferences with Sidney Hillman in Cleveland and considered proposals laid before them by the Amalgamated's president for the establishment of "some sort of national joint council." Early in July the same group, augmented by their labor managers from New York, Chicago, Rochester, and Baltimore, met again to continue these preliminary discussions at a hotel in Rochester.

By September the national men's clothing association was functioning informally. No over-all agreements were ever reached; the whole affair was only in its exploratory stage. Yet as the General Executive Board report for the convention of 1920 observed somewhat later:

> The fact that a national organization of clothing manufacturers was organized for the express purpose of maintaining collective regulations with the union was a matter of the highest significance.

The newspapers, on hearing rumors of these ambitious plans for stabilizing what was then America's tenth largest industry, now frequently published interviews with Hillman. He explained that he was absorbed in continual study of the whole problem of costs and standards of production. Variations in wage scales and methods of operation made for serious conflicts between different sections of the ACWA itself. The employers

> made and unmade standards at their own sweet will [Hillman said]. They created sweatshops and drove men and women to premature death or invalidity. In the name of efficiency . . . they set strong men against weak, young against old, prompted overspeeding and task-setting, with resultant chaos and waste.

Industry had only the rule of thumb. But the union, at Hillman's prompting, was now instituting experimental researches of its own, he reported, with the aid of industrial experts. The task was difficult, for in a study of one shop having 3,000 workers, more than 150 different operations were accounted for in the making of a ready-made suit. Yet with the help of interested shop committees of the workers, and good will on both sides, Hillman said:

We analyzed and timed each operation and determined the normal speed. We then set a maximum speed above the normal and a minimum below. We provided for grades between the normal and the maximum and set special standards of wages for each grade of work. . . . All workers were then classified into grades. Each worker who delivers the output of his respective grade is entitled to the corresponding wage. The grading of workers is . . . subject to approval by the union and the management.

Thus progress was being made, though slowly, in adapting the clothing workers to new machines and new operations, yet without permitting the burden of such improvement to be borne only by the workers, through a "squeeze" or "speed-up." Hillman was strong for the advancement of productivity by scientific methods, but with the restriction that this process remain under the safeguard of union control, in the interests of the workers' health and economic welfare. He said:

We propose to make industrial science possible. We too shall employ experts familiar with all the devices of the stop watch, etc., who will make time studies. . . . We are not opposed to methods of efficiency— but they must be humanized and made subject to democratic control.[5]

In the autumn of 1919 Hillman engaged the services of a young economist recommended to him by Felix Frankfurter, Dr. Leo Wolman, who had taught at Johns Hopkins University and had done statistical research for the Federal Government in the field of labor during the war. Dr. Wolman, very fluent, clearheaded, and vivacious, greatly attracted Hillman and was retained by the union to organize the first full-fledged research department ever used by an American labor union. The printers, miners, and railway workers at periods before this had had only the temporary services of labor economists like W. Jett Lauck. But the Amalgamated now sought precise knowledge of its industry, and Hillman, hereafter, appeared at conferences armed with information more complete than was possessed by any of the industrialists of clothing.

II

The "New Unionism" * was a term much used by students of the labor movement toward 1920 to describe the industrial movement

* Title of a work by Joseph Budish and George Soule, published in 1921.

typified by the ACWA and the plans of its ambitious president. These included regular and friendly conferences with the capitalists of clothing in the interests of co-operation—much to the disgust of orthodox Socialists. One former executive of the ACWA has said:

> We had the "class struggle" tradition then. We believed that even to talk to a manufacturer alone or to have a glass of soda water with him was a crime. We didn't think the capitalist system would last so long that you had to make friends with the manufacturers.[6]

Yet while Hillman on the one hand made every effort to "live with industry," on the other hand he constantly sought expansion in the broad field of labor organization itself. A great trade union, he said in effect, cannot exist by itself, as if on an island. If groups of textile workers went out on strike, then the Amalgamated must aid them. Some of Hillman's best organizers were sent to help the United Textile Workers (AFL), then active again among the silk workers of Paterson, New Jersey. Later in the same year, when a great textile strike broke out at Lawrence, Massachusetts, the Amalgamated contributed large funds for the relief of the strikers, and battle-hardened organizers were loaned to them during their terrible struggle.

In the spring of 1919, a faction among the textile workers, who had long experienced the utmost difficulty in establishing a stable union, decided to apply to the Amalgamated for a charter. Led by the former minister, A. J. Muste, who later founded the Brookwood Labor College, the new union called itself the Amalgamated Textile Workers, and set up temporary headquarters at the ACWA's national office then at 31 Union Square, New York. The active sponsorship of this textile group by the Amalgamated suggested, at this time, a possible plan for a giant textile and clothing-trade federation to be led by Sidney Hillman. This thought was then in Hillman's mind, according to Dr. Muste.[7] But at the moment Hillman advised that it would be in the best interests of the workers to handle the textile group as a separate, that is, unaffiliated, organization.

The textile field employed more than a million workers, and offered immense difficulties to labor leadership; it was to wait long years for its inspired organizer. In the labor boom of 1918–1919 only some 45,000 members had been recruited for the new union.

In an allied field, close relations, naturally, had been maintained between the Amalgamated and its sister union, the International Ladies' Garment Workers—the Amalgamated, in reaching a peak of 177,000 members by 1920, had become almost twice as large as the ILGWU. When Hillman's organizers, gathering in men's clothing workers in small mill towns, found groups of women's garment workers who clamored to be organized, locals would be set up for them by the Amalgamated officers and the members turned over to the ILGWU.

In 1920 an approach was made to an informal needle-trades "alliance" to be composed mainly of these two industrial unions whose work so closely paralleled each other's. The proposal, as first put forth by President Ben Schlesinger of the ILGWU, envisaged autonomy for the separate unions in the federation, but combination for mutual defense—at a time when big strikes were expected. Smaller organizations in related trades, such as the new textile workers' union, the United Cloth Hat and Cap Workers, and the fur workers' union, were also to be included. It was hoped that the entire needle-trades federation would embrace some 400,000 workers and "serve as a powerful instrument for the workers' welfare." [8] Yet the fact that the Amalgamated as an "independent" stood outside the AFL set obstacles in the way of a close combination. The "International's" executive officers of thirty years ago included several men of difficult temperament—"prima donnas" in current parlance—who were not eager to be swallowed up by the powerful Hillman. Nevertheless, though Hillman made no overt moves, he had during many years "in back of his mind a long-range plan for building up the several textile and garment unions into one vast industrial organization." [9]

His union's treasury by the end of 1919 was reported to have approximately $500,000, a large fund for a labor group in those days. The Amalgamated now constantly sought wider fields of usefulness. The resources, as well as the achievements, of the ACWA, as Hillman used to say, were "not for themselves alone, but for the working class as a whole."

When the great steel strike began in the autumn of 1919, with the support of twenty-four AFL unions, urgent appeals were made to Hillman for donations; they came from the Amalgamated's old Chicago friend, John Fitzpatrick, who, with William Z. Foster, played a leading part in this contest. Hillman responded in most spectacular fashion by donating to the AFL, in behalf of the Amalgamated union, the sum of $100,000 for the relief of the steel strikers. It was the largest gift of its kind ever made by any union in this country. The press and the entire labor movement took note of it. This was indeed a case of "paying literally with bread for the stones that were so freely thrown at us," as Secretary Schlossberg remarked.[10]

It was Hillman who had urged this *beau geste* toward the steel workers upon his associates of the General Executive Board. Upon the outcome of this struggle of 367,000 men against the most powerful industrial monopoly depended the progress of the whole American working class. The money was paid over at once, on November 8, 1919, following which an appeal was made to the Amalgamated members to donate two hours of their pay for the steel strikers. The entire sum was thus collected and replaced in the union's treasury within a few days.

III

Convention day came around every two years, in the second week of May. The routine of Hillman's life consisted in meetings and conferences, bitter labor disputes and shrewd peace negotiations. The labor leader lives in the atmosphere of crowds; he lives an intensely *political* life, not for a season, every year or two, but all year round.

The membership had full power under the Amalgamated's extremely democratic constitution to control their executive officers through their delegates to the convention and the referendum vote. But the president and his fellow executives of the G.E.B. also had the administrative power to take action freely and continuously without obtaining the approval of the mass of members at every step. Such power might have been abused in the hands of other men. But the tactics followed were highly democratic, especially in handling the rank-and-file leaders in day-by-day union action, as in drawing up trade agreements for wages and hours. These would always be presented to the local members for approval: objections were heard with courtesy; disappointing features of such agreements were explained with frankness; the hope of further improvements next year or the year after was clearly conveyed.[11]

To be sure, a great international trade union with many thousands of members scattered over the whole continent could not be run like a small New England town meeting. It had to be directed "in an *organized* way," as its leaders held. The office of the president was powerful under the Amalgamated's charter; that of the members of the General Executive Board, raised from nine to fifteen in number in 1920, was only less powerful.* These were in effect "regional bosses," heading large city-wide markets, whose locals were organized under Joint Boards (district councils), of which they were usually the managers; and they enjoyed a large influence in the election of officers and convention delegates for the different local unions in their districts.

Repeatedly some factions among the delegates to the conventions would protest against the privileges enjoyed by some G.E.B. members who were on the payroll both as organizers and as executive officers (thus sometimes passing judgment on their own work). But Hillman and Schlossberg met these objections by arguing that these privileges had not been abused in any way. The added power had been necessary. "We have made progress because we have had power," they said.[12] The majority always had recourse to the referendum vote following each convention.

No opposition worth the name rose against the Hillman "slate" between 1916 and 1922. Yet, despite the president's great personal power, the rank-and-file members were deeply convinced that they functioned as a part of a truly democratic union—as may be seen from the verbatim records of its proceedings.

By 1920 the Amalgamated conventions enjoyed a unique fame among trade unionists; they had become also a focal point of interest for thousands of Americans who gave serious thought to our public affairs.

At Tremont Temple in Boston on May 10, 1920, there were gathered some 500 delegates from 141 locals, hailing from eighteen states in this country and three provinces of Canada. The presence of delegates' wives, of local members from Boston, of social workers, university scholars, and journalists made for an audience of

---

* The general secretary, Joseph Schlossberg, issued charters for locals and, after the first treasurer resigned, handled the treasury funds also. Schlossberg, in addition, because of his particular talents, was the union's most prolific orator and publicist in the early years.

2,500 to 3,000 persons. A symphony orchestra opened the proceedings with selections from classical music; "The Star-Spangled Banner" was sung; then, amid a deafening roar of applause and a steady stamping of feet, Hillman took the center of the stage, a familiar, slender, bespectacled figure, with his mop of curly hair, his straight, jutting nose, his alert eyes. He stood there, neat, trim, quiet, collected, smiling, and very taut—in appearance perhaps a highly successful young sales manager, in fact the successful manager of the most advanced trade union in America.[13]

This display of mass emotion was described by newspaper reporters as having a note of unmistakable personal affection. They saw Hillman saluted as the leader of one of our greatest industrial unions, which on the score of strategic influence and leadership, was considered already as "the most powerful" or "significant" union in the country.

Hillman began in his resonant voice (rolling his *r*'s), very precise, very serious in manner:

Again we meet . . . to legislate for labor in our industry and elsewhere, to promote and protect the interests of labor. We meet to review our work for the past two years, to take account of what we have done and lay out a program for the future.[14]

These words about "legislating for labor" were not idle talk, for it was a fact by now that the Amalgamated convention was truly a "parliament of labor," whose deliberations might lead the way to action by the rest of the American trade-union movement. Once the convention was under way, the delegates grappled with questions as weighty as those which any parliament then sitting concerned itself with. Their subjects of debate touched the daily lives of millions of workers; they concerned the leisure, the education, the very future and security of those millions and their families in a far more vital way than did most of the issues which our political legislatures permitted themselves to debate. Moreover, having discussed and agreed upon the measures to be taken, the union's leadership then proceeded to have them put in force by economic action. It was for this reason that the earlier Amalgamated conventions began to hold such uncommon fascination for many American intellectuals of that era. A newspaper reporter related: "This big, well-clad gathering of clothing workers, despite the noise and jollity, proceeded with complete order and high seriousness, like a gathering of professional people." Men who had not many years before toiled in sweatshops "gravely debated whether they should set aside $1,000,000 or $2,000,000 as a war chest . . . against future strikes." They spoke breezily of $100,000 given to the steel strikers, and made further donations to other unions, schools, publications, or causes of all sorts that enlisted their sympathies.[15]

Adding their knowledge to the debates were men of light and learning such as Professors W. Z. Ripley and Felix Frankfurter, who spoke also of having come to learn here from the men of labor themselves. ("I took a serious course of instruction from Sidney Hillman," said Ripley.) Economists and experts familiar with the problems of co-operative enterprises, such as James P. Warbasse, or of unemployment insurance plans, or of the engineering of factory efficiency, also were heard. A contingent of Socialists, including Charles W. Ervin, editor of the New York *Call,* and J. B. S. Hardman, often took part in the proceedings.

However, this "parliament of labor" would end not in mere talk about Socialist doctrines or hopes, but would usually put its plans into action. The 1920 convention, in fact, at Hillman's insistence, decided *not* to give its official endorsement to the Socialist Party's candidates for office. Nevertheless, as was said then by William L. Chenery (the future publisher of *Collier's Weekly*), one saw here "the vanguard of American labor in convention." To the novelist, Mary Heaton Vorse, author of a book on the steel workers, the story of the Amalgamated held all the drama of a "small group of labor idealists" who had created a union having both a spirit of realism and an ultimate program. To progressive minds of the 1920's this organization was the most effective and promising example of industrial unionism; while to an exponent of liberal capitalism like Felix Frankfurter its great merit resided in the fact that it moved in the path of "peaceful evolution," and that its leadership had the wisdom to use "scientific research" and expert knowledge in dealing with the workers' problems. "You are not only workers, but dignified, eager, and cultivated human beings," Frankfurter said in his speech to the delegates.[16] The industrial-union movement led by Hillman thus appeared to have as many different facets of appeal as there were schools of thought—it attracted revolutionists on the extreme left as well as men who favored the uninterrupted flow of profits.

The emergence of Hillman as an outstanding American labor leader happened to coincide in time with a growing post-war disillusionment among the intelligentsia about the Socialist Party. Socialism had aroused hope in hundreds of thousands from 1908 to 1916; but by 1920 the mere verbal assault upon American capitalism during election seasons seemed to offer too little. However, the industrial-union movement, as typified by the Amalgamated under Hillman, suggested a more *functional* approach to problems of social justice. Its aim appeared to be the "One Big Union" plan for which the IWW agitated; but unlike the IWW, Hillman's organization attached to its economic cause the expert and the engineer. Thus devotion to "the workers' world" was combined with practical "brains" and an approach to scientific knowledge of industry— quite as the philosopher Thorstein Veblen urged. The great hope for the future seemed to reside in the "New Unionism" which appeared to many, by its planned, daily economic action, to be building gradually and peacefully a new society "within the shell of the old." It offered Americans "the vision of a labor union which embraces all of life's activities, instead of limiting itself to shop action." [17]

When called as a witness before the United States Senate Committee on Education and Labor in 1921, Hillman affirmed his belief as follows:

> Our organization . . . is concerned with the everyday progress of the worker in industry, of getting a larger partnership in industry, a citizenship in industry, I call it, and we do hope . . . that at some time labor will be free to answer its own destiny.

He added further that the union's leaders were participating in the conferences of co-operative societies, and considered going into co-operative enterprises such as banking, food stores, and possibly clothing manufacture.*

* In the volume entitled *The New Unionism,* published in 1921, which was largely inspired by the industrial union movement in this country, the authors, Joseph Budish and George Soule, wrote: "An analysis of the strategy of the new unionism will discover in it two fundamental objectives to which all other policies are subordinate. The first is to organize all the workers in the industry; the second

In those days, a quarter of a century ago (long before our present cold war with Soviet Russia), it was not considered unpatriotic or wicked for Americans to declare their purpose of bringing about the peaceful conversion of our society into a system of democratic Socialism. This was assumed to be the "ultimate aim" particularly of the Amalgamated union, as of many other large trade unions. All effective trade unions, including those of limited aims, may be considered "revolutionary" inasmuch as they seek, through control of the job, to interfere with the assumed right of capitalists "to manage their own affairs," to control their property, and to hire and fire.

At the 1920 convention Hillman's opening words were an appeal to the delegates to help direct the organization "into new fields." Thus they were to "plant the seed that will bring forth a new society where there will be no need of a struggle for simple human rights." The first of the "new fields" was to be that of "co-operative work." The second was to be an experiment in establishing security, through unemployment insurance, for workers who were made idle in the men's clothing industry through no fault of their own.

. . . We feel that the time has come when we have a right to ask of the industry that we serve every day in the week that it should protect and safeguard the workers in the industry!

Perhaps, as on other occasions, we will take a new step that will be followed by the rest of the labor movement, by which the terrible evil of unemployment will be . . . abolished.

At a time when most American unions did little or nothing about the problem, the Amalgamated made its first proposals for establishing unemployment funds in the men's clothing industry. These were to be raised through a weekly "tax" on the employers' payroll, in effect an indirect increase in wages. To offset seasonal booms and slack periods, contracts for the various markets were to be drawn up, after 1922, which arranged for sharing of the work so that production might become, as far as possible, continuous. The charge of unemployment benefits on the cost of manufacture was designed

---

is to develop them, through their daily struggles, into a class-conscious labor army, able and ready to assume control of the industry."

to encourage the continuous use of machines and men. As Hillman had said as early as July 1919:

> There is no reason why industry should not assume the task of maintaining workers during the full year. A tax on industry of 10 per cent above total wages will probably be sufficient for the creation of a proper unemployment insurance fund.[18]

As always, careful research was made by the union into the problems faced in carrying out this great experiment in social security—already initiated many years before, under government auspices, in Belgium, England, and other European countries. When practical measures had been worked out on paper, an unemployment fund was then set up for the Chicago market in 1923, with a charge at first of 3 per cent upon the payroll—the worker paying in 1½ per cent and the employer 1½ per cent. (Later, the Chicago employers' payments were substantially increased.) Several years afterward, in 1928, somewhat similar unemployment funds were established in New York, Rochester, and other markets.*

The resolution in favor of unemployment insurance was received with great enthusiasm at the 1920 convention. There was much less agreement, however, about the proposals to launch various co-operative enterprises—to begin with, a co-operative labor bank. The Socialists present argued that the establishment of co-operatives and their successful management meant the beginning of the Socialist way of life—one might say the "co-operative commonwealth" on the installment plan. But there were more radical delegates who denounced such co-operative undertakings as banks, already initi-

---

* In urging at first that the employer exclusively should bear the costs of the worker's enforced idleness, Hillman, in a newspaper interview at this period, presented arguments which strongly reflected the influence of Thorstein Veblen's ideas. He is recorded as saying:

"The interest of the employer in any industry today is casual and relative. It is an interest in the product, and not in production, in the profits from sales, not in the process of workmanship. The employer is ready to transfer his interest to any point of the industrial system where returns are more promising. He willingly plays long or short with his industry . . . his attitude is that of the investor and speculator, not that of the producer.

"On the contrary we workers have a permanent interest in our industry. We spend our lives in it. Our families depend on it. We have no economic interests outside of it. We must keep production going to maintain and improve our standards of living." (New York *World,* July 11, 1927.)

ated by the railway Brotherhoods and farmers' associations, as mere "bourgeois" follies. Some argued that such plans would always fail; others that their success would degrade the Amalgamated, transforming it into a "capitalistic" trade union. Still others insisted that such ventures would give the union members an opportunity to show "that we can work and manage also."

After hearing all sides patiently for some hours, Hillman, presiding, made some pungent remarks which had the effect of bringing the debaters down to earth:

The chairman regrets that the discussion has been so long as to nearly talk the subject to death. If we are going to have a theoretical discussion to establish theoretically whether from the point of view of The Revolution, or something else, the co-operative movement is desirable, I would suggest that we specify another time for that kind of discussion. We are here to say whether the Amalgamated is to approach this subject in the spirit of the Amalgamated. Are we ready to go ahead, or are we going to remain on the outside?

The delegates, he said, sometimes seemed to be riding on an express train

whose only stops are Paris, Berlin, Moscow, and Milan. They forget that our stops are New York, Chicago, Rochester, Baltimore, and Boston. We must sometimes think about the local train. . . .

We feel that when we started the movement for a shorter week, if we had given it as much . . . discussion as to [co-operatives] our people would still be in the sweatshops. . . .

I feel by giving the organization another phase in which to test its abilities, that hundreds and thousands will spring up from the ranks and will make their contribution. . . .

I feel even more strongly that the line of simply talking wages and cost of living will soon pass. I want to be frank with you delegates, I am tired of it. We go into conference and gain another $5.00. Wonderful victory! Another $5.00! and then you find the cost of clothing has gone up enough to take it away—not because of the $5.00 granted you, but because of the tremendous waste in the methods of production and distribution—there is where the high cost of living comes in! We want to go into banking . . . because we have found out that the gentlemen in the banking concerns have close connections with every one of your tailor shops. We want to have our own credit, so that we don't have to go to the gentlemen who control credit to get them to help us establish the co-operative movement.

I have no ultimate program. I have no ultimate program for this convention. In time of leisure—and that time is becoming more and more scarce—I indulge in dreams, but I don't permit them to become the policy of the organization.

The resolution empowering the officers to undertake co-operative enterprises was passed by an overwhelming majority.

When the report of the general officers for the past term was brought in with a recommendation that it be approved, the members were about to accept it in a perfunctory way, when Hillman suddenly called a halt to the proceedings, saying:

Now is the time for criticism. If there are delegates who do not approve of what the officers and General Board have done let them speak at this time. I do not want any delegate to go away and say that if he had had the chance he would have voiced his opposition. Has anyone anything to say?

It was a courageous challenge, for the winds of doctrine blew strongly from all four corners of the earth among this medley of races. Hillman waited, on the alert.

One delegate from the rear said: "I think the general officers went beyond their powers in adopting a plan of co-operation. Was that submitted to the locals for approval?"

Other voices rose to defend the administration, but Hillman avoided calling them, holding that this was the hour for the critics. The fun continued. Another man arose and said he was opposed to Impartial Chairmen.

We find that sometimes they decide for the employers. They have the capitalist point of view. I do not believe in joint dealing. The workers ought to decide what they want and tell the bosses. We don't want any conferences.

A New Yorker then swung in from another tack, asking: "Why did not the general officers show more force in disciplining the New York locals? The general officers should use their authority more vigorously."

The New York bloc of delegates roared in anger, but Hillman would not hear their defense, and called on still another left-winger who said that the General Executive Board had come to Montreal and "put over" a scheme for production standards (at piecework rates) in an agreement. He cried: "What have they got to do with production? Are they doing the bosses' work?"

The shooting went on, until many delegates were weary and called for the vote. Then Hillman made a devastating reply:

The General Board wants criticism, but we want intelligent criticism. Approve of what we have done, or repudiate . . . but do it intelligently on the basis of facts. On one matter criticism has come from two opposite sources. . . . We are blamed for not having exercised enough authority in New York, and for having done too much in Montreal. Let us look at the facts. The general officers have no authority to sign any agreement which has not first been voted on and approved by the membership of the locals affected. The agreements providing . . . for production standards in Montreal were submitted to the locals . . . before they became agreements.

Then he turned his sharp logic upon the delegates who had attacked arbitration:

I do not understand that delegates to this convention want to interpret the class struggle as an everyday petty fight in the shop. We got the 44-hour week in New York by striking for it! Hart Schaffner and Marx conceded it without a struggle. Is the 44-hour week good in New York and bad in Chicago? The purpose of this organization as we understand it is to deal with employers so that the interests of our people will be protected. . . . I feel it my duty to say that we believe in production standards. I want to say that sabotage against the industry comes from employers, not from members of our organization.

Hillman had used no parliamentary tricks, but had simply acted on the conviction that differences of opinion offered no threat to the health or unity of the organization if, instead of being intimidated or suppressed, they were allowed full expression and fully and fairly answered. In the end, those who had spoken up most forcefully against the union's president were smiling or laughing at his sallies. When the motion to approve the report of the executive officers was finally made, it was voted unanimously.

There was less smiling, however, when the issue of piecework versus weekly wages was brought up.

Part of Hillman's "statesmanship," according to many veterans of the union, one of his chief contributions, was the effort he made to redefine the workers' relationship to industry—even when this appeared, in the short view, to win him no favor.

Like Veblen, Sidney Hillman argued constantly that labor had "no quarrel with industry," but that it was the men of business whose policies tended toward mismanagement and underproduction. But when he spoke with employers of standardized wages and standardized operations they insisted, for the sake of incentive, on the adoption of the piecework system. It was always their contention that in the same shop men earning a fixed weekly wage inevitably "slacked" on the job, while those on piecework produced more and also earned more in the same number of hours.[19]

Hillman was aware of the unpleasant fight he faced in his own union when he decided now to advocate the general adoption of a system of wages which he knew was disliked by several of his powerful lieutenants, representing perhaps half the membership. In his opening speech he had urged that "week work with production standards" be accepted as encouraging higher productivity.

Within the Amalgamated, strife over this issue had been continuous for two years, since Hillman had made a similar proposal at the preceding convention of 1918. The piecework scale was in use in the large factories of Chicago and to some extent in Rochester. In New York the Amalgamated locals for long years had nailed the flag of weekly wages to their mast.

What Hillman feared was that the great New York clothing market would be out of line with the labor costs of Chicago, Baltimore, Rochester, and other centers, where piecework had been in force for years. This would make it impossible to equalize wages for all the different sections of the union, and would injure the clothing trade in New York, faced with higher production costs. The New York manufacturers who had made peace with the Amalgamated the year before would therefore be driven to cut wages, or evade their agreements with the union, or, in desperation, break with the union and lock out its members. The outcome, Hillman predicted at the G.E.B. meeting that preceded the convention of May 1920, would be a fearful struggle that might destroy the union. His associates, however, warned him that forcing his own plan upon the union members would split the organization.[20]

But now the issue was joined before the convention. Having

spoken for his proposal, Hillman met the opposition head on. One man after another rose to denounce the piecework system as "slavery" or "class collaboration" on the part of the union. They recalled the sweatshops in which, not many years before, they had worked under the hated "task system," turning out so many pieces a day for twelve hours a day, seven days a week. It was to end all this that they had rebelled in 1913.

Against these emotional outpourings men like Hyman Blumberg, head of the Baltimore Joint Board, cited facts and figures in favor of week work under production standards. He himself had installed such a system in a plant with 3,000 employees, by which men were graded according to capacity for an expected group output—after the union's agents had determined what would be a fair rate of production and payment. "The workers themselves decided what a day's work should be," he said. Their strength was not overtaxed, and they shared with management the gain in increased productivity.[21]

Yet the voices of the opposition spokesmen were vehement and loud; the temper of the delegates was shown by the big rounds of applause they received.

Hillman wound up the debate and spoke with great intensity for almost an hour. He was pale and tense. It was the sixth and most exhausting day of the convention he had presided over; yet he seemed more aroused than at any other time that week. He was aware that the members were bitterly divided, for the proposal of a universal piecework system seemed, on the surface, to offer advantage chiefly to the manufacturers. But he was going to tell them some unpleasant truths; and his courage in doing this was the high mark of his leadership.

If they had large achievements to show now, he said, it was because "we"—Hillman seldom used the singular personal pronoun—"have followed rules of sound judgment and careful plans," not the "prejudices" of the members. Basic was the idea that "labor cannot destroy the house it lives in." Those workers who thought they might win The Revolution by shirking work had the wrong idea. This would mean accepting that "law of the jungle" that dominated our wasteful, ill-managed society. Labor, he urged, "must rise above the morale that prevails in capitalist society today," which demanded only that "they do as little as possible for as much as they can get."

The resolution offered by the Hillman forces had recommended the "week work system with standards of production" to be instituted at once. In conciliatory spirit, Hillman presented this as, in effect, a compromise plan:

I am happy that I can say that we have worked out a middle ground between piece and week work . . . a program that will protect us from "racing," will protect us from ruinous effects upon health. . . . For the first time we will legislate for our organization as a whole and at the same time adopt a program that will help the industry.

Hillman looked worn as he finished, for he had spoken with great emotion, hammering out his ideas with his characteristic, quick gestures of his arm; his head was bathed in perspiration as the vote was taken. It seemed close at first; but the tellers' count showed a clear majority favoring the plan of week work with standards of production.

Some of the onlookers thought it had been a costly victory, for he had been sharp, even ironical, with his opponents, and they expected that when the nominations for the presidency were called for he might have to pay for his bold stand. But at the end

a sudden mass stood on the floor. A mass of hands rose up, stretched out toward the platform. Everybody seemed to want to nominate somebody. Almost everybody did. There was one cry: "Hillman! Hillman!" [22]

Chapter Nine

DEPRESSION AND COUNTERATTACK:

1920-1921

We are at the beginning of one of the greatest attacks
that has ever been directed against labor. . . . Their
attack is . . . not the result of hasty plans, but of
concerted action conceived and planned far ahead,
but postponed until the time seemed to them ripe.
—Sidney Hillman, Speech, Dec. 29, 1920

Up to the spring of 1920, as for two years past, the
mood of organized labor had been of the highest optimism. Union leaders dared to speak as if the battle of labor for a
place in the American sun were almost won.

Almost in the twinkling of an eye this bright picture darkened.
The inflationary post-war boom turned into a slump. The fall in
wholesale commodities from May 1920 to June 1921, from an index
figure of 272 (using the 1913 average as 100) to 148, struck hard
at the clothing trade. The price decline of woolen cloth, which began
at the end of May 1920, was approximately 40 per cent; hundreds
of wholesale clothing firms were caught with large inventory losses
which led to bankruptcy.

Only yesterday there had been a serious scarcity of labor, with
the Amalgamated union, as Hillman testified, struggling to keep its

members from "taking advantage of the law of supply and demand" by changing to jobs offering more pay. Now union contracts which expired were being abandoned in an atmosphere of panic; tens of thousands of men's clothing workers were discharged. Overnight the whole position of the Amalgamated was seriously imperiled. The counterattack of capital upon organized labor, already under way after the summer of 1919, increased in violence throughout 1920. At the cheerful Boston convention of the Amalgamated in May 1920, Hillman had given warning that "the forces of reaction are mobilized as never before to attack progressive labor." A few weeks later he reported confidentially, at a meeting of the General Executive Board, that a very acute situation was developing in New York:

> The employers of this city felt that it would be advantageous to them to have a strike for at least three months. Under these conditions we had to carry on the work. In many cases our temper had to be restrained to prevent strikes. . . . As a result of this state of affairs, we are confronted with many employers who are desperate and will foster strikes.[1]

A concerted open-shop offensive seems to have been organized by leaders of heavy industry at this period. Representatives of the National Association of Manufacturers, the U.S. Chamber of Commerce, and other important business associations conferred together and then opened a vigorous press campaign aimed at the alleged "tyrannies" and "extortions" of the great trade unions. The workers were exhorted to join in various types of "American Plan" unions, which were in fact company unions, often fitted out with elaborate welfare and incentive devices.[2]

This counteroffensive of capital was strongly favored by the anti-Red panic that had followed a series of mysterious bombing outrages in 1919. Sensational newspaper stories at the time attributed these crimes to a nationwide anarchist conspiracy, or to a secret "Bolshevist" organization whose aim was to overthrow our system of government with a few packages of TNT. The great "dragnet" operation carried out by Department of Justice agents, under the direction of the FBI, by which many centers of foreign-born workers and trade-union headquarters were raided and thousands arrested without warrant, was a memorable feature of that season of terror and hysteria. State legislatures also, as in New York, established investigative bodies such as the Lusk Committee to inquire into alleged Bolshevist activities.

American Legionnaires and "Vigilantes" helped to break strikes in many instances. Police officers in some towns arrested on sight union agents who were going about their normal business.

Sidney Hillman himself, on August 13, 1919, had his own experience of the "Red Terror." He had journeyed to the city of Utica, New York, where he was to address a meeting of members of a new Amalgamated local. On arriving there he was met at the train by three policemen, several detectives, and a delegation from the local Chamber of Commerce, who said: "You can't stay in this town."

"But I am here on a lawful errand, as an official of the Amalgamated Clothing Workers of America," he protested.

"That makes no difference to us. You are not wanted here."

He was forced to leave town at once, by boarding the train he had just left, and without an opportunity to see the local officers in Utica—who were likewise ordered to leave town, and did so.[3] *

The Amalgamated, in particular, seemed to draw the attention of overzealous government officials, legislators, or judges. From these quarters came the frequent charges that it was a "revolutionary" organization, bent on "Sovietizing" the clothing business—though more than any other union it had specialized in the peaceful arbitration of the workers' grievances.

In October 1919, Hillman was involved in a perfect cape-and-sword intrigue, complete with secret agents, spies, and counterspies. It would have been merely funny if its repercussions had not been so serious.

He had just then been conducting a vigorous cleanup of some grafters who were officers of one of the New York children's clothing locals of his own union. He felt a deep disgust, though not sur-

* Thorstein Veblen noted extremes of absurdity in the "Red Terror" of 1919–20. The ordinary citizens seemed to be immune to its contagion, he remarks, but "the commercialized newspapers see Red. So do the . . . Lusk Commission, the Security League, and Civic Federation . . . as well as the Workaday Politicians, the Clerics of the Philistine Confession and the Wild Asses of the Devil generally." Bands of "paranoiacs" were everywhere pursuing those men who were considered guilty of "undue sanity." (J. Dorfman: *Thorstein Veblen and His America*, pp. 433–34.)

prise, at discovering among the hundreds of the union's petty officers a few men who had accepted bribes (amounting to $1,000) from dishonest employers who were allowed to chisel away the union's wage standard. One man who was caught had been quickly tried before a committee of the General Executive Board and expelled from the union, together with two other local officers who had been his confederates.[4]

At about the same time two other officers who stood high among the executives of the New York Joint Board and who were considered to have been either incompetent or to have tolerated similar corrupt practices were induced to resign from their offices.

Hillman had handled the affair quietly, though promptly. The letters of resignation of the higher union officials who had been judged untrustworthy were published without comment in September 1919 in the Amalgamated's official newspaper, *The Advance.* Thereafter, it was decided to reorganize the several different Joint Boards, based on old divisions of the trade—coat makers, pants makers, etc.—into one responsible body. For Hillman believed that it was the existence of those autonomous groups within the New York organization that encouraged weakness and corrupt practice.

It was while he was busied with this job of internal reform in New York that Hillman, on October 22, 1919, received a call from a stranger. The visitor gave his name as Loeb and said that he had just arrived in town from Chicago. With an air of elaborate intrigue, he described himself merely as a go-between, authorized by his principals to offer large sums of money to the Amalgamated president if he would come to meet certain persons in a designated law office in New York. Hillman, controlling his emotions, listened carefully and was convinced that this was decidedly a scheme to "frame" him. By alternate pleas and threats, he persuaded the man to make a clean breast of the affair. Affidavits and copies of incriminating telegrams were then obtained from the go-between, who protested that he did not know the identity of the real instigators of the plot, and with these documents Hillman hurried off to the district attorney's office in New York. At the same time he engaged a detective agency to trail Loeb.

But Hillman himself had been shadowed when he went to the district attorney's office. His own detectives trailing Loeb had also been followed by the conspirators' detectives. Then word came to

him that the persons who had been trying to entrap him had taken
fright and fled to Chicago, where the whole scheme, as he suspected,
had originated.

Hillman wrote at once to the union's leaders in that city, and
to the Amalgamated's Chicago attorney, William Cunnea, warning
them to be on guard against similar attempts.

October 25, 1919, New York

My dear Cunnea:
  I am enclosing herewith copies of Loeb's affidavit, together with copies
of telegrams that have been received and sent him. . . .
  We have established upon investigation that an agency was occupied
in trailing Loeb. Two men were working on the job. No doubt an attempt
was made to implicate this office. We consulted counsel and turned over
subject matter to the district attorney's office. . . . This man will be
ready to swear out an affidavit should that be necessary.
  . . . The telegrams received late Friday seem to show that the whole
thing is off; and the efforts to frame up the General Office were frustrated.
Loeb might be on the level. However, the boys should not be too frank
with him. . . .

Ever since the time in 1914 when a large bribe had first been
offered him, Hillman had learned to walk warily. He waited. Two
weeks later the blow fell. In Chicago, where the Amalgamated had
but recently organized the whole market, a dissatisfied element
among the employers apparently still hoped to drive the union out.
It would seem that they wielded extensive political influence, for on
November 6, 1919, the state's attorney's office at Chicago went
into action, and a sudden raid was made on the Amalgamated headquarters. The union's books, records, and correspondence were
seized, and sensational statements were given to the press that evidence of large-scale extortion by the Amalgamated officers in Chicago had been discovered. A week later seven of the leading Amalgamated officers in Chicago were indicted and found themselves
pilloried in the "yellow" press, not only as alleged criminals, but
as "the reddest sort of Bolsheviki." To be sure, the Chicago *Daily
News,* one of the city's leading newspapers, came to the defense of
the accused as honest and responsible trade-union leaders.[5]

The state's attorney, who had been directing vigorous attacks on
other unions in Chicago as well, now released to the newspapers

selections from correspondence between the officers, such as the following:

A few lines to let you know what is going on here in the Children's Clothing situation. K——, against whom charges of graft were made, confessed. It appears now that he was not the only one.[6]

Slanderous charges were now circulated from the state's attorney's office that union officers had been engaged in "gigantic extortions." (The fact that the Amalgamated executives of their own volition had acted months ago to eject the wrongdoers was ignored.) As evidence, a cashed check for $1,000 was finally produced, which was made out by a manufacturing firm, the Stagg Company, and endorsed to the officers of the ACWA's Chicago Joint Board. Upon investigation this pretended piece of evidence turned out to be not that of fraud, but of an act of the greatest honor and generosity on the part of the Chicago union members and their officers. The sum had been received in settlement of workers' claims for back pay, and the members had then voted to donate the money entirely to the relief of other Amalgamated members engaged in a strike at Rochester.

An indictment, nevertheless, was brought against seven Chicago union officers on the counts of extortion and "conspiracy to boycott." But when the defendants, long known in Chicago for their probity, demanded an early trial, the prosecution moved repeatedly for delays. Meanwhile employers mentioned as having been subjected to extortion came forward to testify to the union's honest dealings with them:

Any insinuation or charge that corruption was ever attempted between the officials of the union and ourselves is absolutely without the slightest foundation.

In view of the publication above referred to, and in justice to the union and its officials, I feel that this letter should be published at once, and given the same conspicuous position in your reading matter that the original publication was given.

Yours truly

Kahn Bros., per S. W. Kahn, President [7]

This was the most serious effort made up to that time by public authorities to ruin the Amalgamated in Chicago. Hillman was extremely jealous of the Amalgamated's reputation, which stood high among trade unions in America. With some of his old Chicago comrades, men of the highest character, atrociously accused, he spared no effort to have the whole case exposed in the light of a public court. But after repeated postponements requested by the prosecution, the state's attorney in June 1920 moved to have the case stricken from the docket.

II

The business depression continued unchecked in 1920. Only recently the managers of great business enterprises had been complaining that labor was "underproducing"; today they were shutting down thousands of factories. Hillman asked:

> But after all, America is self-sufficient. Why this great depression in the midst of plenty? Why are people deprived of the opportunity to work, when millions are not provided with the necessities of life?

The only strategy known to the labor-baiting employers, according to Hillman, was to "smash the unions [and] call those who dare to disagree: 'Bolsheviki.' " [8]

Weak unions yielded all along the line in 1921 and 1922; strong unions fought back stubbornly and clung to their "control of the job." The Amalgamated suffered from its share of "smearing." Moreover, drastic court injunctions halted its strikes; suits for immense sums in damages were entered against Sidney Hillman, as president, and against the union.

In their four-year-long unionizing drive the clothing workers had often run into strong points, as noted, which could not be quickly captured. One of these was the factory of Michaels, Stern and Company in Rochester. This firm had stubbornly remained aloof from the Rochester Clothiers' Exchange and its collective-bargaining agreement. The senior partner, Mr. Stern, it was reported, considered Samuel Weill, head of the Exchange, as his chief rival in business. Hillman's persistent missionary efforts had no softening effect. Instead the management exercised an ever-stricter surveillance over those workers who were reported to have joined the Amalgamated in secret. They, in turn, were embittered by having been denied the same conditions gained by the unionized workers. A last straw was an incident in July 1919, when a girl worker was forcibly searched by a forewoman for possession of a list of union members and dismissed. The workers then walked out on Saturday, July 26, 1919, only about 50 of the 700 employees remaining in the shop. Hillman, in response to a telegram, came from New York to confer with Mr. Stern and his attorney, former Judge Robert Sutherland of Rochester, on the Monday following.

The union leader now played his cards very carefully in a supreme effort to win over this obstinate employer. On the one hand he made an earnest appeal to Mr. Stern to join with the other 19 leading clothiers of Rochester in signing a preferential union-shop agreement with the ACWA; while at the same time, in token of his own good faith, he offered to keep the strikers in hand; that is, he would restrain them from going over to the other firms in Rochester, though it was a season of great labor scarcity, in order to give Michaels, Stern time to come to satisfactory terms with the union. The company asked for a delay of several days, which was granted; Hillman then returned to New York and waited for their final reply.

At the end of that week, however, he heard unpleasant news through confidential sources. The head of Michaels, Stern and Company was reported to be in New York negotiating an agreement with the ACWA's old rival—the United Garment Workers—whose members Stern had also driven from his shop in earlier years. Feeling that he had been dealt with in bad faith, Hillman telephoned the plant manager of the firm in Rochester, saying that he considered himself "released from my promise to hold my people back." He was then informed by Mr. Stern that a satisfactory arrangement had been reached with the United Garment Workers. Hillman's reply, cold and abrupt, was: "Good-by, Mr. Stern."

The Amalgamated offer, he felt, had not been honestly considered, for there were not ten UGWA members in that shop at the time. It was to be war then.[9] The place was picketed at once, on a large scale, by thousands of Rochester members of the ACWA, for Mr. Stern's deal with the rival union threatened the stability of the entire market agreement in that city.

On September 29, 1919, the company obtained a temporary injunction from Justice A. J. Rodenbeck of the New York Supreme Court, which forbade all strike action on the ground of anticipated injury to property of the plaintiff, Michaels, Stern. Now that the war was over, the court injunction was once more a terrible weapon for the employers' side in industrial conflicts. At the same time the struck firm moved, through its attorneys, to open suit for damages against the union, on grounds of alleged conspiracy, to the extent of $100,000, later raised to $200,000. This was a new weapon, and its use was imitated at once by a half dozen other large clothing firms who were resolved to fight the union.

Meanwhile in Rochester the Amalgamated pickets were enjoined not to "loiter" or "persuade" or distribute leaflets or even speak to the non-union workers, who gradually filled up the Michaels, Stern plant. The police drove the strikers off the streets.

The labor injunction as used by the courts, at a period when Federal and state governments alike showed marked unfriendliness to labor, had a disastrous effect upon trade unions throughout the 1920's. At this stage, while the suit against Sidney Hillman et al. was pending, the Lusk Committee of the New York State Senate entered the picture by ordering an investigation of the Amalgamated's Rochester locals, raiding their offices, seizing records, and causing the arrest of some of the members. Although the Committee refused to permit Impartial Chairman Leiserson of Rochester to testify about the workings of the union agreement in that center, its agents issued reports to the press charging that the Amalgamated was a "syndicalist" union and had a "revolutionary" preamble in its constitution.[10]

In his extremity Hillman turned to Felix Frankfurter, who, after his distinguished wartime services to the government in the field of labor regulation, had joined the faculty of Harvard University as a professor of law. To Frankfurter this was no mere labor injunction and damage suit but an action that threatened the existence of all organized labor. If unions could, on charges of conspiracy, be enjoined "unreasonably" from all use of their economic power of resistance and ruined by huge damage suits, then the game was up.

On reflection Frankfurter urged Hillman to have the union take up the defense in a broad way, as if championing the rights of all organized labor in America rather than the Amalgamated alone. They could take the lead in this fight, make of it a cause célèbre, bringing in a whole battery of talented lawyers and calling for the testimony of distinguished men of affairs and government officials; experts and economic specialists would also be introduced as witnesses. This would all cost much money, but it was a great opportunity to "highlight" the drastic labor injunction as an abuse of judicial authority found in almost no other democratic nation.[11]

Hillman rose to the idea eagerly. He invited Frankfurter to assume the direction of the defense for the union, to which the professor agreed, with the understanding that he was to serve without compensation, as he considered he was only discharging a public duty. It was a prelude to his gallant service several years later in the cause of the condemned anarchists Sacco and Vanzetti. He was to continue teaching at Harvard, arranging to follow the trial during his week ends and through the Easter recess. The details of the trial work, however, were to be handled by a group of prominent law firms whose service he recommended: these were Root, Clark Buckner and Holland; Max Lowenthal and Robert Szold; Gerard Henderson of New York, and O'Brien and Powell of Rochester. In addition, Frankfurter had Hillman draft the services of the economist, Dr. Leo Wolman, who with a staff of assistants was to prepare an authoritative survey of the clothing industry, showing the effect of unionism upon its working population since 1911. Here was a combination of legal talent and university brains converging on the inland city of Rochester for the defense not only of the Amalgamated but of all American labor.

The trial opened impressively on April 12, 1920, with Mr. Emory Buckner for the defense, a star performer in a courtroom, outlining the history of the Amalgamated and asking for the right to expound its full record. Professor Wolman stood by with charts, graphs, and pictures. But it was not to be. Judge Rodenbeck leaned to the view of his old Rochester neighbor, Mr. Sutherland, attorney for the plaintiff, that the background history of the labor organization and the great social gains it had won for the needleworkers were extraneous matters; and that this lawsuit was brought only "to compel these people to leave us alone and to mind their own business." Sociological and economic data, prepared with great pains, were severely ruled out. (They were used with good effect in other suits.) The issue was narrowed to the question of evidence of "violence," mass picketing, and "conspiracy."

The defending lawyers, despite many objections and adverse rulings from the bench, struggled manfully to introduce masses of testimony on the economic benefits of the union. Buckner also presented evidence showing the deal between Michaels, Stern and the United Garment Workers to be a sham agreement.

The climax of the trial came when Felix Frankfurter introduced Sidney Hillman and examined him as the chief witness for the defense. He was a nervous witness. Under the hammering of the opposing counsel, who made repeated objections to nearly everything he said, Hillman worked himself into a perfect rage at those "evil men" who sought to "smear" his union. The baiting of Attorney Sutherland, who raised questions concerning his "Americanism," burned him up. At one point Hillman exclaimed with spirit, "Real Americanism is not talking about it, but working out in its own sphere of action a system that will create less unrest." Hillman, at times, could scarcely refrain from exploding at Sutherland, and his defending lawyers, Buckner, Frankfurter, and Lowenthal, were repeatedly forced to caution him and cool him down between bouts of cross-examination.

He managed thereafter to testify in more measured tones, and during two days that he was on the stand presented a striking picture of the effort and toil which are the life of a good labor leader. Through his testimony one followed the machinations of this antiunion employer, stubbornly determined that he would "never be a party to dealings with Hillman and his organization"; one saw the narrow little world of spies and informers at Michaels, Stern's shops; one saw "Rosie," the amazon of a forewoman who held the girl workers in terror and sometimes searched their persons for union cards. It was true, Hillman argued, that he had intervened as the advocate of Mr. Stern's employees. But did not Mr. Stern "have his counsel, Sutherland, with him when he met me, while he denied his employees the same privilege?" He continued:

> I told him that this thing has to be met right, in a big way. This strike is not the result of a small grievance. . . . We will either have a condition where the workers have no way for redress outside of stoppages or strikes, or . . . provide for the adjustment of all grievances. . . .

In the course of this trial the functioning of a diligent labor spy system in the plaintiff's factory was fully exposed in court by the defense counsel.

Yet to the mind of Judge Rodenbeck nothing of all this counted in the balance against evidence of a mild scuffle or two on the picket lines, or of a union member having thrown pepper at the coat of a Rochester policeman. The famous "industrial-union" Preamble to the Amalgamated's constitution also played its part in hardening the "Red state of mind" which seemed to grip that Rochester court in 1920. Hillman might point out that such phrases were but the expression of pious hopes for the distant future. But nothing helped. On June 21, 1920, Judge Rodenbeck granted a permanent injunction to the plaintiffs, Michaels, Stern and Company, in which the union men were found guilty of participating in a "national conspiracy" aimed at a "monopoly" of the clothing workers. The terms of the injunction were sweeping, all-inclusive. Later, on appeal, many of its harsh conditions were modified. It is notable also that the claims of the plaintiff for damages against Hillman and the ACWA were not allowed, and only the costs of the trial were assessed upon the union.[12]

The union had expended almost $100,000 for this trial; it had met with a heavy defeat. Though it had hoped to arouse public opinion, in the immediate sense the results were disappointing. However, the affair drew the attention of all factions in the American labor movement to the crisis before them. The American Federation of Labor, thereafter, petitioned Congress unremittingly for legislative relief from the terrible court injunction. In the long view the case of Michaels, Stern vs. Sidney Hillman may be said, therefore, to have been a momentous step toward the enactment of the Norris-La-Guardia Anti-Injunction Act, which came after a ten-year struggle. But in the summer of 1920 the anti-labor camp was heartened by the Rochester decision, and prepared still heavier blows at a union that had its back to the wall.

III

That summer of 1920, in describing the panic conditions that seemed to have developed in the New York City clothing market, Hillman told the members of the Amalgamated's G.E.B.: "Our entire situation is fairly well strained. We have to do everything to prevent a general conflagration." [13]

At the heart of the problem was the demand of the New York clothing manufacturers for the establishment of a piecework system that would permit them to measure and control their unit labor costs in competition with other markets. The union's local organization, however, not only opposed the introduction of a piecework system, but also resisted the compromise plan of "week work with production standards."

Hillman might plead that "you cannot beat the machine"; that labor costs were actually higher in New York than elsewhere. But the leaders of the New York Joint Board, at a stormy session, voted him down, while rank-and-file sentiment at local meetings showed itself bitterly opposed to what appeared to be "class collaboration" on President Hillman's part. He might have beaten down the opposition by main strength; but this was not his way, and it might have split his union following. The compromise plan for production standards to be worked out under a weekly wage, as voted by the 1920 convention, was shelved as far as New York was concerned.

That summer the problem of contract renewal was before the union. In August, Cohen and Goldman, the largest New York firm in the business, employing thousands of workers in its own plants and in the shops of numerous contractors, closed down and dismissed most of its employees, nearly all of whom were members of the Amalgamated. The company also declared that its agreements with the union were terminated and that its orders for finished clothing would henceforth be sent to out-of-town contract shops operated on a non-union basis. The "out-of-town" movement had begun in earnest.

For some years the great majority of the New York clothing concerns, now united in a single trade association, had been doing business with the ACWA. Their agreements were administered under the familiar arbitration system, presided over by Dr. William M. Leiserson, as Impartial Chairman then serving the New York center as well as Rochester. When Dr. Leiserson now summoned the dissident firm to appear before him and proceed to arbitrate its differences with the union, his request was ignored. The Clothing Manufacturers' Association of New York was thereupon induced, though with reluctance, to expel the recalcitrant member from its midst, while the union called its people out on strike against the Cohen and Goldman concern. But this was scarcely an effective weapon, during the depression of 1920, when many manufacturers were shutting down of their own accord.[14]

The contracts of the union with the trade association had terminated in June but had been continued on a temporary basis while negotiations proceeded between Hillman and the manufacturers' representatives. Hitherto the Association's labor manager, Major B. H. Gitchell, had been extremely friendly in his dealings with the Amalgamated. But on October 6, 1920, he wrote a letter to the union on behalf of the Association, declaring bluntly that the business outlook for the coming spring season was poor and that therefore the union and the Association must proceed at once to work out a program

for readjusting conditions affecting the cost of production. We desire to put the New York industry on a basis that will enable the manufacturers to secure the maximum business possible in competition with other markets.

Attached to this letter was a resolution drawn up by the market committee of the Association, which claimed that (1) labor costs were 50 per cent higher in New York than in competing markets; (2) a week-work system without any standard for output prevailed here against piecework systems elsewhere; (3) shop discipline was lax. Meanwhile the public appeared to be holding off buying unless prices were reduced.

The resolution ended with "seven demands" on the union, featured principally by the demand for the "right of the manufacturer to install piecework rates"; to use the scale of wages prevailing in other markets; to set individual standards of production for week workers and cutters; and for "adequate freedom" in hiring and firing and in the introduction of improved machinery.

Hillman had seen the trouble coming. Those "seven demands" were like an ultimatum preceding a declaration of war.

Let both sides, he urged, conduct a joint investigation into the New York clothing trade with a view to determining the best measures for raising output and lowering costs. This suggestion was offered in the union's official newspaper, where Hillman said:

If the union . . . has gained exceptional advantages for the New York workers, we don't propose to give up these advantages; *but if there are conditions you complain of which have nothing to do with the position of labor as such, we are ready to look into them with you and are willing to establish what is proper.*[15]

At a conference on November 14 before the Impartial Chairman, Hillman's final offer was to have the union assume responsibility for the production of its members, to reduce labor costs where necessary, and to work out "adjustments" of wages and prices by joint conference. These concessions might have led to production increases of 10 to 40 per cent, according to expert opinion, and a large group among the manufacturers in the Association seemed ready to accept them rather than plunge into war. Major Gitchell, the Association's labor manager, favored such a peaceful solution and a tentative understanding was reached.[16]

At this stage, according to Dr. Leiserson, who constantly treated with both sides, a small die-hard group among the manufacturers, headed by a lawyer named Harry A. Gordon (whom they had especially engaged for this emergency), took charge of the Association's market committee and came out against any concessions to the union, thus forcing a showdown. In testimony later before a Senate committee Leiserson related:

> The employment of Mr. Gordon as counsel was . . . imposed on the [market] committee by the small group. He is an eloquent agitator, and just as the IWW agitator acts upon the disagreeable things in the wage earner's life to stir up discontent, so he seized upon the irritations caused by union members and business agents in the shops, to stir up discontent and class feeling among the employers. . . . Mr. Gordon emphasized the irritations, harped on them as inevitable consequences of dealing with a union.[17]

In other words, a "war party" suddenly took over at this crisis. It was headed by one of the manufacturers, William Bandler; the conciliatory Major Gitchell was replaced by Mr. Gordon; and a lawyer named Archibald Stevenson, who had assisted the Lusk Committee recently in its attacks on labor unions, was also added to the staff of the Clothing Manufacturers' Association. This was in the third week of November 1920.

The aggressive new leaders of the Association now sent Hillman an ultimatum on December 2, 1920, giving the union four days to agree to the establishment of piecework in the New York trade.

Hillman had made the greatest efforts to avoid a final showdown. If only his union members had listened to him earlier, and if only both sides had been more "scientific," this impending battle would not have been "inevitable."

A call had gone out a few days earlier to all the Amalgamated members in New York to appear at mass meetings scheduled for

December 6 at sixteen different halls. The clans were gathering for battle again in the turbulent garment industry. It was a struggle Hillman had not in the least desired and which he dreaded, as he had told his associates of the Executive Board, for it was ill-timed. His mood was grave as, once more, he rode about the city from meeting to meeting to address excited throngs of workers, men and women, old and young, who looked to him as their leader. He thought then, as always, of the long weeks or months of privation they might face and of how uncertain the outcome was. Yet standing before his people, hour after hour, he took heart and spoke with his characteristic fire.

The keynote of Hillman's talks was: "We stand for peace, but if the employers insist on war they shall have it!" Far from seeking a remedy for the ills that beset their industry—in which the union was willing to help to its uttermost—the Association was acting in concert with anti-labor elements throughout the country to force a lockout and destroy the Amalgamated. "And if they succeed with us they will try it on the whole labor movement of America. They have picked on us first because we are the vanguard," he said with pride.

The mass meetings in each case adopted resolutions rejecting the employers' proposals and voting enthusiastic support of their leaders. Two days later, December 8, the New York lockout began. Thousands of union members were discharged by the larger firms, and this course was followed by the smaller manufacturers, until 45,000 workers (then employed) were made idle. Similar action was begun by employers in Baltimore and Boston also, thus involving the clothing workers of three great Eastern cities in this broad anti-union drive. The Amalgamated was now engaged in a battle for its very existence, the longest and most bitterly fought contest yet seen in the clothing trade.

IV

The prolonged lockout that began in New York in December 1920 became a war of attrition. It was the employers who had chosen the time for this contest, which was one reason why Hillman had tried up to the last moment to avoid it. Never start an industrial dispute in a season of depression was one of the oldest maxims of the labor movement. The Amalgamated was low in funds at the end of 1920 because many members had been out of work for months and had ceased to pay dues. The two preceding years, 1918 and 1919, though without any large-scale strike, had been a period of intense and costly organizing activity, and a total of 101,549 workers had been involved in mostly localized strikes or lockouts in many different cities.

The union's leaders, however, had been preparing for this fight for many weeks before it came. Hillman was planful; he liked to be more prepared than the adversary, and had a flair for organization. His lieutenants and the local leaders under them had been driven unflaggingly to check up on out-of-town contractors in New Jersey, Pennsylvania, and other outlying centers of non-union clothing manufacture. Arrangements were also made to raise large funds, for there would be tens of thousands of hungry families to feed; and the maneuvers of armies of pickets were plotted to the last detail.

One of the first steps Hillman took a few weeks in advance of the contest was to engage a publicity man; he was Heber Blankenhorn, formerly assistant city editor of the New York *Sun,* but in late years a close student of the labor movement, whose investigation of the steel strike for the Federal Council of Churches was a memorable performance at the time. Blankenhorn arranged for Hillman to speak on December 7, 1920, before the congregation of the Church of the Ascension, at Fifth Avenue and Eleventh Street. Not only was this an enlightened congregation, but its rector, Dr. Percy Stickney Grant, was a distinguished leader of the Episcopal Church. By telling his story from the union's side before this important church group, Hillman was sure to gain attention in the metropolitan press on the eve of the conflict.

Hillman, however, had been so busy night and day addressing union rallies that he met Blankenhorn at the very last hour before the church meeting. He had dictated some notes but, as prepared, the speech sounded heavy, and Blankenhorn advised him to throw it away and speak ad lib. Hillman was weary; the meeting at the Church of the Ascension seemed of minor importance in view of its small audience, and he urged that a substitute speaker be called in quickly. But Blankenhorn induced him to go.

He mounted the pulpit, ill at ease in this unfamiliar gathering place. The press had been filled lately with charges by the employers that his union was a "Bolshevik conspiracy" whose alleged extortions had vastly increased the cost of clothing. He said:

Labor is being charged with the intention of revolution. It is labor that stood for order in industry and stands for it and is ready to fight for it. . . . In this city within the next few days, a struggle involving 65,000 clothing workers will begin. Perhaps tomorrow morning what we call our State Department will resign and the Department of War—industrial war—will take its place. It is important to know what are the issues that the fight is about, and I want to say to you that there is only one issue. The issue is for the introduction of government in industry.

Then he said that he would tell them the real story of his union, of the long struggle of his people to climb from the depths of degradation in which they had lived. His arms dropped to his side; he was silent for a few moments; then he came around in front of the pulpit and began again. "If I could only make you understand the tragedy of this situation," he said. He forgot where he was and spoke with an emotion, a blazing sincerity that reached everyone in the church. The union's constructive achievements, the changes it had wrought in the lives of its members, the rise of order and democracy in the sections of the trade where its plan of joint government had been introduced were described. At the end Hillman told about his strenuous efforts to mediate the impending dispute, and the determination of the employers to force the lockout. He gave warning that the manufacturers' association would end by being destroyed in this struggle, but the union "would still be there" when it was over. But it was his word picture of the sufferings which a hundred thousand or more persons would endure through long months of idleness and hunger that most moved his audience and caused one of them to speak of Sidney Hillman, the Jew, as "the one true Christian in that church." [18]

There was little violence in this long contest, though many pickets were out. Yet here and there a striker was slashed with a razor or a girl was arrested for slapping a female "scab." It was an old story to Hillman, this warfare of pickets and their enemies: the plain-clothes men and the "scabs." A friend driving with him on a tour of the garment district pointed to several men scuffling before the doors of a clothing shop. Hillman said with a smile: "Oh well, there you see just some—*peaceful picketing.*" [19]

One feature of the lockout, aside from the widespread use of the court injunction, was the series of suits for damages on the ground of conspiracy brought against the union. Following the example of Michaels, Stern and Company, the Rogers Peet Company sued for $200,000; another still larger concern, J. Friedman and Company, one of the leaders in the "war party," sued for no less than $500,000, petitioning also for the dissolution of the Amalgamated, the first time such an action had been brought against the union. In all fourteen injunctions and suits for damages were entered in 1921 and 1922, until the grand total rose to $3,500,000!

The union's legal defense was then in the hands of the firm of Lowenthal and Szold. Robert Szold was a former United States district attorney; Max Lowenthal had had experience in labor cases as an assistant to Felix Frankfurter on the War Labor Policies Board and in the recent Rochester trial. Mr. Lowenthal, an ingenious and sharp-witted lawyer, handled most of the Amalgamated cases and specialized in maneuvers against the potent labor injunction—then somewhat new ground for most lawyers.

The suits began, as if by a common understanding among the employers, shortly after the lockout started, in January 1921. For the dissolution suit which threatened the very life of the union, the Friedman firm had engaged as counsel Max D. Steuer, one of the spectacular trial lawyers of that period. Hillman, not to be outdone, enlisted the services of former Judge Samuel Seabury, as well as those of Lowenthal and Szold. Mr. Steuer, of course, made hay with the famous "revolutionary" preamble to the Amalgamated's constitution, until Hillman was sick of hearing of it.

To add to his embarrassment, Secretary Joseph Schlossberg, at a huge rally of 20,000 union members in Madison Square Garden in January 1921, permitted himself to speak with the fervor of an old-fashioned Socialist on the theme "the industry belongs to the workers!"

Hearing of this at the time, Hillman sat fuming in his office. There would have been a stenographer taking down the words of that fervent tailor-orator, he knew, and a transcript would show up in court —as it did later in the difficult Friedman case. Hillman exploded: "Think of it! that I should have Joe Schlossberg saying things like that, along with all my other troubles!" From this time on it became a rule in the Amalgamated organization to avoid any ideological utterances that advanced the workers' cause in no immediate way, while exposing them to legal hazards. (The Amalgamated Preamble itself was eliminated by constitutional amendment in 1922.)

Fortunately the dissolution suit was tried in March 1921 before a judge of reasonable temper, Justice Nathan Bijur of New York Supreme Court. Dr. Leo Wolman had an opportunity to present the extensive economic surveys which had been prepared by the Amalgamated's research men for the earlier Rochester trial. The defending counsels, Mr. Seabury and Mr. Lowenthal, were also permitted to parade before the court the favorable personal testimony of numerous distinguished American economists, sociologists, and writers, such as Professor Edwin R. A. Seligman of Columbia University, Mrs. Florence Kelley, and John A. Fitch of *The Survey,* who all declared that the ACWA was civilized and peaceful. Justice Bijur ruled finally that the Amalgamated organization served its members beneficially; as to the phrases of the Preamble, he judged them "innocuous," not inciting to destructive or revolutionary violence but expressing, as he said, merely a pious wish for "an ideal which it is hoped may at some time in the future be achieved." [20]

The victory in the J. Friedman and Company suit for dissolution of the union was heartening, for in the atmosphere of those witch-burning days after the war it was not known how far the courts might go to strike at labor organizations.

At one point in the trial, the opposing counsel, Mr. Steuer, arguing against witnesses who said the union avoided all violence, had spoken with derision of the claim of "peaceful picketing." "Your honor," he exclaimed, "how would you like it if, at a time when you were away from home on business and left your wife all alone in the house, a picket walked up and down before her window all day long, *peacefully?*" The union, he declared, had actually picketed the plaintiff's private residence, disturbing his family and his neighbors.

Many months later, when Hillman had occasion to meet the employer face to face, he discovered that the memory of the episode still rankled in the man.

Hillman laughed and said: "Oh well, you use advertising in your business, don't you? Picketing with us is just our way of advertising." [21]

"It fairly rains injunctions hereabouts," a liberal weekly commented dryly during this fight between New York's unionized tailors and the clothing manufacturers.[22]

In one of the trials of that time a clothier, whose products were a household word to generations of prep-school boys, asked for $200,000 in damages, citing alleged violent actions by the union. The plaintiff pressed hard for production of the Amalgamated books and records in court, and appeared on the verge of obtaining an order for this. But the Amalgamated's "intelligence service" was on the alert. In some way certain confidential information was brought to the union's counsel which reflected unfavorably upon the widely respected concern. Mr. Robert Szold, for the union, charged that the firm had "maliciously attempted to induce others not to employ members of the organization and by illegal means," hence was "guilty of illegal conduct toward each member of the union." Impressive evidence of the employment of professional gangsters and armed guards against pickets was introduced, and suggestions of other still more serious irregularities as well were made. The union's lawyers therefore entered a countersuit for large damages, on the ground that the plaintiff had not come into court with "clean hands"—demanding in turn that his books and financial records be produced together with the union's. The case, which dragged on for a whole year, ended with a decision by a higher court in favor of the union, permitting examination of the company's books. It was at that time (July 22, 1922) a notable victory for the union's resourceful legal defenders—for it not only established important precedents but made "conspiracy" suits against the union hazardous. The employer promptly settled out of court by agreeing to drop his original suit.[23]

But a year earlier, at the height of the lockout struggle, the attacks through the courts seemed unremitting. In one case, Justice Van Siclen of the New York Supreme Court handed down a decision enjoining the union from all picketing. The ground for the action as declared by Judge Van Siclen was that the court "must stand at all times as the representative of capital, of captains of industry, devoted to the principles of individual initiative, to protect property and persons. . . ." [24] This opinion was often cited by historians as showing the high-water mark of class prejudice in the courts' handling of labor disputes during the 1920's.

Hillman's reply was a call to the union members to see to it that while the employers might "succeed in getting injunctions they succeeded in nothing else. . . . As long as they think they can ship customers injunctions instead of pants, let them go ahead."

v

At the outset of the lockout there was much fear that the New York manufacturers would be able to induce the big, well-organized Rochester and Chicago manufacturers to combine with them in fighting the union. In fact, a dispute over the current union agreements flared up in Rochester in January, and there were reports that a complete rupture was threatened. Such a development would have been fatal at the time. Hillman rushed off to Rochester and was closeted for days with the leading figures in the Rochester Clothiers' Exchange, who insisted upon a 25 per cent wage cut. He made concessions that satisfied their demands for the moment; the whole issue, by agreement, was to go to arbitration; and co-operative relations with the union were to be continued. When this news came, on January 28, 1921, the union members in New York were vastly relieved; it was understood that a great peril had been averted.

The negotiations eventually led to a 15 per cent reduction in wages as of October 1921.[25] Yet the Rochester organization, and—thanks to further skillful negotiations on Hillman's part—the Chicago market as well, worked full blast during the long period of stoppage in New York. A lockout by certain firms in Boston and troubles in Baltimore were also settled quickly by the exercise of diplomacy. Thus fully half of the industry's working population remained on the job and helped support their idle union brothers in New York. While the workers had been educated to act with solidarity, the capitalists of clothing were divided against each other.

Solidarity was imperative, for the struggle cost the Amalgamated huge sums in strike relief for thousands of families over a period of twenty-five weeks. In December, Hillman had announced that an International Lockout Resistance Fund of $1,000,000 was to be raised. Relief costs for food and fuel totaled, by June 1921, $1,165,000; in all, about $2,000,000 was raised and expended before the struggle ended.

Hillman and his lieutenants were unremitting in their demands on those union members who had jobs for donations to the New York relief fund. For almost six months a regular assessment of 10 per cent of wages was imposed by many of the stronger locals. The well-drilled Chicago workers, for example, week by week, sent sums as high as $50,000 to New York. No less generosity was shown by the recently unionized Rochester members. These mainly immigrant factory tailors showed a loyalty and a discipline that were to be among the distinguishing traits of the Amalgamated union. The very life of their organization was at stake, Hillman urged repeatedly; let the members who were lucky enough to be employed pay to fight the great "open-shop" drive which tomorrow might be turned against them. The New York manufacturers, who had counted on the early collapse of the union's resistance in the face of such enormous financial burdens, were unpleasantly surprised. The stubborn but orderly struggle continued month by month, a prolonged test of endurance.

One feature of this long conflict was the masterful organization of relief for the locked-out workers. Frederick the Great's dictum, that an army "travels on its belly," had been much in Hillman's mind ever since the dark days of 1910. In the Chicago strike of 1915 two commissary stores had been set up for the strikers. Now, in New York, with more than twice as many to care for, he rented a warehouse with space for over $100,000 worth of food supplies, and seven large co-operative commissary stores were opened in January 1921 in the different boroughs of Greater New York. These provided food at 20 to 25 per cent below average retail prices. Two men who had run such co-operative stores for the United Mine Workers in times of strikes were brought in to organize this department. Thereafter the purchasing of provisions and management of the stores was placed in the charge of J. B. S. Hardman, the union's educational director, and A. E. Kazan, an employee at the general office. During four months the needs of a population equaling that of a sizable city—more than 50,000 persons and their families—were met by the commissary stores, and none starved.

In addition, the union's Educational Department, under Hardman, worked to build up morale by conducting day schools and classes for the workers made idle during long months. Courses in English, literature, history, and economics were given by numerous volunteer teachers. An impromptu "Amalgamated Labor College," which specialized in the theory and practice of trade unionism, was also set up, under the direction of Dr. David Saposs of Columbia University. Finally, an information service, under Saposs, gathered news of developments in the lockout day by day and distributed this through bulletins posted in union meeting halls.

Others devoted themselves to carrying on an organized medical service for the union members. In addition to this, many friends of the union, among them social workers, theater people, or authors, such as Mrs. Mary Heaton Vorse, arranged for free concerts and theatrical entertainments. Thus on New Year's Day there was a memorable children's party for some 10,000 members' children in five halls throughout the city, the program consisting of music and Charlie Chaplin films.

Mrs. Vorse's account of the affair runs:

> There never was such an audience. . . . They were sitting on their mothers' laps, cramming the aisles. Their fathers standing filled up the space behind the chairs. . . .
>
> I don't believe the world has such children anywhere as the East Side children. . . . It was their eagerness that broke one's heart. . . . They took our modest program and transformed it through their magic. They changed it over with their laughter and their singing and with their applause until it became beautiful and significant.
>
> If I could play or sing I would beg to be allowed to play and sing to the children of the Amalgamated. . . . Sights like these children make one dream. What if all the forces of society were bent on developing their gifts? What if society's business was making people instead of profits? [26]

The union's defensive action in this lockout proceeded at times with almost a festive air. The movement of pickets was accompanied by the laughter of children and the peaceful spectacle of members buzzing over schoolbooks in classrooms. The spirit of the tailors seemed indomitable. How could a union that conducted a great industrial "crusade" with music, schoolbooks, and the singing of small children be defeated by the employers?

There were hardly any desertions from the ranks of the strikers. Numerous mass meetings and union rallies, with as many as 18,000 gathered together in the spaces of Madison Square Garden, also helped to keep the pickets at fighting temper.

One of Hillman's famous speeches of that era was given before a union gathering at the Grand Opera House in Boston on December

29, 1920, at the beginning of the lockout struggle. After all the wild charges that had been made against the Amalgamated union, he now turned the tables on the adversary and made serious accusations, supported by considerable evidence, that a widespread conspiracy against the consuming public was under way:

The menace which now confronts us is not the result of hasty plans, but of concerted action by the employers, conceived and planned far ahead, but postponed until the time seemed to them ripe. . . .

Every word I say here this afternoon I shall be ready to support here or elsewhere before you, or before any committee appointed by the government or by anyone else.

The first motive was to *stop production* throughout the country, so that they might continue to profiteer. Nothing else. Under post-war conditions, they raised price upon price, added profit to profit; indeed pyramided profits so high that under the weight of these swollen profits the industry collapsed. . . .

Then the employers, instead of taking a loss, determined to keep down the supply, and to say to the public that "you will either buy clothes at our price or you won't get any clothes at all." This, in short, was the purpose of the seven demands presented to us in New York. I repeat that you . . . are the victims of a conspiracy hatched in New York City. . . .

What is the reason for my charges? First, that as far back as four months ago, feelers came to me, as they had to the national organization, with regard to my position on a friendly strike or lockout—a plan, you understand, for *getting together and holding up the public jointly*. It was not done boldly, it was not done openly, because they knew the characters of your officers. When we turned down these feelers completely, and said we would not be a party to any conspiracy against the public, and they found they could not do in the clothing industry what had been done in the building trades of New York, when they found they could not make an unholy alliance between profiteers and grafting labor officials, then, and then only, did they turn to the seven points. . . .

Once in a conference, as we were sitting together, and I said to them, "Gentlemen, we will grant every one of your seven points. How many factories will you open tomorrow?" they looked around and said, "None." . . . Their purpose is not to produce but to stop production, so that they may realize more on the stocks at hand.

Hillman said that when he, on behalf of the union, had tried to stop overbidding for workers during the war, the industry had called him a "statesman." Today he was a "Bolshevist" because he and the union opposed schemes to curtail production and "sabotage" industry. He closed with a powerful onslaught on the whole campaign of employers for the open shop.

Open shop means arbitrary dictation. Open shop means the un-American way—open shop means employing the methods of the Kaiser, the Czar, and every other autocrat. Open shop means starvation, death. Open shop means the slums, it means crime, it means asylums, it means everything that is rotten, everything that is inhuman. . . . It means a citizenship that has no time to think, the 7-day week, the 12-hour day in the steel mills. It means Lawrence. It means the East Side.

Did the employers want the open shop? Very well, he said, "not only shall they be open, but they shall also remain empty." Starvation held no terrors for the clothing workers, for would they not starve under the open shop while they worked? But then Hillman made the solemn vow: "They shall not starve us." The organization, he said, was strong enough to protect its people in this great trial. However, it must ask great sacrifices of all members.

The organization will ask you to walk instead of paying a nickel carfare. Your lives depend on it. Your future, the future of your children . . .

But we will take care that there is not a single house without sufficient bread. We won't give you meat . . . but the members who are at work will divide with those who are not, and those of you who will go back to work will see to it that the battle is not lost for lack of ammunition. . . . Not revolvers, guns, we don't want them. . . . When I say ammunition I mean ammunition to keep the body in shape, so that your soul and your spirit shall remain independent.

Hillman called on his hearers to remain "true soldiers in the cause of labor. . . . We are 200,000 strong. We will stand the siege, and we will win the battle." [27]

The decisive factors in this long contest were the strong discipline and high morale of the New York tailors who kept this great clothing market tightly shut down—this at a time when there was a great crisis of unemployment throughout the country and 4,000,000 were without jobs. The feeding and provisioning of the mass of idle workers greatly contributed to this result, while showing the hand of a born organizer and planner. Hillman himself was intensely proud of the way the Amalgamated people managed such difficult affairs, and at the same time expressed much contempt for the New York clothing manufacturers of that period. The employers—whom he was to educate a great deal—were then a disorganized group of cutthroat competitors, not united by any sufficient bond of interest and principle. He would say: "The workers have nothing but their hands, their jobs; if they should lose such a fight they and their families would starve. Yet they remained steadfast." The employers had machinery, plants, and millions of dollars on their side, yet they were, to his mind, "a lot of noodles." For once the employer began to fear he was losing his *working capital,* then he was quick to give up the fight.[28]

By April 1921, a whole production season had been lost, and the loss of a second season (for autumn-winter clothing) impended. The smaller businessmen felt the pinch severely; about 400 of them abandoned the Association front and signed agreements with the union. This made a sizable breach in the opposition and brought employment in May to about 20,000 members.

At the end of April, the Bandler-Gordon faction among the manufacturers tried to enlist the political aid of some of our conservative statesmen in Congress. This was made plain when Senator George H. Moses of New Hampshire introduced a resolution in the Senate for an investigation of "the purposes, methods, and tactics of the Amalgamated Clothing Workers of America, and its relations . . . with other political groups."

But Sidney Hillman by now had strong admirers on Capitol Hill. A few days after Senator Moses had spoken, Senator William E. Borah of Idaho introduced a resolution of his own calling for an investigation not only of this union but of "the profits in the manufacture and sale of clothing during the past seven years . . . with special reference to the contracting system and sweatshops." At this point the clothing manufacturers advised that Senator Moses' original resolution be dropped, which was done.[29] It was high time to wind up the affair.

Incessant efforts had been made by Hillman to create dissension among the employers. Finally, on May 19, 1921, news arrived that the Association's president, William Bandler, along with the lawyer Harry A. Gordon, had suddenly handed in their resignations. The break had come when several of the big manufacturers in New York, one of whom alone accounted for 5,000 employees, quit the Association. A newly organized market committee now hastened to treat with Hillman and end the conflict on terms he had offered in November 1920, six months earlier. The employers were forced to retain the 44-hour week, the union shop and the system of joint administration of grievances; in return they were assured of "group standards of production and moderate wage reductions," these to be determined by "joint committee" decisions.

The union had come out on top once more, and the manufacturers' association, as Hillman had predicted, was now broken up. For several years there was no clothing-trade association worth the name in New York, and collective-bargaining agreements were made individually between the union and the different concerns on a year-to-year basis.

Meanwhile Hillman, by his skillful generalship—in a war he had never wanted—had led his people out of a most perilous situation. The Amalgamated had taken some hard blows; however, it still stood entrenched, "controlling the job," in New York, as in the other major clothing markets. The employers had also been taught the lesson that it didn't pay to fight the Amalgamated. From then on, New York saw no more "general strikes" or lockouts.

In another sense, Hillman's judgment had been fully vindicated before his own union members. They had been forced in the end to accept the system of "production standards" which he had warned them a year before to accept in order to avoid a desperate struggle. And though the conflict had come against his will and despite his pleas, he had borne his heavy responsibility loyally and, more than anyone, had helped to save the union from disaster. The peace settlement he had maneuvered for the "victory" of 1921 was, in point of wages and production schedules, a retreat, though a skillful retreat.

The liberal journalist George Soule, who admired Hillman, asked him why, since he had felt he was right, he had not forced his policy on the New York membership at all costs. His reply was: "A union is not like an army or a business organization in which the power of the executive is supreme." Even a correct decision cannot be executed, he said, unless the rank and file and subordinate officers support it willingly.

Now the New York members, having been allowed to overrule

their leader on the issue of piecework, and having seen how devoted had been his efforts in the recent struggle, developed an enduring faith in him which few leaders of men have been permitted to enjoy.[30]

Chapter Ten

NEW FIELDS
FOR LABOR:

1921-1924

The Amalgamated Clothing Workers' Organization had successfully passed through a supreme test of its power in New York in 1921. That year, as Hillman pointed out, "a new period of our organization began, a period when our right to live [was] established." [1] Thereafter a measure of recovery in business in 1922 and 1923 helped the union to consolidate its position, recoup most of the wage concessions it had made, and turn to face both the problems of its industry and of its own internal reform.

The New Era, so-called, arrived with the decade of the 1920's, a time of unprecedented industrial growth and prosperity. Yet, paradoxically, this was a period of steady retreat for the American labor movement as a whole. While the Amalgamated had established its right to exist, that right was denied, Hillman remarked, to the majority of industrial workers in the United States, still without benefit of unions. Indeed the trade-union movement, during this ebb tide, lost approximately 1,500,000 members from 1920 to 1930, or about 30 per cent of its peak numbers. The Amalgamated itself declined from its record membership of 177,000 in 1920 to less than 140,000 two years later, when it began to stabilize itself and recover its membership gradually. Labor leaders as a rule do not like to discuss publicly the loss of membership, but Hillman did this with indirection when he said at the 1922 convention of the union that it represented an "army perhaps not quite complete in numbers."

The decade of the 1920's was the heyday of the all-wise efficiency engineer; output increased as new machine processes were installed, and manpower was reduced in light industries, such as clothing, as well as in steel, machinery, and mining. The followers of Frederick Taylor and Charles Bédaux moved everywhere with their stop watches, directing time-and-motion studies and using more and more unskilled or semi-skilled workers. Immigration had been halted, but women and Negroes entered industry in large numbers and made new problems for labor. Mass-production methods in manufacture made the weaknesses of the old AFL craft unions all the more evident, and these lost strength steadily in the 1920's (with the exception of the building-trades unions). But even the largest of American unions, the United Mine Workers, under its new leader John L. Lewis, progressively lost control of most of the soft-coal fields, and by 1927 "was probably less than half its size of 1920 and . . . steadily losing membership." [2] Meanwhile, the mammoth automobile industry, like the steel trade, became one vast non-union shop. Elsewhere the "American Plan" for company unions, with its incentives of workers' stock shares, group insurance, and other welfare plans, spread into many fields, until by 1930 about 1,600,000 workers were enrolled in such management-sponsored organizations.

The Plateau of Prosperity in the 1920's was in truth a valley of defeat for American labor organization. The leadership of our official trade-union movement committed many errors of judgment, misread the trends and the changed economic conditions of the "new" capitalism. By contrast the "independent" industrial union of the Amalgamated Clothing Workers under Sidney Hillman, during this decade, held dominant control of labor in its industry, which was from 75 to 80 per cent unionized. While other organizations were greatly weakened, the Amalgamated kept the bulk of its membership firmly together and expanded its social program in new directions. It stood forth, in the opinion of many observers of the labor scene at home and abroad, as the most "dynamic" of American trade unions.

Hillman constantly studied the shifting industrial conditions of the post-war period. What was wrong with American labor? he asked himself. He thought the trouble was that it had no new ideas; its leaders "forgot that conditions in this country have changed since 1878." Meanwhile capital had learned many lessons from the past. If one of its great trusts was "dissolved" by law under the Sherman Anti-Trust Act, it merely formed still greater combinations of capital. "Capital adjusts itself. Capital finds a way," Hillman said at this period. "The trouble with our labor movement is that we are not looking for new ways. . . . We will have new problems and we will have to look for new methods." [3]

He had a powerful disposition to be practical, to examine all questions "in the light of the world as the world is today," to determine always "what can be done today and tomorrow and next week." For a workingman could not live only on his dreams of a Co-operative Commonwealth, he maintained. As his friend Clarence Darrow would say: "It is well enough to have your dream and to work for it and hope for it. But in the meantime you must have a living; and we ought to have enough to have some fun in this world." [4]

Nevertheless, as he intimated, his concept of the New Unionism at that period involved ultimate aims toward some "new order." He and his union brothers must work for some better condition of society than the one they were living in now. The day-by-day tactics of collective bargaining were to be used not only to win material concessions "but as a means of solidifying the workers and retaining victories that will make possible further progress along the main highway." When he thought of venturing into new fields, he thought now in terms of large co-operative enterprises. The main direction should be that of "training the workers for assuming control of production and accepting the social and economic responsibility which such control involves." [5]

Before an Amalgamated convention of 1924 he flung out the challenge:

. . . If the Amalgamated, if, indeed, the labor movement, is to make progress, it must have the courage to open new fields, to make mistakes, to pay for them, and learn from experience so that we can grow in strength and wisdom for the future!

For many years the more doctrinaire members of the union had shown a lively interest in experiments with co-operative clothing factories to be run by the union members. Resolutions favoring the co-operative movement had been introduced at the 1916 and 1918 conventions, but were received with no enthusiasm on the part of Hillman or the other leaders. By 1920, however, the union's leadership gave increasing attention to the consumers' co-operative movement, then making large strides in England and Scandinavia, and gaining support among farmers' and labor organizations in the United States. Aroused by wartime inflation and profiteering, many spokesmen for consumers' co-operatives urged that their program offered a logical means of increasing the earnings of farmers and laborers by raising their purchasing power.

In February 1920, Hillman and other national officers of the Amalgamated went to Chicago to attend the All-American Farmer-Labor Co-operative Congress, of which Warren S. Stone, Grand Chief of the Brotherhood of Locomotive Engineers, was one of the leading sponsors. Hillman considered the veteran Stone "one of the master builders" of the American labor movement. Stone, for his part, admired Hillman and told him about the plans of his union to launch a chain of labor banks.

The Amalgamated had hitherto encouraged the formation of small local credit unions for the benefit of its members. Now Stone's idea of a labor bank exercised great fascination for Hillman. The pioneers in co-operative enterprises had discovered that what was needed by the farmers and workers was the lifeblood of credit, and financial institutions of their own. The workers contributed immense savings funds to the keeping of "unfriendly banks" who sometimes used those very funds to fight labor unions in a strike, as Warren Stone said. In the New York lockout struggle Hillman had felt keenly the need of a labor bank to handle the large financial transactions involved in the union's relief and co-operative activities. He had also been aware that the banks had helped the union's adversaries by extending them credit. Why could not able union officers run banks and direct their policies to encourage the establishment of co-operative stores, insurance, and retirement plans, or even of low-cost housing projects? "To enter the banking business seemed the highroad to social control, a peaceful way of penetrating the holy of holies of the capitalist system." [6]

The first large-scale labor bank in the United States was opened by the Brotherhood of Locomotive Engineers in Cleveland in November 1920. By 1927 there were 35 labor banks having deposits of about $128,000,000.

Long before that time Hillman had been haunting the doors of various Wall Street financiers to learn what he could of banking. The union's economist, Dr. Wolman, also gathered all possible information bearing on the launching of such an enterprise. It was foreseen that in the two cities of New York and Chicago alone there would be more than 75,000 union members, most of them, perforce, habitual savers, who would provide the clientage for a banking system.

The convention of 1920, as we have seen, authorized the executive officers to establish a co-operative labor bank. On July 22, 1922, the Amalgamated Trust and Savings Bank was formally opened in Chicago, with a capital of $200,000 and surplus of $100,000. Within a short time it had 6,000 deposit accounts, including the treasury funds of 240 labor unions.

On April 14, 1923, after most painstaking preparations, Sidney Hillman opened the first labor bank in New York State, named the Amalgamated Bank of New York, with capital funds of $300,000 (later raised to $2,000,000). The union's leaders appealed to the members for its support:

> The Amalgamated Bank is bound to be the safest place for the workers' money because of the watchfulness of both its friends and enemies. The latter will be searching for every opportunity to attack the bank. That will be another reason for our exercizing the utmost care in banking transactions. By adhering strictly to the banking laws, in the enforcement of which we do not expect to be favored, and by banishing . . . every possible element of speculation, the fullest protection will be afforded the workers in their savings.[7]

Hillman, in whom Joseph Schaffner long ago had detected a genius for business affairs, faithfully observed the pledges made by the union to its member-depositors. The labor banks grew rapidly, perhaps in many cases too rapidly. Some of the first enthusiasts of labor banking, such as Stone of the Locomotive Engineers, had extravagant notions of what could be done by mobilizing the immense savings of the workers. Others believed it would be possible to finance strikes, to give support to pro-union employers, or even to control certain basic industries in the interests of organized labor. Stone actually prophesied that the day of the strike was over.[8] However, the labor banks founded by the Locomotive Engineers and other unions were to be short-lived. Their investments in Florida real estate and in coal-mining ventures in West Virginia turned out badly. The placement of labor-union bureaucrats in jobs as bank officers, and the making of unsecured loans to "friends" of the unions, also proved unhealthy for labor banks. Nor was the financing of strikes a practical form of business activity.

The Amalgamated's leader set out, in the first place, to find expertly trained and high-minded banking personnel. One difficulty was the question of salary. Hillman himself, as president of one of the country's largest unions, then drew but $5,000 a year. "We cannot have men who think only of large remuneration in the labor movement," he said to several applicants for executive positions in the new bank. Eventually an experienced banking officer was engaged to head the Chicago bank, from which he was later transferred to New York. Hillman, Dr. Wolman, Max Lowenthal, Fred R. Macaulay, and Fiorello La Guardia were members of the first board of directors. Hillman took his responsibilities in this new field very seriously. Leo Wolman was a strong figure in the early years of the bank; while Max Lowenthal, one of the most active of its directors, constantly urged that the union's banks be run primarily as savings institutions, with a view to safeguarding the depositors' funds—by pursuing loan and investment policies more conservative than those of ordinary commercial banks.

Hillman, as banker, proved to be both more practical and more far-sighted than other labor leaders who had ventured into this very competitive business. The New York bank, located (after 1926) in large quarters at 15 Union Square, like its sister bank in Chicago, attracted many thousands of worker-savers and many labor-union accounts—though the great masses did not rush to all the labor banks in the floods some had expected. At the Amalgamated Banks, shares of the capital stock, reflecting ownership, were held by the union and allotted only in small amounts to directors and a few other approved depositor-owners, while being limited in dividends. On the other hand, interest payments to savers were considerably higher than in other banks during the 1920's.

Of immeasurable service to the union members was the early innovation of a small-loan department, by which "character loans" in sums of $50 to $300 were extended on the strength of two satisfactory endorsements. (Afterward the small loan was introduced into general commercial banking on an enormous scale.) Still other important services to workers were the small building loan and home owners' mortgage, as well as the financing of the union's co-operative housing ventures—which other banks were somewhat loath to encourage.

The operation of both banks was successful from the start. Within six years the New York bank alone had more than 20,000 depositors, and the two banks combined had assets of $28,000,000, making them profitable, middle-sized banking institutions. How prudently their affairs were managed was to be shown in the terrible financial crisis of 1929–33, out of which only the two Amalgamated Banks of all the labor banks emerged as solvent, with the funds of the workers fully safeguarded. One unbiased commentator has written: "Amalgamated banking proved more conservative than capitalistic banking." [9]

At the period when the labor banks were started many critics in trade-union ranks opposed such action as leading to the absorption and debasement of the labor movement in "bourgeois" financial activities. (These predictions were not borne out by events.) Sidney Hillman argued that: "The more responsibility the labor movement assumes, the greater will be its power."

In the 1920's Hillman was intensely aware of the giant strides being made by great capitalistic groups such as that of Henry Ford.

What achievements has the labor movement got that can contend with these new industrial forces? A little group here, a little group there! What we want is greater power. What we want is greater strength, and we in the labor movement must wake up to these new conditions.[10]

Not for nothing had Hillman observed the role of leadership played in our industrial society by banking and finance. The bank supported the drive for union standards in the clothing industry. At first a rule was observed that no commercial loans were to be made to manufacturers or employers in the Amalgamated's own industry; but this was modified later to a restriction against employers who were unfriendly to organized labor. On the other hand, pro-union employers were, as far as safety permitted, to be encouraged.

One day when Hillman was visiting Chicago, he saw the head of a large clothing firm who gave him the sobering news that his company (which had always co-operated with the union) was about to liquidate its business. The manufacturer said to Hillman: "Because of our friendly relations and your responsibility to your membership you ought to be the first one to know about this."

It came out that this firm had suffered a heavy inventory loss in the collapse of woolen cloth prices in 1920 and was deep in debt to its bankers, who were calling their loans. The union leader thought the business was essentially sound. What troubled him was that several hundred workers would soon lose their jobs if nothing was done, and the non-union element would exploit such unemployment everywhere.

On an impulse he said to the manufacturer: "I have no authority for this from my board, but subject to their approval, do you think it would tide you over if the union should lend you $100,000, on condition that the banks will extend their loans?" The manufacturer was astonished; he had expected nothing of the sort. He finally agreed to go back to his bankers with Hillman's proposal. The bankers were, at first, dubious about the union's intentions, but finally agreed to extend their loans if the Amalgamated backed up its promise with hard cash. In the end, the Amalgamated union (not its bank) risked the sum of $30,000, all of which was ultimately repaid. The business was saved and has remained in a flourishing condition to this day.[11]

Still another instance of the constructive use of the Amalgamated's new financial resources occurred in the case of a large and well-known Baltimore concern reported in difficulties at this same period. This firm had long observed its collective-bargaining agreements with the union, and Hillman felt acute distress at the thought of its 1,500 workers losing their jobs. By this time a staff of technicians skilled in clothing manufacture was retained at the union's national office. These men were sent in to study the company's plants; they proposed a scheme of reorganization presently which would greatly raise its efficiency. On this basis, bank loans were advanced, secured by the union's treasury, and the business was saved for years to come.

Another story is told of one well-known New York manufacturer of men's garments who had long refused to play ball with the union and whose firm at one point underwent reorganization and passed into the hands of a new management group. Soon afterward its chief executive called on Hillman and offered to sign an agreement for a union shop. Hillman looked at him coolly and said: "We have got along without each other all these years. Why should we change at this late date?"

The man was surprised and pressed Hillman to tell him why he who had sought to unionize every firm in the industry suddenly, in this case, appeared so coy. Hillman replied that, through his financial contacts, he had received definite reports that the firm in question was in serious straits. He would not sign a union agreement covering a thousand employees only to have them thrown out of work soon thereafter.

The businessman then laid his cards on the table, declaring that a skilled production expert had been engaged to redesign their plant, but he had insisted that the company establish sound working relations with the dominant union in the field. At this Hillman quickly shifted his position and warmly agreed to lend his full co-operation. A union contract was signed and the business was set on its feet.[12]

The union moved more warily into other co-operative ventures. For example, proposals for the establishment of co-operative clothing factories were usually sidetracked by the Amalgamated's hardheaded leader. He was conscious of the long history of failure of such enterprises in America. Here also the problems of policy appeared complex and the risks great; nor was the social climate of the period favorable to such plans. But by 1928, under the special circumstances of a lockout contest with a manufacturer in Milwaukee, the union felt justified in attempting the experiment. The old firm of Adler and Sons since 1916 had intermittently provided trouble for the union; on the death of the senior partner, his successors came to a complete break with the Amalgamated's local organization in Milwaukee. The lockout that followed dragged on for six months at great cost to both sides, with the owners, who were of independent wealth, apparently content to see their business destroyed and the workers, mostly natives of the city, reluctant to leave their homes and families to seek jobs elsewhere.

One day in the autumn of 1928 it was made known that the Amalgamated union had leased 15,000 feet of space in the abandoned plant of a great brewing company—for those were the days of prohibition—and was organizing a co-operative clothing factory, under the union's management, for the employment of the 300 workers who had previously been subsisting on strike relief.

Technicians in clothing manufacture soon arrived from the Amalgamated's headquarters in Chicago to take charge of the place. Hillman and Frank Rosenblum, then director of the union's Western Organization, had ensured the success of the co-operative factory in advance through a favorable agreement with Hart, Schaffner and

Marx of Chicago, by which that house contracted to purchase the entire output of the Milwaukee co-operative. The place was to be organized along modern lines, its workers were to be trained carefully by the union's own instructors (who served without pay), and quality of output was to be kept to the high standards of the big Chicago firm.

Rosenblum has related that discipline in this shop was very strict. "The people went into the factory with a spirit of determination that the shop must be a success," he said. "They realized that they were working for themselves and the union." [13] Amalgamated veterans still recall their Milwaukee co-operative as "beautifully run." Gradually more and more of the striking Milwaukee workers were taken on, and the plant operated at a very decent profit. The Amalgamated's official newspaper, *The Advance,* observed that this undertaking had created

. . . the first clothing factory run by the union for the union. We say the first, not because there is a second in sight, but . . . it is within the realm of possibility that what was done in Milwaukee may be attempted elsewhere if and when an emergency will call for such a step.

After more than three years of successful business management of its only co-operative, the Amalgamated decided to sell out the business during the depression of 1932. But the skilled working force developed in Milwaukee was fortunately combined with a group of experienced clothing salesmen who had just then lost their jobs. Thus the workers were able to continue on the job under private management, though on a profit-sharing basis.

From this co-operative venture, so rich in possibilities and lessons for the future, the forehanded Amalgamated leadership withdrew with honor, as well as with discretion. Here again its labor banks, as service institutions, had played a helpful part through the extension of credit.

II

In a time of political reaction, the Amalgamated union, almost alone, continued to function as a "school" for progressive labor action. Hillman and the resourceful types of union officers who were molded by his influence, literally stayed awake while others slept. They pioneered; they broke new ground and accumulated experience and knowledge of immense value for the future.

Though he had little time for study in those days, he courted the friendship of men with expert knowledge in various fields and picked their brains. Thus, as soon as he learned of the large strides being made after the war in England and other nations of Western Europe toward more adequate employment insurance systems, he was all eagerness to introduce similar measures for the men's clothing workers. Though such plans had been inaugurated from ten to twenty years earlier in England and Western Europe, no unemployment insurance worth mentioning existed in the United States. At the Amalgamated's 1922 convention in Chicago, Hillman, in his opening address, spoke—in keeping with the spirit of the time—for the "engineering-efficiency" approach to the unemployment problem:

What is the curse of unemployment? It is not only that you and I and the rest of labor in other industries may be out of work. What is more important is that the very industrial foundation of the country is undermined, and that billions and billions of dollars of wealth are being destroyed. And why? Because of the inefficient way industry is run today. As long as labor and labor alone, I assure you, pays the penalty for unemployment, I can assure you that the employers will do nothing to cure unemployment. Unemployment has to be placed as a definite responsibility on industry. The men and women who are needed in industry must not be discarded as human wreckage. . . .

Two years earlier he had served notice on employers that the question of doing something about seasonal unemployment would soon be brought up. In Chicago an employment exchange had already been created under Amalgamated Joint Board management in accordance with the city-wide trade agreement of 1919. Its function had been to promote the sharing or "equal division" of work. But the employment exchange bureaus had not been effective enough at the start, and various petty abuses had crept into this service. Hillman, as usual with him, now engaged an expert, Bryce M. Stewart, chief of the Canadian Public Employment Service, to come to Chicago in the summer of 1922 and reorganize the system. Dr. Leo Wolman, Hillman's most intimate adviser at this period, was also dispatched to Chicago to explore the whole problem of setting up an unemployment insurance plan. Mr. Stewart, meanwhile, engaged competent clerks for the employment bureaus, enlarged their quarters, and established detailed records of the hours of work and earnings of 35,000 men's clothing workers in Chicago. Wolman found later that the compilation of these elaborate records was what made it possible to launch the union's first experiment in unemployment insurance with some hope of success.

In the spring of 1922, following prolonged negotiations for a renewal of the trade agreement with the Chicago manufacturers, the union had staved off a very strong demand for wage cuts. This time Hillman appeared with his economist, Wolman, armed with elaborate charts and surveys of the clothing trade, which forecast, accurately enough, a return of prosperity. The question of unemployment insurance payments, however, was deferred to the winter of 1923, when it was brought up in earnest by the union's spokesmen before a joint committee of arbitrators headed by Professor John R. Commons of the University of Wisconsin, then the foremost American authority on labor affairs. In these renewed hearings Wolman, having completed extensive studies in this field, presented a notable brief in favor of an unemployment insurance plan as part of a new increased wage scale.

Sidney Hillman by now had got the Chicago manufacturers in a position where they were obliged to accord the unemployment insurance provision if this was approved by the committee of arbitrators under Commons. This was precisely what happened when a 10 per cent wage increase was awarded the Chicago workers, and an understanding reached that part of this increase, amounting to 1½ per cent of their wages, was to be paid each week into an unemployment fund. Management was to pay in an additional 3 per cent—making, together with the workers' share, a total of 4½ per cent of payroll regularly set aside to provide for unemployment.[14] The employers in return reaped advantages in reduced labor turnover and higher morale. Thus, at a period when no social security law was dreamed of in this country, and when the AFL leadership under Gompers' influence still assailed such schemes as "useless barnacles" on the labor movement, the Amalgamated bravely launched its pioneer undertaking.*

* Somewhat earlier, in 1922, the ILGWU Joint Board at Cleveland had established a system of unemployment insurance though on a small scale, with all funds paid out and accounted for at the end of each year—very different from the ACWA plan for continuous insurance.

To Hillman these annual (sometimes biennial or triennial) "peace treaties" between union and management, such as took place in Chicago in 1923, were the high points of the Amalgamated's achievements in the field of union-management co-operation. Here, at joint conferences of thirty to forty persons embracing managerial skill, union leadership, and legal and sociological learning as well, broad measures of economic reform were enacted which set new standards for industrial democracy and paved the way for similar advances by other large groups. Thus unemployment insurance plans were afterward worked out for 13,000 Rochester clothing workers and some 50,000 more in New York, to begin in 1928. Yet at this time, outside of one or two liberal groups in close touch with Hillman's Fabian labors, there was too little awareness of the importance of this determined campaign for social security. It was rare that such nonviolent news reached the front pages of the newspapers as actually happened in the case of the Chicago unemployment plan.[15]

Serious problems of adjustment had to be faced at the beginning of the experiment. The more skilled, more regularly employed groups among the workers objected that the brunt of the costs would be borne by them rather than by the unskilled workers, who suffered more from seasonal layoffs. There was the problem also of turnover of employees from one firm to another, and of the unemployment compensation funds being preserved separately, in trust, for the different firms and their personnel.

Yet all these difficulties were overcome by intelligent and patient effort. The funds were safeguarded by being invested entirely in United States Government bonds and excluded from use in any industrial controversy. Much credit for devoted service in this field was due to Professor Commons, acting as chairman of the various committees charged with care of the funds.

The system was administered, of course, under the limitations of a plan lacking the advantages of tri-partite schemes, including payments by employer, worker, and government or municipality—as in England and Western Europe or, as later, under our own Social Security Act of 1935. Its provisions were too small, and in most cases funds began to be accumulated too late to offer protection in any large way against the mass unemployment that came not long afterward. Even so, the Chicago Unemployment Fund paid out more than $5,000,000 in benefits over a period of six years (from May 1,

1924), while the New York section of the union (though representing a much larger working population and initiating its fund only in 1928) paid out nearly $2,000,000 during the catastrophic depression of 1930–33.

The establishment of the Amalgamated's unemployment insurance funds was considered at the time (1923–28) as heralding the first systematic attack on the unemployment problems of this country. At that period about 48,000,000 workers in Europe and England were already benefiting from various forms of compulsory unemployment insurance. Here, by 1929, only 200,000 were thus insured, and of these, about half were members of the Amalgamated Clothing Workers' Union. Altogether it was "only a drop in the bucket," as Hillman said, when the great depression was upon us. Yet he and his apostles had truly opened up "new fields." Their union members, for the most part, shared the work and received regular, if small, unemployment benefits. None of them was forced to beg for bread. The records and experience of the Amalgamated were available also to those who were to draft the historic Federal Social Security Act of 1935.

III

During the early 1920's, Hillman's campaign for the piecework system, his absorption in labor banking, and his espousal of plans for union-management co-operation led to the accusation by members of his own union that he had turned "conservative." The unemployment insurance scheme evoked similar criticisms of him, this time from leaders of the American Federation of Labor!

To describe Hillman's thinking as either conservative or radical was fallacious then, as later. He was, by disposition, not an idcologist, but a realist (in John Dewey's sense of the word), who believed in functioning through experiments and tests rather than under the rule of fixed dogmas. With Hillman a "conservative" experiment was apt to be followed by a "radical" enterprise, or vice versa.

By 1921 a great right-left controversy raged in the labor world (then, as now) over the question of the Russians. In the needle trades the more class-conscious, foreign-born workers, many of them Russian-Jews, were not unhappy to see the Czar overthrown in 1917.

Many Russian immigrants, like Hillman, had taken part in the popular uprising of 1905 and had their bitter memories of the old regime in Russia. Yet, as in the time of the French Revolution and its Terror, great dispute arose in countries outside the revolution's orbit over the reported virtues or wickedness of the revolutionists. There were men of high authority who asserted that Lenin and his accomplices were assassins and thieves; others, equally authoritative, held that Soviet Russia had now—inspiring thought—a "labor government." Many of the Russian-born in America bitterly resented the invasion of Russia by armies of the Allies in support of the Whites during the civil war.

When Lenin, in the end, emerged triumphant, hundreds of thousands of workers of Russian origin had been without news of their families for years. Stories of sweeping reforms being instituted in "the one land where the workers rule" reached them; also Lenin's appeals to all the world for help in the struggle against famine and disease after the wars. By then many Americans, whether left or right, believers or atheists, were for giving Soviet Russia aid on humanitarian grounds.

Hillman himself was filled with curiosity and doubt about Russia. His own family was in Lithuania, at that time an independent state. He had had scarcely any rest from his union work in ten years. A recent resolution of the Amalgamated's General Executive Board, empowering both President Hillman and Secretary Schlossberg to make a brief tour of observation in Europe and report on trade-union developments there, provided the opportunity for the trip he had hoped to make at the end of the war.

On July 16, 1921, shortly after the lockout struggle in New York was won, he sailed for Europe, saying in an interview:

> I am going away for my first vacation since the organization of the Amalgamated. I am going to see again my father and mother, whom I left in Lithuania fifteen years ago, when I sailed for the United States. I expect to visit en route England, France, Germany, and other countries in Europe. . . .[16]

He spent but a week in England, reached Berlin in mid-August, and there met with the representative of the Russian Red Cross. After hearing from him of the famine conditions which threatened 20,000,000 Russians, Hillman determined to visit Russia himself.

Meanwhile he sent off a cablegram at once to his union headquarters in New York. Quantities of food, clothing, and drugs were desperately needed to save the lives of millions of Russian women and children, he reported, and the Amalgamated members were called upon to donate a day's work to this end. *"Urge our membership to lead way —act quickly,"* the message ended.

The Amalgamated organization, like many other groups, had begun to raise funds for Russian relief even before Hillman's departure. Now some $250,000 was collected and used to outfit an "ACWA Relief Ship," the S.S. *Margus,* with 65,000 bushels of wheat and hundreds of tons of condensed milk, clothing, and drugs. The Russian Red Cross reported later that this gift alone had saved the lives of 36,000 souls.

Nearly three years after World War I had ended Hillman found old Europe still in turmoil. Some of the observations he made then measure shrewdly the cruel aftermath of war and revolution. England, prosperous when he was last there in 1907, had millions of unemployed. France was "full of fear and hatred," demanding indemnities of everyone. In Germany inflation had disrupted the whole economic structure; its people seemed hopeless; a tailor there earned only 2½ cents an hour!

Europe [he reported later] has gone through a frightful operation performed by some of the most ignorant surgeons in the profession. The patient is still bleeding, and there is no sign of recovery.[17]

Each country lived in suspicion of the other—especially in Eastern Europe, which had been carved up into little buffer states. People were still parading about in uniforms, and there were "some very violent insane people running amok," he noted.

It was with considerable difficulty that he made his way into Lithuania—and out again later—for he kept forgetting or misplacing his passport. But at last he was in Zagare and saw again the small wooden house where his parents still lived. They had suffered, they had aged, but they had managed to survive the great war, whose early battle zone had been chiefly in the western provinces of Russia. For a period his parents and their four children (who remained after the others had gone to America) had retreated before the German invaders to an interior city of Russia. But later, when the fighting was over, his mother had insisted upon returning to her home and little shop in Zagare.

Hillman had always loved his mother, and she was full of pride and joy at this reunion. He had never ceased to write his parents through the years and had regularly sent money for their support. But his repeated offers to aid them in coming to settle in America were met by his high-willed mother with a firm refusal. It was too late for the elder Hillmans, she said, to change from their Old World and their old ways to the New World. Yet her brief notes, written from time to time in Yiddish, expressed in almost religious terms her love for Sidney and her sense of his "mission."

He was always a man of sentiment; he relived all the years of his hungry youth during these visits to the place of his birth. On this occasion (or perhaps on a later visit in 1925), leaving Zagare, he passed through Kovno, where he had studied for the rabbinate and later had gone into the service of the underground labor movement. Meeting old acquaintances here and walking with them in the streets, he saw a procession of children singing hymns on their way to a nearby church. Distractedly he left his friends, followed the children into the church, and there sat down and listened to the service and the hymn singing for a long period, as if lost to the world.[18] The return to the scenes of his childhood and youth was a richly emotional experience for one in whom many sensed a hidden religious and messianic spirit, strangely contrasting with his taste for practical affairs.

A few days after quitting Zagare, he crossed the border to the nearby Union of Soviet Socialist Republics. It was a moving and strange adventure. A noted American journalist of that time, Lincoln Steffens, had written: "I have seen the Future and it works!" Could this be true? Hillman related shortly after his return to America:

My friends . . . I found myself at the door of the unknown. I felt very much disturbed before entering Russia. You want sometimes to keep to your dreams in this gray world, in this world where there is very little of the ideal and the beautiful . . . and before entering Russia there is the doubt that perhaps that dream will be shattered. The country has been so much talked about, so much more lied about that you don't know what to expect. I crossed the border and felt a great sense of relief. At least people were dressed! . . .[19]

The head of the great tailors' union in America had been assured by travelers met in other parts of Europe that either he would be followed, arrested, and hanged, or that he would not get through, as no trains ran. He reached Moscow without difficulty. There, he related, he tried to place himself strictly "in the position of the observer and student" and avoid the effects of prejudice of any sort.

He was from the start impressed with the atmosphere of peace and order in Moscow and other cities he visited, contrary to reports heard abroad. He met Lenin at the end of September, at a time when the Amalgamated's relief ship, laden with food and clothing, had just arrived at St. Petersburg, and received thanks from the Russian leader in person for the generosity of American workers. He saw and spoke also with other leaders. Indeed he saw men of every shade of opinion during a stay of a month. This was still possible then, for he said that he even visited "some of the counter-revolutionists who are in jail—for they are all in jail." [20]

Sidney Hillman, by now, though his mind was always open to new ideas, was a professional American trade-union officer heading an "economic movement," concerned mainly with the workers' right to the job and with union-management co-operation, not with something called "The Revolution." He was not at all interested in "the theories of Bolshevism, or the arguments of Menshevism, and all those petty quarrels," as he phrased it. The real question was: would the regime of Lenin *et al.* endure? Did these new rulers of Russia have the support of the people? Were they honest? Were they capable of "doing the job"?

On one of his first days in Moscow he had had the opportunity to attend a session of the Supreme Soviet of Labor and Defense, at which Lenin outlined his plans for the "New Economic Policy," designed to encourage private capital to produce consumer goods. Later, when he met and conversed with the poised but unpretentious man who had led the Russians through foreign invasion and civil war, and heard him speak of his plans for Russian reconstruction, he was deeply impressed. Lenin, a planner above all, entertained visions of a new society in which the scientific knowledge of the technician was to be linked with the energies of millions of organized workers and peasants. There was no denying that he had stirred the hearts of great masses of men returned from the shambles of war. Hillman was convinced at the time that the only force able to hold Russia together was the party of Lenin, whatever one might think of it, and that its overthrow would spread only boundless chaos.

He was particularly impressed with Lenin's realistic spirit, which, at that time of post-war prostration, led him to embrace a "compromise" program, offering concessions to foreign capital as well as to private enterprise at home. Hillman's first conclusions were that the people in power in Russia were able and efficient.

It is my conviction that Russia is facing an era of the greatest economic reconstruction. I cannot say whether the New Economic Policy is a compromise or not; if it is, it is one that is absolutely essential—it is a compromise with life. I believe that it will show results.

One of the first things he had done had been to visit a clothing factory in shell-cratered St. Petersburg, and there he had peppered his guide, the director, with questions about why things were not done in accordance with approved American production methods.

"Mr. Hillman," the man replied, "do you appreciate the fact that practically the whole male population of St. Petersburg is no more?" Only a short time before 700 girls had been working here stoically, with blinds drawn, while the artillery of the White Army, entrenched in the outskirts, poured shells into the city. Hillman said later:

One who comes to Russia cannot but feel a sense of humiliation before that great people. . . . After all, people are no different in Russia than anywhere else. If they are permitted, they will do the noble thing. . . . There is nothing so appalling as the destruction in Russia.[21]

During the famine, Hillman learned, the bulk of relief provisions had come from the Russian people themselves, who regularly donated part of their meager rations of bread for the relief of the famine-stricken regions. Nothing seemed more abominable to Sidney Hillman than the thought that some people welcomed this famine if it would but help to overthrow the new government. He was fully aware that personal liberty was harshly restricted under the Bolshevist regime, but at the time refrained from condemnation of such methods as being perhaps made necessary by the emergencies through which the country passed.

His visit to the St. Petersburg clothing factory and the announcement of the New Economic Policy, with its concessions to foreign investors, had given Hillman an idea of how he could be of help.

The Russians needed food first of all, but also clothing; many of them were in rags, though they bore themselves proudly. They had courage enough, and manpower and resources. What was needed now was that men of good will, and especially the labor movement in America, "help the Russians to help themselves." On his return to New York in the first week of November 1921, he brought home with him a plan for having the Amalgamated union aid the Russians to reconstruct their clothing industry.

IV

His home-coming was an occasion for hearty demonstrations of affection by his associates in the Amalgamated, several hundred of whom chartered a tugboat and met his ship in the outer harbor of New York. An official welcome-home party was also arranged for November 13, 1921, at the Manhattan Opera House, where 4,000 persons, beside themselves with curiosity, foregathered to hear what the returned traveler had seen of the "land of mystery."

The keynote of Hillman's speech at Manhattan Opera House (passages of which have already been cited above) was the phrase: "We cannot separate ourselves from the rest of the world." Sympathy with the Russians in their trials was not enough; it also placed Americans under the obligation to furnish help and guidance. A few days later he repeated the same speech before an enthusiastic audience of Chicago workers. Then, for several months prior to the forthcoming convention of the ACWA, he devoted such time as he could spare from union business to shaping plans for a co-operative industrial corporation which was to organize several modern factories for the production of clothing in Russia. It was to be financed not only by union members but by others interested in promoting peaceful trade relations with Russia. A sizable capital was to be raised through the sale of shares of stock. The proposed corporation would obtain a concession from the Soviet Government enabling it to engage in business in Russia, and in return the Soviets would place a number of clothing factories at the disposal of the corporation and allot personnel to be directed by the American technicians.

Hillman's enthusiasm for this proposed Russian-American Industrial Corporation (which was to produce clothing 4,500 miles from our shores) was so infectious that he succeeded in enlisting the interest not only of many union members but also of several of his capitalist friends, two of whom accompanied him on a second trip to Russia in the summer of 1922. On that occasion the terms he negotiated with representatives of the Soviet Government involved a guarantee of the principal and interest on the capital to be invested—which, in the end, amounted to only $300,000.*

The scheme itself proved to be, for many reasons, fairly Quixotic, though Hillman was able to see to it that no one who invested in it suffered any loss. Hillman's public action, however, and the impact of it on opinion, was of great significance. Like other progressives of that time, he worked to bring about a return to sanity with regard to the problems posed by the recent Russian Revolution. The intervention in Russia of Allied armies (including American forces) had not been popular in America; the economic blockade against Russia was also strongly opposed by many enlightened people, who urged that peaceful commerce with Russia would better serve the interests of civilization. (It must be remembered also by the present-day reader that at that time, thirty years ago, Soviet Russia offered not the remotest threat to the security of the United States.)

The Fifth Biennial Convention, opening at Carmen's Hall in Chicago on May 8, 1922, was a momentous gathering in the annals of the Amalgamated Clothing Workers. The proceedings covered not only the "new departures" of the two years past but also the "burning issue" of aid for Soviet Russia.

At one of the last sessions of the convention Hillman presented his plan for organizing clothing factories in Russia and appealed to the Amalgamated members to participate in the project.

This long extempore speech surely marks one of Hillman's finest hours, for apart from its special theme of aid to the stricken people of Russia, it gave expression, in the terms of his own temperament and in his own pungent phrases, to his sense of human values, his

---

* By 1921 the Socialists in America, who had a strong following among the needle-trade workers of New York, were split over the issue of Bolshevism versus democracy, with the larger faction, under the influence of the *Jewish Daily Forward* and its editor, Abraham Cahan, turning against the Soviets, and the smaller, left-wing faction going over to the Workers' Party, led by William Z. Foster. Hillman was fully aware of this quarrel among the "doctrinaire" element in his union but held that his own project was non-political and humanitarian.

humanitarian faith. His general reflections here on life and labor were made with an unaffected eloquence that lingered long in the memory of those who heard him.

Americans, he began, could no longer isolate themselves from the misfortunes of the rest of the world; and labor, above all, must not permit "the few" to determine both the fateful issues of war and the condition of peace afterward. Our government, which had long recognized the regime of Czar Nicholas, should not now assume, like the European powers, that it had the right to dictate conditions of life in another country. To blockade the Russians, to scheme for their starvation, meant disease and death for masses of innocent women and children:

You do not commit murder only when you go out in the street and kill someone; you commit murder when you make it impossible for other people to live. . . .

The great danger is that the peoples are indifferent . . . and it will all result in part of the world trying to choke the other. When that happens there will be very little left in the world worth living for. It is up to the people in this country, as well as in every other country, to rise and say that . . . the lives of millions of men and women and children are the concern of all the people.

When a great conflagration strikes a community it disregards all petty divisions of groups and classes. . . . Disease and fire have their own laws, and when the community is in danger, it is up to all the people in the community to fight for those who are menaced, regardless of class or group. . . . You cannot fight the Bolsheviks without fighting the men and women and children of Russia.

In short, he chose his ground out of a sense of the common humanity of men in all countries and with no partiality for the particular system of government then ruling Russia. With great emphasis he said that he would consider it *a betrayal of the interests of his union and of the labor movement if he assumed even mentally a position of partisanship.* Here, he said, there was no question of entering into disputes over theories of government "which may be of interest to a few but do not concern the great masses of people." But what was essential was that Europe was in danger, that Europe could not be reconstructed without Russia, and civilization itself was at stake. It was a question not of being

for Bolshevism or against Bolshevism—but of being for or against the slaughter of millions of people, for or against life and happiness for several hundred million people. . . .

I can tell you that we did not discuss revolution in the United States, or even revolution in Russia. . . . I did not care what they thought would happen in Russia twenty years from now. Conditions will rise dictated by life, and not by theoretical speculation. It is much more important to have a proper policy than a great deal of noise. Policies, if sound, have a habit of accumulating more and more strength as they go along.

The question now was that of finding ways to aid in the process of reconstruction. Would men not ask themselves later:

Have we helped the constructive forces that are making for a better future, or were we just a fine bunch of sentimentalists? . . .

There is no patent medicine, *right, left, or center,* of any kind. It takes men and women to build an organization, and not abstract theories. It takes warm hearts to maintain ideals and not phraseology.

The men and women in charge of affairs in Russia were realistic and practical, he went on. They had power and they would hold it, he predicted.

In the history of the world the poets will be remembered more than the practical men, but actual life is made by the practical men, inspired at times by the writings of the dreamers. Life is made by the men who can take hold of life and have the power to mold it. . . . The power of that Russian group . . . comes from the willing co-operation of the peoples of Russia.

Hillman did not pretend to know enough about the Russian Revolution after a four-week visit to be able "to write a book about it," but he did know something about clothing and textile factories and how labor was handled there:

There is in Russia a great understanding of labor. . . . Their purpose is not destruction. The idea of sabotage, the idea that it is the purpose of labor to see how little it can do, is not found there. Labor appreciates that work is not something that one has to undergo as a punishment, but that work is something to be proud of. It helps build the world, because the world is built by work. . . . Labor understands . . . its mission in life is to build.

Hillman then concluded by outlining his project in detail. He asked that the Amalgamated convention authorize the initiation of the project, urging that such action would be a message of courage for men abroad and at home. It would show that constructive economic aid might come through channels other than "Wall Street and the banking combination." He closed with a memorable peroration, full of the flavor of his personality and embodying his philosophy of labor action:

> If we do nothing else, we are at least willing to put ourselves in the front ranks and take the criticism—and I know we will be criticized. I know this proposition will be lied about. . . . I know that we may be misunderstood even by some friends, but I tell you that the world will never make a step forward unless there is a group of people who are willing to stand the brunt, and who, when their effort is successful, will not even be given the credit for what they did. . . .
>
> But we men and women in the clothing industry have said to ourselves: We want to find out what is right, what is our duty, where our responsibility lies, and then go ahead and let the future justify our undertakings. If it had not been for a few people who had the courage of their convictions, we would today be living in the jungle, if the beasts of prey had permitted us to live there. It was due to the rebellious spirit of a few that we made progress. There are some people who are great rebels, although they are of a quiet disposition, although they do not indulge in high phraseology. They stand for and do the things that carry the human race a step forward, and they are greater than those who have all kinds of prescriptions and know how to lead us overnight to the ultimate goal. It is to the credit of our organization that we have always paid attention to what seemed right and we are willing to await the judgment of time.

At this time there was the beginning of some factional strife within the ranks of the Amalgamated between left and right wings. The anti-Communist Abraham Cahan himself, as a guest speaker at this convention, had attempted to carry the fight against the pro-Communists to the floor of the convention. Hillman's words had reference to these incipient quarrels; and as one labor journalist, Benjamin Stollberg, wrote at the time:

> It was then that Hillman showed his statesmanship, first by opposing the introduction of factional strife over Old World political theories, and in the second place by laying before the convention his definite project for aid to the Russians on a non-partisan basis. . . . [This was] the grand stroke which reconciled the right, left, and middling wings of the

convention. . . . Good business and humanity combined to outwit political factiousness.[22]

The end of Hillman's speech on Russia was followed by one of the greatest demonstrations ever made for him by his labor audience, who cheered and paraded for an hour. The right-wing dissenters were silenced as approval of the project was given with such enthusiasm. Yet at the same time, resolutions brought in by left-wingers to support pro-Communist trade-union organizations were quickly voted down, with Hillman's approval.

In September 1922, Hillman made his second trip to Moscow to complete the organization of the Russian-American Industrial Corporation, this time accompanied by his old friends, William O. Thompson and Earl Dean Howard. Details of the agreement between the American investors and representatives of the Soviet Government were worked out: the Americans were to send a few technicians who were to be charged with management of the allotted factories, but the Soviet Clothing Trust made careful stipulations for the right to revise or terminate the agreement in the event of differences arising between the two parties, pledging to repay, in such a case, all sums advanced by investors.

Hillman was back in the United States in November 1922, promoting the distribution of stock in the R.A.I.C., which was sold in shares of $10 each to the extent of about $300,000. Discussion of the plan in the press undoubtedly stimulated various other business groups to resume profitable trade with the U.S.S.R. But investors' interest in Hillman's undertaking soon flagged. Mr. Thompson, incidentally, after his return to the United States—though not questioning Hillman's good faith—expressed fears that difficulties would be encountered in dealing with the Soviet Government, which proved correct. After several factories had been set up by the R.A.I.C. and had been producing for several years the Russians took steps to regain full control of the plants, wound up the R.A.I.C. and arranged to refund all payments made by the American shareholders. This was done before 1928, when the New Economic Policy was supplanted by Stalin's Five-Year Plan.

Hillman's project remained small in scale and did not have the effects he hoped for. But one unexpected by-product of the R.A.I.C. proved to be very profitable and stimulating to trade between the

United States and Russia. During his second trip to Moscow in 1922, Hillman acquired, in the name of the two Amalgamated Banks, an exclusive concession for the remittance of drafts in dollar currency for all of Soviet Russia. Hitherto there had been much confusion and uncertainty in this business, as Americans remitting dollars to relatives in Russia found that payments were made only at an "official" exchange rate that was far below the actual dollar values in the market. But from 1923 to 1928 the Amalgamated Banks in New York and Chicago alone handled the remittance of more than $18,-000,000 of draft or cable payments, in more than 600,000 transactions for individuals, export corporations and banks all over the United States, a profitable banking service. Thus many Americans of Russian descent were enabled to assist their families or relatives in Russia, and peaceful trade was facilitated. After a time the leading commercial banks in America made arrangements for the transmission of dollar currency to Russia.

At this time (1922–24) Hillman came under the fire of the right-wing elements in his union, not to speak of the yellow press, for having extended aid to a country ruled reputedly by a gang of ruthless dictators. (In reality industrial assistance on a far vaster scale came to Soviet Russia from corporations like the Ford Motor Company, General Electric, and other purely capitalistic concerns.) Partisans of Soviet Communism, on the other hand, though only for the moment, spoke in terms of high praise of the Amalgamated and its leadership, of "the joy and pride" aroused by its "inspiring" industrial program and "broadly progressive" policies.

But any notion that Sidney Hillman was now a convert to the official Russian creed of Marxism was knocked on the head almost at once early in the summer of 1924, when his strategy in the political field turned squarely against the Communists in America. Then, like the "regular" Socialists, they had no epithet insulting or injurious enough for him, such as "traitor" or "labor faker" or even "dictator." For this is the common currency of political pamphleteering among the sects and schools. Yet Hillman remained true to his realistic philosophy of labor action in America.

Chapter Eleven

THE "NEW ERA":
THE TRADE-UNION
DOLDRUMS

American labor did not reconcile itself easily to the extreme conservatism that ruled our national politics in the twenties. By 1924 even the American Federation of Labor, after having received rebuffs from both parties, seemed disposed to overhaul its traditional political program of "rewarding labor's friends and punishing its enemies."

Hillman, like many other union leaders, was saying at this period that the labor movement needed a political party of its own, that it could not go far enough with economic power alone. One had only to look at the number of court injunctions being issued, he said, to understand why it was absolutely necessary for labor to turn to political action.[1]

Among the workers in the needle trades there were, to be sure, many old-time supporters of the Socialist Party, particularly in the New York area. The Amalgamated members in New York, like those of the ILGWU, had for years supported some of the Socialist candidates for local office. Hillman, however, did not see the Socialist Party, and even less the newly arisen Communist group, as the political medium for a broad-based party of American labor. The old-school Socialists, Hillman felt, did not merit his respect; many of their leaders "lacked the courage of their convictions," he said.[2] They themselves were torn by factional disputes, and some of them had tried to make trouble in his union.

Nevertheless, the issue of a third party was repeatedly raised after November 1920, especially by John Fitzpatrick, head of the Chicago Federation of Labor. A Conference for Progressive Political Action (CPPA) was initiated in February 1922 and included various independent groups which had supported the Farmer-Labor Party's national ticket in the Middle West in 1920. Several state and city labor bodies, and twenty-eight international unions affiliated with the AFL, sent representatives to this gathering; in behalf of the Amalgamated, Hillman appeared and addressed the conference. The railroad Brotherhoods were the sponsors of this movement, which aimed at launching an independent labor party. At this juncture Hillman felt that prospects for a third party dedicated to a progressive labor program were brighter than ever.[3]

Factional trouble, however, developed in Chicago in the summer of 1923 when Fitzpatrick called a conference of the Farmer-Labor Party of Illinois, which he headed. It was his intention to combine this local group with the larger third-party movement being prepared under the auspices of the Progressive Conference. But representatives of the Workers' Party (as the Communists then called themselves) appeared in force; whereupon the AFL and railway Brotherhoods' contingents walked out, and the conference collapsed.

When the Republicans nominated President Coolidge in 1924, and the Democrats chose as their candidate John W. Davis, a distinguished corporation lawyer identified mainly with J. P. Morgan and Company, the election contest promised to be truly a choice between tweedledum and tweedledee. The leading spirits in the Conference for Progressive Political Action then got their third-party movement under way in earnest after June 1924. The labor unions, together with the various state Farmer-Labor, Progressive, and Non-Partisan League groups in the Middle West, were induced to combine their forces in support of Senator Robert M. La Follette of Wisconsin for President under the banner of the Progressive Party. Surprisingly enough, the AFL finally gave its endorsement to La Follette and his running mate, Senator Burton K. Wheeler of

Montana, though declaring that this established no permanent commitment to a third party.

Hillman, who had been in close touch with leaders of the Progressive Conference, had apparently known two months in advance that a broad third party would form itself around La Follette. For he had warned the Midwestern members of his union not to join with any narrow political group—such as that in which the Communists had earlier tried to insert themselves.[4] As Hillman had foreseen, La Follette was nominated at the Cleveland convention of the Progressive Party, and he read out the Communist delegation there as a condition for his acceptance of the nomination. The Amalgamated gave a generous donation (of $10,000) to the La Follette campaign fund and, with Hillman's enthusiastic approval, its local officers in the larger cities worked hard to rally voters for the third party.

The La Follette movement captured 4.8 million votes, running a strong third to the defeated Democratic Party. Its adherents failed to set up a grass-roots organization to contend with the other parties for seats in Congress. But it was a record-breaking vote for an independent party, and the first presidential campaign in which organized labor had played a leading part, with the aid of farmers, middle-class intellectuals, and Socialists. For the first time virtually the entire mass of organized labor in America had acted concertedly in the political field and shown its power. The Amalgamated, in this case, came nearer to official endorsement of a political party than ever before in any previous election.[5]

Hillman thought that many valuable lessons were learned from the election of 1924. As he said, a few weeks after it took place:

The most important of these [lessons] is certainly the conclusion that an independent political party cannot be built overnight. Considering the circumstances under which the Committee for Progressive Political Action engaged in the last campaign and the speed with which political organizations were thrown together in practically all the states of the Union, no one has any valid reason for being disappointed with the results. . . . A very substantial proportion of the rank and file of the American labor movement were prepared to support an independent labor-political party. And this willingness to participate did not come after years of preparation but . . . after only a very short and swift campaign in which the political machinery showed all the defects that could be expected of machinery when hastily set up.

He referred to the recent success of the British Labor Party, which came into power briefly in 1924, as the culmination of a quarter of a century of hard, preparatory work. Here, where the complexity and size of our country made the problem more difficult still, to expect that an independent party should win at the start, on the strength of "a few slogans and a dominating personality," he said, "is to expect the impossible." An independent party for labor, he emphasized, must embody a program based on the needs of the movement underlying it, and deal with the problems and ends with which the workers were concerned.[6]

Hillman would have gone on working to build a labor party "from the bottom up," if the labor movement as a whole had continued to lend its support. But two years later the railway brotherhoods and the AFL abandoned the third-party movement and returned to their tactics of bargaining with the two professional parties. "The organization of an all-inclusive party of American labor is still a dream unrealized," was the comment of the Amalgamated General Executive Board in its report for 1928.

II

"A union may win a strike and then find out that the workers have lost . . . the industry," Hillman used to say.[7]

After the long lockout contest of 1921 many evils beset the Amalgamated; they were chronic, insidious, difficult of cure, for they were internal. The union's main troubles appeared in the chaotic New York market, where discipline among the members grew relaxed and serious dissensions arose among the local leaders and their followers.

The problem of co-ordinating the intensively competitive garment market of New York would have been difficult and time-consuming enough. It was made well-nigh impossible by the want of solidarity among the different groupings of workers such as the cutters, the children's clothing and the coat and pants tailors. The cutters, for example, being employed at good union wages by New York wholesale firms, had little contact with and indeed looked down upon the main army of operatives employed as a rule in "outside" contract shops. If the cutters made no effort to supervise the shipments of the cloth they cut—consigned all too often to non-union or even "out-of-town" contractors—then the problem of maintaining union standards became all the more baffling. According to clothing-trade authorities, such standards were maintained effectively in less than 50 per cent of the New York clothing shops in the early twenties.

In 1923, Hillman carried out a shake-up of the New York organization, placing Hyman Blumberg, the hard-working Baltimore leader, in charge here as director of Eastern Organization. With August Bellanca assisting him as his chief deputy, Blumberg was to struggle for years with the problem of keeping the small contract shops in line.

With business reviving strongly in the summer season of 1924, Hillman called a special conference of the union's top executives in New York. A group of the veteran leaders from Chicago, including Frank Rosenblum, director of Western Organization, Levin, Rissman, and Marimpietri, were brought in to help reorganize the New York section of the union. Plans were laid also for numerous brief strikes or "stoppages" of one or two weeks, designed to bring pressure upon delinquent employers. Mass meetings of the rank-and-file members were then held in New York and in Newark, New Jersey, at which impassioned union orators sought to raise the workers' morale. They were "mobilized" and then called out for a series of walkouts beginning on June 25, 1924, that closed down many non-union shops.

Meanwhile Hillman had secretly prepared some unusual moves. One of the troubles with the New York clothing trade was that there was no unity among the manufacturers and wholesalers themselves, for their trade association had been broken up in its struggle with the union in 1921. Unless the union could negotiate with a responsible body, there would never be order here.

He had noted that one group of manufacturers with whom he had been doing business for the union retained a lawyer named David Drechsler, who appeared to be able and high-minded. Early in 1924 he approached Drechsler privately, saying that he "hoped very much they would get along together." Mr. Drechsler was astonished when the union president then proposed to him that he take the initiative in organizing a real men's clothing manufacturers' association in New York. Otherwise, Hillman pointed out, it would be impossible to maintain city-wide agreements and union scales. Mr. Drechsler agreed to undertake the project and arranged for a number of conferences to which the city's principal manufacturers were invited. "But this is a Hillman job," some of them protested. Drechsler insisted that it was for the good of the industry and would permit union-management co-operation in a thoroughgoing way.[8]

At the time when the June 1924 strike action flared up in New York the formation of the new Clothing Manufacturers' Exchange was announced. Soon it was learned that the strikes would be halted and that the Amalgamated would sign an agreement with the employers who had entered the new association. This was a bloodless war in which both parties seemed equally determined to inflict no injury upon each other. By July 1, 10,000 workers were back in the shops. Within one month 90 per cent of the union members in New York had returned to their jobs under a new one-year agreement.[9]

There had been an average wage increase of 10 per cent gained by the union in 1923, though it had not been too well maintained. Now the same wage scale was to be imposed on the trade through a city-wide agreement aimed at lowering costs in New York, with the union accepting "production standards" which, it was hoped, would approximate the standards set by piecework systems used in other markets. The Clothing Manufacturers' Exchange, for its part, recognized the union shop, agreed to inaugurate an unemployment insurance plan, and restored the arbitration machinery that had been dropped in 1921. Thus a long stride was taken toward overcoming the weakness of the New York clothing trade: an unfavorable cost differential which prompted employers to evade the union's standards or go out of town.

However, Hillman said at the time that, unless the Amalgamated's New York structure were quickly centralized, all the gains of the recent campaign and strike would be meaningless. There were still three separate organizations within the city, relics of the old craft-union divisions: a Men's Clothing Workers' Joint Board, one for the Children's Clothing Workers, and a Cutters' Organization, each dealing separately with the employers. He pleaded that one joint board must be established immediately in order to carry out their agreement with the employers effectively.[10]

As he feared, the advantages of the 1924 action were indeed "frittered away" or "talked to sleep" by a renewed outbreak of dissension within the union. This time it took a political form, with left and right, Communists and anti-Communists at each other's throats. This new menace tried all of Hillman's considerable patience and diplomacy; it stimulated opposition to his tenure in office for the first time—that is, to the extent of one vote in ten against his re-election.

III

Some squabbling had first broken out in Local No. 3 (pressers) in the summer of 1923, when right-wing Socialists attacked the officers in charge as Communists and urged that they be ousted from office. The accounts of the left-wing faction held that Socialists systematically stirred up trouble in this and two other locals of the Amalgamated, but that the Workers' Party faction at this time actively defended the union's official leadership.[11]

The Communists, under William Z. Foster, former AFL organizer during the great steel strike of 1919, had recently formed the Trade Union Educational League, an organization which was to penetrate or "bore from within" existing labor unions and seize control of them. By 1923 they were busily at work in several of the needle-trade unions in New York and elsewhere, but for a while held their hand in the case of the Amalgamated, whose progressive leadership gave less scope to rank-and-file discontent than in other unions.

Hillman tried to head off trouble by warning the rival groups that "the Amalgamated will not permit outside bodies—right, left, or otherwise—to transact business and make decisions for it." This even-handed scolding was necessary because the Socialists had formed a "Tailors' Council" and were hitting back at the Communist-led Trade Union Educational League.[12]

The left-wing faction was bitterly disappointed when Amalgamated officers participated in the Progressive Party convention at Cleveland in July 1924, and did nothing to prevent the expulsion of the Communists. Hillman and his associates were now assailed as "class collaborationists," and Foster, through the T.U.E.L., pressed the attack with the utmost vigor inside the Amalgamated, in local union elections of September 1924.

In 1923 the right-wing faction had called on members of Amalgamated locals in New York not to pay dues at the recently increased rate; by the autumn of 1924 the Communists were calling for the same measures of opposition. Several months earlier, at the union's biennial convention in Philadelphia on May 12, 1924, Hillman had made renewed appeals for harmony, saying that while the strain of alternate fighting or negotiating with the employers was heavy, it was as nothing compared to the trouble of

bringing together dissenting groups within the organization . . . the most deadly enemy of the whole labor movement is internal dissension!

I wish I could find words, I wish I could find thoughts to convey to you that you are called upon to make the greatest sacrifice for the sake of the organization that is dear to you. I want you to determine to make the sacrifice of personal ambition, of personal differences, for the sake of the greatest weapon, the only thing that makes the labor movement possible, for the sake of unity, unity within our ranks! [13]

Hillman's clear-cut attitude was that the Amalgamated, as an industrial organization, should not favor or antagonize any group of its members because of their political affiliations. But the T.U.E.L. faction, which controlled one of the union's large locals, No. 5 (coat makers), was not to be placated by such moderate views. They called a mass meeting in August 1924, at which speakers such as Ben Gitlow, then a leader of the Workers' Party, had a field day assailing the union's general officers, accused them of wasting the union's funds, and derided the whole system of arbitration as a "betrayal" of the class struggle. The two factions carried their fight into the sittings of the New York Joint Board; their adherents sometimes assaulted each other, but usually confined themselves to a battle of leaflets.

In December 1924, things took a turn for the worse when the leftists controlling Local 5, under one Sam Lipzin, called an unauthorized strike against the firm of J. Friedman and Company, in protest against the dismissal of two workers who had engaged in a brawl. Since the union agreement called for peaceful arbitration of such grievances, higher officers of the union ordered the men back. But the picketing was continued against their orders. Eventually the two discharged men were reinstated, though the local officers were still disgruntled, and new mass meetings were held at which opposition to the union's leadership was urged with great vehemence.

Repeatedly pressed by his colleagues to expel the disaffected local, Hillman said: "I hope we will not have to revoke charters. I do not like it, regardless of how it may appeal to some." He was for full freedom of discussion of union affairs, but through union channels, not through "outside bodies." Yet, when renewed movements of revolt came from the same quarter, threatening to undo all the gains of the recent union campaign in New York, the New York Joint Board, in January 1925, finally suspended the three executives of Local 5, with the approval of Hillman and the other Amalgamated general officers.[14]

Hillman, in sarcastic phrases, expressed his poor opinion of the "political gangs" who were making a football of their union. The anti-Communist "Council" had come out against an increase of dues; and the "Educational league" (pro-Communist) had hastened to do likewise. Did either faction consider whether the 15 cents' weekly increase in dues was for the real benefit of the union members? No, they "played politics," they "played the game" in the hope only of winning popularity. The improved shop conditions, the new scale of wages won in New York were being frittered away by their dissensions. How long could even a powerful union endure such divisive tactics?

> We refuse to be a party to any single group or combination of groups. We will no longer deal with a "good" League or a "fine" Council. . . . Our experience has been that neither faction has the interests of the Amalgamated at heart. We recognize the impossibility of carrying on constructive work if factionalism continues.
>
> The union views the group leading the opposition not as a right or left movement, but as a group organized by outsiders for the purpose of wrecking the Amalgamated. . . . The G.E.B. looks upon these activities as nothing less than dual unionism.[15]

He fully appreciated that the rebels were "boring from within." (At this period the T.U.E.L. faction had seized full control of the ILGWU's New York Joint Board.) But in the first place, Hillman and his friends were not going to help the Communists take over the Amalgamated; and in the second place, he believed that by refusing to give way to panic and by acting in a spirit of fairness and tolerance toward the opposition he would, in the end, draw their teeth.

Hillman had passed through many perils. As leader of his union he had now come round full circle, to confront opposition (though of no great strength) both on the right and the left. He said later that it seemed absurd for these groups to be fighting like fanatics over their opposing beliefs about what kind of social revolution we would have in twenty or fifty years, meanwhile risking the destruction of their union. But it was best to let them talk and "demonstrate" as much as they liked. The overwhelming majority of loyal members could also talk and demonstrate.

At a mass meeting in February 1925, called by the Communist faction to protest the suspension of their leaders, Hyman Blumberg and other Amalgamated officers, accompanied by a score or so of loyal union members who happened to be of robust physique, came down and fought the opposition, demanding the right to speak. There was some scuffling, perhaps even a small riot—as the opposition's newspaper reported—then the loyal union group retired from the scene.[16] On the other hand, the T.U.E.L. faction, in April and May 1925, organized more aggressive demonstrations by holding parades and mass meetings in Union Square before the general offices of the Amalgamated. On one day the demonstrators invaded the union's office and smashed windows and furniture, until police arrived and drove them off. On another occasion the "rebels" threw inkwells at persons who had gathered before the offices of the union, as if to prevent another invasion, ruining their new spring suits.[17]

These fairly unimpressive manifestations did not move Hillman to abandon his attitude of impartiality and moderation toward the political factions. He strove as far as possible to keep the internal squabble out of the newspapers and within the family, for even occasional newspaper reports of minor intra-mural disturbances had the effect of hardening the attitude of employers. The rebels, moreover, had not yet shot their last bolt.

In the last week of March 1925, Hillman, accompanied by Dr. Leo Wolman, arrived in Chicago to negotiate the renewal of the union's agreement with the manufacturers' association in that city. The suspended local officer, Lipzin, together with Ben Gitlow, chose this very moment to appear in Chicago in the hope of recounting his grievances and arousing the union members there to opposition. A mass meeting was announced for March 23, just as Hillman arrived in town.

Sam Levin, head of the Joint Board, decided to attend the "protest" meeting with some 5,000 other faithful union members, since it was plainly to be an affair that concerned all the clothing workers and not merely a small faction among them. "*We* will be the majority at the meeting," he said, laughing. Dr. Wolman went along to see the fireworks. So many thousands of people turned out an hour ahead of time that the manager of the hall, in fear of a riot and damage to his property, decided not to open it. The opposition group, though having paid for the hall in the name of the Workers' Party, seemed somewhat frightened and refused to go ahead with their meeting, though Amalgamated executives offered to post deposits covering possible damage. The thousands of people lining the streets nearby roared for the meeting to begin. Wolman's account refutes later charges that Hillman's faction broke up the meeting by force:

I mingled with every part of the crowd and saw only members of the Amalgamated—no sluggers. I saw the men and women, cutters, pants makers, whom I have seen at hundreds of meetings in Chicago. It was a quiet, cheerful, patient crowd. . . .

Altogether there were no more than a half dozen police. They did nothing but keep the crowd from pushing up against the closed glass doors of Temple Hall.[18]

Levin, however, invited the crowd to come to Carmen's Hall, which was nearby. There the evening was passed in the jovial singing of union hymns and the adoption of various resolutions condemning the Communist faction, whose spokesman, though invited to do so, refused to take the floor.[19]

The weak efforts to "bore from within" by the would-be revolutionists were everywhere countered by patient and ingenious defense tactics on the part of the Amalgamated leadership. Less than a score of members were suspended, and the right of reinstatement was always held open to them; only one local was "disciplined" by having an executive appointed to its command. The union must remain tolerant of divisions of opinion and "encourage free discussion among its members" at all times, Hillman preached, thus enabling those who were in error or misled to rid themselves of their wrong notions. The policy of tolerance, he declared later, had been successful in disposing of the "Communist menace." [20]

That the attempt of the T.U.E.L. to build up a rank-and-file organization within the Amalgamated had met with complete failure, especially in the New York area, was frankly admitted afterward in articles of "self-criticism" published in the Communist press. But in several other cities, where the "rebels" had real grievances against the local leadership, the factional struggle renewed itself in 1926 and 1927.

In Montreal and Toronto certain locals allied themselves with the Trade Union Educational League or later with the "All-Canadian Labor Union Congress," in a movement toward a dual organization. Hillman waited patiently before taking action, while two experienced organizers, Elias Rabkin and Sander Genis, despite the fiercest opposition, carried on an "educational campaign" among the Amalgamated members in the two Canadian cities. False rumors and accusations were countered with sober facts and figures; the opposition was permitted to talk itself out. In a few cases some of the local officers elected by the T.U.E.L. were exposed as having been guilty of improper conduct.[21] Hillman, as usual, arrived at the right moment—in June 1927—and managed to settle a number of "wildcat" strikes on terms most favorable to the union members. By his friendly demeanor he left the members in Toronto and Montreal in a more cheerful frame of mind. When the local union elections came up in September, he was back again, to spur the drive against the T.U.E.L. faction, with the result that the pro-Hillman slate was overwhelmingly elected by a four to one majority in both cities.

More serious and prolonged disorder threatened the important clothing center of Rochester for several years after 1924. There was not only the T.U.E.L. group working among the discontented, but also dissension on racial grounds between the Italian and Jewish workers. The men who were "boring from within" had set up a rival council or committee which, by 1926, threatened to become the controlling agent of the Rochester locals. Grievances arising from incompetent management of the union's affairs by its Rochester officers gave strength to the insurgent leaders, one of whom, Abraham Chatman, a coat maker at the Hickey-Freeman plant, was regarded as a youth of high character by the union members. One of the Rochester employers, however, described him as a "radical, un-co-operative union agitator." Impartial Chairman Leiserson urged Hillman to do something about this young firebrand; while Alex Cohen, a veteran member of the General Executive Board, who had been investigating the trouble, advised that Chatman was "the soul of the organization" in Rochester and that his expulsion from the union might do great harm.[22]

The Amalgamated's Executive Board came to hold inquiries in Rochester and heard grave charges of unauthorized strikes led by the rebels in the union. Hillman called four or five of the ringleaders on the carpet and considered suspending them. One of them was Chatman, a poised young man who frankly confessed that he had been one of the ruling spirits among the insurgents, declared he had good grounds for his actions, and was ready to take the consequences. On Blumberg's advice, Hillman arranged to see Chatman privately at a later date to try to bring him over. His proposal, when they met again, was that Chatman take the post of assistant manager of the Rochester Joint Board, under Blumberg as acting manager. Thus the insurgent leader was to help re-establish order in this market.

"Hillman could have crushed me then and there, but instead offered me the chance to see what I could do to introduce needed reforms," Chatman said afterward. From that day on Chatman was one of Sidney Hillman's most ardent supporters and believed implicitly in his long-range policies.[23]

The following year young Chatman, with Hillman's blessing and the support of the union's administration, was nominated as manager of the Amalgamated's Rochester Joint Board. Hillman himself came down in September 1927, during the election campaign, to take the stump for Chatman, who was elected by a vote of 3,000 to 1,200. Thereafter the stormy Rochester section became one of the most smoothly functioning units in the system; all details of agreements were so scrupulously followed that it became proverbial, in the local clothing trade, that Chatman's signature was never needed for any contract, his word alone being sufficient.[24] The group of Rochester locals made a record of carrying on without a single strike in unionized shops in the twenty-five years since Chatman (now a union vice-president) took charge.

When the Seventh Biennial Convention of the ACWA came round in May 1926 at Montreal, Hillman reported that the Communists were thoroughly beaten. One factor in this result was the continuance of the union's militant economic action and its expanding social program.

With great good humor he remarked that all men "had a right to make a revolution" if they wanted to; and if they won out they could, of course, draw up their own rules.

I said to one of their high priests: "Any time you can take the Amalgamated you are entitled to it, but don't expect us to deliver it to you." I have no fault to find with any outside organization that is ambitious enough to capture us; if they can do it they are entitled to it; but they will probably have to wait a little while. . . . [Laughter.] And when I say a "little while" I speak in geological terms!

In more serious vein he closed the discussion by promising that everyone who was ready to show his loyalty to the union would find its doors open to him again.

I hope that this convention will lay out its policy of tolerance inside our ranks. . . . As to political parties, you can have as many as you like; you can disagree in the union as much as you want; but we will not allow an outside organization to run our affairs.

On the same subject, at a later gathering held in the following year, he spoke with regret of the bitter feelings aroused by recent controversies, saying:

Whenever the Amalgamated is attacked I am here to fight and fight hard. But while fighting, I remember that the fight is to make the labor movement more beautiful, not more bitter.

Chapter Twelve

CONSOLIDATION:
THE MIDDLE YEARS

A series of important conferences between the Amalgamated leaders and representatives of the Chicago Wholesale Clothiers' Association were held in March and April 1925 to negotiate the terms for a renewal of the union-shop agreement. This was at the very time when the union was having its troubles with the Communist faction. Nevertheless, the Amalgamated leadership continued to absorb itself in the immediate, unromantic task of protecting the welfare of clothing-trade labor. Since the country was passing through a period of sweeping technological change in industry, Hillman and his associates were led once more to undertake some remarkable pioneering in order to provide for human readjustment to the shocks of our Machine Age.

During the 1920's the American consumer spent less of his dollar on suits of clothing and more on automobiles. The trend was toward cheaper men's suits to be sold in chain stores. New and improved machinery for pressing suits and for cutting cloth and many other devices were introduced, resulting, at the end of 1925, in sharp reductions of the working force. At Hart, Schaffner and Marx about 30 per cent of the cutters were due to be dismissed.

·

Should the new machines, the new processes be resisted by the powerful union in the field? On the contrary, its leadership co-operated with the manufacturers in meeting their problems of production. "Inefficient shops meant low wages, long hours, and bad conditions," as Frank Rosenblum said at the time. Realizing that it could not fight against technical improvement, the union "directly and indirectly participated in the technical revolution which the industry has undergone since 1920." [1]

But what was to be done with 150 skilled cutters, accustomed to good wages, at a time when employment in men's clothing tended to decline? The Amalgamated leaders improvised a plan by which these men were to be given quittance pay for having been permanently displaced by electrically driven machines. The company, counting on large annual savings by use of the new machinery, eventually agreed to contribute a $50,000 payment, to which the Chicago section of the union added $25,000 from its unemployment insurance fund, making up a capital of $500 for each displaced man, so that he could enter some small business or train himself for other mechanical work.[2] Here was a striking instance of that "economic legislation" which Hillman believed it was the mission of the clothing workers' union to carry on.

Meanwhile, by May Day, 1925, the Chicago members were enabled to celebrate a renewal of their union-shop agreement in that market, a new treaty of peace for three years to come, and upon most favorable terms. The Association had exerted great pressure this time to win concessions that would help them in dealing with the changed condition of their business. Hillman was forced to deliver an ultimatum, carrying the threat of a city-wide strike; the manufacturers had then yielded. That is, all but one of them, who held out against any agreement with the union. He was J. L. Reiss, the largest mail-order clothier in the country and a man of wealth, controlling two firms, the International Tailoring Company and J. L. Taylor and Company, both with branches in New York as well as in Chicago. In New York, where the Amalgamated in June negotiated a city-wide agreement with the newly formed Clothing Manufacturers' Exchange, Mr. Reiss's New York branches held out again. He appeared determined to go ahead without union control of his shops—which, as he wrote Hillman, made for a "high cost of labor."

He seemed to have made up his mind about what a battle with the union would cost and what he would do about it.

In those middle years of the Amalgamated, Sidney Hillman talked peace everywhere.

> Many people outside the labor movement think that [it] is organized only in order to strike. . . . The strike is merely a weapon to bring labor into its rightful place. Unfortunately, with conditions as they exist today, labor is compelled to strike for that which should be properly regarded as its own.[3]

However, employer opposition was hardening again along the borders of the big unionized clothing centers. A bitterly fought strike against a large firm in Philadelphia had been lost recently when the full force of the police and courts was thrown against the union's pickets. In St. Louis a long conflict with the Curlee Clothing Company proved to be hopeless for much the same reason. But those were smaller centers. The challenge of the International Tailoring Company was aimed at the very heart of the Amalgamated organization in Chicago and New York. An "open-shop" breach in the union lines would endanger the whole system of joint government that had taken more than ten years to build. There would have to be a showdown fight with this aggressive concern. For some time the union's agents had been reporting that the managers of International Tailoring had been quietly making preparations of their own for war.

During May and June the union's strategists made elaborate arrangements to assure themselves of victory in the approaching contest with this firm. Few unions in those days conducted strikes with the finesse of the Amalgamated, and once engaged in a fight, its officers fought to win at all costs. Their own view is that they used no special trickery, but depended on elastic or varying tactics designed for different situations. Industry used labor spies against the union men; the Amalgamated had its own sharp-witted intelligence service. This helped them to bring the element of surprise into play with tremendous effect.

In the International Tailoring affair, which was to be known as a "classical" strike action, arrangements were made for very close liaison between the Amalgamated's New York organization and the leaders in Chicago. These careful preparations were all the more necessary inasmuch as Sidney Hillman was planning to leave that summer on a long journey to Europe (with the intention of winding up the affairs of the Russian-American Industrial Corporation). Chief responsibility at the New York end was to be in the hands of Hyman Blumberg. Hillman, after working over plans with his lieutenants, went off on his voyage; and everything worked like a charm.

Mr. J. L. Reiss was described at the time as a man of very determined views. It happened also that he enjoyed strong friendships with men high in the political world; and so it was expected that the police would be staunch in the defense of his property in New York, while his workers in that city were considered weak on the score of unionism. They had all been "maneuvered" hastily into the union during the booming war days. Some of them, spurred by the T.U.E.L., had even refused to pay dues.

On the other hand, Mr. Reiss counted on closing down his Chicago shops, where the Amalgamated was known to be very strong. But against this contingency he had, with foresight, laid plans to shift production to an unused factory in another Midwestern city 150 miles from Chicago.

On June 26, 1925, some 1,500 employees of the International Tailoring Company, about equally divided between the Chicago and New York branches, were called out on strike by the Amalgamated. In Chicago they went out as one man; in New York the picture was somewhat different. Special guards blocked all entrances to the company's building at Fourth Avenue and Twelfth Street as union agents came to enter the shop at the given hour.

The cutters' business agent was stopped at the door when he arrived; but this did not prevent him from reaching the 50 key workers in the cutting room. An alert fellow, he quickly went to a telephone booth and at a cost of 5 cents ordered the whole cutting department of International Tailoring out on strike. The cutters came rushing forth as one man. Thereafter the telephone to the cutting room was disconnected, but it was too late.

However, not all the workers in the other departments came out; many hesitated and then decided to stay at work. The union's pickets then closed in on the International Tailoring's building, only three blocks from the Amalgamated headquarters at 32 Union Square. At noontime as many as 10,000 would gather from the garment center to block all movement in the neighborhood of Fourth

Avenue and Twelfth Street. But the police struck hard; hundreds of them moved in quickly to drive off the pickets. The union men fought back and many were injured and arrested.

The non-union workers, strongly guarded, remained at work. When they went home at night, however, they were met by committees from the union who addressed them in terms so persuasive that "they were convinced they would have to strike." [4] Meanwhile Mr. Reiss, known for his upright and philanthropic character, had made strong statements that were given wide publicity in the newspapers, declaring that the union had called a strike "without cause" and that he stood ready to pay high wages to all who were willing to work for him. After a while non-union cutters were brought in under guard and the company managed to continue operations.

Blumberg, who was in charge of this strike at the New York end, found that high Police Department officers had given orders to the patrolmen to treat the Amalgamated pickets rough. Yet it seemed to him that as long as the pickets were behaving peacefully it was the bounden duty of the police to protect rather than molest them. After a time the persuasiveness of some of the union zealots worked to convince various sergeants and patrolmen (who, in any case, did not enjoy carrying out their orders) of the fairness of the union's case against International Tailoring. Thereafter the squads of policemen not only protected Mr. Reiss's property, but also guarded the Amalgamated pickets from harm. New York's finest did their duty with impartiality.

The strike had run for some six weeks; it was still touch-and-go when on August 13, 1925, the company obtained a court injunction restraining the union men "from picketing the plaintiff's business . . . in any manner whatsoever, and from congregating or standing *within ten blocks in any direction* from the said place of business." It was an injunction, as Hillman remarked—just before leaving on his European journey—that permitted no one in the union to move or breathe without risking a jail sentence, since the order to keep ten blocks away from the strike-bound plant would have obliged him to close up the union's general offices as well as its bank in the Amalgamated Building on Union Square, only three blocks from International Tailoring. Moreover, within the circumscribed area there were about 30,000 members of the union at work in many other clothing shops, which would also have to close up to obey this injunction.

Hyman Blumberg, however, noticed that the injunction referred only to the site of the International Tailoring Company at 107 Fourth Avenue. But next door, at 105 Fourth Avenue, was the J. L. Taylor firm, its subsidiary, about which nothing was said in the injunction order. The next morning five brave little pickets were posted in front of Taylor and Company. The police felt compelled to arrest them, but the Amalgamated's lawyers managed to obtain a ruling from a court that "peaceful picketing" was not forbidden at the building next door to the struck plant. Soon bigger picket lines closed in again next door to International Tailoring and interrupted its traffic. Yet, by transporting his people in taxis under the care of policemen, the obdurate employer managed to keep his business in operation. Strikebreakers were kept on the job in good number, with the help of professional strikebreaking agencies.

At this stage Blumberg, keenly aware of the sufferings of many loyal union men who were out of work in other cities, thought up a plan for helping them earn good wages temporarily. International Tailoring was calling for more cutters from out of town, he knew. Amalgamated agents in other cities were now quietly informed that a certain number of dependable union men might accept strike-breaking offers and were to be given instructions about how to proceed. Indeed a certain strikebreaking agency, recently established in New York, soon approached the company managers and offered to supply non-union workers from out-of-town points in return for liberal fees, of course. This agency's "scabs," as it happened, turned out to be "union-made." [5] Then the fun began.

The new hands proved to be very playful and hard to discipline. From time to time the company's shops were rife with loud arguments and all sorts of high jinks, and this undoubtedly led to some confusion and error either in the cutting, tailoring, or shipment of merchandise. Soon many customers were sending in complaints of fantastic errors showing up in their orders. A size 42 coat would go out with a 36 vest, or a pair of pants would have one side shorter than the other. It was as if a band of gremlins had got into the place. The trouble would be traced to some of the new workers, and many of them were discharged. But soon afterward things would become disorganized all over again, and more time would be lost before the new source of mischief was discovered. Meanwhile the morale of the workers in the New York plant and their output remained very low.

In Chicago the International Tailoring Company prepared to move its managerial staff and machinery to Rock Island, Illinois, where the large unused plant of the Daniel Boone Woolen Mills was to be leased. But the Amalgamated organization for some time had maintained close connections with the AFL and railway unions of that strong labor center. Now, as the International Tailoring made preparations to move into the Rock Island plant, there were numerous pickets on hand and the local workers, under orders of the central labor council, seemed all stirred up against the company. This move seemed blocked before it could be started. Once more the union's intelligence service had been a jump ahead of the employer.

In New York production had gone forward again after considerable trouble and mystification. The foremen were now doing their utmost to train green hands for their work. It was the eighteenth week of the strike; and Blumberg, feeling that it was dragging out too long, thought of another bold coup. There were a score of foremen in charge of manufacturing at the International Tailoring, and the union leaders knew who they were. Now lately there had been several serious outbreaks of violence along the picket lines. These foremen had been under a severe strain as they worked with their clumsy "scabs."

Somehow Mr. Blumberg managed to reach them and convey to them his proposal that they come out on strike, which was something truly unheard of in a labor dispute. The ostensible motive for their action would be the expected discharge of one of their fellows. The foremen seemed fed up and, to the union leader's delight, agreed to walk out.

On the morning of October 28, 1925, the strike leaders arranged to have 10,000 Amalgamated pickets on hand to fill all the width of Fourth Avenue for many blocks surrounding the International Tailoring plant. It was a perfect bedlam; the crowd uttered bloodcurdling yells or roared: *"Injunctions don't make pants!"* The police looked on in bewilderment, unprepared—in fact, unable—to proceed to the arrest of 10,000 persons. Upstairs in the factory, the workers were frightened and restive.

Suddenly the fifteen foremen, as if in disgust at the whole affair, came walking out, declaring they could not keep order under such conditions. Many of the remaining workers followed them. The crowd, seeing this, went wild with jubilation.

The walkout of the company's foremen was the finishing blow. The company had lost much money in this struggle of five months. Every effort to defeat the strike had been balked by the union's superior planfulness. By now public opinion had veered around in favor of the union; the mayor, the governor, and many civic leaders urged Mr. Reiss to end the tug of war at last. Moreover, Sidney Hillman was known to be on his way home from Europe; it seemed to be time to negotiate.

Terms were arranged to the satisfaction of the union at a conference held on November 4, 1925. Blumberg recalls having "held things up until Sidney's ship arrived in New York, so that he could sign the agreement."

There were no dramatics. Hillman had had nothing to do with any of the trick plays that had been used. Thus he could negotiate without heat, in a spirit of sweet reasonableness. The employer, who had shown himself a determined foe, is reported to have said briefly that he would sign Hillman's agreement and hoped he would have the union's aid in restoring order.

Hillman, fresh and tanned after an ocean voyage, in his most jovial humor said: "Your business is in a pretty messed-up state, but I suppose we will have to put it in shape again. We want employment for our people, and on union terms, of course." [6]

For twenty-seven years since then this firm has had no labor disputes; its present head, Mr. Raymond Reiss, son of the founder and one of the leading figures in his industry, is today one of the strongest friends of the Amalgamated union.

II

At the height of the "open-shop" drives in the 1920's the growth of company unions offered the greatest menace to organized labor in the clothing trade as in other fields. In paternalistic fashion management held out usually the inducement of various profit-sharing systems, often in the form of incentive payments in capital stock. However, the largest and most successful company union the Amalgamated ever encountered in its industry seemed to be based, strangely enough, on its religious appeal. It was founded by Arthur ("Golden Rule") Nash in Cincinnati in 1918, and from a small concern with a few dozen ill-paid workers, a sort of sweatshop, grew in six years to be an organization employing 3,000 operatives and 2,000 salesmen. The company specialized in the distribution of cheap suits made according to mail-order specifications.

What was dangerous for the union was the extremely rapid expansion of this concern, and in a time of depression. Its president made claims everywhere that his shops, run according to his "Golden Rule Plan," offered greater benefits to the workers than any plants operating under agreements with the labor unions. The tales of the Nash workers' high earnings, liberal bonuses, and paid Christmas vacations were spread all over the press much like the legends of Henry Ford in the early twenties.

The first efforts by Amalgamated organizers to unionize Nash's firm in 1919 were brought to nothing by his workers, who fervently believed in Mr. Nash as their benefactor. They could not be induced to go out on strike. The company thus offered unusually tough problems which seemed to defy the best efforts of labor organizers working along conventional lines. Perhaps it was all "phony," but the people here seemed hypnotized, as Jack Kroll of the Cincinnati Joint Board reported, by a manufacturer who was a skypilot with a silver tongue. Hillman himself studied this case for long years. Then with the help of skillful assistants he worked out a method of attack, specially adapted to dealing with a corporation whose pecuniary success flowed from its claims to religious evangelism.

According to his own account, Arthur Nash was born in 1870, the son of a poor farmer, in a small Indiana village. He was raised in a log cabin; his parents, fervent Seventh-Day Adventists, bred in him their highly evangelistic faith. After some brief seminary training in his early youth he became an Adventist preacher in Detroit for a year or two; but later he lost his faith and wandered about as a casual worker. At one period he was a salesman for a clothing house in the Middle West; then he tried a small business venture of his own and failed. During this time of crisis he apparently underwent a form of religious conversion and began to preach his own non-sectarian doctrines before various church groups. On again entering the clothing business in Cincinnati toward 1913, he prospered in a small way and, with the help of partners, purchased an additional shop. At the end of 1918 he managed to buy still another clothing shop for $60,000. It was then that the "miracle" took place.

As a lay preacher he had been giving strong sermons lately on the theme of the Golden Rule. Then one day he looked at the payroll of the wholesale tailoring shop he had just acquired and saw that it showed a roster of workers of the poorest class, with women button sewers earning $4.00 a week and pressers receiving $18—the scale of a small Cincinnati sweatshop. He now called his workers together and preached a heart-warming sermon in which he declared that he was going to act as Jesus Christ would have done if he had been a businessman. He would begin by raising the unskilled workers 300 per cent (from $4.00 to $12 minimum), while those receiving $18 would be raised 50 per cent, to $27 a week.[7] In return he would expect his workers to abide by the Golden Rule so far as output was concerned. (The average wage increase during this year of severe inflation was actually about 50 per cent, according to Amalgamated investigators.) Nash discovered now what Henry Ford had learned long years before, that raising the minimum wage improved productivity. His people, in gratitude, "worked like hell," as one of them put it, and the shop was soon turning out and selling more than three times as many suits of clothing as before. At the end of the year its profits were $42,000, or at the rate of over 70 per cent on its capital. By 1920, the Nash Company did $1,580,000 worth of business in its so-called "Christian clothing"; and the dizzy pace continued. The company bought larger factory space and was soon recapitalized at $1,000,000, with Mr. Nash owning half of the stock and the rest being distributed gradually among the workers.

Under "God's Plan" the workers sang hymns, prayed earnestly, and labored swiftly; the salesmen prayed also and sold orders for suits at little church gatherings in small towns, where they preached the gospel of the Golden Rule Shops. Part of the success of this scheme derived from the low price of Nash's Golden Rule ("direct-to-consumer") suits, which sold at $16.50 to $29.

Since most of the Nash workers were women, one of the Amalgamated's best women organizers of that period, Ann Washington Craton, was sent to investigate the Nash Company in May 1921. In the line of duty, Miss Craton attended a church meeting in a small Midwestern town at which Arthur Nash himself preached. He proved to be a strikingly handsome man, with fine eyes and snow-white hair, who spoke with great charm of the spirit of harmony and Christian love ruling his shops. Many who heard him were moved to tears; while they wept several rather ascetic-looking salesmen moved about the room quietly passing out orders for A. Nash clothing, which were quickly filled. It was "a most curious performance," Miss Craton thought.[8]

After six months her reports to Hillman gave evidence of that which he had only suspected till then: wages here were far below the union scale for unskilled groups, while cutters earned about 50 per cent less than in Chicago. Overtime rates (time and a half) were unknown, though long hours were common in the rush season. Mr. Nash explained that he was absorbed in long-range plans to eliminate overtime work altogether at some time in the future. True, bonus payments were made, in what seemed generous lump sums at Christmas, to the accompaniment of much hymn singing and praying, but when averaged over a year amounted to only $1.00 to $2.00 a week in addition to regular pay. Miss Craton's report indicated that Arthur Nash was at once a remarkably shrewd man of business and, in her opinion, "a profound hypocrite." While his office was located in a clean model factory, the bulk of production was carried on elsewhere in Cincinnati "in a large sweatshop" bossed by a tough foreman. Some of the workers in the subsidiary plants had never heard of the Golden Rule in clothing manufacture.[9]

A first unionizing drive was begun by the Amalgamated in the autumn of 1921. Leaflets assailing Nash's methods as constituting a "Golden Fleece" were busily circulated; his workers were urged to seek the advantages of a real labor union.

Nash appeared to be disturbed at the initial thrust of the union organizers under the charge of Frank Rosenblum, Jack Kroll, and Eli P. Oliver. Suddenly he sent word that he would like to see Sidney Hillman privately. Hillman promptly met him in a hotel in New York, bringing with him a briefcase full of letters from nationally known clothiers expressing satisfaction with their union-shop agreements.

He too found Nash like no one he had ever known. At one moment the man spoke with the utmost sincerity of his role as benefactor of his workers, declaring that he himself had once been a member of the Knights of Labor and believed in unions. Then in the next moment he turned bitter at the "misleading" pamphlets of the Amalgamated agents. Hillman was amused, puzzled, and suspicious; but he could be most persuasive in these heart-to-heart talks, and apparently gained Nash's permission to come and speak to his workers during a week at Christmas that was to be given over to "Bible study and meditation."

A few weeks later, to Hillman's intense disappointment, a letter arrived from Nash saying that it would be "inopportune" for Hillman to come and speak at his shops because of his workers' indignation at false statements made by the union about the Nash Company. Soon afterward, at the beginning of January 1922, news came that Nash had decreed a 10 per cent over-all increase in wages and had established the 40-hour week. Union hours then were 44 hours but provided for higher pay for overtime work, not to speak of joint labor-management supervision of working conditions. Yet, placing his hand on his heart, Nash would address his workers at shop meetings as his "brothers and sisters," and make such earnest professions of love and solicitude for their welfare that all acclaimed him. His complaints about his alleged "ill treatment" by the Amalgamated aroused the indignant workers to pass resolutions ordering that members of the Amalgamated be denied employment in the Nash shops.[10] As their "servant in God's shop," Nash felt bound to accept their "order."

A sort of guerrilla war was waged against the company by the Amalgamated over the next three years. The union's leaflets urged that "if fear of unionism has given you the 40-hour week and a 10 per cent increase, think what complete organization will accomplish!" But no further progress was made in this campaign, while the Nash Company kept increasing its business until it ranked among the largest clothing firms in America.

In the period from 1921–25, the Amalgamated, greatly absorbed in fighting the out-of-town movement from Chicago as well as from New York, met with heavy reverses in the Cincinnati clothing center. Police and local court action was extremely hostile during a long series of strike and lockout contests. Meanwhile, the spectacular success of the Nash "Golden Rule" enterprise seemed to foreshadow a time when the Amalgamated could scarcely raise its head in this city. Hence, toward the end of 1924, renewed efforts were made to unionize the company as soon as the union felt conditions favorable.

Hillman turned the problem over to Dr. Leo Wolman, who, after prolonged study, advised that routine methods would bring no results. The key to the problem, in his opinion, was the powerful support Nash had gathered to himself among numerous church organizations; for this reinforced his peculiar hold on the class of workers he had attracted to his Cincinnati shops, people of all denominations, to be sure, but strongly swayed by religious sentiment. The way to attack Nash was on his strong side, that of morality and religion, which might be shown to have vulnerable places. As for the economic side, Wolman had gathered information that in 1924 the company had overextended itself through the purchase of a very large plant in Cincinnati which was now operating at a loss.

At this time there was a young woman named Celestine Goddard, who, owing to her interest in social work, had joined the union's staff. She was a graduate of Bryn Mawr College and had been active in church groups earlier. At Wolman's suggestion she was sent to work in the field in Cincinnati, in connection with the Nash Company case, early in 1925.

After a time the pretty Miss Goddard took special pains to meet ministers and church leaders of the Cincinnati community and before them raised the question of whether Arthur Nash was not using the cloak of religion improperly to advance a large commercial enterprise. She had facts about some of his shops that weren't pleasant. The workers were called "brothers" and "sisters," to be sure, but had no voice in the management of the Golden Rule company. On the contrary, Mr. Nash met with them only twice a year, when he would submit resolutions he wished them to pass, gave them a strong sermon, and left it at that. Many worked up to 60 hours a week in the rush season, and only employees of long standing owned shares of company stock.

The Cincinnati community showed a renewed interest in the controversy over Mr. Nash's business after Miss Goddard came to take up the cudgels for the union. Some of the more orthodox ministers, moreover, had no liking for Mr. Nash's non-sectarian Christianity. In sermons, articles, and letters in the Cincinnati newspapers the question was raised whether it was proper for such a concern to use church facilities in seeking profits, while rejecting the union scale of wages. How "Christian," then, were the pants made by the A. Nash Company? A prominent Episcopalian clergyman, the Reverend William B. Spofford of the Church League for Industrial Democracy, entered the fray with an article in the *Christian Century* asking whether this "Golden Rule" business was not the bunk. The union's regular organizers also grew more active, and more of Nash's workers came to union rallies sponsored by Celestine Goddard and Jack Kroll. Now Mr. Nash was said to be growing uneasy.[11]

Through church workers friendly to organized labor, Hillman and Wolman were able, at length, to have a conference organized by the Federal Council of the Churches of Christ for the discussion of the "Golden Rule" Nash business. It was to be held at Olivet, Michigan, in August 1925, with Mr. Nash invited to speak for his plan, while Hillman, Dr. Wolman, and Miss Goddard represented the union's side.

Nash declined to appear but sent a close friend and business associate in his place. Earl Dean Howard, an old Christian Scientist, on his way to the conference, dropped in on him in Cincinnati and asked for information about his payroll. Nash now at last brought out his records. Howard said later: "I was astounded when I saw those payroll figures, for they were far below our own scale at Hart, Schaffner and Marx. That was the 'pay-off' on the Golden Rule." [12]

At the Olivet conference, the protests of liberal church leaders placed the champions of Mr. Nash on the defensive. Professor Wolman brought much specific knowledge to his analysis of the situation, but spoke in somewhat conciliatory terms of Nash's sincerity and good intentions. Hillman's vigorous speech, drawing the contrast between the definite moral and material benefits introduced by the Amalgamated system of industrial democracy and the dubious character of the "Golden Rule co-operative," received wide attention in the press. Reports of this conference in various church publications bore hard upon Arthur Nash.

Several weeks passed, and then Nash suddenly telephoned Professor Wolman and arranged to meet with him and the Amalgamated's president at a hotel in Washington in the last week of November.[13]

Hillman, with his economist, hastened to Washington to meet the great man. As he recalled it:

I came all prepared with a number of agreements. You know when I travel I have in my satchel the various kinds of agreements our organization will make. . . . Mentally I came with samples and I said: "It is very important for us to organize that shop and I must be quite sure not to get excited." . . . In our organization sometimes even the officers get excited.

"It is your move," Mr. Nash began. "What is it that you want? How shall we do it?" The manufacturer quite took Hillman's breath away when he said simply that he had resolved to have the whole body of his workers, now more than 3,000 in number, brought into the Amalgamated union. There was no bargaining, but only the request that Nash's people be given the best union-shop agreement available anywhere. Nash himself would serve as Hillman's "organizer"!

Hillman could scarcely contain his excitement. From dinnertime until two in the morning he was closeted with this strange character. The only problems he had were in convincing Mr. Nash that the Amalgamated Clothing Workers' Union was not an "irreligious" or "pagan" organization. Hillman gave the clearest assurances that the Nash workers would be organized into locals under officers of their own choosing and could pray or sing hymns as much as they liked.

What had happened was that Mr. Nash had undergone another of his famous conversions. One day not long before he had lectured at some large gathering of manufacturers on the theme of the Golden Rule and co-operation in industry. The audience had cheered him to the echo, and one of their officers said when he had finished: "I move that we go on record as recognizing this as the greatest scheme to lick unionism that we have ever heard of." That, Nash added, was the straw that broke the camel's back. He began to wonder, then, if the Amalgamated, if Hillman, were not right after all. Were not the labor unions trying but to do the job that "the Teacher had when He came into this world, and that is to give the people a larger life"?

It also happened that his business was now getting out of hand. While he wandered about lecturing before Rotary and Kiwanis clubs, some of his managers were turning out orders on their own in his shops. The quality of Nash clothing, too had been deteriorating.

When he revealed to associates that he had decided to turn the whole affair over to the Amalgamated, he was warned that the union's leader was a Jew. To which Mr. Nash answered bravely:

Our great idea has been the Golden Rule, and it was a Jew who propounded that too. . . . Let me tell you something, brethren, Sidney Hillman, to my mind, stands only second to the Carpenter of Galilee in his leadership of the people themselves.[14]

That night in Washington was like a revival meeting; Hillman had his difficulties in restraining Mr. Nash from giving his whole business away either to the workers or to the Amalgamated union. It needed all his tact, also, to dissuade this millionaire from seeking to become a member of the Amalgamated Clothing Workers. But as they wound up their discussion Hillman, too, rose to the heights of the spiritual drama in which they seemed called to play their parts, and exclaimed that this was no ordinary case of just another clothing factory being unionized.

Neither one of us can explain how this has happened, but we have waited until the attention of the world would be attracted to us, and it will be the greatest thing that has occurred in the labor movement for a long time to come when you go back to your people and not only ask them but urge them to come into the union.[15]

The next morning there was to be a sales conference of Nash Company people at a hotel in Washington, and Nash asked Hillman to join them. Hillman accepted the invitation and sat beside Mr. Nash at the banquet table—when a photographer suddenly appeared and took a flashlight picture of the proceedings. Hillman was taken aback, thinking it might be a trap; he could have refused to appear in the picture. But he composed himself almost instantaneously, deciding that he would gamble on it.

Mr. Nash said afterward that he had realized what was passing through Hillman's mind, and that this exhibition of trust on Hillman's part confirmed his own decision to go along with the Amalgamated.[16]

A week later Hillman, with his retinue of production experts, economists, lawyers, and publicity men, proceeded to Cincinnati, arriving there on the morning of December 9. News of Nash's plan, kept secret up to now, had leaked out, he found. A meeting of all Nash employees was scheduled for the day after his arrival, at the Schubert Theatre in Cincinnati, and Hillman had reason to fear that their vote might well go against Mr. Nash's proposal. The foremen and managerial personnel had been going through the shops telling the people that Mr. Nash had "gone out of his head" and that all that they had gained might be lost to the union people from New York. Executives of the company seemed bent on stopping Nash or ousting him.

That night Hillman held a conference with his staff of Amalgamated officers. The whole affair looked bad. They were entirely at Nash's mercy. "We are in his hands," he agreed soberly.

Kroll had reported earlier that the workers would come over to the union only if Nash told them to. "If he fails us," Kroll said, "if he 'double-crosses' us tomorrow morning, this will be a terrible black eye for the whole labor movement. And remember, he has that picture of you sitting in at the sales banquet with him."

Hillman answered hopefully: "He will be with us!" [17]

The meeting at the Schubert Theatre the next day began with prayers and hymn singing by the great throng of workers. Then Nash presented Hillman as virtually a prophet from Israel. Hillman took his cue from the tone of the proceedings; he spoke of the larger, spiritual life which the union had brought to the downtrodden needleworkers, of their sense of brotherhood and their long "crusade."

The audience listened intently, silently, but quite evidently without sympathy for Mr. Hillman, who was given only a ripple of applause. They were "cold." Many faced him with placards in their hands bearing the words: *"Don't Give up the Golden Rule!"*

The executive vice-president of the Nash Company, then Mr. E. T. Clayton, addressed the meeting, attacking the whole plan of unionizing the company's workers with the greatest vehemence and charging that Mr. Nash was being duped. The Amalgamated, he shouted, would wreck "this great ship, manned by the crew of love, friendship, toleration, and co-operation." His appeal to the workers to vote "No!" was received with the greatest ovation of the meeting. Hillman and his friends resigned themselves to defeat.

Arthur Nash then took the chair again. No one knew what would follow now; but, as Hillman acknowledged later, he was a man who practiced what he preached. His manner was tenderly paternal as he appealed to his "dear brothers and sisters" to lay all their doubts or questions before him that he might meet them fully and fairly. Some asked: why bother with the union when all was going well? But here was no question of money; the Nash people must no longer "build a wall around themselves," while ignoring the great army of toilers who called them to take their place at the head of the procession. One worker objected that the Amalgamated was "radical"; but had not Christ been considered "radical" too? Another member in the audience recalled that an Amalgamated organizer had once punched him in the nose, to which Mr. Nash replied: "What does our Great Teacher say? 'Love your enemies! Do good to them that despitefully use you.' "

The whole tone of the meeting changed miraculously. None could resist the persuasive powers of Mr. Nash, the new convert to unionism. When at the end of the meeting Hillman answered satisfactorily various questions put to him by Vice-President Clayton, he too withdrew his objections, and the vote swung in favor of joining the Amalgamated.[18]

At one stroke, 3,000 workers who had known nothing of trade unions passed into the Amalgamated system. Mr. Nash's moral power had prevailed where Sidney Hillman felt his own best efforts might have been in vain. The head of the concern thereafter proved to be loyal to the very letter of his bargain. He was certainly, in some measure, a mystic who lived in his own world of illusion or fantasy, believing that by his own efforts he could move great numbers to do that which was right. And yet with his religious mysticism was mixed a native shrewdness in affairs.

In his own artless, rambling confessions he said later that he knew, in December 1925, that his mushrooming factories were getting into poor condition.

I knew that without a guiding hand that was vitally interested . . . that that thing could not last very long. I had a job that I could not do and I just passed the buck to Mr. Hillman. I unionized them because I could not sleep at nights, because I was afraid that things were not right in my industry, with my brothers and sisters that were working there, and I did not know how to make them right, and I felt that Mr. Hillman and his organization could do it. . . .[19]

Meanwhile the Amalgamated organizing staff had moved into the Nash shops at once to create locals overnight, to hold meetings under union auspices, and educate the people to play their part in the union. As Hillman said, this in itself was an inspiring adventure. The Amalgamated's technical experts also came in to reorganize production routines in the Nash shops. Within a year, earnings of the workers were increased by 25 per cent and prices for the Nash suits were actually reduced. Other employers in Cincinnati hastened to re-examine their position, and most of them also permitted their shops to be unionized.

Two years later Arthur Nash was dead, and Hillman paid sincere tribute to him as one who was truly loved by his workers. As one commentator wrote, "There was never anyone exactly like Arthur Nash." [20] "Golden Rule" Nash had won wide credit for having created one of America's outstanding company unions. That he should have handed it over without a contest to the Amalgamated Clothing Workers was one of the sensations of the day. Hillman himself remarked that it was one of those rare instances where a strongly anti-union position was conquered by "the power of ideas and ideals." Secretary Schlossberg declared that this victory, coupled with that over the International Tailoring Company, helped to save the union from those who had been fomenting dissension within it.

III

Hillman promptly grasped the advantage of the moment to press on with sweeping reforms of the union's New York organization. The separate craft divisions were now merged into one unit, the New York Joint Board, to which the others were subordinate. Abraham Beckerman, business agent of the cutters' local, and at that time a member of the New York Board of Aldermen, was named as manager of the Joint Board, while Abraham Miller, chief of the pants makers and a loyal Hillman supporter, was named secretary-treasurer. The selection of Beckerman was expected to help patch up local quarrels and end the well-known bitterness between the cutters and tailors.[21] He was then considered an intelligent and ambitious union leader, and at the time Hillman thought the choice a good one.

New agreements were drawn up between the union and the New York Clothing Manufacturers' Exchange in the spring of 1926; the city market was now brought into line with piecework standards established elsewhere. Finally the agreement provided, as earlier in Chicago, for an unemployment insurance fund to be started in 1928, based on weekly payments of 3 per cent of payroll, shared equally by management and labor. Thus prospects for the New York clothing workers seemed brighter than in many years. Yet from now on a new element of trouble showed itself in the steady migration of many manufacturers from the strict union regime in New York to the open-shop "paradise" of nearby Philadelphia. This out-of-town movement was at first a small dark cloud on the horizon; but by 1928 the Philadelphia region sheltered the third largest clothing market in the country, made up of determinedly anti-union employers. At no time could the Amalgamated officers feel that their job was done. No sooner did they put out a fire in Cincinnati or Chicago than they had to rush off and put out a still bigger one in Philadelphia.

In the City of Brotherly Love municipal authorities, court, and police had combined to repel labor organization. Only the AFL building workers and a few other groups had been able to maintain their unions there during the early 1920's. The Amalgamated organizers who had been driven from the city in repeated campaigns called it "the graveyard of unionism." There had been a flourishing community of 3,000 members of the ACWA in 1920, but by 1928 their numbers had dwindled to 700.

Not only did large non-union houses flourish in the city itself, but in the country towns surrounding it numerous small contractors had set up shop and worked at low cost for New York and Philadelphia wholesalers. When Hillman, during that period, insisted upon wage scales that New York or even Chicago employers considered too stiff, they would counter with: "Well, then, we will move to Philadelphia."

That great city, only two hours from New York, now offered the most serious threat to the future of the union. Hillman said that the 15,000 men's clothing workers there were drifting into a state of peonage. The struggle to organize Philadelphia must be renewed.

At the spring meeting of the General Executive Board in 1928 a new and more ambitious "Philadelphia Plan" was brought up and discussed at great length. The mistakes of the past were analyzed, and new modes of attack were devised. Hyman Blumberg, the union's crafty tactician, was selected by Hillman to take charge of the proposed Philadelphia campaign. In undertaking this assignment Blumberg spoke in sober terms of the difficulties before them, and gave promise of no speedy results. With the aid of a corrupt and reactionary Republican political machine, an "anti-union stone wall" had been built around Philadelphia which somehow had to be breached. According to his first estimates, the preparatory work would take two years at least.[22]

In June, Blumberg slipped over to Philadelphia and set up a staff of experienced assistants. For the next seven or eight months he worked with them, as if underground; for the program that had been mapped out required that real union support be built up, without noise or fireworks, before the enemy awoke to the danger. Repeated failures of the union had lulled employers here into a sense of security, which Blumberg and Hillman found at the start was one of the few advantages in their favor.

At this stage no attempt was made to gather recruits indiscriminately. On June 29, 1928, Hillman went to Philadelphia to address a first union rally to which mainly key workers had been invited. He told his picked audience how much less they earned than members of the union in other cities, and exhorted them not to be "timid" in the fight.[23]

A few days later, in July, a trial balloon was sent up when one of the smaller manufacturing firms was struck; several days later a second and a third firm were singled out. In one case the sixty men involved went back quickly as the result of a compromise agreement. In the others the people, following careful orders, returned to work after a short walkout without gain. These were the first skirmishes made in order to feel out the situation.

The local manufacturers had their trade association. But how strong, how united were they? The fact that one or two small firms signed union agreements that summer raised some doubts on this score. After a "deliberate feint at an organization campaign" in the summer and fall season of 1928, the union, as if discouraged, called off its action.[24]

It seemed like one more abortive effort. But Blumberg soon pushed forward the work of organizing more people in the field. Huge files with the names and addresses of clothing workers in Philadelphia were steadily collected day by day through various innocent-seeming activities, such as charity drives or lotteries staged to help some neighborhood church—the money raised being turned over to the churches, the lists of workers being retained and classified at the union's office. Even the names of many foremen were obtained by these or other ruses. Finally some of the union's most skillful organizers from Chicago and New York were brought in to carry on the missionary work by calling at the homes of thousands of workers night after night and enlightening them as to the character of the union and its program. By the end of 1928, thousands of pledge cards were being signed in secret. At this point Blumberg reviewed results thus far with Hillman and laid plans for a large-scale attack in the 1929 season.

The plan of campaign, as fixed in conferences held in February 1929, was quite different from other operations and, above all, sought to avoid

the terrible mistake of calling a general strike in Philadelphia. . . . The new tactics did not call for the distribution of circulars, mass meetings, and publicity. . . . The strategy in the present campaign was to conduct strikes against single firms.[25]

There were times when the men running the campaign felt profoundly discouraged by the baffling difficulties of their task. In this sprawling city of three million, the workers often seemed to slip from their hands, disheartened by many previous failures of the union and knowing that to be seen with union people meant the loss of their livelihood. Moreover, all but one or two of the small test strikes in 1928 had been lost. Blumberg was determined to build up confidence in the union's power and saw to it that every man and woman who had been discharged for having walked out was helped to find a job elsewhere. To reach the mass of Philadelphia workers, Hillman said, "every officer, every organizer that could be spared was drafted." A war chest of about one million dollars was accumulated for the campaign and replenished by periodic assessments on the Amalgamated members.[26]

In the late winter of 1929, Hillman himself went to Philadelphia and took charge of operations there, setting up his headquarters at the Sylvania Hotel.

The slogan Hillman set for the 1929 "drive" in Philadelphia was: "Keep out of the limelight." Charles W. Ervin, who did publicity work for the union, was told to see to it that nothing was printed about current activities in Philadelphia. Two of the Amalgamated's ablest Chicago organizers, Charles Weinstein and Michael Di Novi, were brought to Philadelphia to act as Hillman's chief aides. Other Amalgamated veterans arrived from points all around the country, men who spoke Italian, Polish, and other languages. During May and June they were working in squads under Charles Weinstein, shunning the factories, but combing the districts where the workers lived. Hillman, for his part, remained in seclusion in his hotel; yet his presence was known and aroused speculation. At times he suspected that his telephone wire was being tapped and avoided using it, sending out his communications by courier.

One of the first measures Hillman took after his arrival in Philadelphia was to engage as the Amalgamated's counsel the head of one of Philadelphia's largest and most influential law firms—whose partner, as it happened, was then serving as Commissioner of Public Safety, as the police department of that city is called.

Hitherto, in cases of strikes, there had been the most successful teamwork among the employers, the courts that issued drastic labor injunctions at top speed, and the police who enforced these orders.

By early June, at the start of the rush season, the men in the field were ready. Two houses, the Navytone and Goodimate companies, whose key workers had been carefully groomed for their assignments, were selected for strike action, and their people came out solidly. Only 200 workers were involved in each case; but their employers were taken by surprise and seemed not to be in condition to face a long struggle. The pickets were out in force, kept good order, and were not molested by the Philadelphia police. Within three weeks these firms surrendered and signed a union agreement granting recognition and wage increases. Then the Amalgamated production experts came down and helped get the plants running again in jigtime, which made an excellent impression.

Next, the campaign managers struck at a larger firm that was believed vulnerable, kept the action going in highly professional style, and won a very favorable settlement for 500 strikers early in July. Some initial alarm was now felt in Philadelphia clothing circles at signs of a union revival; but Hillman ostentatiously left town at the end of June, telling Charles Ervin to see to it that this was made known, while spreading reports through the newspapers that the union had no intention of proceeding any further with organizing work at present. A few weeks later, at the end of July, he slipped back to Philadelphia again, still keeping himself closely hidden. The pace was being stepped up.

Attacks on the big factories had been reserved for the peak of the summer season. One of these, Daroff and Sons, employing 800 persons, was chosen for strike treatment in August. A well-managed firm it was, and its owner maintained very friendly relations with his seasoned mechanics, whom, as a matter of fact, he had invited to a "get-together" dinner on the Saturday night before the strike was to be called. That night they were all "one happy family," and some of the old hands presented gifts to Mr. Daroff. Nevertheless, on August 1, 1929, they all streamed out of his shops at the given signal, while Daroff looked on in amazement, tearfully exclaiming to some of the workers: "For fifteen years I paid you good wages and now you are leaving me!" [27]

Hillman made no effort to hit the important competitors of Daroff, who, having been "tipped off" that the union would not move against them until Daroff had signed up, hastened to take over Daroff's orders.

Hillman, now working in the open, seemed to be everywhere during that strike. He had seemed weary or ill recently, yet once more, as the industrial warfare broadened, he had the light of battle in his eye. He spoke often at union rallies and gave courage to everyone.

Walk the picket lines smiling. . . . Don't let anything provoke you. Observe the law strictly because that is what the employers don't want you to do. Remember this is a free country. . . . This market is going to be a union market and no longer a menace to good workers in other centers.[28]

One of his happy expressions, struck off at the spur of the moment during a strike rally, was: "Our strikes now are *battles to end strikes*. And we will wage them until we accomplish this high purpose." The Philadelphia campaign became known as the "strike to end strikes."

Now the movement was expanding, swiftly, irresistibly. Small or medium-sized firms were being picked off one by one in this large guerrilla warfare. In such crowd movements, human emotions become contagious and work toward a climax. As Hillman came back to speak day after day in the main union hall, the auditorium of the Labor Institute, droves of new workers kept crowding in, announcing amid wild applause, that they too were out on strike. "They seem to be always coming, I don't know where they are coming from," Hillman cried exultantly. "But I know where they are going!"

In back of the Labor Institute's auditorium were conference rooms where Hillman worked day and night with the union's lawyers, strike committees, and representatives of the manufacturers to negotiate settlements. As in similar contests, he shrewdly played the anti-union manufacturers off against one another. Daroff, for example, was losing business to his rivals. After making the gesture of securing a court injunction, this strong manufacturer suddenly capitulated and, like others, came to the conference room at the Labor Institute to see Hillman. This was in the afternoon of August 28, after a fight of four weeks' duration. The discussion of terms lasted for twenty hours, until Hillman was almost drunk with fatigue. Outside the conference room there was a crowd of two thousand in the auditorium, many of them Daroff's workers, in a continual uproar as files of new recruits kept marching in to join them. Hillman came out of the conference room toward noon the next day, pale, with bloodshot eyes, but smiling nonetheless. He stood before them so tired that he could barely raise his voice above the long cheers that greeted him, and simply held aloft the papers in his hand, the copy of the signed agreement with Daroff and Sons.[29]

The remaining clothing workers in Philadelphia now seemed to be on edge; as Charles Weinstein reported, it was growing hard to keep these men and women from all walking out at once, instead of timing their action against individual firms, according to the union's strategy. It was then that Hillman, sensing this fever for action, suddenly made the decision to delay no more the attack against the group of big clothing firms that had not yet come to terms, and take them all on at once.

The iron was hot. The workers who had won their strikes would call out others, then go back to their jobs and donate part of their wages to those who replaced them on the picket lines. For they were swept by a wave of hope and confidence in the union and saw that its leaders had the winning spirit.*

* In those days the American workers were very much "on the fence," as Professor Selig Perlman wrote at the time, as if trying to guess whether the employer or the labor union had more to offer them.

Late in August a strike was called against one of the largest clothing plants in Philadelphia, that of the Middishade company. Its management, very determined and resourceful, brought in numerous strikebreakers and prepared to throw everything in the book at the union. What was more, a group of the fourteen biggest manufacturers, employing some 10,000 workers, including those at Middishade, banded themselves together in a firmly knit association for mutual defense against the union. This time they vowed not to accept orders for goods in competition with each other, raised large funds and, under legal advice, imposed on their workers a common "yellow-dog" contract by which each employee pledged that he was not and would not become a member of the Amalgamated union, and would not aid in its unionizing work, on pain of being discharged. They also petitioned for a court injunction restraining the officers and members of the union from all strike activity.

The all-out stage of the battle was reached in September, when several other big firms were struck. Hillman concentrated his fire on the Middishade company, a leader in the strengthened clothiers' association.

The purpose of a strike is to cut off the employer's business. When such a result was not easily obtained by picketing, as in this case, Hillman bethought himself of other expedients. In Chicago, as he knew, one of the largest retail merchants in the country regularly bought from Middishade consignments of clothing valued at a million dollars annually. This man had in the past shown a genuine admiration for Sidney Hillman and had acknowledged that the Amalgamated was "different" from other unions. Hillman now got in touch with him by long-distance telephone and arranged to meet him privately in New York a few days later to discuss the Philadelphia strike situation, which was, of course, a serious inconvenience to his business.

The Middishade owners had hardly ever seen this merchant and were accustomed to dealing with him only through his subordinates. They were therefore astonished when he walked into their office one morning in September and asked whether his orders would be filled promptly. They were still more astonished when he firmly advised them to yield and do business with Mr. Hillman or he would transfer his orders elsewhere. This broke their backs and they began to sue for peace on September 16.

The victory over the strong Middishade company was largely due to Hillman's individual efforts along the lines of business strategy. This coup was made all the more effective through being combined with other actions carried on simultaneously. There were continued demonstrations of the Philadelphia tailors (by now well schooled by their hard-working organizers), who were infuriated by the "yellow-dog" contract which seemed to deny them elementary rights as American citizens and, as one newspaper commented, "played right into the union's hands." The workers had come to believe that their employers were "frightened and desperate," and that the union held the upper hand and the end was drawing near.[30]

But the other manufacturers fought back. On September 10, 1929, a few days before the Chicago merchant talked so persuasively to the Middishade management, a great blow had been struck at the union when Judge W. H. Kirkpatrick of Federal District Court in Pennsylvania issued a temporary injunction as drastic as any court order ever known before. It restrained all officers and members of the Amalgamated Clothing Workers, on the ground of "conspiracy," from interfering with the production and shipment of clothing, from picketing, from visiting workmen at their homes, or from using any union moneys or property for strike expense or relief. At once summons servers were out hunting for Sidney Hillman, Hyman Blumberg, and all the other union officers.

Hillman had been working under extreme tension, as always in such struggles. At times he had been forced to remain in hiding for days on end, going out only at night, and with an escort. His associates thought it was dangerous for him to walk the streets unguarded because of the recent appearance of known hoodlums and gangsters among the strikebreaking forces.

Just at the moment when he was to attend hearings for the injunction suit before Judge Kirkpatrick he fell sick, was hospitalized, and underwent a minor operation. His illness was kept secret for "reasons of state." His friends and union associates watched gravely at the door of his sickroom, wondering if he would be able to carry on through the climax of the battle.

"Within two hours after President Hillman came out of the ether he was holding a staff meeting of organizers in his hospital room. . . . In a few days he was up and about, addressing meetings of the strikers." [31]

When the injunction was issued, the Amalgamated's Philadelphia law firm withdrew as counsel, since one of its partners, as civilian head of the police department, would now be obliged to take action against the union's officers. Up to then the Philadelphia police had not been unfriendly, as the Amalgamated leaders recall. Another Philadelphia firm was called into service, and Maxwell Brandwen of the union's regular New York law firm hurried to the scene to help in the defense.

Just before he fell ill Hillman had planned the measures to be taken against the injunction. Charles Ervin was dispatched to Washington, where he saw Senators Robert M. La Follette, Jr., and William E. Borah, and laid before them the order of Judge Kirkpatrick. The two senators were shocked at its terms. The younger La Follette, with Borah's support, on September 16, 1929, introduced a Senate resolution to investigate the "feudal" injunction issued by the Pennsylvania Federal District Court, a resolution which met with no opposition from even the most conservative quarters in the Senate. The newspapers of New York and Philadelphia, which had been following the strike and the recent injunction case with great interest of late, featured the La Follette resolution on their front pages.

When Maxwell Brandwen, the next day, rode out to see Judge Kirkpatrick at his home in Easton, the jurist seemed greatly taken aback at the Senate resolution that had been aimed at him. He agreed to consider the union's petition for modification of the terms of his restraining order—which in fact he granted a few days later, permitting the strikes to continue.

In any case, the fact that the Middishade company had finally decided to come to terms with the union had broken the ranks of the manufacturers' association. Several other large firms also gave way quickly, and 2,500 more members were taken into the union overnight, while resistance seemed to collapse everywhere. The Amalgamated had conquered about half of the "anti-union citadel," and the rest was only a mopping-up job for the aggressive Charles Weinstein. This able young officer emerged as one of the heroes of that whirlwind campaign and was chosen by Hillman to head the Philadelphia Joint Board, which soon included some 20,000 men's clothing workers.

At the end of the contest Hillman dealt with the manufacturers in a most conciliatory spirit, vowing that their prosperity was the concern of the entire union. At the same time he sagely warned the strike-happy union members that they, for their part, must show self-restraint; they "must not expect to get everything at once." He added an appeal for patience and discipline: "As human beings you will have differences. Never allow these to interfere with the building up of a great organization." [32]

The Philadelphia organization of the Amalgamated, under the vigorous leadership of Charles Weinstein, soon became one of the strongest pillars of the union's structure—in a city which had once been a haven of sweatshops. As Hillman said at the time, "If we could break through Philadelphia there is not a market in the whole country where we cannot obtain union conditions."

This spectacular labor victory came at a time when the rest of the American trade-union movement seemed to be in the doldrums. The "dynamic" methods of the Amalgamated leadership, based always on elaborate preparation and planning, were observed with intense interest in labor circles, and their pattern was to be followed in great measure during the "labor renascence" of the 1930's. The cleanup of Philadelphia came, as Hillman said, in the nick of time, for even as they reached the climax of the unionizing drive, in October 1929, a tremendous crash engulfed the financial markets of Wall Street, foreshadowing depression in business and the end of the so-called New Era. An unorganized Philadelphia clothing trade, in the years of mass unemployment that followed, would have been given over to an orgy of wage cutting and price slashing.

Chapter Thirteen

AN AMERICAN
"FABIAN"

*It is the party that has the power to create a new
condition in industrial or political relations that is, in
an important sense, progressive.*
> —Sidney Hillman, *Labor Attitudes*

In the spring of 1927, Hillman had turned forty. He had
reached the years of discretion, of success, of considerable fame. The Amalgamated Clothing Workers' Union was also
mature; entrenched as a "partner" in its industry, it ranked easily as
one of America's most powerful industrial unions and was regarded
by labor, as one leading newspaper remarked, "as a model for working conditions and efficiency." [1]

During the New Era of Prosperity its labor action was essentially
defensive or "corrective," as contrasted with the strenuous years
of expansion in 1914 to 1919. Only from time to time was the
union obliged to turn and crush some individual clothing manufacturer who tried to challenge its power, as in Rock Island, Illinois, or
Vineland, New Jersey. For the most part its progress seemed as
orderly as those regular meetings before impartial trade boards administering the joint government of its industry. The Amalgamated,
in short, had become "institutionalized," and at times almost seemed
to run itself under its experienced officers, like some of the long-
established trade unions in England.

"Soon there will be nothing for me to do!" Hillman would say to his chief aide, Potofsky, during the more peaceful intervals in the 1920's. A picture of Hillman's working day, with "nothing to do," has been drawn for us by Beatrice Bisno, who was his secretary during the 1920's.

Very often he would come to his office in Union Square at eight-thirty in the morning, before the clerks and secretaries on his floor arrived. This might be when he had stepped off a night train arriving in New York at an early hour. A knot of people would usually have congregated in the corridors of the Amalgamated headquarters, waiting to see "the boss." Miss Bisno, coming in at nine, would inform them that the president was out of town. Oh no, they had "heard in the streets" that he was back, which proved to be true. His secretary, after having exchanged greetings with him, would recall that there were many matters needing his attention.

. . . He says yes, he must get at them, and reminds her that Napoleon solved the problem of correspondence by locking up his unanswered mail for a period of two weeks, during which time it invariably answered itself.

The president then asked for news of the New York situation, and arranged to have a meeting with his trade managers that day, as he thought he might have to leave at night for Montreal. He had his home called on the telephone, saying: "I haven't been home for so long, I want to see if it is still there."

His secretary told him that a committee from the knee-pants makers' local insisted on seeing him. Glancing through his mail, he separated the important from the routine matters and received the committee for all of two minutes. They came out smiling, having won a promise that he would speak before their people in a few days *if* he were in town then. A woman with two children arrived and asked to see the president about her husband's having been discharged. She would not be refused, and so he had her come in for five minutes before sending her along where she should have gone in the first place, to the Joint Board. She left his office beaming. "The president is a fine man—if the business agents were only like him! . . ."

A clothing manufacturer arrived in town from Rochester and telephoned for an appointment. The matter seemed urgent and a meeting was arranged for lunch time. The trade managers had come meanwhile, and the president had asked not to be disturbed during the meeting. But while he was closeted with them a newspaper reporter dropped in to interview the president on unemployment insurance. The secretary, though remembering the president's admonition not to disturb him, knocked boldly at his door.

He emerges, apologizing to the group inside, and talks for five minutes with the press, then returns. The telephone rings all the time; people who must speak to the president *personally* are told they must call later in the day. The trade managers leave at last and the president asks for a little lunch to be brought to his room, but is reminded that he has an appointment for lunch. He looks at his watch and asks to have his home called again, saying to his wife that if he does not go to Montreal that night she is to come downtown to have dinner with him and go to a theater. He goes out to lunch, then to a directors' meeting at the Amalgamated Bank downstairs. A big fur manufacturer, after having telephoned for an appointment, arrives at the hour fixed, 3:30, and waits, with an injured expression on his face, until nearly 4. The secretary calls the president and he hastens back. Three other gentlemen wait while he talks with the fur manufacturer. It is 5 P.M., and Montreal calls, saying they will call again before his train is to leave that night at 7:45 P.M. At last he leaves with Bessie Hillman for dinner, when the union's lawyer, Max Lowenthal, calls and says he must come back to the office to sign some papers before his departure that evening. The president returns from dinner, signs some papers, chats with the lawyers, then learns by long-distance from Montreal at 7:15 that his meeting there is postponed. With ill-concealed delight the president rises, puts on his coat and hat, and leaves with his wife. They are going to the theater.[2]

That was the end of a "quiet" day.

Another contemporary description of him (in 1926) shows him being called on the telephone five times within a half hour regarding a small strike somewhere out of town. He would give his orders calmly: "I would have held them for a couple of days. But the strike is on now, so there is no use fussing about that. X will be down tonight; meanwhile you should see Y——" Then he would return at once to the point where he had stopped in his talk with the newspaper reporter before him. Normally he managed to carry on two or three different trains of thought without confusion or fuss.[3]

The Amalgamated was by now like a large corporate institution engaged in a variety of co-operative and financial undertakings for the benefit of its members. Employment exchange bureaus were being administered; unemployment insurance funds requiring collection, investment, and repayment of millions of dollars were in operation. The union's two banks were growing rapidly. Its charitable donations to other unions and social welfare groups, amounting often to more than $100,000 a year, required supervision. (In the two-year period of 1928 and 1929 loans to labor unions totaled $370,000.) Moreover, its educational work was being expanded under J. B. S. Hardman, and publications were being issued, several of them weekly, in English, Yiddish, Italian, Polish, French, Lithuanian, and Bohemian.*

Yet, as if all this were not enough, Hillman announced at the time of the May 1926 convention:

> We are just beginning in the co-operative line. We have initiated a movement in banking. We hope to initiate one in co-operative housing . . . and show the way along all lines of co-operative endeavor.

A severe shortage of housing had been experienced after World War I in our large cities, particularly New York. Despite the building boom of the 1920's, nothing had been done to relieve the slum conditions of the East Side, where most of the needle-trade workers then lived. Conditions here were admitted to be evil, but it was said at the time that nothing could be done about them. When Hillman's brief report on a housing project was made he and various assistants had already been hard at work for six months seeing to it that something would be done.

Many of the union's members had come to live in congested sections of Manhattan's East Side because this had formerly been within walking distance of most of the clothing shops in the city. But now, with higher wages and shorter hours, they could afford carfare and the time to travel some distance over New York's subway system. The underlying idea was to start moving as many of these people as possible out of the slums to less congested uptown areas. Further stimulus to the project came from recently enacted laws providing tax exemption and other privileges for workers' low-cost housing.

In the northern Bronx, adjacent to Van Cortlandt Park and

* The Americanization of the Amalgamated Clothing Workers in the course of about three decades, President Potofsky has pointed out, is well reflected in the fact that the union's newspaper, once printed in seven languages, is now issued only in English, as the overwhelming majority of the members read no other language.

Mosholu Parkway and fronting the Jerome Park Reservoir, a plot of land embracing 42 lots, 25 by 110 feet each, was purchased. The site was attractive also because it could be conveniently reached by two north-south subway lines. To purchase the land and construct the buildings planned for it a special subsidiary, named the ACW Corporation, was formed as a limited dividend corporation. The plan called for building several blocks of co-operative apartments having about 1,000 rooms and giving on common enclosed gardens, with the dwelling space covering only 50 per cent of the land. The tenants were to be co-operative tenant-owners who were to buy an equity in the property through monthly payments, and were to benefit by low-interest cost on mortgages as well as low upkeep and tax remission.

There had been hitherto some small, ill-starred ventures in workers' housing, but nothing as yet on the scale now projected, involving at first 300 to 500 families and an initial investment of more than $1,800,000. Hillman's first question in such a venture was: "How are we going to do it?" To determine this he sought expert advice, with the result that the basic plan incorporated the best architectural thought available then in the field of public or co-operative housing. A number of philanthropic New Yorkers prominent in banking, building, and the legal profession, including Herbert Lehman and Robert Szold, contributed technical, financial, and legal assistance.

Hillman decided at the start that he wanted a man from the union's own ranks to oversee the whole job. He chose Abraham E. Kazan, who had had experience with credit unions, and said to him: "You go ahead and learn this new job." Before many months had passed Kazan became a building expert and personally supervised the execution of contracts for excavation, masonry, plastering, and plumbing amounting to $1,500,000.

The proposed tenant-owners were asked to pay for 50 percent of the equity of $500 per room in cash, in order to take advantage of provisions in the law offering more favorable arrangements under such conditions. Since few of them could provide so much money on the spot, various financial devices were used to lend them money for this purpose through the Amalgamated Banks, on security furnished by subsidiaries and credit unions in the Amalgamated system. In addition to this, the Daily Forward Association advanced a loan of $250,000. Thus about a third of the needed funds, $479,000, was provided in time, and construction went forward rapidly, until it was possible to secure a permanent first-mortgage loan from the Metropolitan Life Insurance Company for $1,200,000 to replace the temporary building loans. By holding costs down, by eliminating all commissions for agents, and by obtaining sound workmanship and good materials, the whole project came to only $1,825,000 and permitted a "rental" of $11 monthly per room for apartments completely modern in construction, provided with public rooms, handsome gardens and playgrounds, and full of space and sunlight. Comparable dwelling space then cost $25 to $30 per room in monthly rent, without any of the extra features.

After two years, Hillman, appearing before his union's convention in May 1928, was able to report that labor co-operative housing "was an accomplished fact and not a theory." Members of the union and their families, scarcely able to believe their eyes, were now moving into the first of 303 completed apartments. The initial results appeared so encouraging, Hillman reported, that plans were already laid for the construction of dwelling space for 200 more families upon adjacent land. He spoke with immense pride as he described the blocks of modern buildings, with their neighboring parklands, gardens, and views of the reservoir before them. "To describe the apartments is almost impossible. One has to see them to realize what has been accomplished."

This was but a beginning at labor housing; only a few hundred families were enabled in 1928 to pass from the East Side slums to this "workers' paradise," as the tailors called it. These apartments represented a construction and dwelling standard superior to that of another contemporary low-cost housing development that had been built by one of the greatest insurance companies at Sunnyside, Queens.

With accumulated experience a new and larger project, Amalgamated Dwellings, Incorporated, was initiated two years later. A solid block of dilapidated tenements on Grand Street, in the heart of the lower East Side, had been purchased and demolished. Under the direction of Mr. Kazan, construction was begun on a group of six-story apartments with full modern equipment and a fair amount of garden space. This enterprise had been originally sponsored by two philanthropists, Herbert Lehman, then lieutenant governor of New

York, and Aaron Rabinowitz, who had decided to turn over their project to the efficient Amalgamated management. In April 1931, Amalgamated Dwellings, Incorporated, was awarded the citation of the American Institute of Architecture for sound city housing construction combining the most desirable light, space, and living conditions with pleasing aesthetic qualities.

These two co-operative developments and Hillman Housing, erected later, eventually provided low-cost residence for a total of 2,536 families, and represented an investment aggregating $20,000,000. As "pilot" enterprises they had the effect of inspiring many other such ventures. The original projects of 1928 included provisions for various community services, such as co-operative stores. Over and above this, under the guidance of tenant committees and educational directors, there was created a neighborly bond, a close community relationship among the "co-operators," which is seldom known in the life of our great cities. These co-owners developed pride in their dwelling projects and responsibility in their maintenance, as A. E. Kazan has related, tending to make them "more independent and self-respecting citizens . . . and even better members of the general community outside. . . ." [4]

At the ground-breaking ceremony for the second group of co-operative apartments, Hillman said:

The [banishment] of human misery for the great mass of the people, and the creation of a rich life for every person is not to be accomplished by the altruism of a few, but by the mass of the people, by the organized power of their numbers to do what each cannot do alone. [5]

II

As early as 1925 Sidney Hillman's growing reputation as a constructive labor leader led to his being invited to address the Academy of Political Science at its annual meeting in New York, March 9, 1925. The Academy, then as now, was an exceedingly conservative body, including in its membership many bankers and industrialists who were believed to embody wealth and learning combined. Nevertheless, the subject chosen for one of the day's sessions was the labor movement in America; besides Hillman, President William F. Green of the AFL and two other AFL officers were invited to speak. Mr. Green, who had continued the late Sam Gompers' feud with the Amalgamated union, chose to wire his indignant refusal of the invitation, indicating that under no circumstances would he appear on the same platform with the leader of a "dual union" which had successfully opposed the AFL. His two AFL associates also refused on similar grounds. Nevertheless, the invitation to Hillman was not withdrawn and he appeared in New York as scheduled to speak on the theme of labor banking.

In December 1928, the Harmon Foundation, a liberal businessmen's body, awarded Sidney Hillman its gold medal and a prize of $1,000 for "outstanding public service in the year 1927" in pioneering the unemployment insurance plan and the enterprises in labor banking and co-operative housing.

He was so often described in the newspapers as a "labor statesman" in those days that the phrase became all too familiar. A writer in one New York daily in 1924 ranked him with Sam Gompers and Warren S. Stone (who were twice his age) as one of labor's three outstanding figures, but accorded Hillman "more social vision" than the others.[6] While the other American labor leaders seemed old and tired nowadays, said another, Sidney Hillman "combined the fire and faith of youth with the practical sagacity . . . of mature years."[7] A publication issued by the National City Bank expressed high approval of the Amalgamated banking experiment, and noted that Mr. Hillman gave no more thought to "violent revolution or change." A Hartford insurance magnate praised the union's housing ventures; while a famous Catholic social worker, Father Francis J. Haas, extolled its pioneering in unemployment insurance.[8] At the other side of the country, the San Francisco *Post* applauded his opposition to communism and his exertions for industrial peace; while at the Antipodes, the *Argus* of Melbourne, Australia, published similar words of praise. In New York, Louis Marshall, a millionaire lawyer, speaking at a manufacturers' banquet, called Sidney Hillman a man of "sweet reasonableness and marvelous tact." In London, H. N. Brailsford, internationally famous Socialist author, eulogized Hillman's strategy in leading the organized workers toward a share in management while maintaining his union's vitality and will to fight when occasion warranted.[9]

More and more often nowadays he spoke before gatherings of churchmen, social workers, and even business associations. It became important for him to set forth his ideas and theories in an effective way before audiences of strangers, something he had done hitherto only on the spur of the moment, or before friendly gatherings of his own union. But he had had no formal education in this country save for a few months of night school; his English syntax was uncertain at best, his foreign accent still very marked, and he was extremely sensitive on this point.

In preparing a public speech he often drew upon the help of his friends and staff assistants at the Amalgamated, such as Leo Wolman and Charles W. Ervin, or sometimes Dr. Horace Kallen of the New School for Social Research. These assistants corrected his English, rearranging his sentences and adding punctuation. But the ideas were his own—hammered into words and phrases by him with intense effort—as he dictated hour after hour with tortured nerves. After his editorial advisors were done, he would go over his proposed speech or article again and again, pondering the possibility of error or misrepresentation underlying each word or phrase. He seemed at such times almost in agony as he struggled for the exact expression or phrase with which to communicate his own distinctive thought. Once the process was carried through and the speech or article completed, he would be immensely relieved, as happy as a child.[10]

Though he was ill trained as a writer, he had imagination and wit and was not afraid of ideas. His original philosophy of labor action is clearly mirrored in his numerous prepared or impromptu speeches, and in passages of interviews published during this period of his growing fame. To Miss Agnes Hamilton, writing in the *Contemporary Review* of London, a half hour with Sidney Hillman seemed well worth the long journey from England:

> We have talked of "workers' control" in Great Britain; the Amalgamated Clothing Workers exercises it. It has welded technicians, shop chairmen, and rank and file into a homogeneous body . . . rendering service so efficient that, in effect, they run the factories. Today the union not only owns bank and libraries, newspapers and educational institutions; it manages, for the industry, unemployment insurance funds and the entire Labour Exchange system, and the employers come to it for statistics of markets, prices, and conditions all over the world.

Hillman's program required that the workers should master their functions in industry, he told Miss Hamilton, increasing their productive power and earnings:

> We have to learn *management* as well as ownership. That is where labor banking comes in. The motive is service, not profit. There power as well as responsibility are being assumed together. At the same time the democratic method, which must penetrate our industrial life . . . is being tried out. We have got to find a way for the introduction of democracy into industry whereby experiments with the popular conduct of industry will be so gradual that mistakes can be corrected without social injury.[11]

At this time, in this epoch of ill-founded, unevenly distributed prosperity, the American labor world as a whole appeared "profoundly depressing" to the eyes of the observant visitor from Europe. "Against the darkness of a movement subdued in mind and method to what it works in, the light of the Amalgamated shines all the brighter."

Hillman himself spoke to Miss Hamilton in skeptical or disillusioned tone of the American labor movement as a whole. Referring to the blatant prosperity of the New Era, he said:

> We are in a materialistic period which has got to be gone through. . . . Here two million workers own automobiles. . . . In New York, Tammany is a democratic institution. . . . We are against capitalism, not against capitalists. . . . As for revolution, we have no particular way of getting it.

To his English Socialist visitor, Hillman seemed as resourceful a Fabian as Sidney Webb himself. "He is no visionary, but he has vision," she concluded.[12]

The hope of "utopian" revolution was put aside. Instead, Hillman, now forty, in contemplative mood at this middle period of his life, devoted himself during such leisure moments as he had to giving form to his thoughts about a realistic but "expanding" program for American labor.

In the autumn of 1927 he had been invited to contribute a paper to be published in a book surveying the labor situation in this country, with contributions by outstanding authorities in the field. Very painfully he composed the piece according to his own light. Though edited by Charles Ervin, the original manuscript entitled "Labor

Attitudes," as dictated by Hillman, appears to have been but little changed and only in the interests of rhetoric.*

In this paper he is very much the *Realpolitiker* of the labor movement, the man of practical affairs who, in his own organization, has successfully beaten off the assaults of the left-wing radicals. His lance is sharply tilted at those doctrinaires who place purity of belief or theory above the value of an effective program of action. In his estimate of American trade unionism, as contrasted with that of Europe, he is now more hopeful than in earlier expressions, despite his dislike of the narrow craft-union spirit of the AFL. The triumphant materialistic spirit of the times indicates, to his mind, postponement of "revolutionary" social trends. But at the same time he is conscious of the speed of social change in the United States, as he himself has observed it in the twenty years since his arrival, and prophesies that the tide in this country may not run forever in a reactionary sense.

"Hackneyed attitudes" and "petrified programs, whether imported or homemade," he urges, must all be cast aside in the attempt to weigh the "facts and forces" of our situation:

Conservative or radical, what is your creed?—how often one hears the question and it is surprising how many people [attach] importance to the answer. . . . There is a very radical labor union around the corner, so radical, indeed, that it recognizes no God or master, nor common sense, either. Yet it wields no power in its industry, and its standards and working conditions have gone all the way down. . . . And then you have another union, notoriously conservative, opposed to all things modern and progressive. But that union is in full control of the conditions under which its people are employed, and high wages and protection of the worker on his job are theirs.

It was not one's doctrines or fine phrases, he would say, but "the line of action one follows" that counted. You could vote Socialist for twenty years and get nowhere; or you could take an active part in an organization like the Amalgamated Clothing Workers, which enforced democracy in the shops every day and built co-operative

* "Labor Attitudes" by Sidney Hillman, published as Chapter XXV of *American Labor Dynamics*, an Inquiry by Thirty-Two Labor Men, Teachers, Editors and Technicians. Edited by J. B. S. Hardman (New York: Harcourt, Brace, 1928). This excellent anthology surveying the labor movement of the twenties includes also articles by John Brophy, James Maurer, A. J. Muste, Harold Lasswell, Leo Wolman, Abraham Epstein, and the editor.

enterprises and a "larger life" for its people. To Hillman a "ready-made terminology, which may be convenient and comforting to lazy spirits," meant little:

It is the party that has the power to create new conditions in industrial or political relations that is, in an important sense, progressive. Such a party [or labor organization] may recondition our social relationships.

There you have, cautiously stated, the essence of Hillman's Fabianism. His union, it was often remarked, actually exercised a considerable "control" of its industry, and in a sense was now confronted by the problem of *which of the good things in life it could safely demand for its members,* hampered only by the backwardness of the rest of American labor. But makers of radical phrases who made promises they could not fulfill, or "amateur idealists" with various recipes for the rapid salvation of the workers—by teaching them the values of literature, music, and such things—Hillman had little patience for. He said: "The great problem of the worker is not appreciation, but the securing of these good things of life."

To him the overshadowing danger was that the American labor movement was terribly weak in point of organization. "Without organization there is no power. And power is the foundation of effective policy and distant goals. . . ." In 1928 only 4,000,000 out of 30,000,000 wage workers were unionized. In this ocean of the unorganized no labor union could stand safely as an island. That was why the realistic leader of the Amalgamated constantly urged his members to help organize the steel workers of Pittsburgh or the textile workers of Passaic.

At any rate, the going trade unions in America, Hillman believed, had done more to raise the standard of living and "protect the worker on the job" than the "politically and sentimentally radical" European trade unions. American labor leaders were much more concerned with industrial and managerial problems than were Europeans. Hence continuity of leadership was important, though it sometimes resulted in a bureaucratic or "autocratic" abuse of tenure, with existing leadership constantly perpetuating itself. ("Few die and none resign," as Thomas Jefferson once said of political officeholders.)

The study of managerial problems, the maintenance of labor-management co-operation were warmly advocated by Hillman. Criticism of such tactics as a form of "class-collaboration"—a term, he wrote, "which means everything and nothing"—was merely so much loose talk indulged in by the extreme conservatives of the AFL as well as by the leftists. It was the want of knowledge of changing business conditions that had led recently to terrible defeats for once-powerful unions. (He did not mention by name the well-known instance of the United Mine Workers' near-collapse under John L. Lewis after 1926.)

On the other hand, the Amalgamated policy—"after we give a stubborn employing concern all the fight they want and we bring them to terms"—was to put the firm into proper shape again. Thus their workers would share in its prosperity; whereas under the opposite policy of avoiding any co-operation with industry "a union may win a strike and then find out that the workers have lost . . . the industry itself." Similarly an employer might defeat a union and also ruin his business.

A very characteristic and keen reflection of Hillman's was:

. . . The happiest solution of almost any conflict is likely to be achieved before all possible resources are drawn into the fight. One is more likely to succeed in getting concessions while on speaking and bargaining terms with the other side than when those terms no longer exist. Once a fight is on, the desire to win develops. . . . The realist[ic] combatant will not disregard this human element in the situation.

A constructive labor policy must be related to the facts of industry, "must be stated *in terms of the achievable,*" he wrote. The American worker did not care much for "promises" which appeared unsupported by responsibility and the real power to carry them out; he felt he had much to lose if his business were mismanaged. On the other hand, Hillman believed that a program of action based upon realities, "if it succeeded in stating large objectives in simple and convincing terms," would one day find a strong response from the mass of American workers.

Thus he prophesied, in the complacent days of 1928, that "American labor is more likely than is generally assumed to go out for economic radicalism." In its irresistible march, American labor might end by destroying "the most sacred taboos."

"Labor Attitudes," published in 1928, is one of Sidney Hillman's very rare literary efforts, highly concentrated in style and coldly logical in its approach. The "messianic" spirit that was also very marked in Sidney Hillman is de-emphasized in this middle period. It was said that the influence of Professor Leo Wolman, his most intimate adviser and almost his *alter ego* during the twenties, was at its maximum then. This paper also reveals how much Hillman's thinking on the labor question had been molded by purely American influences. In these days he used to mock at the Socialists in his organization, exclaiming, "Bah, they sound like the French Revolution of 1848! But this is America in 1928."

Prospects for the advancement of labor here were gloomy as this article was written, New York was agog with revelations of racketeering in the building-trades unions; the country was fat with prosperity, and the fiber of labor leaders as well as of businessmen had grown soft. Yet as Hillman remarked in this article with sober optimism: "Changes in American industrial life are all too rapid." A few years might make a surprising difference.

In the army of clothing workers that he led, there were thousands who had been brought up on red carnations for May Day and the "class struggle." Yet many of them, under Hillman's teaching, were now soberly studying industrial management and production technique. And yet Hillman, though "at times knee-deep in the mud of union politics, never ceased to think of larger aims and yes, even ultimates," one of his friends of those days maintained.[13]

III

Many persons wondered "where Hillman would go from here" toward 1928 and 1929. That he had high ambitions for himself was evident enough; that his ambitions were always closely connected in his mind with service to millions of his fellow workers made them none the less ambitions. He felt keenly at times the limitations of his office as head of an organization of tailors and clothing workers. To be sure, clothing ranked as one of the necessities of life only after food and shelter; yet this consumer-goods industry did not have the decisive economic power of the heavy industries such as coal mining, steel, or transportation. He might have gone very far with his "dynamic" strategy if he had been leader of the workers in one of these key industries, then so ill-organized. He might have gone far indeed if he had been able to rise within the hierarchy of the American Federation of Labor, but this avenue was then closed to him. Its leaders at that period were said to be afraid of Sidney Hillman. And he often reflected that it was a handicap to be a foreign-born American with a foreign accent which he could never wholly correct. Moreover, he was always conscious that he was a Jew and therefore must play his part with all the more honor. But would he be limited always to leadership of a union including only a portion of the needle-trade workers in the country?

The idea of combining all the needle-trade labor—including the workers in women's clothing, hats, and furs—into one organization was repeatedly brought before Hillman and his associates, as we have seen. The first approach to an "alliance," at the time of the 1921 struggle, had ended in little more than a paper organization. Any real combination between the ILGWU and the Amalgamated was always opposed by the AFL. However, the ILGWU came on very bad times toward 1926, when the Communists suddenly gained control of its New York locals, representing then more than half of this union's strength. A general strike in New York in 1926 lasted twenty-eight weeks, was attended with great violence, and ended in complete disaster. After the leftist faction was ousted from office, the ILGWU, rent by dissension, saw its membership fall from about 100,000 to less than 40,000. The union was now virtually bankrupt, and in this crisis President Schlesinger and Secretary-Treasurer David Dubinsky, a local hero of the "civil war" with the Communists, were able to negotiate some large loans from the Amalgamated Bank secured by adequate endorsements. There was much talk at the time of a merger with the stronger Amalgamated organization, whose jurisdictions often touched those of the ILGWU. Officers in the cloakmakers' union came to Hillman's aides in the winter of 1927 and said they stood ready to work out a plan of amalgamation "in a few weeks." [14]

Hillman himself earnestly desired fusion, but held back some of his overeager followers who thought of forcing the issue. "Nothing should be done," he had said somewhat earlier (at the May 1926 convention of the Amalgamated), "that would tend to bring about dissension in other organizations. We have taken our stand, and when they are ready we will be with them."

The existence of separate organizations in the needle trades made no sense, of course. Yet the play of personalities barred the way; at one point events waited only upon the retirement of one particular leader of the ILGWU, to whom the idea of amalgamation was anathema. David Dubinsky, on the other hand, was one of the ILGWU executives who then favored a combination of forces under the seemingly invincible Hillman. The long-range plan of bringing upward of half a million needle-trade workers and several organized groups of textile workers as well under one tent was all but undertaken between 1927 and 1929, then repeatedly, tantalizingly, postponed. After depression arrived at the end of 1929, the whole scheme was abandoned. The crushing debts of the Ladies' Garment Workers by then seemed too heavy a burden at a time when even the Amalgamated staggered under heavy blows.

Meanwhile, Hillman still seemed troubled at not having enough work to keep him busy. He longed to run a movement, not something that was going around in circles. The excitement of directing a great union was strong, yet not satisfying enough. It needed endless care and calculation merely to manipulate the ambitions of the several powerful "Joint Board Kings" who were his own lieutenants heading the different city organizations.

Non-essentials took a great deal out of him. When he felt excessively tired, he would go off on a vacation trip abroad, to attend some labor conference in Europe. But an enforced rest, the quiet of an ocean voyage, filled him with the greater misery of having nothing to do all day. "No, tired is not the word. In fact, he is anxious for more work. He is often short of time, but his energies are not used up," one of his friends observed.[15]

He was groping for ways of expanding his influence in the national scene. Fortunately the union served as a springboard, so to speak. Its publicity staff saw to it that their president made numerous public appearances and was frequently quoted in the metropolitan press on the Burning Issues of the day. When in the autumn of 1929 panic and then depression suddenly engulfed the country, the emergencies and rigors of that time provided scope and opportunity enough for a Sidney Hillman.

BOOK TWO

Chapter Fourteen

THE STRUGGLE
WITH
THE RACKETEERS

The union appeared to have reached the peak of its
power in the summer of 1929, after the Philadelphia
campaign. Then, almost at once (as so often before), grave troubles
beset the Amalgamated from another quarter. Racketeers had begun
to infest the garment trade on a small scale toward 1920, as Hillman
knew, though very much under cover, which made proceeding
against them difficult. But by 1929, when panic conditions struck the
New York clothing market, bringing in their train a long series of
commercial failures, the racketeers grew bolder than ever and worked
openly to "protect" non-union shops. Now the whole New York
clothing trade seemed suddenly to be disintegrating before Hillman's
eyes.

Early in 1929 the New York Joint Board was given a rude shake-
up when Abraham Beckerman was forced to resign as its manager,
a position of great power and responsibility in the union's hierarchy.
Beckerman had at first been charged only with incompetence in the
conduct of his office. He was a clever and well-spoken man and a
local leader of the Socialist Party. In a statement almost tearful in
its extenuation of his poor performance during the five years past,

he pointed out that the five boroughs of New York and its industrial suburbs offered baffling problems to those who would exercise control over its two thousand or more small contract shops. "I defy anyone to give, within one hundred firms, the number of manufacturers of clothing in New York City," he said at the time of his "resignation."

Meanwhile the New York cutters' organization still retained its local autonomy within the union; its officers exercised no real surveillance over contractors who, after paying the cutters their union wages, shipped bundles of cut cloth by truck to be sewn up in nonunion shops. Although relieved of the higher post, Beckerman was still an officer of the cutters' local, still a member of the General Executive Board and the New York Joint Board. There were "too many governments" within the New York section of the union, Hillman said; it consisted, as he put it, of "a number of shells within a shell." But while these local officers played their secret little games against each other, the unionized tailors were losing work to fly-by-night sweatshops. The rank-and-file union members were growing desperate. Manufacturers who observed union-shop standards were now suffering the fierce competition of others who had "solved" their labor-cost problems with the "protection" of racketeers.[1]

Two of the union's ablest trouble shooters, Hyman Blumberg and Sidney Rissman, were placed in charge of a clean-up campaign in May 1929. Rissman, a very amiable man, but powerfully built and quite tough himself, found that nowadays various shady characters dropped in to see him regularly at the local offices he supervised, to ask him for "favors." When he refused, they informed him that he "might get hurt on this job."

"That's all right," he said to them. "Hillman always gives me the tough assignments. Better go away and don't come back again." [2]

By 1930 Hillman knew how much the racketeers were terrorizing the garment manufacturers. The friendly David Drechsler, counsel to the New York Clothing Manufacturers' Exchange, informed him of cases where manufacturers who refused offers of "protection" against the union were threatened on one day, then raided on the next by gangsters. As much as $50,000 worth of suits were destroyed by acid in one instance.[3] Similar threats were reported to have been made to the manufacturers in several cases by Philip Orlofsky, the business agent of the New York cutters' local, No. 4. Behind Orlofsky now stood the sinister figure of Louis "Lepke" Buchalter, over-lord of industrial racketeering gangs in New York. His plundering methods were systematic: manufacturers who might have begun by paying $5,000 a year for "protection" ended by paying $10,000 or $25,000, or even sharing their annual profits with the racketeers, whose accountants regularly went through their books.

To Hillman the worst aspect of the affair was that the gangsters had dug themselves deep into the union's key local, that of the cut-ters, who controlled the underlying manufacturing operations. The vast majority of the cutters were honest and loyal, but when Hillman quietly called in some of them for examination, nine out of ten re-fused to give testimony, for they lived in terror of losing first their jobs and second their very lives. Some of their own officers, such as Orlofsky, worked in secret partnership with the gangsters, but also enriched themselves by stealing from the treasury of this large local, as Hillman suspected.

For several years Hillman had been puzzled over what measures he might take to stop industrial racketeering in the garment trade—though it was on a much smaller scale than in other fields, such as the gang-ridden building industry. Some of the clothing-trade em-ployers had turned to the gunmen in times of strikes and had found themselves later unable to dismiss these plunderers—guests who arrived for a week end and stayed for years. The prevailing moral climate of business encouraged "rackets" and gangsters in our great cities. But hitherto the gangland people, who worked for occasional employers and fought the union men, had never tried, as now, un-der Lepke, to seize control of the union locals themselves. The very existence of the union was threatened.

What was to be done? Here one entered a jungle-like environment where one's life might be in jeopardy at every step. One felt that the employers, as well as many of the union members, drawn into the net, lived in fear. If a strike were called against a gangster-protected firm, the racketeers seemed to know of it in advance; the union's officers received threats of death. Hillman was even warned that high police officers attached to the Industrial Squad were in the pay of the gangsters; it seemed not only useless but an invitation to murder to turn to them for aid. Meanwhile he knew that trucks were rolling out of town by day, guarded by gunmen, carrying large shipments of cut cloth to "runaway" contract shops in New Jersey, Connecticut, and Pennsylvania. The demoralized condition of business after the summer of 1930 in itself encouraged the spread of racketeering and worked to undermine the whole position of the Amalgamated union in New York.

For months Hillman was tormented by the feeling that something must be done, and he did not know where to begin, while he restlessly turned over in his mind the whole terrifying problem. Suspicions, rumors were not enough. To invoke the power of the law seemed vain. The gangsters and their allies had big money, lawyers enough, and even a portion of Mayor "Jimmy" Walker's police force on their side. Irrefutable evidence must be obtained before the plan of action he slowly shaped in his mind could be launched.

He had heard lately that the "Orlofsky machine" had been raising dues and assessments among the relatively well-paid cutters; he knew almost exactly how much of their local's treasury had been passed around by the crooked union officers to "thugs" who kept the cutters in line.[4] At certain wholesale clothing houses the corrupt union officers themselves, acting in connivance with the gangsters, gave orders to the employers about where to ship their cut cloth to be "made up" or sewn into suits at out-of-town contract shops, also under control of the racketeers.

In most instances, as impartial investigation has shown, industrial rackets have flourished in this country because business and the public have avoided assuming responsibility for eliminating the gangsters. Criminologists have agreed that there is no evidence that crime is more prevalent in labor organizations than in business. Approximately 70 per cent of our 200 leading corporations have been cited for violations of the law or even (repeatedly) for criminal action of one form or another. As a means of "keeping labor in hand," many businessmen have tolerated extortion, theft, and murder, notably in the shipping industry, in the building trades, and in the motion-picture field, because, as one recent investigator has said, "morality does not carry over into their business practices," and because in spite of these charges their enterprises show an annual profit. (In the same manner, some labor leaders here and there betray their trust under the spur of the profit motive.)[5]

The more he thought about it, the more Hillman felt he was fed up with the racketeers and must drive them from his industry, though the conscience of the public, of business, and of the rest of the labor movement seemed strangely quiescent. It would be a most difficult and risky affair, he knew. Others deplored gangsterism in industry and in the labor movement but did nothing about it.

He exclaimed to his assistant, Potofsky, at this time: "It's like a cancer. We have got to tear this thing out by the roots before it has a chance to grow deeper." [6] At the same time he held long private conferences with David Drechsler, Julius H. Levy, and Charles O. Jaffee, the heads of the clothiers' associations, who had shown themselves strong friends of the union, so that they might prepare measures in concert. The action of honest employers, according to the general plan he was shaping, was to be timed with that of the union and all the friends among the outside public they could summon to its support.

In May 1931, the general office of the Amalgamated, on Hillman's order, called for the books of Local 4, supposedly for a routine examination. Potofsky then went through the books with accountants and reported gross irregularities to Hillman. Nothing was said as yet; no efforts were made to give the affair any publicity. Meanwhile a new trade agreement was drawn up in June 1931, and Hillman called a mass meeting of 1,500 New York shop chairmen and local officers at Webster Hall, as if to discuss the proposed terms of the new agreement with the membership. The announcement of the meeting referred only in the most general way to efforts to secure rank-and-file co-operation in correcting various evils besetting their industry. On the surface, it looked like just another attempt at "house cleaning," as in 1921 and 1924.

However, when Hillman stepped to the platform he was grave. His mode of expression was blunt: "We might as well be frank here and say out in the open what we have been saying to each other in private. What the New York market is suffering from more than anything else is the racketeering evil!" This was his first public challenge to the racketeers inside and outside the organization, a warning to the men who represented the secret opposition within the union that he meant business now. There must at last be a showdown, he exclaimed, on the question of "who is to run the union." [7]

As the next step, reports were allowed to "leak" to the newspapers that Hillman had gone to lodge vehement protests about the racketeers before Police Commissioner Mulrooney and District Attorney Crain, offering testimony on the gangsters' extortions from various contractors. The Amalgamated union would give its fullest co-operation, he was quoted as saying, in any action undertaken by the city authorities against the racketeers. Strikes were to be called against firms that violated the union's standards under the protection of the hoodlums, and shipments of bundles to out-of-town shops were to be halted at all costs.[8] There was design in this first guarded effort of Hillman to serve public notice on the politicians, the police, and the underworld that he was in earnest. Meanwhile he informed himself thoroughly about certain clothing firms that were known to be working hand and glove with the racketeers and "chiseling" on the union scale.

Five days later, on the morning of June 24, he suddenly struck at one of these houses, ordering Amalgamated pickets out in large force against the clothing shop of Silverman and Turner in the center of the garment district at Fifth Avenue and Fifteenth Street. This firm had suddenly broken its agreement with the union. However, one of the local officers who was to be in charge of the strike failed to reach the scene of action through no fault of his own. Early that morning, as he left his home in Brooklyn, a gunman leaned out of a car that trailed him and blazed away with his automatic. The union man fell seriously wounded with bullets lodged in his leg. A short time later, at the loft building which housed the Silverman and Turner shop, a band of armed gangsters, at a given signal, suddenly rushed out of the lobby downstairs and fell upon the Amalgamated pickets with knives and blackjacks. Two of the strikers' leaders were left wounded, while the hoodlums fled and were lost among the dense crowds in the street.

Thus Sidney Hillman had his answer promptly from the gunmen. He had known that the lives of his people would be endangered by any act of opposition. That was what made it so hard. His loyal union officers, his pickets were under the menace of being carved to bits or shot down at any moment by the monstrous creatures they fought. Unmistakable warnings came to Hillman also that if he persisted in his course he would himself be "laid out in a vacant lot," and his chief lieutenants as well. The same unfriendly message was sent to Mr. Drechsler, the ruling spirit of the New York Clothing Manufacturers' Exchange.[9] The worst lesson learned in the Silverman and Turner affray was that men who held high places in his union—something he could only have suspected up to now—had informed Lepke's gunmen of the place and time of that strike on lower Fifth Avenue and of the names and addresses of its leaders. The whole business looked more and more deadly. Some of the manufacturers Hillman had long done business with begged him to "lay off." Certain of the executives in his own organization urged him to be reasonable, holding that it was impossible to cope with the vast, insidious power of the underworld.

II

Living in a state of contained excitement, and accompanied now by armed guards, Hillman was, nevertheless, keen to see this "war" through. "The best defense is the offense," he said to his associates. They must use "power psychology" against the underworld mob, impress them with the strength and determination of the union, drive them from pillar to post.

On June 25, 1931, a day after the bloody skirmish on Fifth Avenue, Hillman, at the head of an imposing procession of 300 respectable citizens, bore down on the City Hall to lay a petition before Mayor Walker calling for drastic measures against the gangsters who preyed on New York's garment industry. Included in this delegation were various leaders of retail business and manufacturing such as Jesse I. Straus of R. H. Macy and Company, Lessing Rosenwald of Sears, Roebuck, the heads of the Clothing Manufacturers' Exchange, and various officers of the Amalgamated union. Newspaper reporters were out in force to cover the story, and motion-picture news cameras ground out their record of the highly publicized conference between Hillman and the Mayor.

The object of this demonstration, Hillman said, was to arouse public opinion as far as possible to the peril in which they all stood. He spoke for 40,000 honest workers who were trying to preserve law and order. Evidence was in his possession that the underworld people had been going around with "threats, intimidations, and offers" to various firms, and that people were afraid to testify against them or sign affidavits in all but a few cases. "The gangsters boast that they are as strong as the government of the city. . . . A number of manufacturers pay tribute to them," he added. Unemployment was growing as a consequence in New York, and business worth many millions of dollars might be lost to the city. Word had come to him and other Amalgamated officers that they were marked men and would be "bumped off." Were the gunmen to be the rulers of New York? "We do not believe that these racketeers have real power; we believe it is mere cowardly bluff. But they have issued their challenge to our industry and to the government of the city." Hillman called point-blank on Mayor Walker to defend public peace, which the Mayor gallantly pledged he would do with the co-operation of the entire city police force.[10]

That demonstration was, of course, a bit of theater; but it had brought the spotlight of publicity on all the doings of the racketeers; stories of Hillman's bold fight against the gangsters were featured in all the metropolitan press and over the radio and in the newsreels. Meanwhile the Amalgamated proceeded with stoppages of gangster-protected contract shops. At Commissioner Mulrooney's order police cars roved the garment district to protect the union's pickets against assault—a sight for sore eyes!

Within the union Hillman was involved night and day in the struggle to cleanse the local organization of its corrupt officers or those who, out of fear, did the bidding of the racketeers. Before the Joint Board he advocated a more widespread stoppage movement, which he called now "a strike against gangdom." The majority of the clothing manufacturers would support this action and also promised to keep their workers under surveillance in order to check on those who took orders from the criminals. This task would be long and arduous, but the Amalgamated was ready as before, he exclaimed, "to wage a man-sized fight." [11]

A few days later the action was broadened when some 30,000 New York men's clothing workers walked out in the "strike against gangdom." The stoppage began in early July 1931 and was continued through August and several weeks afterward. At this time about 40 per cent of the small contractors were operating without union-shop agreements. With the pro-union firms idle, it was easy to spot the movement of trucks, guarded by gunmen, coming from the non-union shops. Union pickets would then close in on the racketeers' trucks and begin hand-to-hand action. Fighting took place in the streets of New York; some of it flared up suddenly in small towns of New Jersey and nearby Pennsylvania, where the new depression-period sweatshops had been set up.

The gang, which had lately been enjoying a booming business in various trades, was certainly meeting with tenacious resistance from the Amalgamated union. Yet this was not enough. Corrupt union officers were still in full legal possession of their branch organization of cutters and had 1,800 skilled workers paying them toll. Nor did it appear at first that they could be easily or quickly dislodged. Holding complete power over this key local, with the support of the gunmen, they could lie low for a while and then renew their racketeering operations whenever it pleased them to do so.

Hillman was saying to his people that it was only a question of time before the gangsters and their sweatshops would destroy all that had been built up in twenty years. The paramount thing was to drive the racketeers' organization out of the local union they controlled. How to do this was the problem that obsessed him night and day. He did not want to have a long trial within the union, or go to court for three years, during which the crooks could make hay with the industry. Then at last, after long reflection, he had the right "angle"—as he used to say—and made ready to take final action, though he whispered of his bold-handed scheme to only three or four of the old stalwarts on the General Executive Board whose courage he could absolutely rely on.

There were decent men among the union's executive officers in New York, though timid souls also, who hoped that Hillman would take it easy rather than risk a sudden and horrible end. Some of them up to the last, it is recalled, made bets among themselves that in the end he would not have the nerve to go through with his all-out attack on the gangsters within the union.

In the week of Monday, August 24, while the rank-and-file members picketed the city's non-union clothing shops, he opened sessions of the Amalgamated General Executive Board that sat in New York day after day and before them he filed charges against the union men who were in league with the racketeers.

Bluntly Hillman denounced the two top officers of Local 4, Philip Orlofsky and Isidore Machlin, for corrupt conduct. Benefit funds assessed upon their local members to the extent of $89,000, he charged, had completely disappeared during the past year. Potofsky's audit revealed that out of $96,000 received in dues during a recent two-year period, the sum of $60,000 also was unaccounted for. The accused men were summoned to appear and testify, but refused to do so, sending word that they intended to cling to their posts, run their local their own way, and, if need be, their own union. Abraham Beckerman, still a power among the New York union leaders, spoke vigorously in their behalf, declaring that the charges were baseless. Moreover, there were procedural and legal difficulties in the way of action. The hearings dragged on amid unflagging disputes for three more days, while the accused officers were being tried and judged *in absentia.*

Still nothing happened; and there were some who still believed that nothing would happen. It was known that the rank and file of the cutters were tied to their old local officers by powerful bonds. Long dependence on them for jobs or favors, on the one hand, deadly fear of them, on the other, kept them in line. Those workers dreaded and hated the gunmen who guarded their shops, but most of them averted their eyes, bent to their work, and said nothing. The Executive Board, at length, voted to dismiss the accused from office, as Hillman insisted, but no one knew as yet what good would come of this. It was still only a show of action, not action itself. Meanwhile all gangdom in New York was on the alert, waiting. The crooked officers now stayed at their local headquarters night and day.

However, Hillman's real job was being done not at the G.E.B., but in secret, with a small group among the Amalgamated executives, four or five of his oldest associates, including the union's lawyer, Brandwen, who met with him every day that week in a room of the Hotel New Yorker. He had worked out a plan for a real surprise party, an action that would hit the adversary like a bolt of lightning. On the night of Friday, August 28, he was up with his aides until the small hours of the morning, completing all preparations, having all the necessary legal instruments drawn up. Men high in the political world had been sounded out, and the full co-operation of Police Commissioner Mulrooney had been won. He had first offered to send Hillman a detachment of men from the Industrial Squad; but it was known that these were infected and Hillman insisted that a group of detectives from the Homicide Squad be sent over instead to protect the union leaders in the next few days, which was done.

The night of August 28 and the morning following were a time of cruel and unendurable tension, and no one slept. Hillman's proposed coup was highhanded; its outcome could hardly be foretold.

None knew what the reaction of the Lepke mob might be. There would be, according to his strategy, one more meeting of the General Executive Board, as early as possible on the morning following. The executive order for the ousting of the dismissed officers would be presented for a vote, immediate action would be authorized on the spot, and according to the plan evolved, the act of expulsion and replacement of the crooked officers was to be carried out instantaneously— indeed, before the formal voting was done. The supreme danger was that Beckerman, still a member of the G.E.B. and Hillman's unrelenting opponent, might inform the enemy of this decision at once, and there would be violent reaction. Hence all of the little group at the New Yorker proceeded in the utmost secrecy, and their movements were planned to the minute.

On Saturday morning, August 29, Hillman called the G.E.B. members together again to face their zero hour. Throughout this fight "Jack" Potofsky had been working at the side of Hillman, whom he regarded as a combination of father and elder brother. On the night of the final preparations Hillman said to him: "Jack, you're elected to do the job tomorrow." Potofsky, though fully expecting unpleasant and bloody business, possibly even his own demise, loyally accepted the assignment.

At eight in the morning of Saturday, August 29, the tall, bearded, distinguished-looking Potofsky proceeded to his post near the office of Local 4, then at West Seventeenth Street, accompanied by an inspector of police, a couple of plain-clothes men, and a group of picked union members. They waited.

Toward nine, at the Amalgamated headquarters, Hillman opened the meeting of the General Executive Board, his manner cool, his voice very stern and harsh. He reviewed the situation briefly and began reading the resolution to take over the cutters' local. The session then became stormy. Beckerman, surprised at the action, cried out in wrath: "Hillman, I hope you break your neck on this case." He would fight the organization to the bitter end, he said, and handed in his resignation to the G.E.B. Before he could leave the room, however, and while the motion was still being read and debated, one of Hillman's aides slipped away and telephoned orders to the waiting Potofsky. Toward eleven o'clock he and his little column of detectives and union members moved upon Local 4, opened the locked door of its offices with a duplicate key, and burst in upon the officers who had lately been camped there day and night. The telephone wires were cut; books and records of the local branch were quickly gathered up by Hillman's aide and the detectives.

"What does this mean?" cried the chief officer of the local and his assistant, as he tried to stop these proceedings.

"It means you're through! You go right out that door!" yelled Potofsky, who was in a state of high excitement. He exhibited his documents, orders signed by President Hillman and Secretary Schlossberg, with the big union seal affixed to them. For the moment, the detectives and police officers backed him up. Let the others go to court, they advised, if there was anything wrong. Now it was "Jack" Potofsky who barricaded himself in that office at West Seventeenth Street. In an adjacent room was the clubroom of the cutters, filled with adherents of the ousted officers; on the first afternoon—when the police guard was momentarily relaxed—the rebellious union men, with their gangster allies, suddenly surged into the local's office to throw Potofsky out, but Hillman, in response to a telephone call, sent reinforcements in the nick of time.[12]

Several days later a mass meeting of the cutters was called at Webster Hall to hear speeches by Hillman and other Amalgamated national officers appealing for the support of these misled and terrorized workers. En route, Hillman's car was followed by gunmen, it was noticed, though a police prowl car accompanied him. On the other hand, Beckerman, Orlofsky, *et al.*, held their own rival meeting, attended by those who still admired or feared them, and for a few days bristling challenges and accusations were hurled back and forth between both camps.

At that Webster Hall meeting, Hillman declared: "When it comes to a question of the underworld trying to control any part of our organization, there cannot and will not be any compromise." He spoke in a perfect fury at the hard-faced crooks who stole money belonging to the workers and even funds provided for their relief.[13]

Faced by the danger of having his union undermined and destroyed by a few corrupt officers in league with the gangsters, Hillman had acted quickly to effect a *coup d'état* in the cutters' local. This meant, frankly, "cutting corners" so far as the union's established procedure and constitution were concerned, in the light of a terrible emergency. The question now was whether public opinion, the courts, and above all the sentiment of the rank and file in the cutters' local would back up Hillman's coup.

The racketeer faction thereafter fought stubbornly to hold a portion of the men's clothing industry in New York, petitioning for a court injunction to restrain the Amalgamated's executive officers from seizure of their local and its property. An executive committee of the cutters' local for a period withheld its decision in favor of one party or the other, on "constitutional" grounds, while the case was being fought out in court. For almost a year the "Orlofsky machine" was reported to have held a sizable minority of the cutters, some 500 in number, under its guns. It had its gangster-ridden wholesale shops in New York and its own sweatshops in New Jersey and Pennsylvania, where women and girls now worked for $4.00 a week to sew the cloth they still managed to ship out stealthily or at night. Thus the industrial racketeers' ring was able to undersell the union-scale market in a season when all business seemed demoralized. Yet their hold on the men's clothing industry was weakening swiftly.

Happily, at the very beginning, in September 1931, New York Supreme Court Judge Irwin Untermeyer had ruled promptly in favor of the Hillman leadership, denying the injunction sought by the band of Orlofsky and Beckerman. A long delay in court was spared them. There were appeals, to be sure, to higher courts. However, the fight within the union, after dragging on for most of a year, suddenly ended in the summer of 1932, when all the cutters returned to the Amalgamated fold and the affairs of the "rebel local" were wound up. They had been won over thanks largely to the unremitting exertions of one of Hillman's most courageous lieutenants, Murray Weinstein, who now took command of the demoralized cutters' local, reorganized it and helped in the general clean-up of the New York market. The Lepke gang, weary and discouraged, began to look for other fields to plow. This return of the cutters accompanied another spectacular action by Hillman that summer to bring about a powerful revival of the Amalgamated, an upsurge of morale, in a time of almost universal business prostration and despair. No other American labor leader and no leader of business had ever put up such a relentless fight against the underworld as had Hillman in 1931 and 1932. If citizens all over the United States had joined him in this action it would have bid fair to rid the country of its worst social evil.

Chapter Fifteen

THE GREAT SLUMP;
LEADERSHIP
IN CRISIS: 1929-1933

"No one can deny the fundamental correctness of our economic system," said the Republican candidate for the presidency in the summer of 1928. His high purpose, he declared, was to "abolish poverty, to protect labor and maintain its prosperity."

The Bull Market of the 1920's rose to new peaks with Mr. Herbert Hoover's election. It was the heyday of engineers and business "statesmen" and their "yes-men." High-pressure salesmen roved the land, and Americans purchased from them the luxuries of life on the installment plan and worried no more about primary needs. Henry Ford was saying that it was wrong for people to save money. The introduction of new labor-saving machinery would create an abundance of new jobs and endless prosperity, he prophesied.

To those who made claims that the New Era had ushered in eternal prosperity, Hillman used to say: "I just don't believe it!" [1] He himself by 1929 was the responsible head of a sizable financial "empire" composed of the various banks, co-operative enterprises, and beneficiary funds created by the Amalgamated union, with combined assets of some $20,000,000 invested with an eye to safety rather than profit. This, during the greatest riot of speculation ever seen in our history, when the head of the Amalgamated Bank of New York reported:

You ride in an elevated or streetcar and the conductor asks you, "How is General Motors?" Bank stocks are just flying up and down, and everybody is speculating, and this little organization known as the Amalgamated has made up its mind to keep its feet on the ground.[2]

The bursting of the great Wall Street bubble came at last in October and November 1929, shaking the country's financial institutions to their foundations. After the stock market panic had subsided somewhat, there began that steep decline in industrial production which, by the summer of 1931, deprived 60 per cent of the Amalgamated members of regular employment. Wholesale prices also fell at an alarming rate, and pressure to cut wages became irresistible, though the union fought hard against this movement. Two years after the financial crash of October 1929 there were fully 10,000,000 families in such acute distress that they were postponing purchases of clothing, if not of food.

The only industry in America which had installed a system of unemployment insurance upon a large scale was that of men's clothing under the initiative of the Amalgamated union. In the early stages of the great depression, before the 1930 convention of the union on May 12, Hillman spoke pointedly of the strong support a good union gave its members during hard times. The slogan used now was: "Stick to your union—you need it more than ever when hard times come." The manufacturers were pressing him for wage cuts, he said, but he refused at first to consider their proposals. He also referred to the fact that President Hoover, in November of 1929, had called upon our leading industrial captains to pledge that they would avoid dismissing workers from their jobs and try to have all possible work shared.

But what has happened since this pledge of last November? More millions thrown into the army of unemployed. Delegates, this experience is the latest confirmation of our belief that in order to enforce an industrial policy there must be organization of labor, and that in no other way can it be done.

This union long years ago had initiated a plan for equal division of work available in times of seasonal unemployment such as Hoover now advocated. In the principal clothing markets where the Amalgamated controlled the job, its members shared work during the darkest years of Mr. Hoover's Administration. They were cut down to as little as one or two days a week; they suffered, they pulled in their belts, *but they did not go to the bread lines,* as the union's old officers proudly recall.

In addition to the work-sharing, the union's unemployment insurance funds, through the Chicago, Rochester, and New York centers, paid out roundly $8,500,000 to its members who were eligible for such compensation between 1924 and 1933, inclusive. This, Hillman admitted, was far too little. But those meager payments of a few dollars a week helped.*

Hillman remarked:

If all the industries in the United States would have had the same provision for unemployment insurance as we have in Chicago—surely the automobile industry, the steel and other industries like them which count their profits in hundreds of millions of dollars could have made at least the same provisions—there would be today over one billion dollars in reserve to meet the problem of unemployment. We would then have been spared the terrible catastrophe which is confronting so many people.

Instead management was now instituting a drastic wage-cutting policy. Hillman exclaimed: "How are we meeting the problem of unemployment? By bread lines; by crowded poorhouses; by despair in millions of homes? What is the answer? A great deal of *sympathy.*" In our time of prosperity we had utterly failed to plan or legislate for the time of unemployment that we knew was bound to come.[3]

II

We were at the very depths of the depression—or so one thought. The number of the unemployed by now was reckoned at 15,000,000.

* The unemployment plans varied from each other in the three principal markets where they were instituted. The earlier one, in Chicago, provided benefits for 14,000 to 15,000 workers during two layoff seasons at a maximum of 30 per cent of wages: benefits were typically $10 a week, for six weeks of the year. From May 1, 1924, to May 1, 1930, the Chicago Fund paid out nearly $5,000,000 to the union members eligible (ACWA, Doc. Hist., 1930, pp. 42–44). In Rochester and New York, where the same system was installed only in 1928, benefits were smaller, and accumulated reserves were inadequate when the great decline in employment began after only a year.

Many of us still recall the "Hoovervilles" made of tin cans, driftwood, and old packing boxes, whole towns of unemployed established along the docks or in vacant lots of the suburbs of our great cities. In the garment trade, the slump had begun in 1930, and by 1932 the industry was running, as Hillman said, at about 30 per cent of capacity, while membership in the ACWA fell approximately 50,000 below its 1929 figures. During the runs on all banks, the two Amalgamated Banks, which had been thoroughly prepared for the panic by the drastic liquidation of investments in the spring and autumn of 1930, met all demands, but deposits sank steadily. The union officers and staff at headquarters were placed on half pay; most publications were discontinued.

At night Hillman would walk about the city's silent garment district with a union associate and point to the tall loft buildings of the various concerns still engaged in manufacturing men's clothing and say: "I wonder if that house will open up tomorrow morning or go into receivership. I wonder who will be left."

One day he came into the office of Charles Ervin at the Amalgamated's headquarters and, after taking stock of the low state of affairs in industry, government, and the labor movement, said sardonically: "Well, Charlie, when are you Socialists going to do something!" [4]

To an interviewer at that period he admitted that things really looked black. There was great danger that we were going back to the 1890's, the days of the sweatshop, he thought. Wages, he said, were being cut on the average of 40 to 50 per cent, and the union was being forced to make heavy concessions, since the employers would otherwise find means of evading or breaking agreements. And yet, he added: "This depression won't end until mass buying power is restored. I tell businessmen: 'You cannot sell your goods to people earning $4.00 or $5.00 a week.'" He was engaged in a struggle mainly to "hold the line," he said. "But in this game you cannot stay only 50 or 60 per cent, or even 70 per cent, organized, or you are on the downgrade." [5]

Now in this time of supreme crisis for the union, he somehow found new strength, new resources with which to take up the fight again and stem this disastrous retreat. He was dynamic as ever. He exuded fire and determination again. He said to his staff: "We are going to 'call' such-and-such a company in Boston, in Vineland, New Jersey—where the non-union bundles are rolling in by truck."

A renewed strike movement in New York, to bring the non-union firms to book, was organized in the summer of 1932, in which some 20,000 men's clothing workers, still employed in the city, were to help track down and harass those who shipped goods to the out-of-town sweatshops. This campaign was organized under the inspiration of Hillman with an eye to drama and pageantry.

On August 8, during the noon hour, in the garment district of New York, as the "scab" trucks pulled out along lower Fifth Avenue, strikers suddenly flung themselves down in a living line that stretched across the street, barring the path of the trucks with their bodies. It was a strange sight. People at the curb instinctively rushed to pull the men out of danger, then realized that they were witnessing for the first time an application of Mahatma Gandhi's tactics of passive resistance in an American strike.

The truck drivers, not wishing to commit mayhem on a grand scale, jammed on their brakes, then slowly turned back; the passive resisters, together with hundreds of other pickets, conducted them back to their base. The truck drivers became emotional; they refused to proceed any further over the bodies of workers. Hillman, of course, used the incident, which caught the attention of the whole city, to lift the morale of 20,000 strikers. The Lepke mob was being put to flight. At a mass meeting that night he exclaimed: "Every right-thinking person in the community admires persons who will lie down in front of the truck and be run over rather than allow work to go to non-union shops." [6]

This new campaign was timed with some small symptoms of recovery in the clothing trade, which actually was extremely low in merchandise by 1932. On the East Side of New York men still fought with bottles and marble slabs against the racketeer-protected sweatshops. In towns of eastern Pennsylvania and southern New Jersey, Amalgamated pickets, mainly women, held the lines they had set up against "vigilantes" who menaced them with sawed-off shotguns. The 1932 stoppages in the East were firmly clamped down until 235 "outlaw" clothing houses in New York agreed to arbitrate their differences with the union, accept the union shop, and send back 10,000 workers into the Amalgamated's ranks. For the moment Hillman's "offensive defense" seemed to have checked the disastrous retreat.

Was capitalism "doomed"? many Americans were asking themselves. Never was the discussion of human affairs more searching than in the years of the Great Slump. Hillman, while busy fighting racketeers and open-shoppers, thirsted for precise knowledge about the world-wide economic crisis. At night he pondered over the gold and exchange problems. He sought out people who specialized in questions of industry, government, and human relations.[7] The ideas of the technocrats and of the Keynes school were studied; and he picked the brains of those who advocated national planning. A speech he gave before a conference of social workers on November 15, 1930, still seems one of the soundest utterances in behalf of government relief made at that early phase of the depression cycle.

Taking issue squarely with those who, like President Hoover, held that our economy was experiencing only a temporary setback, he said:

We must not delude ourselves into believing that a natural readjustment of business will eliminate unemployment. . . . [Italics added.]

The present depression, like the earlier ones, is the result of our drifting without a policy or plan to avoid these recurrent disasters. Because we have had no policy we again find ourselves on the rocks of industrial chaos.

Palliative measures will not see us through this crisis and will surely not prevent a repetition of the same thing in the future. To justify itself before the country, industry should present a constructive program and provide organization to carry the program through.

His first proposal for relief measures was then similar to that sponsored by the AFL: the reduction of hours by establishment of the five-day week. "What work there is should be shared during a depression." But since industry had failed in the crisis, he urged that the government should step in and use its power to compel reluctant or unenlightened industrial leadership to accept this program.

The second step would be setting aside a 5 per cent tax on payroll for unemployment insurance, which would come to about $1,600,-000,000 annually, and furnish a reserve to cushion the impact of depression on the workers. A third step was *"the establishment in industry of an organization of the employers and the workers for the purpose of carrying through this policy and preparing proper plans for the future."* [Italics added.]

To say to millions out of jobs that nothing could be done for them, Hillman argued, was to invite greater disasters still. Did not our large corporations provide "doles" for their stockholders through reserves for future dividends? Hillman's parting words in this speech were forceful and timely:

> Let us stop drifting. Let industry assume its full responsibility. Let the state, through its power of persuasion or coercion, if necessary, do its share. Let us not, ostrich-like, bury our heads in the sand and delude ourselves that in this way our problems will be solved.[8]

Thus three years before Roosevelt and the New Deal arrived, Sidney Hillman was outlining a national recovery program that foreshadowed the subsequent NIRA. His intellectual approach, it has been observed, was sympathetic to "statism," an attitude formed during World War I, when a constructive policy toward organized labor had been adopted by the Federal Government.

By the winter of 1930–31 the captains of industry and the masters of finance themselves were rather blue. Though bankers like Albert Wiggin of the Chase National Bank still insisted that we must do nothing to "shake confidence" or impede the workings of "natural economic forces," there was more and more clamor for government intervention. Hillman, very active nowadays, spoke in public as often as possible, and his voice was beginning to be heard.

In December 1930 he appeared at a session of the American Academy of Political Science in Philadelphia to debate the question of "Security in Industry" with Gerard P. Swope, president of General Electric, and other distinguished industrialists. (It was on this occasion that Mr. Swope proposed a form of national planning for stabilization by the establishment of "industrial councils," the councils to include some degree of labor representation.) Hillman, that night, spoke bitingly:

> The undue optimism of a year ago makes things worse rather than better. We have exhausted the possibilities of optimistic statements. It is time now to face things as they are. *There must be a way out.* [Italics added.]

Declaring that no one now knew when prosperity would return of its own accord, he insisted that henceforth we must plan our production and our consumption. An obvious first step was to reduce hours; if such measures were not taken, if we continued to "drift," then the vast majority of the people, victims of industrial chaos, would see to it that "coercion" was used by the government in behalf of all the people.

This was a most trenchant speech. One eyewitness felt that Hillman now "was reaching out to a much larger audience outside . . . with the ideas he was presenting so incisively. The response . . . indicated how grave many people consider the present situation." [9]

For long years now, Hillman had marched uphill and down again with the clothing workers. Was this to go on forever? *There must be a way out,* he told himself. The planner and builder in him were outraged at the thought that all that had been accomplished in the struggles of nearly twenty years was being swept away. "Modern" sweatshops were being thrown together in barns or lofts of small outlying towns where the children of the·immigrants of yesterday now worked for 10 or 15 cents an hour. Hillman's testimony showed that by 1931 fully 50 per cent of the men's clothing workers were unemployed, while those employed did not work full time by any means. In the non-union centers workers earned a maximum of $10 a week for extremely long hours. These facts were made known at a hearing of the Senate Committee on Manufactures early in 1932. In the course of his testimony Hillman burst out in anger at those who opposed paying a "dole" to the starving. There were some who held it was not time yet to give Federal relief.

I would ask by what standards are we to gauge that time; must we have hundreds of thousands of people actually dead and dying from starvation? Must we have bread riots? What is necessary to convince them that there is a need for Federal and speedy relief? . . .

I am speaking feelingly today because no one can meet any group connected with labor without realizing, as I do, the terrible distress that prevails, and one must be inhuman to quibble about it. . . .

Everything worth while built up in the last few decades is being annihilated and destroyed. It is all going down at a speed that is just appalling. . . . I am one of those who never believed the conspiracy of silence will instill confidence in a community. There is all this talk of hopefulness, but we know better. In 1929 and 1930 they got away with it.[10]

By now Hillman was in favor even "of a dole for capital." There was a great clothing manufacturer in Baltimore, employing 2,000 workers, who had co-operated with the union for almost two decades. He now fell on evil days, and the Amalgamated struggled vainly to keep him afloat. At this time all Baltimore, as Hillman said, had become "one vast sweatshop." But when Hillman learned one day from the management of Hart, Schaffner and Marx in Chicago that they too were considering—in these darkest hours of the depression—the liquidation of their affairs, he almost broke down and wept. At this point the 4,000 remaining Chicago employees of the Hart, Schaffner and Marx firm instituted a voluntary wage cut, to be considered as a "loan" to the company of part of their contractual wages for a year—later repaid in full.*

Not only was the Amalgamated membership cut to the bone, but its co-operative ventures in banking and housing rode through the storm only because of the utmost vigilance on the part of those who managed their affairs.

In New York in 1932 there were some 862 families housed in the Amalgamated co-operative apartments as "tenant-owners," many of whom, out of work, could pay neither their monthly loan installments nor interest on their obligations. But this emergency had been provided for; the endorsements of certain philanthropists covered these loans, so that the jobless workers were not evicted and in the end survived to pay off all arrears and debts.

One fearful side effect of the financial debacle in Wall Street was the run on banks which began in the autumn of 1930 when the ill-starred Bank of United States in New York fell into difficulties. The Amalgamated Banks in New York and Chicago then had over 30,000 depositors and more than $15,000,000 in deposits, mainly as savings accounts. *All* the other labor banks were going under. But some months before the 1930 bank runs, the Amalgamated Bank, at the insistence of one of its active New York directors, Max Lowenthal, had begun to sell its securities for cash. Although this was at the period of partial recovery from the extreme decline of 1929, it involved a heavy loss of the bank's surplus funds. Dr. Leo Wolman, who for a while had been bitten by the New Era optimism,

* In one month in 1932 the per capita payments into the ACWA's general office treasury were only for 7,000 dues-paying members! This represented the deepest dive in the cycle. However, a few weeks later, the records show per capita payments for over 70,000; and soon afterwards for 107,000.

by now predicted that the depression would last a long time. Hillman agreed with Lowenthal's view that the bank's surplus was "there solely to protect the depositors' holdings" and should be sacrificed if need be. Thus all securities were sold and loans liquidated, even at a loss, until only cash and short-term United States Treasury bonds remained. The first bank runs of December 1930 were therefore successfully weathered. The later bank runs of 1932 and 1933 were also met by payment of all demands. At the time of the Bank Holiday of March 1933, the little Amalgamated institutions in Chicago and New York were on a basis of 99 per cent cash or the equivalent. No savings depositors were ever made to wait for full payment, as the law permitted and as happened with other and far bigger banks. This, as Hillman admitted, was "ultra-conservative," not profitable, commercial banking technique, but it was safer in the end to err on that side. For who would have aided these labor-union banks if they had fallen into straits? Years afterward Hillman recalled that it was "the advice of Max Lowenthal that helped more than anything else to keep our banks open during the Hoover banking collapse." [11]

Hillman never slept in those days. In the eyes of his union associates he showed himself at his best during the misery and stark panic of the Great Depression. During the fat years of the 1920's many trade unionists had been lulled to sleep. But in a sense the depression gave Sidney Hillman a great opportunity, such as he longed for, to raise himself far above the level of other routine-minded labor leaders living out their days in the restricted world of their own union. *"There must be some way out,"* he said. No labor union alone or, for that matter, "no industry alone could overcome the conditions existing in the terrible years since 1929. . . . We urged economic planning. Of course ours were voices crying in the wilderness." [12] After the elections of November 1930 (in which the Republican President lost the support of Congress) Hillman turned his eyes to the national capital at Washington.

III

A real labor leader eats, drinks, and breathes politics every day of his life, especially one with such a politically alert membership as the Amalgamated's tailors. Hillman, in whom the arts of diplomacy and manipulation were instinctive, had up to now interested himself only in a desultory way in organized political action; the economic job had been all-absorbing. He had been attracted only by third-party movements that gave promise of winning a broad national following—such as the elder La Follette's in 1924. However, the extreme backwardness of the United States in all labor and social legislation, compared with England, Sweden, or Germany, was glaringly illuminated by the crisis, and, like other politically sensitive persons, he could feel the ground-swell of anger in all the people. The elections of November 1930, producing a House and Senate majority opposed to Hoover's conservative policies, included a goodly number of "radical" Western leaders. Now was the time, if ever, to press for Federal legislation on unemployment relief, through whatever groups he could work with.

On September 19, 1930, Hillman wired Senator Robert M. La Follette, Jr.: "Heartiest congratulations on the splendid victory of Progressives in Wisconsin." On November 17 he dispatched a similar telegram to the Progressive Republican Governor Gifford Pinchot of Pennsylvania, whose wife sometimes helped man the picket lines of the union. On the same day he wrote Representative Fiorello La Guardia, congratulating him on his re-election to Congress, and urging that he "put unemployment insurance on the agenda of the national legislature." A man interested in political action must keep his name before his political friends.

From the beginning of 1931, Hillman literally hounded men like Senators Edward Costigan, Smith W. Brookhart, Robert Wagner, and even Royal Copeland, to induce them to press for Federal relief measures. In addition to this he also kept watch on the state legislatures at Albany and Harrisburg, arranging through the Amalgamated union to have experts in sociology or economics, such as John A. Fitch, Morris Llewellyn Cooke, or Harlow Person of the Taylor Society, appear before them and give testimony on the need for state relief measures.

Being at the head of a highly esteemed labor institution was a decided advantage in such political work—though of course not as much as if one were chairman of General Electric or General Motors. Hillman used such leisure and staff assistance as he had to organize conferences of interested university professors or economic authorities in Washington, with the Amalgamated union footing the expense. A very effective project was thus launched in the spring of 1931, when he suddenly telephoned Charles W. Ervin, Washington representative of the Amalgamated union, and asked him to approach Senator Robert La Follette, Jr., with the suggestion that a Senate committee be empowered to investigate the causes of the depression and the possibility of setting up a national economic council.

Ervin related:

> I took the idea to Bob. Bob has a very quick mind. He said: "I'll draw up a bill that nobody will oppose, because I won't put teeth in it at first, but it will give my committee power to bring prominent industrialists, financiers, and labor leaders to Washington to give testimony as to the planlessness of American industry." *

The younger La Follette (who, like his father, had been warmly supported by the Amalgamated people in Wisconsin) showed enough interest in the idea to come on to New York to see Hillman. For their conference held at his office, Hillman also invited Professor John M. Clark of Columbia University, Harlow Person of the Taylor Society, Isador Lubin of the Brookings Institution, and George Soule, an editor of the *New Republic*. These men were of the type he so often referred to as persons "who believed in human values more than in property interests." They all worked enthusiastically with Senator La Follette and Hillman over plans for an investigation of the financial crash in Wall Street and for public hearings of some of its dramatis personae. Such an investigation by à Senate subcommittee was to serve, of course, as a platform from which real facts and specific remedial proposals would be broadcast before the entire country. Hillman and his group of experts were by now in thorough agreement that "the only possible solution of the country's problems lay in some measure of national planning," as one of them has related. Therefore, a bill was drafted by Hillman's advisers providing

* Ervin declared further, in an article written in *The Advance* in 1934, "The NRA didn't happen by chance. Nothing happens by chance! It really began to breathe two years before in the testimony gathered from all of the industrial and labor leaders of the country in the hearings on the Economic Council Bill put before the Senate by Senator La Follette! That was the hand that put it in, but the mind that gave birth to the idea was a long-distance message to me by Sidney Hillman. . . .

"You all know the result. It was on that seven weeks of testimony . . . that the National Industrial Recovery Act was built."

for planning through an Economic Council of fifteen members representing "industrial, financial, agricultural, transportation, and labor
interests in the United States." [13] Such a council was to have mainly
a broad fact-finding power and serve as an advisory body formulat-
ing recommendations for action by Congress.

What Hillman hoped was that the inquiries to be conducted by
La Follette's subcommittee would precipitate a great debate on the
contemporary breakdown of private enterprise. To make sure that
the discussion would be comprehensive, he and Lubin mapped out
in advance the various steps that were to be taken, listing the eminent business leaders and experts who were to be called to testify,
and even outlining the questions that were to be put to them. If the
business magnates admitted that they knew of nothing that could be
done, they would be exposed as a weak and defeated group, which
would convince everybody that governmental action must be taken.
At this stage a group of economists with ideas for some positive
action in the line of planning and control by the Federal Government might be brought forward to give their views. Popular discontent over the miseries of the depression might help, thereafter, to
open the way for legislation.

The public had been highly aroused by stories of mismanagement
and dishonesty on the part of big business, told recently before
committees of Congress. There was all the greater bitterness because
of widespread hunger and deprivation in a land which only yesterday
had been a scene of astonishing luxury and sybaritism, and where
the fear of poverty or the need for social reform was held to be
"obsolete." President Daniel Willard of the Baltimore and Ohio Railroad, in March 1931 had declared publicly that if he and his family
were in the position of millions of hungry Americans he would steal
before he would starve!

In this highly charged atmosphere the La Follette resolution for
an inquiry was quickly approved by the Senate, and the subcommittee hearings began at the end of October 1931. To Sidney Hillman,
active behind the national political scene for the first time—since a
brief foray during the war days of 1917—it was like attending a play
in whose rehearsals and stage management he had taken a leading
part.

Before the eyes of an interested public the figures of great money
lords like Charles E. Mitchell of the National City Bank, Eugene

Meyer, governor of the Federal Reserve Board, Alfred P. Sloan of General Motors, James A. Farrell of United States Steel, and many others passed in turn as they gave their testimony, sometimes confused or disheartening, at others downright unpleasant. Albert H. Wiggin (later charged with having betrayed the trust of his own Chase Bank's stockholders), declared that nothing could be done to stabilize conditions in this country. A crisis was bound to come every so often. But was the capacity of human nature for suffering endless? La Follette asked thoughtfully. Wiggin thought it was. "Your counsel is one really of despair, then?" And Wiggin merely shrugged his shoulders at this accusation.

Then the scene shifted and social workers such as Frances Perkins, Industrial Commissioner of New York, and Monsignor John A. Ryan of the Catholic Welfare Conference were on the stand describing the malnourished condition of hundreds of thousands of wage earners' families. Finally Sidney Hillman, whose initiative was principally responsible for this public inquiry, came under the spotlight and took up the cudgels against the conservative leaders of finance typified by Wiggin. He spoke as the first labor leader in the United States who had established unemployment insurance funds on a large scale almost a decade earlier, and as one who, by co-operation with management, had striven for years to stabilize one of the country's largest industries.

Gerard Swope earlier had presented proposals for stabilizing employment and prices through trade associations within individual industries. Hillman, asked by Chairman La Follette for his views on this idea, said:

Not only do I disagree, but I believe that it is not feasible from the whole recorded experience of industry. . . . In the clothing industry we have been unusually resourceful in seeking and putting into effect methods to bring about stabilization. We have gone beyond other industries in putting up unemployment reserves. . . . But even in normal times we did not succeed in achieving real and complete stabilization.

No one industry can stabilize itself. Its prosperity is dependent upon the general state of industry and of agriculture.

The problem today is to find jobs for people out of work, and to maintain a standard of living to match our productive capacity. . . . National economic planning is essential to any constructive program.

He was for national planning through a council in which capital, labor, and the public were represented, not for leaving this to the giants of business and their trade associations. He continued:

We know that we have a population of so many; we have capacity to produce things on a certain scale, and we should run industry accordingly.

He did not accept depressions as "inevitable," as men had accepted plagues centuries ago—and as was being done by the President's committee for "voluntary" action against unemployment. These men were saying, in effect, that the depression was "an act of God," that nothing could be done about it, and that a third of the population would simply have to be wiped out. There had been witnesses who argued that national economic planning would result in dictatorship; but Hillman answered that

the surest road to dictatorship is just not to attend to things that have to be done, or at least not finding out what has to be done. That may result in our drifting into something that none of us will be able to control.

In a challenge to the do-nothing tycoons he went on to say:

In this time of great emergency . . . no leadership has come from industry, finance, or any other source to which we have a right to look. The real trouble is the lack of responsibility. . . .
The tragic situation in which we are all caught is one from which we need not continue to suffer. I do not share the belief that we must stand by hopelessly until good luck or the operation of mysterious forces temporarily brings us back to . . . prosperity.[14]

Those who watched and listened in the audience at the Senate committee hearing "could not help noting a feeling of impatience and even contempt in Hillman toward the men who had failed to take hold of the present crisis." [15] Hillman's words of challenge were now carried far by the nation's press. That season the whole country, literally, seemed to be given over to the discussion of national economic planning, the idea of which touched even the circles of professional politicians such as Governor Roosevelt of New York.

At the hearings in Washington in the autumn of 1931 Hillman had met Hugo Black, the senator from Alabama, who was preparing a bill seeking to limit hours of work to thirty per week by statute. At this period Hugo Black and Senator George Norris of Nebraska were in contact with various liberal groups representing certain farmers, AFL unions, and the railway Brotherhoods, all of whom were interested in recovery legislation.

Hillman pointed out to Black that a drastic reduction of hours, while helping to spread work, would also spread hardship, and some added provision was needed for setting a "floor," or minimum, under wages. The senator held up action while he explored the possibility of enacting a minimum-wage law such as Hillman urged. "At that time," Black said, "the AFL unions were strongly opposed to a minimum wage, holding that it would tend to become a 'maximum.' "[16]

Meanwhile the economic plague raged on in 1932. In New York and the surrounding region the Amalgamated members, as noted above, were making a temporary seasonal recovery in clothing manufacture in the summer of 1932—which, though carried out with high spirit, was, as Hillman knew, hopeless in the face of the massive economic disaster engulfing the whole nation.

The Communists, during the twenties, had made an impressive failure of their campaign to organize the American proletarians. But by 1932 their slogans, aimed at the unemployed and homeless (*"Starve or Fight!"*), were taking some effect. "Sure, you'd be a Bolshevist too, if you were starving," John L. Lewis' Pennsylvania coal miners were saying now.[17]

Those were the days of Communist-led Unemployed Councils, of virtual civil war in the mine fields of Kentucky. Farmers in mobs attended auctions of their foreclosed farms, armed with shotguns to drive off the auctioneer and the sheriff. Hunger marchers besieged state capitols or city halls. Testifying again on the need for Federal relief before a committee of Congress, Hillman assailed those who worked for delay or claimed that more information was needed:

> Talk about information! All you have to do is to go out in any street and look at the faces of the people, and get all the information you want as to what is happening in homes. . . . Thousands of people are standing in the bread lines in the cold and rain waiting for a sandwich and a cup of coffee, and yet it is said we do not know that there is a situation of distress that should be relieved by the government.[18]

With increasing exasperation he read accounts of riots of the unemployed, of the "Ford Massacre" at Dearborn, Michigan, and of General MacArthur's "Battle of Anacostia Flats" against the Bonus

Marchers. In response to an invitation from Scripps-Howard's Washington *Daily News* to comment on this last, he wired his protest on July 29, 1932:

THE MILITARY RUTHLESSNESS AGAINST UNARMED VETERANS AND CITIZENS WAS A BLOW AIMED DIRECTLY AT THE LIBERTIES OF ALL THE CITIZENS STOP . . . HAD THOSE IN POLITICAL POWER ACTED ONLY A YEAR AGO TO MEET THE PROBLEM OF RELIEF TO THE MILLIONS OF UNEMPLOYED THEY WOULD NOT HAVE HAD AN UNARMED ARMY SEEKING RELIEF AT THE DOORS OF THE NATIONAL CAPITOL AND THE DISGRACE OF THURSDAY WOULD NOT HAVE STAINED THE PAGES OF OUR HISTORY.

A few weeks before the Battle of Anacostia Flats, Governor Franklin D. Roosevelt had been nominated for the presidency by the Democratic Party. In his campaign tour Roosevelt spoke as a prudent liberal in the Eastern cities (promising government economies), while pledging radical measures aimed at recovery and relief to his Western audiences. But Hillman knew that he had privately indicated he might support some labor law like Senator Black's 30-hour bill. In his caravan there were, among others, liberal professors who "ghosted" his speeches or acted as his advisers, such as Rexford Tugwell of Columbia University and Felix Frankfurter of Harvard—an old friend and benefactor of the Amalgamated since World War days.

Hillman's interest in the Democratic candidate rose sharply when he read in the newspapers of July 1932 of a proposed program for Federal public works, credited to Roosevelt's adviser, Tugwell, that would result in the re-employment of many millions.

"There is a trial balloon, and *very interesting*," he said.[19]

After the decisive Roosevelt election victory, when the President-elect was secluded at Hyde Park, New York, Hillman tried to get to him through Felix Frankfurter, in order to place his proposals for recovery and labor legislation before him.

This was in January 1933, almost at the height of the banking panic. Frankfurter wrote Hillman that he would do his best to bring the Hillman memorandum to Roosevelt's attention, but that he must realize that the President-elect was besieged on all sides with proposals of every sort. Hillman, the professor suggested shrewdly, would do well to go out and stir up public interest in his ideas in other quarters, in order to reach the attention of Roosevelt with greater effect.

In such matters Hillman needed no prompting. Shortly after the election he had heard that Frances Perkins would probably be named Secretary of Labor. In December 1932, he arranged to meet her, through Dr. Leo Wolman, and soon afterward sent her a memorandum for the attention of Roosevelt (dated December 1932), on proposed labor legislation. This paper clearly reflects his political philosophy at the period, deeply influenced as it was by the experience of benevolent government labor policies during World War I.

In the absence of leadership in private industry, the only way out now, he urged, was through governmental regulation on a nationwide scale:

During the period of war, when the problem confronting the country was the shortage of labor, the Federal Government through its War Labor Board established rules to guide industry, subordinating the interest of the group to the welfare of the country. The emergency today . . . is much greater than during the war and similar action should obviously be taken. There ought to be established a . . . Labor Board whose function it shall be to regulate hours in the different industries in a manner that will not only check further layoffs but will replace part of those who are at this time unemployed. In our industry the enforcement of 30 to 36 hours a week would give employment to tens of thousands. . . . It shall also be the duty of the Board to establish minimum wages for men and women in each industry.

The membership of the Board should be composed of a representative of labor from each industry, of capital and of the public.[20]

In this panicky interregnum between two presidential administrations groups of business leaders associated with the United States Chamber of Commerce, and including also Bernard Baruch and Gerard Swope, were demanding that trade associations be allowed immunity from the Sherman Anti-Trust law so that they might combine to "stabilize" (that is to say, *raise*) prices and foster employment. Labor leaders, including John L. Lewis, William Green, and Hillman were now supporting the pending 30-hour bill. Out of these conflicting pressures of different interest groups there was to emerge the National Industrial Recovery Act.

The intermittent bank runs of 1930-32 were resumed with greater fury than ever before in January and February 1933. On March 6,

1933, President Roosevelt, as his first act in office, declared a National Bank Holiday, closing all banks. The reopening of the banks beginning March 11 was carried out only after Federal Reserve Bank examination and approval of their condition. In all, 15,000, or half of America's banks, were closed down between 1929 and 1933. But on the select list of banks approved for prompt reopening in the New York Federal Reserve District as in Chicago was the Amalgamated Bank, found to be about 99 per cent liquid.

In the banking field, the Amalgamated alone among labor banks had weathered the full force of the depression in a style that few of the country's greatest financial houses could rival. The union's leadership had shown its brains and courage in the world of practical affairs at a time when the "giants" of finance seemed to be in a complete state of funk. In this prolonged crisis only a lamed politician in a wheel chair and a few university professors, or labor leaders like Sidney Hillman and John L. Lewis, were acting as if they had nothing to lose and feared nothing.

Planful and farsighted by disposition, Hillman, after March 4, 1933, saw that the tide was turning; all his thought was bent now on finding the means of passing rapidly from the condition of momentary relief after near disaster to one of aggressive advance.

Chapter Sixteen

THE NEW DEAL:
HILLMAN
IN WASHINGTON

It is not easy to convey to the reader in a later, very different epoch something of the atmosphere of emotional drama
in which President Roosevelt assumed office on March 4, 1933. By
emergency decrees and by acts of Congress passed with lightning-like
speed, enormous powers were tendered the Chief Executive. But
though armed with such great powers, the head of the government in
crisis could not have eyes everywhere; and so he leaned upon the new
staff of assistants and experts who gathered about him. Thus the "New
Deal professors" came into power, as a satirical weekly, *The New
Yorker*, noted,

through no magic recipe of their own, but through the abdication of
their predecessors. Before 1933, men like the Van Sweringens, the Insulls,
the Hopsons, and the Richard Whitneys usually helped to "run" the
country. During the great depression some of these men came to an
untimely end, some skipped the country, and a few even landed in the
penitentiary. The nation was distraught, business had lost its nerve. . . .
Hope, courage, and faith in the future of the nation were wanting.[1]

But not in the new officeholders who administered the New Deal: the professors, economists, agricultural experts, social workers, and labor-union people.

The field had been opened for "extended social action." It was a time for reform; it was a splendid time for Hillman to come to Washington. Nor was he the only one. "Bill" Green, John L. Lewis, and A. F. Whitney were also on hand to speak for labor. The farm bloc sent its spokesmen, and the representatives of great corporations, accompanied by their lawyers, came also to clamor for relief.

The problems of industrial recovery and stabilization which the Roosevelt regime attacked, it must be noted, were of the kind Hillman and the Amalgamated staff had specialized in for almost twenty years in their own field. The schemes now put forward for the regulation of production standards, prices and wages, and for effecting a "concert" of different interests were all familiar devices to Hillman.

Roosevelt "improvised" measures for recovery with a certain inconsistency, it has been remarked, yet unlike other presidents, he placed constructive measures for the relief of labor and the strengthening of trade unions high up in his agenda. Because possible legal difficulties were foreseen, the original Black-Connery (30-hour) Bill was set aside for the moment and, with Roosevelt's approval, Secretary of Labor Perkins appointed a committee of labor authorities who were to confer together on the problems of adjusting wages and hours and make their recommendations to her and the President. Those appointed to participate in this conference were Sidney Hillman, William Green, A. F. Whitney, and Miss Rose Schneiderman of the Women's Trade Union League. Hillman thus found himself at long last sitting down with his erstwhile adversary, the head of the AFL, involved in the common task of shaping new labor legislation for the emergency. Out of this conference came one main recommendation, strongly urged by Hillman, that the government establish labor boards to regulate employment, wages, and working conditions.

On March 31, 1933, the committee of labor leaders, including Hillman, had come to the White House to confer with President Roosevelt and make their recommendations. By his handling of the money crisis of March, Roosevelt had become overnight a national hero. It was Sidney Hillman's first meeting with Roosevelt, whom he found fascinating then and always, as he said. Roosevelt had style, he thought. Hillman enjoyed even the way he waved his cigarette holder and threw back his head and laughed. He did not make the mistake of under-rating Roosevelt's political intelligence.[2]

Meanwhile other advisory groups from the camp of the capital-ists—led by Gerard Swope and Bernard Baruch—were drawing up their own schemes for regulating production and adjusting prices as in the time of World War I. On April 6, 1933, Roosevelt ordered these different groups of advisers to "get into a room and weave it all together." They were to write an omnibus bill combining a huge pub-lic works program with one calling for the control of production, prices, employment, and hours of labor. The writing of the bill was entrusted mainly to General Hugh S. Johnson (a former employee of Bernard Baruch, the financier), who had been "loaned" to the Demo-cratic National Committee during the 1932 election campaign. The business groups opposed demands of the labor leaders for a 30-hour bill, while the laborites were suspicious of the businessmen's plans for raising prices and restricting output. In the end the Chamber of Com-merce element had its way. But this time the wishes of the trade unionists were also consulted and a clause incorporating their demands for a labor code, the famous 7(a) clause, was written into the recov-ery bill.[3] Hillman, as well as William Green and Edward McGrady (a former AFL official who became Assistant Secretary of Labor), had a hand in shaping the labor provisions of the National Recovery Act. Before the proposed law was announced a weekly news magazine reported:

> In and out of congressional committee rooms, hotel lobbies where labor groups gather, and conferences at the Department of Labor, there has moved these past crowded weeks the trim, slim figure of one of the youngest presidents of an important labor union, Sidney Hillman. Serious, almost somber, with no small talk, no glad-handing, Mr. Hillman . . . brings a brass-tacks philosophy of industrial democracy to the labor group in the Administration struggling to devise new economic machinery.
>
> Secretary of Labor Perkins, whose regard for Mr. Hillman's advice is outspoken, has taken over the outlines of Mr. Hillman's proposals and put them into her substitute for the Black 30-hour bill.[4]

Hillman himself, in an interview on May 5, 1933, gave some advance hints of the nature of the new law that would establish an "industry board" and "encourage employment and labor organization." [5]

Two weeks later, May 22, 1933, the provisions of the National In-dustrial Recovery Bill (NIRA, later shortened to NRA) were made public. Under its terms, manufacturing units would be obliged to enter into trade associations for each industry or trade and formulate "codes" of fair competition controlling standards of hours, wages, and working conditions as well as agreements on prices governed by "fair trade practices." The workers, under the 7(a) clause, would be assured of the right to organize and bargain collectively, to designate their own union representatives, and to be free from interference by their employers in such choice.

Hillman was jubilant over the turn of events. Almost three years before he had urged that the government step in to regulate wages and prices. The recovery measure "was like the realization of a dream." He expected that labor unions would be enabled to secure collective-bargaining arrangements covering 100 per cent of their industries. The industries themselves would be forced to acquire a national viewpoint, and Hillman saw at a glance all that this would mean for the American labor movement.[6]

This would be the first time that Congress had passed a law directly encouraging labor organization. On the other hand, the bill *did not ban* individual bargaining, company unions, or the open shop. In a radio address he made in New York on June 9, 1933, Hillman was quick to point out that this great "charter" would exist only "on paper, void of results, unless labor takes full advantage of it." Recovery itself, he said, depended on labor's securing higher wages and diffusing purchasing power among the masses—"otherwise we will not get the benefits of this law." [7]

He soon brought down to Washington a whole "bloc" of his own to support the national recovery bill. At his suggestion leading capitalists of the clothing trade who had long co-operated with the Amalgamated union wired their congressmen from New York, Chicago, and Rochester, urging its passage. To Hillman, as to John L. Lewis and other alert labor leaders, the advantages of the 7(a) clause outweighed those provisions of the bill permitting the establishment of cartel-like trade associations having immunity from anti-trust laws. This Hillman did not fear for the moment, so long as his union might keep control of the job in its industry. John L. Lewis, like Hillman, hastened to the lobbies of Congress, where there was some opposition to the labor provisions of the bill, and brought pressure for its passage.[8] This was obtained after only two weeks of debate. At once Lewis hurried off to the coal fields, where the mine-union organizers were engaged in a whirlwind drive to win back members. Hillman, too, many weeks before the law was passed or codes were set up, sent forth all the Amalgamated officers and staff organizers available to open the greatest unionizing campaign the union had attempted since 1919. The people were told something they had never heard hitherto: that the new President "wanted them to join the union." In the coal fields the United Mine Workers' organizers bellowed that "John L. Lewis was eating ham and eggs with President Roosevelt."

Much ground had been lost for the clothing workers during the depression years: the very promising shirt workers' department, for example, had been cut down to some 5,000 members, centered mainly in New York City, while huge non-union plants producing the bulk of the industry's output flourished in Pennsylvania, Connecticut, and upstate New York. Foreseeing new opportunities in this field, Hillman assigned Assistant President Jacob S. Potofsky to head the shirt workers' "drive" in the towns of eastern Pennsylvania and upper New York.

Potofsky pointed out that he had had no real experience in organizing work.

"Remember, I will be standing behind you wherever you go," Hillman reassured him. Potofsky, with squads of veteran organizers, took the field. In New York, Louis Hollander led a massive walkout of 35,000 union members in July in an effort to strengthen the local organization, while Hillman stayed in Washington to see to it that a satisfactory men's clothing code was drawn up. As a result of this teamwork the New York employers' group was persuaded to grant the desired concessions, thus ending the walkout.

The renewal of aggressive organizing action was indispensable in view of the loopholes in the NRA law permitting employers to do much as they pleased about union recognition, or about the observance of the new labor standards—save where the union men themselves enforced the 7(a) clause.

The man chosen as administrator of the NRA was General Hugh S. Johnson, former Army judge advocate and lately a Wall Street statistician. He in turn appointed an Industrial Advisory Board to aid him, composed of representatives of business, while Miss Perkins, Secretary of Labor, on June 19, 1933, selected a Labor Advisory Board which Johnson agreed, somewhat reluctantly, was to be consulted by him. Of the five-man labor board two members came from the Amalgamated Clothing Workers: Sidney Hillman and Dr. Leo Wolman, whom Miss Perkins named as chairman. The other members were John L. Lewis of the miners' union, Joseph Franklin of the boiler-makers, and John Frey, of the AFL metal-trades department, while Edward F. McGrady sat in for the government. Hillman's reputation at this period stood higher than that of the AFL leaders on the board, including John L. Lewis. At any rate, as a dollar-a-year man in Washington, he was now in an excellent position to help improve labor standards in many industries.

The AFL men were reported as none too happy at the presence of the unorthodox Hillman in their midst. But the man who was plainly the strongest member of their group in Washington (as Hillman quickly perceived), John L. Lewis, from the start of the New Deal gave Hillman his warm support and friendship.

Lewis, head of the country's largest industrial union since 1919, was then fifty-three, seven years older than Hillman. With his powerful barrel-chested figure, his deep-set dark eyes, and his huge black-maned head, he was a virile figure of a man, with a natural power of eloquence. Yet while Hillman during the 1920's had made himself noted for progressive and constructive leadership, Lewis had undergone a decade of disaster.* The recent history of the United Mine Workers, as John Brophy wrote in 1929, was one of "broken faith, lost hopes, bitter defeats, and the almost total destruction of a once powerful union." A large group among the members had rebelled against the "reactionary" policies of Lewis to form an insurgent organization of their own. But in the crisis of 1932–33, Lewis had undergone a decided change of heart. He called back to his side the insurgents he had expelled from his union, such as John Brophy and Powers Hapgood. In the first summer of the New Deal, as if reborn, he launched one of the most spectacular unionizing campaigns ever seen in the coal fields, returning to Washington in the autumn with the UMW's membership restored to 400,000, and gaining for himself the reputation of the country's strongest organizer of labor.

---

* "The contrast between the two men is most instructive," one of Lewis' former associates has said. "Hillman had taken a rabble of poor immigrants and organized them into the most advanced trade union in the country. During the depression he had held their ranks together. Lewis, on the other hand, in 1919 had risen, by political cleverness, to the presidency of the country's greatest labor union, which others had organized into an army of 500,000. Ten years later it was in ruins, and down to about 80,000 bona fide members." (John Brophy to M. J.)

With his old-fashioned oratory John L. Lewis had dramatized the resurgence of labor in 1933 as no one else could have done. The miners, having seen the entire economy of the coal fields collapse, had been on the verge of revolutionary action. At Lewis' powerful call they joined the union en masse. Lewis, the erstwhile political supporter of the Hardings and Hoovers, now saw himself as a progressive leader. His own explanation for his change of heart was: "It takes every man some time to find himself in this world. It took me longer than most people." [9]

Meanwhile Hillman was immersed in the turbulent politics of Washington during the early phase of the New Deal. Codes for more than 400 different industries and trades were being hastily drawn up to the accompaniment of much high-voiced argument, swearing, and table-thumping by "dictator" Johnson. The oaths of Johnson, as Hillman perceived, were usually much stronger than his bite. Hillman's job as a labor adviser and, soon afterward, as a member of the Clothing Code Authority, was to serve as labor's watchdog. His influence in setting the terms of the industrial codes was to be decisive, not only in men's clothing, but in women's garments, textiles, and many other industries.

Every hour of labor that he was able to cut down in those noisy and wearisome sessions with the representatives of industry at the NRA meant work for tens of thousands who were idle, and almost as many new union recruits for all labor organizations. David Dubinsky, who that year became president of the International Ladies' Garment Workers, declared that Hillman was the ILGWU's "best organizer." This union, like that of the coal miners, made a spectacular gain, bringing its membership up from about 50,000 to 200,000 by 1934. Dubinsky at this time said that it was Hillman who showed him how one could "take advantage" of the NRA, adding:

. . . To a large extent, the credit that I receive today, the praise that my new organization receives is due to Hillman. He was the driving force in the early stages. He would say, "When are you starting the [organization of the] dress industry?" He talked like a teacher would talk to his pupil. I consider him as such.[10]

The unionizing campaign of the Amalgamated itself was less spectacular than that of other unions, *only because it had never gone down so far as the others during the depression.* Even so, in actions that were still far from peaceful, some 25,000 newly organized shirt workers were swiftly added to the union's ranks in the 1933–34 drives in Pennsylvania, New York, and Connecticut. Elsewhere the tailors' union increased membership about 50 per cent. In the Pennsylvania towns where the coal miners' union was potent, much help was tendered the Amalgamated and the ILGWU by Lewis' men. In return the Amalgamated officers in many towns gave strong assistance to the miners also, as even William Green (a former officer of the UMW) gratefully acknowledged. The success of this interdependent action turned, to a great extent, upon Hillman's decisive influence in the enactment of labor codes for the mass of 400,000 to 500,000 or more needleworkers and textile workers, for whom he appeared now as the chief spokesman in the national capital.[11] On the other hand, the intense activity of organizers and the reviving spirit of the workers vastly strengthened the bargaining position Hillman, Lewis, and other labor advocates held in the Washington sector.

There were, meanwhile, many vexations and disappointments suffered even from the start of the NRA. Yet Hillman, established in a little office of the Department of Commerce Building, bubbled over with good spirits, and assured all who came to him that labor was on the march, that Roosevelt had given labor this golden opportunity, and that the United States, after being twenty years behind other nations, was catching up at last in its labor laws. He went so far as to say:

I have no patience with those who minimize the NRA. Only people who in my judgment have a sinister purpose say that the NRA has not been a great gain for labor. . . . Also, those who haven't the patience to think things through.[12]

II

In the spring of 1933 hope returned and recovery from panic began under the smile of the confident Roosevelt. Half of the NRA program, it will be remembered, called for huge public works expenditures. In anticipation of this, wholesale prices rose quickly and employment mounted, while Roosevelt's noisiest deputy, Johnson of the NRA, bellowed: "We're going to put millions back to work, pay them living wages, cut down production." He roared for ever more and faster codes. Trade-union leaders and leaders of industry and their agents thronged to Washington, to harvest what they could for their clients or followers. Excitement over the hundreds of codes, such as those of the diaper, millinery, or hosiery industry, filled the government offices and the lobbies of Washington hotels. "Hoover made monkeys of the American people during the depression," one wag said at the time, "but Roosevelt has them climbing trees." [13]

When the industrialists of steel and motors ignored the NRA, Johnson vowed that the government would "crack down" on them. He growled and heaved himself about and in the end brought forth the device of the Blue Eagle as a certificate of honor to be awarded only to those who complied with the emergency law. Blue Eagle parades were held in our cities; indeed the whole country was placarded with Blue Eagles. Yet the coal miners found that their code was enforced only when they had unionized the coal fields.

Perhaps Hugh Johnson was a good deal of a fraud. Perhaps the Blue Eagle was part fraud, and under its frowzy wings too many business chiselers raised wages 10 per cent while marking up wholesale prices as much as 50 or 100 per cent and scheming to curb production.*

"We must use the instruments that are at hand," Hillman would say in extenuation of the more dubious features of the NRA.

Almost from the start, on June 20, 1933, in hearings for the first code, that for cotton textiles, he locked horns with the mighty John-son, who had rushed through an ill-conceived agreement allowing the 40-hour week and a low minimum wage. Hillman, in his severe criticisms of the administrator, declared that such a code did nothing to encourage re-employment or increase purchasing power, thus defeating the object of the NRA law. It would all have to be done over again, he predicted—and rightly. By taking a strong hand thereafter in the writing of the women's garment code, Hillman obtained a 35-hour week, a great boon for the Amalgamated's sister union, the ILGWU.

The men's clothing code, as worked out a few weeks later, providing for 20 per cent wage increases and a 36-hour week, was declared at the time to have been the most enlightened of the NRA codes. This was not, however, an easy victory. To be sure, Hillman had brought into the picture his old capitalistic friends in the clothing industry, such as Earl Dean Howard and Mark Cresap of Hart, Schaffner and Marx;

---

* In some industries it was reported that manufacturers' associations entered into collusive agreements to raise prices, lower quality, and restrict output. Thus instead of expanding the country's productive capacities, as was intended by this act, many used it in a contrary sense.

in addition, David Drechsler, for the New York Clothing Manufacturers' Exchange, and Max Holtz and Jeremiah Hickey of Rochester were there to back him up. These allies were badly needed; for, in drawing up the men's clothing code, Hillman came into collision with William Green, head of the AFL, who supported the claims of the old United Garment Workers for a large share of jurisdiction in this field.

The fight soon became a three-cornered one. Against the majority group of clothing manufacturers who had worked in co-operation with the Amalgamated for years and who were marshaled by Hillman to support his program, there now appeared a minority group headed by clothiers long known for their anti-union policies, such as Francis Curlee of St. Louis, Michaels, Stern of Rochester, and Greif and Company of Baltimore. This faction, calling itself the "Industrial Recovery Association of Clothing Manufacturers," opposed the pro-Hillman group, the American Men's Clothing Manufacturers' Association, which it charged was dominated by the Amalgamated union. Taking advantage of various legal loopholes in the NRA law, the rival faction insisted upon the "right" of their workers to choose company unions "of their own free will"; or, in some cases, to sign agreements with the small United Garment Workers' Union, AFL, instead of with the Amalgamated. The rival group, moreover, had mustered strong legal and political support through their lawyer, ex-Senator James Reed of Missouri.

The clothing firms that had resisted the ACWA for more than a decade were now being supported by Green and Thomas Rickert of the AFL, though Hillman, in their common interests, had been working unsparingly to help the AFL unions. Thus disheartening prospects of "dual-union" strife were opened up at the very beginning of the New Deal. In a statement assailing President Green of the AFL before the NRA's Advisory Labor Board (where they sat together as members), Hillman charged that Green had written letters to factory owners offering "scab" labor in recent strikes.[14] The Amalgamated, he threatened, would fight the AFL on this issue just as before.

Hillman was in top form in the all-day hearings for the men's clothing code, beginning July 27, 1933; by force of argument, by the weapons of logic and marshaling of facts, he made a tremendous impression and had no trouble besting opponents such as the Curlees and their lawyers. A spreading strike action of the Amalgamated was being directed at this time against his union's die-hard opponents in St. Louis, Rochester, and Baltimore. The chief obstacle, however, was the renewed rivalry of the AFL's union, which, Hillman said, was almost defunct and represented only 10 per cent of the workers. How much longer would the official labor movement of America—in the light of the swiftly changing political situation—continue to treat the great Amalgamated union as an "outlaw organization"? Confronting the hostile Mr. Curlee of St. Louis, he ventured the prediction that in the near future organized labor would cease to be divided against itself for the benefit of those who hoped to undo the NRA. "The groups of labor by themselves will get together. . . . The representatives of labor will take care of that," he predicted.

An accommodation of some sort seemed the only way out of this impasse. At a number of recent meetings of the NRA's Labor Advisory Board, the majority of those present—to Green's surprise—refused to sanction the AFL's interference in Amalgamated strikes. The most powerful of the AFL leaders of that day, John L. Lewis, now moved over to support Hillman.

Lewis had observed with growing admiration Hillman's zealous labors at the NRA code hearings. It was he and Daniel Tobin, veteran president of the Brotherhood of Teamsters, who were mainly instrumental in bringing about the rapprochement between the Amalgamated Clothing Workers and the AFL's United Garment Workers. All questions of jurisdiction between them were to be settled by negotiation, and the big independent clothing union was to become affiliated with the Federation after a divorce of nearly twenty years. News of this momentous compromise agreement leaked from Washington on August 18, 1933.[15] It foreshadowed the swift defeat of the anti-union manufacturers' bloc who opposed Hillman at the NRA code hearings for clothing.

Three weeks earlier the end of dual-union strife was sensed by Amalgamated officers, although they had not known of the secret conferences going on in Washington. In Rochester a strike was being carried on by Hillman's lieutenants against the Keller, Heumann, Thompson plant, which had at first announced an agreement with the AFL affiliate, the United Garment Workers. The police here used tear gas to rout the crowds of Amalgamated pickets. Chatman, the Rochester Joint Board manager, then created a sensation by telegraphing to Secretary of Labor Perkins a request for a loan of 500 gas masks from the War

Department. The Rochester pickets, led by the ACWA's "Joan of Arc," Dorothy Bellanca, swelled to the number of 5,000, and excitement ran high in the city.

But on the night of July 25, 1933, word came at last from Washington to the union leaders in Rochester that the Keller, Heumann, Thompson strike was settled. The firm's executives in Washington had just signed a collective-bargaining agreement with the Amalgamated, and the other union was out of the picture. This news was communicated at once to the crowds of workers in Rochester, who gave themselves over to jubilant demonstrations.

Despite the assignment of a few ready-made clothing plants, such as that of Michaels, Stern and Company, to the UGWA, the Amalgamated was to have jurisdiction over about 90 per cent of its industry, including all men's clothing and shirt workers, while the UGWA was to confine itself almost entirely to the manufacture of work clothing and overalls. Had this agreement with the American Federation not been reached at the time, many manufacturers would have hastened to sign agreements with the UGWA, and chaotic fighting might have spread throughout the industry. Instead, Hillman had skillfully worked his way out of the dangerous jurisdictional problems posed by the NRA law. The men's clothing code was completed and approved by President Roosevelt on August 29, 1933, and was in line with Hillman's program.

Meanwhile, at conferences among the labor magnates, arrangements for the chartering and admission of the Amalgamated into the American Federation of Labor were completed. The formal announcement of this event came at the AFL's national convention on October 13, 1933.

Through his coming to Washington and his work there with the leaders of the AFL, Sidney Hillman had won the unstinted praise of some of the "official" labor body's old-line executives. With his help, the International Ladies' Garment Workers had been restored to full strength and solvency. In the councils of the AFL, it was believed, he would speak not only for his own industrial union, but also for the ILGWU and other apparel and textile organizations embracing almost 500,000 workers. It was foreseen also that he would tend to become the natural ally of the industrial-union bloc now led by John L. Lewis. Perhaps there would soon be a New Deal even in the American Federation of Labor, some observers permitted themselves to hope.

III

In the autumn of 1933 the impetus of the recovery movement in markets and industries began to slow down perceptibly. This was attributed, in part, to the tardiness with which public works programs were developed; also to the poor standards of wages and hours set by most of the NRA codes, and the failure of the government to enforce compliance with such codes of fair labor standards and prices. Roosevelt was warned by his legal advisers that any real tests of the NRA law in the Federal courts would result in its being declared unconstitutional; hence such tests were postponed, and enforcement was timid.

Hillman, at any rate, centered his efforts upon improving the NRA codes as far as possible, while trusting that the growing strength of the labor movement would force compliance.

On January 7, 1934, both Sidney Hillman and John L. Lewis appeared as guest speakers before the American Academy of Political Science at Philadelphia. Lewis, always a natural orator, spoke in far more serious vein than in former years on the critical situation of labor even under the New Deal recovery laws. By contrast, Hillman was less eloquent than Lewis, though very cool, reasonable, and precise. To him the significance of the NRA lay in the fact that it led the country away from the old concepts of laissez-faire economy. For the first time it was recognized that hours of labor must be regulated to spread employment, that minimum wages must be fixed to foster mass purchasing power. But there was a debit side he said, for alas "too many are still unemployed, and too many who are employed receive inadequate compensation." On this occasion he sharply assailed General Hugh Johnson for permitting the earlier codes, such as that of cotton textiles, to be established with standards so low that "opportunities for economic liberalism were frustrated by a bad start."[16]

The NRA was a sort of impromptu parliament of industry, and those who understood the arts of political manipulation could go far in such a situation. Hillman, by instinct, was as skillful as anyone in playing this game. He noted one day that a code for the woolen trade had been written virtually at the order of the largest corporations in the field, and remarked to one of his associates: "It's a rotten code. I'd like to find someone who could blast it."

A young, rosy-cheeked economist named Leon Henderson, employed then in a minor capacity by the Consumers' Board of the NRA, was unearthed for this purpose by Charles Ervin. At first sight he seemed like a mild type of Socialist intellectual. But Hillman briefed him on the woolen industry and, at the code hearings, Henderson proved to be so aggressive and even profane—as if in imitation of Hugh Johnson—that the labor members were pleasantly surprised. The code was revised and Henderson was used effectivly again in similar emergencies.

However, the labor movement often fared poorly under the NRA; where the unions were weak, labor standards were ignored. In the mass-production industries such as steel and automobiles, where some efforts were made to set up "outside" or legitimate unions, labor organizers were simply driven out or thrown out. Even in coal mining, John L. Lewis met with serious checks when he attempted to organize the "captive mines" controlled by huge corporations like United States Steel and Bethlehem. Mr. Henry Ford completely ignored the existence of the NRA.

Since the Roosevelt Administration was still loath to enforce the new emergency laws, the only hope for the moment lay in militant labor action. By the summer of 1934 a great wave of strikes broke forth, centering especially in the coal fields, the textile industry, sections of the garment trades, and even to some extent in the fields of automobiles, rubber, steel, and electrical appliances. These first stirrings of labor in the unorganized heavy industries under the New Deal, as Hillman and Lewis observed, were largely frustrated because of the rigid craft-union character of the various AFL unions, whose officers assumed jurisdiction in these areas.

To Hillman the most vexatious problem at this time was the cotton-garment code, the first one hastily authorized by Johnson, providing for only a $12 minimum wage and a 40-hour week. Many thousands of members of the Amalgamated and of the ILGWU came under its provisions, all those who worked in the manufacture of shirts, cotton clothing, and cotton dresses throughout the South and also north of the Mason and Dixon line. In this trade there was also much complaint of the "stretch-out" system as tending to reduce employment.[17] Unrest in the related textile field also led to growing strike action. By June 1934, it was reported that the Amalgamated and the ILGWU would combine in bringing about a concerted walkout of more than 200,000 garment workers.

Once a revival of union action had begun and employers were trying to stop strikes or organizing campaigns, the need for some mediation agency became acute. A National Labor Board (of sorts) was set up in August 1933 with Senator Robert Wagner as its chairman and Dr. Leo Wolman as one of its members, the others being all representatives of industry. But it had no real power. General Johnson sometimes rushed in to mediate strikes and "speed recovery," with indifferent effect; the Labor Department also attempted conciliation, though its authority was very limited.

For months Hillman prodded Johnson and Miss Perkins to have the case of the cotton-garment code reopened. But the textile firms fiercely resisted all efforts to revise the previous agreement. Going over the heads of Johnson and Miss Perkins, Hillman at length managed to see President Roosevelt and warned him that a terrible wave of strikes by textile and garment workers would soon burst forth in many cities, and that "things people were not looking for would happen!" Following this conference at the White House, Roosevelt issued an executive order on August 22, 1934, requiring that cotton-garment workers' hours be cut to 36 a week and their minimum wage be raised 10 per cent. It was the first time that the President had intervened in such a deadlock and used his emergency powers under the National Recovery Act.

The reply of the manufacturers came promptly. They would defy the President's order. They had consulted their lawyers and received assurance that the law would uphold them; the Roosevelt Administration then was eager to avoid long court processes.

Hillman stepped into the breach again, declaring that the Amalgamated and the Ladies' Garment Workers, almost 400,000 strong, would strike, if need be, to support Roosevelt. "Labor will help the NRA administration uphold the President's order." [18]

Roosevelt liked Hillman's spirit at such a juncture. In fact, he said that Hillman was one of the "longest-headed" individuals he had ever met. He was also struck by Hillman's great skill as a negotiator. Roosevelt enjoyed having people throw ideas at him, a sport in which Hillman excelled.[19] This incident marked the beginning of a strong political friendship.

Although some delay in enforcing the new order was wrung from the President, the order slashing hours of labor for an immense number of garment and textile workers was imposed in October, chief credit for this being attributed by the newspaper columnists to "the canny Sidney Hillman." [20]

At times Roosevelt wavered badly on the labor issue. But early in 1933, when signing the NRA law, he had told Raymond Moley that he was convinced that "the historic American policy of laissez-faire" was done with. He had certainly no great understanding of the trade-union field but was very set, in 1933 and 1934, in his determination to have the power of workers increased.

At this stage, late in September 1934, General Johnson, who had been taking a pounding from all sides, resigned, to the regret of almost nobody. President Roosevelt then did what he was so often to do in the future; he reshuffled the NRA by setting up a new commission, a seven-man board, to direct it in place of its would-be "dictator." Its members were: S. Clay Williams of the Reynolds Tobacco Company, Arthur D. Whiteside of Dun and Bradstreet; Leon Henderson; Professor Walton Hamilton of Yale Law School; Professor Leon C. Marshall of Johns Hopkins University; Donald R. Richberg, lawyer for the railway workers; and Sidney Hillman. The appointment of Hillman as labor's sole representative on the National Industrial Recovery Board, or NIRB, was a reflection of the increasing favor in which he was held by Roosevelt. "The Administration turns to Hillman for advice on labor problems rather than to any old-line AFL leader," a well-informed Washington correspondent wrote at this time.[21]

The NRA codes were under heavy attack now; unemployment was not being reduced. The AFL leaders, Lewis, Green, John P. Frey, and George Berry, frequently clashed with the industry representatives on the NIRB and pressed Sidney Hillman to urge new measures to bring about a shorter working week and wage increases.

During the big strikes of 1934, mainly called in order to secure union recognition, the need for an authoritative government agency or labor board which could oversee union elections and decide who was to represent the workers had become apparent to all. The first version of a National Labor Board was reshuffled, but extreme individualists like Henry Ford still defied it. When labor trouble mounted in the Detroit motor center, a special Automobile Labor Board was appointed, with Hillman's old friend Leo Wolman as its chairman. Professor Wolman, by then, was having quite a career as a New Deal bureaucrat. There were times when some observers, Hillman among them, thought he might make an excellent Secretary of Labor someday. But Wolman chose rather to take the path of other "reformers" before him and since:

while wielding his bureaucratic authority and working to regulate interest groups with immense wealth or power, or both, he grew disillusioned with the possibilities of "reform."

After having cleaved to Sidney's side for long years, he had begun to walk alone in 1934, and the two old friends gradually drifted apart. Wolman felt that in instances where he had honestly judged the claims of labor as less strong than those of capital Hillman had criticized and opposed him unfairly. Hillman, on the other hand, gathered that Wolman nowadays listened with far greater deference to the views of the Standard Oil or General Motors magnates, who were his new social acquaintances, than to those of labor's spokesmen.

The break between the two men came soon after Wolman's appointment as chairman of the Automobile Labor Board. Wolman, sitting between a management and a labor representative, cast the deciding vote in favor of "proportional representation" plans that gave fullest scope to the company unions set up at General Motors and Chrysler's and offered no chance for the new United Auto Workers to serve as bargaining agent. The "outside" or workers'-sponsored unions, Wolman held, were as yet too weak in numbers. The tactics of violence and espionage that kept their numbers so small were to be revealed not long afterward in the labor spy investigations conducted by the La Follette committee of the Senate. They were to be revealed as well in the published confessions of Harry Bennett, the hard-boiled chief of Henry Ford's "Service Department," who commanded a battalion of a thousand ruffians.

Wolman's rulings aroused a storm throughout the labor movement. Hillman himself had appealed to his old friend in vain. He was now profoundly chagrined, for he had loved Wolman like a brother and felt forced to speak of him as one who "betrayed" labor. After the November congressional elections, which marked a tremendous victory for the New Deal, Hillman joined with Green and Lewis in exerting pressure upon the Administration to give the unorganized workers in the giant motor companies a square deal.

On November 9, 1934, the Washington press correspondents reported that Roosevelt had called Hillman to the White House for a private conference lasting half an hour. Their talk was said to have been in connection with the crisis in automobile labor. During this conference, in fact, Hillman urged a revision of the existing automobile code and a showdown on the company-union issue. He asked for

Wolman's head. At the same time he brought forward a typical Hillman device, that of a commission of inquiry, to be headed by Leon Henderson, which was to report on the labor situation in the motor industry. That very day the automobile code was to expire, unless the President extended it. Alfred P. Sloan, Walter Chrysler, and S. Clay Williams had been girding at the President earlier that day, demanding that he continue the present order of things under Dr. Wolman.

Shortly after Hillman left the White House, Roosevelt announced that he was extending the existing automobile code for three months as the industrialists desired, but also that, despite the manufacturers' contrary wishes in this matter, he proposed to "institute a study which may contribute toward improvements in stabilizing the [automobile] industry." [22]

The man in charge of this investigation was Hillman's choice, Leon Henderson, whose report, several months later, was at great variance with the previous literal-minded rulings of the Automobile Labor Board in favor of company unions. But long before that, Dr. Wolman had handed in his resignation and quietly departed from the turbulent labor scene. He declared himself "disgusted" with the politics of the New Deal and opposed to its program of national planning.*

Hillman, as a rule very detached in his judgments of people's behavior, was heard on many occasions thereafter to speak with extreme bitterness of Wolman, who for fifteen years had been one of his closest associates. After the day's business was over at the NIRB, it was Hillman's custom to return to his living quarters at the Wardman Park Hotel, gather together several convivial friends, and spend the dinnertime and evening in the only way that ever provided him with distraction—plunged in "shop talk" of labor and politics. Leo Wolman always used to sit on his right at the table, and with his quick wit served as a spur to Hillman's own vivacity.

On the evening after the final rupture with Wolman had occurred (in the autumn of 1934), Hillman returned as usual to dine with his cronies at the Wardman Park Hotel. He sat down at the head of the table, glanced about distractedly, then noticed the empty chair beside him. He stared, then motioned to it, saying sadly: "Well, Leo is really gone from us now." [23]

---

* In later years he served as a labor consultant for the National Association of Manufacturers.

IV

In the eighteen months since he had come to his unsalaried office at the national capital, he had shown his mettle as "labor's politician." "Hillman is just about gone with fatigue, excitement, and everything else. What can you do?" his secretary observed at the time.[24] There was no doubt that he was enjoying his new role.

After the new Board had been in charge of the National Recovery Administration a month or two, Hillman was described in the press as its "strong man," though experienced and conservative men of business, such as Whiteside and S. Clay Williams, really dominated the picture. Hillman, however, as the only labor representative, worked on very friendly terms with them.[25] But Donald R. Richberg, the Chicago labor lawyer who had long served the railway unions, was becoming a problem now that Dr. Wolman was gone. His heart also bled for justice to company unions nowadays; and Green and Lewis were reported to be in a fury at Richberg and the NIRB.

The NRA had lost much favor not only with trade unionists but with the consumer public as well because of its tolerance of price raising. This led to an investigation of the NRA by a Consumers' Review Board, headed by Hillman's old friend of Chicago days, Clarence Darrow. In the House and Senate, attacks on the Recovery Administration were most popular among the partisans of small business. The aged Mr. Justice Brandeis, in private conversation with Hillman, warned him at this period that the NRA's procedures were unlawful and unconstitutional by their exemption of "trusts" and trade agreements from the provisions of the Sherman Act. But Hillman could only see that the NRA was an "instrumentality" favoring the advancement of labor.

To be sure, the NRA was national economic planning in a bedlam. Yet, amid the confusion, Hillman managed to snatch at advantages for the trade-union camp.

In March 1935, the Senate failed only by the narrow margin of ten votes to pass amendments to the NRA law nullifying most of its provisions. It now looked as if Congress might soon undo the NIRB if the Supreme Court did not get there first.

On March 21, 1935, the Senate Finance Committee held hearings on the NRA, to whose excesses Clarence Darrow testified at great length. Later that day it was Hillman's turn to defend the Administration which, Senator King of Utah believed, was virtually handing the country over to the Bolsheviks.

Hillman began by citing figures showing the increase of production and employment since 1932, when Senator King interrupted him rudely:

SENATOR KING: You organized the Amalgamated Clothing Workers? . . . I have here a copy of your preamble and bylaws. . . .

He read from the old constitution of Hillman's union the phrases concerning the working class eventually taking control of the system of production.

SENATOR KING: That is part of your creed?

MR. HILLMAN: That preamble has been out of our constitution for probably over ten or fifteen years——

SENATOR KING: You put that into your constitution? You put that into your program after you had come from *Russia*. . . .

MR. HILLMAN: Of course, I come from Russia.

SENATOR KING (interrupting): No. That was put into your organization here after you had come from Russia? Please answer that.

MR. HILLMAN: Of course it was. I was born in Russia. . . .

The questioning went on in this vein for some little time. Hillman was extremely sensitive about his race and origin, and had his pride. At length, very red and angry, he exploded at the senator:

MR. HILLMAN: Instead of permitting me to give what I believe is my honest opinion of the policies of the NRA, the question is: "Was I born in Russia?" As if I had anything to do with where I was born. At least I can say, Senator, that this country is with me not merely a matter of accident [of birth], but it is the country of my choice!

It was a protest noble in conception and voiced with deep emotion. There followed a long moment of dramatic silence on the part of the hundreds of persons who packed that committee room. Then from the crowd came a spontaneous burst of applause and cheers. The New Deal senators, Black, Costigan, and Barkley now intervened, protesting that the hearings were being conducted like a court trial, and took up the questioning of the witness in a more judicious manner. Hillman now spoke with great ardor as he assailed those who prated of "freedom for industry" when there were girls who were forced to work for a dollar a week and others who could not even find a job. Arguments for the freedom of the employer might be carried on, he said, for a hundred years, but "the 15,000,000 men and women out of work cannot afford to wait." [26]

The audience at the hearing had felt that Hillman had shown qualities of real greatness as he faced the senator from Utah who baited him. "Long after the adjournment some of those who had witnessed the scene could not discuss Mr. Hillman's appeal without tears brimming in their eyes." [27] He had merely done before the Senate Finance Committee what he had done many times before his old audience of tailors—swept them off their feet under the inspiration of the moment.

Right after that hearing, still flushed with his triumph over the Senate's reactionaries, Hillman hastened to the White House at the head of a delegation consisting of himself, John L. Lewis, and William Green. Donald R. Richberg also came to the conference with the President. He and the labor contingent in the NRA were now at swords' points. At this session Hillman succeeded on the one hand in composing the quarrel between the labor leaders and Richberg, and on the other hand in persuading President Roosevelt that he must continue to support the NRA law at all costs. If Congress or the Supreme Court quashed it, then new legislation protecting labor's rights, as in Section 7(a) of the NRA law, must be enacted. The conferees agreed that Richberg be appointed chairman of the NIRB as a measure of compromise; but to offset this another labor representative was to be added to the Board. That was a day of "tense work," Hillman recalled afterward. For the moment he was full of joy at having saved the NRA and brought about an accommodation, especially since Lewis had seemed on the verge of rebellion.[28]

On leaving the White House, the three labor leaders issued a press statement declaring that labor was determined to have the NRA codes continued and strengthened. But the system had not long to live.

The Supreme Court moved at last on May 27, 1935. In handing down a decision in the Schechter ("Sick Chicken") case, the justices declared the National Recovery Act null and void. Hillman that day was in a room of the Hotel Willard with some old friends listening to news of the decision over the radio. The whole affair struck him as ludicrous. He was lying down on a couch, with a highball glass in his hand, and began to laugh so hard that he rolled off the couch to the floor, still holding his glass without spilling it. "And we knew this would happen all along!" he exploded.

Rooseveltian Washington was in a state of high befuddlement that day, when the President made his angry protest at the "horse-and-buggy-age" opinions of the Supreme Court justices. At the NIRB headquarters various officials moved about in a daze, discussing the crisis that had arisen in their affairs, and wondering what they were expected to do. Were all the hundreds of codes, with their controls of hours and wages and child labor, to be junked?

Leon Henderson went into Hillman's small office and found him busily ransacking the drawers of his desk and throwing the few papers he kept there into his bags.

"Well, what are you going to do, Sidney?" Henderson asked.

Hillman said: "What am I going to do? We're all through here. I'm packing my bags and taking the next train to New York. I'm going to raise a war chest of a million dollars through my union to see to it that we hold onto the gains labor has won." [29]

Chapter Seventeen

THE RISE OF
THE CIO: 1935-1937

*Up to a few years ago, in this country, we had no
labor movement. . . . I consider that the CIO is the
beginning of a real labor movement.*
— Sidney Hillman, April 1936

The Supreme Court decision had plunged the whole country into one of its recurrent constitutional crises. Foreseeing the breakdown of the NRA codes, Hillman and the other labor
leaders had already obtained the promise of Roosevelt's support for
the Wagner-Connery labor-disputes bill (in its earlier form), providing governmental machinery for the election of the workers' union representatives.

So far as the high court was concerned, Hillman had some tart things
to say to his associates about the "dictatorship of the nine old men,"
once he had got back to New York and his union headquarters at 15
Union Square. He had always set great store on having government
sanction for labor's rights (as in World War I). Some of his own associates thought he talked "too much NRA," or, at any rate, was over-
enthusiastic about a program that still tolerated company unions and
low wage scales in many trades. Yet he continued to show the strong-

est faith in Roosevelt's leadership. Roosevelt, he said in an off-the-record talk of June 1935 before his union's Executive Board, was fully agreed that it was "the responsibility of government to give work to every able-bodied man or woman who wanted work." They would have to come back to something like the NRA very quickly, he predicted. The President would now support a minimum-wage law and the restriction of working hours. "But if the government will not do it, we will!" Whatever "paper decisions" the Supreme Court might make, the Amalgamated members had the 36-hour week and they were going to hold onto it come what may. "These are days when we have an opportunity to change our social system. These are days when we have an opportunity to reach the goal of our movement—security for all!" [1]

For Hillman the NRA was dead but not forgotten. In its Labor Advisory Board, from 1933 to 1935, men like himself and John L. Lewis, working together, had learned to think "in terms of the whole labor movement," he said in afterthought. This experience in itself was of immense importance. Taking our cue from Hillman's incisive phrase, we might say that the next ten years of trade unionism would witness the conflict between those who thought in terms of the labor movement as a whole and those who thought only in terms of its parts, the parts most useful to their own power and place.*

On the collapse of the NRA, Hillman had dispatched telegrams to all the Amalgamated's 600 locals in the country, warning that

we may expect immediate attacks by some employers on the 36-hour week and upon minimum wages provided in the codes. You are instructed to see that wages and hours under which our members are working are maintained. You are hereby authorized to call strikes if necessary against any employer who attempts violation.[2]

The ACWA, having kept the core of its organization solid throughout the depression years, had taken a leading part in the great "resur-

---

* Where very strong labor organizations, as in coal mining and clothing, took advantage of the protection of workers' rights incorporated in Section 7(a) of the NRA law, results were most favorable. But on the other hand, many powerful industrial corporations prodded their employees into company-sponsored unions. In the two years of NRA, the AFL gained some 500,000 new recruits, reaching a total membership of 3,600,000 in 1935. Company unions, however, grew twice as fast, rising from 1,263,000 to about 2,500,000 in this same period! (Millis & Montgomery, *Economics of Labor,* Vol. III, *Organized Labor.* McGraw-Hill, 1945, Vol. IV, p. 194, n.)

gence" of labor unionism after 1933. Within the two years that followed some 30,000 shirt workers, mostly employed in factories of the Eastern states, had been brought under the Amalgamated jurisdiction. To these were added eventually about 30,000 laundry workers and many thousands of cleaners and dyers, glove workers and salesmen in retail clothing stores. The union's return to the AFL also opened the way to affiliation in 1936 with the fine old Journeymen Tailors' Union, having then a membership of 7,000 custom tailors; this was a long-delayed marriage, almost consummated in 1915. The union's executives also directed powerful organizing drives against non-union clothing concerns in the upper South, as in Virginia and Tennessee; a large penetration was also made into the cotton-garment industry of the South's backward regions where ill-paid women made up the chief working population. Finally, in New York, during a secondary organizing drive, under the new co-managers of the New York Joint Board, Louis Hollander and Joseph Catalanotti, some 1,500 small contractors' shops were fully organized and a tighter control of labor was established there than ever before.

But at this period Hillman and many of the Amalgamated's veteran officers were not worried about their own union and more concerned with the fairly revolutionary developments taking place in the national labor movement as a whole.

The revival of unionism after the proclamation of "labor's Magna Charta" in May 1933 under the NRA had appeared spectacular enough at first. "There was a virtual uprising of workers for union membership," the AFL's Executive Council reported in 1934. Workers in the mass-production industries, such as automobiles, rubber, steel, and textiles, in haste to avail themselves of their new rights, held mass meetings, set up organizations, and applied to the AFL for charters and for help without loss of time. Yet though the Federation had talked for twenty years of organizing the millions of unorganized in our mass industries, only a handful of old-style craft-union officials were sent out into the Midwestern industrial centers where there was a great clamor for unions. No funds of any size were provided for this work, though the opportunities seemed immense.[3]

At the Amalgamated Clothing Workers' May 1934 convention, President William Green of the AFL had come to speak in celebration of the union's entrance into the Federation after a schism of nineteen years. In introducing Green, Hillman spoke with a courtesy that was obviously restrained. The ideals of the clothing workers' industrial union and those of the AFL craft unionists were, after all, still far apart. Green, a personable, well-spoken man, very much the middle-aged officeholder, in a passage of his speech welcoming the Amalgamated into the AFL admitted that the American Federation of Labor had perhaps "not been as aggressive as we would have liked to be." [4] No one knew this better than the Amalgamated people and Hillman.

John L. Lewis, however, was something quite different from Green. In 1933 he had found the workers aflame with the will to "do something" after their sufferings in the depression years. But his first appeals to the AFL's Executive Council that everything possible be done to sweep together hordes of unorganized workers under Section 7(a) met with a poor response. The old labor body had no facilities for such a huge and complex task. Its officers clung to the tradition of "voluntarism," according to which groups of the workers themselves must come forward to seek unionization. Moreover, the principle of organization by crafts, which looked for union strength chiefly among the skilled and steady workers, barred the way to vigorous action. Daniel Tobin of the teamsters' union, one of the more liberal figures among the AFL chieftains, was credited with having said in 1933 that the semi-skilled laborers in the mass-production industries were only "rubbish" and not worth organizing.

The AFL did undertake, as a provisory measure, to organize "federal" unions among the new locals of rubber and auto workers during the hectic summer of 1933. They were to be granted temporary or "federal" charters, and officers appointed and salaried by the AFL, pending the reapportionment of the new members, according to strict craft jurisdiction, among the established unions. At the insistence of leaders like John P. Frey, head of the AFL's Metal Trades Department, Wharton of the machinists' union, and "Big Bill" Hutcheson of the carpenters', the most experienced or "organizable" of the new recruits were to be drawn off and parceled out among thirty or more different craft unions. What was to happen to the rest of the unskilled workers was uncertain.

These highly bureaucratic arrangements were heartily disliked by the new flock of rubber, auto, and steel unionists from Detroit, Akron, and Pittsburgh. For one thing, they wanted officers of their own choosing to represent them. In their own shops they had been accustomed to working in plant-wide rather than craft groups; some of them, during a single day, might work at five different crafts. The AFL orders threw them into confusion and promised no effective means of collective bargaining in their gigantic factories.

By 1934 a reversal of the union boom of the early New Deal days had set in. "Paper" unions, which had gathered up pledges of as many as 300,000 members in the field of autos and textiles, melted away almost overnight. Much of the trouble was due to the "devitalization" of the protective labor clauses in the NRA law, helped by rulings such as that of Dr. Wolman's board in favor of company unions.

Hillman, who had observed this process with extreme distaste, said:

It was only during the period of the NRA that the organized rubber workers began to achieve real power. They attained a membership of over 40,000 and became a factor in the industry. Then the American Federation of Labor, through its Executive Council, stepped in and started to divide those organized workers among the different international unions claiming jurisdiction over them. As a result of that procedure, the membership of the rubbers workers' union fell as low as 3,000.[5]

The AFL was using the tactics that Gompers had shown to be sound in the 1880's, Hillman used to say. But these no longer applied. A marvelous opportunity to gather in many millions of industrial workers was being frittered away. It was the unpredictable weight of these millions of new members, however, that the old-time AFL leaders feared and were determined to control, so that they might, as in the past, hold their positions of power in the labor movement. For in later emergencies the craft-union leaders, by changing their tactics, showed that they themselves did not regard craft traditions as sacred.

At the 1934 convention of the AFL, John L. Lewis raised the issue of industrial unionism with great force of argument, and among others, Charles Howard, head of the typographers—one of the most famous of craft unions—warmly supported him. But their protests were in vain. At the next AFL convention at Atlantic City in 1935 it was apparent that labor's organizing impetus was steadily losing force. The Lewis faction, somewhat strengthened, introduced once more a resolution protesting the organizing methods then being used, and proposing that industrial unions for the mass industries, with full rights of self-government, be chartered instead. Hillman, who was present as a delegate at this convention, took an active part in the floor fight of the industrial-union minority.

Behind the stubborn opposition of the old-guard leaders, as he knew, was their abiding fear that their voice, their power in the councils of the Federation might soon be overwhelmed by the hordes of mass-production workers. These craft-union men also made much of the alleged menace of "Reds" introducing themselves into the labor picture. Hillman, as was his wont, spoke in conciliatory tones, urging that the clashing labor factions compose their differences and concentrate on the paramount task of winning over the employees of the giant motor and steel corporations. Let us have a moratorium on craft jurisdiction, let the "young men" of labor have their day, he said. The common struggle was against "the kind of arrogant industrial control that is Fascism in all but form." There, he said, was the real enemy, in Detroit and Pittsburgh, whose cruel belt-lines made men old and worn-out at forty and then cast them aside. The AFL's failure to organize the country's largest industries was evident to all; unless effective action to remedy this was taken, labor in the United States would remain fundamentally weak.[6]

Lewis, determined upon a showdown, gave no thought to the usages of diplomacy, but spoke with the extreme passion and bitterness that were to be the characteristic style of the "new" Lewis in these later years:

A year ago I was younger and naturally I had more faith in the Executive Council. . . . I know better now. At San Francisco they seduced me with fair words. Now of course, having learned that I was seduced, I am enraged and I am ready to rend my seducers limb from limb, including Delegate Woll. In that sense, of course, I speak figuratively.

The miners' union, he said, could not go forward so long as the "captive" coal mines and the steel industry, so closely linked with coal, remained strongly defended non-union centers. The same was true of unions in other industries, struggling to set up new locals in sections dominated by powerful anti-union corporations. He ended with an eloquent appeal to the Federation to

heed this cry from Macedonia, that comes from the hearts of men, and in doing this make the American Federation of Labor the greatest instrument that has been forged to befriend the cause of humanity.[7]

The industrial-union resolution was voted down by 1,820,000 to 1,090,000. But Lewis, Hillman, and Howard were impressed by the fact that a third of the delegates had supported their resolution. This was a far better showing than at earlier trials of strength.

The debate over this issue was highlighted by an exchange of bitter invectives between Hutcheson and Lewis—following which Lewis, considering himself insulted, suddenly smote Brother Hutcheson with a mighty blow to the jaw. It was a most calculated thrust, according to many eyewitnesses, delivered with an effect that not only felled the huge Hutcheson to the platform but also dramatized the cleavage between the industrial-union and craft-union camps in spectacular fashion.[8]

Even before this convention had adjourned Lewis had called together an informal conference at his hotel, in which he was joined by Sidney Hillman, Charles Howard, David Dubinsky, and Thomas McMahon, then head of the United Textile Workers. Lewis' union associates, Vice-President Philip Murray and John Brophy of the UMW, were also present. On this occasion, at the beginning of November 1935, the first tentative plans for a committee to encourage the formation of industrial unions were broached by Lewis and the other labor leaders.

A few days later, on November 10, after the AFL convention was adjourned, a second conference was called in Atlantic City by the same initiating group and was joined by representatives of the Mine, Mill and Smelters Union and of the new organizations that had sprung up among the steel, automobile, rubber, shipyard, and radio workers. Out of this meeting, where about 900,000 workers were represented informally, there came the first public announcement of the launching of the Committee for Industrial Organization.[9]

The program of the Committee, soon to be known to fame as the "CIO," had been made clear in a resolution offered at the recent AFL convention by Charles Howard:

In the great mass production industries and in those in which the workers are engaged as composite mechanics, specialized and engaged upon classes of work which do not fully qualify them for craft-union membership, industrial organization is the only solution.

Such workers, after being assisted in forming new industrial unions of their own, were to be encouraged to affiliate themselves with the AFL. The CIO, therefore, was going to help the Federation in spite of itself, and to this end proposed to raise $1,500,000 for the expense of organizing the unorganized mass-industry workers. It was a project that Sidney Hillman had been advocating for nearly twenty years.

Hillman's ideas on craft and industrial organization had been fully formed as far back as 1919, when he predicted the failure of the old method of craft organization. At that time he said in a speech at Chicago:

An industry must be organized completely under unified leadership. It is impossible to find a way out when every small part of an industry has the power of inflicting damage upon the [whole] industry. Through a combination of all the people in the industry a great responsibility is invested in the workers.

For him the attitude of the AFL leaders after 1933 constituted a betrayal of the workers' real interests; and he had been warning his associates that a great chance would be missed again, as in 1919.

He predicted the failure of the old methods of craft organization.

During the NRA days [wrote Potofsky in 1936] he talked with Lewis and others of the need and opportunity of reaching out into other spheres. He saw the opportunities in the automobile and other industries that had for years gone by default for lack of leadership. Industrial unionism was clear in his mind as the only basis for organizing the large industries.[10]

Now that the break had begun from the AFL policies, Hillman was again sanguine. He had long been thinking and dreaming of just such developments. He said:

To organize the workers of America is one of my fondest dreams. Now I can see the possibilities of this. Lewis is sincerely interested in doing the job.[11]

In John L. Lewis he had found a comrade in arms who was a man of great imagination and magnetism. The famous miners' union had of course been built up by organizing all the workers around the pits and not in accordance with craft divisions. Lewis had long believed that industrial unionism was "the only way." But now he seemed like one "converted" to a burning faith in his new mission of reform. None could mistake the immense ambitions that beckoned him to lead millions of new unionists, nor his iron resolution. From an early stage he foresaw that this action would precipitate a complete rupture with the AFL.

On the other hand, Lewis' progressivism was fairly recent, whereas Sidney Hillman had enjoyed a liberal and progressive following for nearly twenty years. Hence Lewis needed Hillman for his movement, and it was he who approached the clothing workers' leader and eagerly invited him to be his ally. Hillman gave him his hand in partnership without hesitation. The UMW was once more the country's biggest union, but the Amalgamated was considered the most advanced; it was also "seasoned" and financially one of the solidest. Thus Hillman was the strongest ally that Lewis attracted to his side; for after Howard's death in 1938, the typographers withdrew from the CIO.

Lewis had seen his own industrial union, like Hillman's, go up and down in boom and depression. The sense of history had come to him at last, after many errors and wanderings. Like Hillman, who always seemed to be moving in step with history, Lewis perceived the turning of the tide for labor in 1933. He had gained new confidence from the hundreds of thousands of miners who had rushed to join him in the 1933 "crusade." And he saw also how his colleagues of the AFL Executive Council, fearsome of change or risk, hesitated and drew back from action.

Both men saw the boundless opportunities opening before them, the massed labor power that lay ready to be gathered up and organized by those bold enough to bring real leadership, at this very hour, to millions of workers, embittered, disillusioned, and restive almost to the point of rebellion.

II

One might have searched far and wide and not found two men who offered more contrast outwardly than Hillman and Lewis, whom the AFL magnates considered the two strong men of the CIO. It was they who, together, made the largest contributions to the launching of the industrial-union movement in 1935. Lewis, aged fifty-five, the native-born son of Iowa coal miners of Welsh descent, was still all massive bone and flesh, exuding the magnetism of sheer physical power. His beetling brows, outthrust jaw, and flamboyant gestures served to dramatize his sense of his own power as the leader of armies of rawboned coal miners. Hillman, the Russian-Jewish immigrant, was seven years younger, soft-spoken, unostentatious in gesture; with his expressive gray eyes and finely shaped forehead, suggestive of subtlety rather than exuberant force, he reminded one in appearance of an accomplished musician or an artist. Lewis was by instinct the "rabble-rouser," the stump orator who stunned or excited crowds with his torrential eloquence, whereas Hillman, the self-educated intellectual, worked on men's minds by his crisp logic and his finesse. He did not dazzle those who heard him speak, but he grew on them and left them with food for thought.

The former coal miner excelled in histrionics. "Labor leading is 90 per cent showmanship," he is reported to have said at this period. As an actor, he was superb; he was grand opera and in no sense provincial. He could, when he had a mind to, rant and roar, with his blue eyes flaming, smashing the table with his fists; or keep his temper under the strongest provocation; or lower his wonderful voice to a stage whisper for emphasis or to create tension. He could turn comedian and mimic Roosevelt, Miss Perkins, "Bill" Green, and John Garner, until everyone present collapsed with laughter. And his speech, now extremely apt, vivid, and racy, now studded with quotations from Shakespeare, Milton, Bunyan, or Whitman, was like a swiftly flowing stream that beguiled his listeners—and he, behind the mask, ever watching and weighing the effect. For inwardly he was no less calculating and planful than a Sidney Hillman.

John L. Lewis' very complex character had been molded by the rough-and-tumble fighting of the labor movement, which had instilled in him a fund of animal cunning. He knew well the byways of politics and the secrets of big business. And he was instinctively a gambler of the boldest sort. Yet in private conversation Lewis could show himself a man of great charm, or assume an air of light and learning. Hillman, on first meeting him in Washington, was immensely impressed by his varied talents.

The two men, in the contrasting qualities they suggested, seemed at first to complement each other perfectly. Lewis, for his part, fully appreciated Hillman's mental resourcefulness. He particularly noted Hillman's political skill as exhibited in the period of the NRA. At an early stage of their friendship he is said to have proposed to Hillman a division of labor between them: he, Lewis, was to proceed at the head of the labor army wielding a battle-ax, while Hillman was to use the lighter weapons of finesse and strategy on the flanks of the enemy. Hillman (to change the metaphor) was to be the quarter-back; Lewis would crash through the line.

Henceforth Lewis in his forthright expressions and bold actions appeared as a dauntless "radical," and drew to his support all the radicals and left wingers whom he had once fought tooth and nail. Hillman, on the other hand, in the early years of the CIO, was seen as the cool counselor and strategist of the movement. "Hillman wrote the lines of the play and Lewis acted them," was the quip of Thomas F. Burns, vice-president of the United Rubber Workers. The imperious Lewis did not have the habit of listening to other people, yet he hearkened to Hillman with respect and also, as some observed, with a gently protective attitude, as of an older man listening to a brilliant youth. Each was very conscious of the other's power.

The less "dramatic" and more reasonable Hillman thus seemed to resign himself to being second-in-command under one who possessed extraordinary talents for mass leadership. Hillman had had visions for years of the millions of marching men who were ready to stream into new unions. But he, as a naturalized American, stemming from a minority racial group, was not destined, as he realized, to be their leader. The premier role was to be reserved for Lewis, who seemed so well cast for it. There was irony in this situation, since Lewis had formerly lived only for the fleshpots of the old-style labor movement in the days when Sidney Hillman had been as a voice in the wilderness crying for true industrial unionism. Yet now they were intimate co-workers in a tremendous enterprise, for which whole battalions of organizers were thrown into the field. Large sums were drawn for this from the treasury of the United Mine Workers by Lewis. The ACWA, traditionally generous, was the only union that could fairly match such contributions in the formative years of the CIO.

In those days Lewis used to address Hillman affectionately as "son" or "young man," or sometimes "Sid." When his younger colleague fell ill in December 1937, Lewis wrote him:

Dear Sid—
It has been lonely without you. I am glad you are better and are going South. You have had a hard fight, but I counted on you to win. In all important matters I have tried to consider what you would think. Our affairs are in sound condition. No worries for you. "Go South young man." You know my wishes and hopes go with you.

John L.[12]

"When Lewis and Hillman worked together as close allies the CIO rose to its greatest heights, and Lewis himself enjoyed his hours of greatest triumph," one of their observant co-workers, August Bellanca, said in after years.[13]

There was no talk, at the beginning, of a rupture with the AFL, or of forming a rival labor body, though that was always in the cards. The program of the CIO, it was announced, was to be "advisory and educational." The provisory executive council named Lewis chairman of the new organization, and the progressive-minded Howard secretary, with the former insurgent miners' leader, John Brophy, as the executive director.

Lewis' clarion calls to the unorganized soon began to be heard among industrial workers in many parts of the country and aroused memories and hopes of the militant One-Big-Union movement of earlier days. The AFL magnates were disquieted. A fortnight after the CIO had opened for business, Mr. Green issued a warning to the AFL unions sponsoring the CIO, and spoke of his "apprehension and deep concern" lest the new grouping turn into a dual union or rebel movement. The dissidents were urged to work for their program through the AFL alone.[14]

Lewis' answer was to resign his office as vice-president of the AFL, a significant gesture in itself. His accompanying letter contained expressions of extreme ridicule of the "Old Guard" of the Federation.

Hillman also replied to Green on December 12, 1935, by way of interviews in the press, using more moderate terms—though in private he expressed disgust at the narrow policies of the AFL's craft-union leaders.

A second warning was sent to the dissident unionists in May 1936 by the president of the AFL. Hillman, addressing the Amalgamated convention at Cleveland at this time, replied by declaring that the organization of the steel, motor, textile, and other mass-industry workers in industrial unions was "a matter of life and death." There was something profoundly wrong, he felt, in the methods pursued by the Federation hitherto. As for the jurisdictional rights they were always quibbling about, "what good were these rights as long as the people were unorganized?" He said:

Less than 15 per cent of the workers in trade, commerce, service, and industry are members of any organization of labor. This 15 per cent is confined, for the most part, to a small selected group of industries. . . . And the mass-production industries have gone back to long hours and wage-cutting, while we still have ten or twelve million people unemployed.

I know that some people say that the workers in the mass-production industries cannot be organized. Professors have even written theses showing why they cannot be organized. But those who are old-timers in our industry will remember that twenty-five years ago the same story was told about the clothing industry. And only five years ago that was the story we heard about the shirt industry.

Well, we went ahead and organized, didn't we? [15]

The original nine component unions in the CIO had undertaken to raise $500,000 to unionize the steel workers. Although the Amalgamated claimed no jurisdictional rights whatsoever in this field (as did other CIO unions), it contributed $100,000 for this drive. What was more, the Amalgamated, like the UMW, lent its most experienced executives, speakers, and organizers to the new movement, in this and other mass-production fields.

The affairs of his own union, Hillman said in 1936, were flourishing. What did the members want to have money in their treasury for, he used to ask, if not to spend it in the interests of labor? For no union could stand by itself if other trades were unorganized. "It is not a question of helping others," Hillman said with unassailable logic. "It is a question of helping ourselves by helping others." [16]

The spring and summer of 1936 saw the real beginning of the CIO drives, in which the young men of labor Hillman had called upon started moving into the fortress-like factories of the steel and motor corporations. But at this time the quadrennial election tournament at which our Chief Executive was to be chosen overshadowed everything else in importance.

III

The collapse of the NRA in May 1935 had left a great void so far as labor legislation was concerned. Immediately thereafter all the labor factions were united in urging Roosevelt to exert the utmost pressure on Congress for passage of the long-prepared Wagner labor-relations bill. This he did, though, it was said, without great enthusiasm for this epoch-making bill, which was enacted on July 5,.

1935. Under the power to regulate interstate commerce Congress now established fair labor practices guaranteeing workers the right to form their own unions without suffering discrimination and to engage in collective bargaining. This act continued the usages adopted under the NRA's labor clause. A National Labor Relations Board, moreover, was empowered to supervise union elections, check lists of workers, and determine which unions were to represent them, such decisions being subject to court review. But the attitude of the Supreme Court in 1935 created great doubts that the new "charter" for labor would be sustained; many employers were advised to ignore the rulings of the National Labor Relations Board.

To Hillman, as to Lewis, everything now turned on the re-election of Roosevelt in 1936. For how else could the Wagner Act be enforced and added legislation controlling wages and hours be enacted? As early as January 31, 1936, a large gathering of CIO leaders in Washington was suddenly turned into a "tumultuous demonstration" for Roosevelt's re-election in the course of a speech by Hillman warning his hearers that the party of Herbert Hoover must be defeated once more if labor's recent gains were to be preserved.[16a]

A few days later, Hillman and Lewis learned that James Farley, in his role as Roosevelt's campaign manager, had arranged to have Daniel Tobin, president of the International Brotherhood of Teamsters and a powerful opponent of the Lewis faction, appointed chairman of the Democratic Party's Labor Committee for the approaching election. This was plainly a scheme to hold the conservative AFL leadership close to the throne, while keeping the CIO element at a distance.

At once Hillman spoke to Lewis of the need for putting the CIO into the 1936 election campaign in a big way and forestalling the Farley-Tobin arrangement. The two then approached George L. Berry, head of the Printing Pressmen's Union (AFL), who had been on the NRA's National Labor Board and held office subsequently in the Roosevelt Administration. Hillman said to Berry:

> George, the organized labor movement is failing in the performance of its duties. . . . Here we are with the [National] Manufacturers' Association, Liberty League, Talmadge's Grass Rooters or something, the Crusaders and all those people who have organized to fight the President, and we are standing by waiting.[17]

Overnight, by agreement among these three men, it was decided to form a nationwide political association which was to be the vehicle by which the growing labor movement would participate in the campaign for Roosevelt's re-election. Berry, who was in high standing in the AFL and "not on either side," as Hillman said, agreed to serve as its chairman, with Lewis as its director and Hillman as treasurer and fund-raiser. The name "Labor's Non-Partisan League" was chosen to indicate, as Hillman explained later, that it was "nonpartisan" only in that it sought the support of the two wings of labor, but not at all with regard to the re-election of the New Deal President. Hillman said afterward that he and Lewis had "cooked up" Labor's Non-Partisan League and that was how they had got into national politics:

Not a single person in the Administration knew about the formation of the League until it was announced. . . . The Administration was not notified because some of us believed that pressure would be used to stop it. . . .[18]

The setting up of Labor's Non-Partisan League was announced on April 2, 1936, "as if from Administration circles in Washington," to the great vexation of Farley, Tobin, and William Green.

A constantly recurring motif in Hillman's career was his pre-occupation with the idea of putting American labor into politics through its own political organization, as in England and other countries, instead of leaving everything to our professionals. For Lewis, a life-long Republican, who had once felt himself flattered at the passing attentions of a Harding or a Herbert Hoover, the venture was a novel one. However, he threw himself into it with his characteristic ardor, proclaiming that "labor has gained more under President Roosevelt than under any President in memory. Obviously it is the duty of labor to support Roosevelt 100 per cent."

National headquarters for the LNPL were quickly established in Washington under Lewis' direction and staffed with numerous old United Mine Workers' officers. However, Eli P. Oliver, formerly an Amalgamated organizer in Cincinnati and a "Hillman man," was made executive vice-president of the organization, his salary being furnished by the ACWA. His chief assistant, salaried by the UMW, was Gardner Jackson, who had championed the cause of the condemned anarchists, Sacco and Vanzetti, in 1927. Contacts were established with 35,000 local labor-union officers all over the country, as with the Farmer-Labor and Progressive Party in several states and various other liberal groups, including church and university organizations. Meanwhile Lewis and Hillman both hit the highroad to raise funds needed for the new political vehicle. A flood of letters, more than 100,000 in number, came from all parts of the country to the LNPL headquarters in the first few weeks, strongly endorsing its program.

For Hillman the first and most important task was to "sell" the idea to his own union people. The Amalgamated "school" had long studied the possibility and the difficulties of labor political action in this country. Many of the union members, especially in New York and Chicago, had grown up in the tradition of supporting the Socialist Party, at least locally, and shunning our Tammany Halls. What Hillman advocated now was a distinctly *opportunistic* approach. The new League, unlike La Follette's Progressive Party of 1924, was to function mainly through one of the two major parties, and particularly the Democratic Party, in order to ensure Roosevelt's re-election. Some left-wing unionists had their doubts about Mr. Roosevelt, though he had done well by labor. As an "honest broker" in politics he often gave the effect of facing both ways, especially on the company-union issue. Moreover, in the Democratic Party's Southern stronghold CIO organizers were still welcomed by armed mobs of vigilantes or Klansmen. Yet Hillman wanted his union to make a very large contribution to this same Democratic Party's campaign fund through the LNPL and expected the various Joint Boards in different parts of the country to send forth all their local officers to canvass for votes for the Democratic Party.

At a two-day meeting of his union's fifteen-man General Executive Board in late April, at a hotel in Atlantic City, Hillman conducted a discussion of the New Deal and the new League that lasted for hours on end. Once more he assumed the role of teacher before his associates, most of them men who knew the ways of the world. The whole labor-political problem in this season of swift change was analyzed by him in the most painstaking way. This eternally hurried man of action expressed some of his best and deepest ideas spontaneously in the privacy of these off-the-record talks before his old comrades; and he had extraordinary gifts for political analysis. He said:

We have had a policy, which was not to endorse either of the two political parties, and that if we took a position it should be along Socialist lines. The position of our organization is known: that we are for a labor party. We are today bound . . . to help bring about a labor or farmer-labor party—what is commonly known as independent political action.

But in the last two years things have happened . . . since the coming of the Roosevelt Administration. *We have participated in making the labor policy of this Administration.* [Italics added.]

We know that the NRA meant the revival of our organization. . . . Anyone will agree that these things would have been totally impossible without legislation. Our condition, pre-NRA, was almost as bad as in all industry. Although we were still carrying on, there was a question whether we could have carried on as a successful organization for even another year. . . .

Well, we had the Supreme Court decision. And we know what has happened in most industries since, and how it affected our own organization. . . . I am rather hopeful about what we can do this coming season, but in the long run the absence of such legislation as the NRA is a real threat.

We know that the defeat of the Roosevelt Administration means no labor legislation for decades to come. . . . I don't know whether legislation would put all the unemployed back to work, but we do know in our industry that the reduction in hours took in 50,000 . . . and with improvement in business and farm income we would have 175,000 in our industry. A change in the Administration raises a definite question whether the Amalgamated would have to fight completely on its own and not get the support which it enjoyed under the NRA.

Here Hillman disclosed that he had been informed of the President's intention, if re-elected, to find ways of curbing the "power of review" of the Supreme Court. The President had also promised Hillman that he would support the proposed minimum-wage bill, which Senators Black and Wagner were preparing.

I believe if the demand is strong enough a way will be found to pass new legislation. When the AAA was declared unconstitutional, they found a way to do the same thing under another name. The NRA was not re-passed because labor was supine. The usefulness of this legislation had not been sufficiently explained to the workers. Some even joked about it and undermined it.

But besides economic power, Hillman now believed, there must be the political power to safeguard labor's rights. If you were permitted by the police and courts to picket, you could win a strike sooner than otherwise, he pointed out. Or if you had the minimum wage, you didn't have to fight to get at least a miserable 25 cents an hour.

In my judgment, up to a few years ago we had no labor movement in this country. Even in our so-called radical organizations we paid lip service to the need for organization, but what did we actually do toward making a real labor movement? *I consider that the CIO is the beginning of a real labor movement.* [Italics added.] That, I am sure, would have been impossible without the NRA. . . . In the Labor Advisory Board, people thought in terms of the whole labor movement. Now people who can influence the labor movement are doing something about it, not merely passing resolutions. They are giving financial support. . . .

Now . . . are we supposed to let the chance go by and wait until the Socialist Party comes into power? There is no labor party—let us not fool ourselves about that. And since there is no labor party, are we just to sit down and admit that we cannot do anything? . . . You talk labor party. But can you have a labor party without an economic labor movement? I do not mean to criticize the Socialist movement, but it is composed of intellectuals. . . . I say to you that the defeat of Roosevelt and the introduction of a real Fascist administration such as we will have is going to make the work of building a labor movement impossible. . . .

I know that . . . all the forces of Fascism are opposed to him. The election of Roosevelt will not solve all our problems, but it will give us a breathing spell.

He also hinted that out of the new groupings of labor in politics there might come at last a true labor party. Not through the speeches of "outsiders" like Norman Thomas, but through practical efforts such as had been made recently to unite the needle-trades unions of New York, embracing some 400,000 members, in support of labor's new political organ. The sum of $10,000 had been donated by the group of garment unions in New York, and more would be forthcoming. This was better than "always taking the same Socialist group and naming it a labor party. As I have said, the more progress the CIO makes, the more the logic of the situation drives them into politics." [19]

The honest old Schlossberg and other doctrinaires on the Executive Board who had opposed formal support of the Democratic Party were overwhelmed by Hillman's arguments. At the ACWA convention in Cleveland on May 25–30, 1936, the CIO as well as its political league and the Roosevelt ticket all received the enthusiastic adherence of the delegates and officers. In his opening address Hillman promised that Labor's Non-Partisan League was going to meet the challenge of that "holding company of the big interests," of the Du Ponts and Raskobs, which was the Liberty League.

This convention had a highly political flavor. Emissaries of Roosevelt and the Democratic Party addressed it. When it was over Hillman forwarded to Roosevelt by telegram the resolution pledging the support of all the clothing workers, but also stating most explicitly what this group expected from the President in return:

Labor anticipates your support for decent labor legislation . . . the guarantee of the right to organize and the enactment of minimum labor standards. . . . Your re-election as President will provide a bulwark against the threat of fascism.

From Washington, Roosevelt telegraphed his thanks, adding, in a letter to "Dear Sidney," that the action of the Amalgamated gave him "new strength and courage." [20]

Labor's Non-Partisan League in 1936 cemented the alliance of the Rooseveltian democracy with what was nowadays called Big Labor. In that heated election season the President earnestly courted the aid of the Lewises and Hillmans and Tobins and Greens.

Although the League, unlike third-party ventures of the past, functioned mainly within and through one of the two major political organizations and made no effort to set up a precinct and county system of its own, it opened up serious possibilities of an independent labor party. Organized labor was abandoning its bi-partisan traditions. Lewis, who treated the League as if it were his own affair and staffed it mostly with "loyal Lewis men," gave numerous hints that a "political realignment for 1940" was being kept in mind.[21]

Hillman took the stump often during this campaign and with marked effect, especially in the New York district. In a speech at New York on September 15, he said that Labor's Non-Partisan League was "not supporting the Democratic Party," but was mainly interested in re-electing President Roosevelt. Fifty-nine international unions with a membership of more than two million had joined in this movement, "organizing for the first time the political power of the men and women who toil." The separate tickets of Norman Thomas and of William Lemke's Union Party were strongly assailed

400 , *Sidney Hillman:* STATESMAN OF AMERICAN LABOR

by him as representing false friends who served only to divide labor's strength. Norman Thomas' statements, he said, were merely "love letters to Alfred Landon." Hillman's own thinking seemed to be directed toward turning the Democratic Party eventually into a farmer-labor party:

> After November 3 [he said], Labor's Non-Partisan League will remain a permanent political organization. In this state it is organizing under a separate emblem as a separate party, known as the American Labor Party.
> The interest of the country as well as of labor demands a realignment of all progressives into one party, and the basis for that kind of realignment ought to be the reorganization of labor in the political field.

Through its state and national organizations LNPL, with Hillman as treasurer, raised and expended the very considerable sum of about $1,000,000 for this campaign, according to statements of Executive Vice-President Eli P. Oliver. Of this fund, $500,000 was contributed by Lewis in one lump sum, drawn on the treasury of the United Mine Workers, at a moment when the Democratic Party was hard pressed for cash. The Amalgamated Union, in addition, contributed more than $100,000, according to contemporary reports.[22]

A very important development was the belated decision of the CIO leaders to launch the American Labor Party in pivotal New York State as a local affiliate of LNPL. The thought was to channel the "regular" Socialists into the Roosevelt camp. This was done in hasty fashion on July 16, 1936, principally on the initiative of Hillman, David Dubinsky of the Ladies' Garment Workers, and Alex Rose of the Millinery Workers. Joseph P. Ryan, the conservative leader of the International Longshoremen's Association, brought to the American Labor Party the support of the AFL's Central Trades and Labor Council of New York City, which he then headed; while George Meany also helped the new party through the AFL's state body. The new grouping included the right-wing faction of the Socialist Party in New York, but also enjoyed the support of Governor Herbert Lehman, A. A. Berle, and Mayor La Guardia—all in all a remarkable amalgam of AFL and CIO unionists, as well as Republican Fusionists, New Deal Democrats, and Socialists.

The importance of Hillman's role in the Roosevelt camp was reflected by the serious attention paid to him in the Hearst press, which turned up with the stunning revelation that Hillman, and David Dubinsky as well, were the reddest of Communists. Taking to the hustings at Madison Square Garden, New York, before an immense mass meeting on September 23, 1936, Hillman turned the Hearst charges to ridicule, and defined them as "the lowest kind of political clowning." Hillman's collisions with the Communists in his union were too recent and too well remembered in this city. Dubinsky, who spoke from the same platform, registered indignation and shock at having the methods of "character assassination" practiced upon himself, in view of his well-known attitude toward communism.[23] By 1936 the red herring was flourishing in the political fishpond, and yet exploitation of it was slight compared to that of later years, when its usage was to be extended to the uttermost by men who had been themselves the victims of the red herring.

IV

The landslide proportions of the election returns in November 1936 were undoubtedly swelled by the LNPL's exertions in Ohio, Illinois, Pennsylvania, and especially in New York, where the new American Labor Party mustered about 300,000 votes. Lewis, who had been referring to Roosevelt almost as "his man," was said to have been disconcerted by the size of the President's victory. It would naturally lessen F.D.R.'s dependence upon labor.

Nevertheless, Chairman George Berry of LNPL on November 11 wrote to the President extending him congratulations on behalf of John L. Lewis, Sidney Hillman, and himself. He took occasion also to remind the President that the three directors of the League wished to discuss with him matters relating to forthcoming labor legislation and the office of the Secretary of Labor, "before final determinations have been made." [24]

On November 21, Hillman, Lewis, and George Berry were seen climbing the steps of the White House together to confer with Roosevelt, who had just returned from a vacation cruise. After a long visit they reappeared, smiling at the press and movie cameramen, but saying nothing. The conference was not an unalloyed success, and it is believed to have marked the beginning of some strain between those two power-minded gentlemen, Roosevelt and Lewis.

This was a meeting of victorious allies; but allies often, on the morning of their common triumph, show differences in ulterior aims. For the head of the rising labor "empire" it was an occasion to remind the politician Roosevelt that he had political partners who had come to stay; that the United Mine Workers had contributed $500,000 to his campaign fund; that he, Lewis, expected to be consulted frequently on many questions of national policy; and possibly that the office of the Secretary of Labor might fairly be treated as a patronage plum for the Lewis wing of the labor movement. Judging from recorded statements of John L. Lewis, it was his view that when one gave money to politicians one had a right to expect something in return.*

In CIO circles much discontent with the Department of Labor's mediation service as being slow and "bureaucratic" had been voiced at this period.[25] Lewis often alluded to Miss Perkins as a mere "social worker." But Miss Perkins was loyal to Roosevelt above all things, and the President liked that. The gentleman from Hyde Park, though truly democratic in spirit, felt himself irked by this imperious son of coal miners almost from the start of their uneasy alliance. Lewis was authoritative, even arrogant, sometimes bluntly interrupting the President when his conversation sounded evasive to ask: "Well, will it be *yes* or *no?*" But whenever Lewis pounded at Roosevelt, Hillman would make all possible efforts to compose their differences. To him it was clear that Roosevelt, after having challenged the billionaires of the Liberty League, was not going to be subservient to John Lewis.

While Lewis and others made loud complaint at Roosevelt's periodic lapses with regard to labor's interests, Hillman was voicing another point of view, as Raymond Gram Swing reported:

> Labor . . . cannot expect Roosevelt to win its battles. If it is not strong enough, coherent enough, nor modern enough to walk through the door the President is opening, that is its fault, Hillman says quietly, not the President's.[26]

Roosevelt sensed that he and Lewis might have their troubles in the future. On the other hand, he showed a most decided liking for Sidney

---

* Lewis is quoted by his friendly biographer, Saul Alinsky, as saying on this subject: "Everybody says I want my pound of flesh, that I gave Mr. Roosevelt $500,000 for his 1936 campaign, and I want quid pro quo. The United Mine Workers and the CIO have paid cash on the barrel for every piece of legislation that we have gotten. . . . Is anyone fool enough to believe for one instant that we gave this money to Roosevelt because we were spellbound by his voice?" (Alinsky: Lewis, p. 177.)

Hillman. In this Trojan War between labor and capital, in which Franklin Roosevelt sometimes appeared to be involved far more than he desired, Lewis seemed to have both the reckless courage and the excessive pride of Achilles, while Hillman, by his spirit of diplomacy, his wise counsels and stratagems, seemed to be of the stamp of Ulysses. Hillman, for example, was still conferring privately with leaders of the AFL, such as Matthew Woll, in the hope of ending the rift between the two labor-union camps—though these persons assailed him in public. But John Lewis and Bill Green, as Hillman wrote to his daughter after the elections, were having nothing but arguments, and there was little hope of peace.[27]

At the late November conference between Roosevelt and his labor allies, new labor legislation was discussed, though Roosevelt did not tell them at that time how he intended to enforce it. Meanwhile they warned him that very serious industrial conflicts were impending in the motor industry and in steel, and expressed the hope that Roosevelt would stand by his labor allies.

On December 22, 1936, Hillman was at his office in New York in a conference with several of the Amalgamated executives when he was called to the phone. The voice that spoke to him was that of the President. "How are you, Sidney? When can you come up to see me for a chat?" Hillman was surprised but made no sign to his colleagues, and agreed to an appointment with Roosevelt for the following week.[28]

A tremendous wave of strikes had swept the country after the elections. Since the grievances of labor were not being treated in a conciliatory way, men turned to industrial war. Thus industry, which had enjoyed a marked recovery lately, faced paralysis. But neither the President nor Congress could do much about all this since any remedial legislation they attempted might be nullified by the Supreme Court.

When Hillman went to the White House on the morning of December 29, 1936, the General Motors strike was in progress at Flint, Michigan, and the President talked with him intimately and at length about what should be done. He left without any comment to the newspaper reporters; no one was more closemouthed than he in those days. But to his daughter at Oberlin he wrote privately:

I had a very satisfactory conference with the Chief in the W.H. about labor legislation. . . . I have been very busy the last couple of weeks. I have given most of my time trying to be of help in the G.M. muddle.

Right now the situation in Motors is at a standstill. It may change at any moment.[29]

They had talked also of action to support the wages-and-hours or "fair labor standards" bill, sponsored originally by Senator Hugo Black and later by Senator Robert Wagner. After Hillman left, Roosevelt, in his press conference that afternoon, declared that urgent efforts were now to be made to eliminate child labor, long hours, and starvation wages; but he did not say as yet whether he would make specific recommendations to Congress, for the Supreme Court's consistent hostility to legislation in this field provided a terrible dilemma still.[30]

However, Roosevelt told Sidney Hillman in advance, under pledge of secrecy, in their talk of December 29, what he proposed to do about the Supreme Court. He was going to introduce a bill to reform the Federal judiciary; that is, to increase the membership of the Supreme Court and bring about the retirement of those justices who were over seventy. This world-shaking news was imparted by Roosevelt to only two other persons besides Hillman. Hillman kept the secret well, and mentioned his previous knowledge only when news of the court-packing bill was given to the press five weeks later, in February 1937. He said at the time to Jacob Potofsky that Roosevelt had a great spirit and courage and "was more reliable than some of our own labor people." [31]

At this period and afterward the newspaper gossips often spoke of Hillman as Roosevelt's "chief labor consultant," and there were frequent rumors that he was slated to succeed Miss Perkins as Secretary of Labor. These rumors were undoubtedly circulated in order to cause jealousy between Hillman and the tempestuous Lewis. According to some reports, Roosevelt did consider Hillman for this post on a number of occasions, but was made aware that Mrs. Roosevelt would not have liked having her old friend, the only woman member of the Cabinet, superseded; and Eleanor Roosevelt's influence counted for much in such a case. The growing split between the CIO and AFL factions, moreover, made it more diplomatic to continue the well-intentioned neutral Madame Perkins in office. Hillman therefore served as an unofficial, or auxiliary, Secretary of Labor during these trying years, often consulted by telephone and constantly at the beck and call of the White House. The adept Roosevelt on numerous occasions showed Hillman flattering attentions, as on March 23, 1938, when he telephoned him to extend congratulations on his fifty-first birthday, or when he wrote to inquire about Hillman's health during an illness.

Nor is it surprising that the President, who attached to his personal service men without political weight, like Harry Hopkins or Rexford Tugwell, should have sought out the veteran unionist with his legions of devoted followers in New York, Chicago, and Philadelphia. Moreover, Hillman was loyal and trustworthy as an ally. Many old-line labor leaders talked all day long and held their whisky fairly well but never got things done the way he did. By December 1936, Roosevelt badly needed Hillman's expert advice, for the whole country seemed to be shaken by the storm of labor's revolt. And as even the adulatory Miss Perkins wrote of the President, "there was a great deal about trade unions he never fully understood."

v

Earlier that same year, amid the excitement of one of the bitterest presidential election campaigns in our history, a contest strongly colored with class feeling between the haves and the have-nots, the CIO movement had engendered a rolling offensive that swept into the "mass-production industries" of steel, motors, rubber, aluminum, textiles, and many other fields. Freed from the restraints imposed by the old AFL organizers, the rubber workers of Akron, for example, in January 1936 had improvised a "sit-down" strike, in which they occupied the factories of their employers day and night. Their action had an immense significance; it symbolized the bond between the workers and those great silent machines; it bespoke their intense belief in their proprietary "right to the job" and their will to exclude strikebreakers, even at the cost of their lives, until union recognition was granted them. This tactic, whose legality was questionable, as it appeared to violate, at the very least, the law of trespass, was so much feared by capital that it was not much talked about in the press at the time, but caught the attention of labor leaders, always eager to learn from each other's experiments.[32]

All during the summer and autumn of 1936, the country was filled with the alarum of the first great CIO drives. Everywhere the stentorian voices of organizers or their loud-speakers in sound trucks stationed at the gates of America's factories seemed to be calling the people to "Organize! Organize! Organize!" Caravans of trucks carrying militant trade unionists rode from town to town to spread the word of a strike, in festive spirit, singing jubilantly and waving their banners or placards,

Within the year that followed the launching of the CIO as an "educational" movement, its 900,000 members had grown to more than 2,000,000. The numbers were to be doubled again in the next year, 1937.

The irresistible momentum of the drive was noted by Hillman with enthusiasm. The rubber workers' union, almost defunct the year before under the AFL, had mushroomed again in 1936 until they had nearly 40,000 members and were spending tens of thousands of dollars, raised among themselves, on new drives. The same development could be felt at last in the great non-union automobile centers. "What has happened in this one year?" Hillman exclaimed. "The CIO . . . is making its contribution."

Of the first anniversary conference of CIO union representatives, in October 1936, Hillman wrote his daughter Philoine:

> We had a splendid conference. The CIO came of age. It is now an organization with a policy. Before the conference it was hard to tell whether the different groups could be made homogeneous. The leadership is fully accepted by the rank and file. We did not have to compromise our positions.[33]

This furious drive for industrial organization seemed to gather *élan* constantly until it appeared as the most formidable mass movement of Americans into unions ever seen. One strike action after another convulsed the heavy industries, where such developments were almost unknown before. And Lewis was everywhere as the inspirational leader of the mass movement.

He was like Danton in the early days of the French Revolution crying for "Audacity! Audacity! Ever more Audacity!" The crowds of workers loved him for his huge and animated eyebrows, his theatrical explosions of wrath and hate, his "revolutionary" tone.

Appearing before a gathering of the rubber workers in Akron, he would say:

> What have Goodyear workers gotten out of the growth of this company? [A significant pause; then in sneering tones] *Partnership!*
> Well, labor and capital may be partners in theory, but they are enemies in fact. . . . [Then pounding the speaking pulpit he roars] *Organize! Organize!* [34]

After the New Deal triumph in the November election, the workers were in no mood to brook opposition of the old sort. In the United

Auto Workers' Union, unknown young leaders arose, such as Homer Martin, the Reuther brothers, George Addes, Richard Frankensteen, and Robert Travis. All through 1936 the armies along the automobile belt-lines of Detroit and Flint were being steadily organized by their new leaders.

By November and the early part of December brief test strikes, during which the workers "stayed in" several General Motors plants in the Middle West, revealed the employers as confused or uncertain in their attitude. In a number of cases active union members who had been discharged were reinstated as a result of strong demonstrations in their behalf by the rank and file. Lewis said at the time that he was following this spreading action (which he had not initiated) with intense interest. Then, shouldering aside young Homer Martin, the UAW's president, Lewis himself took charge of this movement just as it "jumped" to Michigan.

His entrance into the picture was well timed. On December 18, 1936, he issued a public statement appealing to William S. Knudsen, executive vice-president of General Motors, to join in a collective-bargaining conference on the auto workers' demands, which, he held, must be dealt with on an industry-wide basis. Knudsen ignored this appeal. The company held to the position that relations with unions among its members must be limited only to the local affairs of separate plants. But on December 28, 1936, union members at Fisher Body Plant Number One, in Flint, Michigan, took matters into their own hands by "sitting down" and stopping the shipment of tools to G.M. factories in other, less unionized cities. From that day on it was "war," and the union members were as soldiers holding the fort.

The aspect of this historic industrial struggle that is of point to this narration is the unusual deadlock that developed throughout January 1937 and created a political crisis for the Roosevelt Administration. Normally General Motors, one of the world's richest corporations, would have shut down part of its business and starved out the strikers. But its directors were highly incensed at the "capture" of one key factory after another in Michigan and immediately called on the local sheriff and the newly elected Governor Frank Murphy to eject the workers by force. The managers of the company, whose success in maintaining completely non-union shops up to now depended largely on the use of force and constant espionage, had at once obtained an injunction.*

To enforce the court order, the entire Flint police force attacked the Fisher Body plant with shotguns and tear-gas shells on January 11. The 400 workers entrenched behind its walls replied with a tremendous volley of steel nuts and bolts, and completely routed the police in a skirmish in which a score of the strikers were wounded.

Governor Murphy, a fervent liberal and New Deal Democrat, then called 1,500 National Guards to the scene to preserve order. But he was a man of humane feelings, the son and grandson of Irish rebels. As mayor of Detroit in 1932 he had witnessed the terrible privations of the unemployed workers and made strenuous efforts to succor them. Now, despite the unremitting pressure of the motor industrialists, he refused to "shoot it out" with the strikers—Roosevelt supporting his stand covertly.

The heat was on President Roosevelt at this stage. Everyone now looked to Washington, where several preliminary conferences were held in which Governor Murphy, coming in from Detroit, talked with chairman Alfred P. Sloan of General Motors and with Lewis separately. Miss Perkins also conferred with these two separately and reported to President Roosevelt.

On January 20, 1937, Lewis, in a front-page newspaper interview, issued an appeal for Roosevelt's aid, declaring that whereas labor had helped to repel the attacks of the Du Ponts and Sloans upon the Administration, now

the same "economic royalists" have their fangs in labor. The workers of this country expect the Administration to help the workers in every reasonable way.[35]

It was a blunt reminder of the debt that Lewis felt was owing to the CIO. But Roosevelt keenly resented this open pressure upon him at this moment. Moreover, Congress and the press were in an uproar over the alleged "anarchy" in Michigan. There were cries for Federal Government intervention, even, if need be, by the use of the United States Army. The embarrassed Roosevelt promptly issued a statement

* General Motors expended $994,855 on private detective service from January 1, 1934, through July 31, 1936, according to a Senate committee's report on civil liberties. (U. S. Senate: Committee on Education and Labor, 74th Cong., 2nd Session. Violations of free speech and the rights of labor. *Hearings,* 1936–40. Pt. 6, p. 2175.)

in reply to the CIO's chairman, which the newspapers interpreted as a rebuke: ". . . I think, in the interests of peace, there come moments when statements, conversations, and headlines are not in order."

Lewis insisted that Roosevelt was still the ally of labor; but in private vented his rage at the President, whose hesitation in this difficult affair he called ingratitude or worse.

Roosevelt was fairly caught in the squeeze between capital and labor. In those days the magnates of motors still refused to stay in the same room with men like William Green, let alone the "revolutionary" Lewis. They insisted that the United Auto Workers held but a numerical minority of their employees and had no right to an exclusive bargaining position for all of them. But on this point Lewis was adamant.

On the one hand, Roosevelt was not going to desert his industrial union friends; but on the other, the Red Specter of property seizure by the proletarians of Flint and Detroit was being invoked by the nation's press every day. In the midst of the peace negotiations that had been initiated in Washington, Mr. Sloan suddenly left town, breaking off all contact with Miss Perkins, as if to underscore his view that capital could expect no fair treatment from what he regarded as a "pro-labor" government. At this point the President turned to the man he most relied on as his adviser on labor affairs, Sidney Hillman—just then absent on a brief vacation in Florida—and asked him to come to Washington. A few days later, on January 26, 1937, there was a conference at the White House to which Hillman, it was reported, at the President's request, brought John L. Lewis and Charles Howard, general secretary of the CIO. Roosevelt asked Lewis and Hillman to "get the men out of the G.M. plants." But the most that could be wrung from Lewis was the promise that the men would leave "when the company begins to bargain with them or even with me, in good faith." [36]

It is highly probable that this White House conference was called by Roosevelt, as one of Hillman's aides reported, "in order to offset the impression that the President is 'off' the CIO." Lewis, it was related, had "made a mess of things, and in the long run Hillman will have to clear the mess." [37] After having rebuked Lewis, the President sought to balance the scales by spanking Mr. Sloan in the press the very next day for leaving Washington and breaking off negotiations.

"Let Roosevelt Do It!" front-page newspaper editorials (as in the Detroit *News*) now thundered, almost in unison. But what Roosevelt

had decided was precisely that he was *not* going to handle the affair in Washington, through the national Administration, if he could help it. The General Motors people had obtained a court order setting a deadline for February 3, 1937, when the strikers were to be expelled from the company's property by the state militia. Governor Murphy had already hastened back to Detroit; and John L. Lewis, according to the President's plan, was to follow him a few days later. Roosevelt was going to request that the heads of General Motors begin negotiating with representatives of the strikers and Lewis *in Detroit*. To have handled this affair in the atmosphere of Washington would have been a political disaster.

Roosevelt's strategy in this crisis was, above all, to keep the sit-down fight out of Washington and in Michigan. It was a brilliant move politically and psychologically, and reflects clearly the pattern of Hillman's habitual strategy in such affairs: to force negotiation first at lower levels of authority, and keep the supreme arbiter in reserve, only for the last contingency. Governor Murphy, by dint of his local authority, with General Motors and the strikers, personified by Lewis, were to settle their affair out in Detroit at all costs. Only if they failed would Roosevelt come in.

Lewis swaggered through the headlines of the nation's press and departed for "the front" in Detroit on February 3, 1937, to face no one knew what. What was not revealed at the time was that Roosevelt had asked him to go. On receiving hints that the General Motors executives might welcome some exit from their deadlocked position— if he, as President, applied pressure upon them—Roosevelt had telephoned Knudsen a few days earlier and appealed to him to meet with "a committee of the workers," which meant John Lewis. Knudsen, after consulting with his colleagues, agreed to do this, saying that the request from the President left him with no other alternative.[38] By now time was short. The law, the Michigan National Guard, even the kindly Governor Murphy, could wait no longer.

The day after Lewis departed was the occasion for an official reception at the White House by President and Mrs. Roosevelt. Among the many invited guests, chiefly Cabinet members, diplomats, congressmen, and government officials, were Edward McGrady, Miss Perkins, and Sidney Hillman, resplendent in white tie and tails. Hillman held no office, but as one CIO official said at this period: "A whisper from

Sidney Hillman of the Amalgamated is louder than the loudest shout of almost anyone in the national Cabinet." [39]

Roosevelt, as usual, left the party early for his upstairs study, where he could be free for telephoning, it was reported. Miss Perkins, Mr. McGrady, and Mr. Hillman followed him and also spent the evening speaking on the telephone to Governor Murphy and conciliator James Dewey in Detroit. Now and then one or another would come downstairs, quietly exchange greetings with some of the guests, then go back to his telephoning. Below, the party carried on with great good cheer; there were champagne and music and dancing. Meanwhile the anxious people at the telephones above were in touch with the actors in the greatest industrial conflict of that era at Detroit and Flint, where thousands of desperate men waited that cold night in the plants of General Motors among the huge, silent machines. [40]

The reports received at the White House hour by hour indicated that Lewis was holding out stubbornly for recognition of the United Auto Workers as the exclusive bargaining agency for the G.M. workers. The heads of General Motors were also complicating things by insisting upon similar recognition being given to a pretended dual union, the so-called "Flint Alliance," recently sponsored by the company—which Lewis refused.

Late that night President Roosevelt spoke to Lewis himself in Detroit:

Hello, John, how are you? We're having a sort of party up here at the White House, but I'm talking to you from my bedroom upstairs and things are very quiet here. As a matter of fact, Sidney Hillman is here, and I've asked him to come upstairs. He's sitting right alongside of me. I've had a long talk with Sidney about this situation out in Detroit and we came to an agreement. John, I think I can get an agreement for you with General Motors to give you recognition for one month. What do you say, John? [41]

Lewis refused this compromise proposal, saying: "Mr. President, my people tell me it's got to be six months. One month is not satisfactory." The President then suggested a two-month period, but this, too, was firmly refused, and the talk was broken off.

An aid of Lewis recalls that, putting down the telephone, he said with a scowl: "Do you hear, Sidney's sitting right there. What is he doing in the President's bedroom—it's a bad thing!" [42] In Lewis' mind Hillman stood too close to the President's middle-ground position.

To others it might appear that Hillman's ingrained moderation disposed him to counsel avoidance of a possible explosion of violence whose consequences none could foretell. Lewis, however, with his attitude of complete indifference to danger, held out for the full terms he had stipulated—although even Governor Murphy and President Homer Martin of the United Auto Workers appeared hysterical with the strain. Bluffing Murphy into delaying military action beyond the court's deadline, February 3, Lewis wrangled on with the General Motors executives for another week.

The CIO leader played his hand with amazing brass, even though it was Roosevelt who had forced the powerful General Motors people to do that which they had never done before, to treat with labor-union representatives. And the auto workers' shock troops, still holding possession of the key plants under their young leaders, in those forty days, by their unshakable determination to stay in to the bitter end, played a decisive part in the outcome.*

Then Roosevelt delivered what must be regarded as the final stroke. On February 5, 1937, the bill for the reform of the Supreme Court by the increase of its membership, the so-called "court-packing bill," was suddenly announced and sent to Congress, creating a sensation surpassing almost everything that had gone before under the New Deal. After all, the big employers such as General Motors were being fought by their workers, as the sit-downers proclaimed, because they still refused to "obey the law and engage in collective bargaining." The Wagner Labor Relations Act, after nearly two years' delay, was still not being enforced; and Roosevelt had moved with the directness and logic of a road-building machine to settle the problem by reforming the Supreme Court.

A few days later, on February 11, the General Motors executives at Detroit hauled down their flag and signed an agreement granting exclusive recognition to the United Auto Workers for a period of six months to cover the seventeen plants affected by the strike. It meant that the rising auto workers' organization was inside the mammoth corporation for good. This was unquestionably the greatest and, by all

* The "sit-down" strikers' message to Governor Murphy and the world outside was an eloquent one: "Unarmed as we are . . . we have decided to stay in the plants. We have no illusions about the sacrifices which this decision will entail. . . . Many of us will be killed, and we take this means of making it known to our wives, to our children, to the people of Michigan and the country that . . . you must be held responsible for our deaths."

means, the most strategic victory ever won by American labor and, in effect, opened all of America's heavy industries to unionization.

On March 3, 1937, only three weeks later, there came also the astonishing announcement that the United States Steel Corporation had agreed to recognize the CIO's Steel Workers' Organizing Committee as collective-bargaining representatives for its employees—following direct personal negotiations between John L. Lewis and Chairman Myron C. Taylor of United States Steel. Chairman Philip Murray of the SWOC and other CIO leaders had been directing a number of key strikes with great effect. But this appeared as a great personal triumph for John L. Lewis. Behind the surrender of "Big Steel" lay the conviction of its bankers (the Morgan group) that labor was in the "wave of the future" and that Roosevelt would have his way in the reform of the Federal courts and the enforcement of the new labor laws.

"This was a great day in the history of labor," Hillman said when he learned that U. S. Steel had entered into an agreement with the CIO. It meant a complete break in the traditional policy of the strongest financial groups in Wall Street. The road lay open to the unionization of those "20,000,000 wage workers" that the old AFL leaders so often talked about as their objective.[43]

In the climactic year, 1937, more than 1,800,000 went out on strike, most of them members of new CIO unions.

Around mammoth modern mills and at bleak old factories, on ships, on piers, at offices, and in public gathering places, men and women roared "CIO! CIO!" with the gathering velocity of a massed football cheer. . . . Millions of CIO buttons sprouted on overalls, shirtwaists, and workers' hats and caps. They became badges of a new independence.[44]

For democracy now entered the great motor and steel factories. Men who had been intimidated, spied on, and "driven" for twenty years, or who were known to have been actually fired for "smiling," walked with their heads up while their own shop committees and shop stewards looked to their rights and interests.

That year the fame and power of John L. Lewis was at its zenith, and fear of him also filled the pages of our press. The CIO, by October 1937, reached a reported membership of 3,700,000, surpassing that of the AFL, then at 3,400,000. When the workers saw also that their pay checks were substantially increased, their idolization of the man-with-the-eyebrows passed all bounds.. "I have a $16-a-month increase and pay $12 a year in union dues—should I 'hate' Lewis?" a typical automobile worker wrote to his newspaper. And others declared that it was worth $12 a year only to be able to walk about the streets of their steel towns in Pennsylvania "just like free American citizens." All over the country, in the homes of hundreds of thousands of workers, the photograph of Roosevelt was taken down, to be replaced by a portrait of the frowning John L. Lewis.

The persistence of sit-down strikes during the early months of 1937 alarmed Congress, which threatened to investigate the growing labor trouble. In late March 1937, Hillman was called to the White House and asked by Roosevelt to see to it that the CIO used restraint in applying the sit-down tactics. Hillman, it was said, was able to give the President assurance on this point, and the proposed investigations were dropped.[45]

There was much talk in these days of Lewis as a would-be dictator, marching at the head of ever-larger masses of men into the White House itself. It was the season for dictators: Huey Long was dead, at the hands of an assassin, but Hitler and Mussolini were still flourishing. Hillman repeatedly felt compelled to come to the defense of Lewis against such accusations, declaring that instead of offering "something for nothing," like Huey Long, Lewis was working effectively to improve the condition of the masses. With the rank and file becoming "more free and articulate," a dictatorship was unthinkable to them.[46]

Yet the vast expansion of Lewis' ego these days was something to behold. He saw everything in terms of personal power; he directed the CIO as his personal organization. He himself seemed naïvely unaware of the inflation his pride was undergoing when, addressing CIO gatherings, he would talk for hours on end about his own contributions to labor's "renaissance" and about his own fearlessness and courage and even that of his Welsh ancestors far back in time. It was true, nonetheless, that 1937 witnessed the "greatest mass maneuver" of labor in all history and that, as Lewis said: ". . . It was no little achievement, and I have reason to be proud of the part I played."

More and more Hillman was forced to act as moderator between Lewis and Roosevelt, whom Lewis seldom visited. A Washington correspondent wrote now:

It is through Mr. Hillman that the President now deals with Mr. Lewis, and through Mr. Hillman that Mr. Lewis now deals with the President. Their personal relations are concededly strained.[47]

This was only one more chore for the unresting Hillman, who, early in 1937, took command of the most difficult sector of the CIO's organizing campaign, that of the entire textile field, embracing America's largest manufacturing industry in point of labor force.

Chapter Eighteen

THE TWOC--

LABOR'S

CIVIL WAR: 1937-1938

Almost without pausing for breath, the CIO leaders, following their victories in the automobile and steel industries, after February 1937, turned to the job of unionizing the ill-paid workers in the textile field. These numbered roundly 1,250,000, and were widely dispersed over 29 states in many thousands of units ranging from small mills using 100 to 200 hired hands, to gigantic, highly mechanized factories with 10,000 or more workers. The textile industry was not only immense and highly varied in its products —chiefly cotton, woolen, silk and rayon cloths, and carpet fabrics— but it was also notoriously a "sick" industry. Most of this sickness stemmed from the migration of Northern and New England textile capital to the South, where a working population (of whom half were women and children) labored for about 25 per cent less in wages than their counterparts north of the Mason and Dixon line. The "poor whites" in the mill towns of the Deep South were almost wholly unorganized as late as 1937, and lived in their hills and valleys in what was often described by investigators as a state of peonage. Moreover, regional, racial, and religious differences deeply divided the labor force of this sprawling industry.*

Since the famous "turnout" of the Lowell girls in New England in 1834, its history had been one of recurrent struggle and heartbreaking defeats. As in 1919 and 1929, so in 1934, under the stimulus of the NRA's labor charter, the textile people had risen again in a great general strike that had rallied 400,000 to the picket lines of the United Textile Workers. Yet the results of the 1934 movement had been disheartening. Within two years only about 60,000 bona fide members were left in the union, half of them centered in one strong, autonomous unit, the American Federation of Hosiery Workers, headed by Emil Rieve. The textile workers' leaders had then turned to the CIO for help, as to a last hope. At conferences held in 1936 between the United Textile officers and the CIO executives, it was decided that the CIO must take over the whole job of rebuilding and expanding the shattered union.

On March 7, 1937, the formation of the Textile Workers' Organizing Committee, or TWOC, was announced in the press, and Sidney Hillman was named by Lewis as its chairman. His own clothing workers' union and the ILGWU stood closest to the textile industry. The other executive members of the TWOC were Thomas J. Kennedy of the United Mine Workers (serving as secretary-treasurer), Francis J. Gorman, president of the United Textile Workers, Emil Rieve of the Hosiery Workers, Charles Zimmerman, a vice-president of the ILGWU, Thomas F. Burns of the United Rubber Workers, and Charles Weinstein of the Amalgamated.

Under a firm agreement similar to that of the Steel Workers' Organizing Committee, Hillman and the other TWOC executives were to be in full control of the new organization for the duration of the projected campaign. Hillman was reported to have said to Francis Gorman, the textile union's leader:

Let us have no misunderstanding about this. In an important project of this kind, there must be no divided responsibility. If the TWOC runs this campaign, it must have full charge. . . . If you don't like this arrangement, the TWOC will step out of the picture and leave the job to any other friendly union.[1]

* "From the point of view of numbers involved and complexity of economic problems, organizing the textile industry was the biggest of the tasks assumed by the CIO," wrote Edward Levinson in *Labor Marches* (1938).

In truth, most of the funds for this huge drive were raised through the exertions of Hillman, since it was his persuasive tongue that led the Amalgamated members to donate $500,000 to the TWOC. To this the ILGWU, under Dubinsky, generously added $112,000; while the coal miners gave $100,000 in addition. The cost of the campaign during two years mounted to considerably more than these sums—in all, upward of a million dollars was said to have been contributed by the Amalgamated alone. In appealing to his own union members to support such heavy drafts, Hillman argued that their interest in unionizing textiles was immediate. No union could be safe when such a large and closely related industry underpaid its labor and continued as "a feeding reserve for open-shoppers everywhere." Throughout the South, and in other centers of textile manufacture, often located near factories employing men's and women's garment workers, the non-union cloth mills exerted a most depressing influence upon the union people through their maintenance of substandard wages and working conditions.[2]

The press was soon spreading reports of the new movement in sensational headlines: *"Hillman Reported Seeking a Labor Empire of 1,000,000 Textile Workers!"* It was not to be as clear and simple as that; and Hillman, at any rate, unlike others, seldom estimated the value of trade-union groups or labor leadership in terms of the gross quantity of followers or dues payers. The real task was arduous enough: that of conquering new frontiers of unorganized industry, where men and women had labored for a century in thousands of cotton mills, in silk-weaving and -throwing plants and bleacheries and rug factories, without benefit of unions.

For many weeks Hillman and the staff he gathered around him plotted out a many-pronged campaign. The walls of the TWOC headquarters in New York were hung with maps of 29 states, dotted with little flags denoting textile mills, as in any large-scale war. But as the "generalissimo" of the textile drive afterward explained it, the program worked out in March and April 1937 was, to begin with, "educational" in character. An intensive drive was to be launched in which the pledge cards of hundreds of thousands of workers were to be gathered up. By means of widespread publicity, pamphleteering, house-to-house canvassing, and mass meetings, this two-million-dollar campaign was to combat the deep-rooted prejudice against unions among textile workers in the towns of New England as in the Deep South. In the South, for example, the abiding fear of the people that a weak organization would be set up for a while, only to retreat again, as had so often happened, leaving them worse off than before, was to be overcome by confident and aggressive action on the part of regional organizers.

The second phase of the operation would be devoted to stimulating a widespread demand in the factories for the election of union representatives under the supervision of the National Labor Relations Board. Hillman planned to use Federal Government support to the fullest extent, in the light of the more vigorous labor-law-enforcement policies now promised by Roosevelt. The final phase of the action would involve negotiating union agreements with employers as a consequence of strike activity from below and political pressure from above.[3]

The field was divided into five regional fronts: New England, the Middle Atlantic States, the upper South, the Deep South, and the West. Seasoned Amalgamated organizers such as Hyman Blumberg, who was named New England regional director, and Joseph Salerno, who served as his deputy, were drafted for the TWOC campaign. Frank Rosenblum at Chicago headed the action in the West; Abraham Chatman handled the upstate New York region; while Charles Weinstein of Philadelphia directed operations in the Middle Atlantic States with the assistance of Carl Holderman, New Jersey organizer for the United Textile Workers.

The great stumbling block in all previous textile campaigns had been the South. Here Hillman, fortunately, obtained the services of A. Steve Nance of Atlanta, a courageous AFL leader, formerly president of the Georgia Federation of Labor, who now came over to the CIO. While Nance was to center his efforts upon Georgia and Alabama, John A. Peel, who, like Nance, was a Southerner, was to direct operations in the upper South, from Richmond.

By 1937 the bulk of America's cotton and rayon mills was concentrated in the Southern states, where some 450,000 unorganized men, women, and children, white and Negro, were employed at substandard factory wages. Hence it was to this section that Hillman assigned the new type of men and women who were flocking to the banner of the CIO: college graduates and young ministers, such as Franz Daniel (an able Amalgamated organizer in recent years), T.

Witherspoon Dodge, Lucy Randolph Mason, and numerous other churchmen and social workers of Southern birth. All this was arranged in full awareness of the fact that the Ku Klux Klan would ride again at reports of alleged Yankee intrusions or alleged "Communist" labor organizers arriving from "outside." [4]

A small army of 650 organizers was assembled and allotted to nine regional headquarters and 74 local offices. Most of them were very young and received only $25 to $30 a week, but they were fired with a crusading *élan* and, like missionaries, went forth on house-to-house canvasses to bring in union pledges. Old-time AFL organizers scoffed at such tactics.[5]

Operations began promptly in April 1937 on a broad front, in the South as in the North, as if Hillman were in haste to follow quickly upon the CIO's great victories in motors and steel. His public statements, however, were temperate and calculated to lay stress on the constructive value of the TWOC campaign. The textile industry, like the clothing trade of yesterday, he said, "needed organization in order to stabilize itself, and to save itself from cutthroat competition." Far from opposing the new high-speed machinery being installed in textile and rayon mills, the CIO desired to co-operate with management in seeking to "adjust" conditions burdensome to the whole nation's economy.

We do not claim to have a sovereign cure for all the ills of industry. But we do claim a democratic willingness to discuss our plans and hopes with other men of larger experience in such matters. We ask that they believe in our good will . . . and join with us in eradicating the evils. . . . If we can agree upon existing evils, I shall lack for neither patience nor confidence in the adjustment of details or of methods.[6]

Hillman wisely chose the big manufacturing units in Pennsylvania, New Jersey, and New England, the producers of carpets and rayon cloths, as the scene of the first skirmish. Within a month many contracts were being negotiated, providing for wage increases, vacations with pay, and a 40-hour week—with concerns whose working hours had run as long as 55 per week recently. In April 1937 the great Viscose Company, employing 20,000 workers, was won over to a union agreement calling for a 10 per cent wage increase. Soon afterward another huge company, North American Rayon, with 8,000 workers, came into the fold. The campaign in this region proceeded almost without opposition until the end of July, when a general strike of silk workers was called in New Jersey and Pennsylvania. The focal point of resistance in Pennsylvania was the big Duplan Company, with more than 5,200 workers, and the strongest measures were used by the TWOC leaders to bring the employers to terms.

By mid-August, through the pressure of state authorities, a conference between the Duplan management and the TWOC representatives was opened at Harrisburg in the offices of Thomas J. Kennedy, who was then both lieutenant governor of Pennsylvania and secretary-treasurer of the TWOC. Kennedy's dual role was symptomatic of the changed political climate in which the CIO campaigns were being conducted that season. Yet the company officials held out obdurately against the TWOC's terms—until Hillman arrived in town. He had been working "twenty-four hours a day," as Emil Rieve said, constantly on the move from Washington to the New England front at Boston, and down to the danger zone in Atlanta. It was late at night, and he was pale and spent when he turned up at Harrisburg.

At once the atmosphere of the conference changed for the better. The Duplan executives, who had refused to treat with the other union spokesmen, showed marked deference toward Hillman. He, for his part, was his old reasonable self, very mild in argument, and willing to settle for a 10 per cent wage increase, though insisting on union recognition along with it. After an hour or so of discussion, he won his point, and at midnight more thousands of textile workers were marched into the CIO ranks.[7]

In New England, Hillman and his associates sought to create the impression everywhere that the CIO was moving with irresistible impetus. Advantage was taken of the recent change of heart in the Supreme Court—as a result of which the Wagner Labor Relations Act, after two years' delay, was sustained—to enlist the support of the National Labor Relations Board.

On May 23, 1937, a gigantic open-air meeting was staged by the TWOC in a baseball park outside Lawrence, Massachusetts, with more than 50,000 workers in holiday mood turning out to hear John L. Lewis and Sidney Hillman. Young Joe Salerno of the Amalgamated's Boston branch, who was to be chairman of the meeting, received a careful briefing from Hillman as to procedure: "You must devote at least twenty minutes to your introduction of John L.— and make it strong! You can make it short for me."

Salerno obliged by preparing a long speech in terms of the most extravagant panegyric he could conceive for "Big John," whom he portrayed as a "composite of all the heroic qualities of Brutus, Robespierre, Tom Paine, and Abraham Lincoln"; in short, "the great industrial emancipator of the American masses." When he came to writing a few introductory remarks for Hillman, he said later: "I felt as if I had no breath left." These, at any rate, were the usages of diplomacy estimated by Hillman as needful to keep the much-adulated Lewis in good humor.

Hillman, who spoke first, was all vibrant with enthusiasm, exclaiming: "The South is going to be organized as well as the North. . . . This is a fight for everything worth while!" He spoke simply but with great fire that day.

But Lewis was the idol whom the thousands had come to see and hear. His confident gestures, his tone, his inflection were, as always, those of the consummate actor. Yet somehow it was not one of his good days. The honors for oratory really went to Salerno.

Driving back to Boston with Hillman and Salerno after the meeting Lewis expressed himself as well pleased with the young chairman and asked him how he had learned to speak so well.

Hillman said: "Why, Joe is one of our own Amalgamated boys, a Boston clothing worker; and besides, he has managed to study elocution and win a law degree in his spare time."

But Salerno interposed: "It was Mr. Hillman and the Amalgamated that helped me through college. Mr. Lewis, everything I am, everything I have learned about the labor movement, I owe to Mr. Hillman."

At this Lewis frowned noticeably. The big TWOC campaign was not his show.[8]

The demonstrations at Lawrence, historic site of many struggles against the huge American Woolen Company, ended later that summer, after NLRB polls had been held, with the unionization of America's greatest textile concern, employing 20,000 people. The workers in about half of New England's woolen, worsted, and cotton textile mills, some 90,000 in number, were swept into the TWOC during 1937. In the carpet, silk, and synthetic-yarn factories of Pennsylvania and New Jersey the CIO drive was even more successful, bringing 85 to 90 per cent of the workers into the union by the end of 1938. Wages which had been, on the average, as low as $750 annually in 1936 began to climb gradually toward the levels of other industries.

In the South the going was much harder, with best results reached in the Piedmont region (of the Carolinas, Georgia, and Alabama), where 100,000 textile workers, almost 40 per cent of the working force, quickly moved into the union during the first big push of March to September 1937. As earlier, in the 1934 United Textile campaign, the TWOC's agents were given a warm reception by the white-shrouded fanatics of the KKK and by surreptitiously organized Citizens' Councils, which operated as armed mobs against the mill-workers in the Georgia and South Carolina towns. Franz Daniel reported that on evenings when the TWOC called people to union rallies fiery crosses would regularly be set burning. Then, to make things worse, religious revivalists suddenly appeared in mill villages where a strike or an organizing rally might be in progress, and put up large new tents in which they preached sermons full of fire and brimstone, threatening eternal damnation for all who dared to sign for the TWOC. Everywhere fear was generated; in all the local press hate was spewed forth against the Jew, Hillman, and the "godless Bolshevik" Lewis. Daniel and Nance were assailed and threatened constantly.

Early in 1938, amid the strain and excitement of the organizing struggle at Atlanta, Regional Director Steve Nance, only forty-three years of age, suddenly died of a heart attack. Before his death he had helped to bring about a large penetration of the Georgia-Alabama cotton textile region; 25,000 workers were unionized here in the first year of the TWOC campaign. Hillman paid high tribute to Nance as no less a martyr of the CIO crusade than those who had fallen in the Memorial Day massacre at South Chicago.

By early October, the TWOC could report that almost 450,000 workers had either enrolled as union members or signed pledge cards. (These estimates, however, may have included many duplications.) In any case, approximately a quarter of a million people were now covered by union-shop contracts with 905 concerns, which is a clearer index of actual results. The campaign had begun with about 65,000 members in the United Textile Workers, and only half of these under union-shop agreements. A good start had been made in organizing, what was for labor, one of America's most demoralized industries.

Hillman had followed the characteristic Amalgamated strategy of trying to rationalize the whole situation, and of viewing the industry as a whole instead of merely organizing quantities of workers. Some attempt was made also to educate the employers by encouraging them to form trade associations and thereby take labor out of competition.

Some criticisms of Hillman's work in this field were voiced later by various authorities on the labor movement, such as John L. Lewis, who felt that he had "spread himself too thin." It is true also that many of the new recruits in the blighted areas of New England did not stay long in the union ranks. Hillman made it his policy to sound optimistic in public about the coming organization of "one million" textile workers. But he knew that he was working in America's "industrial back yard." The problems of the highly dispersed textile industry were far more complex than those of industries concentrated in a few giant factories of the industrial belt of the Middle West, as in the case of steel and motors.

Hillman's conviction was that this industry would never really raise its labor standards without Federal legislation fixing minimum wages and maximum hours. For this reason he was hard at work in Washington, even during the TWOC drive, lobbying for the passage of Senator Wagner's wages-and-hours bill, when his health collapsed and he was forced to relinquish command of the TWOC for six months. Furthermore, the sharp business recession that began in the autumn of 1937 brought the textile drive to a halt for the time being.

In September, the TWOC officers in New England had joyously celebrated the signing of a union-shop agreement with the American Woolen Corporation of Lawrence. One month later this giant corporation shut down most of its plants and discharged 75 per cent of its 20,000 employees. The renewed deflationary trend affected nearly all industries. Hundreds of thousands of workers lost their jobs, and dues payments to union treasuries declined everywhere. Even John L. Lewis appeared baffled, as his associates noticed, by the return of business depression and the ebbing of the great wave of union organization.

Were the armies of labor to march uphill and down again forever, with each cycle of boom and slump? The recurrence of depression, the fall of markets, the renewed spread of unemployment were disheartening signs. The Roosevelt Administration in 1937 had begun to cut down on spending and had balanced the Federal budget. Hillman agreed with the views of many economic experts that this action was premature, that more Federal relief and public works expenditure was needed now rather than less. More than ever, new laws establishing a floor under wages and a ceiling over hours were needed to eliminate substandard wages—as low as $1.20 a day for a 12-hour day—which the Textile Workers' drive had uncovered in the South. But how could such great goals be reached when the American labor movement itself was embroiled in a "civil war" between the AFL and the CIO? The recession made it more urgent than before to bring to an end these hostilities that seemed as grotesque as they were useless.

II

There had been a war of words between Lewis and Green throughout 1936, the first year of the CIO, in which Lewis easily took the palm for belligerent language. (Hillman cared less for ultimatums and adjectives.) The tone of disgust and of mockery adopted by Lewis from the start strongly suggests that there was in his mind always the fixed intention to bring about a complete rupture between the two camps of labor. By the autumn of 1937, after the CIO had made its spectacular advances in the mass industries, Lewis seemed convinced that the CIO would swallow the American Federation of Labor in its own good time.

Other leaders had conceived of the CIO as a phase of more or less friendly separation, after which the two wings of labor would reunite. Yet behind the jurisdictional strife that flared up in many an industry lay the fierce passions of leader-egos reckoning their power in terms of so many hundred thousand or million union members' votes "in their pockets," and jealous of their "national" sovereignty over great industries or crafts.

That the issue of craft versus industrial unionism no longer counted for much in this conflict was shown by the haste with which the AFL's agents now threw together industrial unions of their own under "Federal charters." An unexpected turn of events was the great stimulus given to the growth of the AFL unions by the intense activity of CIO organizers. As the CIO miners and steel workers planted new unions in, for instance, the Pennsylvania towns formerly run by the "coal-and-iron police," and even elected friendly local governments in 1936, the organizers of the AFL teamsters, who had never penetrated these sections before, now moved in, and theirs and other AFL unions expanded tremendously. With the rank and file helping each other, this "civil war" of labor revealed itself as primarily a conflict of leading personalities at the top for supreme power in the American labor hierarchy. The Old Guard in the AFL, typified by Hutcheson of the carpenters' union, Daniel Tobin of the teamsters', and Frey of the Metal Trades Department, closed their ranks in fear of the masses of new industrial-union members being assembled by Lewis, Hillman, and others.

As a first measure, warning letters had gone forth from the AFL's Executive Council to the heads of the original unions in the CIO, who were summoned to appear for a hearing in June 1936. Hillman, like the others, refused to appear, though his letter was written in a tone of civility contrasting strongly with Lewis' philippics. The unity of labor, he said, was for him a "matter of life and death," and it was his earnest hope that differences between the two blocs would soon be composed.

On August 6, 1936, following a "trial" of the dissident unions before the AFL's Executive Council—at which the defendants put in no appearance—the ten original unions constituting the CIO were formally suspended. Lewis, in one of his angry tirades, declared it "an act of stupidity." Hillman was silent. The legality (as well as the wisdom) of the Council's action in suspending 38 per cent of the AFL's membership was questioned at the time, for the constitution called for a two-thirds vote of the annual convention in such cases. Thereafter revocation of the charters of the condemned unions overhung the dissidents as a final draconian measure.

One result of the growing split was especially disliked by Hillman: at the height of the struggle to establish the TWOC in the South, agents of the AFL turned up in Alabama and Georgia to offer the services of a rival textile union. And yet in September 1937, he was reported to have joined David Dubinsky of the ILGWU in efforts to bring about peace. In the older labor body, the AFL vice-president, Matthew Woll, and George M. Harrison, president of the Railway Clerks, also headed a "peace party" that put out feelers to the CIO.[9]

A week later, however, on October 1, 1937, the annual convention of the AFL in Denver finally authorized its Executive Council to expel the CIO unions by an overwhelming vote, in which the opposition, of course, did not participate. The Council thus was empowered to revoke the charters of those unions affiliated with the CIO which had not returned to the fold by a date set at the Council's discretion. "The die is cast for war against autocracy, against rebellion, against the alliance of American greed and alien Communism," the resolution of the Denver convention declared. At the same time the delegates voted to continue the standing committee which was negotiating for peace with the rebellious organizations.[10]

Within the high councils of the CIO, as was known to the press, there had lately been serious friction between John L. Lewis and Dubinsky, and between Dubinsky and Hillman. "The CIO prima donnas are pulling each other's hair backstage," wrote one Washington correspondent.[11] Hence the AFL's Denver resolution against the CIO sought to exploit these known differences by observing that Mr. Dubinsky and the ILGWU were being "ignored and belittled" by Lewis and Hillman. The errors of the International Ladies' Garment Workers up to now were censured but mildly, and they were entreated by the AFL leaders to return to the true faith and be pardoned.

On the other hand Hillman, who was pictured as playing Machiavelli to Caesar (or Cesare Borgia?) Lewis, was singled out for severe condemnation. He was accused of "burdening" his union members "with undue and special assessments . . . for purposes of political aggrandizement."

In language which was a crude imitation of Lewis' wind-blown rhetoric the AFL's bill of accusation ended in an epopee that pictured Lewis and Hillman, in their different ways, as the personification of all that was evil and abhorrent in the secessionist movement:

We find, on the one hand, the dominating and fulminating Caesar of the CIO marching his Roman legions to the White House at Washington with bludgeoning threats, while on the other hand, we find the Machiavelli of the same CIO pursuing the methods typical of that old master of cunning and conniving, working through the catacombs of politics, pouring oil upon the troubled machinery of national politics, so that where the one smashes through in ruthless effort at conquest, the other follows with soft words, with the trappings of intellectualism and the tenuous and slandering tactics of the ancient masters of deception and ensnaring. We refer to one called Sidney Hillman.[12]

This was gross caricature, to be sure; yet it served to perpetuate a fearsome myth of the two ruling CIO leaders working together mysteriously—in short, the lion and the fox of the children's tales— a fable calculated to terrify all those who had reason to dislike the tendencies of progressive labor.

In the labor movement it is quite customary, however, for the rival politicians to call each other the worst names and then sit down to a peaceful conference together. A few days later, on October 12, a proposal of the CIO's Executive Board for a meeting of a joint committee (initiated by Hillman and made with Lewis' approval) was forwarded by telegraph to the AFL and accepted with alacrity.[13]

The conferees met in Washington on October 25, among them Charles P. Howard, Philip Murray, David Dubinsky, and Sidney Hillman for the CIO, with George M. Harrison, Matthew Woll, and G. M. Bugniazet representing the AFL. Both Lewis and Green stayed away from this conference, though keeping in close touch with its participants.

The principal demands of the CIO were that the Federation declare its support hereafter of industrial unions for workers in certain specified industries; establish a CIO Department that was to be autonomous within the AFL; reinstate the CIO unions with full rights; and work out and ratify this program at a joint convention of affiliates of both labor bodies.

The Federation representatives indicated their willingness to receive back the ten original CIO unions in toto and to set up an autonomous CIO Department to rule the industrial unions. But at first they refused to accept the twenty new unions added to the CIO since the beginning of 1936 upon the same terms as the original ten, several of these new unions like those of the automobile workers and the steel workers being very large numerically. The question of an adjustment of craft and jurisdictional rights in the case of the newer unions remained a thorny issue—and yet here, too, the conferees showed some indication of reaching agreement under a compromise formula using the joint conference method.

At one point the negotiators showed willingness to approve and initial the compromise plan as a "basis of agreement" uniting the two movements. But on the afternoon of the next day Philip Murray of the Steel Workers' Organizing Committee, then the faithful lieutenant of Lewis, was absent, and the meeting was adjourned. Murray, who seemed keen for unity, had retired to consult with his chief. The next morning his attitude appeared entirely changed, and he raised the question of whether the AFL representatives had any specific authority to see that the terms of the provisory agree-ment were carried out. Some of those present for the AFL later recalled the complete change in Murray's tone; some CIO representatives also remember how Lewis, on meeting them in the afternoon, at the adjournment of one of the daily conferences, stormed: "What authority do they have? Who is there to agree with?" [14]

Unfortunately, after the first day of these negotiations, Hillman was not on hand to reason with Lewis or try to calm him. That afternoon he had felt ill and gone back to his hotel to lie down. The next day, feeling no better, Hillman took the train to New York, managed to crawl home, and went to bed with a fever. Jacob S. Potofsky took his place in the capacity of an observer.

Later reports from the AFL side gave details of the tentative oral agreement reached, and attributed the breakup of the conference to Lewis' rigid opposition to any agreement.[15] The AFL leaders had given assurances that they were properly authorized to make recommendations to their Executive Council. The terms of affiliation tentatively agreed upon, at a time when the CIO claimed the larger membership, might well have resulted in the industrial-union faction becoming the preponderant force.

Philip Murray, on the other hand, like Lewis, reported that no real basis for agreement on the question of the twenty newer CIO unions had been reached. Hillman's own references to the affair were unusually evasive, but he said nothing at the time to contradict the more positive statements of Lewis and Murray that agreement, under the circumstances, was impossible. In any case, these first peace parleys broke up a few days after Sidney Hillman fell sick. The results, when he learned about them, did not surprise him, for he seemed fully aware that John L. Lewis was less than serious about reunion with the AFL. Reports that President Roosevelt keenly desired the reconciliation of the two wings of American labor may have counted for something in hardening Lewis' resolution to oppose this.

In January 1938, the Council of the AFL finally moved to revoke the charters of the CIO unions, while Lewis announced plans for a constituent convention in March, at which the "Committee" was to become the permanent "Congress of Industrial Organizations."

David Dubinsky, speaking a few months later before the Amalgamated Clothing Workers' convention on May 15, 1938, hinted that, in this case, Hillman's wishes had been overborne by Lewis. He said:

I, more than anyone else, regret the unfortunate fact that President Hillman was not able to participate in those conferences because of his sickness. I had faith and confidence that *if he had participated the situation might have been entirely different.* [Italics added.]

I happen to know his position in this matter, and I have good reason to believe that . . . with his influence and his ability to negotiate, the results would have been different.[16]

Chapter Nineteen

LOBBYING:

1938

*Sidney Hillman was after all the driving force behind
many of the measures attributed to the New Deal. If
it had not been for him there would probably have
been no Fair Labor Standards Act.*
                                        —John L. Lewis

This time Hillman was a thoroughly sick man. For several days after he had come home to the apartment at East Twentieth Street near Gramercy Park in Manhattan, where he resided after 1936, he stayed in bed and rested. It was believed at first that he had the grippe, for he was quite feverish. Then his temperature shot up to 106; a lung specialist, Dr. Alexander Miller, was called in, and Hillman was placed in an oxygen tent for most of a week. His illness was now diagnosed as double pneumonia. For many days in November his life was in extreme danger, and he was attended night and day by physicians and nurses. Mrs. Hillman and his daughters Philoine and Selma were beside themselves; his lifelong associates at the Amalgamated, in great anxiety, called every day to inquire about his progress. The distraught family might have suffered even greater strain if the news of Hillman's critical condition had not been kept out of the newspapers.

Up to the time of his collapse, Hillman had been working for at least two years at what was perhaps the maddest pace of his life. He was a man in a hurry in 1936 and 1937; as the second-in-command, he was immersed in all the problems of the CIO; he directed the most difficult organizing campaign of that period, the textile workers' drive, and handled his own union's considerable business in his spare time. He also took an active part in the campaign for the re-election of his old friend Mayor Fiorello La Guardia of New York in the autumn of 1937. On top of all this he acted as President Roosevelt's confidential adviser on labor affairs, mediated between the President and the difficult Lewis, and headed a powerful lobby for the passage of a minimum-wage law (to which we shall revert later). This last highly important campaign in Washington ground to a halt when Sidney Hillman's health collapsed. Without him the President made no further moves in this difficult affair and took time to write Hillman on November 15, 1937:

My dear Mr. Hillman:
    News has just come to me of your illness. I feel certain that you need no assurance from me of my deep personal concern and my genuine sympathy. To be deprived of your counsel, even very briefly, at a time like this is a serious loss to the labor movement and to the people of our country. I do hope you will be well again soon.
    With my very best wishes,
                                        Sincerely yours,
                                        Franklin D. Roosevelt [1]

Always very high-strung, propelled by a tremendous, unresting nervous energy, this man of frail physique, who had borne real hardship in his youth, had expended himself completely in the TWOC drive, which perhaps more than anything else had helped to break him down. Collaboration with Lewis at the helm of the CIO was in itself a cause of considerable nervous strain. Lewis conducted the affairs of the CIO with a high hand, consulting his associates only when it pleased him to do so. On one occasion earlier in 1937 he named Harry Bridges, president of the West Coast Longshoremen's Union, director of Western Organization—without consulting anyone among the CIO executives. Hillman, who did not see eye to eye with Bridges, learned about this appointment through the newspapers. His own close associates were up in arms at Lewis' action and asked Hillman what he was going to do about that so-and-so.

He said quietly: "It's all right for you to swear at Lewis. But as for me, I have to try to live in the same world with him."

Hillman's greatest talent as a political personality in the world of labor, or that of national affairs, resided in his special ability to bring men and groups of opposing tendencies together to work in a tolerable accord for some common end. He had been doing this, in effect, since 1911, at Hart, Schaffner and Marx in Chicago. Thus we see him persuading the conservative unionists in the CIO to work with the progressives or radicals (whom Lewis then welcomed as devoted aides). We see him trying to reconcile the AFL and the CIO; we see him cajoling the Southern Democrats to go along with the Northern New Dealers in Congress. But this role was, by its very nature, fearfully exhausting.

One felt the never-ending tension in Hillman as he tapped his hands together constantly, or drummed with his foot, or rode his chair like a taut jockey; one sensed an incessant effort to keep himself in hand. A man of action, one who literally lived in action, he was forever manipulating difficult people, forever receiving and dismissing callers, giving orders, making plans, speaking on the telephone, attending meetings, or hurrying off somewhere by train. The haste was necessary, for there was always another task. Then one day, under all these accumulated strains, his system collapsed; he lay as one dead. Everything stopped while his family and friends waited in despair.

At last, late in November, his fever subsided, and the worn invalid looked out at the world again with cool brows and eyes rested and clear. Hope flowed back into his worn body, and the love of life, and renewed interest in men and things.

On November 30 he was well enough to dictate a reply to President Roosevelt's kind note, which, he declared, "definitely contributed to my recovery." He said that he expected to leave for Florida within a week, to recuperate there, and hoped to be himself again in a very short time after that. His convalescence was to take much longer than he thought.[2]

The recession of 1937–38 was in full swing. Lewis and Philip Murray were stopped cold in the drive to organize "Little Steel"—as Hillman had been halted at the halfway mark in the textile field. Thus only about half of the steel workers were organized. Pressure upon Roosevelt for action against the "independent" steel companies brought no results, especially with Hillman sick. The rift between "Big John" and F.D.R. widened visibly that season. It was at this stage, in December 1937, that Lewis wrote the tenderly solicitous letter to Hillman (cited

previously) in which he said that it had been "lonely" without him at
the CIO.

At the end of December, in the company of Mrs. Hillman and his
daughter Selma—Philoine being away at college—Hillman went to
Miami, where, at a comfortable hotel fronting the beach, he submitted
himself with some reluctance to a strict regimen of rest, medical treatment, dieting, and sun-bathing. There was much congestion in his chest
at the beginning; and his doctor examined him three times a day. In
the afternoon he would walk a bit, or converse with his fellow invalids
or with friends arriving in Miami to call on him—sometimes in droves.

In mid-January, Mrs. Hillman reported in a letter that her husband
found Miami Beach much too noisy; that union people and businessmen and politicians who forgathered in Florida at this season came
to visit him and wearied him. He had counted on remaining in Florida
for a month at the most. But the doctors issued strict orders that he
was to stay in the South until spring. This bad news had to be divulged
to him in installments, for it was known that the very idea of a prolonged vacation or rest was hateful to him. He moaned bitterly at his
enforced "exile." But since he was "sentenced" to stay longer than
he had counted on, he decided to move to a quieter spot, the Miami-
Battle Creek Hotel, a sort of sanitarium located in Miami Springs,
about seven miles from the center of the town. Mrs. Hillman, after two
weeks, returned North with Selma, for with the children grown up
she was busy once more organizing shirt workers, cotton-garment and
laundry workers.

He was aware of how weak he was and how close the call had been,
for he wrote to his family in late January:

> I am practicing CAUTION—this is the watchword. We are all so sure
> of ourselves; and then something happens and it may be too late to
> mend it. It will take a little time before I am myself again.

At the Miami-Battle Creek Hotel he became interested for a period
in following a strictly vegetarian and high-vitamin diet. There was a
Dr. Kellogg at the same place, as he noted, who, thanks to a diet of
wheat germ and carrots, was able to ride a bicycle for hours on end
at the age of eighty-seven. He too consumed many carrots, although he
had no ambition to ride a bicycle.

One day Senator Robert Wagner, with a friend, came over to call
on him. Hillman offered his guests a vegetarian luncheon which, he

said, "they scornfully refused. I don't blame them. It's supposed to prolong life. But what a life!" After a while he gave up his vegetarian fad.

He grew so bored with the company of invalids that his letters became almost a continual lament at his enforced isolation from the world of high politics and red-blooded labor action.

> Frankly, I am about as tired as one can be of this whole summer in winter affair. Of course I am resting—and I am restless. I am longing for the good old days of Clothing, Textiles, CIO, and what have you. Can I get some assurance about the weather up your way in March? Well, it is just a mood.

And later again:

> It is a lazy and lonely day. A bit of rain outside turned me in. . . . I am benefiting by my stay here. That I am sure of. I look far better than I have for a long time. But there is an urge to get back—and still a fear that I may not be able to stand it.[3]

His restlessness so alarmed his family and friends that he was now bluntly informed that, on strict orders of his physicians, he must resign himself to a complete rest of four months. Mrs. Hillman, moreover, wrote sternly that she would "have him picketed" if he dared to leave Florida. Plaintively he replied that he felt himself the victim of a plot "organized in New York City to keep me in the After-March Club," but that he would stay on. In his state of enforced idleness he distracted himself somewhat by what was, for him, a voluminous correspondence with the members of his family, his friends and associates.

The home life of the small Hillman family was, as a matter of principle, marked by an extreme simplicity verging on austerity in the earlier years. During the early twenties the Hillmans had lived in a small $30-a-month apartment, a long subway ride uptown in the west Bronx. Later, from 1924 to 1936, they lived in a modest suburban cottage at Lynbrook, Long Island. After 1936, however, they moved to the modern apartment building at East Twentieth Street, whence Hillman could walk to his office at Union Square in ten minutes.

Back in 1920, during the Amalgamated convention of that year, at a moment when Hillman was absent from the chair, he had been voted an increase of salary, from $5,000 to $7,500 (plus expenses), which he said was quite ample for him. Unlike some trade-union leaders of his time who handled far smaller affairs than he, Sidney Hillman never accumulated any wealth, and was to leave an estate of no consequence. "I do not believe in getting too far away from the standard of living of a pants cutter," he used to say.

At one period, for several years after 1926, he and Jacob Potofsky shared the ownership of an old farm at Flattersville, New Jersey, in the foothills of the Poconos, which they and their families together used as a summer camp or at week ends. Shortly after his illness of 1937–38, Mrs. Hillman, in the belief that sea and sun-bathing would be most beneficial to him, purchased a very small summer cottage at Point Lookout, Long Island, about thirty-five miles from the center of New York. It was so modest and diminutive in appearance that some of his more property-minded colleagues remarked that the place was not suitable for him. He said firmly: "It is just right for me." The place did not front the sea, but had a spacious garden full of bright flowers, which Bessie Hillman cultivated, and where he loved to rest on a lounge chair in the sun.

As husband and father Sidney Hillman was affectionate, even sentimental. He was deeply attached to his two daughters. After both were full-grown, his daughters and Mrs. Hillman made a high-spirited female trio in whose midst the powerful union president was often outvoted. "He was no president or king to us at home," one of his daughters used to say. Here the quick-thinking leader of the clothing workers, usually so formidable in argument, found himself freely criticized and lovingly teased. Mrs. Hillman, he used to say good-humoredly, could always squash him by reminding him, as she often did, that "it was the women workers who first came out on strike, long before the men" at Hart, Schaffner and Marx in 1910, and so started the movement that led to the founding of their union. "It is not always the men who lead the women," Mrs. Hillman would end up. And he, alluding to this feminist theory of the origin of their movement, on one occasion before an Amalgamated convention remarked jocularly:

> I want the delegates to know that we mere men never got over the incident. We are reminded of it all the time—that we were working while they were striking. [Laughter.] It has given what I consider a completely unfair advantage to Bessie Hillman over me, even in our household. [Laughter and applause.]

He would listen to the forthright views of his wife and his daughters, hang his head with pretended meekness, and protest: "But you seem to

know all the answers!" Then he would bury himself in the many newspapers he read every evening. But there was hardly enough of this fun
and teasing for the Hillman ladies, since he "lived in trains" almost half
his life.

His public career for many years past had left him, then, with arrears
of private life of which now, in meditative and penitent mood, he became more aware. For too long he had been away from his family, and
now the urgent need was upon him to write to his wife and daughters
and stand closer to them than before. Every day during his convalescence his letters flowed forth.

Philoine, for instance, was the "intellectual" of the family (according to her attractive younger sister Selma). She resembled her father
in appearance and was very pretty. Sitting in the sun, her father now
wrote her of the books he read (chiefly works of history, biography,
and economics), of the talks he had with cranky invalids or with
friends who visited him, and of the gardens and tropical flowers of
Miami in which he took great pleasure. He described in detail a "tree
bearing seven different kinds of citrus fruits," and his delight in the
masses of red and yellow poinsettias all around him. Quite seriously he
took up again the oft-interrupted role of mentor to his two daughters.

The year before, early in 1937, after Philoine Hillman had gone to
study at Oberlin College in Ohio, her father, at her insistent demand,
had begun to write her a few notes on "inside politics" as he knew it.
Philoine, in the spirit of an idealistic student, earnestly questioned
whether her father's or President Roosevelt's policies followed a middle
course which perhaps led away from the path of true progress. Sometimes she chided her father on his "conservatism." Meanwhile, she
owned up, she had become so absorbed in outside student activities
that her lessons had been neglected and she had met with reverses in
mid-year examinations.

With the utmost tenderness her father wrote her:

Dear Phil,

Do not be discouraged on account of temporary setbacks. Life is full of
them and one can profit a great deal by them. One, of course, must learn
from experience. . . . Temporary defeats can be turned into ultimate
victories. . . . I am enclosing a newspaper clipping about the White
House reception. It may interest you. Much love.[4]

Now, during his convalescence in Florida a year later (in February
1938), he resumed this intimate discussion with Philoine, referring

to himself in one bantering letter as a "Royalist," yet with some experience of life. In pragmatic spirit he declared that for him ideas and programs were valid only when they could be tested through actual experience. Philoine would always find his experience at her disposal. Reverting to the subject of his health, he wrote that he had gone through many severe "tests" himself of late, adding: "I have passed my *exam* satisfactorily—which means I will soon be in good working order again." He closed with the suggestive reflection: "Biological living is a matter of faith." For this faith he had finally given up smoking cigarettes, which he used to consume in an endless chain. Now he spoke of his intense longing for the coolness and freshness of the North, for it had turned hot in Florida in March.

This interlude of quiet, as his strength returned to him, became an opportunity for meditation, for collecting his thoughts on human affairs at home and abroad. These thoughts were in fragmentary form, expressed in passages of his letters, or sometimes in conversation with visitors. He reported that "John L." was in touch with him regularly and once came over to Miami Springs accompanied by none other than the Postmaster General and Democratic Party chairman, James Farley. But this permitted no opportunity to talk of anything but the weather and one's health, Hillman said.

A friendly soul among the members of the AFL's Executive Council then meeting at Miami slipped over one day to see the invalid at Miami Springs and bring him news of recent developments in the opposing camp. Leon Henderson, economic adviser to Roosevelt, and Dr. Isador Lubin, then an official in the Labor Department, also dropped in for several days, and Hillman felt himself in touch with all the world of Washington politics. Of Henderson he wrote: "We talked of the good old days of NRA. We talked about everybody. We came to the conclusion that we were the only two nice fellows around there." [5]

Hillman had always exercised a very powerful attraction upon intellectuals of all sorts. Having great imagination himself and a nice analytical spirit that showed itself in his spontaneous talk, he was stimulated by the company of men of ideas and often "picked their brains." On the other hand, intellectuals found him fascinating as a "man of action" who was not afraid of ideas or theories, but showed uncommon resourcefulness in putting them into practice.

One day at Miami, a writer named Joseph Gollomb, whom Sidney Hillman had met many years before, hove up on the beach. As they strolled off to a quiet spot, the writer began to examine Hillman's mind and try to "take him apart." Hillman wrote friends that for a whole week Gollomb "took up all my afternoons" and never stopped talking.

Joseph Gollomb was a large, stout man of great personal charm, well known in New York literary circles at one time, who had also emigrated from Russia in his youth and participated in the American labor movement as a member of the IWW some twenty-five years before. Later Gollomb had begun to write novels and detective fiction which were eventually sold to the movies. Fat and prosperous in his later years, he tended to neglect the Class Struggle. Yet he could not forget his own experiences in the romantic fringe of the labor movement; and recalling that Sidney Hillman had been the *beau ideal* of the young radicals in New York and Chicago two decades before, he strove to learn what had really happened inside the man in all the years that had passed. What was his philosophy of life and labor? What were his goals? Had he clung inwardly to his earlier ideals, or had he "sold out" to the capitalists and the practical men of politics? What, in short, was the "mystery" of Hillman's complex personality?

Every afternoon Gollomb took Hillman off for a walk on the beach and dissected him. The next day he would begin over again, so that their talk went on interminably like that of characters in a novel by Tolstoy. Later he wrote a memoir of their conversations during this interval of repose that was so rare in Hillman's life:

I tried to pin him down to the espousal of some social philosophy, by repeating the charge that he leads labor into collaboration with capital to the detriment of the "social revolution."

But he is a pragmatist to the core, abstract theories affect him like mist on the eyeglasses, and he snaps: "Labor unions cannot function in the atmosphere of abstract theory alone. Men, women, and children cannot wait for the millennium. They want to eat, mate, and have a breath of ease *now.* Certainly I believe in collaborating with employers! That is what a union is for. I even believe in helping an employer function more productively, for then we have a claim to higher wages, shorter hours, and greater participation in the benefits of a smooth industrial machine."

In the last sentence I heard intimations of the fairly long view that Hillman, either consciously or implicitly, has in the back of his mind. The industrial machine he envisages may be owned by private capital or the state, so long as the lot of the worker is improved. If capitalism should break down Hillman could consistently espouse a Socialist economy, but until capitalism shows itself utterly unable to feed its workers, it is my guess, he will help it function, because to him the imperatives of the workers' daily life are first and foremost.

Gollomb's conclusion was that Hillman was neither the "Benedict Arnold" that the Marxist press called him at this period nor the "matinee idol of the social workers" that conservative laborites had sometimes named him, but the strategist, the "engineer" of American labor.[6] By March 1938, he was feeling so much more like himself that time lay always heavier on his hands. Mrs. Elinore Herrick, New York regional director of the NLRB, visiting Hillman at this time, reported that he looked tanned and healthy but had not yet recovered all his strength, which was chiefly "mental energy." He was thinking of the need for peace between the AFL and CIO because of the return of business depression; and of the textile workers' union job, which many felt would be his monument. He hoped, as he said now, that when he returned there "will still be enough of the CIO left to keep me busy."

In the last days of March he was strong enough to go swimming, and wrote, in one of his happy phrases: "I greet the ocean before breakfast." [7] The doctors now declared him fit to return; and he was off to the North like an arrow, stopping at Washington to confer with President Roosevelt on April 6, 1938.

II

Almost the first business on hand after Hillman's return to active life was that of preparing for the Twelfth Biennial Convention of the Amalgamated union at Atlantic City, beginning on May 9, 1938. He had been "on loan" to the TWOC for most of 1937 and had been on sick leave for five months after that; his old friends among the tailors had seen little of him. On this occasion their general officers and convention delegates planned an ovation to end all ovations. Besides, the Amalgamated had reason to celebrate: its membership, now at 225,-000, had broken all past records; the combined local and national revenues for the two-year period were between eight and nine million dollars, as Hillman remarked. A large part of this had been expended for the various political and organizing activities of the CIO, and notably for the Textile Workers' Organizing Committee.

The strategic influence of the Amalgamated union, as a sort of "rich uncle" to the CIO in its early years, was surpassed only by that of the larger United Mine Workers. (The steel and automobile workers had not yet been built up into the giant organizations which they became during World War II.) At Atlantic City, the ACWA convention was not merely the "parliament" of the men's clothing workers, but also a sort of national political forum. John L. Lewis, "the great leader of men," as Hillman flatteringly called him, was on hand as a guest speaker, as were also the newer leaders of the various CIO organizations, such as Philip Murray, Michael Quill, Sherman Dalrymple, and Emil Rieve. In addition there was an assortment of New Deal senators and congressmen, as well as Mayor La Guardia and Secretary of Labor Frances Perkins, who spoke as the President's emissary.

Hillman, on taking the chair again, was hailed as a man who represented and served "close to one million workers organized, as well as any number of unorganized from coast to coast." [8] The bands played, the crowd of delegates paraded about the hall, laid flowers at his feet, or made other gift offerings. It was by now an old ritual, and yet Hillman stood there before his old friends and wept unashamedly. He never forgot that he was anchored to his union. For a half hour or longer the return of their leader who had been all but lost was celebrated in the exuberant manner of labor conventions, before the meeting turned to transact its business.

An observer of the period would have found the core of the New Deal faith in such gatherings as that of the ACWA in 1938. The recession had brought home to everyone the need for dealing basically with the problem of unemployment, estimated just then at more than 11,-000,000. Hillman, like John L. Lewis, urged that mass purchasing power must be raised by the concerted action of government as well as organized labor. "If Congress had enacted a wage-and-hour law . . . millions of men and women who are today unemployed, who are today on the relief rolls of state and Federal agencies, would be today at work," Hillman said. Lewis, in his speech before the convention on May 12, hinted at preparations of the CIO to organize the armies of the unemployed who were on the rolls of the WPA. He too stressed the need for "increased participation by labor in the political field." [9]

For a year or more the CIO, through the Washington office of its political affiliate, Labor's Non-Partisan League, had been conducting one of the most remarkable lobbying actions ever seen in order to win passage for the Black-Connery bill for minimum wages and maximum hours. This bill, a variant of the 30-hour law proposed originally in

1933, had been set aside during the interval of the NRA and the later struggle of Roosevelt for the reform of the Supreme Court. After April 1937, when the Supreme Court, reversing its earlier position, sustained the Wagner Labor Relations Act and the Social Security Act, the effort to supplement these great reform bills with a Federal minimum-wage law was resumed, this time under the direction of Sidney Hillman.

The Supreme Court, though the scheme to "pack" it had been defeated, had begun to change its complexion by the summer of 1937. Senator Hugo Black, the New Dealer, had become one of its associate justices, while Wagner of New York sponsored his old bill in the Senate. When Representative William Connery died soon afterward, Mary Norton of New Jersey took up support of the bill in the House. The proposed law was rewritten somewhat, with the advice of Hillman, and renamed the Fair Labor Standards Bill. Its essential provisions were for a Federal commission to enforce a minimum wage and a limitation of hours in all industries engaged in interstate commerce; the minimum wage was to start at 25 cents per hour, rising to 40 cents by 1942; hours were to be fixed at 44 per week and reduced gradually to 40. By a further provision the labor of persons under sixteen was to be eliminated in interstate commerce.

Hillman had set his heart on winning passage of this bill in 1937, despite the formidable opposition it aroused in many quarters, including part of the labor movement. The TWOC drive in the South (and elsewhere) had uncovered broad areas of industry where it seemed hopeless to unionize men, women, and children who worked for $6.00 or $8.00 a week in textile and garment mills and whose employers were stoutly defended by all the local authorities. Only a political attack on a nationwide scale could correct this situation.

During his convalescence in Florida Hillman had been doing a heap of thinking. To a friend who called on him there he admitted that the direction of his union, the control of its industry, would henceforth not satisfy his need for action. To right things in one or more industries would never be enough, he believed, if things continued to be ill-ordered in the rest of the American body politic. Labor, he said, must constantly widen its horizons and play an ever-larger part in national politics. Action for such a measure as the pending Fair Labor Standards Bill, for example, was paramount. It would increase solidly the earning power of millions working at substandard wages and lessen the downward drag of these marginal workers upon the organized.

Lewis, for his part, had shown considerable indifference to the proposed wages-and-hours bill. Its scale seemed fixed too low to benefit the coal miners or Northern mass-production workers, who were demanding $1.00 an hour. There were provisions in the bill to which he objected. Hillman argued that "if we can only get the elephant's trunk in the door, then later things can be improved." He certainly agreed that 25 cents an hour was wretched pay, but insisted it was good bait for millowners in the South and their political allies. After a spirited passage with Hillman, Lewis finally proposed that he take over the minimum-wage-bill campaign as his "baby." Lewis wanted no part of it.

In 1937 the AFL and the railway Brotherhoods opposed this bill because of its low minimum pay. The farm bloc also fought its passage in Congress; likewise the Southern conservatives in both Houses, who worked to hold wages low in their section, under the fixed notion that the differential in labor costs benefited the people of the South. Roosevelt, who had met his first serious defeat in Congress in the case of the court bill, was at first reserved in his support of a minimum-wage bill, though it had been promised in the Democratic platform in 1936.

While directing the TWOC campaign with one hand, Hillman with the other kept pushing the wages-and-hours bill during the summer of 1937, when it was making little progress in committee. The object of the bill, he said when he appeared to testify before the Senate on June 15, 1937, was to help the "submerged third of our working population," especially in the textile, cotton-garment, and shoe industries of the South and West, where unionism was weak. A minimum wage of $800 a year and the 40-hour week would be no great boon, but would at least "provide a bottom" from which collective bargaining could start.[10]

But why only 25 cents an hour as a minimum wage, many friends of labor asked? Would not this minimum become the maximum? At another hearing, before a joint committee of the House and Senate, Representative Clyde H. Smith of Maine pointed out that such a scale, in view of seasonal unemployment, might mean only $500 to $600. Why did Hillman not advocate more than that?

MR. HILLMAN: Because, Senator, I believe that progress should be made slowly. I believe that we ought to move very cautiously. It is, after all, a field that we have not got sufficient administrative experience in. During the NRA we were in a great emergency and . . . were compelled to do things that have shown themselves ultimately as unwise. Now, if we start in with something, in my judgment, we ought to go slowly.

The next thing is, I do not believe we can get a higher wage from you gentlemen, and I would rather advocate something with the hope of getting it than put myself on record for a much higher minimum wage and walk out with nothing. . . .

I think what is necessary is to lay as a foundation the principle that we are going to guarantee American labor a minimum. Time will show if our minimum is too low, and if it is we will come back to you, or industry itself will agree to pay more.[11]

Throughout the regular 1937 session of Congress, Hillman's lobby, directed by Eli P. Oliver of Labor's Non-Partisan League and Charles Ervin, the Amalgamated's Washington representative, worked for the passage of the bill, which the House Rules Committee refused to report out on the floor of Congress. In August, Representative Cox of Georgia made a fierce onslaught on Sidney Hillman because a petition "instigated" by him had been circulated through the House demanding that the bill be called back from the Rules Committee. "Sidney Hillman . . . now assumes to speak for the Democratic Party," exclaimed Cox, "and with his usual effrontery undertakes to exercise leadership in this situation." [12]

Only by the sternest efforts was the bill finally brought to the floor in that session, when it was amended and, to the dismay of its sponsors, defeated by ten votes at the close of the regular session.

Oliver later gave a most interesting report of how a majority of the House had been pledged to support the bill and then, after all the noses were counted, a number of them reversed themselves. According to Oliver's estimate, 20 per cent of Congress was pro-labor; another 20 per cent "will do anything they can to defeat labor and progressive principles"; while another 60 per cent had no convictions of any kind except that they intended, at all costs, to be re-elected. When the CIO's spokesmen came to these "doubtful" congressmen, one could perceive how "a certain look came into their eyes"—a look of cold calculation. Would a vote for the wages-and-hours bill increase the chances of re-election or defeat in the next campaign? Would the possible loss of money contributions from the employing class really be outweighed by the strength of organized labor? But these were the days when big labor was moving into the political field in earnest; and so the vote was close.[13]

Hillman was desperately sick when the wages-and-hours bill was defeated. As Congress adjourned on December 17, 1937, President Roosevelt, in observance of his election pledges and his promise to Hillman, summoned a special session for the express purpose of reconsidering the minimum-wage law. Again the Rules Committee of the House, dominated by the Southern Representatives Cox of Georgia and Smith of Virginia, refused by a single vote to report the bill.

At this stage, following a suggestion made by Charles Ervin, the New Deal supporters of the measure decided to make an earnest attempt to revive the old, seldom-used petition method, whereby a vote of 50 per cent of the representatives may discharge the Rules Committee from further consideration of a bill and force debate on it on the floor of the House. From all over the country delegations of CIO and other union representatives, gathered together by the ACWA local officers, journeyed to Washington and, day after day, pleaded with their congressmen to support the bill. Thus, after weeks of agitation, more than 220 representatives were persuaded to sign petitions to the Speaker calling the bill to the floor. Yet once again it was defeated by a small, stubborn handful in December 1937. Hillman, then very sick, was not told about this setback until later.[14]

Most people believed that the wages-and-hours bill was finally buried now that it had been killed in two sessions of Congress. Yet in January 1938, President Roosevelt, spurred by appeals that came to him from the invalid in Florida, once more, in his State of the Union Message, urged passage of the law. Not long afterward the nomination of Lister Hill of Alabama as candidate for the Senate in the Democratic Party primaries broke the solid ranks of the Southern opposition, for he had pledged himself to back the minimum-wage bill. Sponsorship of the bill was now in the hands of Representative Mary Norton and the House Labor Committee. Hillman, at the climactic period of this new offensive, arrived in Washington from Florida, his health fully restored, and saw Roosevelt at once, on April 6, 1938. More than a year had passed since the bill had begun its slow, painful journey through Congress; it was more than two years since Hillman had first laid the idea before Roosevelt.

The opposition was still formidable, with various Southern businessmen's associations in its forefront. Behind the scenes, it was said, lurked the powerful John Garner, who had helped to defeat Roosevelt in the Senate fight over the court bill. The President now hesitated to engage himself fully in this hazardous contest. But Sidney Hillman (it was reported later) "changed his mind for him."

Hillman took the position that the American government, like other civilized nations, must protect labor by guaranteeing a minimum wage. The measure would even help the Southern capitalists, in spite of themselves, by raising the buying power of our lowest economic groups, and thus, in the end, would be not a liability but a feather in the cap of the Democratic Administration.

Two days after seeing Hillman, at a moment when the bill was once more blocked in the House Rules Committee, Roosevelt sent a strongly worded telegram to Representative Norton, declaring that he earnestly favored the petition being circulated then for recommitting the bill. Hillman stayed in Washington this time, working with infinite patience to mobilize the full power of labor and the New Deal elements behind the Wagner-Norton bill. Even the American Federation of Labor now came out in its support.

Once more the petition method had to be used to tear the bill from the hands of the powerful Rules Committee, which was resolved to delay action indefinitely. On May 6, 1938, 218 congressmen marched to the well of the House to hand their signed petitions to the Speaker, praying that the bill be brought to the floor. With this remarkable demonstration of labor's full power, backed by all-out presidential support, the grip of the conservative bloc seemed finally broken.

The Fair Labor Standards Act was passed by the House by a large majority on May 24, 1938, with many congressmen now jostling each other to vote for it, on the eve of another election season. There was still the Senate to reckon with and the danger that the bill would be "amended to death." Hillman left Washington only to attend the Amalgamated Convention at Atlantic City on May 9–15, then returned to his post.

"As late as June 9," Hillman related, "it looked as though the bill would be killed once again" in the Senate. The country's most powerful business leaders, not to speak of senators like William E. Borah, and Vice-President Garner, would be in there fighting at the last hour. Still uncertain of Roosevelt's interest, Hillman decided to forgo a request for a formal appointment through the White House secretary and telephoned Roosevelt directly to report on the gravity of the situation.[15] The

President responded by sending further urgent messages to Congress, and on June 11, 1938, the Joint Conference Committee of the House and Senate voted unanimously to report out the completed bill in quite the form that Hillman had hoped for.

Up to the end Hillman was in close communication with Roosevelt through "Tommy" Corcoran, the President's representative on Capitol Hill. Corcoran, who was helping him with the minimum-wage bill during the last phase, noted (in his memorandum to Roosevelt) that Hillman seemed at times "a little unnerved," owing to the great pressure upon him, and that at this very moment he seemed to be having his hands full holding back John L. Lewis from an open break with the Administration.[16] The White House, however, never slackened in its efforts to see the measure through.

On June 14, 1938, the bill at last came to the end of its laborious journey, when it was passed by both Houses. The industrial lobby and the veteran politicos had used every device of parliamentary delay known to such groups for a hundred years past to check reform. Yet they had been overcome by the organized power of the labor bloc and the almost inhuman tenacity of Hillman. Roosevelt, skeptical at the start, had decided to give help in the end and take all possible credit for this historic reform law, which was to have a great impact on our whole economy. In signing it, he declared that the American people were indebted to no one more than to Hillman for its passage. Lewis, a year later, wrote that if it had not been for the "driving force" of Hillman "there would probably have been no Fair Labor Standards Act." [17]

This law supplemented the Wagner Act (which sought simply to ensure the right of labor to collective bargaining through its own representatives) and brought 12,000,000 workers of the lowest wage bracket under its minimal protection. Though the minimum of 25 cents an hour appeared pitifully low and reflected a compromise on the part of Hillman with Southern politicians, it forced immediate pay increases for 750,000 workers, chiefly in the Deep South, in the lumber, fertilizer, and cotton-textile trades. Not only did this humane measure help the most depressed sections of the working population, but it also removed the blot of child labor, as Hillman said. Under procedures fixed by law the minimum wage was raised to 30 cents per hour in 1939, and to 40 cents by 1941–45. On January 25, 1950, the minimum was raised again, to 75 cents.

However, no law is better than the government officials who administer it. On the score of personnel to enforce the Fair Labor Standards Act there was much parliamentary scuffling in Congress following passage of the law. Finally, in July 1939, the threat of disabling amendments loomed up in Congress. Behind these moves, Hillman and Lewis clearly saw the maneuvering of Vice-President Garner.

At an Executive Board meeting of the CIO, Hillman proposed that Lewis appear in defense of the law at a forthcoming hearing before the House Labor Committee considering such amendments. Lewis, with many doffings of the hat, deferred to Hillman, saying, "Ah, no, Sid, it is for you to speak. I know little of all this. It is your specialty and the honors of the occasion must go to you." Hillman, however, insisted that Lewis accompany him and give a prepared speech, in view of his great influence over Congress and the powerful impression he would make. After some fencing and parrying, Lewis, as reported by one of those present, said: "Well, if I get up to speak before the Congress, you know, Sidney, I am a man of strong impulses and warm feelings. *Something may happen.*" [Italics added.]

But since Hillman seemed ready to take a chance, Lewis finally overcame his scruples and agreed to appear. On the morning of July 27, 1939, while on his way to the hearing, Lewis almost collided with Vice-President John Garner in one of the narrow paths of the park outside the Capitol. Both men came to a halt, while the friends accompanying each of them fell back respectfully. There was no exchange of greetings. "Heh," grunted Mr. Garner contemptuously. Lewis stared him down. "Heh!" he trumpeted in return, and passed on his way to the caucus room where the hearing was to be held.

A large public, including many newspapermen, was on hand to hear the testimony of the labor leaders against the proposed amendments to the Fair Labor Standards Act. Hillman spoke first. Then Lewis followed with a prepared statement in defense of the existing measure, well reasoned and temperate. But as he finished reading, it was apparent that he could no longer contain himself. In a spontaneous concluding paragraph he burst out at the Vice-President, to whose machinations he attributed the attempt to hamstring the minimum-wage act, as "that whisky-drinking, poker-playing, labor-baiting, evil old man." [18]

Hillman was appalled. But in a few moments, as scores of newspaper reporters rushed from the room to send the CIO chairman's withering remarks over the wires, to be headlined that day on the front page of every newspaper in the country, he realized that the effect would be salutary. Garner, labeled by Lewis once and for all in the public mind as the enemy of reform, slunk off to his home in Uvalde, Texas, and thereafter played no part in the high councils of the Democratic Party. Efforts to emasculate the Fair Labor Standards Act were defeated.[19]

III

During the period defined afterward as the "first New Deal," from 1933 to 1937, the country's economy appeared to be decidedly on the mend. Many believed then, perhaps with too great optimism, that there was almost no social problem that could not be attacked successfully by intelligent planning and courageous leadership.

Then, from the autumn of 1937, after all the talk of "pump-priming" and economic controls, we were in a business depression again, and many who had pinned high hopes on the New Deal tactics suffered a strong shock of disillusionment. Even so ardent a Rooseveltian as Professor Rexford Tugwell commented upon the obvious failure of the Administration's domestic policies to effect a radical cure of the country's chief sickness, unemployment. The government's sudden reduction of deficit spending for relief in 1937, coming at a time of active speculation in the commodity markets, was said to be a contributing cause of the renewed movement of deflation. The Roosevelt Administration spent too little rather than too much, as its own economic experts confessed. Roosevelt himself now seemed puzzled and hesitant. In reality he had no consistent program in mind for our economy. During the NRA period combinations of business interests had been encouraged; but by 1938 the "second" New Deal was supporting a vigorous trust-busting campaign designed to help small business and increase competition.

From the labor wing of the New Deal there now came a sharp protest at the recent economies in relief expenditures, typified by Sidney Hillman's speech before his union convention on May 9, 1938, in which he said:

As far as labor is concerned, as far as the progressive forces of the country are concerned, we will not permit budget balancing at the expense of hungry, starving men and women and children.[20]

Similar protests came from Lewis, Philip Murray, and other labor leaders. In the spring of 1938 the Roosevelt Administration resumed the policy of "compensatory" deficit spending.

It was while pondering over the famous American paradox of poverty and rags in the midst of plenty in early June 1938 that Hillman suddenly had an inspiration to do something about it. Recently the government had organized the Federal Surplus Commodity Corporation to keep the "oversupply" of agricultural products out of the farmers' markets and distribute it gratis to persons on relief rolls. Hillman thought: Why not do the same thing with surplus clothing products, especially cheap utility clothing which the millions of people on the WPA also needed badly?

At once Hillman, who was in New York, telephoned to Charles Ervin in Washington, asking him to sound out Harry Hopkins and arrange for an appointment with him. On June 10 Hillman, back in Washington to watch over the final stages of the contest for the minimum-wage law, saw Hopkins and laid his proposal before him. Let the WPA, of which Hopkins was then still administrator, purchase a mass of clothing direct from the manufacturers, at wholesale cost, during the slack summer season that was now approaching. The market was weak; there was much distress merchandise on hand and few orders for fall business were being placed by large buyers. Such an operation would cost the government little more than current arrangements for relief, would help hundreds of thousands who were destitute, and also stimulate business and employment in the clothing trade.

Hopkins rose to the idea at once. Two days later the newspapers published announcements of his plan to purchase approximately $10,000,000 worth of men's clothing and a similar amount of women's clothing, which were to be distributed to persons on the relief rolls.[21]

The effect of this action was most beneficial for employers and workers in both the men's and women's garment trade. The allotment of government orders was carried out by arrangement with a committee of manufacturers under the fairest possible procedure. Thousands of clothing workers went back to their jobs, and confidence was revived somewhat in this and other industries which hoped that the government would now act to check the deflationary trend.

The affair of the WPA's free-clothing distribution, like that of the minimum-wage law, shows how constructively Hillman used his personal influence in Washington for the benefit of the whole labor movement and the underprivileged. In this case we see also that whatever missions he might be performing for the President, or for the CIO, as a whole, the legitimate interests of the Amalgamated, his own "constituency," were never out of his mind.

After the NRA codes were quashed by the Supreme Court in May 1935, Hillman, amid all his other activities, had set in motion a program that was to lead to a similar form of stabilization under a union agreement throughout the men's clothing industry in the United States. A necessary preliminary step, however, was to stabilize the manufacturing process itself, as far as possible—a problem that Hillman had been pondering since 1919. The question of fixing a fair day's work for a fair wage on a nationwide scale, though it was present in nearly all other industries, was immensely complicated in clothing, whose different manufacturers and localities allowed for a great many "differentials" in labor time and cost, as in details and modes of construction of garments. Even the separate regional branches of the union competed with each other to some extent in allowing for small "differentials" in shop standards, processes, and wholesale cost of a garment, as for instance between a metropolitan factory and an out-of-town plant.

To consider remedies for all these perplexing matters Hillman, back in 1936, had arranged to have a committee of four representatives of industry, together with several experts from the union, tour the principal clothing centers throughout the country and survey the problem of standardizing their processes of manufacturing. As a consequence of their detailed report it was proposed to classify all men's suits into six categories, ranging from Number One, the cheapest, machine-made article, to Number Six, incorporating the highest standards of craftsmanship and hand-tailoring possible in ready-made garments. The program of standardizing costs and labor time was begun throughout the industry in 1937. On this basis relatively uniform wages and piece rates were to be established throughout the Amalgamated's economic field. The problems were human as well as technical, and of extreme complexity (indeed, never fully mastered to this day). Yet impressive progress was made toward intelligent solutions.

In February 1937, following steps initiated by Hillman several years before (under NRA) to organize the American Men's Clothing Manufacturers' Association, the Amalgamated, for the first time, signed a nationwide union agreement with the employers representing about 90 per cent of the industry. Its terms provided for the program of standardization of manufacture, for a nationwide increase of 12 per cent in wages, and a basic 36-hour week, effective May 15, 1937. Thus there was introduced into the markets of the clothing workers a stability which greatly mitigated the impact of renewed hardship during the business slump beginning in the autumn of that year.[22]

While Hillman was away in Washington, or occupied in directing the CIO's nationwide campaign for the textile workers, or "troubleshooting" for Lewis in other large CIO unions, the ACWA carried on successfully under the veteran officers who had long served as his lieutenants. On most of these men Hillman had placed the stamp of his own philosophy as a labor leader. Yet they were in no sense "yes-men." On the contrary, it needed much shrewd diplomacy at times to handle the high-willed, often stubborn personalities who made up the Amalgamated's Executive Board or headed its regional organizations. Within the group were men who were as aggressive or hard-boiled as any administrators to be found in the business world; others among them were of an intellectual bent, given to reflection and the reading of serious books.

In any formal organization or bureaucracy the problem of conflict always arises between individual ambition or will-to-power and the interests of the whole organization. On seeing that one of his lieutenants, for example, felt that there was not enough scope for his ambitions in the particular niche he occupied, Hillman would nourish the man's self-esteem by encouraging him to enter politics and helping him win honorable office in the community. Another who began as a dissident radical would be converted into a loyal organization man by being charged with the responsibility of his local branch. Working usually in the spirit of what has been called (in political-party machines) the "easy boss," Hillman almost always pursued the conference method of settling difficulties within the organization.

On one occasion Hillman laid before one of the union's most important joint boards in a Western city a proposal which several of his colleagues did not favor. He argued firmly and at great length, then called for a vote. He was defeated.

An assistant who saw him immediately after the meeting heard him laugh over the episode. "They voted me down, me, their president—but I'm proud of them." [23]

On another occasion, as the story is told, Hillman was forced to judge between the claims of two of the union's most powerful executives who were bitter personal rivals. One of the two was his lifelong friend; the other, though one of the ablest of the Amalgamated leaders, always exhibited his independence by acting as one of Hillman's severest critics within the union's councils. Hillman settled the affair by demoting his old friend and elevating his most persistent critic to an authority above the other's—for the good of the union, as he said. There had been high words and bitter argument; Hillman, emotionally exhausted on leaving the conference table, was seen to burst into tears. He was heartsick at having been forced into a position where he must rule against one of the friends he loved best.

In the decade that followed the end of the NRA, the Amalgamated membership rose to more than 300,000; at the end of World War II it approached 375,000. Most of the increased membership was gained in the newer jurisdictions of shirt workers, laundry workers, and in the growing cotton-garment field generally.

In 1940, Joseph Schlossberg, then sixty-five, retired from the post of general secretary after twenty-five years of distinguished service. Jacob S. Potofsky was elected in his place.

As a group the Amalgamated leaders, virtually all drawn from the workers' ranks, showed considerable talent for public and administrative life and, because of their varied experience in co-operative business enterprises, appeared more broadly educated than most American trade unionists. As one of them said, Hillman was no "dictator" among them. "We were a symphony orchestra and Sidney was our conductor." [24]

IV

The alacrity with which Harry Hopkins had responded to Hillman's proposals for the distribution of surplus utility clothing reflected the high credit now enjoyed by the Amalgamated leader in the Roosevelt Administration. Hopkins, by 1938, was the favorite in Roosevelt's "kitchen cabinet." But the intimacy between the President and

Sidney Hillman also grew during the late 1930's until, though he had no public office, he was numbered among the dozen or so of Americans who were the President's most trusted political friends.*

With business depressed in 1938, there was much talk of the need for establishing an accord between the President and the country's alienated business leaders. Efforts were made to hold conferences among representatives of government, big business, and labor that would lead at least to a temporary cessation of the conflict among them. Oddly enough, it was Hillman whom President Roosevelt selected in June 1938 to serve as his emissary in approaching persons like Thomas W. Lamont of J. P. Morgan and Company, Joseph P. Kennedy, and other persons of similar financial standing, and laying before them a "program of rapprochement between government, capital, and labor." Hillman attempted to perform this confidential mission discreetly enough, but found that what capital wanted mainly was an abatement of taxes and Federal expenditures and a relaxation of irksome government controls, while labor seemed not yet strong enough, in his opinion, to assert its own views.[25]

He also took an active part in the so-called "purge" campaign of 1938, by helping Hopkins and Thomas G. Corcoran in the struggle to defeat, among others, Representative John J. O'Connor of New York, a leading opponent of the New Deal in Congress.

It was at this period also that a rather tentative movement developed in the newly formed American Labor Party of New York State to run Sidney Hillman as candidate for the United States Senate. At one stage, early in July 1938, it was reported that President Roosevelt himself "wanted Hillman to stay in the race." [26] It was hoped that, besides the ALP, one of the two major parties might agree to accept the Hillman candidacy. He himself scarcely pursued the matter seriously, though he pretended that the idea of taking a seat as the junior senator from New York intrigued him a great deal. On the other hand, he said in private that he had no intention of retiring

* The closeness of their relations in the ten years after 1935 has been somewhat underestimated or belittled by others in Roosevelt's circle who have already published their memoirs. It has also been grossly exaggerated by persons or groups who had their reasons for hating the Roosevelt Administration and the New Deal policies. The numerous Roosevelt papers and memoranda addressed to Sidney Hillman fairly reflect an alliance for mutual advantage, in a very decent sense of the term, based on mutual esteem and trust.

from the labor movement and doubted that he would enjoy quibbling with the lawyers in the Senate.

On July 5, 1938, however, following a conference at the White House with Roosevelt, Hillman, and Postmaster General James A. Farley, it was reported that Hillman had cheerfully withdrawn his name as candidate for the Senate and that the ALP in New York would support the Democratic ticket of Robert Wagner and James Mead for the two Senate seats, and Lehman for re-election as governor.

This very fleeting senatorial "boom" for Hillman, in any case, brought down upon him vehement attacks in the press, one of them by David Dubinsky, President of the International Ladies' Garment Workers and also a leading figure in the American Labor Party at the time.[27] The attacks on Hillman from Dubinsky's quarter signalized the beginning of a split in the American Labor Party and a struggle between the two largest labor groups in New York for local political influence. The ILGWU membership was heavily concentrated in New York City and in sheer numbers outranked the Amalgamated there. This union, in the phrase of John L. Lewis, "had taken on a lot of meat" in recent years. Its ambitious president not only came forward as a rival of Hillman, but was making preparations to take the ILGWU out of the CIO and into the American Federation of Labor. Dubinsky also used the augmented resources of his union at this time to intervene in a bitter factional dispute that had arisen in the Executive Council of the United Auto Workers, by helping the group opposed by Lewis.[28]

While the ill-starred "purge" campaign of Roosevelt and Hopkins created intense bitterness among the Democratic politicians, quarrels flared up among the labor factions as well. The 1938 congressional elections registered sharp losses in the ranks of Roosevelt's supporters in House and Senate. The so-called New Deal "revolution" had apparently reached limits beyond which its adherents seemed for the time unable to advance. Such an ebb tide had often shown itself before at a certain stage of political revolutions or of popular political movements. Where yesterday men from all walks of life seemed resolved to work together to feed the hungry, employ the idle, and save their country from disaster, now it was as if the *élan* produced by the crisis were gone and the momentum of leaders and followers alike were slackening. In the reformed labor movement called the CIO, fierce dissensions now burst forth over personalities and alleged differences in ideology, reminding men of that phase of the French Revolution of which it was said: "The Revolution is now devouring its own sons!"

V

John L. Lewis often assigned some of the most difficult tasks facing the CIO to Hillman and Philip Murray. At the beginning of September 1938, Hillman, in the company of Murray, went to Detroit, at Lewis' request, to negotiate some settlement of a dispute that had been simmering among the United Auto Workers' Union ever since the summer of 1937 and now threatened to explode into civil war.

This lusty young organization was at the time headed by Homer Martin, the former minister turned automobile worker, who had won his post in the early days of the union through unusual gifts of popular oratory. But within two years the auto workers' union had mushroomed from a membership of about 20,000 to nearly 400,000, and was eventually to become a giant union of more than a million workers. Here the stakes in terms of labor power, centered in America's key industry, were enormous. It was therefore not long before a fierce struggle broke forth between Martin and the other young men who had risen from the ranks to the Executive Board. The complaints against Martin were that he had shown himself too ready to yield both in the sit-down strike of 1937 at General Motors and in subsequent negotiations with that company and with the Ford Motor Company, which the UAW was now struggling to organize. The maneuvers of a small but articulate faction of Communists, the counter attack of self-proclaimed anti-Communists headed by Martin, and the intrigues of labor spies added partisan passion to the conflict. After denouncing all his opponents indiscriminately as Communists in June 1938, President Martin summarily suspended five members of the Executive Board, namely Richard Frankensteen, George Addes, Wyndham Mortimer, Ed Hall, and Walter N. Wells, leaving only his own adherents on the governing board of the union. In this action he openly defied the orders of John L. Lewis. The opposition leaders, who called themselves the Unity Faction, assailed Martin's procedure as unlawful and "dictatorial," and attempted to run the union themselves through control of its large local branches, embracing about 80 per cent of the membership.

Hillman and "Uncle Phil" Murray arrived in Detroit in the midst of this brute struggle for power in the first week of September and opened conferences with the separate factions in their rooms at the Statler Hotel.

As Philip Murray has related, he took on one group and Hillman took on the other. Negotiations continued for two weeks. "The union was young and undisciplined as yet. . . . The boys were loud and rough and tough," Murray recalls.[29] In those gangster-ridden days the moral tone of Detroit was far from exemplary. There was often a suggestion of riot and imminent homicide in the air. At one point during the negotiations with Martin and the others—late at night— a group of hard-faced hoodlums, with guns bulging from their armpit holsters, suddenly entered the rooms shared by Hillman and Murray and significantly exhibited their artillery.

Hillman, who had been so sick the year before, had been lying down on one of the twin beds in the room. He rose from bed, pale and angry, and began to walk up and down the room. Everyone was silent, waiting. Finally he exclaimed impatiently: "*Guns, always guns!* Why is it there are always guns in Detroit? Now you, please go away!" The gangsters were persuaded to depart, and the conference continued.

Martin and his friends complained to Hillman and Murray that Lewis attempted "dictation" of the auto workers' union, and took the part of the Unity Faction. Hillman's and Murray's view was that Martin had shown a certain "dictatormania" himself in suspending the five Executive Board members who, they insisted, must be reinstated. The times, Hillman observed in referring to this and similar affairs, were full of "large and small dictators," and "all sorts of immature people aspire to be dictators." [30] In the end he and Murray induced Martin, as they declared, to accept a compromise agreement under which the suspended officers were to be reinstated and R. J. Thomas, apparently a neutral figure among the union's officers, was to be nominated for president at the forthcoming convention.

A few weeks later, however, Martin repudiated this agreement in a statement bristling with denunciations of Lewis, Hillman, and Murray. Hillman meanwhile had returned to New York at the end of September. In January 1939, he hurried back to Detroit with

Philip Murray, to deal with a new crisis which had arisen as a result of dissatisfaction among the members at Martin's secret and unauthorized negotiations for a union agreement with the Ford Motor Company. His purpose, it was reported, was to arrange for the withdrawal of the United Auto Workers from the CIO. At this stage the union's Executive Board rose up and impeached Mr. Martin, installing R. J. Thomas, whom Hillman and Murray had recommended, as acting president. Thomas and his supporters made peace of a sort —after Martin had departed with his tiny minority faction—and the UAW remained to grow and prosper in the CIO.* [31] Much credit for this outcome was given to Hillman. In a speech of November 1939, Philip Murray generously attributed to him "most of the success which attended the efforts of the CIO to establish peace within that union." Lewis also paid homage to his "feat of negotiation and statesmanship" in saving this gigantic new labor union from deterioration.

The disposition of leadership and power during the formative period of these new CIO unions was unpredictable, and tenure very fluid. Ambitious young men, seeing new labor "empires" being carved out overnight, longed to possess and enjoy them. Even in the relatively stable periods of the American labor movement, in the oldest of AFL unions, all the arts of demagogy and undemocratic violence were brought into play as rival labor politicians fought for power.

At the very time when Hillman was occupied with the trouble in the auto workers' union, in the autumn of 1938, an intense factional fight arose in the textile workers' camp. President Francis J. Gorman of the United Textile Workers' Union, who was subordinate to Hillman as chairman of the TWOC, rose in rebellion against the Hillman leadership. There had been trouble with a branch of the textile union at Providence, Rhode Island, and its local leader, Joseph Silva, had been dismissed by Hillman. Silva sued in the courts and managed to tie up the funds of eleven textile locals in Providence. President Gorman now chose to come to the support of the Silva faction, although the entire Executive Board of the United Textile Workers

* Not long afterward Mr. Martin, having tried working with the AFL and the group of dissident Communists headed by Jay Lovestone, turned up in the employ of Harry Bennett, head of the Ford Motor Company's Service Department!

and the great majority of their 700 locals repudiated his stand and lined up with Hillman. Gorman, whom Hillman described as unstable, then ruled that the executive officers who opposed him were all ousted, declared their offices vacant, and moved his own headquarters to Washington, taking with him a "shadow union" of about 2,000 members, with which he proposed to return to the AFL.

On December 15, 1938, Hillman, under the authority vested in him by the agreement between the Textile Workers' Organizing Committee and the component unions, removed Gorman as a member of the TWOC, charging that he had obstructed negotiations for increases of wages in New England's woolen and worsted industry and violated the terms of the contract between his own organization, the United Textile Workers, and the CIO—which by now had expended nearly $2,000,000 in this campaign. By this brusque action Hillman decreed Francis Gorman's "descent into obscurity." [32]

Except for a few small blobs of dual unions in the South, sponsored by the AFL, the Textile Workers' Organizing Committee founded by Hillman still ruled this field. In time, the component labor groups were welded together by the TWOC leaders into a going labor organization which, because of litigation instituted by the Gorman faction over the old name, assumed the new name of the Textile Workers' Union of America, CIO. Emil Rieve of the Hosiery Workers became its president, but for almost two years more Hillman served as chairman of the Executive Board.

The break between the AFL and the CIO was now complete, and labor's civil war flared up sporadically at many points. In November 1938, the CIO, now entirely on its own, held its first convention at Pittsburgh, when a constitution was drawn up and the permanent name, "Congress of Industrial Organizations," was adopted. Lewis, of course, was elected president. He in turn took the platform to nominate Sidney Hillman as vice-president, eulogizing him as "a sword and buckler" for the labor movement, and adding:

I have found him a constant inspiration . . . a thinker, a philosopher and statesman, a great son of a great race, wise in counsel, terrible in war. . . . I give you the name of that man, my friend, Sidney Hillman.[33]

In those earlier years of the CIO, Lewis and Hillman, so different in temperament, worked together as partners, the planful tactics of the one supplementing the fierce driving power of the other, to bring about veritable miracles for the reborn labor movement. But under the mask of their mutual admiration, shown in public, the growing strain between them was already perceptible to discerning eyes at the very moment when the CIO organized itself as a permanent and separate federation.

Chapter Twenty

"THE BLIND
GIANT"

The autumn of 1938 had witnessed not only the reverses
of the New Deal at the election polls but an intensification of the crisis in Europe, provoked by Hitler, and the consequent
signing of the Munich Pact. The Western democracies had thus
yielded before the threats of the German dictator and offered "appeasement" in the form of free Czechoslovakia. Hitherto the Roosevelt Administration had shown a marked indifference to the political-
military problems of Europe; but after September 1938, President
Roosevelt arrived at the conclusion that war in Europe could no
longer be avoided. The seizure of the rump of Czechoslovakia by
Germany a few months later, on March 15, 1939, hardened his
conviction. Henceforth the question of American security in the face
of world war absorbed his mind, and he now "began his long battle
to turn the American people toward the enemy." [1]

For almost a decade the American people had been overwhelmingly concerned with their domestic problems and all the strenuous
controversies these had aroused. Public opinion in America following World War I had become "isolationist" and decidedly favored
neutrality in the event of resumption of European warfare. Hillman,

like other public men here, had had time to give only an occasional glance at the European and Far Eastern scene, where wars had actually been in progress since 1935. And yet he was bound by many ties to Europe and during the 1930's maintained friendships particularly with leading figures of the British Labor Party, many of whom came to call on him during visits to America.*

His own union following, moreover, was then largely made up of European immigrants. Since 1924 a big anti-Fascist Italian contingent in the Amalgamated had repeatedly brought forward resolutions condemning the regime of Mussolini, which had regularly been voted at conventions. Then came the persecution of Jews in Germany and Austria, many of them relatives of clothing workers who had emigrated to America. Hillman, though very conscious and proud of his Jewish heritage, had never participated in any active sense in the Zionist crusade for a Jewish state in Palestine, declaring privately that he felt his particular mission was to serve as an American labor leader and not as a Jewish nationalist. Yet once the pogroms had begun in Germany in 1938, he felt the greatest anguish for his kin, and the Jewish problem was constantly in his mind thereafter.

The Amalgamated resolutions condemning Fascism (and later National Socialism) at regular intervals from 1924 to 1940 described these movements as extreme modern examples of imperialism fostered by the prolonged economic depression afflicting Europe. Where governments were weak and demoralized the Nazi-Fascist system, engendering hatred, fear, and racial and religious divisions, throve best. The tragic upheavals of Europe must be regarded as a warning to freedom-loving America and not as "a remote, theoretical danger." For America herself was not safe from Nazi-Fascist encroachments. "That danger is right in our midst." [2]

The thoughts expressed in these resolutions were pursued further by Hillman. Various "splinter groups" of Fascists, he pointed out, such as the Silver Shirts and the organization of Father Coughlin, were trying to spread the detestable doctrines of the dictators in our midst. Hillman was for peace, he said, but the greatest vigilance

* Hillman was perhaps better known in British labor circles than any other American trade unionist. Dr. Harold Laski was an old friend since 1919. Since the twenties, Ramsay MacDonald (before his famous defection from the Labor Party), Jenny Lee (Mrs. Aneurin Bevan), Professor R. H. Tawney, and later Ernest Bevin sought him out during visits to this country.

might be needed henceforth to safeguard American institutions providing for "free discussion through democratic organization." It was well, he said, for labor everywhere to realize "that one of our major objectives is to defend freedom and liberty." As if to emphasize his difference of opinion with other public figures who had associated themselves with the America First Committee in 1940, Hillman added: "I know of course that we in America are neutral, but we cannot help but be horrified by what is going on abroad." [3]

These words were spoken on May 13, 1940, during the Battle of France. Hillman undoubtedly shared Roosevelt's conviction since the beginning of 1939 that the United States stood in danger of involvement in foreign war and would do well to prepare for it. In this view he was in accord not only with many liberals and progressives but also with conservatives like Henry L. Stimson, who, after the Munich Pact, had begun to call for a revision of our neutrality legislation embargoing arms shipments to nations at war, a measure which, as in the case of Republican Spain, worked to the advantage of the Fascist aggressors. For Hillman the major problem was how —in view of the chances of war—to conserve labor's gains and the new rights and instruments of social justice established under the New Deal.

The evolution of John L. Lewis' ideas about the threat of the "totalitarian" powers was less simple and logical than Hillman's; in the end (though by a somewhat tortuous path) he was led to the point of complete rupture not only with Roosevelt, but with Hillman, the firm ally of the President, on this ground.

In March 1937, Lewis had addressed a great mass meeting of protest at recent Nazi outrages, held at Madison Square Garden, New York, under the auspices of the American Jewish Committee. In an impassioned and eloquent speech, Lewis, as liberal and humanitarian, voiced his indignation at the persecutions borne by Jews and other minority groups in Germany, while 20,000 persons in the audience cheered or wept at his words.[4] Yet at the same period, in the councils of the CIO, Lewis firmly opposed the introduction of resolutions censuring General Franco, which were sponsored by Heywood Broun of the Newspaper Guild. The CIO, he held, could not afford to commit itself too deeply in the Spanish situation.

He pointed out that Catholic members might be offended. So disturbed was he by this possibility that he compelled one of his appointees to resign from affiliation with a Spanish Loyalist committee before joining the CIO staff. [5]

The cause of the Spanish Loyalists, after 1936, stirred the compassion of labor groups throughout the world. Hillman, in contrast with Lewis, openly manifested his sympathy for Loyalist Spain by attending a dinner in New York in honor of her wartime Foreign Minister, Alvarez del Vayo.[6]

The growing tensions in Europe, the mounting difficulties experienced at home, especially by those who struggled to organize the unorganized for the CIO at this period, evoked from Lewis nowadays no utterances that stirred men's hearts with hopes of bolder or more inspiring programs. Indeed many observers friendly to Lewis remarked with surprise that the man who had generated the greatest mass movement of labor ever known in this country had really no long-range program or philosophy of his own. To be sure, he urged always a broader extension of industrial democracy and declared that as a "by-product" of such a development the workers must soon acquire a "greater participation" in the government. From time to time he threatened to organize the 10,000,000 or more of the unemployed into a vast auxiliary army of the CIO. He would assume an air of knowing mystery about what a more powerful labor movement might try to achieve someday, and on one occasion was heard to remark, with no little wit: "It would be unwisdom to paint a picture that would only alarm our adversaries of tomorrow." But when questioned persistently by journalists like Louis Adamic and Dorothy Thompson as to what form such an enhanced industrial democracy was to assume, his replies were indefinite, or touched only on improving the workers' material standard of living in the way of food and clothing.

Meanwhile, though the United Mine Workers had fared well in late years and by the end of 1937 had accumulated a reserve fund estimated at $8,000,000, Lewis then did not favor experiments in co-operatives or improved schools or housing in the drab miners' villages where his constituents passed their arduous lives. On the other hand, he himself drew the highest salary of any labor leader of that time ($25,000 a year and expenses); his suite of offices was luxurious; a large limousine bore him about everywhere, and doubtless to meetings at which he assailed "men of privilege." Unlike the more modest Hillman, he would justify his way of life, saying: "The miners pay me to live well and eat well."

In practice he was what Professor Laski would have called one of the labor movement's "benevolent despots," though by no means the only one. Democratic representation in his own union was much restricted by what he termed the need for "efficient organization." In the CIO nearly all the officeholders were "Lewis men." After Eli Oliver, a Hillman appointee, resigned from Labor's Non-Partisan League in protest at Lewis' policies in 1940, Big John cleaned house thoroughly, saying: "I expect anyone who takes my money to be loyal to me."

He thought always in terms of power, personal power. Through his leadership of the coal miners and the great CIO unions commanding the basic industries of steel and motors he had attained a key position in the nation's economy which a Hillman, with his influence over mere hundreds of thousands working in light industries, could not rival. From this eminence he treated men like Myron C. Taylor, chairman of the U. S. Steel Corporation, as his equals and sat down to negotiate contracts affecting the lives of millions of workers. "Mr. Taylor and I understand each other very well and speak the same language," he once remarked to William Hammatt Davis, chairman of the War Labor Board. "You never said a truer thing in your life," Davis snapped back.[7]

There was, moreover, in those years of success the unending adulation of vast crowds (the "ocean of faces"), which had turned many a stronger head than his. Petty demagogues who bobbed up here and there with schemes for leading shirted mass movements of a few thousand morons were as pygmies compared to this veritable idol of the millions. He had counted, it has been said, upon an irresistible march of men and women under his leadership toward heaven knows what promised land of milk and honey, or well-being and security. Many of us forget, in these later years, what a colossus John L. Lewis appeared to be toward 1937 and 1938 when he spoke confidently of organizing "twenty millions"—nay, "thirty millions"—under the banner of the CIO. Roosevelt feared him much as he had feared Huey Long and his share-the-wealth slogan.* Lewis' attempts

* Max Lerner, after an off-the-record interview with the President in 1939, related that Roosevelt regarded Lewis as one of the Administration's most serious "problems" and grimly likened him to Huey Long.

in 1938 to reach an understanding with Harry Hopkins by which the CIO was to organize the WPA workers evidently impressed Roosevelt as a very sinister intrigue. At any rate, the plan (if ever seriously entertained) is said to have been repudiated by Hopkins after the November elections, because of Roosevelt's abiding fear and hatred of Lewis.[8] At any rate this was what Lewis believed.

Many who approached him after 1936 alluded flatteringly to the possibility that he might succeed Roosevelt, who was expected to retire as President in 1940, by placing himself at the head of "a powerful alliance of dissatisfied farm and labor elements." With an air of modesty he is said to have remarked that such a development was improbable, but that he would run for the presidency only if he felt it "a good thing for labor." One of the journalists who discussed such ambitions with him, however, observed: "He would like to be President. . . . The prospect of leading perhaps 30,000,000 voters does not frighten him." [9]

But the fact was that the "tidal wave" of the CIO began to ebb after 1937, and Lewis was much disconcerted. After reaching a membership of 3,700,000 within two years, the CIO gained only 400,000 more recruits in the next two years. Lewis was still balked by the "independent" steel companies; Ford remained unorganized; even the coal fields were not yet conquered, since the "captive mines," owned by the steel and railroad interests, still held out against the union shop.

It was Lewis' conviction, after 1938, that the CIO's reverses in these quarters resulted from President Roosevelt's deliberate refusal to give stronger political support to the CIO unions. The fact that Roosevelt had virtually lost control of Congress in November 1938 and faced the most serious opposition of his career in no way diminished Lewis' mounting resentment against the President, whom he privately called a "double-crosser." Neither the imminence nor the outbreak of world war in 1939 impressed Lewis with the thought that some change of policy, some trimming of sail, might be in order. He continued to besiege the President (though in formal correspondence) with proposals for drastic Federal legislation designed to disfranchise corporations that still closed their doors to union labor—proposals whose great legal and political difficulties Roosevelt merely hinted at in politely evasive replies.

Lewis had won command of a vast independent labor movement

and felt himself "on the threshold of gaining a nation," one of his most ardent apologists has said. Roosevelt, however, appeared to his mind as the prime enemy barring his way.

By 1940, the same admiring biographer of Lewis relates, he

passionately believed that Roosevelt was determined to get us into war. On the basis of pure power politics, certainly Lewis recognized that Roosevelt would be . . . more vulnerable to attack in this area than almost any other. "Peace" is a cause of perennial popularity.[10]

The touch that completes the picture of this remarkable and contradictory personality was the revelation in 1940 of Lewis' close connections with the international oilman, William Rhodes Davis. The Mexican Government, not long before, had confiscated foreign oil properties in Mexico, notably those of the British, who thereafter attempted to discourage the export of Mexican crude oil. Thanks to John L. Lewis' earnest recommendation of Davis to persons high in the Mexican Government, the oilman obtained a concession in the form of an export contract for the shipment of petroleum to refineries in Germany, where he also enjoyed special favor. Thus Lewis, who in public described himself as a Quaker, abhorring all violence and eager to save Americans from Roosevelt's alleged "warmongering," in private seemed to lend himself to the designs of an international financier who furnished oil for the hungry Nazi war machines.[11]

Such maneuvers, so extremely contradictory in principle, were typical of Lewis' unhappy later phase (from 1939 on), during which he constituted one of the Administration's largest domestic headaches. Yet outwardly he was all candor, all sincerity. One feels that never for a moment did he doubt the rightness of these and other, still more compromising, actions which shocked persons in his own entourage, forcing them to leave his service in protest.*

In extenuation of his Mexican adventure, several years later Lewis blandly explained that he had had many warm friends in the political and labor movements of Mexico and had sought only to help their "progressive" government dispose of its surplus oil. As for the ethics of Mr. Davis' selling this material of war to the Nazis, with whom we

* Gardner Jackson, an official of Labor's Non-Partisan League, in resigning his post, wrote to Lewis: "These are days when, more than ever, men seem to become captives of their personal ambition for wealth, social position, and influence, and when their adventures in power politics, both at home and in the international field, also make them captives."

were then at peace, many of our best families or best corporations were doing likewise, he pointed out.[12]

II

Early in 1939 President Roosevelt made cautious preparatory moves aimed at shoring up the country's military defenses. Some naval building was initiated. All preliminary surveys of any larger program for arms production forecast a high volume of industrial activity, instead of the half depression ruling in that year, and even eventually a shortage of labor. It was therefore imperative to bring about peace and unity in the labor camp.

On February 25, 1939, Roosevelt wrote identical letters to John L. Lewis and William Green urging that they appoint committees to negotiate terms for the reunion of the two great labor federations. This was in line with Hillman's insistent advice to the President that he assume the initiative in such action, even if he must bear affronts from Lewis. Two weeks later Lewis, Hillman, and Murray appeared at the White House in the company of Matthew Woll, Daniel Tobin, Harry Bates, and Thomas Rickert, representing the AFL. A few days later the conferees met again at the Biltmore Hotel in New York, where Lewis brough forth a proposal that a new all-embracing American Congress of Labor be established which would absorb the AFL, the CIO, and also the railroad Brotherhoods. The railway unions, always very jealous of their independence, had not even been consulted about this elaborate project. It was said at the time that Lewis could hardly have been very serious about his proposal. Hillman and Lewis were reported to have been in violent disagreement on this occasion—though they did not "come to blows," as rumor had it.[13]

Returning from one stormy session with Lewis at this period, Hillman was met by an old acquaintance who asked whether any results had been reached. Wearily Hillman shook his head and said: "No. Too much John!" [14] Nevertheless, he refused to abandon the efforts to reunite the AFL and CIO, which were continued at further conferences during the spring of 1939. But on July 1, Lewis finally declared: "Peace is out."

On August 9, 1939, Hillman spent the day at Hyde Park with the President. After lunch Roosevelt in person drove Hillman all around the estate in his car. Mrs. Roosevelt's account of the visit was guarded:

August 10, 1939. The President spent yesterday afternoon as usual going around the place. Sidney Hillman, who was with him, at least saw a good deal of the countryside. Whether he had an opportunity to talk about the things he wanted to talk about is quite another question. The President has always greatly enjoyed his trees.

They chatted about the trees, to be sure, but from Hillman's very brief disclosures to members of his family—he was always most discreet about his relations with the President—they also talked a good deal about the Lewis problem. Hillman had previously urged that the umbrageous Lewis be mollified as far as possible; at his suggestion (somewhat earlier) Mrs. Roosevelt had written inviting Lewis and his daughter Kathryn to tea at the White House. Lewis had replied through his secretary on June 2, 1939, with a polite refusal.

Nevertheless, Hillman urged the President to make further efforts at conciliation by taking the first opportunity to write or telegraph him in friendly spirit, as when Lewis would have made some public statement he approved of. A while later Roosevelt did send messages to Lewis urging him to telephone or come to the White House whenever he felt the need to do so.[15]

It was known among the President's intimates at various periods in the summer and fall of 1939 that he was considering the possibility of running for a third term. But if he were to stand again, in view of the growing conservative opposition even in his own party, he would need the support of all labor factions, notably of the millions of CIO workers who, it was said, loved Roosevelt "as their President," but adulated Lewis. The rift between the two was by now fairly well publicized. If this continued it might work great injury not merely to whatever plans or ambitions Roosevelt entertained as being in the country's best interests—in the event of war—but to the cause of all labor. Roosevelt feared greatly that the CIO, which had given him such mighty aid in the campaign of 1936, might be turned against him through the enormous influence of Lewis.

In his dilemma, Franklin Roosevelt, with keen intuition, turned to Sidney Hillman for help. In Hillman the President sensed a rival force within the CIO, one that might be used to divide the growing opposition in the labor movement or wean it away from Lewis. Hence the marked personal attentions shown to Hillman at Hyde Park and elwhere. No one of that day possessed deeper political acumen than Roosevelt.

Hillman, on the other hand, was scarcely less the skillful opportunist than Roosevelt, and had also a "long nose" for what might lie ahead, politically speaking, for labor and for himself. He believed that his close working alliance with the President was a good "investment," so to speak; it represented to his mind the best way to advance the interests of labor while at the same time strengthening his own position in labor and in the political field.

Certainly Hillman was human and ambitious; he was no doubt affected by the attentions shown to him by the President, though neither deluded nor dazzled, as Lewis thought. But then, the happy thing about Hillman's own career, and especially about his ambitions, was that he habitually directed them within the frame of the labor movement and in line with labor's long-range interests. To be sure, Roosevelt, though labor's friend, often showed himself disposed to compromise with its enemies. But Hillman, far more than Lewis, appreciated the fact that the President faced many other "battalions of opinion" than those of the trade unionists. He was decidedly in favor of co-operating with Roosevelt rather than battering at him, especially in a season when the threat of world war weighed upon everyone's heart.

A few days after Hillman's visit to Hyde Park, the German-Soviet Pact of Friendship was announced to the world on August 22. The halfhearted Anglo-French overtures for the Russian alliance had failed. The invasion of Poland followed promptly, and World War II began in Europe.

The production of Army and Navy munitions in the United States now underwent a moderate expansion; orders from the British and French governments also came to our steel, motor, and aircraft companies in quantity. But on Labor Day of 1939, John L. Lewis, in a speech before a huge audience of workers, served solemn warning on all his hearers that they must beware of statesmen who might attempt to solve difficult domestic problems by plunging their countries into war. It was a shaft obviously aimed at Roosevelt.[16]

The second annual convention of the CIO was due to open in San Francisco on October 10. A week earlier the all-important Executive Board began its sittings, and Lewis, with all the dramatic emphasis at his command, informed his colleagues that he had recently been requested by Roosevelt to "step down" in order to permit peace in the labor movement. He had therefore determined to resign as president of the CIO. The other members of the Board, including Hillman, quickly talked him out of it, Hillman assuring Lewis that he was the "greatest labor leader this country has ever produced"; and so he was "drafted," which was as he wanted it.[17]

No record of such a request by Roosevelt seems to have been found. The important pre-convention issue, before the Executive Board, was really Lewis' anti-war resolution by which he strove to embarrass Roosevelt. Lewis argued that labor would do "most of the work and most of the dying" in the event of war. The anti-war resolution was adopted by the Board, as later by the convention. It declared that organized labor opposed any involvement in the European war, and demanded at the same time, in behalf of labor, "adequate representation in all governmental boards or agencies set up to cope with the war situation and mobilize national defense."

Hillman had bent all his efforts to keep Lewis from effecting an open breach between the CIO and the Roosevelt Administration. There was no firing at Roosevelt at that CIO convention; nor was there any open quarrel as yet between Lewis and Hillman. In deference to Hillman's views the anti-war resolution had been expanded by the Executive Board to include a paragraph declaring that the members of the CIO stood ready always "as Americans to defend our country and our free institutions against foreign invasion." [18]

It was fascinating to watch these two very power-minded gentlemen, especially at the council table where the audience was small. As yet they fenced with foils, meanwhile plying each other with compliments. Lewis was lavish in his praise of Hillman, referring to him as "statesman" and "philosopher" and stressing his own "growing admiration" and friendship for him (as in the article he wrote in the *CIO Daily News* on Soule's biography of Hillman). At about this time Hillman was invited to appear a few weeks after the CIO convention as guest speaker at the forthcoming United Mine Workers' ("Golden Jubilee") convention in January 1940, while Lewis, in return, was invited to speak before the Amalgamated's (twenty-fifth anniversary) convention in May. Yet at heart they no longer trusted each other. One of Hillman's aides, in a letter of this time, noted privately that her "boss" and John L., despite public manifestations of friendship, were actually "on the warpath" by October 1939.[19]

The issue between them was Hillman's determination to support Roosevelt's policies and the movement for his renomination in 1940. Lewis, for his part, deeply resented the favor shown Hillman by the

President, and sensed that Roosevelt's great influence stood behind Hillman to strengthen his hand in the CIO councils.

After the CIO convention at San Francisco was over, Roosevelt sent Hillman an urgent message asking him to join him on his private train in order that he might be informed as to what had really happened at the convention, especially with regard to the question of reunion with the AFL.[20] Roosevelt was quite worried about Mr. Lewis.

One development at the recent convention had been the beginning of serious controversy over the Communist faction within the CIO. The Communists had provided a powerful nucleus for the Unemployed Councils organized in various cities during the worst days of the depression. Thereafter, they had established themselves also as a small, hardworking minority both in the AFL and the CIO unions. Authorities on the labor movement have seldom estimated their numbers, including followers or sympathizers, at more than 5 to 10 per cent of the CIO's membership. Indeed at the time when the Steel Workers' Organizing Committee was being built up in 1936 and a few of the small steel locals set up by the Communists in the Pittsburgh area were brought into the CIO fold, it was noted that their actual numbers were pitifully small; that is, they had but a few hundred followers. Yet in view of the rather casual system of representation functioning locally in most labor unions, by which only a small fraction, in the neighborhood of 10 per cent of the membership, regularly attend local branch meetings or even special meetings for voting on agreements or strike settlements, the influence of these diligent Communist members could become disproportionately large. Indeed, the more "corrupt" or lax a union was, through the indifference of the leadership to rank-and-file participation, the easier it was for zealous Communists to penetrate the organization from below.*

* To be a good labor leader, especially at the local branch level, a man must possess the moral equivalent of religion. The local business agent is much burdened with quantities of routine, bureaucratic tasks of handling workers' grievances, complaints of foremen, helping the jobless, and door-to-door canvassing. Reserves of moral fervor are needed in such a situation, lest the local union officer sink into apathy or cynicism. It is not surprising, therefore, that Communist zealots, with their vision of a Socialist paradise buoying them up, should make good union material. Their cult of energy also stands them in good stead at periods of violent conflict.

Hillman, after having effectively subdued the Communist threat during the 1920's within the Amalgamated, expressed himself as indifferent to the private beliefs of union members so long as they were loyal in the service of the organization. John L. Lewis declared that the Communists made "superb organizers," and inasmuch as they went along with the CIO's policies, he too was not disposed to examine their doctrines about the ultimate reformation of the body politic. This is the view followed to this day by the great British trade unions.

After the Russo-German "peace pact" of August 1939, however, the picture changed completely. The political character of the American Communist movement now required a brusque about-face from the anti-Fascist or anti-Nazi position to one of neutrality and isolationism. In New York fierce dissension broke out within the American Labor Party between the right- and left-wing factions. Anti-Communists in the New York unions, especially those of Jewish and European descent, felt most bitterly about the treaty between the Nazis and the Soviets, and attacked those who condoned Soviet policy. In the end the American Labor Party was split asunder, its State Committee coming under the control of Mr. Dubinsky and his faction, its New York County Committee being captured by the left wing under Vito Marcantonio.

At the October 1939 convention of the CIO the same fierce divisions arose. In the contest over the election of two added vice-presidents of the CIO, the Amalgamated delegation now threw its influence against those who were alleged Communists or their allies, so that the "pro-Hillman" Emil Rieve of the Textile Workers and R. J. Thomas of the UAW were chosen over proposed left-wing candidates. Resolutions condemning the Communists and the German-Soviet pact, however, were firmly blocked by Lewis, who said jestingly: "If we start removing people *merely charged* with being members [of the Communist Party] we will have to remove Lewis and Hillman and Murray!" There must be no "witch hunts" in the CIO, he held. "If the Communists are good enough to work for General Motors, we have little choice but to accept their dues in the United Auto Workers." [21]

The little bloc of Communists and fellow travelers gave impassioned support henceforth to Lewis' "peace movement." Sidney Hillman, on the other hand, was in the Communists' bad books for the next two years, the duration of the Soviet-German pact; in the *Daily Worker's* well-known vocabulary of vituperation, he was a "lackey of the imperialists" and a "tool of the warmonger, Roosevelt."

III

Before 1939 was out various labor groups around the country had endorsed the "draft-Roosevelt" resolutions. On January 6, 1940, Hillman, speaking before a labor gathering in New York, declared that the Amalgamated Clothing Workers would give hearty support to Roosevelt for a third term if, in view of the world-wide emergency, he should decide to run again.[22]

Lewis remained silent for the moment. It was as if he feared to precipitate the final break between the President and himself. The much-rumored quarrel between them was profoundly disturbing to the labor movement, which owed so much to both.

On January 19, 1940, the President asked Lewis to come to the White House to see him. Rearmament was in its preliminary planning stages. The CIO leader had been writing the President letters in which he urged that he use his authority to prevent the award of contracts to companies standing in violation of the Wagner Labor Relations Act. It was on this occasion, early in 1940, that Lewis may have made his proposal that Roosevelt and he join forces again—but upon terms that fairly startled the President.

According to the account given by Frances Perkins, Lewis, after touching upon the difficulties in the way of a third-term campaign, said:

> Mr. President, I have thought of all of that and I have a suggestion to make for you to consider. If the vice-presidential candidate should happen to be John L. Lewis, those objections would disappear. A strong labor man would insure full support, not only of all the labor people but of all the liberals who worry about such things as third terms.[23]

In Miss Perkins' account Roosevelt was both amused and incredulous, but promised to give some thought to this extraordinary counsel.*

Lewis' proposal of himself as Democratic candidate for Vice-President was as incredible as anything he ever did in those years. He had

---

* Miss Perkins has fixed the President's statement as being made to her in late March or early April, "about two months" after John L. Lewis' visit, at a time when Roosevelt still refused to commit himself even to his intimates on the third-term question. His mind was made up, however, by April, the time of Hitler's invasion of Norway, heralding the campaign in the West. Lewis, years later, denied the veracity of Miss Perkins' "gossip"; but Philip Murray recalls having heard an account of the affair in 1940 from Lewis himself.

been privately calling Roosevelt a "traitor to labor" and a "double-crosser" (though this was known in the White House). Yet now, it was said, he offered to help re-elect the alleged "double-crosser" and "war-monger" for a third term by lending his own name, for Vice-President, to the Democratic ticket. (It must be noted also that there was much interested speculation touching Roosevelt's health in 1940.)

Lewis' next move was his opening address at the miners' "Golden Jubilee" convention at Columbus, Ohio, on January 24, 1940, a thunderous broadside at the whole Democratic Administration of the past seven years and its leader. The Democratic Party, he argued, was only a "minority party" which had won in 1936 because of its coalition with organized labor. But it had not kept faith.

In the last three years labor has not been given representation in the Cabinet, nor in the administrative or policy-making agencies of the government. The current Administration has not sought nor seriously entertained the advice or views of labor. . . . Labor today has no point of contact with the Democratic Administration in power, except for casual and occasional interviews which are granted its individual leaders.

The Democratic Party is in default to the American people. After seven years of power it finds itself without solution for the major questions of unemployment, low income, mounting internal debts.

Labor and the people are losing confidence. They fear for the future, and rightfully so.

In further remarks on the forthcoming election campaign, Lewis added: "Let no politician or statesman dream that he is going to solve the unemployment question . . . by dragging America into war with foreign countries." His advice to the miners was that endorsement of any party be withheld for the present.

I am one who believes that President Roosevelt will not be a candidate for re-election. Conceding that the Democratic National Convention could be coerced or dragooned into renominating him, I am convinced that . . . his candidacy would result in ignominious defeat.[24]

Lewis' philippic against Roosevelt came with the effect of a bomb. But some still hoped that his real intention was only to place the CIO in a good bargaining position for the 1940 campaign.

Hillman was to address this same miners' convention on the following day. He feared that the meeting at Columbus might degenerate into an open brawl in which Lewis would bait him before his audience of coal miners, and being very sensitive, instinctively shrank from such a head-on collision. Yet despite his aversion, he resolved to go before Lewis' people and address them in the spirit of cool reason. Two observers, moreover, had preceded him to Columbus and reported that the miners' delegates were by no means in accord with their president, many of them having tried to present pro-Roosevelt resolutions which Lewis' machine had voted down in committee.[25]

Shortly before Hillman was to speak, Lewis, in discussing the question of unemployment before the convention, said as if gibing at him:

Let's let some gentleman who has some profound belief in the politicians rise up and tell me why that politician or statesman has not concerned himself with this problem. Oh, he may tell me that that politician or statesman is a great friend of labor and that he is lying awake at night worrying over the problems of Europe and Asia. But that does not put my men to work. . . .[26]

Advance reports had promised a knock-down and drag-out fight between Hillman and Lewis. But this was not Sidney Hillman's method. His tone was conciliatory, and he had generous compliments for the great leader, as usual. The miners and the clothing workers, he declared, had the same fundamental objectives, and he voiced the hope that, while they might come to honest disagreements on ways and means, there would be no major differences between them. Then without direct reference to Lewis' address which had "blasted" the Roosevelt Administration, he dwelt on the great advances labor had made under the present regime and the increased power it now wielded in the field of politics. His closing words were an appeal for continued unity of action, for support of the New Deal, and, plainly enough, for support of Roosevelt, who had known how to rally diverse groups of progressives, farmers, and workers to his cause:

This year, my friends, will be a crucial year, when a decision must be made whether . . . the vested interests . . . will again take hold of the destinies of the nation, or whether through the power of labor, *joined with all the other progressive groups,* we will make sure that, after November 1940, there will be a progressive government in the nation, which will mean a great deal to labor and to the country. . . . None of us must shirk the great responsibilities placed upon us.[27]

The miners' greeting to Hillman as he took the platform had been hearty; the applause, as he ended, was also warm and prolonged. On that day Hillman gave a long interview, widely quoted in the press, that was much less reserved and diplomatic in its espousal of the Roosevelt Administration than his speech at the convention. He did not wait for an account of the days' proceedings by Lewis' publicity men to go to the newspapers.

All that season Lewis continued firing broadsides at the President, while Sidney followed hard on his heels and poured out words of common sense. On April 6 they both spoke before a meeting of the United Auto Workers. Lewis, by implication, charged that Roosevelt labored under the delusion that the American people were going to send their sons to be butchered in another foreign war, but he added that he would prove to be thereby "nothing more or less than a fool." Hillman followed him up briskly with a refutation of Lewis' statements that Roosevelt had done nothing for labor, by recalling how the minimum-wage law and other reform measures had been enacted, in spite of fierce congressional resistance, largely through Roosevelt's "stubborn support." Then turning to the subject of the war in Europe, he warned his labor audience that they could not hope to live isolated or unmolested in a world gone mad. He flayed "this rotten thing called dictatorship," which seemed bent upon destroying unions of free people everywhere, and declared that such issues would have to be faced.

Wherever Lewis went, Hillman dogged him. He had earned the wholesome respect of men of labor during long years, and particularly those of the big auto workers' union and the textile and rubber workers. In a very large degree, his defensive action softened the blows struck by Lewis and helped to contain an incipient uprising in the CIO against the party of Roosevelt which Lewis, with all his heart, strove to encourage.

The two principal antagonists in the labor camp were to confront each other again before the Amalgamated convention in May, in their strange duel for the loyalties of the millions in the CIO family. This was at the twenty-fifth anniversary, or "Silver Jubilee," convention of the clothing workers, held in Madison Square Garden before an immense gathering of 20,000 persons. Hillman, Secretary of the Interior Harold Ickes, Senators Wagner and Mead of New York, Governor Lehman, Mayor La Guardia, and other Administration stalwarts were all to address the New York crowd and turn the occasion into a festival for the New Deal and a carefully timed call for a third term for Franklin Roosevelt. Lewis alone was expected to introduce his jarring notes, which, it was hoped, would be drowned in the prearranged New Deal orchestration.

On May 7, Hillman met with the Executive Board of his union, in preparation for the convention the following week. His thoughts flowed forth freely, swiftly, in those jagged sentences of his, yet compact with insights fascinating to the men and women who had listened to him for a quarter of a century. We were living through a time of growing crisis, he told them. There were not words enough to impress people with the gravity of the crisis.

People love to not perceive danger. People love to believe that things are not bad because if things are really bad we have to do something about them.

The Battle of France was on, he continued. If it were lost, if the "totalitarians" won, then everything dear to us would be gone, and for generations to come. All freedom was at stake. "Remember," he cried, "that totalitarianism means, especially for labor, actual slavery."

Here, before his old union comrades, Hillman said that he cared nothing for the Democratic Party as such, nor for its professional politicians. But Roosevelt still meant everything to him—was it not he who had united so many different groups and held them together during the great upheavals of the past seven years? Labor had its working alliance with Roosevelt. Hillman's colleagues knew well that they and he had had some voice in framing recent labor legislation. Was all this now to be cast away? When Hillman thought of the possibility of some reactionary politician taking Roosevelt's place —as a result of divisions among the labor men and liberals—then he had an intuition that we might be faced not with mere political conservatism, but, in view of the world emergency, with some native form of Fascism.

It will be a sorry day for labor and the nation if at this critical hour we permit division among the liberal groups whose unity made these gains possible. *The reactionaries never divide. They always hang together. The great misfortune in the past has been that liberal groups could not remain united.* It is our great obligation to keep progressives and liberals united or we are going to lose a great deal of what we have gained in the last few years.[28] [Italics added.]

In his opening address at the convention itself, on May 13, after the usual viewing-with-pride of past achievements of the Amalgamated, he proceeded to the principal business on hand, which was to "draft" Franklin D. Roosevelt. The way was prepared by the reading of a telegram from the President, congratulating the union on its Silver Jubilee, which was the signal for a great demonstration all over Madison Square Garden. Hillman's closing words were:

Now, my friends, I speak only for myself. I hope that before two weeks are over this will also be the action of the convention. . . . We must demand the one leadership that has proven itself in the last seven years; we must demand of our Chief Executive that he permit the nation to vote for his return to the White House in 1940.

We must do it to safeguard the beginnings we have made. We must do it to assure further progress on the same road. We must do it . . . *to make sure that democracy emerges victorious in the years to come.*[29] [Italics added.]

Mayor La Guardia followed Hillman on the platform, and, as if challenging Lewis, said bluntly: "No one man can deliver the labor vote today!"

At one moment Hillman asked Lewis jestingly: "When would you prefer to make your speech, John, before or after we pass our third-term resolution?" The other man smiled wryly and said that that was up to "Sid."[30]

The overlord of the CIO took the floor when his turn came, in serious mood. Accustomed to mastery of the crowds, like a William Jennings Bryan, he faced an audience which, if polite, refused to be spellbound, and in fact at times seemed downright skeptical. At one point when Lewis chanced to mention the name of Roosevelt the sharp-witted New York tailors broke into a tremendous round of cheers, which disconcerted him momentarily, though he stood smiling patiently through it. There were some here also who heckled him for "playing the same tune as the Nazis and Communists," but Hillman put a stop to this. Yet if Hillman continued to maintain a courteous attitude, Lewis, too, was most courteous in his references to the Amalgamated members. He was too wise to repeat, before this gathering, his wild charges that Roosevelt had done nothing for American labor. His most spirited arguments were in defense of his own position in rejecting unity with the American Federation of Labor, whose old labor magnates he covered with ridicule. And in raising certain issues which stood between labor and the Administration, he made several points of considerable force. A national defense program had been announced by the President a short time ago. Lewis said that before the working people of America could regard such a program with confidence, they might rightly ask:

First, if the social legislation now in effect was being protected . . . Second—Will the collective-bargaining rights and the wages and hours of the workers, both in national defense and in other industries, be protected fully?

Would labor-union standards be maintained in industries that were being given contracts for arms production? Would our civil liberties be safeguarded? And finally :

Will labor be given a voice in the determination of national defense policies and in the discussion of national defense production? If not, why not? Who is more entitled to a voice? If the country wants the co-operation of labor to do the work of . . . war, and in the event of war to do the necessary dying, what is wrong with a little co-operation on policies?

There was applause as Lewis concluded his speech, but it was soon obvious that he had convinced no one. The first resolution passed by the convention, unanimously, was one in favor of a third term for the incumbent President. These words, however, convey nothing of the roof-lifting "pageantry" with which this political manifestation was staged by 20,000 enthusiastic partisans of the New Deal. Hillman had long been almost unrivaled in the arts of drafting petitions and resolutions, or organizing demonstrations, and in employing all those little devices by which the effect of an irresistible current of public opinion can be generated under our system of popular rule. Labor had spoken forth in the metropolis of Roosevelt's home state, the most important, electorally, in the country.

From the White House, President Roosevelt called Hillman while he was on the platform during one of the convention sessions and eagerly asked how things were going. What he learned was reassuring. Evidently even John L. Lewis was not going to take New York away from him.

The President had delayed making his own decision public, though the political season was advancing and many were impatient. As Edward J. Flynn, a keen student of the political animal, has written in his delightful memoirs of this era, the big New Deal officeholders, such as Harry Hopkins, Harold Ickes, and Henry Wallace, were convinced that the current regime must be continued, not only because they were idealists, but also because they did not like to relinquish the positions of power they held to others less deserving or reliable than themselves.[31] Even the big city bosses, Kelly of Chicago and Flynn himself, were not cheerful at the alternative prospect of having John Garner, or even James A. Farley, head their party ticket. Aside from Lewis, big labor, as typified nowadays by Hillman in the CIO and Tobin in the AFL, also desired that the advantageous relations already established with the White House be maintained.

It was on May 17, 1940, as reports arrived of the German breakthrough at Sedan and it was known that Paris was doomed, that Roosevelt made up his mind to succeed himself and asked Harry Hopkins to take charge of the approaching Democratic Party convention.[32]

Fear and hysteria swept the United States as the French Army collapsed under the blitzkrieg. Anyone who visited Washington at the time recalls the terror felt everywhere, even in official circles, lest the French fleet pass to Germany and the swift conquest of England follow. (Many persons, recently escaped from France, went about soberly predicting the appearance of the Nazi invaders, like "men from Mars," upon our own shores "within two weeks.") It was in those days of panic that Roosevelt called for "50,000 airplanes," and on May 28, 1940, announced the establishment of the National Defense Advisory Commission, a body of seven members, who were to help plan the production of vast armaments sufficient to protect the country against all possible eventualities. Among the members of this all-important Commission, along with William S. Knudsen of General Motors, was Sidney Hillman, who was to be in charge of labor under the defense program.

A few days before news of the NDAC was released to the press, Roosevelt had called Hillman on the telephone and informed him that he was to be appointed as one of its commissioners. Hillman expressed surprise and asked: "Are you sure, Mr. President, that you are doing the right thing?" The President replied that he had "thought all around the matter" and was certain that Hillman was the best man for the post.[33] Hillman accepted the appointment with a sense of gratitude at the trust the President showed in him.

At this period Harry Hopkins, Roosevelt's most intimate adviser, installed in a room of the White House itself, had begun to take a leading part in the preparedness program and in planning for aid to Britain. Hopkins greatly admired Hillman. Ever since the days of the NRA in 1933, Hillman had stood out in the eyes of the public as one of the two strongest labor leaders of the time. The other was mistrusted by Roosevelt and regarded by Hopkins as "the worst Roosevelt-hater of them all."[34] As for the Old Guard in the AFL, none of them seemed, by comparison, as fit as Hillman for the arduous tasks Roosevelt and Hopkins already envisaged. The management of labor and its "co-ordination" for the defense program appeared as one of the toughest assignments during this emergency.

Like John L. Lewis, many persons had been asking what would happen to labor's rights in just such a situation, and whether the trade unionists would be given a voice in the shaping of policies— as had been done in England in the new ministry of Winston Churchill by the elevation of Ernest Bevin as Labor Minister. Roosevelt's answer was to name Sidney Hillman as a member of the Defense Commission. To be sure, the American Federation of Labor would consider itself snubbed in favor of the CIO. But Hillman was known to be working overtime, despite Lewis, to reunite the two labor bodies. In discussing the appointment of Hillman at a press conference, the President jocularly described him as really a "middle-of-the-road labor leader [standing] between Lewis and Bill Green."

There was at first a hullabaloo of the labor baiters in Congress at the appointment of the foreign-born Hillman to direct the training and the allocation of labor. Representative Edward Cox was all for launching a "Don't-Trust-Our-Children-to-Hillman" movement in response to an alleged "nationwide clamor from America's fathers and mothers.* [35]

* Numerous letters from frenzied "racists" came to Roosevelt, which he would turn over to Hillman with good-humored jests, as in the case of the following telegram from a person in Litchfield, Connecticut, dated June 20, 1940:   .
   "As Patriotic Citizen object most strenuously you appointing ex-Bolshevick Russian Jew Sidney Hillman for drafting American youth. Is this country so short of red-blooded genuine American stock for us to call on foreign blood and mentality?" In the case of more shocking or insulting letters, Roosevelt had replies written by his secretaries in terms of dignified reproof.

But the angriest man of all was he who was most silent now, John L. Lewis. In naming his chief lieutenant as a member of the NDAC without consulting him, Lewis, the President had mortally affronted him and, he believed, with deliberate intent. In the view of the pro-Lewis and left-wing faction, Roosevelt, by honoring Hillman and ignoring Lewis, sought to divide the growing opposition in the CIO in the interests of his 1940 campaign.

To Lewis, who calculated always in terms of personal power, Roosevelt was not content to be President of the United States, but was also trying to gain control of the CIO! He is quoted as having said in September 1940:

He [Roosevelt] has been raiding the CIO for the past three years. He has been carefully selecting my key lieutenants and appointing them to honorary posts in various of his multitudinous, grandiose commissions. He has his lackeys fawning upon and wining and dining many of my people. . . . He has been engaged in a deliberate conspiracy to wean away the primary loyalty of many of my lieutenants from the CIO to himself.

Take the appointment of Sidney Hillman to the National Defense Council. Why, the first I knew of that appointment was when I read about it in the morning papers at breakfast. . . . Roosevelt could just as easily have called me on the telephone (and I can see him doing it) and said to me: "John, I want Sidney Hillman on my . . . National Defense Council." My answer would have been: "Mr. President, your choice is a wise and prudent one, and I shall . . . call in Sidney Hillman tomorrow morning and . . . tell him that in this new position he would have the full and unreserved support of the CIO and myself. . . ."

But instead of that, what does Roosevelt do? . . . He approaches one of my lieutenants . . . overpowers him with the dazzling glory of the White House . . . under such circumstances that his prime loyalty shall be to the President and only a secondary, residual one to the working-class movement from which he came. . . . Of course Sidney's head was so turned by Roosevelt's personal attention that he didn't think it worth while consulting with his associates.*

* Alinsky, *John L. Lewis,* pp. 182–184.

Throughout this work Lewis is quoted at great length. Since many of the statements contained therein were made under stress of emotion, they are frequently not in accord with known facts or reasonable assumptions. For example, the author quotes Lewis as saying that Hillman told him how much, as a former immigrant, he was "dazzled" by the President's inviting him to the White House and calling him by his first name. Mr. Alinsky has since written me that he is not certain that this was a literal transcription of Lewis' statement on this occasion. That Hillman, a man of great pride as well as astuteness, should have

Henceforth Lewis seemed to regard Roosevelt as his personal devil and Hillman as the devil's advocate.

President Roosevelt was fully aware of the differences between Hillman and Lewis at this time, but this in no way deterred him from choosing Hillman as his aide. Hillman was the man he needed now. Sidney Hillman was by nature intensely loyal. Having determined to ally himself with Roosevelt and support the defense program, he could not regard the arrangement as one-sided. For the first time in his life he would have obligations transcending the labor movement. His relations with the AFL would be difficult; those with the CIO, thanks to Lewis' enmity, would be, at best, precarious. Roosevelt said to him at an early conference with the members of the NDAC in the White House: "Sidney, I expect you to keep labor in step." Under the circumstances, this was to be a heartbreaking job. During the first five months of his term on the Defense Commission, however, he was called upon to act not only as labor adviser to the President but also as Roosevelt's political aide in rallying labor's support for the current election campaign.

IV

In the first week of July, Philip Murray, head of the Steel Workers, and Thomas J. Kennedy, Secretary of the United Mine Workers, with R. J. Thomas and Richard Frankensteen of the Auto Workers, Dalrymple of the Rubber Workers, and Rieve, head of the textile union, arrived at the Chicago offices of the CIO to help the draft-Roosevelt movement at the Democratic Party convention. In this campaign the outstanding CIO leaders, with the exception of Lewis, were lined up with Hillman from the start. Rumors were current that Lewis would launch a third-party farmer-labor movement, based on a peace platform. Other rumors suggested that he might swing over to the Republican Party.

The Republicans at their 1940 convention, however, chose as their candidate for President Wendell Willkie, the "dark horse," over the professionals, Dewey and Robert Taft. Undoubtedly Willkie had political "sex appeal" not unlike Franklin Roosevelt's, and

opened his heart to Lewis under the circumstances of concealed, yet no less intense, hostility that had developed is considered extremely doubtful by those who knew Hillman well.

it was for precisely this reason that he was selected to challenge Roosevelt in the presidential race. Moreover, Willkie was considered "safe" by the interests backing the Republican candidacy, having served for years as a lawyer for the public utilities of the Morgan and First National bank interests. In later years he was to prove himself a sincere liberal (to the intense vexation of his conservative Republican friends). But to those who in 1940 urged a policy of strict neutrality toward the warring powers in Europe, Willkie, by his statements on foreign policy, appeared scarcely less the "interventionist" than Roosevelt. How, then, could the radicals of the labor movement and the isolationists vote for Willkie, "the barefoot boy from Wall Street," in lieu of Roosevelt?

Lewis sulked in silence during the early summer months. When he finally brought himself to speak out, it was to attack the pending selective-service bill, sponsored by Roosevelt, as an act that would deprive labor of all its gains under the New Deal. Addressing the auto workers on July 31, he charged that profitable defense contracts were being awarded to companies that violated the Wagner Labor Relations Act.

The indefatigable Hillman, as always, was on hand to give the riposte to Lewis. He boldly advocated "preparing up to the hilt." If it needed conscription, he was for it. If it needed longer hours of work, he was for it too. "No man can say he is for labor if he is not ready to defend democracy to the utmost." As for the question of enforcing labor-law standards in defense contracts, he insisted that President Roosevelt was co-operating with him to the full. "I see him once a week. . . . Never has anyone said, 'Hillman, don't do this,' or 'Don't do that.' " [36]

In the hard-hitting debates of the 1940 campaign, Roosevelt tried to take care of the vivacious Willkie, while Sidney Hillman looked after the labor-union voters. On this front he was a tower of strength that summer and played no small part in persuading the conventions of the auto workers, the textile workers, the rubber workers, and numerous other unions to endorse Roosevelt again.

In New York there was a spirited brawl between the left-and right-wing factions for control of the state's Industrial Union Council (CIO). Hillman's followers, it was charged, used strong-arm methods to silence the pro-Lewis minority, and Lewis himself made loud complaint. In the end this important New York labor body also gave its endorsement to Roosevelt, as did the state committee of the American Labor Party, despite the opposition of the Communist group.[37]

The campaign went well for the Democratic Administration; the Democratic lead seemed commanding—up to the last three weeks before Election Day, when confidential polls showed that Willkie was rapidly gaining on Roosevelt. At this stage of affairs, in October, with Lewis still sulking in his tent, there was much uneasiness about what he might do. He had lately brought great pressure upon the President and upon Hillman to stop awards for ordnance contracts to anti-union corporations such as Bethlehem Steel—which still resisted all efforts of the steel workers' union to obtain a union-shop agreement. Hillman, in fact, had applied himself with great ardor to winning compliance with Federal labor laws in such contracts, despite the fixed tendency of military procurement officers to treat the question of union recognition as a minor issue, compared with that of speed in output. The solution of this problem, as Hillman knew, waited upon the outcome of the election contest itself. Yet, by his determined appeals both to the White House and to the War and Navy Secretaries, he obtained letters from both departments declaring that, as a matter of policy, compliance with existing labor laws would be required hereafter—save in emergency situations demanding all possible haste. These letters, signed by Secretary of the Navy Knox and Assistant Secretary of War Patterson, he made public on October 1, 1940, declaring that they marked a notable advance in the government's defense policy.

Lewis, however, answered that he was not satisfied with mere statements of policy, and noted their serious qualification. He directed the fire of his criticism with increasing bitterness at the President and Hillman as well. On Hillman's advice Roosevelt made a final effort to placate the great man, and he was induced to call at the White House to see the President on October 17, 1940. They discussed the issue of labor-law compliance and defense contracts; then with a good deal of rancor Lewis complained that he had lately been "shadowed" by the FBI and that his telephone had been tapped, which the President angrily denied. Their parting was on terms unfriendlier than ever; the last attempt at reconciliation had come to nothing. Roosevelt's lieutenants, especially Harry Hopkins, were in great fear that Lewis would abandon his silence and strike hard at the Administration by coming out for Willkie at the psychological moment. Indeed the President, through his private sources, learned in advance (on Sunday, October 20) that radio time on three national networks had been reserved for a Lewis speech on the evening of Friday, October 25, 1940.

In his mood of injured pride, the "good hater" Lewis could not forbear making a supreme effort to defeat Franklin Roosevelt. As an "isolationist" he assailed the President and Hillman unremittingly at this period, though some of his criticisms of the defense program were well founded and well aimed. Lewis might have persisted in his dignified silence toward both parties—or said that on foreign policy here was but a choice between tweedledum and tweedledee. Instead he seemed to be in anguish at the thought that Roosevelt might win again, and he not have struck the massive blow that would surely have destroyed him. He had the vanity to believe that by raising his voice, his voice alone, millions of workers would be moved to desert Roosevelt and the New Deal in favor of Mr. Willkie. He had told none of his associates in the CIO, not even the long-faithful Philip Murray, what he was going to do.

Some twenty-five million people heard the deep baritone of Lewis that Friday night in his powerful onslaught on the President. He attacked, he attacked; he stood forth alone in the role he instinctively loved. Roosevelt meant war, he said over and over again; he had been scheming for years to involve us in war.

The present concentration of power in the office of the President of the United States has never before been equaled. . . . Personal craving for power, the overweening abnormal and selfish craving for power is a thing to alarm and dismay. . . .

America needs no superman. It denies the philosophy that runs to the deification of the state. . . . Are we now to cast away that priceless liberty which is our heritage? . . .

I say "no." It is time for the manhood and womanhood of America to assert themselves. Tomorrow may be too late.

After all, Americans are not a nation of guinea pigs, constantly subject to the . . . experiments of an amateur, ill-equipped practitioner in the realm of political science.

If not Roosevelt, whom do I recommend to do the job of making secure our nation and its people? Why, of course, I recommend the election of Wendell Willkie.

He is a gallant American. He is not an aristocrat. He has the common touch.

Hillman was in Washington that night, at his apartment in the Wardman Park Hotel, with a group of friends, listening, like millions of others, to Lewis' impassioned tirade. With astonishment he heard Lewis' closing words, spoken with supreme arrogance, calling on the men and women of labor and their leaders, upon whom, as he said, he had "bestowed honors," to follow him once more:

> It is obvious that President Roosevelt will not be re-elected for the third term unless he has the overwhelming support of the men and women of labor. If he is therefore re-elected, it will mean that the members of the Congress of Industrial Organizations have rejected my advice and recommendation. I will accept the result as being the equivalent of a vote of no confidence and will retire as president of the CIO, at its convention in November. This action will save our great movement . . . from the embarrassment and handicap of my leadership during the reign of President Roosevelt.[38]

Hillman exclaimed when Lewis had finished speaking: "Now why did he do that? John Lewis is through—this is really the end for him!"

Lewis had done something that men wise in politics always avoid; he had gambled on an ultimatum from which there was no retreat. It was to be Lewis *or* Roosevelt. To his immense labor following he said: "Sustain me now, or repudiate me." Or in effect: "If you take Roosevelt, you lose me." He truly believed they would not risk losing Lewis.

Early in the next morning Hillman hastened to the White House, which nowadays, by special permission, he often entered by the back door; that is, as an off-the-record visitor. Roosevelt received him in the spacious bathroom, where he was being shaved as he sat in his wheel chair. The wan Harry Hopkins was there beside him too. Both seemed very sad and low. Roosevelt asked: "What now? What does this mean?" Hillman had never seen them so "thoroughly scared."

He said: "What are you worried about? It will be all right! So what if John Lewis made a speech for Willkie?" Lewis, he insisted, could not deliver the labor vote.

"I felt it was my job to help the President and Hopkins keep their chins up," he said afterward.[39]

What must be done now, he said, was to get to work at once to repair the damage. He would leave for New York immediately to prepare a "counterblast" at Lewis from the labor camp.

These were the last ten days before Election Day; Willkie was reported, by various polls, as moving up fast. The blow had been well timed for the campaign's eleventh hour.

Hillman rushed to New York by airplane with Maxwell Brandwen, now acting as his law counsel at the NDAC. All that day, at the Amalgamated headquarters, they worked over a reply to Lewis, completed that Saturday night after long telephone consultations with the White House. Within twenty-four hours the counterstatement of Hillman, in behalf of the Amalgamated and many other CIO unions, was being broadcast over the radio and through the press. It ran:

Mr. Lewis did not speak for any significant part of the CIO. . . . He did not even speak for the membership of his own United Mine Workers' Union . . . who introduced 47 pro-Roosevelt resolutions at their last convention.

No enlightened American worker can support the anti-Roosevelt forces which are backed by the Girdlers, the Weirs, and the Henry Fords. . . . Unless labor wishes to crucify itself at the polls, which it will not, the labor vote will prove to be a landslide for Roosevelt.[40]

With Sidney Hillman, one of the most enlightened of American trade unionists, leaping to Roosevelt's defense, it was hard for the public to conceive of the President as a labor-crushing dictator. More money was raised; more and bigger election rallies were ordered.

Spurred by Hillman, officers of the Amalgamated and the Textile Workers' Union and many others took the stump in New York, Pennsylvania, Missouri, and Ohio in a final electioneering drive. No gibes were spared at Lewis' expense, the alleged "Benedict Arnold" who had "sold labor down the river for a Republican Cabinet post." [41]

It was not a polite campaign. The debate over national policies became a travesty in which both parties shamelessly strove to "sell" the best slogans. Willkie was both for eternal peace and for military aid to Britain against the Nazis. Roosevelt was for conscription while also promising that our boys "are not going to be sent into any foreign wars." In the final week the President spoke with his old vigor. The fight had become a "personal issue" between himself and Mr. Lewis, and, as Harry Hopkins remarked, he now put his heart into it if only to discredit Lewis.[42]

When Roosevelt was in such a mood he was hard to beat. In Pennsylvania and Ohio even the coal miners voted three to one for Roosevelt. On November 5, 1940, the President was re-elected by a wide enough margin, and John L. Lewis was in deep trouble.

v

The weeks that followed the election were a decisive period for those who were directing the country's defense program. The air battle above England was on; submarine warfare was increasing in fury; the Nazi-Fascist armies were advancing in the Balkans and in Africa. Now decisions were to be made on plans already under consideration for aid to Britain (by Lend-Lease), the accumulation of raw materials, industrial controls, priorities, the allocation of labor, and the fixing of labor standards. For Hillman at his post in the Defense Commission an incredibly busy period began. Yet developments in the labor movement itself seemed no less critical than the military procurement problem in their immediate bearing on the whole defense program. Much depended on the course of action of one man who still held sway over millions of workers in our heavy industries.

One of the key problems that had been assigned to Sidney Hillman was that of bringing about the unification of the two rival labor camps, for it appeared impossible to speed production and build great arsenals and shipyards—in short, mountains of war matériel—while the CIO and AFL workers kept fighting or raiding each other in vital industries.

As one of his first steps in office Hillman had organized a Labor Advisory Board for the Defense Commission, representing the AFL, the CIO, and the railway Brotherhoods. These were to set forth a labor policy which Hillman would endeavor to put into effect through the NDAC. Yet no such policy could be made to work, there would be no end of labor strife, so long as Lewis threatened to raid the AFL unions by setting up dual organizations such as the huge catch-all union called "District 50," a branch of the United

Mine Workers which was entering building construction and other AFL territory.

Lewis had made his great gamble and vowed that if he lost he would retire as president of the CIO at the approaching convention in November. But would he really step down in favor of Vice-President Philip Murray as he had promised? Would the unification of the CIO and AFL be accomplished at last, as Roosevelt and Hillman desired, thus diminishing the stature of Lewis and the threat he offered to the armament program?

It happened that the General Executive Board of the Amalgamated was holding meetings in Atlantic City at about the same time that the CIO's Executive Board was in session, the week before the convention was to open. On entering the government service Hillman had resigned from the Executive Board of the CIO but still held his old post in the Amalgamated. The rival leaders thus encountered each other on the boardwalk and chatted together amicably enough, much like lawyers on opposite sides in a court trial. However, the reports of Lewis' tirades against him and of his determination to have the CIO pass resolutions condemning the government's labor policy under the defense program made Hillman wary. Lewis was scarcely acting like a man resigned to quitting the powerful office he held in the labor movement.

Among the executives of the Amalgamated conferring at Atlantic City there were several warm-tempered men who were thoroughly fed up with Mr. Lewis. Some wanted to leave the CIO if he remained at its helm. But Hillman argued that the Amalgamated, as one of the founding unions, had a real responsibility to the CIO and should not consider leaving it under any circumstances. It ought to participate in CIO affairs more effectively than before, should Lewis resign, he urged. Plainly, neither he nor the others were as yet certain of that. He agreed that steps should be taken to curb the powers of the CIO's president and unite with the AFL upon acceptable terms. The Amalgamated men were indignant at the fact that Lewis had published his own speech against Roosevelt in full in the *CIO Daily News* while excluding articles defending the other side. Scarcely any mention was made in the *CIO Daily News* of Roosevelt's re-election! It was also proposed, with Hillman's approval, that the constitution of the CIO be amended to exclude Communists, Nazis, and Fascists from holding office in the organization.[43]

Meanwhile, out of the meetings of the Executive Board of the CIO came rumors of a resolution, advocated by Lewis, condemning the labor policy of the National Defense Commission and declaring that "labor had been offered no voice." It was a lawyers' brief aimed at Hillman particularly.[44]

Hillman hurried back to his office in Washington on November 17. There he received a copy of the proposed CIO resolution, read it through, and prepared a vigorous rebuttal, reciting the actual facts about the Labor Division he had set up, and tracing the development of the NDAC's relatively enlightened labor policy. He had planned to absent himself from this CIO convention and was about to send his written reply to the accusations against himself, when he received news by telephone, on November 19, of sensational developments on the floor of the convention that made his presence there imperative.

From the very start of the convention on November 18, Lewis was seen to be using every trick in his bag in order to whip up the passions of the union delegates to a climax of his own shaping. He was, after all, an artist of crowds. This was a great human drama being played out in a hotel ballroom by a superb old Shakespearean actor with a golden voice, the most animated features, and the bushiest of eyebrows. Indeed it was more theatrical by far than any ordinary political or institutional gathering, because labor men are less inhibited or machine-like in their emotions than, for instance, lawyers or businessmen, and more disposed to healthful orgies of fraternal love or hate.

In the lobbies, before the curtain rose, many of the 2,600 delegates appeared wearing huge buttons with the legend: *"We want Lewis."* Placards with the same device seemed to spring up everywhere. There were also visible all those little signs and warnings of what political scientists in America characterize as a "stampede."

Would Lewis resign or be "drafted"? Would he actually let fall the toga upon the shoulders of his old lieutenant, Philip Murray—who moved about looking like a pale, tormented soul? Could Roosevelt or Hillman's people do anything about this? These were the questions on everyone's lips as that seething crowd rose, upon Lewis' impressive entrance, to give him an ovation lasting forty-three minutes. The faithful mine workers, the Communists, and others raised up high their draft-Lewis placards, paraded, yelled, sang, wept, and embraced each other. For a long time the chanting and roaring went on—*"Lewis is our leader! Lewis is our leader!"*—while he smiled and waved and drank in the intoxicating sight. While all this pandemonium was going on, many delegates went up to the rostrum and entreated Lewis to reconsider his pledge to resign.

Meanwhile reports were circulated that Philip Murray had definitely declined to stand for the presidency, though he had been designated from the throne as the heir apparent. He had been thoroughly worn out by raging disputes with Lewis, who had refused to give him a promise of full support and a free hand. Informed labor journalists were saying that if Murray, despite the pleas of his friends and spiritual advisers, stuck to his decision to retire from this strange contest, then the draft-Lewis campaign would gather all the greater momentum. "Personally, I don't want the presidency," Murray said miserably.[45]

During the long uproar over Lewis' entrance, only the group of Amalgamated delegates and a few of their allies sat impassively in their seats. Amid all the surface excitement it was observed how some of them, as well as important spokesmen for the auto, steel, and shipyard workers, went about quietly "caucusing" with known opponents of Lewis, as if in haste to arrange for his retirement.[46] Now if the pro-Hillman bloc, a sizable minority of the CIO, could be suppressed or driven out, the road would be open to the Lewis steam roller. As the convention proceeded it became apparent that this was Lewis' intention.

He was in rare form; his opening address began, rather pompously, with a paraphrase from Lincoln's Gettysburg speech: "Threescore months ago a new union was formed, conceived in liberty . . ." The panorama of CIO triumphs during the reign of Lewis was unrolled. Now the real issue in America, he said, was not foreign war, but "fifty-two million shrunken bellies." Then came what seemed his swan song, executed with much feeling:

> Now, my friends, I came to this convention to make a report of my stewardship as your president and to listen to anybody who wanted to criticize, or traduce, or vituperate, or just rave. It is quite all right. I won't be with you long. I have done my work. In just a day or two I will be out of this office which at the moment I occupy. [Cries of "No! No!"] I shall hope that whoever you elect as my successor . . . you will give him your support without stint . . . because he will need it. I ought to know. But

this is the way of life. Some are able to carry through and some fall. But there is nothing to worry about. . . .

Here Lewis' voice broke, tears rolled down his cheeks, and slowly, with dignity, he drew his handkerchief from his pocket and brushed them away. Then he resumed:

Some great statesman once said the heights are cold. I think that is true. The poet said, "Who ascends to the mountaintop finds the loftiest peaks encased in mist and snow." I think that is true. It is just as true in the ranks of labor . . . and we cannot stop to weep and wear sackcloth and ashes because something that happened yesterday did not meet with our approval, or that we did not have a dream come true.

For sheer pathos this was better than *The Lady of the Camelias* and its farewell scene of renunciation by the dying mistress. Many of the audience sobbed openly—not so the Amalgamated delegates.

On the second day the order of business included first a discussion of the officers' report and then the resolution censuring the Roosevelt Administration and the Labor Division of the NDAC for permitting the award of defense contracts to anti-labor firms. Hillman's associates, Blumberg and Salerno and George Baldanzi, vice-president of the Textile Workers' Union, then asked for the floor, to protest at President Lewis' iron censorship of the *CIO Daily News,* by which almost all reference to a political party headed by a man named Roosevelt was omitted and only the political speeches of Lewis printed.

Lewis answered with aplomb that no blame could be attached to the editor for this, but only to himself, since he had requested that the editor, Len De Caux, follow such policies.[47]

Frank Rosenblum next entered the fray by introducing a resolution ordering the incoming officers of the CIO to begin negotiations for union with the AFL immediately. The leftists, such as Michael Quill, came to Lewis' defense with violent attacks on the Hillmanites. An anti-Communist resolution was offered by the Amalgamated delegates and blocked by Lewis. Now he seemed fully aroused by the opposition voices that seemed to come from many sides. His replies grew more cutting, until it seemed as if he were trying to goad beyond endurance the people who spoke for Hillman.

There was to be no "dishonorable peace" with the AFL, he insisted:

Five years ago a little group of men representing some eight organizations . . . highly resolved that come high or come low they would go forward. . . . Some of them did so, and they have kept the faith, while others have fallen by the wayside.

And one of those men was Mr. Dubinsky, representing the Ladies' Garment Workers, who swore by every god that ever sat on high that he, Dubinsky, would never waver in the cause, and he signed the scroll, and by book, bell, and candle vowed to affiliate to this movement. And where is Dubinsky today? He has crept back into the American Federation of Labor. . . .

And Zaritsky, he was the man representing the Cap and Millinery Workers. . . . And now above all the clamor comes the piercing wail and the laments of the Amalgamated Clothing Workers. . . .

There is no peace because you are not yet strong enough to command peace on honorable terms. . . . And I am not weary of the fight. And after all, I come from those who have fought through centuries and I do not yield to any men. [Then, his voice almost a whisper] In addition to that, I do not have any inferiority complex.

The Lewisites were yelling with joy, calling for more blood. At the suggestion that the mind of the AFL be "explored," he made a thrust that drew a roar of laughter from the crowd:

I have done a lot of exploring in Bill Green's mind and I give you my word there is nothing there!

Mr. Green says there will never be peace until the shadow of John Lewis grows less. Well, the official shadow of John Lewis is growing less. [Cries of "No! No!" from the floor.] That shadow is diminishing. And yet, if I read the temper of this convention aright and if I understand what is in the hearts and minds of the millions of members . . . you are not going to dishonor yourselves or sell the rights of these people that you represent. I don't care about some of the delegates of this convention who dissent from the tenor of these remarks. It annoys me not at all. I have [no] great concern for those who are possessed of little faith and whose courage is waning. If they find the night too dark, if they find the way too rough, let them sit by the wayside . . . while those other valiant spirits go on in this great movement. They will carry on! . . .

Dubinsky took the easy way. Zaritsky took the easy way. If there is anybody else in the CIO who wants to take the easy way, in God's name, let them go! [48] [Italics added.]

His face livid with emotion, and pouring forth insult and injury, and even, by innuendo, race hatred, Lewis "slammed the door on

peace with the AFL and challenged the Amalgamated and other pro-
Hillman unions to clear out of the CIO." As he finished, a great
roar of applause came from the crowd, which burst into a renewed
"draft parade" around the hall. The whole convention seemed on
the verge of riot and bloodshed. The Amalgamated delegates sat
"grave, immobile, furious." [49]

Order was restored with considerable difficulty by Murray, who
was in the chair. When this session adjourned soon afterward, the
Amalgamated delegation, headed by Potofsky, repaired to their
hotel rooms and took counsel with one another. It seemed clear
enough to them that the stage was set for a Lewis "stampede" on
the day following. Some of those present were for "bolting" the
convention. After some discussion it was decided that Potofsky was
to call Hillman in Washington and urge that he come to Atlantic
City at once to deal with the crisis. Mrs. Hillman added her plea
over the telephone: "You *must* come at once, Sidney. Things look
bad." [50]

He was terribly busy: there was a strike at an aircraft plant, of all
things, and many other problems needed his constant attention. He
agreed, however, to come that night, and proceeded at once by train
to Philadelphia, where toward nine o'clock he met his wife and the
Amalgamated delegates at a hotel. There, during a conference that
lasted until long after midnight, he learned what had happened and
how strong were the chances for a Lewis "stampede" as against the
nomination of Philip Murray. He grasped at once that Lewis' theatrical outburst had been deliberately calculated to drive the Amalgamated people into leaving the CIO, and urged that such an outcome
would only ensure Lewis' complete triumph and must be avoided at
all costs. He would address the convention the next day.

"It looks bad in there, like a lynching bee," Jack Kroll warned
Hillman. "You'll have to hit hard."

"That's all right," Hillman said quietly, "I'll be there."

Late that night he drove to Atlantic City from Philadelphia and
went to a hotel for a short sleep. He rose early, and well before nine
o'clock strolled into the almost deserted convention hall. When the
delegates trooped in somewhat later they found Hillman already on
the platform calmly chatting with the other CIO officers, and there
was no chance for a hostile demonstration, as there might have been

if he had made an entrance later before the full assembly. It was only a small detail, but worthy of Hillman.

The operations of that day, November 20, were later described in the press as "a dramatic duel between labor's greatest showman and labor's greatest strategist." [51] Hillman was terribly tired when he arrived in Atlantic City. In fact, he would have loved to be somewhere else. He hated brawls and, in fact, violent explosions of any kind, such as had been going on here for two days and promised to flare up again because of his very presence. Yet here he was once more when the chips were down.

It was a time of supreme danger, he knew, the crisis hour in which control of the organization of millions of industrial workers was at stake. Indeed, Hillman's very physical safety, many thought, was in jeopardy here among this crowd intoxicated by the wine of Lewis' oratory.

He had come, as his friends observed, with no fixed plan of action mapped out in advance but had seemed, as he listened to their reports, to be feeling his way. He had no time to prepare a speech, save for some written notes on the work of the Labor Division of the NDAC. But his friends felt sure that he would *improvise* something under the inspiration of the crisis—for he had "slept on his problem" and in the morning was ready to attack it with the resources of a fresh mind. (Many workers in the sciences and arts have related that, when faced with seemingly insurmountable difficulties, they have learned to depend upon their powers of spontaneous improvisation.)

Lewis had roared like a hungry lion. Hillman had moved in quietly and unobtrusively; he had, so to speak, walked into the arena to deal with the lion before a crowd that was literally crying for blood. Lewis had vaunted his own deathless courage, even that of his ancestors (!), and by inference belittled the fighting spirit of his opponents. But there are other kinds of courage, such as that which Socrates is said to have defined as "the knowledge of the grounds of fear and hope."

The CIO was faced with two alternatives: accepting the leadership of Lewis again (despite his pledge), by way of the "stampede," or turning to that of Philip Murray, as promised by Lewis. Neither alternative looked too good as yet to Hillman, for so far as he knew then Murray was the loyal vassal of Lewis. Yet the second alternative seemed more promising than the first. Some cautious overtures had been made to Murray offering support from the Roosevelt-Hillman side; but he had held himself aloof up to now, fearing a painful rupture with his old leader. Yet Murray was also tormented by anxiety about what Lewis would do, and the prospect of himself becoming a "captive" president. To the mind of the Odysseus-like Hillman, nevertheless, there came the hope that the irresponsible power of John L. Lewis might yet be curbed if he could be forced to keep his pledge and step down in favor of his lieutenant. Perhaps the lieutenant would become a captain in his own right one day? It was toward this end that Hillman felt he must move while doing all that was possible to close the breach between the warring factions.

As soon as Lewis came in, amid loud cheers from the partisan galleries, Hillman went up to him, shook hands, and said grimly: "John, I want the floor at eleven o'clock." Lewis assented. The newspaper photographs afterward showed them holding each other's hand, Lewis frowning, Hillman looking startled, his face tired and drawn. Many persons in the audience showed surprise and no pleasure at seeing Hillman there.

Some resolutions were read off at the start of the day's session while Hillman waited. Then it was his turn to speak. He began amid a great hush, his voice deep and harsh. Hillman was no Daniel Webster of the working stiffs; his speech was not studded with quotations from Shakespeare or Tennyson or Robert W. Service. But his thought was clear as a bell. To many whose brains had become overwrought, he recalled that personal power was not enough in itself, that organizations, like human communities, must see to it that power is contained within the frame of a responsible program.

I hope that whatever remarks I make will not be misinterpreted. I have no feelings of bitterness toward anyone in the Congress of Industrial Organizations. I have enjoyed my association with all of them. I have considered it a privilege to be given the opportunity to do my part, little as it was. . . .

This is a momentous convention. *I hope every delegate recognizes his responsibility.* . . . Remember that the eyes of the workers throughout the nation are on this great assembly.

Not only labor but everyone who is concerned with the future of our nation hopes and prays that *responsibility will prevail,* that we will do our duty as we see it, and not indulge in the kind of thing that we might regret in the days to come.

I speak to you as a man with thirty years' experience in our great labor movement. I have watched this movement. *I have seen men, leaders, come and go. We have the great obligation to lay out policies and follow them, no matter what the cost, no matter what the reaction of groups here or there may be.* [Italics added.] We may not be given many opportunities to organize. You know what division of labor has meant; every time there is division it destroys everything we have built. Those of us who love labor and those of us who have given our lives in the fight for labor know this to be true.

Lewis was not to be permitted to divide and rule the CIO by driving out the opposition:

Now let me say to you . . . there are misunderstandings, misinformation about the . . . Amalgamated Clothing Workers. As the responsible officer of the ACWA I say to you that there has never been a suggestion of our organization leaving the CIO. The Amalgamated will stay in the CIO! There has been some wishful thinking outside and maybe inside of the CIO. The Amalgamated will, without indulging in any boastfulness, without defying anybody, state its position firmly. . . . The Amalgamated will submit to the democratic process of a majority decision of our organization; but we will continue to fight for what we believe are constructive policies. . . . We are going to fight for industrial organization. We were willing to do so even when we had to stand alone.

Hillman then proceeded to give some report of his activities as head of the Labor Division of the National Defense Commission. He declared that all were free to criticize him; that was the democratic way.

It will be a sorry day for America, for the labor movement, and for all the people if it ever comes to pass that we are afraid to state our opposition or discuss our differences. . . . But, delegates, I find no difficulty in reconciling the objectives of labor and the objectives of national defense; they are intertwined, they are inseparable.

Those who would use the national emergency to undo the humane legislation for labor enacted in the past eight years were in effect working for "the dictators," he said; they were "undermining that which gives labor and the common man a stake in our nation." And Hillman was fighting them. Despite the fact that the law still required the award of government contracts to the lowest bidder, he had persuaded President Roosevelt to set forth an enlightened policy with regard to labor-law compliance in defense contracts. His Labor Division, to be sure, had moved slowly. But the Defense Commission to which it was subordinate had been in existence only five months. He reminded his hearers that

During that time, a little political debate, as you know, was going on in our country, and a number of people did not have their minds on the details of national defense and were out in the field trying to influence the electorate of America.

Factious strife in the field of labor as well as politics had delayed events. But Hillman did not wish to enter into a lengthy debate on this question. He still hoped that whatever differences he had with John L. Lewis were "not personal and will not be personal. I tell you from my heart that I do not put it on a personal basis." He went on:

I do not need to tell you of the need for national defense. . . . I hope you are not resting under the illusion that "it cannot happen here." Where is free labor in France? In concentration camps. . . . The only thing that can stop us from getting involved in this massacre is to be ready to meet the totalitarians if they choose to invade this hemisphere, and to help democracy abroad. . . . Bombs are exploding in the workmen's sections in every part of Britain. Labor in Britain is fighting. . . . Who wants to live in a world dominated by scoundrels?

Hillman then turned to the problems of the CIO again:

Let no one say that the Amalgamated or its officers are either scared or tired of doing the job. In every city our dead are buried. . . . We have not built our organization the easy way. . . . No organization that amounts to a tinker's damn was built the easy way. . . .

I also know from my experience that you don't make progress just through power. You have to have a constructive policy. A powerful locomotive put to use with no good rails over which to run will just be smashed up. And so I am concerned with policies. I hold to no formula. Life cannot be fitted into any formula. What is right today may be wrong tomorrow. What I have learned is to look at the objective and try to utilize whatever strength we have to reach that objective. And our objective is no secret. It is a happy America where no child will cry for the lack of milk and no man will go hungry. And our aim is to achieve this objective through the democratic process. No short cuts to heaven will do.

At this point Hillman spoke in favor of the anti-Communist resolution presented by the Amalgamated delegates, saying that he had observed the Communists for long years and refused to be misled by their doctrines, whether they assailed him or praised him. The miners' union, he pointed out, had, in its bylaws, erected safeguards against penetration by Communists, and "I say, what is good enough for the United Mine Workers is good enough for the CIO." On this issue he was aware that he differed with Lewis, yet he spoke of him with the utmost gallantry. Here, to illustrate that he meant what he was saying, he strode across the platform to where Lewis was sitting and shook his hand vigorously, saying:

I have considered my association with John L. Lewis the greatest privilege. There came a time when we had differences, honest differences of opinion. And I give him credit at all times for having treated our differences with respect. . . . I regret more than I can tell you that these differences arose. I think it is bad for the labor movement . . . but I don't question John Lewis' right to speak. . . . And I know when John Lewis speaks he speaks effectively. . . . And when I can be in agreement with him I like his effectiveness. And when I am in disagreement with him I am afraid of his effectiveness. Because I know that when he undertakes something there are no reservations. . . . I hope that out of this convention there will come a stronger labor movement . . . and as to the differences of opinion, time will prove whether we were right or not.

After these compliments (which brought forth loud cheers), after these moves toward conciliation, Hillman turned to deliver his swift finishing stroke. The great man, before 50,000,000 radio listeners, had pledged himself to resign and Hillman, reminding the whole world of this pledge (not yet consummated), was going to accept Lewis' resignation in advance (!) with thanks, and in effect nominate the successor he had chosen before anybody in that convention could wake up from his surprise.

I regret that John L. Lewis will not be the leader of this organization. I know there is nothing else that he can do and will do and will agree to do but what he believes to be the best for the organized labor movement. I have greater respect for a man who in a crisis stands by his guns. . . . I hope to be present in your convention at the election of your officers, but I may be called away. You know I will not serve as vice-president. My work on the NDAC will not allow me the time for that. I hope you will thresh out your differences and you will elect such officers as will command the confidence of the membership you represent, and *it is my considered judgment that when John L. Lewis steps down there must be a demand for Phil Murray.* [Italics added.] [52]

Hillman had thus managed both to "praise Caesar and to bury him," as one observer reported. To this feverish gathering he had brought the cooling breath of common sense. Everything had been brought out in the open; the issues were clearly drawn. "Hillman coldly, logically killed any hopes for a draft-Lewis movement," as well-informed accounts in the press recorded, by nominating Murray, as it seemed, three days ahead of time.[53]

Now an organized demonstration in honor of Hillman and Murray got under way. King Lewis was dead. Long live King Murray!

On the next day, his hand forced, Lewis hastened things by nominating his old assistant, and Hillman, who had stayed on, seconded the nomination. The newspaper headlines were substantially correct in reporting that "HILLMAN SAVES CIO FROM SPLIT— QUELLS LEWIS." Though Lewis had held all the trump cards, packed the convention, and led in oratorical flourishes, the soft-spoken strategist of the tailors had seen to it that control over the big labor federation was taken from him. Philip Murray, who had been so dejected by the ambiguous attitude of his old chief, now, at any rate, had the promise of strong support from the Hillman faction and behind him, of course, President Roosevelt. There was, however, to be a difficult transition period of a year in which Philip Murray struggled to consolidate his power in office and, in his own words, assert his "manhood" against a terrible adversary. But Hillman's admirers were convinced that he had saved the CIO from its "rule-or-ruin" leadership in a time of national danger. He was the only man in the labor movement who had successfully challenged the power of Lewis in his heyday. He himself later could scarcely explain how he had managed the whole affair, except to say that "it just came to me while I was up there talking." [54]

Chapter Twenty-One

NATIONAL

DEFENSE

COMMISSIONER

*Sidney Hillman's was a very distinctive contribution
to our national defense program which has never
been properly estimated.*
                                        —John Lord O'Brian

The picture of America's preparations for defense after
May 1940 is essentially that of a democracy, geared to the
ways of peace, now turning awkwardly and hesitantly to discipline
itself for the crisis of war. Roosevelt, earlier, had both chided the dictator governments and told them that we were not going to be drawn
into war. When Poland was invaded in September 1939, he had declared: "There is no thought of . . . putting the nation, either in its
defense or in its internal economy, on a war basis." But after the collapse of the French Army in May 1940, with the world balance of
power shifting overnight—when, as the President said, Christian civilization itself seemed to be coming to an end—it needed that this neutral
policy be reversed. Yet Roosevelt felt his way cautiously. As many
commentators agree, the "isolationists" were, up to then, in an overwhelming majority among the American people, who "would have
been glad to see the war end on almost any inconclusive terms, so
that America would not be drawn into it." [1] Moreover, the eve of a

presidential election campaign was not the best time to inform the public of what unpleasant medicine was in store for them.

We were, after all, a democracy. Our businessmen were free to do business as usual or to attack the head of the state. Our millions of unemployed were free to do nothing. Everyone was free to plunge into an election contest that tore the country apart for four months. The New Dealers and the dollar-a-year men who now descended upon Washington were free to bicker with each other, as were the different factions in Congress. The country moved all too slowly to prepare for the emergency, and mistakes were made. But in a democracy as fortunate as ours mistakes need not be as final and fateful as those arrived at by a Mussolini.

Some preliminary surveys of our military resources had been made the year before, and scarce raw materials were quietly accumulated. On May 16, 1940, when France seemed doomed, Roosevelt suddenly asked Congress for a huge increase of Army and Navy appropriations and called for 50,000 airplanes. Many sober-faced visitors had been trooping into the White House to offer the President their advice in these dark days. Bernard M. Baruch, who had been chairman of the War Industries Board in World War I, emerged from a conference with Roosevelt on May 22 and declared, apparently in line with the President's views, that an organization with the sweeping powers of the 1917 Board was not needed as yet.[2]

Roosevelt had been working with his White House advisers all that week on plans for a defense program; and on the day after he talked with Baruch he telephoned William S. Knudsen, president of General Motors, inviting him to be a member of a proposed National Defense Advisory Commission that was to be in charge of production. At about the same time he telephoned Sidney Hillman, to whom was assigned the task of co-ordinating defense labor. Roosevelt had not forgotten that his friend Sidney had been one of the most energetic officials of the old NRA. The other members appointed to the new seven-man commission were Ralph Budd, in charge of transportation; Edward Stettinius, industrial materials; Leon Henderson, prices; Chester C. Davis, agricultural products; and Miss Harriet Elliott of the University of North Carolina as consumers' representative.

The new Commission, like earlier New Deal organizations, was set up as an adjunct of the Executive Branch of the government. Roosevelt apparently had some special political reason for not using permanent Federal departments such as Commerce and Labor, and asked Congress only for "temporary" or emergency appropriations. The NDAC, moreover, was to be merely advisory and was to function under a law of 1916 setting up a peacetime-emergency National Defense Council (within the Cabinet) under Woodrow Wilson. The public was not yet ready, the time had not yet come for more drastic procedure, Roosevelt felt. There was not even a chairman for the NDAC. Knudsen, who had been warned by his associates at General Motors that he might run into trouble trying to work with the Roosevelt Administration, at the first gathering of the defense commissioners in the White House asked bluntly: "Who will be the boss around here?" Roosevelt answered firmly: "I will be the boss." William McReynolds of the White House staff was designated as the Commission's presiding officer and secretary and was to maintain liaison with the President.

At his first conference with the commissioners early in June, Roosevelt gave them a serious little indoctrination talk. Stressing the gravity of their task, he said that all that had been accomplished for business and labor and agriculture in the past seven years was now endangered. He suggested that the commissioners meet twice a week, unless emergencies prevented them from doing so, and outlined a plan for the division of their labor, by which each was to be responsible for his own job. Knudsen, for example, was to advise the Army and Navy ordnance officers on industrial production and, because of his specialized knowledge, expedite the making of airplanes, tanks, and guns. Hillman was to see to it that labor-management relations were maintained in good balance, while existing labor standards were also preserved. The others were to gather information and furnish advice in their respective fields of transportation, raw materials, agricultural products, and price maintenance. The directives and the policies they established for the defense program were to be transmitted to the National Defense Council (consisting of all the members of the Cabinet save the Secretaries of the Treasury and State), who were to guide themselves by such advice. Our advisory commissioners thus had no executive powers. But Roosevelt explained that they would exercise a real authority, because he would back up their recommendations, assuming, of course, that he agreed with them. This was what he told Knudsen, who was also to be given some power of review over all defense contracts costing over $500,000.

Hillman's was in many ways the meanest assignment, as soon became apparent. At a subsequent private conference with Roosevelt on June 12, 1940, he was told that he was to assume "complete responsibility for the labor policy of the whole defense program, and that he was to see to it that it was enforced." The President would back him up, he said, and as Hillman related afterward, "Every department of government affecting labor in defense [was to be] under my jurisdiction. He gave me the further responsibility for the labor supply, and the whole training of labor defense industries." [3] This meant that he would supplement and, where necessary, supersede the Secretary of Labor, Madame Perkins.

It had been one of Roosevelt's characteristic tricks to set up overlapping government bureaus, ever since the establishment of the NRA in 1933. On a number of occasions he confessed that he rather enjoyed seeing his executive assistants competing with each other and thought that it "kept them on their toes." [4] That this method led to considerable duplication of work and no little bureaucratic confusion disturbed him not at all.

The appointment of Hillman as "employment manager" under the defense program was, on the whole, not too badly received in the press. It was attributed to his having brains, if no old school tie. The presence of Hillman, a lifelong progressive of the labor movement, along with Leon Henderson and one or two of the other appointees, made for a strong New Deal representation in the NDAC, indicating, as Arthur Krock commented, that the "social gains" of the New Deal, in the form of wage-and-hour limitations, were to be conserved. [5]

Lewis, of course, was enraged at not having been consulted. Mr. William Green likewise reflected the vexation felt in AFL circles at the choice of one of the top CIO leaders. Matthew Woll remarked that a leader of clothing workers was an unfortunate selection for the task of war preparation. Roosevelt, however, early in June, called Green to the White House and, it was reported, did his best to placate him. A few weeks later Daniel Tracy, president of the International Brotherhood of Electrical Workers (AFL), was named an Assistant Secretary of Labor. Thereafter Mr. Tracy and Hillman (who, incidentally, had recommended his appointment) worked hand in hand in dealing with many labor troubles. Indeed Hillman had very little difficulty with the AFL people.

His influence was supposed to be large among the heavy-industry unions of the CIO, so vital for defense production; and yet it was here that he ran into the worst snags. Lewis was still reigning over the CIO in 1940, and at that very season was waging his personal campaign to unhorse Roosevelt. From June to November 1940, amid the uproar of the third-term battle, the progress of rearmament was slow. Some of our captains of industry were curious to know whether Roosevelt would be defeated before undertaking the drastic conversion of their factories into aircraft-engine or tank plants. Mr. Knudsen, acting as Roosevelt's emissary in these quarters, suffered a good many snubs at the start, while Hillman was regularly called away from his plans for the allocation and training of defense labor to take to the hustings in behalf of the Democratic Administration and return the blows of Lewis and other opponents.

On being appointed a member of the NDAC, Hillman had asked his friend, Maxwell Brandwen, the lawyer who had handled the Amalgamated's court cases for nearly twenty years, to accompany him to Washington as his counsel and liaison officer. While Hillman delayed his departure for Washington for about ten days, during which he underwent medical treatment at a hospital—for he was suffering again under a painful arthritic attack—Brandwen began to set up shop for him in the luxurious new marble palace of the Federal Reserve Board at Washington, where space was assigned to the NDAC. From the start Brandwen was joined by the labor economist, Dr. Isador Lubin, who was to act as Hillman's deputy. As head of the Bureau of Labor Statistics of the Labor Department since 1933, Lubin was an expert in his field. He afterward was appointed a White House aide, attached to the service of Harry Hopkins, but he maintained close liaison between Hillman and Hopkins, who directed Lend-Lease.

In the second week of June, Hillman came bustling down to Washington and tackled his job with great zest. With his restless temperament, it gave him a deep sense of relief to be able to do something instead of merely waiting to see what dreadful things the Nazi-Fascists would do next. "The biggest lockout against civilization" was being carried on, he told his Amalgamated associates. It was a war of terror, when one thought of the refugees from Paris being bombed along the roads of France. But it was also "a war of workshops" and that, he pointed out, "was fortunate for us," because he was sure America would do a splendid job along those lines.[6]

By disposition an organizer, he looked always toward the over-all plan and was sometimes negligent of details—often the tendency of good administrators. By contrast, Knudsen, though a successful builder of vast automobile assembly lines, tended to lose himself in details.

Hillman's job, whose scope had first to be explored and mapped out carefully, involved much research and gathering of information, as well as administrative work and the settlement of industrial disputes. To set up the Labor Division within the NDAC, numerous experts and dollar-a-year-men were engaged, until, by the end of 1940, a personnel of about 300 was retained in Hillman's division alone out of about 1,500 serving under the NDAC. The duties and powers of his office gradually defined themselves, though "in a rather haphazard way . . . sometimes by presidential requests, usually verbal, for something to be done," or, at other times, by Hillman's bringing the suggestions to the President in the first place and having him make a formal request for the needed action. Sometimes added duties were staked out "through the assumption of authority by Hillman and his energetic liaison officer and legal counselor, Maxwell Brandwen, as occasion arose for some special action." [7]

Miss Perkins testified later, in her memoirs, that Sidney Hillman tended to "encroach" on others' offices. Under the NDAC this "poaching" was done mainly on the preserves of the Labor Department, in the field of mediation—and *with Roosevelt's authorization at the time* —a point which she has evidently forgotten.

A sudden inspiration or afterthought on the part of Franklin Roosevelt sometimes led to a considerable expansion of Hillman's duties. Thus, a week after he came to Washington, a Red Cross ship was suddenly struck for extra pay by seamen belonging to the National Maritime Union (CIO) because it had changed its destination from Bordeaux, France, to a port in Franco Spain. This union, under Joseph Curran, was known then to be left wing in its sympathies. Noting this, Roosevelt turned over what he called this "ideological problem" to Sidney, asking him to "do something about it." Sidney proceeded to mediate the affair during his first week in Washington, and from then on was occupied intermittently with strike-conciliation work, formerly the exclusive province of the Labor Department.[8]

Or again, in August 1940, Roosevelt received a letter from a very enlightened consulting engineer in Philadelphia who, foreseeing a shortage of factory space, made the ingenious proposal that unused plants be taken over in "ghost towns" of Pennsylvania and New England, where certain industries had moved out in late years, though many skilled workers still remained. Roosevelt turned this matter over to Hillman also. The engineer, Morris Llewellyn Cooke, proved to be an old acquaintance whom Hillman had known since the 1920's. Mr. Cooke was promptly put in charge of a very useful little office of his own, whose function it was to locate abandoned factory space or put to use outworn rolling mills and plants where parts of defense orders could be farmed out, as was done in England under the "bits-and-pieces" plan.

During the first small-scale strikes that broke out in 1940—when defense production was mostly in the blueprint stage—Hillman had a team ready to take up the work of mediation where the Labor Department indicated that its efforts were blocked. To represent industry in his Labor Division he engaged the services of Edwin D. Bransome, president of the Vanadium corporation. Mr. Bransome has been described as a very conservative type of business executive, but, as often happened with such people, he grew very fond of Hillman. Whenever trouble in some labor dispute was traced particularly to the employer, the respectable Mr. Bransome was sent out to reason with him. Mr. Bransome, it was found, often had a "softening effect." When the trouble seemed to come from the labor side, then Hillman and Dr. Lubin took over the task. Under them in the NDAC Labor Division's mediation bureau worked John Owens of the United Mine Workers, who represented the CIO, and Joseph Keenan for the AFL. Between them they divided up the field.[9] During the troublesome strike at the Vultee Aircraft company in November 1940, after the Labor Department had given notice that it had failed to win agreement, Hillman sent John Owens to California to negotiate with the United Auto Workers' Union, CIO; he himself remained in Washington close to the telephone day after day until the dispute was adjusted.

To know where and how much labor force was needed, one had to know the size of the planned defense program. But the budget was constantly being changed, starting at about nine billions for defense in 1940, and rising to many times that sum in 1941. Nevertheless, Dr. Lubin and two Labor Department economists serving under him proceeded to make statistical studies of the quantities of labor and types of workers available in various sections of the country. Estimates were also prepared showing the amount of skilled and semi-skilled labor that would be required in accordance with the rising tempo of defense production. Preliminary studies were made, too, of a project for training and re-employing some 4,000,000 persons.

There was still, in 1940, an enormous number of unemployed in the country—approximately 10,000,000, it was estimated—partly supported by the WPA, the CCC, and the National Youth Administration. Hillman's experts brought him the forecast that, under the impact of the big war-production drive, there would soon be a marked *shortage* of skilled labor and even of semi-skilled labor. Knudsen at first scoffed at the idea that any such shortage was possible, saying: "I never have trouble at General Motors getting workers." [10] That he had underestimated the situation was shown several months later, when Roosevelt sent an urgent letter to Knudsen and Hillman requesting that something be done at once about the severe scarcity of skilled machine-tool men.[11]

For ten years the slump in industry had permitted armies of skilled mechanics to die off without being replaced, or to lose their skills in non-mechanical work. Hillman's assistants were fully aware of this and predicted, as early as July or August 1940, not only that manpower would have to be directed or allocated as we approached the 1929 production levels, but that millions would have to be trained as well. Warned in advance about the need for labor training, Roosevelt, early in June 1940, ordered that this problem be turned over to Hillman as soon as he arrived in Washington to take up his new post.[12]

Following a suggestion from the White House, Hillman enlisted the aid of the "elder statesman" and financier, Owen D. Young, who had had some experience in organizing labor-training projects in World War I. Mr. Young conferred with Hillman and Roosevelt and soon produced an excellent and compact memorandum surveying the whole problem. He proposed a system of training-within-industry, to be coordinated by the government's defense agencies; and that training shops for apprentice mechanics be established mainly in going factories. Two professional personnel experts, Channing R. Dooley of the Socony-Vacuum Company and J. W. Dietz of Western Electric, were drafted to execute this program, after Hillman, Dr. Lubin, and Professor Floyd W. Reeves of Hillman's staff had worked it out to their satisfaction.

The training project was carried on through arrangements with hundreds of trade schools, engineering schools, and universities where the training of workers was to be initiated, and from there extended into defense plants. In addition, training groups, equipped with machine shops, were set up at numerous Civilian Conservation Corps and National Youth Administration camps throughout the country.

As early as June 26, 1940, at a meeting of the Defense Commission, Hillman had presented his preliminary plans for the labor-training program as his first undertaking, proposing that an appropriation of $17,000,000 be made to subsidize it at the start. The money, it was suggested, should be drawn in part from the budget of the WPA and in part from the funds of the United States Office of Education. His plan received the hearty approval of the Commission. By the late summer and autumn of 1940 it was under way in earnest.

Incidentally, Hillman encountered some serious resistance from the AFL metal- and machinery-craft unions, whose officers and members were disturbed at the idea of having many thousands of new workers hurriedly trained to enter their industries. The upgrading of mechanics is a legitimate concern of trade unions, and William Green was not slow to protest that the new program threatened their hard-won privileges. The President thereupon called Green to the White House and gave him assurances that Hillman would see to it that the armies of new apprentices would be employed and upgraded with due regard to seniority rights and in co-operation with the unions in the field.[13]

The importance of this program proved inestimable. It was launched none too soon. By the time Pearl Harbor was attacked, 1,500,000 workers had received, or were receiving, training so that they could be upgraded for skilled or semi-skilled mechanical labor.

Hillman's special administrative tasks at the NDAC were both novel and complex, calling forth all his imaginative and dynamic qualities. It took about three months of preliminary work during the summer of 1940 before he had his functions clearly marked out, in view of the uncertainty about jurisdiction and authority always prevailing in Washington under Roosevelt. Eventually it was determined that the function of the Labor Division, with its growing staff of economists, personnel managers, and labor experts, was not to find jobs, not to train people, but to co-ordinate the placement and training activities of existing Federal agencies, such as the U. S. Employment Service, the CCC, the NYA, and others. It was also to be a center for information about the changing supply of manpower, with its agents helping in the recruiting of needed workers, often by contacting local union offices all around the country. Here liaison with Professor Stacy May's statistical "clearinghouse" in the NDAC was of great help. In the third place, Hillman and his organization were held in readiness to mediate serious labor disputes either by teaming up with the Labor Department's Conciliation Service, or superseding it where necessary. A fourth function would be to safeguard the housing conditions of workers, who by the end of 1940 were beginning to swarm in great cavalcades toward towns or even sparsely populated country regions where arms production had been hastily begun, only to find no decent shelter of any kind available. (A special housing co-ordinator was soon appointed to deal with such problems, and Hillman's assistants worked in liaison with his office.)

From an early date Hillman favored decentralization, urging that concentration of defense industries in thickly populated areas be avoided. He also pleaded for the construction of low-cost housing for workers, a subject of which he had considerable knowledge. But over and above all this effort of co-ordination, Hillman was greatly occupied in seeing that under the emergency defense program the great social and legal gains won by labor during the past seven years should be maintained and, if possible, extended. To this end, as he realized, he must first build a bridge between the AFL and the CIO.

II

How should he go about this? He remembered well the War Labor Policy Board of 1917–19 and its good services. Its members and agents, however, had been businessmen, lawyers, and college professors. What he had in mind now was something like the very useful Labor Advisory Board of the NRA. Having been charged with establishing a labor policy for the defense program, he decided not to lay down such a policy by himself, but to set up a Labor Advisory Committee that would be a cross section of the labor movement as a whole and, with its members working in accord, would shape the labor policy. He would consult with this group at regular intervals, and it would lend its broad authority to the policies laid before the NDAC and President Roosevelt for adoption. There would be, according to his scheme, outstanding union officers from the CIO, the AFL, and the railway Brotherhoods. The advantage of such a "joint advisory board" would be its establishment of a working unity between the CIO and AFL factions. His own notes for a verbal report to Roosevelt indicated: "Policy will be not to cater to the extreme right or the extreme left of either camp." [14]

For several weeks he busied himself in organizing this joint labor board that was to serve under him, conferring with Vice-President Murray of the CIO, Daniel Tobin of the AFL, and on several occasions with Lewis, who made proposals unwelcome to Hillman. Lewis desired that certain persons, known as left-wing CIO leaders and then rigidly loyal to his own views, should be included. Hillman flatly rejected them on the ground that the persons in question might be out of sympathy with the President's defense program. Lewis thereupon protested bitterly by letter, and later vented himself in tirades before the CIO's Executive Council at what he alleged were Hillman's policies of demanding "political conformity" of labor-union leaders and suppressing freedom of opinion.

In his letter of protest to Hillman, on July 29, 1940, Lewis indicated his belief that unless Hillman selected for his Labor Advisory Committee persons satisfactory to Lewis, his procedure must be considered undemocratic:

> It is most disturbing to read some of the statements in the letter of X . . . with respect to your charges of practical disloyalty and political non-conformity. I sincerely hope that the administration of the defense program will not be influenced by such considerations.[15]

Hillman held his ground, denying that he had made such charges and pointing out that representation on his joint labor committee was to be determined not by the size or character of a union, but by the fact that "this committee was set up to aid me—as a member of the NDAC—on matters of labor policy." [16] (Lewis, on the eve of his marriage of convenience with Mr. Willkie, was being very quick to find fault with the man he had so recently extolled.)

Ignoring Lewis' wishes in the matter—and this was to be a very sore point between them in that election-ridden summer—Hillman went ahead and selected his own committee members and persuaded them to serve. As one Washington correspondent noted:

> Mr. Green of the AFL and Mr. Lewis, head of the CIO, were sulkily refusing to have anything to do with each other or with Mr. Hillman at the time Hillman picked his Labor Advisory Committee. . . . Out of nothingness Mr. Hillman established an informal united labor front.[17]

The Labor Advisory Committee, as announced on July 2, 1940, was composed of six AFL union executives, six from the CIO's mass-production unions, and four representatives of the railway Brotherhoods, just as Hillman had planned.

On July 3, 1940, the newspapers published a picture of the sixteen union executives sitting around a long council table, with Hillman presiding. It was a heart-warming sight, for many of those present headed organizations that had long been at war with each other. They were to meet once a week during the emergency period and work together for common aims, Hillman said: In a radio broadcast he gave at this time he stated: "We meet regularly. What is more to the point, we agree regularly. . . . American labor is at work to defend America."

The first thing he asked of this committee was that a labor policy for the defense program be framed which he would recommend for the approval of the NDAC and President Roosevelt. A memorandum with tentative provisions for the maintenance of existing labor-union standards in all war-material contracts negotiated by the Army and Navy was now presented to the committee members and approved.

Hillman had his "social view" of the labor movement and was determined to place its stamp on the great defense organization rising within the government. In talks before the Defense Commission he insisted that labor was not a "commodity," and that he was not a mere "processor" of workers for production purposes. Instead of regarding himself as the medium for channeling labor's energies and sentiments into the defense program, he seemed to consider himself "the personification of labor's viewpoint." [18] His hope and aim was to see to it that labor might gain a position as full working partner in government councils, a position commensurate with its decisive role as a producing class. The mountains of copper and steel being gathered together, the blueprints of weapons and machines of all sorts were important enough; but the mobilization of millions of human beings to extract these ores and process them was no less important. We would prove to the world, he said, "that the skill, the initiative, and the co-operation of free workers, together with American management and mechanical genius, can create an efficiency greater and more enduring than . . . the totalitarian system." [19]

We had many millions of unemployed still, he pointed out. Whereas Germans and Englishmen were forced to work long hours, there was no reason why Americans should not preserve the 8-hour day and 40-hour week, while drawing upon the rolls of the idle for increased output.

However, Army quartermaster and Navy ordnance officers were disposed to order matériel from those who could produce it most promptly and efficiently without regard to standards of hours and wages or recognition of unions. To the military mind the question of training or utilizing the unemployed, or avoiding congested industrial areas, or furnishing adequate housing for workers, seemed secondary to that of speed of output.

On July 19, 1940, Sidney Hillman addressed a letter to Secretary of the Navy Frank Knox, urging that every effort be made to have defense contracts distributed where unemployed workers might be re-hired, instead of loading overtime work, for instance, upon skilled mechanics already busy at Navy arsenals:

> I am thoroughly convinced that one of the most important factors that we must bear in mind . . . is the expeditious re-employment of those persons who are now without jobs. . . . When [a jobless man] is returned to work, as a result of the National Defense Program, we give him not only a feeling of worthiness, but also a sense of making a contribution to the protection of his country.[20]

The Navy Department, however, like the Army, was slow to adjust itself to Hillman's ideas of labor policy.

Outside Washington the spirit of business-as-usual still ruled the country. Henry Ford, for example, held that the British Empire wasn't worth saving, and at first refused to accept orders for British munitions of war. Other large concerns likewise showed no great haste to lend themselves to Roosevelt's plans. Some of them were disturbed by rumors that the President had said: "There will be no millionaires coming out of this defense program." Were profits, then, to be limited to something like 6 or 8 per cent by way of a severe excess-profits tax? Another thing disquieting to the industrialists was the fact that the labor leader Hillman sat high in the councils of the government. A report of something he had said in condemnation of profiteers "leaked" to the press; this led to his insistence that members of the NDAC and their staff treat the subjects of discussions at their meetings as completely confidential.[21]

During that earlier "cold war" of 1940–41 the characteristic attitude ruling in big-business circles was that defense orders should be taken up purely as a "sideline." Mr. Ford, for instance, eventually showed himself willing enough to turn out $122,000,000 worth of aircraft engines—but not if Sidney Hillman insisted upon recognition of the United Auto Workers' Union in his plants. Other heavy-industry spokesmen proposed that various anti-trust suits be dropped, such as that aimed at the Mellon family's Aluminum Company of America. In general, it was desired that the normal supply of "butter" remain undisturbed while guns were being manufactured as a part-time job. Above all, it was said in these quarters, defense production should be *superimposed* on existing arrangements of trade and commerce without causing drastic dislocation of the peacetime order of things. For Roosevelt this made a cruel impasse. He could use only "persuasion and money." [22]

Knudsen, after approaching his old friends in Detroit on the question of conversion of their automobile plants to arms production, soon learned that they were bent on having guarantees against loss—resulting from overexpanded plants—once the emergency was ended. What they preferred were new factories to be built for tanks and airplane parts, which were either to be paid for wholly by the government and leased to them cheaply, or built by them and "depreciated" (for tax purposes) in a very brief period of five years—which was almost the same as having Uncle Sam's Treasury pay for these new plants. Once Roosevelt, in a momentous conference with Knudsen on July 10, 1940, conceded these terms, promising he would support a bill in Congress providing for such advantageous leasing or depreciation rates for defense plants, things began to move faster.[23]

From then on one could perceive, particularly at the NDAC headquarters in the Federal Reserve Building, a great change coming over the Washington of the New Deal. The plates on government office doors now featured more and more names like Harriman, Stettinius, and Rockefeller. Their advisers and assistants were typically smooth, well-groomed executives from General Motors, Standard Oil, and other giant corporations, or neatly pressed lawyers from Wall Street. Though Hillman and Henderson continued to hire numerous professors and labor-union officials of the more threadbare New Deal type, the horde of well-heeled dollar-a-year men literally kept coming in through the windows, the doors, and the floor.

The new business contingent in Washington regarded themselves as

"Machiavellis" in their own right, for many of them had done a great deal of politicking in order to climb the ladder of giant corporations. They were wary of the "dynamic" laborite Hillman, who seemed always to be asking them: "Well, what have you got to give in return to labor —if I am supposed to ask labor not to strike and adjust all differences peacefully?" [24]

The representatives of business, on the other hand, were now asking whether the labor boys couldn't be called off for the duration of the emergency, on the ground that great munitions plants like those of Bethlehem Steel should not be hampered by the demand for fair labor standards. At times Hillman grew quite angry at the effrontery of certain big-business groups who, though defeated at the polls and bested in Congress, now, during the emergency, tried to come in "by the back door" and bend the Roosevelt Administration to their will.

At the NDAC, Knudsen tended to be very secretive and in the early days seldom consulted Hillman or Leon Henderson about what he was doing. Knudsen, a modest, likable giant of a man who knew production lines, was in reality rather bewildered at finding himself plunged in the dark mazes of Washington's political intrigues. Like Hillman, this native of Denmark had been an immigrant factory worker in his youth; he too was animated by a fervent patriotism and deeply believed in the urgency of the task being undertaken now. Knudsen, though no admirer of labor unionists, showed a certain esteem for Hillman; but behind him there stood always his deputy, John D. Biggers, head of the Libby-Owens-Ford Glass Company, a man of very different temperament, who, with the lawyer Fredrick Eaton, did the thinking on policy in Knudsen's division.

The mood of suspicion was a prevailing one in all quarters. Each of the commissioners on the NDAC had his own lawyer . . . who prevented agreement of their principals. . . . In Knudsen's case, the lawyer he depended on most heavily was Fredrick Eaton; in Hillman's case it was Max Brandwen. . . .[25]

Hillman and Leon Henderson were the only real New Dealers in the group. Henderson had just recently come from his work on the Temporary National Economic Committee hearings, during which the operations of industrial cartels had been revealed as naked and unashamed. He now felt, or had the air of feeling, much animus or resentment when he saw these same men suddenly appear in positions of great Government trust.

In this transitional council, Knudsen was a key figure, if only because of the battalion from the National Association of Manufacturers that had gathered behind him. The stout, ruddy Leon Henderson had a quick wit and a loud voice, but only Roosevelt's oscillating favor and no weight of money or armies of union members behind him. Stettinius, a well-intentioned person, who was to have gathered stockpiles of raw materials and prepared a system of priorities, was no genius of administration. It was Hillman who showed both force and resiliency in this difficult, formative period of the rearmament program.

All that summer of 1940 John L. Lewis, in behalf of the CIO, pounded away at Roosevelt with demands that the President issue an executive order requiring all bidders for government contracts to show that they were not in violation of the National Labor Relations Act. Otherwise, as Lewis rightly said, the worst labor-crushers in the country could easily underbid firms that scrupulously observed Federal labor laws and win the most profitable defense contracts. However, Roosevelt had been advised by the Attorney General that serious legal objections might be raised to such an order, and turned the problem of working out this Lewis headache over to Hillman.

The two men were still on good enough terms then to take lunch together on July 11, 1940, when Hillman suggested that Lewis write him a letter outlining definite proposals for government measures against violators of labor laws bidding for defense contracts. This Lewis did several days later by sending Hillman a proposed draft for an executive order, together with copies of his recent correspondence with the President on the subject. Hillman, in reply, wrote that it seemed bootless to urge the President to disregard the opinion of his legal counselors but that his Labor Policy Committee was now preparing similar recommendations which it was hoped would be adopted by the NDAC.[26]

Lewis kept up his pressure by publishing in the newspapers all his correspondence with Roosevelt and Hillman on labor-law compliance under the defense program, together with his own critical observations. More than thirteen billions in government contracts, he charged, were being awarded mainly to anti-union firms such as Bethlehem Steel. Moreover, Philip Murray wrote Hillman early in August that the CIO was preparing strike action against the Bethlehem Steel Company's

Allegheny plants and gave warning that "a general breakdown of our national defense program" impended.[27]

From the start of the Defense Commission, Hillman had urged that it issue a formal declaration on labor policy on which all seven members might agree. In July 1940, he and Leon Henderson were appointed as a subcommittee to work out a proposed statement of such policy. But winning unanimous agreement was not easy. Hillman grew impatient, and on August 7 and again on August 23 jolted the meeting of the commissioners by his vehement demands for prompt action on the issue of labor-law compliance. He made the point that big armament firms like Bethlehem Steel, having been ruled in violation of the Wagner Act by the NLRB, simply appealed against such rulings to the Federal courts and dragged the affair out for years while refusing to permit labor-union elections among their employees. Yet John D. Biggers, Knudsen's deputy, urged prudence and a careful "hedging" of every statement by the NDAC before he would grant his approval. It was "probably not true," he said, that observance of the minimum-wage and eight-hour law or of good collective-bargaining practice made for maximum efficiency of production.[28] At every step, moreover, the War and Navy Departments had to be consulted.

The question of labor policy was deadlocked throughout August. But Donald Nelson, vice-president of Sears, Roebuck and Company, who had been appointed Stettinius' deputy in the division of raw materials and priorities, was then added to the Hillman-Henderson subcommittee on labor policy and leaned to a compromise with labor's demands. Hillman also went to Roosevelt with the problem; his pleas, backed up by the CIO organizers' serious preparations for big strikes, brought the President around. On August 30 the Defense Advisory Commission adopted a statement of policy favoring the re-employment of idle workers and compliance with existing labor statutes that was, in substance, the same as the recommendations made earlier by Hillman's Labor Advisory Committee.

How long it took to get things done in Washington! Hillman used to complain. He never could reconcile himself to the endless delays. This document had needed ten weeks of negotiating and palavering and "was entirely Hillman's work," as authoritative accounts indicate.[29]

The Defense Advisory Commission's directive on labor policy, released to the press on August 31, 1940, declared:

This program [of industrial mobilization] can be used . . . as a vehicle to reduce unemployment and otherwise strengthen the human fiber of our nation. In the selection of plant locations for new production . . . great weight must be given to this factor.

In order that surplus and unemployed labor may be absorbed . . . all reasonable efforts should be made to avoid hours in excess of 40 per week. However, in emergencies or where the needs of the national defense cannot be otherwise met, exceptions to this standard should be permitted. . . . Overtime should be paid in accordance with recognized local practices.

All work carried on as part of the defense program should comply with Federal statutory provisions affecting labor wherever such provisions are applicable. This applies to the Walsh-Healey Act, etc. There should be compliance with state and local statutes affecting labor relations, hours of work, wages, workmen's compensation, safety, sanitation, etc.

. . . Workers should not be discriminated against because of age, sex, race, or color.

Adequate housing facilities should be made available for employees.

A week later the NDAC also voted approval of a further directive entitled "The General Principles Governing the Letting of Defense Contracts," containing a very important paragraph, the fifth, which was distinctly Hillman's contribution:

Adequate consideration must be given to labor. This means compliance with the principles on this subject stated by the Commission in its release of August 31, which is attached hereto.[30]

On that day, September 6, the two documents were transmitted to President Roosevelt for his approval.

The President had just then gone to Hyde Park. Hillman, who had been in touch with him constantly, had received his promise of concurrence, but evidently felt it necessary to remind him of that fact in forwarding the NDAC resolutions, which he also reported had been unanimously endorsed by his Labor Advisory Committee. On the morning of September 9, Assistant Secretary William McReynolds handed the papers to Roosevelt, reminding him of Hillman's request that he sign them. The President signed.[31]

That afternoon Hillman, who had been having his troubles convincing Robert P. Patterson and James Forrestal, Under-Secretary of the Navy, of the merits of his policies, went around to call on them and triumphantly exhibited the NDAC's statement with President

Roosevelt's signature on it. It had its "hedges" and compromises (concerning exceptions for emergencies), but constituted an answer to the polemics of John L. Lewis during the current election campaign. Hillman also communicated promptly with Lewis, pointing out that his demands for an executive order on labor-law compliance were now fairly met. Lewis, however, very properly raised the question of how this policy was to be enforced.[32]

Hillman next hastened to see Patterson and Secretary Knox and urged that they write letters expressing their full agreement with the President's policy and their intention of enforcing it. This too was done, on September 30, though not without stipulated reservations in case of national emergencies. Attorney General Robert Jackson also furnished an informal "curbstone" opinion declaring that the policy and procedure outlined in the NDAC resolution were lawful and that the National Labor Relations Board findings of non-compliance with the Wagner Act would be considered conclusive and binding upon other agencies of the government unless and until reversed in the courts. These official letters and the favorable ruling of the Department of Justice were promptly announced to the press by Hillman on October 1, 1940. What it all meant, Hillman said at a press conference that day at the NDAC offices, was that "Army and Navy contracts will no longer be given to companies violating the Federal labor laws." [33]

Lewis still remained very hard to please. These directives, he admitted to Hillman, marked "a notable forward advance for organized labor," but he feared they would not affect large contracts already awarded, and wondered to whom labor unions must apply in cases of violation.

Hillman, in a soft answer, assured Lewis that aggrieved labor groups might continue to apply as before, "respecting any of these matters, to me." [34] It was too late, however, to turn aside the wrath of Lewis at Roosevelt. He was already preparing to go to the microphone for Mr. Willkie.

III

The week end after Attorney General Jackson had given his favorable oral ruling on defense-contract labor policy Hillman went home for a few days' rest at his beach cottage on Long Island. There news came:

to him that a tremendous storm had been blown up in Congress at the pro-labor policy he had literally forced on the NDAC and the War and Navy Departments.

The press was now full of headlines denouncing Hillman. Mr. H. W. Prentis, head of the National Association of Manufacturers, rushed to the newspapers with a bristling statement charging that Hillman was engineering "a plot to use the defense program to bring industry to heel at the Wagner Act." Then the immitigable Representative Howard Smith of Virginia entered the fray, hurling charges that were remarkably similar to those of the NAM's Prentis. Representative Smith, who headed a special committee of Congress investigating the National Labor Relations Board, now summoned Hillman, Secretary of the Navy Knox, Assistant Secretary of War Patterson, and Attorney General Jackson to appear and testify before his committee on October 8. Knudsen himself chose this moment to deliver an anti-labor speech before a businessmen's gathering in which he declaimed: "We don't want any part of the Russian system over here!"

In trying to set the defense labor policy on high ground, and thus ward off Lewis' political attacks, Hillman had inevitably come under the cross-fire of the anti-labor bloc in Congress. From the White House there now came prompt orders that he was to go into reverse and "soft-pedal" labor-law compliance until the elections were over. Harry Hopkins, it was said, now feared that large employers might decide to shut down their plants and throw hundreds of thousands of men out of work on the pretext that "the government was refusing them contracts." [35] Hillman himself was concerned at the danger of a break in the Democratic ranks during the closing days of the campaign.

Hailed before Congress under the stern inquisition of Mr. Howard Smith, Messrs. Jackson, Knox, and Patterson all backtracked on October 8. Jackson avowed that he had given only a "curbstone" opinion, which meant nothing save in a "legal-technical sense." The Army and Navy could make contracts with anyone they chose to.

Hillman, very nervous and uncomfortable, had a rather bad hour at the hearing, during which he tried to confine himself to generalities about the value of good labor morale for defense production. He alluded to the strong protests that were being constantly made by labor unions at the award of profitable government contracts, entailing almost no business risk, to firms accused of violating Federal labor statutes. Against charges that he was showing favoritism to labor he simply kept his lips buttoned. The four lieutenants of Roosevelt crept out of that hearing room like a bunch of wet hens.[36]

At this very moment the CIO's United Steel Workers, led by Philip Murray and Van Bittner, were on the verge of launching a great strike, long prepared, against Bethlehem Steel—which meant, unfortunately, against guns and warships. Hillman made prodigious efforts to delay their action and was successful for the moment; for Van Bittner suddenly canceled a large press conference on October 18, indicating that everything was off for "political" reasons, until the elections were over. Hillman had promised the CIO leaders that those who violated the law would be properly dealt with after November 5, 1940.[37]

Lewis, however, took grim joy in reminding everyone that Hillman and other lieutenants of Roosevelt had been forced to eat boiled crow before Congress, after making so many "pious declarations" in favor of a sound labor policy. (It was shortly after the humiliating Smith-committee episode in Congress that Lewis, on October 25, delivered his thunderous radio broadside against the President.)

Hillman nursed wounds received in this struggle, and took consolation in the hope that good tidings at the election polls would free his hands again. Blocked by the opposition, often deflected from his goal, he resumed his campaign for an enlightened defense labor policy with the unwearied tenacity he had often shown before in such hard contests. The Roosevelt victory in November gave him new strength.

It was at this point, as related in the preceding chapter, that Hillman was suddenly forced to drop everything else and hurry to the CIO convention at Atlantic City to put down the threat of the Lewis "stampede."

In the course of that speech before the convention, on November 20, 1940, he dwelt upon the good beginnings that had been made during the first five months of the defense program, in words that were optimistic, indeed almost soothing. He and his staff of the new Labor Division had assumed "the responsibility to put the unemployed back to work and give them a chance to rehabilitate themselves."

Contracts were being diverted to "idle labor and idle communities" in many cases. There were, to be sure, serious difficulties in enforcing the provisions of the Wagner Act, but he hinted that he was "watching things" and might soon be ready to come to grips with stubborn characters like Mr. Eugene Grace of Bethlehem Steel and Mr. Henry Ford.[38]

However hopeful a face Hillman might put on matters in public, the fact was that he still confronted stern opposition in the Defense Commission as in the War and Navy Departments—for though Stimson and Knox, like Patterson and Forrestal, were fervent patriots, they were distinctly not New Dealers. Hillman had repeatedly been forced to remonstrate against the

lack of co-operation on the part of the Army and Navy in awarding contracts to concerns which do not maintain the labor standards established by law and adopted by this Commission.[39]

The unionization of workers in the defense program was "not paramount" to the War Department, Robert Patterson told Hillman.

"But you will only have more strikes and delays if you take that position," Hillman argued.[40]

It seemed as if his influence were waning, for only twenty-four hours after Election Day the War Department announced the letting of a $122,000,000 contract to the Ford Motor Company for the manufacture of aircraft engines. Hillman raised most vigorous objections but was told that this was an "exceptional" case, based on the emergency needs of Britain (whom Henry Ford was now willing to help). Overruled, Hillman decided to do no debating in public this time but to fight on behind the scenes. Such incidents, however, were undermining his influence in the labor movement, whose leaders were accusing him of being too "soft" with the defense contractors. As "personnel manager" for the government, he was becoming a punching bag for labor as well as capital. There was everything to be gained by pounding at him. At the NDAC meetings, W. L. Batt, head of S.K.F. Industries, one of Knudsen's chief assistants, would say pointedly: "Our defense program cannot tolerate holdups by either side." In the event of a serious strike the Army and Navy and Roosevelt must be ready to use any expedient to curb organized labor, Batt maintained.[41]

In November the outbreak of a strike by a CIO union at the Vultee aircraft plant in California—which Hillman and his aides helped to settle in quick order—was made the occasion by the anti-labor bloc in Congress to broach the idea of a bill prohibiting all strikes in defense plants. (At the time of the Vultee strike there were many cries in the press for Hillman's head.) On the other hand, if the unions were deprived of their principal economic weapon, the strike, then every labor-baiter in the country could crush out unions in the name of patriotism.

While he wrestled with his terrible dilemmas many letters of criticism were directed at Hillman by those who regarded themselves as labor's friends. On October 24, 1940, there came one such letter from Dr. J. Raymond Walsh, the liberal writer and radio commentator, who greatly admired Hillman, but now deplored the unfortunate impression made by his recent testimony before the Smith committee and regretted that he had not even attempted a "strong public statement" in his own defense. What was worse was that Hillman was forced to remain silent under such reproaches, which took no account of the opposition he faced on every side.

It was only after the elections that he replied to Dr. Walsh, assuring him that he held it to be one of his principal tasks "to safeguard . . . the social and labor gains of recent years," in the best interests of our national defense itself. All of this took time, alas:

You can be assured that I have been most active in implementing the labor policy announced by the Commission. That this has not been accompanied "by a strong public statement"—as you suggest—is due solely to my desire to devote myself to the accomplishment of results and not to engage in any activity which might interfere therewith. Frequently, public statements serve to delay the accomplishment of desired objectives. In such circumstances, the urge for public statement, however persistent, must yield to higher objectives. To announce now what is being done is premature. Although great progress is being achieved, it cannot be the subject of a strong public statement, unless and until greater progress has been obtained.[42]

What he wrote to Walsh was true. Right after the election he went to work on Roosevelt again. On November 14 the President finally took a strong stand by addressing a letter to Patterson and Donald Nelson (the chief of Priorities and Purchasing) saying, among other things, that he had numerous complaints about the labor policy of Bethlehem Steel and two other concerns. "I am told that these three concerns have had definite trouble with labor and have been judicially held to be in the wrong. I am wondering what has been done to assure full compliance with the Federal laws before these contracts were awarded." [43]

But then, as was his way, Roosevelt departed on a cruise in the presidential yacht, leaving his "boys," Hillman and Patterson and Nelson, to "weave everything together." The War Department, up to this stage, had held that violation of the Wagner Act was not the same as a "crime," since most of these cases were subject to court review.

In mid-December there was another brawl inside the Defense Commission over a new order that had been allotted to Ford, this time for only $1,387,000 worth of midget scout cars. Knudsen argued that the Commission must not be turned into a "labor-law-enforcement agency"; he was upheld by Biggers and Batt, who vehemently opposed Hillman's efforts to hold up the contract. Hillman was outvoted.

This time Hillman was thoroughly riled and vowed that "this sort of thing must not happen again." A small order of this type could easily have been handled by another motor company, he said, instead of the Ford Company, which had been ruled in violation of the Wagner Act in nine cases. From the NDAC meeting he walked out to call a press conference in which he issued a public statement vigorously criticizing the War Department.[44]

The aging but obstinate Henry Ford, it was reported, had refused to see Hillman about composing his labor troubles—despite Knudsen's earnest appeals to him. The "old man" had friends in every department of the government, and "especially in the Quartermaster's Department," one of the Ford executives said jestingly, and there was nothing Mr. Hillman could do about it.[45]

Once more Hillman went to the President. Roosevelt, having done a heap of thinking since Election Day about the dissension among his lieutenants and the ineffectiveness of the seven-man Defense Advisory Commission, took drastic action shortly before Christmas. The NDAC was abolished by presidential decree, and the Office of Production Management, or OPM, was created to take its place, but armed with far greater authority. William S. Knudsen was named director-general of the new defense organization, and Sidney Hillman was placed beside him as associate director-general, with powers equal to his. Hillman's position was thus enormously strengthened; indeed, he ranked with Stimson and Knox. The effect was instantaneous.

The next time the Army procurement officers turned up with a contract to be awarded to Ford—this for Army trucks valued at $67,000,-000—Hillman went on the warpath. He roared: "The hell with 'em—we'll get the stuff from some other firm, and it may cost more, but it will be done under a fair labor standard." The War Department was deeply annoyed. Apparently nobody but Hillman was willing to make a stand against both the "Ford empire" and the United States Army, which had an almost superstitious faith in Ford's famous efficiency. But now Patterson yielded to Hillman, and the contract was assigned to the Chrysler company.[46]

Hillman said nothing, but rumors circulated in Washington that the mighty Ford had been humbled—that is, wounded in his pocketbook— in an affair of a large defense contract owing to Hillman's intervention. This, as one informed Washington correspondent wrote, represented "the greatest victory won by labor in the defense program." [47]

A few days later an appeal from an NLRB decision in an important labor case was lost by the same Ford Motor Company before the United States Supreme Court, and this showed the handwriting on the wall. The Ford employees by now were walking out on strike in large numbers and preserving perfect order. At last the company reversed its long-established anti-union policy and, early in May, began negotiation with the CIO's United Auto Workers' Union. Thus it came about that the army of 140,000 Ford workers were swiftly enrolled in the ranks of organized labor in 1941. The CIO men, to be sure, despite the physical danger they ran, had been waging an unremitting campaign within the factories. But the political-financial pressure applied from above by Hillman in Washington helped enormously to hasten the result desired.

Meanwhile a strike that would have constituted the most serious setback suffered as yet by the defense program threatened at the Lackawanna, New York, plant of the Bethlehem Steel Corporation. Here, too, the CIO people under Murray and Bittner had been slowly fighting their way into the shops. In February 1941, strikes began spreading because of the discharge of many union members. Hillman and his mediation aides were told by the Bethlehem executives in Pennsylvania that there would be no compromise: "We are calling out the troops and will break the strike." [48]

He had previously found it very difficult to approach the president of the Bethlehem Steel Corporation, Eugene Grace, a man noted for the fabulous salary he received, on the matter of improving his employees' status. The operating vice-president of Bethlehem, Joseph Larkin, however, was something quite different. Hillman saw him in Washington, in New York, and in Pennsylvania, and "talked his arm off," it was said. Mr. Larkin perceived that with the danger increasing of our being involved in war, the government would be disposed to give labor ever larger concessions, and that it might be better to yield to the inevitable.

Philip Murray, head of the steel union, wired an appeal to Roosevelt on February 20, 1941, to which the President had Hillman draft a reply. (That week Hillman saw Van Bittner, who was directing the CIO action in the field, then rushed off to confer with Roosevelt again.) The terms of the letter to Philip Murray hinted at presidential sympathy with the union workers in this dispute and the hope of a "lasting adjustment." [49] This, too, undoubtedly helped Grace and Larkin see the light. On March 1 the announcement was made that the Bethlehem Steel Corporation, non-union throughout its history, had agreed to hold an NLRB election in its shops. This event soon opened the way to negotiations for an agreement between the United Steel Workers and the country's second largest steel firm, with more than 140,000 employees. Here, too, Hillman had played his part well.

"Hillman saw there was a chance to break through those two great bottlenecks of union labor, Bethlehem and Ford, and was determined to do this at all costs during the wartime emergency," Dr. Lubin has said. Of course this also gained him powerful enemies in big-business circles.[50]

But though controversy raged about him incessantly he had emerged, by the end of 1940, as one of the strongest figures in the whole defense organization.

At the beginning of 1941 he made ready to take up the much heavier responsibilities entrusted to him by the President in the OPM. He was often overwrought and ill at this period; yet, in his hurried life, he knew also moments of deep satisfaction. Labor was winning great victories all along the line in 1941. In this time of world danger it was, somehow, permitted him not only to help the national defense, but also to carry on his chosen lifework: the advancement of labor organization throughout America. In an off-the-record talk before his old union comrades he said:

My friends, it is no accident that the greatest opponents of labor in this country are accepting collective bargaining. Ford will sign an agreement before two weeks in my judgment; Bethlehem is negotiating with their union. Every opposition against the right of labor to bargain collectively has been broken down, and, my friends, it wasn't an accident. It is because we have carried through a policy. . . .[51]

Chapter Twenty-Two

THE OPM

The eighteen months that followed the capitulation of France were not only a period of rearmament but also one of "cold war." In the heat of the election campaign the possible imminence of war had been soft-pedaled by the Democratic Administration—yet Congress had enacted the Selective Service Act in September 1940 as a measure of defense. And once the elections were over, Roosevelt moved again to strengthen our military preparations and give aid to Britain. Winston Churchill, in letters to the President, had promised that England would never yield; to help England, now carrying on alone, unlimited aid in material must be furnished, and the system requiring cash payments for American food and munitions must be changed. On December 17, 1940, Roosevelt announced the plan of Lend-Lease, which at the lowest estimates implied a doubling of the current defense budget and meant, as Secretary Stimson candidly said, "a declaration of economic war." [1]

It was obvious also that the President must now clean house at the Defense Commission. Not only did it lack authority, but, constituted as it was with seven commissioners and their seven watchful lawyers, it made for a good deal of confusion and duplication of effort, as one of its members, Leon Henderson, had recently reported.[2]

On the day after Roosevelt's press conference announcing the Lend-Lease project, Stimson, Knox, Patterson, and Forrestal went to the President and urged that the NDAC be reconstituted as a one-man organization with Knudsen as its responsible director. Bernard Baruch added his voice to the others', arguing that if business had to be regulated for industrial mobilization only a leader of business could do it. But Roosevelt instinctively resisted the idea of appointing a "czar" to wield immense power over the country's industries, and least of all one drawn from the General Motors Corporation. His New Deal advisers had not neglected to warn him against the growing influence of the Chamber of Commerce "crowd" in the NDAC.

Meanwhile, Roosevelt and Harry Hopkins considered it vital that Sidney Hillman be included at the top level of any defense organization, as the spokesman of organized labor. The problem of mobilizing labor presented fully as great difficulties as the mobilization of industry, and could not be safely entrusted to some "czar" drawn from the managerial class, nor to the War and Navy Departments with their traditional anti-union bias.[3] In England, Ernest Bevin had been discharging similar functions in the Churchill Cabinet with great effect. Hopkins had favored the original appointment of Hillman to the NDAC and had worked well with him.

On the other hand, the reorganization plan urged by the Stimson group turned out to be a three-man defense council made up of Stimson, Knox, and Knudsen. After several days of reflection, Roosevelt decided to add Sidney Hillman to this trio. This President, it must be recalled, saw himself always as one destined to play the "honest broker" between the different classes and groups. If businessmen were to be asked to "convert," then it was no less true that labor would also be called upon to make heavy sacrifices—and here Hillman, as the man of labor, could be most useful. Though Madame Perkins expressed strong disapproval of the plan to include Hillman in a two-headed OPM, the President firmly rejected her counsels, and his mind seemed shut on this question.[4]

Roosevelt was aware that Hillman had been a powerful political ally in the recent election and a tower of strength for his Administration in the labor movement. Hillman's intense activity at the NDAC, his shrewdness as a negotiator or in the work of mediating threatened strikes were also appreciated. In a letter to Professor Harold Laski during the war, Roosevelt wrote of Hillman: "He saw the whole range of our economic problems as perhaps only four or five other men in the United States." [5]

On December 20, the President issued a decree establishing the "Office of Production Management" as superseding the National Defense Advisory Commission; William S. Knudsen was to be its director-general, Hillman its associate director-general, and Secretaries Stimson and Knox its two other members. He had rejected the idea that a single "Pooh-Bah" must dictate all defense production. At the head of the new organization, Roosevelt himself would be in command, ready to make decisions if the others disagreed.[6]

The appointment of Hillman to a position in which he shared equal authority with Knudsen over the mobilization of our defense industries made a famous sensation in the press. Most newspaper comments were unfavorable, holding that the OPM would be a two-headed concern and Knudsen and Hillman "a pair of Siamese twins." However, all those who believed in the objectives of the New Deal were pleased, feeling that by this action Roosevelt had reaffirmed his own democratic faith, unlike Woodrow Wilson, who, in the last war emergency, had turned our war industries over to big-business management exclusively. In conservative business circles people were saying gloomily that a "labor government" was in the offing, although Hillman's was to be but one voice out of four at the OPM.

He had learned about a week or two ahead of the public announcement that he was to be retained after the shake-up in the defense organization. Recently he had been ailing again, suffering from a sinus infection and also from various arthritic aches. At Christmas he went away for a week's rest before undertaking his new duties.

The President's order establishing the OPM had been given to the press in outline. Its drafting in final legal form was assigned, according to routine, to Harold D. Smith, Director of the Budget, who was attached to the White House staff; aiding him in this task were the presidential assistants William McReynolds and Louis Brownlow, sometimes called the "architect" of the various Roosevelt emergency commissions. For some reason Mr. Smith freely consulted Knudsen's legal aide, Fredrick Eaton, in writing the executive order for the OPM, while shutting the door in the face of Hillman's Mr. Brandwen. (Hillman, in the meantime, was absent at Boca Chica, Florida.) Mr. Brandwen, acting as Hillman's deputy, grew more and more worried at being thus ignored. At length, through a well-informed Washington correspondent, he found out what was going on behind those closed doors. Soon thereafter, on December 31, 1940, the secret was out when the *Wall Street Journal* published an exclusive front-page story by Eugene Duffield under the headline:

KNUDSEN RECEIVES BROAD POWERS
IN TENTATIVE EXECUTIVE ORDER
IN DEFENSE SETUP—
A CURRENT DRAFT MAKES HIM
"DIRECTOR-GENERAL" OVER HILLMAN,
STIMSON, AND KNOX

Though the President had "put Hillman on a par with Knudsen" in announcing the new office, this order relegated him "to the position of 'adviser' to Knudsen, with no administrative authority," the report ran.[7] The pro-Knudsen draft was the product of long years of preaching, by Bernard M. Baruch, one of our so-called elder statesmen, and the Army-Navy "M-Day" planners, that in the event of a war emergency businessmen should be placed in entire charge of industrial mobilization. The written order, though "tentative," would, like a *fait accompli,* have tempted Roosevelt not to adhere to his previous plan, and perhaps yield rather than struggle.

Hillman was ill and in Florida. But Brandwen called up Budget Director Smith and angrily demanded that he be shown the draft of the order. He also managed to reach Hillman by telephone at his isolated camp and tell him of the proceedings of the White House "cabal." Then he went to Harry Hopkins and Attorney General Robert Jackson and roused them up. Hillman and Knudsen must be equals, he insisted. He raised the alarm everywhere until it reached the President, for the Roosevelt Papers contain a memorandum from Grace Tully dated January 3, 1941:

Mr. Brandwen, executive assistant to Sidney Hillman, phoned. He says before Sidney Hillman left for the South, he arranged that Mr. Brandwen and Director Smith would work together on the executive order involving the four-man committee. He has tried to do this, but without success. It was not until this afternoon that he was able to reach Director Smith, who told him that a draft of the executive order was on the President's desk.

Mr. Brandwen is in daily touch with Mr. Sidney Hillman, keeps asking what is the status of the executive order? The question now is—does the President want to see Mr. Hillman before he signs the executive order? If so, he will return immediately.

Hillman finally reached Roosevelt by telephone and informed him that under no circumstances would he serve under the arrangements indicated by the Smith-Eaton draft of the OPM order. Another message from the President's secretary notes that Hillman was "to come back, leaving Florida January 5, for appointment Monday or Tuesday." [8]

Here we have one of the hundreds of palace intrigues carried on incessantly by the "Machiavellis" of Washington throughout the Roosevelt Administration, in the White House itself, in the Federal departments, or on Capitol Hill. One of the principals in this affair, Mr. Fredrick Eaton, has been described as a young corporation lawyer eager to do his bit for his client, Mr. Knudsen. Roosevelt's aide, Louis Brownlow, on the other hand, was reported at the time to have been somewhat disconcerted by the form in which the tentative order had been cast, and complained about Budget Director Harold Smith's very broad misconstruction of the President's order. Knudsen himself is said to have known little or nothing of all these doings. Roosevelt, on the other hand, seemed to enjoy a bit of intrigue and missed none of the full flavor of the affair. Mr. Brandwen's exertions, as Hillman's loyal aide, can scarcely be overestimated.

Roosevelt, warned by Hopkins, held things up for a few more days and then saw Hillman and Knudsen together on Monday, January 6, 1941. A memorandum from Budget Director Harold Smith shows that the whole order was redrafted to Roosevelt's entire satisfaction: in the end Knudsen was named director-general of the new organization, and Hillman was right up there beside him as associate director-general. Knudsen accepted this arrangement in good part. He saw no great difficulties in working with an associate director. As a president of General Motors he had always had a board chairman to deal with. As for Hillman, he had been accustomed to co-operating with management since the days of the original Hart, Schaffner and Marx Plan in 1911.

The next day the President held a large and memorable press conference and appeared in fine fettle as he fenced with the Washington correspondents. He read all the clauses of the executive order establishing the OPM and commented on them so that the newspapermen would suffer from no misunderstanding and indulge in no more gossip. The four members of the OPM were to fix its policies, and Knudsen and Hillman were to carry them out, just "like a law firm," he said. There was to be no boss.

Would they be "equals," a reporter asked? "A silly question," Roosevelt replied. "Is a firm equals?" he asked sardonically. One member of a law firm handled the contract cases, another specialized in tort cases, and there was no quarreling. Citing the instance of what he jocularly referred to as a "famous law firm in its day"— Roosevelt and O'Connor—he said he would never have known if he and Mr. Basil O'Connor had been equals, but they would usually be found in agreement.

But would the two director-generals be able to avoid clashing over the opposing interests of great corporations and their workers? he was asked.

President Roosevelt said: "*I* think they will. *They* think they will —that's an interesting thing." He had given them broad authority, he declared. "After this they won't have to come to me." But he would be available always to use his decisive power as arbiter, whenever this was needed.[9]

II

Hillman, who had barely managed to pull himself together and fly up from Florida to see the President, went at once to the Johns Hopkins Hospital in Baltimore. The winters were hard on him, though he was only fifty-three; the pressures, the palace plots, the endless trouble-shooting were harder still. He had drawn recklessly on his prodigious nervous vitality, and now, since 1937, was forced to husband his remaining strength and seek rest and medical treatment whenever the press of work permitted.

Sitting up in a hospital bed while underging diathermic treatment for his arthritic condition, with a telephone beside him, he began his work in the reorganized defense council called the OPM.

At the insistence of Secretary of War Stimson a single general counsel had been named for the new organization, who was to co-ordinate its legal affairs and end the rivalries of the various pro-New Deal or pro-industry lawyers under the previous setup. He was for-mer Judge John Lord O'Brian of Buffalo, an experienced and ac-complished lawyer and friend of Stimson's, who had served in high posts in the Justice Department under previous Republican admin-istrations. In mid-January Mr. O'Brian (who was to be one of the key figures in the OPM, as in the later War Production Board) has-tened to see Hillman, still in the hospital, in order to seek an under-standing with him about his problems and duties.

He found Hillman rested and calm, and after a long talk the two reached a very clear understanding which, O'Brian has said, was never breached. Hillman asked only that Mr. O'Brian settle all legal questions in consultation with his assistant, Maxwell Brandwen. But on all questions of plans and policies he showed himself extremely fair, detached, and frank. O'Brian had heard all sorts of curious tales about this "militant" laborite, but soon found himself deeply impressed by Hillman's tact and disinterestedness. Instead of seek-ing only privileges for his own followers, he appeared "willing at times to take his life in his hands, so to speak, by administering re-buffs to organized labor where they seemed to be required," that is, for the sake of the larger objectives of the defense program. As arms production was now to be greatly accelerated, Hillman realized that he was going to be asked to use his good offices to demand of labor more output, longer hours, and the avoidance of strikes.

One day Secretary Stimson appealed to Hillman for approval of orders requiring union mechanics in Army arsenals to work a 48-hour week instead of 40, and Hillman readily agreed— though at the time he was trying to spread the re-employment of the idle else-where. The next day the new hours were in force. Stimson thought he showed great breadth of vision as well as energy.

On the other hand, when a serious strike broke out at a great air-plane factory in California in the spring of 1941, Hillman said: "But this is not a wild impulse on the part of the people out there. There are always grievances, causes behind all this trouble. We must be patient, we must look into them."

O'Brian, who became devoted to Hillman, was also very fond of the "other immigrant," Knudsen, who seemed to him happiest when lying flat on the floor of his office poring over endless blueprints. "Many people said that Knudsen and Hillman quarreled, which just isn't true," O'Brian has related. The two agreed in seeking the same results, though Hillman insisted they must be obtained under union rules. Sometimes they expressed vigorous differences over policy within the councils of the OPM, but they did not air their disagreements in public.[10]

Besides a new general counsel, the OPM was staffed with an executive secretary, Herbert J. Emmerich, a specialist in administration problems, who was supposed to be "neither pro-labor nor pro-management." His job was to co-ordinate the growing OPM organization, which took over the existing Production, Priorities, Materials, and Purchasing Divisions, as well as the Labor Division of the NDAC. He too recalls the personal good will shown each other by Hillman and Knudsen. On one occasion Representative Hatton Sumners of Texas came to see Knudsen and found the General Motors magnate in earnest talk with Hillman, each with his arm draped around the other's shoulder in most friendly fashion.

Judge Sumners stood before them dumfounded. Finally he said: "I read in the papers that you gentlemen are at swords' points. But I come here and find you are corrupting each other." [11]

However, having heard about the friction between the New Deal and big-business faction in the NDAC, Emmerich began by stipulating to each of his chiefs that he was not to share with either one of them any secret information that was to be withheld from the other. This was his solution for the problem of a "two-headed" organization. Knudsen agreed, saying that of course he wanted Mr. Hillman to know everything. But now and then he would forget and begin saying something in strictest confidence. On being reminded of his agreement, Knudsen would show some vexation. Hillman also respected Emmerich's stipulation that there be no secrets between the co-directors; and he would also, quite humanly, forget at times and begin telling a story in confidence.

"But remember, I am supposed to tell Mr. Knudsen about this!" Emmerich would exclaim. Hillman would laugh and quickly change the subject.

The OPM council meetings were regularly attended by Hillman and Knudsen with their aides, Secretaries Stimson and Knox and their understudies Patterson and Forrestal, as well as Donald M. Nelson, chief of the Priorities Division, Professor Stacy May, who headed the OPM's statistical bureau, and other staff members.[12] Harry Hopkins, as director of the Lend-Lease Administration, General George Marshall, Army Chief of Staff, and other Army and Navy "brass" also took part in these conferences from time to time.

The discussion here was businesslike, but also of great inherent interest, as it ranged over all sorts of novel problems being met at the industrial, human, political, and military levels. In these councils Stimson, with his gift of brief and trenchant speech, was one of the strongest personalities. Hillman, too, was vigorous and forthright of expression, but on occasion tended to extend himself in elaborately analytical and fine-spun argument. Once, after listening to him with some impatience, Stimson said dryly: "Sidney, I was with you in the first place, but you have argued yourself out of your case, and so I am going to vote against it." [12a]

By a de facto agreement on the division of labor, Knudsen applied himself mainly to production management and Hillman chiefly to the co-ordination of manpower supply, the enforcement of labor-law standards, and the mediation of strikes. The Knudsen faction, however, sometimes intervened suddenly in strike situations, to Hillman's great annoyance. He, on the other hand, often took the aggressive in demanding the cancellation of certain defense contracts where a firm departed from the labor policies now established.

A basic difference between Knudsen's camp and Hillman's was over the issue of converting and expanding heavy-industry plants. The industrialist group in the OPM, in fear of being left with excess capacity in peacetime, was cautious in dealing with this question. Hillman repeatedly assailed them on this score and (often with Roosevelt's backing) led the clamor in high government circles for the long-range expansion of steel and aluminum plants.

The OPM was a decided improvement over the preceding seven-man Commission in the view of some of its officials and, though much criticized in the press and Congress, was actually one of the strongest of all the government boards of that period.[13] It began to deal in earnest and on a very large scale with the problems that were to be faced by later wartime agencies.

Industrial activity was picking up very sharply, and as it approached 1929 levels, bottlenecks in vital raw materials and in processing showed themselves. After the long years of unemployment, the labor market grew "tight" as 1941 drew on and 400,000 workers went back to jobs each month. Contractors in shipbuilding, aircraft, steel, and defense construction now pirated or "scamped" labor at rising wages as profit opportunities were multiplied, with our business-as-usual democracy turning itself into an "arsenal." In some regions whole towns and cities were blighted by the imposition of priorities halting their peacetime industries, as happened in the silk and rubber trades. In other sections there was no proper housing or shelter of any kind for the swarming masses of workers drawn to new jobs. Now the union organizers of the rival CIO and AFL camps raced each other to win command of armies of laborers in the expanding defense industries, and the first serious defense industry strikes began.

III

The Allis-Chalmers Company of Milwaukee, a major producer of electrical engines and turbines, with 7,800 employees, had been awarded a Navy contract for $40,000,000 worth of turbines for destroyers. These destroyers were desperately needed in view of the growing menace of German submarine warfare. On January 21, 1941, following a dispute arising from the dismissal of two workers who were members of a CIO local at Allis-Chalmers, a strike vote was called and thousands of workers walked out.

The procedure for government mediation at this stage was that the Labor Department, through its Conciliation Service, headed by John Steelman, first undertook to adjust the dispute. If this effort met with a check, then by authorization of President Roosevelt, Hillman's Labor Relations team in the OPM, made up of Dr. Isador Lubin, John Owens, Joseph Keenan, and Edwin Bransome, went into action. Actually Hillman and his staff often tried to prevent strikes before they began, and often succeeded. Sometimes they did not wait, as Miss Perkins complained, for the Labor Department conciliators to get to work. Dapper young Army and Navy "labor adjusters," on occasion, also hurried to the scene of trouble, which snarled things up still further.

President Roosevelt, on receiving complaints of such conflicts in authority, would always appear surprised and say: "Go straighten it out. See the Secretary of Labor. Confer with Hillman. Come to an agreement. That is your job, not mine." [14]

When the Allis-Chalmers strike broke out, the Labor Department sent in Dr. Steelman as mediator. In truth, Dr. Steelman had no easy job, for the Allis-Chalmers situation had been a mare's-nest since the autumn of 1940. The CIO's United Auto Workers' local had fought its way into the plant, despite AFL rivalry and ruthless opposition by the management. Labor relations in this old non-unionized corporation were described as thoroughly unpleasant. The union local, led by an ambitious left-winger, Harold Christoffel, fought determinedly during the defense emergency to strengthen its position in this large concern and won the support of most of the workers. These felt strongly that the country's crisis should not be used by the employer, President Max D. Babb, to deny labor's rights under existing law. Mr. Babb, on the other hand, who was said to be a leading contributor to the America First Committee, was stubborn in his opposition to organized labor. To combat the threat of the CIO, however, the Allis-Chalmers management attempted to bring AFL craft unions into some of their shops, which heightened the bad feeling. Meanwhile Dr. Steelman and some of his Labor Department conciliators, described by one official of the OPM as "a lot of retired AFL walking delegates," found that the CIO union members refused to talk to them. They insisted on the closed shop. More than three weeks passed before Hillman took the case away from the Labor Department, brought both Mr. Babb and Harold Christoffel, with his strike committee, to Washington, and got them into a room together.

From his long experience as a negotiator Hillman brought forth an old plan which would overcome the obdurate resistance of the employer to a closed shop and of the union to an open shop. It was a compromise formula providing for "maintenance of union membership"—a variation on his old preferential union-shop plan. Thus the existing status was to be "frozen," with substantial union recognition granted and union wages and standards established for some of the workers. The management promised not to interfere with or discriminate against employees because of their choice of a union; the union promised not to force non-union members out of their jobs, but remained in a position to advance gradually toward the full union shop it hoped for. The announcement that both sides had come to a compromise settlement was made by Hillman and Knudsen at a press conference on February 15, 1941.* [15]

It was true that representatives of both sides had agreed verbally to accept Hillman's written memorandum. But as soon as Christoffel returned to Milwaukee he boasted indiscreetly before his followers that "union security" had been won, and constituted, according to his interpretation, an advance toward the closed shop. Mr Babb, on hearing of this, was up in arms. He refused to accept any such interpretation, and the quarrel was resumed at once, as the men quit their jobs for two more weeks. Christoffel, by his impolitic behavior, had let him down, Hillman felt. At this point, with the help of President R. J. Thomas of the UAW, the workers were at length persuaded to abide by the original memorandum worked out by Hillman and without further "interpretations."

But now their employer, Mr. Babb, kicked over the traces in his turn, insisting upon a written "explanation" or amendment of the original agreement, which would guarantee that it was never to bring about "maintenance of union membership" or a closed shop. This Hillman, as representing government, refused to grant, insisting that Allis-Chalmers be held to its original agreement. For a whole month longer, throughout March 1941, it was the company and its president, Mr. Babb, who were on strike.[16] This witches' brew simmered on for almost eight weeks, until Hillman was sick at heart. There were fanatics on both sides, he remarked.

What he most feared was that Congress would now pass legislation outlawing all strikes in defense industries. From the start of the Allis-Chalmers trouble there was an uproar over Hillman on Capitol Hill. It was actually charged by Representative Clare Hoffman of Michigan that he "encouraged" the Communists in the Allis-Chalmers strike, to delay our defense preparations. (The Communists charged that Hill-

* Testifying on April 8, 1941, before the House Military Affairs Committee, Hillman explained: "In the interests of national defense I recommended on behalf of the OPM that this [union security] clause be accepted by the company and the union with the understanding that it is not to be considered or used as a device to promote the closed or all-union shop, or to make a man's job depend on union membership." (House of Reps., Military Affairs Com., 77th Cong., 1st Sess. Inquiry as to national defense construction. *Hearings,* Pt. 2, pp. 92–147.)

man was trying to destroy their union.) The War Department also reported at this time that a "slow-down" movement was going on in many industries.

On February 20, 1941, Hillman was called before the House Judiciary Committee, whose chairman, Hatton Sumners of Texas, was preparing an anti-strike bill. Secretary Stimson and Under-Secretary Patterson, for the War Department, favored such legislation; but Hillman was able to persuade Knudsen to join him in making a stand against it.

According to reports gathered by his Labor Division, he said, there had been almost no important strikes save for the one Allis-Chalmers case (which he hoped would be quickly adjusted). Less time had been lost as a result of strikes than from the common cold in the past year. Proposals for lifetime prison sentences for sabotage, a ban on strikes, or laws to guarantee the "rights" of non-union workers, he argued, were not the best way to inculcate a spirit of co-operation and patriotism in labor. One could not raise output by depriving free Americans of the right to leave their job:

It would get the feeling abroad that labor cannot be depended on to help defend the country, that it must be coerced. . . . The self-discipline of a free and independent people will always enable them to outthink, outproduce, and outlive any system of totalitarian slavery.[17]

What he was trying to do, he intimated, was to work out a gentlemen's agreement with both the AFL and the CIO, by which the unions were to abstain voluntarily from strikes in defense industries.

Hillman had given a lot of thought to the wasteful duplication of effort by government agencies concerned with labor. He had confronted both his AFL advisers and Philip Murray, the new President of the CIO, with the proposal that a more authoritative government mediation board be set up to handle disputes in the vital defense industries. Murray, though eager to speed defense production, at first opposed a government mediation board as an instrument that tended to favor the side of the employers. But by March 1941 (with the costly Allis-Chalmers deadlock still continuing), Hillman felt that he could afford to wait no longer, that the time to set up an impartial or tripartite mediation board was at hand.

At this point he ran into opposition from Miss Perkins, when he told her that the Labor Department's mediation machinery had been ineffective and that a new system must be set up, lest repressive laws be enacted by Congress.

Madame Perkins assured Hillman that there was no need for any new mediation setup, and that Steelman's outfit was adequate. Hillman came back with the reply that if she didn't move to face the facts of life he was going to the White House with a demand that something be done. . . . Madame Perkins still refused to budge—and wondered afterward why the Department of Labor lost control of so many functions.*

Once more Hillman went to Roosevelt and, on obtaining his support for the scheme of an authoritative labor mediation board, announced this news to the press on March 14. Three days later he returned to the White House again to confer with both the President and Frances Perkins and arrange for the personnel for the proposed National Defense Mediation Board, which was to bypass the Labor Department's mediation service.[18] Miss Perkins, who was most loyal to the President, made no difficulties.

The tri-partite membership of the NDMB consisted of Philip Murray (who had also yielded on this matter), Thomas J. Kennedy, George Meany, and George M. Harrison, representing both labor federations; four men to represent industry: W. C. Teagle, Cyrus Ching, Roger Lapham, and Eugene Meyer; and three persons representing the public: President Clarence Dykstra of the University of Wisconsin, President Frank P. Graham of the University of North Carolina, and William Hammatt Davis, New York patent lawyer with some experience of labor mediation. Incidentally, Dr. Dykstra, the first chairman, though a man of very robust physique, found the work so wearing that he quickly resigned, and the capable Mr. Davis replaced him.

The NDMB (which became the War Labor Board in 1942) bore the stamp of Hillman's lifelong thinking on labor relations. Its purpose was to relieve the OPM of mediation work. Hereafter, Hillman's Labor Division would try, as far as possible, to locate sources of labor trouble *before* strikes broke out. Where this could not be done in time the

* H. J. Emmerich, "The War Contributions of Sidney Hillman" (Memorandum). Frances Perkins in her memoirs relates, "We decided that one of the best things . . . was to set up a board of mediation for the defense industries. . . ." Apparently this was decided for her by Sidney Hillman, for Dr. Leiserson, then a member of the NLRB, also recalls preliminary discussions of such a plan several months earlier, in 1940. At that period, November 1940, Hillman had said to him: "You have to time such things. It isn't time yet."

Labor Department was to go into action; but if that body failed, then the case was to be certified to the Defense Mediation Board as a "higher court." Though armed with no drastic powers, the Board gained authority from the fact that President Roosevelt stood behind it, ready to take emergency action if need be. In practice the new Board frequently asked to have important labor disputes certified to it promptly by Miss Perkins, and so by-passed the slow-moving Labor Department conciliators.[19] Incidentally, Chairman W. H. Davis, a shrewd and philosophical character in his own right, worked in very close liaison with Hillman, for whose talents he conceived the highest admiration. Hillman, he declared, would continue to use the arts of persuasion when everyone else had given up hope.[20]

Ill-health dogged him that trying winter of 1941. In late March, amid the excitement of the Allis-Chalmers and Bethlehem fights, his arthritic condition returned. Under doctor's orders he left again for Boca Chica on March 26 to seek rest and sunlight. The Allis-Chalmers dispute, he felt, was on the road to peaceful settlement through the new Mediation Board.

But during his absence Max D. Babb suddenly came to Washington, saw Under-Secretary of the Navy James Forrestal (a good hater of labor unions) and Knudsen, and handed them what he deemed was clear evidence that the strike vote taken at Allis-Chalmers two months before had included more than 2,000 fraudulent ballots. (Mr. Babb's investigators included two known as strong opponents of the union; even if their report were true, it was pointed out subsequently, a large majority of the workers had still voted for the strike.) On March 27, Secretary of the Navy Knox and Knudsen, impatient to "do something," and without consulting any of Hillman's assistants, wired abrupt orders to the executives of Allis-Chalmers and to the union officers that the plant must be opened at once.

It was "like a coup d'état effected while Hillman was away," said one of his associates. The next day only 1,200 returned to work out of 7,800 hands; whereupon fighting broke out, Governor Heil of Wisconsin ordered out the militia, and bloody rioting went on for three days in Milwaukee. Feeling in the city ran so high that the quick-triggered Governor Julius Heil withdrew the militia and ordered the plants closed once more.[21]

Hillman was "brokenhearted," as his friends recall, at this violent outcome of Knudsen's and Forrestal's intervention. It was exactly what he had warned against. On March 31 he interrupted his vacation to fly back to Washington.

The Defense Mediation Board now took over the Allis-Chalmers dispute and in less than a week recommended the form of agreement originally laid down by Hillman two months earlier. This time both sides accepted, and the strike came to an end on April 6.

However, labor troubles were spreading, not diminishing. Union organizers who had been held back since the recession of 1937 moved into the field again to recruit hosts of shipyard and aircraft workers. Testifying before a congressional committee on April 8, Hillman said with great detachment:

> When large profits [for industry] are reported in the press labor justly feels it is entitled to some fair share of them. When labor is denied various rights guaranteed to it by law, labor cannot be expected to sit by without protest. . . . No one can reasonably assume that these stoppages are entirely the fault of labor.[22]

Early in June 1941, a big strike began out at the North American Aviation Company's plants at Inglewood, California, when local officers of the United Auto Workers called for a walkout. This action was taken in defiance of appeals from the new Defense Mediation Board that the men continue at work while attempts were made to negotiate a settlement. The North American Company, a subsidiary of General Motors, had 11,000 employees at the time and produced about 20 per cent of the country's military airplanes.

Hillman had known that the strike was brewing and for several weeks made strenuous efforts to forestall it. What made things difficult was that the AFL machinists' union had come in as a rival body. The CIO union, however, a few weeks earlier had won an NLRB election by a narrow margin, and its leaders were in great haste to build up their strength in this big plant. There was undoubtedly a nucleus of Communists at work here, as Hillman learned, to whom—at this period of the Soviet-Nazi "friendship" pact—the output of bombing planes was a matter of less importance than unionizing the plant. A committee of the union local had been summoned to Washington by the NDMB, but after promising that they would allow time for investigation, they had suddenly ordered the strike on June 5, and powerful picket lines, fighting off the police of this Los Angeles suburb, closed up the great plant.

"A small band of irresponsibles" who defied their own union's international executives were at the bottom of this trouble, Hillman declared,
though he was well aware that serious grievances of the workers were
a contributing cause of this outlaw strike. Most of the men earned the
minimum wage of 50 cents an hour and worked on a belt-line all week
for $20, where other plants producing for government contracts paid
a minimum of 75 cents an hour. "A bunch of scared rabbits could have
been led out on strike," one official of the NDMB admitted.[23]

In Washington the President's Cabinet meeting of June 6 was largely
devoted to a discussion of this strike. Stimson urged stern measures.
Attorney General Jackson likened it to an insurrection. Harry Hopkins "would have thrown the whole labor movement overboard at this
stage if it would help Lend-Lease," his aide, Dr. Lubin, said. And even
Hillman, "who had been minimizing the importance of strikes and
urging a course of restraint and government non-interference, felt that
a showdown was necessary and the government must take a firm
stand." [24]

It was the week end; the President went off on a short cruise along
the Potomac while they all waited for further news. Richard T.
Frankensteen, the UAW's international vice-president, had gone to
Los Angeles and, at a union mass meeting on June 8, called for a return
to work in response to the appeals from Washington. Warning had
been given that this time President Roosevelt would order the War
Department to intervene if this government-owned plant was not reopened promptly. It was hoped that the warning would suffice. But
Frankensteen was repudiated at the union meeting, which voted to
continue the strike and resist government intervention. (It was not the
first time, of course, that local strike feeling proved too strong for a
union's international executives.)

The next day, when news of Frankensteen's failure, accompanied by
reports of violent rioting, reached Washington, Hillman went to the
White House and met with Roosevelt, Robert Patterson, Attorney General Jackson, and Assistant Secretary of War John McCloy. Under
powers assumed at the time when he had decreed an "unlimited national emergency" (May 27, 1941), the President now ordered the
Army to take over and open the North American plant on the following morning. Hillman expressed full approval of the President's decision. To an old union man there can be nothing more abominable

than the calling of the Army to put down a strike. Yet these were crisis days; the British were being driven back in Greece and Africa; Jugoslavia had surrendered; the Japanese were on the move toward South Asia. As Hillman said: "What is right today may be wrong tomorrow." Here, at any rate, was the darker side of his job as the labor director of the defense program.

At dawn of June 10 scores of Army trucks bearing 2,500 troops roared into Inglewood, California, under the command of Colonel C. E. Branshaw. The soldiers dismounted before the North American plant and with fixed bayonets drove back the pickets, who offered no resistance, one mile from the plant.[25]

This was the first case in which a property was seized by the United States Army during the defense-production emergency, and the only one in which the union side had been held at fault. The custodian (Colonel Branshaw) had been given instructions not to treat with the strikers' representatives as such, but to require that they return as individuals. Persons who were willing to work were to be escorted in and out of the plant and even protected from molestation in their homes.

After the UAW's international executives, R. J. Thomas and Richard Frankensteen, had reorganized the North American local and ousted its officers, negotiations for a settlement were resumed. These ended with substantial increases of wages up to the prevailing union scale recommended by Hillman's representatives on the scene, and other concessions. However, the Southern California workers could not easily forget the grim scene of that morning of June 10, and the production schedule was not restored for many weeks. Soldiers with bayonets cannot make air frames; nor do they improve the morale of free American workers. Colonel Branshaw, as custodian, had his troubles. An added grievance in the eyes of the men was General Lewis Hershey's threat to reclassify workers under the Selective Service Act when they refused to go along with the defense program. And during all that dire season, John L. Lewis filled the air with his clamor against Roosevelt and that "betrayer of labor," Sidney Hillman.

On June 22, 1941, less than two weeks later, the German armies suddenly burst over the Russian frontier. With the Soviets fighting to defend their soil, resistance of the Communists in the North American local of the UAW folded up; soon everybody was hard at work and output improved.

IV

The play of power politics still troubled the CIO throughout 1941. Philip Murray was that rare thing, the man who had *not* wanted to be a president—at least not as Lewis' "rubber stamp." Yet president he was (though in that first year some still pretended to look for the CIO's real leader at the Washington office of the United Mine Workers). On the other hand, Murray, an experienced and able union officer in his own right, was determined not to bow needlessly before Roosevelt and his lieutenant, Sidney Hillman, who both urged the CIO, in the interests of national defense, to take steps toward unification with the AFL. When Lewis, at the November 1940 convention, had finally placed the symbolic crown on Murray's head in a scene full of theatrical artistry, Murray had declared:

> Many of the news organs in this country . . . suggested that if this terrible man Lewis were pushed out of the way this mild man Murray, this moderate, vacillating, weak individual, would immediately rush somewhere to perfect an agreement with the AFL.
>
> Well, I just want you to know, my friends—as I told you the other day—I think I am a man. I think I have convictions, I think I have a soul and a heart and a mind. And . . . with the exception, of course of my soul, they all belong to me.[26]

Thus "Uncle Phil" made it plain that he would go along with the independent labor policies of Lewis, his old chief, and would make no "dishonorable peace" with the AFL. Moreover, he had dealt with Hillman—though he owed much to him—somewhat at arm's length. For the former clothing worker represented government, the big employer of 1941, and it was legitimate to put all possible pressure upon him in the interests of CIO labor.

Up to the fateful summer of 1941, the left-wing nucleus in the CIO vigorously supported proposals for the establishment of labor-management committees for defense plants, made by Walter Reuther and Philip Murray, which, it was urged, would adjust grievances, raise worker morale, and increase output. Hillman had made an approach to this system in the shipbuilding field but did not force the issue, knowing that the idea of active worker participation in management was held in horror, as a "revolutionary scheme," by the OPM's big-business faction. Hence the legend was fostered in CIO circles that

Hillman was too "reasonable," too "timid," too yielding as labor's spokesman in the government's councils. And yet Murray earnestly desired to speed our military preparations, and was intelligent enough to see the danger of restrictive labor legislation looming up in Congress. In this way he found himself trying, as the official leader of the CIO, to work both with Lewis and with Hillman.[27]

John L. Lewis, on the other hand, regarded the period of emergency, featured by a mounting demand for coal, chiefly as an opportunity to advance union power in the Southern coal fields and elsewhere. The Southern miners' strike of April 1941 had won him new laurels and had the important result of tending to equalize pay between Northern and Southern zones. Now he designed a rapid expansion of the mine workers' union through development of its "catch-all organization," called District 50, which took in workers in chemicals, coke, building trades, and many other fields. In these operations, Lewis, more the "lone wolf" than ever, gave little thought to the needs of the defense program. The breach between himself and Roosevelt and Hillman was wider than ever.

On July 7, 1941, shortly after the North American Aviation strike had been broken, a body of 250 CIO executives met in Washington to discuss the government's coercive measures. Lewis, seething with rage, assailed Hillman as a "traitor" who "was standing at Roosevelt's side when he signed the order to send in troops . . . to stab labor in the back. . . ." Jacob Potofsky was on hand, however, and with voice high-pitched with emotion cried out that he was "tired of coming down here to hear Sidney Hillman attacked and the Amalgamated invited to leave the CIO." [28] Murray, presiding, struggled to calm the partisans of Lewis and Hillman, who seemed ready to come to blows. But there was always method in Lewis' public outbursts of choler.

It was still his purpose to lead the CIO in a grand onslaught against the AFL unions and force the rival federation to terms. The heart of the AFL's strength, he knew, lay in its building unions. Hence, since the beginning of 1940, he had been organizing the United Construction Workers (CIO) as a dual organization in this trade, making it part of the catch-all "District 50" (of the United Mine Workers), under the command of his brother, Dennie Lewis. This was just the sort of thing that made Hillman despair of Lewis.

He had been working for a de facto truce between the two federations and an end of jurisdictional fights. Rules of fair play had been laid down at the beginning of the NDAC's Labor Division, and both sides were invited to observe them: thus, if the AFL unions controlled 90 per cent of the New York building laborers, the CIO was to keep out; the AFL, in turn, would be expected to show a similar restraint in comparable situations, as in coal mining or steel.

In September 1941, the Lewis-sponsored United Construction Workers suddenly announced that, following a successful poll, a union-shop agreement had been signed with the Currier Corporation, makers of prefabricated houses in the vicinity of Detroit. At once the AFL building-trades unions in Michigan were in an uproar and threatened to call a general construction workers' strike throughout Michigan, which would halt factory and defense-housing construction in the country's most vital production area.

As co-director of the OPM, Hillman had authority to review all contracts for defense construction that might give rise to labor disorders. Months before, on hearing of the CIO's proposed arrangements with the Currier firm, he had given warning to both union and employer that their plans were ill-advised and would be disapproved by him. On October 7 he urgently recommended that a contract to the Currier firm for 300 low-cost houses be withheld by the Federal Works Administration in the interests of labor peace, since the AFL had long ago unionized about 85 per cent of the Michigan building trades. Any other course, he said, might lead to a "reign of terror" and tie up five billion dollars of defense-construction plans. The Currier company, meanwhile, was shown to have had a strongly anti-union record and appeared to have become converted to CIO unionism overnight under the persuasion of John L. Lewis himself. On the other hand, Hillman, many months before, through the OPM, had worked out a very satisfactory agreement with the AFL building-union representatives, of which he had informed Roosevelt.[29]

Another storm promptly broke over Hillman's head when Currier, seconded by Lewis, rent the air with charges that a collusive agreement had been entered into by Hillman "which forced everybody concerned with construction of defense projects to pay tribute to the craft unions of the AFL." [30] Assistant Attorney General Thurman Arnold also entered the lists with a statement that Hillman was abetting a "labor monopoly." The Communists had abruptly ceased their attacks on him; but now conservatives, such as Senator Owen Brewster of Maine, raised an alarm about Mr. Hillman's "labor government."

Finally the Truman committee of the Senate (investigating arms production), on receiving vigorous complaints from Lewis, summoned Hillman to appear at a hearing on October 22.

At the time he was called Hillman was making an airplane tour of the Pacific Coast, partly for the purpose of inspecting defense plants, but also to make speeches designed to raise the morale of the workers —which, in the autumn of 1941, he considered a matter of vital importance. "More arms, more arms!" he cried. "We are two years behind!" The men fighting for democracy must never again be left without arms in their hands to face tanks and dive bombers. "This is a war of workshops," was his refrain.

At Seattle, on October 2, he had a curious experience which illustrates the incredible difficulties he faced in dealing with a divided labor movement. He had been invited that day to address the convention of the AFL's Building and Construction Trades Department, whose president, J. P. Coyne, served on his Labor Advisory Committee in Washington. As Hillman began to speak, the huge Bill Hutcheson, president of the carpenters' union, rose to his feet and yelled: "I object most strenuously to the presence of this gentleman addressing this convention!" Although Hillman had been ruling in favor of the AFL building-trades unions, Hutcheson denounced him as a "dual unionist" and the arch-conspirator of the CIO. Hutcheson could scarcely have been following the trend of recent events. Mr. Coyne quickly came to Hillman's defense, declaring that he had shown himself very fair to the AFL and patriotic in conducting his office, and that he now represented the national government. Hillman then went on with his talk, coolly disregarding the unfriendly interruption, and paid his respects to the building-union members for the co-operative spirit they had shown.[31]

Much in the public view after the elections of November 1940, Hillman flew everywhere, literally, on inspection and trouble-shooting missions. In city after city that passed rapidly before his eyes like the scene of an endlessly unrolling film, great crowds of workers came out to greet him and hear him speak during his October 1941 journey along the West Coast. In the months before Pearl Harbor men's minds were greatly troubled by all they read of British reverses and the gigantic defeats suffered by the Russians. Was Roosevelt leading us into war? —as the Hearst and McCormick newspapers shouted every day. Or was he merely striving to prepare our defenses against future danger?

But then, could anyone make peace with Hitler, many were asking, now that Russia had been attacked without provocation?

At Seattle, Hillman had been given a hearty welcome and made a guest of the city. At San Francisco, where he addressed a large gathering on October 8, 1941, before the Commonwealth Club, he received another tremendous ovation. An urgent note was sounded in his "morale speeches," for he was aware of Roosevelt's tremendous exertions just then to bring help to General Montgomery's armies in Africa:

We cannot wait, we dare not wait until the Eastern and the whole Pacific Coast become another line of flaming cities. We have to stop talking about national defense and act it, live it, be it! A great deal has been done. But have we done enough? My answer is no! [32]

Those were high moments, when the applause of unknown crowds came to him in great waves and the courtesies of local authorities along his route signalized the pleasures of power and fame. Yet for him it was also a time of great stress; for, after Roosevelt, perhaps no man in public life was more bitterly assailed than Hillman by the vituperative fraternity of newspaper columnists and radio broadcasters of the stripe of Fulton Lewis, Jr., and Westbrook Pegler. In the Hearst newspapers one read of Hillman as of some "sinister conspirator" who "plotted" to turn over the government to a diabolical gang of "professors," such as Leon Henderson(!). While such demagogic attacks were at their height he returned to Washington from his Western tour, to be grilled by the Truman committee on October 22 and 23. Patiently he explained that he had engaged in no conspiracy to restrain trade or commerce or any other collusive actions. He had been trying mainly to hold the scales even between the AFL and the CIO. Harry Truman, however, delivered a little sermon in which he censured Hillman's measures to avoid labor strife in the Currier case as having cost the taxpayers some $431,000 (or 8 per cent) more than was necessary— since the low Currier bid had been rejected on his insistence. The fact that dangerous delays, involving billions of defense contracts, had been avoided, was passed over.[33] *

* At the very time when the Hearst newspapers were busily smearing Hillman, the executive vice-president of Hearst Publications, Colonel Merrill Meigs, was working very closely with Hillman, as well as with Knudsen, at the OPM's division of aircraft production. Later, in private conversation, Meigs declared that he had found Hillman a "moderate" labor man of strongly patriotic views. Why, then, he was asked, did the Hearst newspaper chain,

There were so many newspaper headlines assailing Hillman toward the end of 1941 that one day the OPM's counsel, John Lord O'Brian, came in to commiserate with him on these unjust attacks. Hillman remarked philosophically: "Well, Judge, I don't even read those things. They don't matter. I always say that any man in this sort of world who assumes some public post of responsibility and power should expect to be misrepresented and attacked. If he isn't prepared to face all that he ought not to accept such a post." [34]

v

Hillman wrote a report of his West Coast trip for the President and the OPM council, covering his tour of Tacoma, Seattle, San Francisco, Sacramento, Los Angeles, and San Diego, including his visits to large aircraft plants and shipyards and the Kaiser aluminum and magnesium works. He had talked with men in all walks of life: executives, plant managers, engineers, small businessmen, labor leaders, and field agents of the OPM. Noting both good and bad conditions, he reported:

I found a marked trend toward greater stability in labor. The stabilization agreement in the shipyards has already proven its worth by cutting down labor migration and pirating. . . . In the aircraft industry, the experience of management and labor in dealing with each other has built a new mutual confidence. . . . At the same time the friction between the AFL and the CIO is definitely on the decline. In Seattle *I met with spokesmen for both groups jointly.* And in San Francisco I met with the leadership [of the AFL and CIO] separately in a series of closed sessions. All of them pledged themselves to . . . a greater degree of co-operation and to stay out of each other's territory, and thus end stupid and senseless jurisdictional rows. [Italics added.]

Urging that more subcontracting be used in defense industries, he noted:

The ruling fear of the smaller businessman, with whom I talked during my West Coast trip, is that he is being frozen out of the defense program. I can state this unequivocally, after a heart-to-heart session with groups of small businessmen from 41 of the smaller communities in the state of Washington.

---

with ample opportunities to learn what Hillman was really like, through Meigs himself, persist in pillorying him as an alleged "Red conspirator"? Mr. Meigs laughed and said: "Oh, *that*—that was *just politics!*"

Severe shortages of steel were developing in the West Coast. But workers and employers were wondering how long this "recovery" would last. Everywhere he went, among diverse groups, he says:

I found a vast amount of "business-as-usual" psychology. Some employers were fearful of expansion at this time, and fearful of the aftermath during the transition back from a defense economy to a civilian economy. Some were dogmatic in their opinion that our danger from Hitlerism is unduly exaggerated. There were, I am afraid, some obvious indications of an appeasement tendency among some of these men.[35]

In November he made a similar tour of the Detroit-Chicago industrial area and helped stabilize the building situation in Chicago, for which he received the warm compliments of General Brehon Somervell.

The NDAC and the OPM took up the first great shocks of America's transition from a peacetime to a wartime economy. It is almost a convention among those who observed the haste, the dissension, the apparent extravagance of that interval that was neither peace nor war to assail the Roosevelt Administration for its bureaucratic ineptitude, the two-headed OPM defense organization being especially singled out as a horrid example. Yet the judicious Mr. O'Brian said later: "The interesting thing about this whole arrangement is that in many respects it succeeded." Donald Nelson, later chief of the War Production Board, declared that while the OPM because of its divided authority, was "not a good organizational setup. . . it signalized a desire on the part of government to emphasize labor's responsibility and make use of labor's contribution." Nelson adds: "It did make possible the full use of Hillman's many talents. . . ."[36]

The country's military leaders faced a huge task of recruiting, arming, and training some 12,000,000 soldiers, sailors, and airmen—but their course was clearly charted for them. Knudsen had the job of leading the way toward the conversion of the country's factories to a war footing. Hillman was entrusted largely with the job of *human conversion* of some 15,000,000 workers who, it was estimated, were to go into war industries.

Modern warfare is a collective action; the "bureaucratic" tasks involved become ever more immense and far-reaching. America had a real labor movement now. No government bureau existed that could deal with such problems as Hillman and his aides confronted in 1940–41. As Donald Nelson predicted, the real effectiveness of their work would be appreciated much better in retrospect. (It was to be studied with great respect a decade later, at the time of our "police action" in Korea.)

One happy example of the planning job carried out by Hillman and his staff is the all-important shipyard stabilization agreement. Shipbuilding was to expand fourteen-fold in four years, employing the largest group of workers after agriculture; its mushroom-like growth presented extremely difficult problems of labor supply, training and industrial relations. These troubles, however, were minimized, as Paul R. Porter has related, through Hillman's foresight in setting up a comprehensive labor policy for this vast industry well in advance of its major growth.

At an early stage of the NDAC, he called together Navy and Maritime Commission officers and shipyard management and shipyard labor representatives (both for the AFL and CIO) for a conference out of which emerged, late in 1940, the Shipbuilding Stabilization Committee. One of Hillman's chief aides, Morris Llewellyn Cooke, was named chairman of this tripartite committee; it proceeded to stabilize basic working conditions in each of four shipbuilding zones —the Atlantic, Gulf, Pacific, and Great Lakes—through voluntary agreements of the three interested parties. Strikes and lockouts were to be banned; grievance adjustment and arbitration machinery was set up; pirating and scamping of labor were eliminated. Collective bargaining relations were in the charge of the AFL unions where they were dominant (as on the West Coast and Great Lakes) and of the CIO on the Atlantic Coast. The pattern of the Pacific Coast Zone conference's master agreement, in January 1942, providing for a complete wage schedule and closed shop, was followed throughout the industry and used, thereafter, as a model by President Roosevelt for other large war industries.

Mr. Porter, summing up his survey of wartime shipbuilding, declares: "The full balanced story is that labor relations were unusually satisfactory . . . collective bargaining agreements stood up well and that . . . both labor and management shared with the government a responsible and influential role in policy-making and administration; and that the production record was magnificent." *

* Paul R. Porter: "Labor in the Shipbuilding Industry," in *Year Book of American Labor,* Vol. 1, pp. 345–360, *War Labor Policies,* New York, 1945.

By the autumn of 1941 the defense budget made the earlier New Deal deficit spending look like small potatoes. Reporting to a committee of Congress at this period, Hillman said that the rate of production of defense materials was up to $11,700,000,000, six times that at the end of 1940; and by Pearl Harbor Day more than 5,300,000 workers were employed in war industries, an increase of over 400 per cent in approximately a year. This number would be tripled in another year, he forecast. It was a picture of a tremendous economic shift (from the previous state of semi-depression) and meant that whole industrial communities were convulsed and dislocated. For example, in May 1941, a cut of one third was ordered in the output of rubber tires for private cars, affecting the livelihood of 100,000 workers in Akron, Ohio. Priority orders also blighted a whole army of people who made refrigerators at Evansville, Indiana. In Detroit some 400,000 auto workers were to be displaced while their employers tooled up for Army and Navy contracts. The cost of retooling was provided for by government contracts. But these armies of workers, dropped from their customary jobs and facing months of poverty, might leave their home and drift away, their skills being lost to the reconverted plants in their home towns. It was with such perplexing human and social problems that Hillman's Labor Division at OPM constantly grappled in 1941.

The flow of labor supply must be directed incessantly into the expanding war industries. More workers were to be supplied as new demands for labor arose in different regions. Millions must be trained for new mechanical tasks in aircraft and tank manufacture and shipbuilding. Displaced labor must somehow be provided for or regrouped. Strikes must be eliminated and, wherever possible, before they got under way. The spread of unemployment because of priority orders, now being applied with greater rigor, must be prepared for in advance. Wages and labor relations must be stabilized, as was being done in the booming, chaotic shipyards by a team from Hillman's Labor Division, headed by Morris Llewellyn Cooke. These were the varied activities, so novel under our *laissez-faire* economy—still regulated very little by New Deal "controls" before 1941—that were carried on by Hillman and the staff he had set up under the NDAC in the summer of 1940.

Under the OPM, the Labor Division was considerably expanded and new branches created to deal with new problems as they arose. Eli P. Oliver, who had worked as one of Hillman's aides before, in 1941 was placed in charge of the OPM's Labor Relations Branch, which helped mediate strikes. This branch, as well as the Labor Supply Branch and the Labor Training Branch, usually worked in co-ordination with existing Federal Government bureaus but sometimes also assumed independent authority handed down through Hillman from the White House.

Hillman had so many diverse interests and such a lively imagination that he sometimes gave the impression of being an erratic administrator who, whenever he was seized by new ideas, set up new committees and engaged more personnel for them.*   •

Of course he had had an extremely varied administrative and business experience at the Amalgamated Union. Knudsen said that he had "a good head for business."

In the summer of 1941, Hillman, after conferring with Reuther and R. J. Thomas of the United Auto Workers, became greatly concerned over the problem of displaced labor in the automobile, tire, and accessory industries. At once he set up a new Labor Priorities Branch, headed by Professors J. Douglas Brown and Fred H. Harbison, who conducted surveys of the effects of priority shutdowns in twenty states. On the basis of their report a plan was outlined by Hillman and his staff that called for government assistance to these masses of displaced workers during periods of retooling and retraining. The provisions of this plan, which would allow weekly benefit payments to supplement state unemployment benefits—up to 60 per cent of previous wages, but not totaling more than $24 a week— were incorporated in the Doughton bill, introduced in Congress in the autumn of 1941, and calling for appropriations of $300,000,000.

Here, at any rate, was an example of intelligent planning and foresight that sought to prevent much of the confusion and hardship suffered during the war-industries boom. The supplementary unemployment benefits of $6.00 to $9.00 a week in most cases were to be offered only to those who agreed to accept training for defense jobs, but denied to those who remained idle or sought jobs elsewhere. The latter would thus receive only the usually small unemployment re-

---

* Nelson, Knudsen-Hillman's successor, noted, however, that some of the Labor Division's work, such as training-within-industry, was "carried forward by some of the ablest personnel men in the country. I cannot overestimate the value of this work," he adds. "I am sure without it the manpower shortage would have become extremely serious." (Nelson: *Arsenal of Democracy,* 96–97.)

lief of about $15 to $18. The bill therefore provided for some partial "direction" of labor, but stopped short of compulsory regulation as used in England.

With Roosevelt's support, Hillman carried on a vigorous campaign to have the bill enacted into law. When he testified before Congress in behalf of the Doughton bill early in 1942, with the country at war, some of the Republican members, such as Mr. Knutson of Minnesota, accused him of "trying to socialize the whole country." Hillman, however, debated the issue with much skill and denied that there was to be actual coercion of labor, saying:

The Federal Government owes something to these people from whom we have taken away their employment, just the same as we have made provisions for the employers . . . to finance themselves in their retooling processes.

But what of General MacArthur's men then fighting at Bataan day and night? Should not their pay be supplemented? Knutson cried.

Hillman's answering thrust was:

I do not think it is enough. I think that the only thing you can pay these men who are giving their lives is in what the country will think of them in ages to come. Not with medals, but in the admiration of the country for the kind of thing they are doing.

But Representative T. A. Jenkins of Ohio (Republican) interposed that Hillman was helping to put the laboring man's head "into a yoke" by this bill. "Your primary interest should be the interest of the workingman, should it not?" To which Hillman replied coolly: "No, our primary interest here is war production. If we lose the war, labor has lost everything." [37]

The Doughton bill was held up in Congress and ultimately defeated by a close vote. However, other emergency measures were devised to deal with displaced labor.

A growing shortage of skilled mechanics, especially tool-and-die workers, as predicted a year before by Hillman and his economists, was experienced in the spring of 1941. Roosevelt (at a suggestion originating in Hillman's office) wrote a mandatory letter on May 28, 1941, to both Knudsen and Hillman, urging that the OPM do something promptly about getting more skilled workers into defense industries in order to speed the output of tanks. Wherever needed, he said, labor should be transferred rapidly from consumer to defense industries. Hillman thereafter was empowered to direct such transfers, by agreement with Knudsen, though he used this added authority to provide manpower for national defense very cautiously.[38]

In a subsequent mandatory letter of July 9 the President addressed himself to Hillman, in order to prod the OPM to efforts for a rapid increase in tank production by

immediate action to utilize for defense purposes a substantial part of the large durable-goods factories that are still manufacturing for consumer use. . . . I am prepared to take whatever executive actions are necessary in order to accomplish this objective. . . . Some of the cost will have to be borne by the government.[39]

The whole industrial situation seemed to be growing very "tight" throughout that tense summer of 1941. At the end of August, the President, finding Knudsen "not able to instill in all his manufacturers the necessary sense of urgency, shook up his defense organization once more." [40] He now superimposed still another overlapping agency upon the OPM, called the Supply, Priorities and Allocations Board (SPAB), headed by Vice-President Wallace, but with Donald Nelson as executive director. More power was thus delegated to Mr. Nelson to impose priorities upon industry and allocate materials.

By the end of 1941 the rolls of the unemployed were cut in half, standing then at only 4,600,000. As Hillman's Labor Division in the OPM had predicted in 1940, it was apparent now, in the spring of 1941, that every able-bodied American would soon be needed. In view of the prospective labor shortage, the question of discrimination in the employment of Negroes, Catholics, Jews, Mexicans, and many other minority groups became a very live issue.

Hillman was among the first to raise this touchy question before Roosevelt, and the President asked him to help establish a new government agency to deal with it.[41]

In order to acquaint the country with the new policy in regard to discrimination, an exchange of letters on the subject between the two men was arranged for and made public.

On June 25, 1941, Roosevelt also issued an executive order affirming the policy of full participation by all men and women in the work of our rearmament program without discrimination against any race, creed, color, or national origin, and establishing the committee that was to enforce this policy. Thus the Fair Employment Practices Committee, or the FEPC as it was known, was launched— a "side show" of the defense movement, but a most heartening development—with the help of Hillman's old friend Mayor La Guardia. Mark Ethridge was named by Roosevelt as its first chairman.[42]

In sponsoring the non-discrimination policy, Hillman, who always felt very strongly on this whole subject, declared that

Americans are Americans not because of their birth and ancestry, but because they believe and support what America stands for. . . . If we care about democracy, we must care for it as a reality for others as well as for ourselves; yes, for aliens, for Germans, for Italians, for Japanese. . . . The rights of Anglo-Saxons, of Jews, of Catholics, of Negroes—all are alike before the law.[43]

Among Hillman's many-faceted activities at this period, not the least notable was the help he extended Leon Henderson in his efforts to deal with the problem of price control. Hillman was highly aware of the difference between wages and "real wages" as affected by changed buying power. He remembered well the inflationary cycle of 1918–20. From the autumn of 1940, at the Defense Commission, he urged that prices and wages be regarded "as a whole," since one affected the other. In the spring of 1941, Roosevelt had set up still another government board as part of the congeries of emergency defense organizations, the Office of Price Administration. To take charge of this the bouncy economist, Henderson, who had been temporarily dropped from the defense organization, was brought back into the picture.

The problem now arose of co-ordinating the work of this new board with that of Hillman's Labor Division of the OPM, which was concerned with wages, and it was worked out in a series of conferences by Hillman, Henderson, and Bernard M. Baruch. Out of their preliminary studies came the scheme for wage-and-price control made famous later as the Little Steel Formula. Leon Henderson has related that such hold-the-line plans, adopted in the period of shooting war after 1942, were "actually sketched out even earlier by Sidney Hillman and myself in the autumn of 1940, when we were on the Defense Advisory Commission." [44]

The danger of inflation was much in Hillman's mind by 1941. When during his absence Lubin worked out an agreement for a 12½ per cent increase in the wages of the Textile Workers' union, which his chief had done so much to organize, he was astonished to find that Hillman, on returning, far from being pleased, severely criticized the agreement, exclaiming: "Why, this is inflationary!" [45]

When the threat of anti-strike legislation and anti-sabotage legislation, as well, appeared again in Congress, Hillman was quick to raise the alarm. Roosevelt might have been inclined to yield to the pressure of the congressmen who worked unremittingly for the passage of a bill outlawing strikes, but Hillman again was consulted and firmly opposed such measures. Roosevelt is shown, in deference to Hillman's views, holding off the persistent Representative Howard Smith once more, at the end of October 1941, in a note to Hillman which reads:

> I do not think in view of our conferences on Monday night that I plan to send any message to Congress on the subject [of an anti-strike bill] at this immediate time. However, if I do . . . I shall have your suggestions before me.[46]

Secretary of War Stimson and OPM counsel John Lord O'Brian both favored passage of an anti-sabotage law in 1941, but Hillman, with much tact, was able to forestall them.

At the OPM the business contingent generally opposed long-range expansion of heavy-industry plants in steel and aluminum. When Hillman felt that prodding them might expedite the defense program, he would suggest to Roosevelt that a formal letter on the subject be written to himself by the President. Roosevelt would then write to him and Knudsen: "I am concerned about additional future steel-production needs. . . ." [47]

In directing the defense organization, Hillman did not confine himself to labor questions alone but worked with other officials to strengthen the entire civilian establishment there. Toward the end of 1941, as O'Brian relates, there was a search on for a good person to replace Donald Nelson (who was being shifted again) at the difficult post of chief of priorities. Hillman said jestingly that "what we need is some tough s.o.b. This great country of ours must be full of hundreds of thousands of them. Surely we ought to be able to find one to do this job."

After a while he came to see Mr. O'Brian, his face beaming, and said: "I've found our s.o.b." Julius Krug, who had been with TVA, had been recommended, and to him the post was assigned. Later Krug was much amused on hearing why Hillman had joined with others in recommending him. Flying about the country to give orders to unhappy industrialists who were being induced to "convert" their plants or have their material cut off, he would explain why he was chosen for this unpleasant assignment. "It's because they needed an s.o.b.!" he would explode, laughing heartily.[48]

VI

In August 1941, Secretary of War Stimson told Harry Hopkins that progress in arms production was not lagging too much, considering that the country was neither at war nor at peace. The spirit of businessmen was not roused up as it would be by the dangers of actual warfare, he held. Our defense organization, however, suffered, in his opinion, from being "an organization without a single head," another cause of our tardiness being "the persuasive handling of labor." [49] This was an example of the type of criticism aimed at Hillman and the OPM in high government circles. Meanwhile, in the camp of organized labor, John L. Lewis was demonstrating that he, for his part, would be immune to any efforts at persuasion used by Hillman or Roosevelt.

In reality the position of Lewis, who still believed himself the power behind the throne in the CIO, had been greatly changed at the time of the sudden invasion of Russia by Germany. The little nucleus of Communists in the CIO had abruptly dropped their agitation for neutrality in the so-called "imperialist" war and were now keen for aiding England and, above all, Soviet Russia with arms. Lewis, at the July 1941 Executive Council meeting of the CIO in Washington, had not even noticed that some of the young union leaders who habitually followed the "party line" in those days now listened in stony silence to his tirades against Hillman and Roosevelt.

It was not long before the left-wing groups began passing resolutions censuring the once-idolized Lewis for his alleged appeasement of the Nazis and Fascists, while Hillman, so long abused in the Communist press, was extolled in the *Daily Worker* (New York) as a hero of the workers. Lee Pressman, the general counsel of the CIO, then considered to have the best brains of the leftist group, attempted to reason with Lewis, though in vain; the CIO's general secretary, James Carey, now attacked him fiercely for his stubborn isolationism. Thus the balance of power within the CIO shifted away from its former president, who had alienated not only the moderate elements in the organization but also the Communists. Meanwhile Philip Murray had been doing what most men with brains and ambition would have done in his position. He had been building up his presidential machine and gathering support for his own policies, as distinguished from those of Lewis. His conviction that the defense program must be supported, the logic of the whole situation, drew him away from Lewis' side, so that now he was on his own—an outcome that Lewis might well have foreseen.

Lewis was alone and in an exposed position; but he had visions of more bold-handed adventures, including a grand onslaught on the Roosevelt Administration that would provide a front-page sensation for days on end. The national defense emergency was only another opportunity for him to show his mettle.

All that autumn, when he was still on terms of peace with Philip Murray, he pressed Murray to join him in his fight against Roosevelt's foreign policy. With organized labor in revolt against Roosevelt, the President, he believed, would be forced to draw back from further challenges to the Axis powers.[50]

He now sent forth an ultimatum to the mine operators, demanding closed shop contracts in the few remaining "captive" coal mines not yet unionized. These were owned by U. S. Steel, Bethlehem, Youngstown Sheet and Tube, and other great steel firms producing arms. It must be recalled that more than 95 per cent of the workers involved here were already employed under union-shop agreements. Yet Lewis insisted upon his "pound of flesh"—complete closed-shop contracts, even though stoppage of soft-coal mining would paralyze the country's key industries. When his terms were not met he called a strike of about 50,000 mine workers in the "captive" mines, and production was held up for ten days. Then a temporary agreement was reached with Chairman William H. Davis of the National Defense Mediation Board by which the men were to go back to work (during a thirty-day truce) while their claims were considered.

During this interval, Lewis conferred with Murray during the week end of October 18 at Atlantic City, when the agenda for the approaching CIO convention were being prepared. He wanted a resolution condemning the Roosevelt foreign policy; Murray now firmly insisted upon the opposite course: all-out support for the defense program. Thus, in a stormy scene, the two men came to a parting of the ways. William H. Davis, who had come to confer with Lewis on the coal-mining dispute, overheard his last words to the man who had worked by his side for more than twenty years: "It was nice to have known you, Phil!" From that day, Lewis, who felt he had "conceived and built the CIO," as he told a confidant, determined to leave it.[51]

The intermittent coal strikes, twice halted and resumed, contributed to the nerve-racking tension of that grim season in October and November 1941, when Moscow was under siege and the Japanese were momentarily expected to enter the war on the side of the Axis. Newspaper headlines reporting that *"Lewis Defies the President— Defense Steel Threatened"* alternated with others featuring news of military disasters for the Allies. Lewis freely denounced the Defense Mediation Board and Sidney Hillman as well, since he knew that Hillman stood behind it. On the government's side it was a question of refusing to change the rules of the game for Lewis' benefit and holding to the present status, as agreed, or having every union in the country strike for a 100 per cent closed shop. Thus the Board finally rejected the closed-shop demand for the "captive" mines by a vote of 10 to 2, with only the two CIO members, Murray and Kennedy, in dissent. These two members of the UMW resigned from the Mediation Board in a gesture of solidarity with the miners. This meant that the Board was wrecked for all practical purposes, since it no longer had any influence over the 5,000,000 members of the CIO. It was a heavy blow at Hillman, who had struggled for eighteen months to bring about a labor truce and had largely succeeded, save in the vital industry controlled by Lewis. Now Lewis called 150,000 miners out again on strike.

At this there were loud cries in Congress for the Army to be brought in to settle the matter. On November 22, however, Roosevelt capitulated to John L. Lewis completely. Mr. Myron Taylor, head of U. S. Steel, was induced to come to Washington to negotiate face-to-face with Lewis; and it was agreed that he, Lewis, and a third man, Dr. John Steelman of the Labor Department, were to constitute a committee to settle the affair peacefully among them. Steelman was known to be favorable to Lewis, and the settlement, in fact, was to be entirely on Lewis' terms.

The reason for Roosevelt's haste in surrendering to Lewis and having coal mining resumed at once may have been the fact that on the same day he had learned, through intercepted messages, that the Japanese government considered war with the United States might begin at any moment. But Roosevelt's attitude toward labor inevitably hardened from now on. He would not forget for a long time those whom he characterized as "a small but dangerous minority of labor leaders who are a menace . . . to labor itself as well as to the nation as a whole."

It was harder than ever to keep Congress from passing anti-strike bills, in view of Lewis' behavior. William H. Davis described Lewis' actions, in this case, as a display of "sheer arrogance." Hillman was in New York consulting with Davis, as negotiations for the new "captive" coal mines' agreement were drawing to an end. Despite his habitual restraint of speech, as an observer of the incident recalled, he burst forth into an impassioned denunciation of Lewis for his "irresponsible" and "evil" behavior during this time of national crisis.[52]

The CIO convention began its sessions on November 17. Though both Lewis and Hillman were absent, their cohorts brawled lustily with each other, thus reflecting the divided loyalties that still rent the younger labor federation. Lewis was reported to have said at the time that he would "lay out" Hillman and drive him from public life.[53] His brother, Dennie Lewis, called for a vote of censure of Hillman at the CIO convention because of his ruling in favor of the AFL in the Currier case. A resolution to this effect was passed, though without naming Sidney Hillman specifically.

On the other hand, Hillman's ardent followers were there also to denounce Lewis' "sabotage of the defense program." Chairman Murray made heroic efforts to keep order, despite fist fights on the floor of the convention, and in the end managed to have some anti-Hillman resolutions buried while others pledging the CIO's unstinted support of Roosevelt's foreign policy and of the national defense program were carried. This change of front sounded the end of Lewis' dominance of the CIO.

The great man himself was in Washington during the first week end of December completing final arrangements for the new contract to be enforced in the captive coal mines. That Sunday afternoon, when Lewis came out of the conference to report to the waiting newspapermen that all the union's demands had been granted, he was told that Honolulu had been attacked from the air by the Japanese. "I don't believe it. It's impossible!" he exclaimed. It was December 7, 1941.[54]

Chapter Twenty-Three

THE WAR
MANPOWER
COMMISSION

After the bombing of Pearl Harbor, Hillman and Knudsen, as directors of OPM, like everyone else, had taken emergency measures at once. They began the reorganization of their bureau in the interests of greater efficiency, and outlined a four-point program whose purpose was to speed up the conversion of civilian-goods plants to a war basis. Arms plants and machine-tool shops were to be run as far as possible on a three-shift and seven-day basis; many forms of consumer-goods production, such as cars and radios, were to be stopped; even the manufacture of clothing and food was to be cut down in part; the training program for workers was to be expanded rapidly.[1] Hillman reported to Roosevelt on December 12 that labor's response to the Axis attack was "splendid and spontaneous." Disputes in war industries were now at the zero point.

On January 6, 1942, Hillman flew to Detroit in the company of Knudsen, Robert Patterson, and James Forrestal, to attend a conference with the leaders of the Detroit automobile industry in order to bring about full conversion of its plant to munitions, tank and aircraft production. Edsel Ford, C. E. Wilson of General Motors,

Paul Hoffman of Studebaker, and other automobile magnates were present. It was a tribute to Hillman, however, that Walter Reuther as well as other high-level officers of the United Auto Workers (CIO) also participated in the talks on an equal footing with that of the motorcar industrialists and presented their own ideas of the most effective ways of converting plant and tools to war purposes. Mr. Reuther in particular spoke with considerable technical knowledge—being a skilled mechanic and self-taught engineer, much like Knudsen—of the need for pooling machine tools and dies and a more rapid scheme of conversion that would reduce the expected layoff of 300,000 workers in Detroit. Labor desired more than an "advisory" role, both Reuther and Addes indicated, and wished for a chance to contribute fully its practical mechanical knowledge and its understanding of personnel problems.

The motor magnates were now belatedly stirring to action. However, neither they nor the Navy's Mr. Forrestal cared much for the CIO leaders' ideas of labor-management committees to oversee the conversion process. They insisted on working through the existing controls and machinery—which was actually the way it was done.[2] Lewis' behavior in the recent coal-mining dispute had created a crisis in the relations of government and labor. Now that war had come, Representative Howard Smith and his allies in Congress were shouting louder than ever for measures to curb the irresponsible elements in labor. It became necessary for the Roosevelt Administration, therefore, to do more than assume a negative attitude toward anti-strike bills and offer sensible proposals for labor legislation on its own. This Hillman and William H. Davis, at the President's request, were now preparing.

On the eve of the war, in late November, Hillman had written a long memorandum to Roosevelt on the question of the control of labor in a time of emergency which is an excellent example of the sort of counsel he furnished the President.

A way must be found to stop defense strikes. We are all agreed that "strikes as usual" can no more be tolerated than "business as usual." . . . In this respect Congress is right, though many of the remedies proposed in Congress are unworkable.

Both the AFL and the CIO have pledged unstinted support to the defense program. If this support can be translated into a concrete program to stop interruptions of defense work, much of the labor legislation now under consideration may prove unnecessary.

Unless every resource of argument is first exhausted, such legislation may impair one of the nation's priceless assets—growing consciousness among all workers of labor's stake in this nation's defense of labor's liberties against aggression.

. . . Labor is now awake to this emergency. The time has come to capitalize upon this freshly awakened loyalty.

Not only can this loyalty be used to stop defense strikes. It can serve to enlist the constructive co-operation of labor. . . . It can provide us with enormous new sources of national energy. . . .

May I, therefore, suggest that you, so to speak, call on labor and industry to make good their promises? Concretely I should suggest that you confer, this week if possible, with Mr. Murray and Mr. Green. . . . More particularly you might suggest the possibility of a national conference of industry and labor, inviting representatives of the NAM, the Chamber of Commerce, the AFL, and CIO.

The primary purpose of the conference should be the formulation of policies and procedures to eliminate work stoppages in defense industries.

Its secondary purpose should be to obtain constructive suggestions from labor and industry on all aspects of the defense effort.

If this suggestion fails, or if labor and industry fail to meet their responsibilities, then they cannot blame government for their failures.[3]

In his advice to the President, as in his testimony before the Senate Committee on Education and Labor (on December 12), Hillman took the position that a freely given pledge on the part of organized labor guaranteeing against any interference with war production was the most desirable solution. Some of the bills aiming at labor control, such as the Smith bill, were really "anti-labor bills" and would not contribute to our defense, he held. He fought to avoid any legislation, but conceded that if it must be passed, then it should be limited only to the necessities of the war effort. The forthcoming labor-industry conference that Hillman, Davis, and Madame Perkins were preparing was to be made the occasion also for the establishment of a war labor board (in place of the wrecked Defense Mediation Board), which would be armed with emergency powers as in World War I.

Largely through Hillman's efforts at persuasion, the Senate Committee on Education and Labor postponed action, for the time being, on strike legislation until there had been an opportunity for the impending industry-labor conference to work out a voluntary program for avoiding work stoppages in war industries.[4]

The conference opened in Washington on January 14, 1942, with Senator Elbert Thomas of Utah acting as moderator. The contingent of industry spokesmen chosen by the U. S. Chamber of Commerce and the National Association of Manufacturers included personages like Walter C. Teagle and Cyrus Ching. The labor delegation included William Green, Matthew Woll, and George Meany for the AFL, and Philip Murray, John L. Lewis, and Julius Emspak for the CIO. (By then Lewis had pledged full support of the government, in behalf of the mine workers, on December 7.)

On the opening day the conferees were invited to meet with President Roosevelt at the White House, where he bade them welcome in an unusually frank and earnest talk. Now that war had come, he seemed like a "changed man" and a "dedicated" one as he addressed the labor-industry delegates in one of the most moving speeches of his career. To both sides he appealed for an end of all divisive action, pleading that they forget old scores and combine in the common task of saving the country. He did not "hate" business, he declared, nor did he hold any grievances against labor for trying to improve its position. But all would be asked to make sacrifices at a time when many of our young men were going to their death.[5]

The conference, after five days of discussion, gave its approval to resolutions banning strikes by labor and lockouts by management for the duration of hostilities; both sides agreed to settle disputes by negotiation and collective bargaining and to leave all issues that were not resolved thus to an emergency board appointed by the President, by whose decision they were to be bound. There was a deadlock, however, over the question of whether the proposed wartime labor board should have power to rule on the open or closed shop. This was left in abeyance when the President, having received the recommendations of the industry-labor conference, established a twelve-man National War Labor Board (representing public, employers, and labor) with authority to mediate labor disputes certified to it—as a sort of high court of appeal. Its chairman, once more as in the NDMB, was William H. Davis.

Lewis had been on his good behavior during the conference. But at its close American labor's "bad boy" threw a bombshell into the whole situation when on January 17, during a press conference at his union headquarters, he announced that he had taken steps to bring about the long-desired unification—"accouplement" was his quaint phrase—of the CIO and the AFL. He also made public letters to William Green and Philip Murray in which he declared that an end of the division in labor's house would now be in the public interest if an "accouplement" could be achieved with unified and competent leadership.

It was an astonishing performance, and only a man with Lewis' brass could have attempted, in secret, to do that which he had so long prevented others from doing openly. It was true that he had been a member of a standing CIO committee, set up almost three years before, consisting of himself, Sidney Hillman, and Philip Murray, to conduct negotiations for reunion with the AFL. Now without warning to Murray or to Hillman, acting as a committeé of one, he had entered into a secret (though "unofficial") bargain with "Big Bill" Hutcheson of the carpenters' union and other AFL executives, including Tobin, Woll, Meany, and David Dubinsky. By its provisions Mr. Green was to be pensioned off; George Meany was to be president and Philip Murray secretary of the combined organization. However, there were indications that Lewis, through his new alliances, expected to dominate the councils of the combined federation of 10,000,000 workers.[6]

When he heard the news, Philip Murray exploded: "I will not be Pearl-Harbored!" Roosevelt, mystified by this sudden move toward a united labor federation under the guidance of the most unpredictable of men, asked Hillman to find out what it was all about. Hillman, after quick inquiries, sent word that it was a maneuver to wrest control of the CIO from Philip Murray.*

On Hillman's warning that labor unity at such cost should not be encouraged now, the President quickly moved to block the scheme. Green was called to the White House, as was Murray, to whom Roosevelt gave assurances that he would back him up with all his influence in opposition to the Lewis-Hutcheson plan. Though the

* From other well-informed sources Roosevelt learned that David Dubinsky, Hutcheson, and Woll negotiated this Lewis business. Murray of course had no idea of it. (F.D.R. Papers: Hillman Memo to Roosevelt, Jan. 20, 1942; also CIO File, Jan. 20, 1942.) The N. Y. *Times,* Jan. 19, 1942, gave an advance account of the scheme that was filled with precise details given by the "insiders."

idea itself was a laudable one, none believed that Lewis' intentions were wholly disinterested, and it all fell through.

The breach between Lewis and Philip Murray, hitherto somewhat concealed, now seemed irreparable. With the United Mine Workers, Lewis was soon to make his grand exit from the CIO, which he had done more than anyone else to organize.*

During the first fortnight in January 1942, Roosevelt was absorbed in military talks with Prime Minister Churchill and his staff, who arrived in Washington soon after our entrance into the war. When the all-important question of America's war-supply organization was discussed, Churchill and Lord Beaverbrook joined with Henry L. Stimson and Bernard M. Baruch in urging that the President appoint a one-man authority in place of the two-headed OPM.

Roosevelt had received numerous accounts indicating that Knudsen, though a "wizard" of mass production, was not an effective public administrator. Moreover, it is quite evident that the President was reluctant to abdicate much of his wartime authority over civilian affairs to another man—least of all to the persistent Baruch, who repeatedly hinted that he was available for such a post. When the President finally was persuaded to reshuffle the defense setup again under a single administrator, he chose Donald M. Nelson for the job, on the earnest recommendation of Harry Hopkins. Intelligent, liberal-minded, and mild in disposition, Nelson was described as "the only big-business executive whom the New Dealers could talk to." [7] These qualities may have contributed to Roosevelt's decision.

On January 13, 1942, Roosevelt suddenly called in Nelson and informed him that he was to be director of the new War Production Board which was to replace the OPM. During their talk the President spoke in terms of lavish praise of both Knudsen and Hillman, who were being supplanted. It was perhaps owing to the tragic confusion of that season of military disaster that Roosevelt said nothing

---

* He was thereafter to make a whole series of ill-advised moves, though none of greater folly than those which led to his forfeiting control, in 1940, of a vast labor constituency of 5,000,000 members and so being left with no more than he had brought to the CIO in 1935: the United Mine Workers' Union. Lewis' opponents and critics declared that he had now "reverted" to the character he had been in the 1920's.

to warn Hillman and Knudsen of the impending change. Knudsen learned about it the following day, when a piece of ticker tape was brought to him. Five days more were to elapse before someone in the White House thought of softening the blow by having Knudsen transferred to the Army, in which he was to serve as an adviser on production matters, with the rank of lieutenant general. As for Hillman, he too only heard of the change when he read of it in the newspapers, and it came as a shock to him also.

The New Dealers still remaining in the President's entourage had been urging Knudsen's removal. The big-business element, on the other hand, wanted Hillman fired. It was true that Hillman had made sweeping concessions to the business point of view, but "he always insisted upon having something in return for labor, and business didn't like that," as Dr. Lubin said. Some leaders of business also had misgivings about labor's assuming a position of power in government that would make it difficult to reckon with after the war. But if Knudsen was to go, then it was to be expected that Sidney Hillman would go too. Yet in view of his devoted service, the manner of this dismissal was singularly lacking in grace. Roosevelt, deep in his military conferences, seemed more and more aloof even to those he regarded as his friends.

Hillman's associates were indignant at the President's action and urged him to leave Washington "rather than be used by the Administration to preserve the appearance of a pro-labor government." [8] Yet he seemed to take the affair with outward good humor, saying that the President's position was a difficult one, and "if he had asked me, I would have perhaps advised the same thing myself, as the best way out."

On January 9 (a few days before the OPM was abolished) Hillman had sent a message to Roosevelt saying that he wanted to see him about "the whole labor situation and War Labor Board." But more than two weeks passed before an appointment was fixed, for January 27. The shift of authority in the defense organization, already announced, was then discussed between them in friendly fashion. On this occasion Hillman is reported to have offered his resignation. The President, however, made it plain that he wished Hillman to continue as his top labor adviser, and to remain as head of the Labor Division, which was to be carried over intact to the new War Production Board. In fact, before this interview took place, on

January 21, 1942, Roosevelt had announced that Hillman was to be retained as a member of the WPB, in charge of labor policy and civilian manpower employment. Hillman agreed to stay on as a matter of duty.

II

In wartime the problem of labor supply or civilian manpower promised to become even more difficult than in the defense period. It was estimated that 2,000,000 men would be drafted into the armed forces during 1942. These would have to be replaced on the home front, while at the same time 10,500,000 additional workers would be needed in war industries under the tremendously expanded budget, now fixed at about $100,000,000,000 annually. As in the case of Ernest Bevin, wartime Labor Minister of England, the man in charge of war manpower would be forced to deal with immense dislocations of citizens, though in a country with a population three times as large as Britain's. The War Department's planners in considering all future emergencies, foresaw the possibility that authority might be needed to draft labor and move men and women about, wherever the national service required. There was preliminary discussion now, both at the White House and in the War Department, of the idea of converting the Labor Division of the WPB into a war manpower commission with far-reaching authority.

At his conference with Roosevelt on January 27, Hillman evidently received the impression that the President intended to entrust this office to him. His associates spoke afterward of the President's having "promised" the war manpower directorship to him. But the reminiscences of Henry Stimson and others have shown how vague and indecisive Roosevelt could be in the administrative field. Often when talking with a caller the President preferred that no third person be present and no record of the conversation be preserved, for the reason that he and his visitor would feel more at ease under such an arrangement. Hillman, moving always at a fast pace, kept neither notes nor diaries, and left only fragmentary memoranda of the most important conferences he attended.

At any rate, he seems to have had no doubt about the President's intentions with regard to the new responsibilities and powers to be vested in himself. But on the day following their interview, he wrote Roosevelt a note, as if to remind him of their understanding:

Jan. 28, 1942

Dear Mr. President:
    Before going away for a week's rest, I want you to know how deeply I appreciate our talk of yesterday. You know how fully you can count on my willingness and determination to help you to the best of my ability in this grave emergency through which we are all passing.[9]

Once it was agreed that authority over manpower was needed, the next question was in whom or what it should be vested. Reasonably enough, Hillman urged that control of the flow of labor into war plants should be bound up closely with the authority controlling war production, that is, the WPB. What the President apparently required now was firm assurance from Donald Nelson, the new chief of war production, that he desired such authority for his Board, under his jurisdiction.

Before leaving town, Hillman spoke with Donald Nelson, who at the time seemed to agree with his view. If the direction of all wartime labor should be relegated to the War Production Board, it would of course be turned over to Hillman and his Labor Division— hitherto armed with only a limited control handed down when needed by the President.

A letter was then drafted at the WPB that was to be addressed to Roosevelt by Donald Nelson, who apparently approved of the letter. It was left with him for his signature as the tired Hillman departed for Florida. The letter stated:

Jan. 28, 1942

. . . My experience in the industrial field, with the Defense Commission, and the OPM convinces me that all such labor problems relating to war production must be concentrated in one place and in one individual. Diffusion of such authority is bound to create unnecessary problems. . . .
    I respectfully suggest to you that full responsibility and authority for determining all such labor questions, as they bear upon war production, shall be vested in Sidney Hillman. Such an arrangement will serve to assure to labor direct participation in the war effort. . . . I believe that our effort will be greatly furthered, if it is clearly recognized that he is

charged with full responsibility for all such labor questions effecting our war-production program.

Respectfully yours,

Donald M. Nelson [10]

Donald Nelson never sent that letter. He never put up a fight to keep the "controversial personality" of Sidney Hillman on his Board.

In the meantime a message from Philip Murray and George Meany of the AFL, asking the President to "do nothing about the War Manpower Committee appointments until they have had a chance to talk with him," was relayed to Roosevelt by General Edwin Watson and Mrs. Anna Rosenberg, now acting as a White House assistant.[11] Rumors that the establishment of a war manpower commission was being considered had appeared in the newspapers shortly before.

Late in January, Roosevelt also went into the problem of a war manpower commission with Paul V. McNutt, former governor of Indiana, who was now Federal Security Administrator. McNutt, whose agency dealt largely with labor, brought forward a scheme of his own for placing the manpower job in the Federal Security Administration under his care. A committee of presidential advisers, consisting of Budget Director Harold D. Smith, Supreme Court Justice William O. Douglas, Judge Samuel Rosenman, and Mrs. Anna Rosenberg, was also studying the problem.

Early in February there were rumors afloat that Hillman was to be superseded and that a new shake-up impended in the WPB's Labor Division. On February 4, Hillman saw Roosevelt in connection with his work in forming a joint AFL-CIO committee, which was to maintain a de facto accord for the duration of the war. With Hillman on this visit to the White House were Murray, R. J. Thomas, and Julius Emspak for the CIO, and Green, Dan Tobin, and George Meany for the AFL. After the conference was over, Roosevelt told Hillman he wanted to see him and would call him. A week later Hillman inquired whether the President was ready to see him, explaining that "he just wanted the President to know he is available and waiting." But General Watson reported that the President was not ready.[12]

However, Roosevelt talked further with Mr. McNutt; and on February 9 he also had occasion to see David Dubinsky, according to White House records. (In those emergency days, marked by tremendous opportunities and hazards for organized labor, its power-minded leaders, unfortunately, were far more jealously divided than were the leaders of the business community.)

Certain CIO leaders, such as R. J. Thomas, then president of the United Auto Workers, are said to have boasted not long after this period that they helped "pull the carpet from under Hillman" in connection with the war manpower post.[13]

The President, it was clear, had almost made up his mind about who was to head the new board, but could not bear to tell Sidney. Meanwhile palace intrigues and the rumors they inspired buzzed about the White House. The gossip about Hillman's forthcoming demotion embarrassed him and made it difficult for him to get anything done. What was tormenting was not knowing where he stood and being forced to wait, while the time for action passed.

On February 13, 1942, Hillman, flanked by his deputy, Eric Nicoll, went thoroughly into the question of the manpower post again with Donald Nelson and his chief assistant, A. C. C. Hill. Nelson, while asking for more time to study the matter, now agreed that Hillman and his staff were to write a draft of a proposed executive order to be issued by the President, establishing a national war manpower board as a division of the WPB, with Hillman as its chairman. The draft of such an order outlining the powers of the proposed board was indeed sent to Roosevelt.

In an accompanying memorandum which he prepared for a conference with Roosevelt, Hillman pleaded that he be given full authority in his field or be permitted to resign. He said:

Up to three months ago . . . my responsibility for labor policy in the defense effort was not questioned. It was taken for granted that an appeal from me would go to you. Now, with the picture changed, Nelson has properly the full power and responsibility for production. It is necessary for labor to be in the same position.[14]

But there was no answer from the White House for more than three weeks, and Hillman could not even get through on the telephone to Roosevelt. This weighed on his spirits more than anything else.

In March there were rumors that Hillman had "quietly slipped his resignation on Nelson's desk." [15]

The March 3 and March 10 sessions of the War Production

Board were held on days when grave news came from Bataan and Singapore. Nelson presided; Vice-President Henry Wallace, Knox, Patterson, Harry Hopkins, Jesse Jones, Leon Henderson, and Sidney Hillman were present. Before this council Hillman stoutly waged his fight for manpower control. His new deputy director of the Labor Division, General Frank J. McSherry, reported on a chaotic labor situation, with a scarcity of workers shown in some vital arsenal areas, but an overabundance of idle workers elsewhere. Housing and even rubber tires to carry the workers to their jobs were lacking. Hillman then spoke about the efforts his division had long made to ward off the evils flowing from the geographical maldistribution of contracts. Unless labor problems were dealt with *before* contracts were placed, he warned, it was going to be all the harder to meet the President's production quotas.[16]

At the next session Nelson himself described the labor situation as constantly worsening; and Hillman added that with the armed forces, private industry, and farms all competing fiercely for manpower, mere talk of co-ordination was no longer enough.

Nelson, though expressing agreement with Hillman on the urgency of the labor-supply problem, stated that he was reluctant to ask for greater responsibilities than were already assigned to the WPB.[17]

III

At this stage of the bureaucratic tug-of-war the New Deal leaders, Hillman among them, were conducting a vigorous campaign to force heavy industry to expand its plant and speed the conversion of consumer-goods factories to war production. The business-as-usual advocates fought back hard. Steel-industry leaders denied the wisdom of building additional hearths and foundries that would take two years to construct; and purveyors of refrigerators worked stubbornly to delay the conversion of their plants into units for machine guns or gun mounts, their influence reaching not only the lobbies of Congress but the councils of the WPB itself. Hillman, the labor man in government, became one of the principal targets of those who for profits' sake strove to delay conversion.

A number of dollar-a-year men had lately been the subject of complaints brought before the Truman committee, charging that they served the interests of their corporations primarily, while employed

in the government's war-industry organizations to distribute contracts involving hundreds of millions of dollars. In defense against
such attacks their champions bethought themselves of an expedient
which, according to the prevailing ethical standards, is considered
"good politics."

On March 2, 1942, as if to forestall further attacks on delinquent
business elements by the New Deal group, Representative Albert J.
Engel of Michigan rose on the floor of the House and, in a vitriolic
speech, charged Sidney Hillman with diverting large Army and Navy
clothing contracts to employers favored by his own union—that is, to
manufacturers under union agreements with the Amalgamated—
while denying such contracts to firms employing the International
Ladies' Garment Workers and to non-union contractors in clothing.
This scheme, Mr. Engel charged, was being carried out by agreement with Chairman Nelson of the WPB and various War and Navy
Department officials. The weight of his accusations seemed to rest
upon a report that a certain small manufacturer of women's garments in Michigan had been denied the chance to bid for Army uniforms, on Hillman's "order," as it was alleged. Mr. Engel asked:

> Is Sidney Hillman interested in production for war purposes, or is he
> interested and devoting his energies to production of war materials for
> his own union? . . . Is Mr. Nelson merely an automaton sitting on
> the Production Czar's throne, while Sidney Hillman sits behind the
> throne pulling the wires and pressing the buttons which manipulate the
> automaton called Donald Nelson? [18]

With a nice sense of timing, Fulton Lewis, Jr., now began a series
of attacks on Hillman over a nationwide radio network, the purport
of which was that Hillman, while pretending to serve his government, drew a salary of $12,500 from his union and saw to it that his
union profited through Army-uniform contracts awarded to its
friends.

At this same period, as if by coincidence, Mr. Dubinsky, always
zealous for the interests of his union, no doubt, lodged vehement
protests with Under-Secretary of War Robert P. Patterson to the
same effect: that Hillman was discriminating in the award of Army-
uniform contracts against manufacturers of women's garments, who
were now threatened with priority orders reducing their output.
Patterson recalled later that Dubinsky's rage had its comical side.
The War Department instituted a thorough investigation into the

affair, which proved that there was not the slightest substance to his charges, nor to those of Mr. Engel or Fulton Lewis, Jr. "We found that Hillman had nothing whatsoever to do with those contracts," Mr. Patterson said.*

The barrage of mud that was being hurled at Hillman emboldened certain elements in Congress to institute an investigation of his recent services before the House Military Affairs Committee on March 16. The irony of the affair was that it was conducted by Committee Chairman Andrew May of Kentucky, who was not long afterward to be impeached and sentenced to prison for corrupt behavior in office. Hillman, indisposed, submitted only a written statement. The hearings completely cleared both Hillman and Nelson of accusations that had been made against them.[19]

Meanwhile, by the end of March 1942, the White House advisory committee of Douglas, Rosenman, Harold Smith, and Mrs. Rosenberg, having completed their studies of the manpower problem, had worked out a draft of an executive order establishing a war manpower commission and made recommendations for its personnel. It was reported at the time that Director of the Budget Harold D. Smith, who had failed to overreach Hillman the year before in the little intrigue touching the establishment of the OPM, was resolved to have him dropped. Mrs. Rosenberg, the labor consultant, who had been serving under Paul McNutt as head of the New York office of the Federal Security Administration, was partial to her chief. With Mr. Smith she recommended the appointment of McNutt as director of the new War Manpower Commission, which it was hoped would be able to co-ordinate the work of twenty different government agencies now dealing with labor.[20]

Hillman had made many powerful enemies in the business world, among labor leaders, and in Congress during his two years' service in Washington. Neither Mr. Green of the AFL nor Mr. Murray of the CIO spoke up for him at this point (though Murray soon after-

* A memorandum dated March 9, 1942, by John Ohly, who investigated these charges for the War Department at the time, shows that awards of uniform contracts, in the cases of alleged discrimination against the ILGWU, were made by Army procurement officers, "on the principle which had been in effect for many months, namely, that awards would not be given to companies which had not been previously making the type of goods wanted, provided there were facilities available in companies making that type of goods."

ward was to form a very friendly working alliance with him against the still formidable Lewis). According to a statement of Joseph Keenan of the AFL, who expressed great appreciation of Hillman's work:

> Once the most powerful labor man in government, he was at his "nadir" from which it was generally believed he could not rise politically. Even at the White House he was in eclipse as big businessmen gained more influence and obtained strategic positions.[21]

He had tried to make labor a "working partner in war production," yet labor was unsatisfied. He was now regarded simply as "Roosevelt's man." What progressive labor wanted—and it showed a far more militant spirit than in World War I, as was reflected in many union resolutions and numerous letters from Philip Murray and Walter Reuther—was to have a *functional* part in war production through the establishment of joint labor-industry committees; in short, an "equal voice."

Hillman had gone far to meet such demands, especially in the shipbuilding stabilization agreement; and some fourteen labor-and-industry "advisory" committees had been established by 1942, thanks to his efforts. Yet here, too, the AFL and CIO men often persisted in their non-co-operative attitude toward each other, and the results as yet were insignificant. Most representatives of "management" detested the very idea of such joint committees and dreaded their portent for the future.

In the circle of Harry Hopkins and in the War and Navy Departments, the top offices were now manned by Republican lawyers like Stimson and Patterson, or bankers like James Forrestal, of Dillon, Read and Company, Robert A. Lovett of Brown, Harriman, and Artemus Gates of the New York Trust Company. The War Department had in view, for possible emergencies, a plan for the conscription of labor—which, in the end, in 1944, though by a scant margin, was dropped as unnecessary. At the time Sidney Hillman was scarcely considered in such circles as the right man to administer such unpleasant medicine to the laboring masses.

Yet it was Hillman who had made some of the most important contributions to the new "technique of manpower" utilization, as the well-informed Herbert Emmerich, executive secretary of both the OPM and the War Production Board, wrote somewhat later:

. . . The War Manpower Commission inherited a ready-made organization. The groundwork for training within industry, for labor supply, for the federalization of the employment service, and for all the other steps that had to be taken in the field of civilian manpower had been laid by Sidney Hillman's Labor Division in the NDAC and the OPM. . . . In spite of sparing twelve million men to the armed services, the U.S. labor force produced the greatest crop on the farm and the greatest production in the factories and the greatest volume of transportation on land, sea, and air ever known. The groundwork for the technique of manpower utilization that was laid before Pearl Harbor can be credited directly to Sidney Hillman's efforts.*

Hillman waited all through March in tormenting uncertainty as to how his case would be decided. He was aware of enemies around him on all sides, and aware that his much-rumored replacement would be regarded as a defeat—which in his heart he felt was undeserved.

On March 22, he addressed a long memorandum to President Roosevelt, in which, in effect, he pleaded with him to make up his mind. In this document his proposals for the mobilization of labor supply in war production were set forth in detail as he had submitted them to the WPB. It was to represent an intensification of the work he was doing: basically a system of labor priorities, with control of hiring and recruitment through the U. S. Employment Service, under direction of the WPB.

In orderly fashion workers were to be moved out of consumer industries into war plants, while wages were to be stabilized, though by use of a flexible scale. He concluded in fairly emotional terms:

I am ready to put this program into operation. Without your specific approval, I cannot do this job.

Other agencies and departments have suggested to you that this responsibility be taken away from the War Production Board and placed

* Herbert J. Emmerich, op. cit. This writer also notes that the War Manpower Commission, vested eventually in the FSA, was "not the most successful of the improvised war agencies," had "fuzzy and tenuous relationships" with the Selective Service and draft board organizations, and never acquired a large authority to direct labor. It was related also that the director made various political appointments of AFL and CIO men, in equal amount, and played no important part in the war-production setup. The decision to cut back Army recruitment in 1944 also made compulsory "direction" of labor unnecessary in the end.

elsewhere. These suggestions have created doubts in government and among labor and employer groups as to where this task is to be performed. Such doubts do not make for effective action. Consequently, I cannot obtain that unreserved co-operation necessary to put over a program of such magnitude and difficulty. Today, when I urge these things, men doubt that I speak with the authority that comes from your wholehearted support—a support which I have never found wanting.

This program of labor mobilization cannot abide longer delay. Unless drastic measures are taken now, we shall find the production effort seriously impeded for want of manpower. Every day's delay is costing us guns and planes and lives.

I am not pleading for the responsibility of this task. I am only asking you to decide quickly where and by whom you want this job done—and to make your decision known in terms that cannot be mistaken by government, labor, or management.

In your decision, there are no personal feelings of mine which you need consider.[22]

But this memorandum was never sent. There was no answer to his repeated requests for an appointment with the President (who was certainly much occupied then). This was a bad omen and greatly depressed his spirits. In the first two weeks of April, Hillman did not attend the WPB meetings. He seemed to be ailing.

The draft of the executive order for the War Manpower Commission was handed to the President on April 13 by Harold D. Smith. By the next day news of its contents began to spread in White House circles. On that afternoon of April 14, Hillman's daughter Philoine, who had been working as one of his secretaries, observed when he came into the office after lunch that he looked fearfully pale and drawn. She begged him to leave at once and go to bed. He consented and was taken to his apartment at the Wardman Park Hotel, where he collapsed under a severe heart attack. He was then removed to the Doctors' Hospital in Washington, where his condition was pronounced very serious.

It was just before his collapse that definite word had reached him at last that the President had decided to pass over him and assign the mobilization of America's civilian manpower to McNutt. (From a purely political point of view this was, for Roosevelt, an easier appointment, so far as dealing with Congress was concerned.) The news hit Hillman very hard. He had tended almost to "identify" himself with Franklin Roosevelt. Now, as one newspaper commentator observed, he was being shelved after two years of furious effort in the public service which had wrecked his health and exposed him to being "ground to pieces between powerful, rival labor advocates." [23]

The news was out in the late evening newspapers of April 15, though the President still had said nothing.*

At the end of a week Hillman was sitting up and resting comfortably, his friends, his wife, and his daughters by his side. From New York his union associates hastened to the scene and with them his old secretary, Tecia Davidson, who recalls his saying sadly: "Well, Tecia, I'm finished, I'm through. I'm no good for anything any more." But she laughed and assured him that he would soon be up and around, and up to his old tricks also. He was then but fifty-five years old.†

Four days after his heart attack there came a belated message by telegram from the preoccupied Roosevelt, who now tried to let Hillman down softly:

THE WHITE HOUSE

WASHINGTON

HONORABLE SIDNEY HILLMAN,   April 18, 1942

DOCTORS' HOSPITAL

WASHINGTON, D.C.

AFTER LONG CONSIDERATION, I HAVE SIGNED EXECUTIVE ORDER SETTING UP WAR MANPOWER COMMISSION UNDER MCNUTT AND THIS OF NECESSITY

* "Paul V. McNutt, the tall, handsome, gray-haired Indiana politician is the choice of the four-member committee to whom the President turned over the job of picking a man and drafting the set-up of the manpower agency. Smith and Mrs. Rosenberg are the big McNutt rooters. Both have personal peeves against Sidney Hillman. Mrs. Rosenberg is anti-Hillman because he didn't bring her into the defense picture." (Drew Pearson in the Washington *Post,* April 16, 1942.)

† A distinguished psychiatrist who knew Sidney Hillman and saw him at this period declared that his fatigue, his chronic illness, and finally his heart attack (April 14, 1942) were typically "psychosomatic"; that is to say affected by the nervous stress under which he labored. That he was "neurotic" in the ordinary sense she did not believe to be true; for though he lived always under fearful tension he managed to balance himself successfully, recovering and renewing himself after each setback. "The only trouble was that he received the blows of life full force. Though he would not admit it, he would be badly hurt. But if he had only known how to 'roll with the punches' he might have saved his health." (Dr. Flanders Dunbar to M. J.)

TAKES TRAINING FUNCTIONS AND LABOR SUPPLY FUNCTIONS AWAY FROM LABOR DIVISION OF THE WAR PRODUCTION BOARD. I AM CHANGING THE LABOR DIVISION PRESENTLY INTO A LABOR PRODUCTION DIVISION, WITH THE OBJECTIVE OF HAVING IT FUNNEL LABOR INFORMATION AND NEEDS PRIMARILY TO NELSON WITHOUT GOING THROUGH OTHER DIVISIONS OF WPB. I FEEL VERY STRONGLY THAT YOU PROPERLY WILL NOT WANT THAT KIND OF WORK WITH WPB, BUT IT IS VERY IMPORTANT TO THE GOVERNMENT AND ESPECIALLY TO ME PERSONALLY THAT I HAVE YOU AS LABOR ADVISER TO ME. I AM THEREFORE APPOINTING YOU "SPECIAL ASSISTANT TO THE PRESIDENT ON LABOR MATTERS." THIS WILL MEAN THAT YOUR RELATIONSHIP TO ME IN THE GOVERNMENT WILL BE VERY SIMILAR TO THAT OF HARRY HOPKINS. NATURALLY THE FIRST THING FOR YOU TO DO IS TO RECUPERATE AND BUILD UP YOUR HEALTH, AND AS SOON AS YOU FEEL WELL ENOUGH I WANT YOU TO UNDERTAKE THE NEW WORK WHICH WILL NOT ONLY BE EXTREMELY USEFUL AND NECESSARY BUT WILL ENABLE US TO WORK CLOSELY TOGETHER.

FRANKLIN D. ROOSEVELT [24]

Hillman made no haste to answer this message.

After a while, when it was learned that he was somewhat recovered, a presidential assistant came to the hospital to inquire whether he would accept the appointment to the White House staff. Hillman said no, declaring that he intended to retire from the government service. However, an official announcement to the press stated that Mr. Hillman would "assume his new post shortly after he had recovered from his present illness." Hillman said nothing in public at the time, nor did he speak of any disappointment in the President. "Well, I can take it. I'm a rough-and-tumble fighter myself," he jested to his old comrade, Blumberg.

John Lord O'Brian, then general counsel of the WPB, hearing that Hillman intended to leave Washington, came to see him at the hospital and found him sitting up in bed, looking calm and rested and receiving a good many visitors. Mr. O'Brian expressed the view that it would be a great pity for the government to lose Hillman now, though he agreed that the way in which the President had removed him from his post was "extremely cruel." Was it because of the attacks in the radio, the press, and Congress that he was determined to leave?

No, Hillman replied, that was all part of the game. But as for going on in Roosevelt's service, he said: "Well, Judge, I'll tell you. If a man has the support and full confidence of his chief he can go ahead and do anything—but once he feels that the chief's confidence is weakening, then it's time to get out." [25]

Roosevelt's action in this case may be analyzed as having been conceived in a spirit of extreme political "realism"—but it was also compromised by his instinctive dislike of hurting people who had been close to him. (In this way he managed to hurt the feelings of a great many persons.) He did not warn Hillman; he did nothing to soften the blow. It has been observed that he needed Hillman greatly in 1940 as the strongest man in the labor movement after Lewis and as one who could do most to check Lewis' powerful opposition moves. But now, after the invasion of Russia, and after our own country had been drawn into the war, all the different labor factions, right and left, seemed tolerably united—and the controversy-provoking Hillman was no longer so necessary at Roosevelt's side.

By now Washington was a city of "war lords"; even that old liberal, Harry Hopkins, who had helped to bring Hillman into the defense organization, depended more and more exclusively upon the abilities of financial and management leaders to speed war production. (At the War Manpower Commission, Paul McNutt, after taking over the "labor direction" post, generated no great authority nor great power in his office.)

The AFL and the CIO leaders alike had helped to pull Sidney Hillman down. Thereafter their agents, as before, haunted the lobbies of Washington, or visited Roosevelt, and tried to exert their influence in the usual ways. But the passing of Hillman was to bring about a sharp decline in labor's direct influence in the high councils of the war government.[26] When Hillman was removed, there was no one of his stature to replace him. None did.

After two weeks Hillman replied to the President with good grace:

Doctors' Hospital
Washington, D.C., May 1, 1942

Dear Mr. President:

I deeply appreciate your telegram in which you state that you are appointing me "Special Assistant to the President on Labor Matters." While lying here in the hospital, I have thought and thought about the problem of how I can best serve our war effort. I fully recognize the growing burdens which are placed on you with the passing of each day. There is nothing I would not do, if thereby I could help ease—in some measure at least—your tasks. Yet I find that I always come back to the same conclusion: namely, that I can help you most and serve the country best if I actively resume my participation in the counsels of the labor movement. I honestly believe I can be of greater service to you if I return to the presidency of the Amalgamated Clothing Workers of America. In that role, I can effectively influence the direction and the activities of labor. I know that you agree with me that the pursuit of sound policies by the American labor movement is one of the most vital factors in the success of our war effort.

Mr. President, you have honored me deeply when you permitted me to serve under you—as I have during the past twenty-two months. For this privilege of service I am and shall always be sincerely grateful. . . . That period was most critical, because a considerable part of the country, as well as labor, was not fully alive to the dangers menacing us. It was your clear and early recognition of the seriousness of the threats to all that we hold dear that made it possible for us to be as well prepared as we are, and to help our valiant allies to the extent that we have. I want you to know that I stand ready at all times to render you any service that you feel I can perform.

Respectfully,

Sidney Hillman [27]

We were at war. Roosevelt, of necessity, spent all his days absorbed in global plans with generals and admirals and forgot some of his friends for long periods. Then after a while he remembered poor Sidney Hillman, whose moving letter he had not answered; and in reply sent him a mass of flowers. Hillman responded with a brief note thanking him, and declaring that he was certain that the flowers had a perceptible effect in aiding his recovery.

In the first days of June, after six weeks in the hospital, Hillman returned to rest at his hotel, then rode northward to New York to resume his old life as a union man.

Chapter Twenty-Four

LABOR

IN POLITICAL

ACTION: 1944

At all times sincere friends of freedom have been
rare, and its triumphs have been due to minorities,
that have prevailed by associating themselves with
auxiliaries whose objects often differed from their
own.
—Lord Acton, *The History of Freedom in Antiquity*

In July 1942, he was back at his cottage at Point Lookout, the small, sedate seaside resort on the southern shore
of Long Island. Here he loved to lie in the sun on the sparkling white
sand, looking out to sea, or watching the swift tide race between the
tiny promontory of Point Lookout and the Jones Beach reef, or to
lounge in the walled garden beside the cottage, reading. Under this
restful regime he slowly regained his strength. His wife was by his side
again, and his two daughters were often with him.

The Amalgamated "clan" also gathered about him as faithfully as
ever in this period of illness and retreat. Nearby was the house of
Vice-President Hyman Blumberg, an irrepressible wit who knew
how to keep the "boss" in good humor. Jacob Potofsky, who had been
the intimate of Hillman since the age of nineteen, was also a constant

visitor. It was Potofsky who, as general secretary of the Amalgamated union, presided over its executive councils during Hillman's long leaves of absence. With these and other old associates, such as Maxwell Brandwen (who had resigned his post at the WPB when Hillman left) and August and Dorothy Bellanca, Hillman relaxed by talking shop, labor, politics, war—or simply playing cards or chess.

One of his old friends, Mrs. Blumberg, asked him at this time if he would be able to reconcile himself to his "little union affairs" after the years among the heavers and shakers at Washington. He protested: "But the Amalgamated, my people, mean everything to me!"

On another occasion, when he was still very ill and scarcely knew if he would ever recover, he said to one old intimate: "The labor movement owes me nothing. I owe it everything." This thought dominated his later years completely.

By the end of the summer he was back at his office in New York. The Amalgamated had become, for those days, a "giant" among labor unions, having reached an approximate membership of 300,000 in 1942, with its network of locals and regional organizations spreading over thirty-four states. Its most important expansion movement in recent years was devoted to the growing cotton-garment industry and to organizing in the Southern "frontier" country. This department was headed by Dr. Gladys Dickason, the union's director of research, who had also become a member of the General Executive Board. Other rapidly growing departments during the war years were those of the shirt workers and the laundry workers (centered chiefly in New York and Philadelphia).[1]

There were, to be sure, numerous unions that were much bigger in numbers than the ACWA, especially in the mass-industry, building, and transport fields. But there was none that carried on such large or varied social-welfare activities in the interests of its members. Because of its success in low-cost housing, the Amalgamated organization was in great demand for the management of additional co-operative housing projects whose investment value, on completion, stood at more than $20,000,000. Still another large recent venture was the Amalgamated Life Insurance Association of Chicago, launched at the end of 1940, which provided death benefits of $500 as well as health and accident insurance to all ACWA workers in men's and boys' clothing, the cost being borne by a contribution of 2 per cent of payroll charged to employers. The grand total of banking, insurance, housing, and other co-operative enterprises managed by the Amalgamated, or held in trust for its workers, came to about $200,000,000 in the years after World War II. To Hillman's great satisfaction the war years also saw the final unionization of several powerful manufacturing concerns that had long resisted the Amalgamated's entrance into their shops, such as L. W. Greif of Baltimore, with 3,000 employees, and the great Cluett-Peabody and Manhattan Shirt companies with an aggregate of 8,000 workers. These last operations, chiefly among women workers, had been carried out by a very experienced and skillful organizing staff under Potofsky, Chatman, Dorothy Bellanca, and Gladys Dickason while Hillman was in Washington giving them counsel occasionally by telephone.

It was good to be back at the general offices of the Amalgamated, Hillman said. Since 1926 these were located in the solid, old-fashioned building that had formerly been occupied by Tiffany's, at 15 Union Square. Its generous windows gave a cheerful view of crowded Union Square in the heart of New York's garment district. This was home to him, his old orbit, with all its familiar stir, its conferences and committee meetings going on all day. Downstairs in the same building was the thriving Amalgamated Bank, with its throng of worker and small-business clients; and a few blocks north on Fifth Avenue was the office of his old friend, David Drechsler, executive head of the New York Clothing Manufacturers' Exchange, virtually the nerve center of the city's clothing market. Within the space of those few blocks many vital issues affecting the nation's billion-dollar men's clothing industry, in peace or war, were settled during brief strolls along Fifth Avenue, or luncheon talks between Hillman and Mr. Drechsler. There was always trouble-shooting; but the clothing industry had by now grown "civilized" in a degree known to few other American manufacturing trades. What Hillman had often prophesied, with an air of good-humored foreboding, had come to pass: the great union literally "ran itself." There was not enough for Sidney Hillman to do here nowadays. For long years, moreover, he had become accustomed to thinking in terms of the national labor movement as a whole. His mind ranged beyond the limits of the clothing and garment industry over the whole American scene, which now gave him much cause for anxiety.

He had promised his family and friends that he would take things easy in resuming his old life; also that he would rest or take vacation trips for the sake of his health. But it was plain enough that he was not made to enjoy the easy life. In the year that followed his illness and departure from Washington he often seemed, as Philip Murray observed, bored, restless, and despondent.[2]

The first year of the war, with its many disappointments and military reverses, was the hardest. In the 1942 state and congressional election the Democratic Party met with heavy reverses. Pro-Administration congressmen were defeated by Republicans in one district after another, or lost ground in the primaries to conservative Democrats. A contributing cause of these setbacks at the polls was the movement of almost 6,000,000 young men into the armed forces, with a resultant fall in registration among those who were most disposed to vote for the party of Roosevelt. It was not that the Republicans made any impressive gains in 1942, Hillman observed later, but that the progressive element stayed away from the polls; only 28 millions actually voted, against some 50 millions in 1940.

Roosevelt was passionately absorbed in the African landing operation scheduled for that autumn; his political advisers were somewhat maladroit in managing the 1942 elections. For the New York governorship, the naming of a Tammany Hall selection, John J. Bennett, as Democratic candidate proved to be far from a shrewd choice. Labor stayed away from the polls. Instead of endorsing one of the major party candidates that year, the American Labor Party of New York State offered a third candidate in Dean Alfange, who had been chosen by the Dubinsky group.

Since February, Hillman had not been in touch with the President. At no time, however, so far as his intimates knew, did he express any disappointment or anger at the President—certainly none of that "extreme irritation and even condemnation of Roosevelt" attributed to him by Miss Perkins in her memoirs.[3] On the contrary, Mrs. Eleanor Roosevelt has said: "There was no break in the friendly relations between my husband and Mr. Hillman at any time." [4]

It was Roosevelt, moreover, who made the first approach to his old friend. In mid-September 1942, when his mind turned for the moment from war to the current election campaign, he wrote to Hillman:

Dear Sidney:
I am delighted to hear from Mac [MacIntyre] that you are feeling all right again. You have certainly had a long siege of it, and I hope the trouble is gone forever.

Very confidentially, I am going away on a bit of a trip, but I hope to see you as soon as I get back. You will note that date from the newspapers.

Always sincerely,

Franklin D. Roosevelt [5]

But the African campaign suffered delays, and his voyage to Casablanca, alluded to in this letter, was postponed from week to week. Meanwhile Hillman and the Amalgamated union showed a notable apathy in the New York State campaign of that year.

On October 9, Roosevelt sent an urgent message to Hillman, as if written by his secretary, stating that

some people in New York, so the President understood, did not think that the President's endorsement of John J. Bennett was wholehearted. The President said when he gave his endorsement he included the three men running for governor . . . and thought Mr. Bennett was the best qualified. . . . The President said Mr. Hillman was very free to say to anyone that the President's endorsement of John J. Bennett was thoroughly unqualified.[6]

Here we have Franklin Roosevelt, the political artificer, revealing himself in carpet slippers. What his communication no doubt meant, when translated into non-technical terms, was that he wanted Hillman to swing the Amalgamated's "battalions of opinion" in New York to the support of the uninspiring Democratic choice for governor. The chances of a Democratic victory in New York were not improved by rumors that Roosevelt himself was cool about Mr. Bennett, and it was hoped that Hillman would now set these at rest by tactfully releasing news of the confidences he had received.

Several weeks passed, and Hillman did not budge. The incident is illuminating in that it shows Roosevelt seeking the help of Hillman in the vexing New York situation. Unlike those "court favorites" who rose and fell as presidential assistants at the White House—a role which Hillman could not possibly have stomached—he wielded a large political influence in his own right through his labor constituency.

Meanwhile the ALP leaders also tried to persuade Hillman to commit himself to their candidate, Alfange. His friends remember that it was impossible to get him to say a word. Indeed Mr. Flynn, as Democratic National Chairman, was obliged to write Roosevelt urging him to induce Hillman to release the President's letter endorsing Bennett. It was a minor political comedy, which came to an end when the Amalgamated union, on October 29, 1942, too late for it to have any effect, rather lamely announced its endorsement of the Democratic candidate.

From the Administration standpoint the election results were very sour; Mr. Thomas Dewey was voted into office by a decisive margin, since the ALP's independent candidate merely helped to cut down the Democratic vote.

That season was one of political and mental depression in the country. The War Labor Board, under W. H. Davis, tried to stabilize wages through application of the "Little Steel Formula," July 1942, developed in negotiations between that group of steel firms and its workers. These resulted in provisions for "maintenance of union membership" and a 15 per cent increase in wages, based on official estimates of the rise in the cost of living from January 1, 1941, to May 1, 1942. The government pledged itself to combat inflation and stabilize prices under the President's directive of April 27, 1942. In the various war agencies AFL and CIO representatives sat as members of "advisory committees," such as the War Manpower Commission, the OPA, and the WPB; Green and Murray also enjoyed an advisory capacity in the Economic Stabilization Board under Director James F. Byrnes, who had become Roosevelt's second-in-command on the civilian front. Yet despite all this there was really no direct participation at top levels of government by representatives of organized labor after Hillman left Washington. Spokesmen of the National Association of Manufacturers successfully opposed the introduction of joint labor-management committees in most war plants as "revolutionary experiments" for which the need had not yet arisen. Meanwhile prices were rising faster than controls could cope with them; despite high wages in some fields, a third of the nation's families earned, on the average, only $1,500 a year in 1942; and housing conditions for war workers remained wretched in areas of intense war production.

In a forthright interview he gave in July, Hillman declared that our output of war matériel could have been advanced 30 per cent if management had been willing to co-operate fully, as labor had done in waiving the right to strike and forgoing many other advantages. Somewhat later, in another interview, he noted also "a feeling of frustration among union men in recent months—a feeling that their unions might not be serving any function as wages gradually became stabilized." [7]

The CIO, whose membership had swollen to more than 5,000,000 during the war boom, was severely shaken when John L. Lewis withdrew the United Mine Workers' Union from its ranks in October 1942. Lewis' next move was to embark on one of his most extraordinary adventures, when the UMW's District 50 undertook to unionize 3,000,000 farm workers. Yet no glory was won in this enterprise, soon afterward abandoned by the miners' chieftain. This fiasco was commemorated by a famous cartoon of the period drawn by Fitzpatrick of the St. Louis *Post-Dispatch,* entitled "The Return from Elba." The scowling Lewis is shown in the uniform of Napoleon, riding past a lonely farmhouse in the dead of night, mounted on a sad and scrawny old cow.

As Hillman had prophesied, Lewis' quest for power without program or policy had driven from his side union officers of intelligence and ability, and brought him to a long series of misadventures that dissolved forever the myth of his infallibility. One important effect of Lewis' abandonment of the CIO and of his "lone-wolf" tactics was that President Philip Murray felt inspired to join forces with Sidney Hillman. One well-informed labor journalist observed in 1943 that, because of the threat offered by Lewis, Murray was now bent on working out a friendly alliance with the resourceful Hillman, "and both may try to cement the CIO against any future storms that the miners' chief may whip up." [8]

The labor movement as a whole, though prosperous, was as far from unity as ever in 1943. When one looked back at the scene of revolutionary agitation in the thirties and contrasted that with the attitude of labor during World War II, one might have said that the unions were merely marking time. Now, at the beginning of 1943, Lewis was making arrangements to re-enter the AFL (though he did not tarry there very long either).

One consequence of the congressional campaign of 1942 was the election of enough anti-labor-minded members to assure the passage of the Smith-Connally bill, called the War Labor Disputes Act, over Roosevelt's veto in the late spring of 1943. Although the no-strike pledge was being observed by labor in good faith, the Act, under emergency wartime powers, imposed a cooling-off period of 30 days before strikes could be called and gave statutory authority for the seizure of struck plants by the President. Among its other provisions was a very significant one restricting the payment of money contributions to political parties by labor organizations.

II

After the great "labor wave" of the 1930's there had come to the CIO, as in every popular movement for political or social change, a period of consolidation. To be sure, the momentum of the CIO's earlier days still generated big organizing drives during the war years under the leadership of Philip Murray, a steadier, less spectacular figure than Lewis, though by no means lacking in native ability and shrewdness. These operations were conducted along lines marked out previously and without the apocalyptic fervor of the sit-down strikes. Indeed, with the AFL pursuing industrial-union methods in the booming war industries, there was increasingly less real difference between the two rival federations. In the CIO the leaders were as a rule younger men; and more progressive young intellectuals, including economists, journalists, and lawyers, sought to make their careers in its constituent unions and central organization.

By the winter and spring of 1943, the younger element in the CIO showed much concern at the New Deal's setbacks and seriously discussed measures for the expansion of the CIO's political department, previously consisting mainly of Labor's Non-Partisan League, now vanished with Lewis. The Smith-Connally Act gave point to their discussion. At the time of its passage by Congress, certain emissaries came to Philip Murray with the proposal that Hillman's varied talents be pressed into service again in the political field. Meanwhile others discreetly approached Hillman too with the same idea.

He himself had been saying that the 1942 defeats showed that labor must make renewed efforts to mobilize the country's voters during the war period. One day in July 1943, when the CIO Executive Board was meeting in Washington, Murray asked Hillman to lunch with him. It was on this occasion that the CIO president first proposed the scheme which was to bring Hillman back on the national stage. He said: "I have an idea that I would like to form a political action committee in the CIO, and I would like you to head the committee. I wish to know how you feel about it before I take it up with the Executive Board this afternoon."

Hillman seemed to kindle to the idea at once, as if it were something new, as Murray recalls. A renewal of vigorous political action by labor throughout the country might well turn the tide of reaction that seemed to be rising during the war, as in World War I. If nothing were done on the political front, labor unionists would be obliged to fight again and again for rights and advantages which would promptly be taken away from them by the politicians in Congress. Hillman was full of ideas for making such an organization part of a new advancing movement by the CIO, and promised to support Murray's proposal with all his heart before the Board. But, he suggested, it was better not to mention his own name in connection with the new committee, for he felt that he had become too controversial a figure to be at the head of it.

After lunch that day the two men went into the meeting and Murray laid his plan for a CIO political action committee before the Executive Board, explaining that it was to back the Roosevelt Administration and support legislation in the interests of labor. Murray then called on Hillman for discussion of the plan and he, warming to his subject, as Murray relates, "gave a most wonderful talk," which evoked a hearty response from the assembled CIO executives. In the enthusiasm of the moment, Murray exclaimed (pointing to Hillman): "And there is the man who ought to run this whole thing!" [9]

Murray recalls also that he suggested to Hillman that they both go to see Roosevelt and tell him of their plans. Hillman said: "No, I think we had better not talk to Roosevelt just yet. Let us first try and make something of this, then tell him about it."

At the time, it was said, Murray may have felt that it was a kindly action to give Sidney "something to keep busy with." In CIO circles the tradition lingers that Murray later was amazed at what Hillman proceeded to do with his assignment. After all, the CIO itself had also been started in 1935 as a mere "committee."

Hillman had been very much the tired warrior in the year that followed what was in fact his dismissal from the war government. While holding his exalted position as one of Roosevelt's chief lieutenants, he had been forced to "swallow many a toad," as the French say. He had been in the position of the government's labor manager for war industries, a spot where he was exposed to fearful pressure or even abuse from both sides, the employers' and the workers.' The affair at the North American Aviation Company was surely the low point in his government career. He had found himself, for a period, moving fairly far over to the right, helping the big aircraft industrialists against their recalcitrant workers, if only in order to speed the output of arms. Then after his "fall" and his departure from the Washington scene, in his state of illness and despondency he had believed that his active life was ended—to the "dynamic" Hillman, surely, the most terrible thought of all. He was only fifty-five, and when well and rested looked very young and spruce for his age.

The formation of the PAC marked Hillman's return to a leading position in the councils of the CIO, at Murray's side, after an absence of two years. Once more he was all vibrant nervous energy, fairly glowing with hope and the joy of battle.

Within a few days he had organized a meeting of 127 Eastern labor leaders, associated not only with the CIO, but with various AFL and railway unions, and several state and city labor councils. It was his way to consult as many persons of different mind as possible before he made an important move. There was also the strong hope of forming a united front with the AFL through the new political league. Hillman presided at this meeting, which was held in Philadelphia on July 11. Following a full and frank discussion of the proposed program of the Political Action Committee, a public announcement was made of its formation. Its declared purpose was not only to mobilize the millions of the CIO's cohorts for active participation in state and national elections, but also church and women's groups as well as farmers, consumers, and "community organizations" throughout the United States.

Sidney Hillman, it was now announced, had been named chairman and director of the PAC; the other members of the committee were Van Bittner, R. J. Thomas, Sherman Dalrymple, and David MacDonald. A statement of policy worked out at this gathering was issued by Hillman and reflected the highly practical spirit with which the labor men approached their task. The country faced a political crisis, he said. The election of many isolationist and conservative congressmen in November 1942 was a dire warning of what might happen in the presidential contest of 1944. Recalling the intense political reaction and post-war depression experienced in 1918–20, he said that one of the prime objects of the new committee was to see to it that our war veterans this time would not "go back to selling apples after peace came." He stated:

We are opposed to the organization of a third party at this time because it would divide the forces of the progressives throughout the nation. We are here to mobilize our power for political action now—not to wait until a few months before the elections of 1944.[10]

Then he hastened to New York to set up national headquarters and assemble a skeleton organization. The Amalgamated's young law counsel, John Abt, was lent to the PAC, in which he functioned as Hillman's assistant and legal adviser. J. Raymond Walsh, a former Harvard University instructor and radio speaker with a wide following, who had lately been serving as a research assistant on Philip Murray's staff in Washington, was also brought into the PAC as its director of research and, with the aid of a few writers, began to turn out political pamphlets.

At the end of September, Hillman went off on a four-week tour across the country, accompanied by his daughter Philoine. In the Middle West he stopped at the principal industrial cities, such as Cincinnati, Cleveland, Detroit, and Indianapolis, to confer with labor leaders and representatives of divers progressive organizations. In Chicago he called a large regional conference of CIO union leaders at which there was extensive discussion of the PAC program. Then, after visits to the cities of Wisconsin and Minnesota, where gatherings of as many as 150 union officers received him, he proceeded by train to Seattle. There again he presided over a regional labor conference representing four Northwestern states. A week later he turned up at similar gatherings in San Francisco and Los Angeles.

Mr. Green of the AFL had been approached by Hillman a few weeks earlier with the proposal that the CIO and AFL join hands for the forthcoming election contests. After taking up the question with the AFL council, Green sent Hillman a reply in the negative. But on the Pacific Coast a working alliance with AFL unions and city councils at the local level was brought about.

Sidney Hillman's fame was nationwide. The labor movement took pride in him and gave him warm welcome at many a long-winded union banquet along the route on that first PAC "junket." He was enjoying himself hugely among his own crowd of working people. But he had not made this long journey just for the fun of it. He listened to people of every sort; he observed everything, asked many questions, and busily shaped his plans.

For example, he remarked to his daughter Philoine that in many important regions, as in Michigan, Ohio, southern Illinois, and Wisconsin, he had noticed that the Democratic Party's "grass-roots" organization had "just about withered away." The local Democratic leaders did their work in routine fashion and were accustomed to defeat. Something would have to be done about that, he reflected. By the time that the "off-year" elections of November 1943 were over, he had his plans for 1944 fairly well mapped out. They were in scale quite breathtaking.[11]

Since the days of La Follette's Progressive Party movement in 1924, he had often thought about the problem of building a third party for labor. But in many sections of the country, state primary laws made it well-nigh impossible to organize a real third party. Moreover, during the long period needed for the building of an independent party, the risk of a breakdown of advantageous political relations were incurred. Now Hillman still believed that labor's "investment" in Roosevelt and his political apparatus was worth while; that a friendly alliance with the Roosevelt Administration represented the best way in which the interests of labor could be advanced in the immediate sense. As early as September 1943, he had sent up a few trial balloons in favor of a fourth term for Roosevelt, declaring that the CIO would support the wartime President if he ran again.[12]

But the problem of organizing a broad class-conscious group that would function in the political field as an independent and coherent force still remained. There were so many clashing sectional forces in the labor movement itself; even in the AFL there was the Socialist minority; there was the rising Negro movement to be taken into account; there were old ties between union leadership and professional party machines; and there was even a vigorous pro-Communist minority moving in another direction. At this time, in 1943, we were the military allies of the Communist fatherland.

Hillman's improvisation, therefore, took the form of a nationwide political league which, while representing labor primarily, was *not* to be a third party or an independent national political party, and yet was also to be autonomous. That is, it was to function as full partner in a coalition, mainly with the Roosevelt Democrats, but it would also lend its strength to progressive Republican candidates for Congress. This was the over-all plan and represented a sort of halfway stage between a third party for labor and an auxiliary of the old professional parties. In its details, in its development of a "grass-roots" organization affiliated with the network of thousands of CIO local union offices dotting the map of the United States, the PAC reflected Hillman's highly imaginative and inventive spirit. The PAC, he insisted, was going to pay its own way. Large sums of money would be needed. In the preliminary conferences with the CIO executives he had asked that seven of the biggest unions donate at least $100,000 each to the PAC treasury.

Appearing before the November 1943 convention of the CIO at Philadelphia after his Western tour, Hillman enjoyed again the long ovations of the union delegates. This convention was a sort of love-fest at which Philip Murray—after excoriating the departed John L. Lewis—publicly celebrated his alliance with the returned Hillman, upon whom he lavished much praise. Hillman, he said, had "never swayed in his loyalty to this cause"; having lent his wisdom and energy to the government in the war emergency, he was fortunately "back in the labor movement to put his shoulder to the wheel in building and building this mighty organization." Then Hillman, in a powerful speech, appealed to the delegates for support of the PAC, arguing that labor had lost much ground politically since 1942. In that year the picture had been dark; it had seemed almost as if we would lose the war. Now, he prophesied: "We will win the war."

He had instinctively felt that a lag had opened up between the emotions, the sorrows and hopes of a people involved in a great foreign war, and the commonplace things our professional politicians were doing or saying. While serving the government at Washington he had been forced to speak discreetly. But now he was no longer inhibited.

Labor must have a voice in the peace, he declared. Today the three great nations, America, Britain, and Russia, were working in full accord, as shown by the recent diplomatic conference at Teheran. "If there had been such accord earlier between the same nations there would have been no Axis and no Fascist powers to throw humanity into this great slaughter."

But when the fighting ended, he asked, would Americans who had witnessed the marvelous expansion of all our industries in wartime be willing to go back to a state of industrial depression? Was there to be only economic "chaos" again? The CIO-PAC was being organized now to see to it that the voice of labor and the common man was heard in the nation's political councils and in the determination of the peace and of our post-war plans. Hillman was for national economic planning in the interests of "full employment" after the war. In this fighting speech keynoting the PAC program, he moved to a position at the head of labor's advance guard, one that he had held for long years before. We were at the crossroads of history. "Make up your minds," he cried, "that we are either going to get a better world or we are going to be thrown backward. We will not stand still! . . . Make 1944 a year of decision for the common man here and everywhere." [13]

Philip Murray, too, reflected the preoccupation of progressive labor with the building of a lasting peace when he initiated a resolution (voted by the convention) calling for a world conference of trade-union representatives hailing from all the nations allied to us in this war, including Soviet Russia, to be held in London in 1944.

The upshot of this enthusiastic gathering was that by vote of the delegates Hillman got the $700,000 promised for the PAC. Not all the CIO chieftains were really eager to part with all that money, but Hillman was a hard man to stop when it came to fund-raising. As news of this got around the professional politicians in both parties began to have the jitters. The newspapers, magnifying Hillman's political "war chest" about tenfold, reported that he was being armed with a "slush" fund of $7,000,000.

III

From the start of the Political Action Committee, Hillman had his eye on New York State's American Labor Party as a pivotal local organization that fitted well into the frame of his larger plan. Thrown together hastily for the campaign of 1936, the ALP had lived a fairly troubled life since then, while trying to gather in the independent, labor, and left-wing voters who balked at the Tammany tickets. At times this party enjoyed a "balance of power" between the two major parties in the state. But the brawls of the right and left wings inside the party had been frequent and loud. The left wing, then led by Congressman Vito Marcantonio, and CIO leaders like Joseph Curran and Michael Quill, was strong in the New York and Brooklyn section of the party. But by 1940–43 the AFL faction, headed by David Dubinsky, Alex Rose of the milliners' union, and Professor George Counts of Columbia University, held control of the ALP state committee and hence ruled the state party organization.

David Dubinsky, it will be recalled, had recently "run away" from the CIO, as Philip Murray phrased it, and had brought the ILGWU back into the fold of the AFL. His now powerful union competed with the Amalgamated for local political influence in New York, as sometimes in Washington. Old rivalries and not a few jurisdictional quarrels lay at the bottom of the conflict between the two unions at that period. Yet in July 1943, Hillman had gone to Dubinsky and to his lieutenant, Alex Rose, who presided over the ALP's State Executive Committee, to urge that they combine forces. What he had proposed specifically was that the ALP's controlling state committee be reorganized to permit a fairer representation of the different CIO and AFL groups, thus encouraging unity between the right- and left-wing factions and ensuring victory for the New Deal in the event of a close election in New York. His proposal was promptly rejected by Dubinsky and his allies.

But Hillman had not come as a mendicant in this case. Through his own influence that could reach tens of thousands of voters who were Amalgamated union members and their "sisters and their cousins and their uncles and their aunts," he was in a position to bring about a decided shift in the composition of the ALP's state committee. He soon began to use public pressure, in the form of an open letter to the newspapers which stated:

> My proposal, in brief, is that all the trade unionists in this state, CIO, AFL, railway Brotherhoods, and unaffiliated unions, be invited to affiliate themselves with the party and to pay to it a per capita tax based on their membership in the state. . . . All state and county committees will be made up primarily of representatives of the participating unions, with a composition fairly representative of the numerical strength of such unions.[14]

Hillman's plan resembled roughly that under which British labor unions were apportioned representation in the British Labor Party. It appealed to him as eminently fair and democratic. Mr. Dubinsky and Mr. Rose assailed his proposal, however, on grounds set forth in vehement polemic articles published in the ILGWU's newspaper, *Justice* and in the Socialist *New Leader:* it would result, they said, in placing "notorious" pro-Communists in control of the ALP. Hillman himself was not a Communist, the *New Leader* pointed out, yet, for the sake of some momentary advantage, he "coolly proposed to take over the American Labor Party" by combining with the alleged Communists, who would doubtless wreck the organization when it suited the party line to do so.[15]

The Hillman proposals met with quick defeat before the ALP's state committee, as it was then constituted. Dubinsky also favored Hillman with a rather mocking letter commenting on this setback. But that was not the end of it. There was a temporary halt in the local hostilities for a few months (during which Hillman made his Western tour for the PAC): then in the early winter of 1944 he was back again in New York, driving hard to wrest control of the ALP from his opponents.

New York (and not only New York) has often seen the most hideous local political brawls, and all the air thick with mud or rotten eggs or dead cats. Yet Hillman had much logic on his side in making the decision to see this fight through. In a close presidential election the whole outcome might turn on the disposition of New York's massive vote in the electoral college. There were three parties now: the American Labor Party covered about 10 to 15 per cent of the state's voters, with the two older parties in fairly even balance, owing to Mr. Dewey's great strength upstate. But if the ALP were torn by dissension, if the CIO left-wing union members were discouraged from making the most intense efforts for the ALP election canvass—as seemed inevitable under the leadership of his opponents—then the state might well be lost to the Republicans in November 1944.

The difficulty was that Mr. Dubinsky, having risen to power in his union through his bitter fight with the Communists in the late 1920's, was implacably opposed to "collaboration" with them in the ALP. Hillman in this time of war emergency was for using everyone, and believed that denying any minority faction its democratic right to share in the work of an American political party was the wrong way to uphold freedom and re-educate or improve the Communists.

His opponents had ample funds and strong support, especially in the large foreign-language press of New York. To lead off the battle Hillman in January 1944 quickly threw together a Committee for a United Labor Party, headed by Hyman Blumberg. The Amalgamated's forces in New York were drawn into the fight, as was every CIO union in the city. Big rallies were held, pamphlets were circulated busily, and there was a mad ringing of doorbells throughout the city. Hillman and his aides had long been masters at stirring up powerful movements of public opinion by such measures. The Hillman faction in the ALP demanded a "broad-based" representation of all groups in the party's state committee and the replacement of the right-wing machine that sought to perpetuate its control. Their impact was so powerful that soon loud cries for help went from Dubinsky's headquarters by telephone and telegram to Roosevelt (who was seriously ill in January 1944). A. A. Berle, Assistant Secretary of State, served as the emissary of Hillman's opponents before the President.

In the Hearst press Westbrook Pegler attempted to come to the rescue of the Dubinsky faction by reviving the old canard of the Amalgamated union's alleged connections with racketeers. He said nothing, to be sure, of Hillman's very creditable and courageous action in 1931 and 1932 (described in Chapter XIV), in driving the gangsters out of the men's clothing trade of New York—an action that other labor leaders in New York might well have emulated.*

Following the intervention of the labor-baiting Pegler, Representative Martin Dies of Texas, chairman of the House Un-American Activities Committee, entered the game. On January 26, 1944, he announced that the PAC, its chairman and officers were under thorough investigation and would soon be called to Washington to testify before his committee.[16]

After some days had passed during which he deliberated over the problem raised by Dies, Hillman made a statement to the press declaring that the Un-American Activities Committee had no legal authority whatsoever to investigate the PAC or to call him for a hearing before it, and that he would have no truck with it. His defiance of the powerful Dies, it was said at the time, won him great credit in the eyes

* At this time Louis Lepke, so-called, languished in a Federal penitentiary. The sensation-mongering Westbrook Pegler related that Governor Dewey had been demanding that Lepke be turned over to the jurisdiction of the New York State authorities for punishment but that Attorney General Francis Biddle refused to permit this, at the order of President Roosevelt himself. This, according to Mr. Pegler, was done in order to protect Roosevelt's friends in the labor movement.

With remarkable indiscretion or naïveté Pegler then added that Governor Dewey's eagerness to have Lepke in his hands and hold him in terror of the death chair was inspired less by fear that justice might not be done than by the desire to induce Lepke to "sing" about his alleged dealings with *both* Dubinsky and Hillman. (New York *Journal American,* December 20, 1943.)

A report of an investigation by a well-known labor reporter of Hillman's fight to drive the Lepke gang out of the garment trade in 1931 was given in much fairer terms in the New York *Evening Post,* December 21, 1943.

Lepke was eventually transferred to a New York State prison, to be questioned by Dewey and his aides and, at length, executed. No "confessions" such as Mr. Dewey, it was said, hoped to wring from him were ever obtained while he waited for his death.

of New Yorkers, many of whom thoroughly disliked the patrioteer from Texas.

By mid-January the fight was going very well for the Hillman faction, when suddenly, in characteristic fashion, he came forward with a proposal for a compromise plan which would offer assurance that neither the left- nor the right-wing groups would gain control of the ALP's state executive committee. At a conference with Alex Rose on January 20, attended also by other CIO and AFL representatives, Hillman proposed that

a joint slate of candidates [for the state committee] be mutually agreed upon. I suggested that . . . all trade unions desiring to participate in the work of the ALP should be entitled to representation in the party leadership in proportion to their membership, *with adequate provision for representation of the liberal and progressive forces who are without trade-union affiliation and who support the program of the ALP.*[17] [Italics added.]

The concluding phrase indicated that Hillman offered to divide the party's control fairly between the CIO or left-wing groups and the right wing, and would give special representation to the former Socialists. But the offer was refused by Alex Rose.

Two days later Hillman made further concessions. Rose had said that he objected to certain "personalities" and in particular to "the placement of certain Communist leaders on the governing body of our party." Hillman now sent emissaries to the left-wing group led by Quill and Curran and, in the interests of labor harmony in New York, induced them to retire; in short, to "relinquish their right as individuals" to participate in the leadership of the ALP, through membership in its state executive committee. This sweeping concession was also refused by Dubinsky (through Alex Rose and George Counts). Dubinsky, as one of his former aides said at the time, "did not want Hillman even as a junior partner in the concern."

After an exchange of letters between Hillman and Rose, published in the newspapers on January 22 and January 25, efforts at an accommodation were finally abandoned by Hillman. His opponents, he said, showed a desire only to perpetuate their "narrow leadership" at all costs and were determined to deny any system of fair representation to other groups. Therefore, he proposed to reorganize the ALP without the aid of Mr. Rose *et al.*[18]

President Roosevelt, somewhat recovered in health, made anxious appeals by telephone to both leaders, asking that they compose their quarrel. After considerable effort to have an appointment fixed, Mr. Dubinsky went to Washington and made his complaints to the President during an off-the-record visit on February 6. Roosevelt, however, had insisted on seeing *both* Mr. Dubinsky and Hillman, though "not together." Soon afterward, Hillman, who had been resting awhile in California, hurried back to Washington in response to a White House call, saw Roosevelt on February 10, and set his mind at ease. Somehow, Hillman's visit to the White House was recorded in the newspapers (while Mr. Dubinsky's was not), leaving the impression that he continued to enjoy the President's favor in this contest—much to the discomfiture of his rivals.[19]

Mayor La Guardia finally intervened as a would-be peacemaker and invited both Hillman and Dubinsky to his office. In the course of a somewhat heated session the mayor urged that Hillman's final compromise offer be accepted, since it would have the desirable result of placing persons like Jacob Potofsky, Dorothy Bellanca, and Louis Hollander, whom La Guardia had long known as respectable folk and no Communists, on the ALP's executive committee. But Mr. Dubinsky was obdurate. The next day a full-page advertisement appeared in the metropolitan newspapers in which Sidney Hillman was denounced by his rivals as a "collaborator" of the Communists. This was their final thrust on the eve of the primary elections.

Hillman indicated at this time that he did not in any sense "hate" Mr. Dubinsky, but admitted that he was pained by him. What he most resented was the "Red smear" tactic, and he vowed that the American Labor Party would be taken away from Mr. Dubinsky's control in the primaries on March 28.

As for the charges that he was a "collaborator" or "tool" of the Communists, Hillman thought the situation was just the reverse. That is, he permitted those whom he had often opposed in the past to work with him toward the desired objective of engendering support for the war government. He used to say that he was very well aware of who was a Communist and who was not. His real attitude toward the doctrinaire or extremist factions of both the right and the left was one of "realistic" detachment or "moral neutrality" (as noted earlier). He had worked also, in much the same spirit, with the Knudsens and Forrestals. Such detachment could be observed in other men of great political talent, such as Roosevelt and Churchill, who were certainly "collaborating" mightily with the Communists of Russia to defeat Hitler's armies. In 1944, moreover, it seemed politically stupid to "wave the bloody shirt" of old left-right quarrels.*

In the final week of March, impressive demonstrations were organized by the Hillman faction, while the war of words and pamphlets rose to its hottest pitch. Hillman, in a final statement before an audience of 5,000 at Manhattan Center, New York, reviewed the issues of the dispute with his customary logic and, more in sorrow than in anger, reproached his opponents for their use of the "Red smear."

On the next day a huge turnout of more than 80,000 went to the primaries and registered a thumping victory for the Hillman slate by a three to two margin. The right-wing faction, still spurning all offers of conciliation, seceded to form the new American Liberal Party, under ILGWU auspices, while Hillman was elected state chairman of the American Labor Party.

IV

By 1944 the American people were feeling many of the discomforts attendant upon a great war in modern times. Wages were frozen, while great stores of consumer goods, especially beefsteaks, tires, and nylon stockings, were passing into the black market. Millions of workers saw their earnings fixed by agreements written for them in a room in Washington under the procedures of the powerful War Labor Board, an arrangement scarcely calculated to inspire them with a sense of participation in their own affairs. Meanwhile their sons and brothers were being called up to the Army day by day. Though the workers were fully employed and prospered somewhat, practical observers of the political scene reported that they felt themselves alienated from the Roosevelt Administration and were of a good mind to stay away from the polls.[20]

It was at this psychological moment that Hillman inserted himself into the picture with the PAC "crusade"—indeed, he and Philip Murray were among the few outstanding labor leaders who offered strong

---

* It must be recalled that the United States was not involved in a "cold war" with Russia then. On the contrary, a Gallup poll in 1944 indicated that most Americans believed that it would be possible to work out a peaceful coexistence after the war with the Soviets.

support to the wartime government. Hillman, particularly, was instrumental in making labor a coherent, highly efficient force in the political field; he gave a voice to the common men who were doing most of the producing and fighting. He raised issues which the former New Dealers, absorbed in military and supply problems, were neglecting. What kind of peace would we have after the fighting was over? Would there be full employment and security after the war? Above all, the PAC pounced upon the issue of the soldiers' ballot—which the Republican-Dixie bloc in Congress had obstructed for a time. Soon the widespread discussion of human affairs inspired by the distribution of millions of bright little pamphlets by the PAC and by the busy marshaling of voters everywhere for registration in the primaries began to make itself felt in all parts of the country. Hillman said: "Everyone was gloomy when we started the PAC. Then liberals seemed to spring up from the ground everywhere!" *

"One thing we know in the labor movement," Hillman said later, "is *organization.*" The PAC showed his organizing hand everywhere. As he explained:

We got up an organization of fourteen regional centers in the United States and from these centers organized downward into states, cities, wards, and precincts. On a door-to-door basis we are registering voters, persuading them that unless the 1944 vote is a mandate for peace and full production, 1932 will seem like a picnic.

Regional offices were located in large cities such as Detroit, Chicago, St. Louis, San Francisco, and Los Angeles. At the national headquarters in New York (located at 205 East 42nd Street), 135 persons were employed full time under the direction of Assistant Chairman

* Political organizations set up by labor in the past had sometimes been rather narrow in their objectives, which were usually limited to trade-union demands not of immediate interest to citizens outside the labor movement. Now, as Philip Murray himself declared, a nationwide organization was being set up not only to protect the political rights of the workingman but also "the rights of the returning soldier, the farmer, the small businessman, and the so-called 'common man.'" Joseph Gaer: *The First Round,* pp. 60–61, New York, 1944. From the start the PAC made a broad appeal to many different white-collar, farmer, and professional groups. Hillman said: "We are calling for a dynamic program to make full production possible after this war—for a Chief Executive and a Congress committed to full utilization of our economic resources. This is not a 'labor program.'" (Chicago *Daily News,* July 17, 1944.)

Calvin B. Baldwin, who joined the PAC in November 1943. Baldwin, a native of Virginia, had served under Henry Wallace in the Department of Agriculture and later, from 1940 to 1943, as head of the Farm Security Administration. Philip Murray called him a "brilliant young administrator." Others described him as "politically wise." Baldwin also worked in close liaison with 75 full-time employees of the PAC at the different regional offices around the country. These men and women in the field, in turn, were in close touch with local union groups and other organizations affiliated with the PAC. As Hillman pointed out, the PAC (besides having a sizable paid personnel) was assisted by thousands of part-time volunteers and union officers assigned to its service by their labor unions at many points throughout the country.

As the PAC got under way there were many mocking comments in the press to the effect that it might do more harm than good to the cause it hoped to serve. Mr. Martin Dies, at any rate, made ready to blast the whole organization with a few flourishes from his "Americanist" trumpet. But for him the PAC was to be no easy game.

Many months before primary elections were to take place in the Southern states CIO local union officers, in contact with the PAC's regional and national headquarters, had begun to canvass all their union members and urge them to register and vote. "Every worker a voter" was the slogan. In Martin Dies' own district in Texas (Jefferson County), where the poll tax severely restricted voting, usually to about 10 per cent of the population, thousands of shipyard and oil-field workers in the towns of Port Arthur and Beaumont were rapidly lined up to pay their poll tax and register for the primaries.

No sooner did Mr. Dies hear of all this than he began his attack on the PAC, as we have seen, in a torrential speech before the House on January 26. He had at that time an enormous influence in Congress, most of whose members stood in dread of his possible attacks on their "Americanism." Now he warned his fellow congressmen that "gigantic slush funds" were being raised by the CIO to defeat them. A few weeks later, agents of the Un-American Activities Committee appeared in New York and sought permission of the banks used as depositories by the PAC to examine the new organization's records and expenditures. This step was taken at the height of Hillman's struggle for control of the ALP in late February.[21]

His first reaction had been to proceed with caution. The Dies committee was armed with all the authority of Congress; Roosevelt himself had failed to terminate its career. For several days Hillman examined the question of what course to take toward Dies, with some of his advisers urging that he permit the PAC books to be examined while others argued strongly that the Un-American Activities Committee had no legal authority whatsoever to examine the PAC. There were, however, other standing committees of Congress empowered to investigate possible malpractice in election campaigns, before whom he could more properly appear. At length Hillman resolved to "fight back at Dies" and try to make the affair a popular issue. "I have wanted to do that all along," he said.

On February 19, in a statement to the press, he announced that he had given orders denying access to the PAC's bank accounts by the agents of Dies, adding:

Mr. Dies has no right to any of our records. The PAC . . . will refuse any demands he may make on it for records, files, documents, or materials. . . . It is high time that someone challenged Martin Dies' abuses of congressional power.

The PAC, he held, was an "educational movement" characterized by a "profound Americanism." Far from advocating any subversive ideas, he argued that

it is mobilizing millions of Americans *to do their duty as American citizens at the polls*. It is a perversion of reason and common sense to hold that it is un-American or subversive to ask these millions of American citizens to give their support to a program of political education.

The CIO and its friends believed that a large vote would most accurately reflect the democratic will of the country. It was the Economic Royalists who desired that "as few as possible might vote"; it was they who were the real "un-Americans."

Up to then virtually no one had dared refuse to testify or furnish records to the Dies committee in fear of a citation for contempt of Congress.

Hillman's old antagonist in Congress, Mr. Howard Smith, had also threatened to take action against the PAC, charging that it had violated the Smith-Connally Act in expending union funds for election purposes and should be cited before a Federal Grand Jury. To forestall this, Hillman and his lawyers went to Attorney General Biddle and voluntarily submitted the PAC's record for examination by FBI agents. On March 4 it was reported that the PAC would be "cleared." Under existing law any labor organization could legally expend money in "educating" people on political issues or in persuading them to register and vote in the primaries. In this case, Biddle's report indicated, funds had not been paid out to politicians or their agents, but only for pamphlets and lecturers. Once the candidates were nominated by their parties, however, different measures would be called for and the labor unions would have to step out of the picture. By then, of course, Hillman would be ready with appropriate arrangements for the next phase.

Within the Un-American Activities Committee of Congress there was now much dissension between Dies and a minority group who held that he had not been authorized to move against the PAC. Nevertheless, he rushed forth with a large 215-page report on the PAC which charged (under congressional immunity) that Sidney Hillman aspired "to become the Red Chief" of America in place of Mr. Earl Browder(!). Hillman, the report admitted, had been "actively and effectively anti-Communist" in the past, but now, it was alleged, he was building up the CIO-PAC by entering into a coalition with the Communists.[22]

A terrible power of slander was lodged in the hands of Mr. Dies, and few men had faced him in public without being besmirched. Yet Hillman bluntly challenged him by declaring to the press: "When Mr. Dies calls men like Philip Murray and other members of the Political Action Committee Communists, he lies and knows that he lies." Dies had made no investigation. He was only "peddling the same shopworn smears." Recently the PAC had been broadcasting the actual attendance and voting records of congressmen like Dies. Was Mr. Dies, then, afraid of having his public record made known? Hillman's parting shot was a telling one and caused a sensation: "Dies is obviously aroused to a frenzy by the possibility of his defeat in the Texas·primary election."

Mr. Dies had in fact grave cause for alarm. In his congressional district, embracing Orange and Beaumont, thanks to the current campaign run by the CIO and AFL local union officers, registration had risen 30 per cent higher than ever known before in that region. The PAC workers in Texas had done their job thoroughly. Indeed, in a thousand precincts local union officers who acted as field representatives for the PAC recorded exactly how many union members had voted in the last election, how many had moved from their homes, and how many held residence permitting them to register. Thus in Jefferson County, Texas, the registration of the union workers in the new war industries reached figures astonishing to hack politicians.

In May came news that seemed miraculous beyond belief: Mr. Martin Dies had withdrawn from the Democratic primary contest for renomination in his old district, admitting openly that he had done this because of the jump in registration stimulated by the PAC. It showed, he said, that "the CIO has captured control of the Jefferson County, Texas, Democratic convention." [23] In quick succession Representative Joe Starnes of Alabama and John Costello of California, two other members of the Un-American Activities Committee, were also defeated in their primary election contests. Sidney Hillman was elated. "This was the biggest thing the PAC had accomplished thus far," he said, "and made the whole effort seem worth while."

Many liberal Americans at this period made great moan about the emergence of characters like Dies, the stentorian-voiced demagogue from Texas. But Hillman and the CIO in 1944 *did something* about him and several of his apostles. As in the early days of the Amalgamated union, when its members used to lament the injustices done them by the police and courts, so now Hillman said that it did no good to utter mere protests or pass resolutions; what was needed were hard work and careful organization.

Earlier there had been some rumors in high Democratic Party circles that the PAC was "too hot," that Sidney Hillman was stirring up too many factional feuds which were likely to injure the chances of the ruling party in the coming elections, and that President Roosevelt would have to speak to Sidney sternly about this. The ailing Roosevelt also was in pessimistic humor at various periods during 1944, especially when a confidential poll made by the Democratic Party showed that he was losing favor with Catholic voters.

But by early June, when Hillman came to see him at the White House, the President had begun to cheer up and there was no more talk of "toning down" the PAC. This young organization was already showing its strength in strategic areas such as Ohio, Illinois, and California. The knockout of Congressman Dies was a feat whose importance the potent Roosevelt himself fully appreciated. Hillman's position was now wholly different from that of 1942, when he had been unceremoniously ushered out of the war-production organization. It was strong enough for him to be able to "change the President's mind on occasion." [24]

What the two men talked about very confidentially at this meeting on June 9, 1944, was the selection of a running mate for Roosevelt in the approaching campaign for a fourth term. It was a subject of enormous interest, for the President had been very ill recently.

Chapter Twenty-Five

"CLEAR IT

WITH SIDNEY"

For generations in this country, president-making has been something like the "sport of kings." But usually it has been the kings of banking and industry who would enter the race to put their favorite contender in the White House, never trade unionists or laborites.

In July 1944, however, as preparations were being made for the opening of the Democratic National Convention at Chicago, Sidney Hillman and Philip Murray arrived on the scene with a large and imposing party representing the CIO, and opened headquarters of their own at the Hotel Sherman. The CIO-PAC was reported to have some 200 Democratic Party delegates in its pocket—though this was greatly exaggerated. Nevertheless, Hillman and Murray seemed determined that the spokesmen of organized labor should take a hand in the president-making of that season, or rather the vice-president-making—which proved to be the same thing.

The war in Europe was in its climactic phase, for the invasion of France had been recently launched; but who could tell how soon the end would come? Roosevelt, with much less hesitation than in 1940, had resolved to run again for the presidency and thus see the war through. None in his party opposed him. The third-term taboo had already been broken, and many persons and organizations (including the Amalgamated at its May 1944 convention) had favored "drafting" Roosevelt once more.

But those who saw the President in the winter and spring of 1944 were quite shocked at his changed appearance. It was not known to the public that in mid-April he had gone to rest at Bernard M. Baruch's estate in South Carolina for two weeks, during which he "looked like a case of walking pneumonia," and had been too weak and ill to return to Washington until four weeks had passed.[1] Roosevelt's intimates and the party leaders were aware that he might well die in office during his fourth term. This led to some ferocious intriguing among the Democrats interested in the vice-presidential choice, all of it very distressing to the weary President.

Mr. Baruch, an old hand at inside politics, used every opportunity while the President convalesced, to urge the cause of his old political alter ego, James F. Byrnes, former senator from South Carolina and Supreme Court Justice, now serving as Director of War Mobilization. Vice-President Henry Wallace (then on a mission to China) should normally have been renominated, for he was supposed to hold great appeal for millions of liberal and labor voters. But powerful opposition to him had arisen among the Democratic Party's big-city bosses such as Edward J. Flynn of New York, Edward Kelly of Chicago, Frank Hague of Jersey City, and Robert Hannegan of St. Louis, the Democratic national chairman. The Southern politicians also were opposed to Wallace, and Roosevelt was "inundated" with advice from anti-Wallace Democrats that the incumbent Vice-President, if renominated, would "hurt the ticket" in a close election.[2]

The party bosses leaned toward Byrnes, a Southern conservative with much political experience—though some, like Flynn, noted that, as a former Catholic converted to Protestantism, Byrnes would be objectionable to one large religious group. Roosevelt was depressed and, according to Flynn, hated to discuss or argue with anyone about who might succeed him at his death. In the end he agreed that Byrnes would be his first choice for Vice-President.

Hillman, hearing of the Byrnes movement, on several occasions in June made plain to the President that Byrnes was considered unfriendly to organized labor and would be ill-regarded by the Negro voters in the North.[3]

It was at this period, in an off-the-record visit with Roosevelt on June 9, that Hillman learned that the names of others being definitely considered for the vice-presidency included Supreme Court Justice William O. Douglas, Senator Alben Barkley of Kentucky, and Senator Harry S. Truman of Missouri. Philip Murray strongly favored the renomination of Wallace. Truman, on the other hand, in view of the sectional conflicts within the Democratic Party, was a more conciliatory figure, coming as he did from a "border" state, and having an excellent record with regard to New Deal and labor legislation.

While in the OPM in 1941, Hillman had been subjected to some searching inquiries on the part of the Truman committee. But a former associate of Hillman's, Max Lowenthal, once an attorney for the Amalgamated, had been closely associated with Truman for years, as counsel to a Senate subcommittee investigating railroad finance, and knew him well. According to Jonathan Daniels' account, Lowenthal, in the spring of 1944, strongly urged Harry Truman to accept the vice-presidential nomination if it were offered to him.[4] Although Lowenthal himself did not go to see Hillman at this time, his very favorable appraisal of Mr. Truman certainly reached the chairman of the PAC.

In his talk with Roosevelt on June 9, Hillman had stressed the large part that the CIO-PAC would play in the approaching campaign and pointed out that it had given the strongest endorsement to Henry Wallace for Vice-President. Hillman therefore, though never keen for Wallace, would give him full support as the CIO's first choice. What worried him most was the determination of the "Big Four" Democratic city bosses, Flynn, Hague, Kelly, and Crump, to block Wallace and push through the nomination of Byrnes.

It must be noted that while Henry Wallace was much idolized by liberals as a man of high principles and humane ideals, and stood forth as a most enlightened figure in Roosevelt's Cabinet—as if symbolizing the New Deal movement itself—he was an aloof man with few close friends, none of them among the professional politicians or the trade-union fraternity. Wallace had been editor of a farm journal and then Secretary of Agriculture for eight years: actually he knew very little about organized labor. It was said that when he was in-

vited to address a big union convention some years before he had
even neglected to reply to the invitation—something a Roosevelt
would never have done. Neither John L. Lewis nor Sidney Hillman
had ever felt close to him. There were others also who found this
"plumed knight" of the New Deal at times very hard to reach when
immediate help was needed to fight off some low intrigue by the political bigots in Washington. Hillman, who had worked with Wallace
during Defense Commission days, had sometimes found him difficult,
and on one occasion said as much to Roosevelt. Roosevelt had remarked: "Well, what can you expect of a *yogi*?" It was an allusion to
Wallace's known disposition for mystical religious cults and the
rather odd letters he was reported to have written on this subject
which, during the 1940 campaign, had led to his being ridiculed by
the Republican opposition.[5]

Meanwhile Hillman was kept well informed about the growing
prominence of Harry Truman as a dark-horse candidate for the vice-
presidency in behind-scenes discussions between the President and
the party leaders during June and early July. Much of the confusion
surrounding the choice of a running mate flowed from the fact that
Roosevelt, as always, wished to avoid hurting the feelings of his old
political associates, Wallace, Byrnes, Barkley, and Douglas, each
with friends near the throne pushing his claims. In the end, when
he was forced to make his decision, he would outrage all of them.
For there was not one among them whose wildest hopes or anticipations had not been aroused by something the "cagey" President may
have said to him at some time or other.

By July 10, 1944, the situation (as far as we can piece it together
from the incomplete and conflicting recollections of all parties concerned) was as follows: Roosevelt had Edward J. Flynn's reports
from the field indicating that Wallace was unwanted by the Democratic Party bosses; he had meanwhile committed himself, in some
measure, to sponsoring Byrnes, but had noted the vigorous objections of Hillman on behalf of the CIO and of Negro leaders and
Catholics as well; and finally he had asked Flynn to get a group of
the Democratic bosses together and "inject Truman into the picture"
as the best possible alternative to Byrnes. On the evening of July
11, a committee composed of Flynn, Hannegan, Kelly, George
Allen, and Frank Walker came to dinner at the White House and
discussed the whole affair with Roosevelt. Justice William O. Doug-

las was mentioned as a possibility by the President, though without evoking enthusiasm. In the end Roosevelt is said to have handed Hannegan a little penciled note saying: "Bob, I think Truman is the right man." [6]

On the day before this (July 10), Henry Wallace had at last returned from his mission to China and closeted himself with the President for two hours. The next day they had another long session, during which Wallace asked for Roosevelt's support for his nomination, saying he would not withdraw from the race unless Roosevelt wanted him to. The President then expressed doubts about Wallace's chances for success, but offered his friendly support. He went so far as to promise to write a letter to the permanent chairman of the Democratic convention, stating that he would vote for Wallace as Vice-President if he were a delegate to the convention.[7]

Two days later Wallace was back again at the White House, and Roosevelt is said to have written the letter for him on that occasion in the terms (more or less) that Wallace desired.

The Wallace supporters now showed increasing confidence, which was reflected in the newspapers on July 13. Hillman and Murray, at a press conference that day in Washington, declared they were standing firm for Wallace. When Hillman was asked if he had talked with the President about Wallace's candidacy, he said cryptically: "I would say no; but if I had, I would still say no." Hillman and Murray both stated: "We have no second choice." [8]

But Hillman did talk with Roosevelt the next day, July 14, about who was to be nominated for the vice-presidency, according to Arthur Krock of the New York *Times*. What Hillman was most worried about was the effort to nominate Byrnes, against which he entered the most vehement objections. But now he gathered that the President had come to the conclusion that Truman was the man who would "least hurt the ticket." True, Roosevelt had written a rather lukewarm letter in support of Henry Wallace, which he showed Hillman. But when Hillman went to the White House on July 14 he found that the President on that day had written still another letter, this time to Robert Hannegan, national chairman of the Democratic Party, in which he stated with much more positiveness that "Truman and Douglas" would also be acceptable as his running mates. The President's secretary, Grace Tully, has related that originally Douglas' name preceded Truman's, but that Mr. Hannegan had the order reversed with Roosevelt's approval. That made, in all, four persons recommended by Roosevelt for the vice-presidency! Hillman was also shown the letter about Truman and Douglas, and it was obvious to him that Wallace could not win.

At this point, when the Democratic Party bosses were buzzing around the White House and the choice was really being made, Hillman reached a clear understanding with Roosevelt, according to which the PAC group was to continue to support Wallace, as it had committed itself to do; but when it became plain that Wallace could not get the nomination, then Hillman would do his best to keep the friends of the CIO at the Chicago convention from opposing the choice of Truman as an alternative.*

On the night of Friday, July 14, the President boarded his private train for a destination on the West Coast, his movements being kept secret according to wartime regulations. The next day the train halted at Chicago, where preparations for the opening of the Democratic convention five days later were in full swing. Democratic Chairman Robert Hannegan went on board the train and received his last instructions from Roosevelt, who did not show himself in Chicago. He is said to have related afterward that Roosevelt said that, as to the final choice of Byrnes, Wallace, or Truman, he and the other Democratic leaders must first "clear it with Sidney." [9] The phrase "Clear it with Sidney," picked up by the New York *Times'* Arthur Krock (through Byrnes and Baruch), was to echo and re-echo through the country (suffering increasing distortions) after the convention was over. What it definitely signified at the time was that a veto power was given to Hillman, as the CIO's political leader, only over the final choice for Vice-President at the convention. Roosevelt wanted labor's wholehearted support.

Truman was in Independence, Missouri, when Byrnes called him by telephone on July 14 and asked him to make the nominating speech on his behalf at Chicago. Truman agreed and proceeded to

* Roosevelt was not himself during the long periods of 1944. At intervals, as in the autumn campaign, he recovered his strength; at others he appeared confused about what was going on around him. Thus in October 1944, addressing a letter of felicitation to the International Ladies' Garment Workers' Union, he inquired of one of his secretaries "if this is Sidney Hillman's or Dubinsky's outfit—and should I send one to the other organization?" (F.D.R. Papers, memo of Oct. 6, 1944.) Here we have a mixture of Roosevelt's political shrewdness and failing memory, affected by his ill-health.

Chicago. But Hannegan, and soon Kelly, Hague, and Flynn, knew that Byrnes would never go down with the Democratic Party's powerful labor ally, and that Truman was the biggest of dark horses.

Hillman, who had a decided flair for high political intrigue, had already discovered as much about a week before, when Truman was still in Washington, and he had arranged to have the senator from Missouri come to meet him, as privately as possible, at the New York apartment of Maxwell Brandwen on Sunday, July 9. He would have liked to sound out Truman. But the senator, for his part, decided that such a meeting was too risky and, at the last moment, canceled the appointment, promising to see Hillman in Chicago.

The stage was set; the roles were all assigned. But one never knew how the play would be performed or received by the audience.

II

At Chicago the eyes and ears of all the press and radio were turned on Sidney Hillman and also on Philip Murray, who nowadays cleaved to his side as closely as possible during the convention. From the day of his arrival, on Sunday, July 16, the chairman of the PAC gave out interviews hour by hour at crowded press conferences attended by as many as three hundred reporters from all over the United States, before whom he outlined the policies of the CIO-PAC:

· We believe that Mr. Wallace will strengthen the Democratic ticket and that any other candidate will weaken it.*. . . We have no second candidate. We are not here to trade with anybody for any other vice-presidential candidate, but to put over Mr. Wallace.[10]

This convention seemed like a mixed salad of labor leaders, city bosses, and Dixie boys, of New Dealers and "Bourbons." As usual there was a sizable list of favorite sons and dark horses of various hues, while rumors of operations in "smoke-filled" hotel rooms were inspired by all the comings and goings of Sidney Hillman and the "Big Four" bosses, Flynn, Kelly, Hannegan, and Hague. On Monday, July 17, Edward J. Flynn told Hannegan that he was out for Truman. Mr. Hannegan, though hailing from Missouri, seemed to have clung to the original plan to have Byrnes nominated. But on that same evening Hillman and Murray told Chairman Hannegan that they would fight the Byrnes nomination tooth and nail. And later that night Roosevelt telephoned from the West Coast and made the blunt request that Byrnes drop out of the race, which was the finishing stroke for the gentleman from South Carolina. Now Wallace, beginning with some 350 pledged delegates, appeared to be the leading contender. This was really illusory, since 589 delegates were needed for the nomination, and various large blocks of delegates held by favorite sons, such as Bankhead of Alabama and McNutt of Indiana, were ready to be traded over to Truman as soon as clear orders came from the professional leaders.

At the early reports that Henry Wallace's chances appeared the strongest, the conservative press thundered against Hillman. The rumor that he and Murray had doomed Mr. Byrnes' candidacy caused newspaper columnists to lament:

The shifting sources of power . . . have produced the anomalous situation wherein a James Farley is on the sidelines and Sidney Hillman is in the forefront of events.[11]

The Chicago *Tribune,* which had known about Hillman since his youth, observed that this former clothing cutter had now returned to Chicago as a "king-maker," and that all the world wondered that "a man who was not even a delegate was consulted by everyone here." Yet he sat "tapping his hands together nervously," smiling, talking about all sorts of things, and saying little.[12]

Westbrook Pegler, writing in the chain of Hearst newspapers, exclaimed as if in a paroxysm of passion:

Hillman! In God's name! How came this non-toiling sedentary conspirator who never held American office or worked in the Democratic organization to give orders to the Democrats of the United States! [13]

Louis Bromfield, a novelist turned political commentator, also expressed his passionate indignation at the thought of the "New York city-bred and Latvian-born Hillman" [sic] dominating this convention. Mr. Bromfield had prophesied recently that the United States would soon exhaust its reserves of food and fodder under the New Deal. Though this prophecy had not been borne out, he now confidently predicted that Hillman's intervention in national politics would cause a widespread revolt against the Roosevelt party. "What do these people know about America?" he exclaimed.

More informed press comments credited the CIO political action in Chicago with being "shrewd, intelligent, and resourceful." Whereas labor leaders or reformers in the past had tried to insert themselves into political conventions in an idealistic spirit, Hillman's organization, as one paper put it, was no amateur outfit, but "had cash, skill, plus discipline." [14]

On Tuesday, July 18 two days after his arrival in Chicago, Hillman, who was stopping at the Ambassador East Hotel, had Senator Harry Truman as his guest for breakfast.

The luxurious suite of rooms in which Hillman received the senator was at some remove from the busy Loop. Here there were restful vistas of parkland and of Lake Michigan from its wide windows. He had often gone back to Chicago on business since 1914, but how different was this return to his own city—for he was also Chicago-bred, despite Mr. Louis Bromfield—where he had begun his toilsome life in America at Sears, Roebuck's and Hart, Schaffner and Marx. Here he had launched upon his career as a young union organizer; here he had won the friendship of his fellow immigrants and of the pretty, dark-eyed Bessie Abramowitz; and with his comrades, on visits to Hull House in the slums, he had sat at the feet of the inspiring Jane Addams, who had long ago seen greatness of soul in the young apprentice cutter before her.

Today, when the newspapers called him a "king-maker," he only laughed, for it was his way to be unassuming and refuse to take his own importance seriously. Yet the man who had now come to see him privately might soon have "only one life between him and the presidency of the United States."

Mr. Truman, according to his own recollections (as given later to Jonathan Daniels), said that he came to see Hillman at that "fancy hotel" as a "Byrnes man." He therefore asked Hillman whether he could depend on his support for Byrnes.

"No," said Hillman . . . He was serious that morning. "No. We're for Wallace, but we might accept two other men. Our second choice after Wallace would be Douglas. I'm looking at our first choice now." Truman protested, "I'm not running. Byrnes is my man." Hillman smiled as he went with him to the door.[15]

Truman's recollection of Hillman's attitude seems to be borne out by the account of another insider, George Allen, who later told of a conference held early in the convention preliminaries between Sidney Hillman and the Hannegan-Flynn-Walker group, at which the CIO leader was told that Wallace's cause was hopeless and was "offered" first Byrnes, then Douglas, but turned them down. When they "offered" him Truman, however, he said cautiously that "he had nothing against him." [16]

By the evening of Tuesday, July 18, it was common knowledge that Hillman had been entertaining Harry Truman at breakfast, and guesses were being made that he was the CIO's next choice after Wallace. The wily Edward Flynn had thrown out hints also that the delegation from New York, though committed to Wallace, would shift to Truman after the first ballot. The whole South was solid against Wallace.

On the next day, Wednesday, Hillman was kept busy denying all these rumors. A front-page cartoon in the Chicago *Tribune* showed him placing the vice-presidential crown on Mr. Truman's head. Another newspaper asked:

What had Mr. Hillman been doing having breakfast with Senator Truman? Mr. Hillman referred this question back to Senator Truman. He was most discreet about this strange breakfast right in the midst of the pro-Wallace crusade. Mr. Hillman could talk for hours without saying anything.[17]

In truth, the Missouri senator and the former clothing worker had come to a pretty clear understanding at their breakfast together, according to accounts preserved by Hillman's intimates. The CIO's political friends at the convention would come out fighting for Wallace. Both President Philip Murray and Secretary James Carey of the CIO were still ardently for Wallace's nomination. But when it was seen that Wallace's progress was definitely checked, then the swing to Truman would be on—and Hillman hoped to maneuver things so that the CIO bloc would not be left in lonely opposition. Indeed, he felt that the problem was to keep the Truman movement from coming up too fast. When the "break came," the CIO influence would be needed also, he believed, as a reserve force that could be used against any sudden thrust for Byrnes or some other "reactionary."

There was much confusion in everyone's mind by now, but on the night of July 18, Roosevelt's letter endorsing Wallace conditionally was released to the press. Its expressions seemed decidedly cool and showed that no sanctions would be taken against those who opposed Wallace:

For these reasons, I personally would vote for his [Wallace's] renomination if I were a delegate to the Convention.

At the same time, I do not wish to appear in any way as dictating to the Convention. Obviously the Convention . . . should—and I am sure it will—give great consideration to the pros and cons of its choice.[18]

But in 1940 Roosevelt had "dictated" the nomination of Wallace.

On July 19, the Hannegan-Flynn group announced that they would also release a letter from the disingenuous President, this time endorsing Truman and Douglas. There was alarm in the Wallace camp, and an emergency meeting was held at the Hotel Morrison. Wallace himself had arrived to lead his fight, but, as his own friends admitted, he had no real organization behind him in the Democratic Party save the PAC. He had not even a campaign chairman until the last hours. At the conference with Wallace, Hillman, Murray, Francis Biddle, Harold Ickes, C. B. Baldwin, and James Carey were present. Ickes that afternoon raised the alarm in the press, declaring that the Democratic bosses were conspiring to defeat Wallace; he also dispatched a telegram to Roosevelt warning him that such an outcome would be "your greatest political mistake in twelve years." Yet Ickes was said to be working for William O. Douglas!

That night Roosevelt telephoned National Chairman Hannegan from the West Coast saying there was a war on and he was to "get the convention over with quickly" and nominate Harry Truman.[19]

On the following day, July 20, Hannegan released the note of July 15 from Roosevelt to himself, reading:

Dear Bob:

You have written me about Harry Truman and Bill Douglas. I should, of course, be very glad to run with either of them and believe that either of them would bring real strength to the ticket.

Always sincerely,

Hillman had finally hinted to Murray that Wallace might lose out. But Murray now seemed greatly agitated at the way in which the party bosses had combined in the end to "put over" Truman, and talked of having the CIO-PAC bolt the convention. The prestige of the CIO was at stake, he said. Hillman went to his hotel room and managed to calm Murray down, urging that the CIO must go along with Roosevelt and continue to act with unity and discipline. Truman, he urged, would be an acceptable alternative.

On Thursday night, July 20—after all these puzzling preliminaries —the convention opened at the Chicago Stadium, where 33,000 persons were gathered, and Roosevelt addressed them by radio. Henry Wallace himself nominated Roosevelt for President in a powerful speech. The stadium crowd, said to have been packed with CIO followers, set up a mighty roar. "We want Wallace!" It continued for twenty minutes. Since the hour was late and the crowd seemed somewhat out of hand, the chairman chose not to proceed with the formal nominations of the numerous candidates for the vice-presidency and gaveled the meeting to a close.

The next morning, before a smaller gathering, made up mainly of convention delegates, the last act was played out swiftly. Sidney Hillman sat in a box of the convention hall with his daughter Philoine and a party of friends, including James Reston of the New York *Times.* The names of Bankhead, McNutt, Lucas, Truman, and finally Wallace were put in nomination. Wallace made his strongest showing on the first ballot with 429½ votes, while Truman registered 319½ and Bankhead 98. On the second ballot Truman was even with Wallace at 473 votes. Then the Southern contingent swung to Truman, as did McNutt's following, making a majority. Whereupon the New York delegation, as well as that of Iowa, passed over to Truman.

When the "break" came in the balloting, James Reston, sitting beside Hillman, exclaimed: "What do you say to that?"

Hillman replied instantly: "We were for Wallace always, but *not against Truman.*" [20]

Then he expressed satisfaction at the convention's choice, saying that Senator Truman was "eminently qualified" and would make "a splendid running mate for the President." Murray, much disgruntled, contented himself with saying that "the liberal elements of the Democratic Party made splendid progress in the convention."

It was said at the time that the labor group had permitted themselves to be "outgeneraled" by the professional politicians; and also that Hillman had in some way "dominated" the convention. Neither conclusion was true. It was President Roosevelt who had fixed on Truman (as was the presidential candidate's traditional privilege), and Hillman had known that all along. The left-wing element in the CIO in private, expressed much discontent at the way in which Hillman had accepted a former protégé of Boss Pendergast of Kansas City instead of trying to "ram Wallace down." But in reality Roosevelt was quite uncertain about his election prospects in that year of war, and desired both to conciliate the South and to satisfy his party's professional workers.

The CIO's bid for Wallace had been defeated, yet the Political Action Committee had been the talk of the convention. Its chairman had, in effect, won for labor, for the first time, something like a veto power over the composition of the Democratic national ticket.

III

At the time when the PAC's field organization in the Texas primary contest of May 1944 had brought about the downfall of Martin Dies, fantastic charges were made about the "unlimited funds" used by Hillman's agents. When Hillman, soon after, was called before a senate committee investigating campaign expenditures, he stoutly maintained that only "our bringing of the facts before the voters is responsible for what happened." The people had come out in force: that was the main idea of the PAC, "an idea at least as old as this country, that political power resides in the people. There are a reactionary few who fear this idea." It was Abraham Lincoln's doctrine that he propounded—in antithesis to Dr. Goebbels' axiom of the repeated lie—that if you told the truth to the people over and over again they would not be fooled for long by those whose interest it was to fool them.

He protested also at the manner in which labor was "singled out for attack" when it entered into primary contests, while the "royalist families," such as the Du Ponts, who gave $186,000 at one stroke to the Republican Party treasury in 1940, were passed over. The financing of the PAC, he added, was an open book which all could examine. Its records and bank accounts, presented before a House committee subsequently, on August 28, showed that this nationwide organization operated on a surprisingly modest budget, running under $50,000 a month. (Estimates of total expenditures for the Republican Party in 1940 had been as high as $17,000,000.) Nevertheless, one clause of the Smith-Connally Act forbade the use of funds of labor unions, as well as corporations, in political campaigns.* Therefore, the PAC had

---

* The PAC's legal counsel rightly pointed out, at the June 13 hearings in the Senate, that a narrow interpretation of the law "would stop every news-

now to give way to some other corporate entity.

The Senate's Campaign Expenditures Committee had rendered no opinion on the PAC. But Hillman, at a meeting of the CIO's Executive Board in Washington on June 18 said that after the primary nominating contests and the national party conventions were over, the PAC's funds were to be frozen—that is, held in escrow—and a new organization would supplement it and take part directly in the election campaign itself. At the end of the Democratic convention in Chicago, he made public announcement of the formation of the National Citizens' Political Action Committee (NC-PAC) as an auxiliary body which would draw its support from associations of farmers, consumers, professional groups, university people, and churchmen. Thus the PAC's "educational" program, designed to encourage the most widespread participation in the national elections, would go full steam ahead.

The NC-PAC had no official connections with the labor movement, though unofficially they were intimate enough, since Hillman served as national chairman of both committees. It would support a very broad program appealing to the common man in every walk of life, he said, not only to trade unionists, but to small businessmen, dentists, and doctors. Its main objectives were: a lasting peace, full production and full employment after the war, a domestic social security program, and aid to economically backward nations.

For Hillman, who had been co-operating for thirty years with social welfare groups all over the United States, it was a simple affair to put together such an organization as the NC-PAC. The honorary chairman was the aged progressive Republican senator, George W. Norris; James G. Patton, head of the National Farmers' Union, was named vice-president, together with Miss Freda Kirchwey, publisher of *The Nation,* and Bishop R. R. Wright, Jr., of the African Methodist Church; while Professor Clark Foreman, former president of the Southern Conference for Human Welfare, was named secretary. The Executive Committee was an amalgam of wealthy philanthropists, progressive political figures, and Catholic and Protestant church leaders; its membership included Elmer A. Benson, former governor of Minnesota, James H. McGill of the McGill Manufacturing Company of Indiana, former Governor Gifford Pinchot of Pennsylvania, Mrs. Emmons Blaine of Chicago, Dr. Robert C. Weaver, a leader of Negro organizations,

---

paper and magazine in this country from spending money on editorials favoring a presidential or congressional candidate."

and A. F. Whitney, president of the Brotherhood of Railway Trainmen.[21]

One side of Hillman's political genius was his extraordinary skill (as catalyzer) in bringing together the most diverse groups of people, stemming from many different classes and social levels, and marching them all toward a grand common objective. It was not easy to hold these people in hand, either in the labor movement or in the political field. The job wore him down slowly. When Hillman was gone, many of those he had held together under his command, fell to quarreling with each other (especially after 1946, when the political skies darkened). But while he was at their head all these different individuals who toiled for the NC-PAC, from Bangor, Maine, to Hollywood, California, worked together ardently; and they loved it, and it was exhilarating.

The objective of the National Citizens' body was to raise a fund of $1,500,000 for the current campaign in support of Roosevelt and Truman nationally, and locally of certain progressive Republican as well as Democratic candidates for Congress. Not more than half the hoped-for sum was raised that year, much of it by house-to-house convassing of workers under the slogan: "A buck for PAC." (The funds of the entire CIO-PAC contributed by the big unions also fell somewhat below their full quota of $700,000; and of this only about $371,000 was spent up to August 1944, when the balance of $289,000 was placed in escrow.)

All the wild charges of huge "slush funds," or of the CIO's "squeezing the workers" to contribute money lest they lose their jobs—made by Thomas Dewey, the Republican candidate for President, and others as well—were answered by Hillman when he opened the PAC's books to a committee of Congress on August 28, saying:

> I think it apparent from these financial statements that the real asset of the two committees is not the money in their treasuries. If that were so, we would be poor indeed and would hardly have merited the interest and attention which our work has aroused. . . . What we have and what [our opponents] lack cannot be measured in money. It cannot be bought and paid for. It is the enthusiasm and energetic co-operation of millions of Americans.[22]

It was as if, during the trying days of the great war, the people were waiting for some movement of this sort to come along, one that marched toward an enduring peace and an era of reconstruction and social justice. Hillman himself expressed astonishment at the numbers in which men and women of every class came forward to join in the work of the PAC, at national headquarters or in its local chapters. They included laborers and capitalists, university presidents and students, distinguished writers and artists, ministers and their congregations—and even "glamorous Hollywood stars" and "pushful night-club personalities," as the opposition spokesmen said. Nothing like this "crusade" had been seen since 1936, or perhaps since Bryan's Free Silver campaign of 1896. Approximately 18,000 persons joined the NC-PAC, which, after a time, actually discouraged further enrollment in order to avoid becoming an unwieldy organization.

The freshness and novelty of the Hillman organization's program, as contrasted with the routine methods of the regular politicians, contributed greatly to its success.

At the national headquarters on the fifteenth floor of 205 East 42nd Street, New York, in a small private office, Hillman as policy-maker presided over a beehive of political workers and volunteers. Assistant Chairman C. B. ("Beanie") Baldwin at the opposite end of the floor was actually in charge of the day-by-day administration. With the aid of J. Raymond Walsh, research director, a program of nationwide propaganda was mapped out, especially for sections of the country found to be weak in local Democratic action. The main job, in the late summer, was to get millions of people registered in time, so that they could go to the polls on November 7. In New York, for example, Walsh reported that 900,000 young men had gone to the armed services, while 600,000 more workers (most likely Roosevelt supporters) had moved to other states in search of war-industry jobs. It was imperative that every person eligible to vote be contacted, precinct by precinct, ward by ward, and door to door. This grueling task was performed with the aid of the American Labor Party, the Amalgamated, and other CIO unions, as well as the railway Brotherhoods.

In Ohio, Vice-President Jack Kroll of the Amalgamated union, a man with much native political skill, headed the regional PAC organization. In the Chicago center, former Congressman Raymond McKeough worked effectively with officers of the Amalgamated union and the United Steel Workers to speed the registration drive. In Michigan, where the Democrats had shown themselves extremely weak in 1942, many hundreds of United Auto Workers' volunteers went out to ring the doorbells of prospective voters and see to it that they registered in time. Thus an improvised "grass-roots" organization was set in operation, based chiefly on the local union offices dotting the country from New England to California. Its effectiveness was soon perceived at many points and "sent chills up Republican spines," as one experienced political reporter wrote:

The CIO-PAC has been hard at work since February and should play a big part in the November result. There are 328,000 CIO members in Illinois—with 250,000 concentrated in the Chicago area.

Raymond McKeough . . . has had a list of all CIO members in the state prepared and checked against lists of registered voters, in order to see that every CIO man and woman votes. A tedious job is being carried out thoroughly. Test samples indicate that about 40 per cent of the potential CIO vote is not registered—135,000 voters—who are the object of the PAC drive. . . . Roosevelt looks stronger in Illinois in 1944 than in 1940. . . .[23]

Reports of record-breaking registration came to the PAC headquarters in New York from Chicago, Los Angeles, and St. Louis during the summer. In St. Louis as many as 36,000 voters were brought in for registration on a single day, and one early result was the defeat of the "isolationist" Senator Bennett C. Clark in the Democratic primaries. In Wayne County, Michigan (which embraces Detroit), only 722,000 persons had registered for the 1940 elections. But now 100,000 or more of the younger workers were in the Army and less registration was expected. However, in a whirlwind campaign directed by the CIO leaders, 1,000 canvassers went out day and night in early October, so that when registration closed on October 18, the record-breaking number of 800,-000 had been enrolled as voters. Michigan "was stirred up as never before" in any election. The same was true of other populous states, such as California, Ohio, and Illinois, whose votes counted heavily in the election results.[24]

By October, Roosevelt's fairly expert field surveys showed that the turnout of voters would be unusually heavy, and he felt easy about the November outcome.[25]

Behind the political army working in the field there came also a rolling barrage of pamphlets, leaflets, stickers, and throwaways, produced mainly at the New York headquarters of the PAC. Dr. Raymond Walsh directed this propaganda with the aid of a small staff of writers and journalists, including Joseph Gaer and Wilbur Ferry, the pamphlets being illustrated by a group of artists under the direction of Ben Shahn. The titles of some of the pamphlets were: *A Political Primer for all Americans*; *This Is Your America*; *The People's Program for 1944*; *The Negro in 1944*; *Catholic Press Supports PAC*; *Every Worker a Voter*; *Back to the Breadlines with Dewey*; *Jobs for All after the War*; etc., etc. In all, some 83,000,000 pieces of literature were distributed throughout the country, their promotion among organizations of all kinds being pushed by Walsh's assistant, Dr. Frederick Palmer Weber. *Time* magazine, though pro-Dewey, glumly acknowledged that this part of the PAC job was "far and away the slickest political propaganda in a generation." [26]

Over the radio, in parades and "caravans," and at great public gatherings, the PAC used the technique of "prestige advertising," with the aid of famous movie stars such as Humphrey Bogart, or popular radio-script writers like Norman Corwin. Incidentally, the PAC canvassers, according to their instruction book (reflecting the Hillman touch), were advised to speak softly, give the facts, and above all, "never to argue with people."

From the start of the campaign, the Republicans were advised by an old student of politics, Frank R. Kent, the Washington columnist of the Baltimore *Sun,* to focus their attack on Hillman and the "Reds."

The clearer it is made that Mr. Hillman and the PAC are not only running but financing Mr. Roosevelt's campaign, the greater will be the reaction among the voters who resent . . . the professional labor bosses.[27]

The Republican propagandists, commanding about 85 per cent of the country's newspapers, fastened on the phrase attributed by Arthur Krock of the New York *Times* to President Roosevelt in his orders to Hannegan on the vice-presidential choice: "Clear it with Sidney." But the words were soon converted into the slogan: *"CLEAR EVERY-THING WITH SIDNEY,"* which was placarded all over the United States. Study of the propaganda technique used by the Republican supporters of Dewey and John Bricker has shown that the ideas they stressed mainly were: (1) the "menace" of labor's entrance into politics; (2) the use of "huge slush funds" by labor; (3) alleged communistic influences back of the CIO; (4) the vague irrational appeal of anti-Semitism, directed against Sidney Hillman in particular.

Our election-time "debates," to be sure, are usually pointed at the lowest common denominator among the voting population. But the contest of 1944 has probably never been surpassed for abusive violence of language, for hysterical appeals to prejudice, or for slanderous whispering campaigns used by the party of the "outs." For four months the name of Sidney Hillman scarcely ever left those verbal pillories erected for it in the front pages of the chain newspapers of Hearst, McCormick-Patterson, and Gannett.

Governor Dewey had begun mildly by offering his own "me too" version of a Republican New Deal. He ended by centering his attention on the alleged "Roosevelt-Hillman-Browder plot" to subject the United States to a Communist dictatorship. An example of one of the opposition party's slogans was:

Sidney Hillman and Earl Browder's Communists have registered. Have you?

The nation was declared to be in instant peril of capture by "Sidney Hillman, the pants presser." President Roosevelt and Mrs. Roosevelt were pictured in our yellow press as surrounded by the gangsters of Murder, Inc. Mrs. Clare Boothe Luce, in mid-October, discovered that Hillman's PAC was spending dollars "like confetti" in order to defeat her in a Connecticut congressional district. "If my head is to roll in a basket," she exclaimed, "at least it's a more American head than Sidney Hillman's"—thus joining the brave company of those who aroused the passions of race hatred. Hillman's reply was that Mrs. Luce was overestimating both the PAC's resources and her own importance. He added gallantly: "I hope she carries her pretty head around for a long time—but not in Congress." On one occasion during this explosion of slander, Governor Earl Warren of California, one of the leading Republican speakers, admitted that he had censored one of the "Clear-it-with-Sidney" pamphlets used by Dewey's aides as being obviously libelous or defamatory.[28] Another Republican campaign pamphlet circulated in an edition of 4,000,000 was finally barred from the mails in October by the Postmaster's Department on grounds of libel and provocation to violence.

Stoically Hillman endured all this calumny and all the hideous caricatures of him that were being disseminated. To friends who urged that he open suit against those who grossly libeled him, he declared that he would do nothing of the sort; he trusted that the slander of his opponents would serve as a boomerang against them, if only "the facts" could be put strongly enough to our people. He said:

Neither the CIO, nor the PAC, nor its chairman is an issue in this election. But the right of workers and the other common men and women in America to organize for full . . . participation in politics is an issue. The torrent of reckless slander and abuse is but a foretaste and a warning of what is in store if those forces should prevail in the election.*

One would have thought that not Roosevelt and Truman but Sidney Hillman were running for election, and that the office involved—as Horace Greeley once remarked on a somewhat similar occasion—was the penitentiary, not the presidency. Inwardly Hillman suffered keenly under this torrent of abuse, though he did not choose to show it. As he said later in reviewing the campaign:

I was not surprised at the attacks. I rather considered them a testimonial to the effectiveness of our work.

Our opponents attempted to cut us off from the main body of the American people. No slander was too base, no appeal to prejudice too bigoted. They failed because we voiced the aspirations of the great majority.[29]

He was always intensely conscious of the fact that he was a Jew. Had he not been born under a regime in Russia made hateful by its religious, racial, and political persecutions? Now in America, he perceived, to his sorrow, the truth of that which a great English political philosopher, Lord Acton (a Catholic), had once said: that democratic societies are not always distinguished by self-restraint and seem at periods to have a veritable "affinity" for religious persecution and for the oppression of minorities. In his long public career as a labor leader Hillman, for the very reason that he was a Jew, subject to the attacks of the beetle-browed and chuckle-headed, had always tended all the more to conduct himself with extreme probity and bear himself with pride.

* Note the striking coincidence of the following:

Now . . . with the aid of Sidney Hillman, the Communists are seizing control of the New Deal . . . to control the Government of the United States. (Speech of Thomas Dewey, Boston, Nov. 1, 1944.)

The CIO-PAC is under the complete domination of the Communists . . . fighting for the re-election of Roosevelt and the dissemination of Communist ideas. (*Pariser Zeitung,* Paris, July 23, 1944, issued during the Nazi occupation of France.)

But there are all sorts of Jews, as there are all kinds among all other races. One prominent Jewish member of the New York Bar, known for his self-advertised devotion to the cause of civil rights and liberalism, actually came to Hillman and advised him to give way as chairman of the PAC "because you are a Jew." Hillman invited the man to clear out. Instead of retreating, he gave vigorous answer to his defamers in at least one public statement:

> Red-baiting and Jew-baiting go hand in hand. It is not surprising that Hitler has been calling President Roosevelt a Jew . . . and the native-American Fascists have been screaming about the "Jew Deal." and the Hearst-McCormick-Patterson papers' Axis rarely misses an opportunity when discussing the PAC to drag in the fact that I am a Jew and was born in Lithuania. I don't apologize to anybody for it.[30]

Called up for investigation again before a committee of Congress, he appeared good-humored and sharp-witted as always. The PAC, he explained, was supporting Roosevelt in a "non-partisan" spirit.

Representative Clarence Brown (Republican) of Ohio asked why, if Mr. Hillman was so non-partisan, he had not paid more attention to the Republican National Convention, and was told that one PAC executive, Van Bittner, had been sent there.

MR. BROWN: We missed you.

MR. HILLMAN: You must have missed Mr. Willkie too.[31]

It was a neat thrust at the Republicans who had eliminated the candidacy of the liberal Wendell Willkie earlier that year.

The extremists among the Republicans seemed to have overreached themselves in focusing their attacks on Hillman and the PAC. Millions of Americans were affronted by the unfairness of their tactics and its resemblance to Dr. Goebbels' method of the Big Lie endlessly repeated. In the frantic search for issues the Republican propagandists even assailed President Roosevelt's dog, Fala, for whose public journeys or medical care, according to rumor, large public funds had been "squandered."

In October, Roosevelt, in good form again, made some hard-hitting speeches, especially the famous one before the Teamsters' Union in Chicago in which he mercilessly ridiculed the "scandal" of Fala and called attention to some of the real issues facing the country as the war neared its end.

Vindication came on November 7, 1944, when 45,000,000 went to the polls. The populous states of Ohio, Michigan, Illinois, and California were carried by the Democrats, though many soldiers in foreign service (despite the simplified soldiers' ballot) failed to vote. In New York the contest was close, with Roosevelt ahead by only 300,000 out of 6,000,000 votes. Hillman's vigorous fight to broaden the American Labor Party in that state by bringing in *every minority group* that might have been disgruntled and stayed at home was fully justified. The ALP had enrolled all of 485,000 voters under its banners, while some 300,000 also voted for Roosevelt under the new Liberal Party ticket.

Roosevelt had figured on a very close race. In the final weeks the PAC campaign all over the country wound up with a strong finish. Numerous political "experts" were all in agreement that Roosevelt's margin of victory, reduced to only 3,100,000 in excess of Dewey's 21,-300,000, could not have been gained save for "the strength of Hillman's PAC drive." Republican newspapers saluted Sidney Hillman as the "Number One labor politician" who had emerged triumphant over bitter attacks, and "as the mobilizer of millions of labor votes that were Mr. Roosevelt's margin of victory." The great turnout, the rise of the PAC, the "Hillman Blitz" were "providential for Roosevelt." [32]

From the PAC headquarters in New York, on the night of the election, Hillman spoke on the air, a few minutes after midnight, to the PAC workers throughout the country, announcing the news of certain victory for the party of Roosevelt. He was weary but elated as he congratulated them, saying that labor had come of age and a "phalanx of liberalism" had rallied to its cause. "This election was *cleared* with the American people!" he wound up.

Only two years before he had been, as many thought, at his political "nadir" when he left Washington. Now Roosevelt wired him on November 8:

> I cannot delay longer telling you how deeply I appreciate the splendid job which you did from start to finish. Hope to see you soon. Affectionate regards.[33]

A fortnight later Roosevelt made his acknowledgments by letter more handsomely still:

> One thing I want to make perfectly clear to you, Sidney, is my appreciation. It was a great campaign and nobody knows better than I do how

much you contributed to its success. I was glad to learn that the CIO in Chicago authorized the continuation of the PAC. I can think of nothing more important in the years to come than the continuing political education and political energy of the people who do the jobs in this land, in the determination that the American nation shall do the great job it can do for all. I send you no condolences for the licks you took in the campaign. You and I and Fala have seen what happened to the people who gave them.

Hillman's reply, less modest than usual, was intended as a reminder to the sometimes overburdened President that labor would be a force to be reckoned with in the political arena:

Dear Mr. President:

Your letter was most heart-warming. As old campaigners you and I have come to accept the "licks" as a tribute to the effectiveness of the job. But I am delighted to learn that Fala too took them like the true thoroughbred that he is.

The enthusiasm, determination, and deep political understanding with which the CIO convention moved to put the PAC on a permanent basis is a good augury for the future. I came away from Chicago confident that we can look forward to the continuance of intelligent and effective participation in American political life by millions of the men and women who do the work of the nation. I know you believe with me that this is the best guarantee that we can move forward with assurance to attain the great goals which our people have set for themselves and for the world.

I do not need to tell you how greatly I have deemed it a privilege to have made some contribution to the recent campaign and how deeply I and my associates rejoice at the result.[34]

Chapter Twenty-Six

THE LAST
CRUSADE

On November 22, 1944, at the annual convention of the CIO in Chicago, Sidney Hillman stepped to the rostrum to give his report on the PAC. As the familiar figure was recognized, the audience of 1,500 delegates and guests burst into a mighty ovation that continued for more than half an hour, with much parading and chanting of "Hillman!" and "CIO Forever!" It was a welcome to whose warmth Hillman responded with unfeigned sentiment, one such as the crowd of CIO union officers were accustomed to give to their old hero John L. Lewis in his time of glory. Only a few years before, in 1940, Lewis had denounced Hillman before this same audience, many of whom had received him with stony suspicion. And he had suffered something approaching political eclipse in Washington in 1942. Now Lewis was a fallen idol, while the resurgent Hillman seemed to overshadow all others in the American labor scene. In his career this point of triumph marked a tremendous rebound for Hillman. At last President Philip Murray brought the long demonstration to a halt, and the reading of the report proceeded.

It had been a great fight, Hillman began, and he gave unstinted praise to Murray and his CIO colleagues for their powerful support.

During the recent political campaign the men of the CIO, he said, had made a contribution of "their special skill as organizers" in the service of all the people. A mighty instrument had been forged in the form of the city and state political action committees, established through the CIO's local unions; these community organizations, he urged, were of the highest importance. Thus it had been shown that labor and all the various democratic groups that had worked together could at least express their will through "the two-party system [used] as a framework." Instead of seeking to form a third party, the CIO, he advised, should keep to "the mainstream of American political life . . . and work in a non-partisan way with forward-looking members of both parties." Then he added the warning that this victory had not destroyed labor's enemies, but had administered only a serious setback. "They are well financed and powerful. They will strike back with the fury of desperation." [1]

Hillman was quickly reappointed as chairman of the PAC by the CIO Executive Board. The continuance of the PAC as the CIO's permanent political arm was voted unanimously and with great enthusiasm by the convention. To be sure, there were some misgivings expressed in high-level labor circles about the danger of the political committee eventually overshadowing the economic role of the CIO. Yet the PAC seemed then too potent, too well launched as an engine of labor power in the political field, for any to question its usefulness. Hillman himself, in the autumn of 1944, as peace drew near, was looking elsewhere; he was already preparing to take up another great enterprise that appealed to him as the most important task of his life, indeed, in many ways, as the logical culmination of all his effort and life work; this was nothing less than the organization of world labor unity in the interests of a true peace.

He had long ago, after the end of World War I, lamented that the workers and the common people "permitted the few to manage the world," and it was to this that he attributed the rise of Fascism and Nazism and the renewal of mass slaughter in Europe and Asia. After this long holocaust of World War II, surely mankind would clamor for the guarantees of an enduring peace; and labor, by seeking and fashioning an international accord at its own level, might contribute greatly toward such an end.

It was Philip Murray, as Hillman always acknowledged, who, as early as the autumn of 1942, initiated the CIO's efforts, in concert with national trade-union bodies of the allied nations, to bring about an effectual world federation of labor. There had been in existence up to then among the Western nations the old International Federation of Trade Unions (IFTU), founded in 1900, sometimes called "the Amsterdam organization," but more lately an appendage of the British Trade Union Congress. It was a non-political body quite distinct from the Socialist or Communist "Internationals" and having the purpose of fostering the exchange of information and co-operation on humanitarian grounds among the different national labor groups. The AFL was a member of the IFTU, as it was also of that other labor body at Geneva, the International Labor Organization, or ILO, which had a consultative status under the old League of Nations.

The IFTU was unrepresentative, since it excluded not only the Russians, but the American CIO with its 5,000,000 members. Therefore, during the war President Murray had repeatedly urged that steps be taken toward real international labor co-operation, and had maintained a frequent correspondence to this end with the British Trade Union Congress and the IFTU. The AFL, however, had blocked efforts of the British to widen the scope of the International Federation of Trade Unions by including the CIO. As Hillman remarked, while Secretary of State Cordell Hull might freely meet with European and Russian statesmen, the representatives of the great CIO could not meet with those of the European or Russian trade unions, even for co-operation in benevolent and charitable activities in the international field.[2]

In the autumn of 1943, Philip Murray had had a conference with Sir Walter Citrine, who was general secretary of the British Trade Union Congress—then visiting the United States—and tentative arrangements were made that were to lead to a form of "three-power" co-operation between representatives of American, British, and Russian labor. Such co-operation was, of course, in effect in the military sphere between the three great powers. We were in the heyday of the "united front" movement, through which Soviet Russia joined with the United States and England at the Dumbarton Oaks Conference in the summer of 1944 to organize what many then hoped would be a truly effective world league, the United Nations Organization. Though Sir Walter Citrine earlier had been reluctant to invite in the Russians, such a step was now in accord with Churchill's foreign policy.*

In November 1943, the CIO received an invitation to send representatives to a world conference of national labor bodies to be held in London in June of the following year. The invasion of France at the time arranged for the conference and the excitement over the American elections had led to a postponement until December 1944. As originally planned, Murray was to have attended it with Hillman, but withdrew at the last moment, owing to ill-health. It was agreed, therefore, that Sidney Hillman should go as chairman of the CIO delegation, which included also R. J. Thomas and Emil Rieve.

The entrance of the CIO into the international picture had resulted in the AFL's promptly refusing to participate in the conference in any way, since its leadership desired no meetings with Russian representatives and no co-operation with the CIO at the international level. But Murray, who shared with Hillman the conviction that this time "the world labor movement must make its voice heard at the peace table," declared that the AFL's withdrawal would in no way affect the determination of the CIO to rejuvenate the International Federation of Trade Unions. It was hoped that this might become a companion piece or an auxiliary to the proposed United Nations Organization, and that the IFTU might eventually win a consultative status under the UNO.[3]

Hillman, preparing to attend the London conference, was urged by his friends and members of his family to consider his health and avoid this exhausting journey. What he needed, they said, was rest in a warm climate such as that of Arizona, which had seemed to benefit him during a few weeks in the winter of 1943. But he had visions of "parliaments of man" and "federations of the world," and would not be dissuaded.

He said simply: "I know this may shorten my life, but I have to make up my mind either to live ten years longer as an invalid, or do what I can now."

It was understood in advance that the proposed federation would be, at best, a loosely knit affair, with its official action restricted (as

* Philip Murray wrote in an article published in February 1945, in *War and the Working Class* (Moscow): "Workers in free countries the world over, and more especially those who are in trade unions, are united by a great common bond—the fight they are waging against Fascist aggression."

before) by the veto of each of the large national groups who were represented in it. Perhaps, then, only another "talking shop"? Yet that was what many had predicted for Sidney Hillman's Political Action Committee.

In a sense Hillman, as catalyzer, had worked for the unity of labor all his life, and in a constantly widening circle, starting from his first efforts to unite the factions among the Chicago clothing workers in 1910 and ending with the two PACs of 1944, a remarkable synthesis of liberals and radicals, Protestants and Catholics, Northerners and Southerners, Jews and Gentiles. Now that the suspicious Russians themselves had turned again, after 1941, to the policy of the "united front," was it not time to strike out for an effective world labor organization? Hillman had always abundant confidence in his powers of persuasion, in his ability to overcome profound disagreements and fuse the most diverse groups into an accord of some sort for common action. Thus it was to be, for him, one more "crusade": this toward a world labor unity that might foster world peace. It was perhaps a dream, but a dream that possessed him in the days and months that remained of his life. He had been practical and opportunistic enough in recent years. But had he not also said oftentimes that it was "a good thing to live for your dreams?"

He hoped, above all, that the preparatory meeting in London might become labor's "Dumbarton Oaks." This could also be made an occasion for helping to revive the ruined trade unions of the liberated areas of Europe, many of whose officers had been executed or imprisoned, though many also had been fighting in the underground against the Nazis and Fascists and their collaborators.

Hillman had certainly been cast in the American mold during more than thirty-two years. Domestic problems had been all-absorbing in this period. Yet his youth and his early struggles were bound up with memories of old Russia; and after her revolution he and the Amalgamated union had maintained, for a period of time, friendly relations on a humanitarian or philanthropic plane. Now everything that was happening overseas in these culminating days of the war seemed of enormous interest. The upsurge of the Russian armies had astonished the world ever since 1943; only a little time was needed, apparently, for the final defeat of the German arms. Hence, the postwar problem that was paramount to many minds was that of establishing good working relations, a *modus vivendi*, among America and Britain and the reviving Russian giant.

A second problem that now haunted Hillman was the fate of the Jews of Europe. Lithuania had again become Russian territory in 1939. But now the first horrifying rumors were abroad of Nazi atrocities committed against the civilian populations of the lands along Russia's western borders, densely populated with Jews, across which the Germans had first advanced and now were retreating, destroying everything as they went. There was scarcely a Jew hailing from Europe who did not fear for some member of his family. Hillman's father had died several years before the war. But of his aged mother, who was over seventy-five when war came, and of two sisters and a brother, he had heard nothing since 1941.

One of his younger sisters, Leah, he had managed to bring to the United States in 1940. But his mother, whom he had long supported by regular remittances, had firmly refused, then as before, to transplant herself, in view of her advanced age. A year later, in 1941, the Germans had poured into Russian-occupied Lithuania in the first hours of their eastward advance. And now Hillman feared that his mother and an elder sister, Sarah, who with her husband and three children had been living in Kovno, had fallen into the hands of the Germans. Another younger sister and brother, Minna and Mordecai Hillman, he learned, had managed to get to Moscow and were believed safe.

In the winter of 1941, when he was in Washington at the head of the OPM, he had made strenuous efforts to have an American visa granted his mother and sister and her family, so that they might enter the United States. The State Department and the American consul at Moscow gave all possible help; but it proved to be very difficult to move his mother and sister to Moscow, where they were obliged to go to obtain a Russian exit visa, because hundreds of thousands were then trying to flee eastward out of the border lands, and severe restrictions had been placed on such movements by the Soviet Government. Hillman's efforts to bring his relatives out met with delays of several months, for correspondence with Russian territories moved very slowly. Then suddenly, on June 22, 1941, it was too late. All he could do now was hope that his family had managed to move back and escape; but he feared the worst, for he could learn nothing whatsoever of their fate.

The fight was on now for the establishment in Palestine of a national state for the Jews who would survive the genocidal crimes of the Nazis. Though Hillman had not been overtly or actively a Zionist in any sense, he had helped, through his union, to raise large sums of money for the relief of his unfortunate fellow Jews. He had held always that his course was to help all people by strengthening the healing power of labor organization everywhere rather than taking his stand as a Jewish nationalist. But in the past two years, when no longer holding government office, and on learning of the immense catastrophe that seemed to have overtaken the Jews, he had become increasingly active both in seeking aid for the survivors and in urging the establishment of a Jewish state in Palestine.

On December 1, 1944, he took the plane to London. The transocean flight in those arduous days of war was neither a swift nor an agreeable journey, often requiring time-consuming stopovers or lengthy detours via Brazil and Africa. After three days the press reported his safe arrival in London on December 4 with his party.

He was received with great cordiality by the British Vice-Premier Clement Attlee and Labor Minister Ernest Bevin (who had met him earlier in Washington) as something like an elder statesman of the American labor movement. On the day after his arrival one of the largest press conferences ever held for any foreign visitor took place in the council room of Transport House, the Labor Party's headquarters, with some three hundred journalists in attendance on Sidney Hillman.

During the election campaign in America just ended, the British had heard as much about Sidney Hillman as about almost any other American of that season and were curious to know what this "benevolent-looking missioner" had to say of our strange American politics or about American labor. Hillman, though "infinitely discreet," as one journalist remarked, declared that he wanted labor to "do in the international scene" what it had done in the national scene in America recently; that is, organize itself. What was the meaning of the PAC? he was asked. That "labor in the United States had become politically potent," he replied. American workers, he assured the British, were no longer "isolationists," adding emphatically: "Every reactionary is an isolationist. Every labor-baiter is an isolationist." As for the rightness of co-operating with Russian trade unions (which many believed were but "captive" organizations), Hillman held that

Roosevelt's good-neighbor policy favored such action. "We feel they are one of our great allies. Their internal arrangements are their own affair," he said guardedly.

When the questioning turned to the American political scene, he felt on safer ground. Beaming with pleasure at their previous bewilderment, Hillman responded to the queries of the Britishers on the mysteries of American political life. When asked why Mr. Dewey's platform had been the same as Roosevelt's he laughed. "Political platforms are not taken seriously in the United States. Politicians' promises don't mean much." He also denied that he was a "labor baron" or any of the other evil things said of him in the recent election campaign. Those were but the statements of opposing politicians who also "were never taken seriously." As for his mission in London, it meant that the CIO was resolved "to arouse mass interest in international relations" as had been done through the CIO-PAC in America's national politics.[4]

The small gathering that began its sessions on December 6, 1944, and called itself the Preliminary World Trade Union Conference, included only representatives of the Big Three nations (the United States, Britain, and Russia). It was to restrict itself to the discussion of organization plans and rules for procedure. For the Soviets, V. V. Kusnetzov was on hand with a Russian delegation. This in itself was something of a new departure, the Russians having previously confined their international labor activities largely to meetings of the revolutionary Third International, or "Comintern." Now they were working with an old "bourgeois" opponent of Communism, Sir Walter Citrine, and the scarcely less "bourgeois" Sidney Hillman.

Sir Walter had been the real directing head of the old International Federation of Trade Unions, then reduced to only a few unionists in exile. He showed extreme caution about undertaking any actions that might finally alienate Mr. William Green and the AFL (which had refused to participate in this gathering), and seemed less than eager to form ties with the new trade-union people who had arisen out of the resistance movement in Europe.

Hillman argued that the CIO now dominated America's key industries and the problem of AFL participation could wait. He wanted a plan worked up quickly for a permanent organization that could be presented for approval to a larger international labor gathering to be called later. But Sir Walter worked for delay. Hillman, after trying hard to win agreement of the other parties to his project, bethought himself of going to see Ernest Bevin, the real boss of the British TUC. Past master of the art of persuasion, he gained Bevin's assent to the plans he had in view. The stubborn British veto on any organizing action was then withdrawn. The Russians also fell into line.

German V-2 rocket bombs were now falling over London, one arriving with a hideous uproar about four blocks from the meeting room of the labor conference, thus underscoring the urgency of their task. Within three days the organizing group reached a working agreement on "provisional agenda and recommendations for Standing Orders." Highly pleased with results thus far, Hillman flew back to the United States, where he arrived on December 18, 1944, to give his report to Philip Murray. He had acted in full accord with the Roosevelt policy, he felt, of building a "bridge" of unity between the British and the Russians. Some efforts were now made by Hillman and Murray to bring the AFL into the reorganized international federation, but in vain.

In February 1945, Hillman was designated by Murray to head a CIO delegation to a second overseas conference on this matter, this time including the labor-union representatives of half a hundred nations, most of them allies of America in the war, a few of them neutrals. The so-called World Trade Union Conference, which began its sessions at County Hall, London, on February 6, was a gathering of 204 persons who were to carry on the preparatory work begun two months earlier. Along with the British, American, and Russian delegations there were now Louis Saillant and other representatives of the French Confédération Générale du Travail, Lombardo Toledano of the Latin-American Federation, and, in all, the representatives of 53 national trade-union bodies, hailing from all parts of the world, including Asia and Africa. There was a confusion of tongues. The Poles even had two competing delegations! (At this very time Roosevelt, Churchill, and Stalin were conferring on the conditions of peace in a palace in the Crimea.)

The silver-haired Sir Walter Citrine, a skillful parliamentarian, dominated the proceedings at the beginning—for Hillman was late in arriving and only a part of the American CIO delegation was present. Bringing to the surface the strong differences already felt among the several national groups, Sir Walter strongly opposed the acceptance of some of the new trade-union bodies that seemed to have come down from the hills with the underground armies in Western and Southern Europe. He also refused to agree that the pro-Communist "Lublin Poles" had more legitimate claims than the rival anti-Communist delegation from the Polish London Committee. Italians, Finns, and Bulgarians were also to be barred. Since war aims were to be discussed here, trade unionists from former enemy countries could not properly be included in such debate, he argued. Finally, he raised the question of the preponderance of the Russian delegation, which he strongly feared might dominate the new organization in the event that membership was to be based on mere numbers of trade unionists claimed—of which there were more than thirty million in Russia.

The purpose again was plainly to delay action on implementing the new organization. Sir Walter also proposed that voting on the steering committee's proposed plans be held up until it was known on what terms the old IFTU was to be merged into the new World Federation of Trade Unions, or WFTU. Let the old IFTU's paid secretariat be continued in office, the British delegate urged, so that it might carry on the work of the new organization.[5]

The meeting now seethed with dissension; the French and the Russians vehemently attacked the British spokesmen, the former defending the heroism of the "underground" labor unionists, the latter invoking the name of their "beloved Marshal Stalin" and calling to witness the millions of Russian dead and their ruined cities. R. J. Thomas, acting as chairman of the American delegation, appealed for unity, but since he and his compatriots seemed to lack parliamentary experience, that was more easily said than done. The sessions approached a breakdown amid much ill feeling. Everyone seemed to be waiting for Sidney.

He arrived four days late, on February 9, 1945, but at first avoided speaking on the floor of the conference, limiting himself to more private negotiations in committee rooms, in which he tried to iron out basic differences among the contestants. The British (who still acted as if they had been dragged into this affair against their will and better judgment) stubbornly insisted on keeping the machinery and personnel of the old IFTU. Hillman was willing to concede that, but was determined also that they should not delay the writing of a new constitution and the calling of a constitutional convention. Meanwhile he wrung from the Russians very important concessions that went far to remove some of the British fears.

On February 12 he took the floor and in a prepared speech proposed a four-point program. First, the conferees must agree to establish a new federation to succeed the old IFTU without delay. Second, all true national labor organizations must be united with the new world federation. Exceptions, Hillman said, should be made in case of the existence of divided authority, as in that of the AFL and CIO in America. (A place would be reserved in the councils of the new organization for the AFL, which, Hillman believed, would feel forced to come in later.) Third, the World Federation of Trade Unions was to be "democratically constituted." As to the question of Russia's preponderance, Hillman observed:

I am confident that any attempt to control an international labor organization by virtue *of mere size or weight of numbers,* or in any other way, would be fatal to the purpose we seek to accomplish. [Italics added.] [6]

In the fourth place, an executive or administrative committee must be set up and armed with broad powers to take action and carry on the business of the WFTU, pending ratification procedures.

Organized labor has not lacked good programs in the past. But the best of programs is useless if it is not implemented by an effective organization . . . fighting for the realization of that program . . . translating it from paper into action.

We, the leaders of the labor movement, have it within our power to create a mighty instrument for the expression of the people's will. We would betray our trust if we failed to do so. We must not—I know that we shall not—fail.

The historic conference at Yalta had ended harmoniously. Hillman pleaded that his labor associates must try to do no less than their Prime Ministers and President. He seemed positively "mystical" on the subject of labor unity, it was said in London.

In the discussion that followed he now proceeded to work out his compromise solutions. The Russians, who might have dominated the new labor federation, were induced to accept a far smaller proportion of votes than their claimed trade-union membership would have allowed. The British were given certain assurances, for the time being, about the continuance in office of the old (British-paid) secretariat of the IFTU during the period of transition. In return, they ceased their delaying action and agreed to the formation of a strong administrative committee of thirteen members, which was to write a constitution and call a founding convention.

The British press observed that this conference, for which many had predicted failure, had ended "with a notable success"; the clear agreements drawn up by the labor groups from so many different lands represented "a victory for the CIO." [7]

At the invitation of French labor leaders, Hillman flew to Paris to observe something of the poverty and suffering the workers of France had endured; he also spoke before a great labor gathering in the Salle Pleyel (by way of an interpreter) on the new federation. Thence he returned by plane to New York to address a "World Unity" rally at Madison Square Garden early in March. The UNO was also being launched at this time and was to convene in April in San Francisco.

Hope ran high after the Yalta Conference that the crude weapons of power politics would be set aside in favor of economic and military co-operation for world security. Hillman's New York followers therefore received him on March 12 with an outburst of mass enthusiasm. But he spoke to them soberly, declaring that powerful interests were already at work to undo President Roosevelt's constructive program; they were people who sought "only domination of markets and dreamed of an 'American Century.'" Labor must be on guard everywhere, he urged, to check "a new imperialist scramble for power." He reported also that a committee of the WFTU, headed by Philip Murray and himself, was to meet soon in Washington and prepare to present the views of world labor at the opening meeting of the United Nations Organization at San Francisco in April.[8]

He was in Washington a good deal during late March and early April, often conferring with Philip Murray on the work both of the PAC and the new trade-union international. There were, of course, new attacks on him for seeking to organize what some timorous souls were already calling an "international political action committee" that aimed at winning "world political power." [9] But ignoring the bigots, he worked on at a furious pace. At this period also he was in close touch with President Roosevelt, whom he visited at the White House on March 20 and found looking very poorly.

Three weeks later, on April 12, he was in Washington again, attending a press conference at the CIO headquarters. Philip Murray was presiding and talking to the newspaper correspondents, with Hillman sitting beside him, when a messenger hurried into the room and whispered something into Murray's ear. Murray was silent, his face impassive as he heard the news of President Roosevelt's sudden death, which he then very gravely reported to the others present.

Hillman turned extremely pale; he seemed to be struggling with his emotions; his grief was obvious. A reporter hastened to ask him if he had any comment. He exclaimed: "No, no. Not now, please!" and left the room.[10]

The death of this one man that shook the world was felt by Hillman in all its impact. Labor had built so much upon its alliance with this most powerful of American presidents—not to speak of Hillman himself as labor's political leader. None could measure better than he all that might now be endangered or lost. Then also, his own emotional and sentimental attachment to Franklin Roosevelt had been very marked. He mourned his friend; and the thought of the weakness of human flesh was borne in upon him with special force now that he himself was far from a well man, and extravagantly spent the last small hoard of strength left him.

One remembers how, even in these "Babylonian" United States, where the incidence of death is so often observed without dignity and the expression of emotion or sentiment upon such tragic occasions often comes without grace, a great hush fell upon the land that lingered for many days after the sudden demise of Roosevelt. It was as if a huge oak tree had fallen in the forest with tremendous reverberations of sound, followed by a prolonged, painful silence.

Three days later, on April 15, Hillman, like many other notable Americans, attended the funeral ceremonies at the White House, passed before the President's bier and paid his respects to him for the last time. Then, feeling very faint, he went out alone, tottered across Pennsylvania Avenue, and sat down on a bench in Jackson Park. To a friend who came to look for him and discovered him there he said later: "I just sat on that bench alone for hours, it seemed to me. I thought I would never be able to get up and walk again." [11]

Sidney Hillman had found Roosevelt endlessly "fascinating," as he said. "For all his faults," he had been unswervingly loyal to the President. In memorial ceremonies conducted in 1946 in Roosevelt's honor, before his union convention, he said that he had admired, above all, the late President's breadth of view, his courage and sense of "compassion." It would not be easy to find his like among our politicians. Labor would carry on along the road that had been charted, "though some fire and zest have gone with him." [12]

At the time of the President's death a statement issued by the Amalgamated union read:

Roosevelt was one of us. He was the friend and guide of labor. He saved us in 1933. . . . We have been running to him with our problems ever since. Now we are on our own.[13]

At Roosevelt's death, Mr. Truman, as was usual, vowed that he would continue his policies. The CIO had been of powerful assistance to Harry S. Truman's vice-presidential campaign in 1944. Sidney Hillman himself, as it happened, had given the final sanction for his nomination. Yet it was significant that, with Mr. Truman in the presidential chair, labor considered that it was now really "on its own."

II

A few weeks after the passing of Roosevelt the belated news reached Hillman of the death of his mother. A letter that had been many weeks en route, dated March 2, 1945, arrived at last from his long-missing younger brother, Mordecai Hillman, who reported grimly:

The fate of our family is too tragic for me to describe. Mother and Sister Sarah and her entire family were annihilated in beastly fashion by the German executioners in Kovno, October 28, 1941. Sister Minna with her little son also perished tragically.

These evil tidings, long awaited, long feared, were authenticated by the Soviet Government after the reconquest of Lithuania. His aged mother had been shot during the early weeks of the German invasion, when a series of mass executions had been carried out.

Hillman, grief-stricken, wrote to his brother on June 25, 1945:

I need not tell you how shocked I was by the terrible news concerning our family. I knew that a similar fate had fallen upon millions of families. Nevertheless it was a great shock.

I do not understand why Minna was in Lithuania. What was she doing in Lithuania? I wish you would write me in detail about that. . . .

If there is anything I can do for you, to be of help, please let me know.[14]

He learned later that through mischance his younger sister Minna had been in Kovno visiting with her mother at the time, and so perished with her. This grim news, as his daughter Selma recalls, depressed him so greatly that he was ill and took to his bed for several days. Now he too mourned with millions of Jews, Poles, French, and Russians, and all others whose kin the Nazis had murdered en masse. In these days he was terribly in earnest when he pleaded that all who labored for their bread, all the common people who suffered in our great twentieth-century wars should be given a voice in the drafting of the peace.

The members of the WFTU's administrative committee and their aides, by previous arrangements, arrived in the United States early in April and were welcomed by Hillman and Murray in Washington. Among them were Sir Walter Citrine, and V. V. Kusnetzov and D. M. Tarassov, the Russian delegates, as well as Louis Saillant of France, Lombardo Toledano of Mexico, and H. T. Liu of China; also Walter Schevenels of Belgium and J. H. Oldenbroek, of the Netherlands, the veteran secretaries of the old IFTU. This committee hoped to appear in some advisory capacity before the UNO, Hillman and Murray declared, though no one had invited them.

Two days before Roosevelt's death the executive group of the World Federation of Trade Unions had announced plans to meet on April 25 at Oakland, California, just across the bay from San Francisco, where the UNO was to hold its inaugural sessions.

Arriving in Oakland on the appointed day with the other members of their committee, Hillman and Murray not only proceeded to the consideration of their own agenda, but made it known that, as the American representatives of the WFTU, they would be available to Mr. Edward Stettinius, the United States representative to the UNO, for consultation on questions affecting world labor.[15]

Hillman's conception of the WFTU was as a great sounding board projecting the voice of labor throughout the world. It was as "one voice for sixty millions," he said, that the new world labor federation spoke:

It is a movement by organized labor, but will not work for the interests of labor alone. It includes men of every political faith and party, from the most conservative of trade unionists to Communists. It can and will be one of the most potent instruments of world peace and a tower of strength to the United Nations in their effort to make peace durable.[16]

The idea of bringing the WFTU's executive committee to conduct its sessions at Oakland, face to face with San Francisco, where the far more auspicious launching of the UNO was taking place, was a superb symbolic gesture made under Hillman's inspiration. The spokesmen of world labor had come to petition the United Nations to admit them into their councils, and awaited their decision. Among the public at large the fact that such a federation was being founded at the same time as the UNO was overshadowed in the news and aroused very little interest for the moment, as Hillman admitted. To be sure, several of the UNO delegations spoke favorably of inviting in the WFTU committee as an advisory agency on labor matters; but the majority, urged on by Senator Vandenberg, chose to exclude it. It made no difference, Hillman remarked; the WFTU would continue to organize and grow. He wrote at this time:

We were representing no country, merely the common people of all countries on whom the penalties of war had fallen heaviest.

Our request was denied . . . on the technical ground that the WFTU was not an "intergovernmental agency" and hence was not eligible to participate. But it is worth keeping in mind that three of the Big Five—France, Russia, and China—dissented from this narrow view . . . and voted to invite us, at least as observers.

At any rate, the Steering Committee barred us. That, as they probably knew perfectly well, settled nothing. It did not put an end to world labor's demand for the right to participate in making the peace, as we helped in winning the war.[17]

Those who hoped that "Sidney Hillman's international side show" at Oakland would be a "flop" were disappointed. The WFTU committee members and their aides worked out the agenda and the full text of a constitution to be voted upon at the forthcoming Paris convention in September 1945. This task was accomplished successfully despite the widely divergent views of the committee members, which were expressed in four different languages: English, French, Russian, and Spanish. Hillman constantly admonished his colleagues that all who opposed their ideas hoped they would break up in deadly strife. Everybody, consequently, behaved very well.

In these last years of his life, Sidney Hillman, liberated from the routine duties of a union president, gave himself over almost completely to the role of a "crusader," a tireless missionary for labor and world peace. Rebuffs had no power to affect his beliefs. Acting nowadays as a leader of world opinion, in his ripe years, Hillman preached everywhere the "religion of labor" and its constructive mission. The WFTU might appear decidedly utopian. Yet, as the philosophers have shown, utopian ideas have played a considerable role in the development of man and society. If some men are permitted to dream of ever more perfect and fantastic machines of death—which eventually we seem to attain—then others may also aspire to create what appear as yet "impossible" or utopian vehicles of civilization.

Shrewdly enough, Hillman saw that if men talked peace and worked constantly over the techniques of conciliation, something much better might come of it than if they lived only in mutual fear and hate, while busily preparing to exterminate each other. The WFTU had a post-war program which it was going to "talk up" all over the world: it embraced the elimination of Nazism and Fascism; plans for the reconstruction of the war-devastated regions; the revival of trade unions in the occupied countries; the dissemination of the "Four Freedoms" in the colonial lands. If the representatives of many countries, despite differences in faith, language, and degree of development, could work together in a world labor federation, Hillman was saying, it would provide incentive for their governments to go and do likewise. Americans were going to be international-minded henceforth. To be sure, there were Secretaries of State and diplomats to take care of our foreign relations, but, Hillman warned:

"We the People" . . . must be back of them with all our power if we want them to follow correct policies, and we must be on the job to keep them from drifting. . . .[18]

The founding convention of the World Federation of Trade Unions was fixed for September 1945 in Paris. In the interval since the committee meeting at Oakland, earth-shaking events took place: Hitler died and Berlin fell; the Labor Party won the elections in England, turning out the Churchill ministry; and Japan surrendered. The world was suddenly at peace—but the detonation of the first atom bombs over Japan a month before filled the minds of those who worked for world unity with a sense of terrific urgency.

Once more the unresting Hillman flew to London and then Paris, this time appearing several weeks before the WFTU convention opened. The French capital was filled with delegations of trade unionists from all parts of Europe, who appeared from the mountains and forests, where they had been fighting in the resistance movement. They were in high spirits; the new age of freedom could not begin soon enough for them.

In the week preceding the formal opening of the convention there was much caucusing; many of the tensions shown at the early gatherings were felt again. The blueprints for the organization had all been completed, but there was haggling still over details and personalities, with the reluctant Sir Walter Citrine, chief of the British delegation, at the center of it. "Fear of Communist domination haunted Sir Walter," it was said.[19]

Unfortunately, after each global war—as those who do nothing to prevent them should be reminded—there are usually two or three times as many Communists in the world as there were before.

The WFTU held its first session on October 3, 1945, with the serious attention of the world's press focused upon it. The large gathering of more than 500 delegates and their assistants was said to represent the central labor bodies of 56 countries and 70,000,000 union members. Two days later, after the constitution had been voted, Louis Saillant of the French Confédération Générale du Travail was elected general secretary, while Sir Walter Citrine was elected president. Hillman was named one of the six vice-chairmen and a member of the executive committee, which was the WFTU's highest council. His shrewd negotiations were reflected in these arrangements, very surprising to many observers, by which "British Labor's ultra-conservative, Red-hating Citrine" was chosen president. The Russians and their friends from the satellite countries had been persuaded to accept a reduced voting power (considering their larger union membership) of only 41 votes against the 22 for the American delegation and the 23 for the British Commonwealth. The Russians also yielded on the issue of continuing the old IFTU's paid secretariat for two years as an "annex" of the new organization. Indeed, the Soviet's representatives were described as "most conciliatory." "Between the Communists and the Citrine group the wily Sidney Hillman threaded a complex skein of compromise," one American correspondent reported. "The sweetness and light were almost unbelievable." [20]

At the end of that big day's work, at the third session, Hillman, quite in character, was found in one of the lounge rooms of the hall, cheerfully drinking toasts to world peace with General Charles de Gaulle on one side of him and Tarassov of the Russian trade-union delegation on the other. What he was doing at the time (as he often maintained afterward) was pursuing a policy paralleling that of Roosevelt, which he called an "independent American policy, neither pro-British, nor pro-Russian." [21]

One of the main items of business was Hillman's report urging that the WFTU continue persistently to seek representation in the Economic and Social Council of the UN, and appoint commissions to visit conquered Germany and Japan to survey conditions there. These recommendations were adopted.

The proceedings of the Paris founding convention left one thoughtful commentator, J. Alvarez del Vayo, with the hope that a new international labor leadership had emerged. Referring to Hillman, he wrote:

His share in the creation of the labor international was, in a certain sense, decisive. He has proved an able and skillful diplomat at a time when diplomacy's stock is very low indeed. Without his patient intervention it might have been impossible to hold the British and Russian delegations together. But his historic contribution has been to introduce the American labor movement into world affairs. From time immemorial American labor has been all but absent from the international movement. . . .

It is the CIO leaders who have put an end to this position. . . . American labor . . . in the international crises that lie ahead can play a decisive role. . . .[22]

III

One resolution of the WFTU convention authorized a small committee, which included Hillman, to make a brief, preliminary tour of inspection in occupied Germany. They obtained permission from the Allied Control Commission and set off on October 12, 1945, for Berlin. The purpose was to study the results obtained thus far in the process of denazification being applied by the Allies in the four separate zones, and to report on the prospects of rebuilding a free German labor movement.

From Berlin, Hillman flew to Frankfurt, where he was cordially received by General Dwight Eisenhower, to whom he presented the proposal that the WFTU be granted some consultative status on the Allied Control Commission. Since this tour was necessarily brief, Hillman made arrangements for a longer return visit to Germany early in 1946. After a week spent in that bewildered and devastated land, he flew back to New York.

In the autumn of 1945 there was rising criticism in America of the policy pursued by the American military government in Germany, now under the direction of General Lucius T. Clay. On January 18, 1946, Hillman called on President Truman at the White House and had a friendly talk with him on the question of the world labor federation having a voice in the UN councils. He also told the President of his intention of paying a longer visit to Germany at the end of January with a WFTU delegation.

Truman, aware of recent criticisms of our military-government policies, invited Hillman to report to him frankly on what he saw of the AMG's work and of the progress of denazification in Germany.[28]

Five days later, January 23, 1946, Hillman was off to London again, by transatlantic plane, and completed arrangements to go with a party including Sir Walter Citrine, Léon Jouhaux of France, and Kusnetzov of Russia on a five-week tour of Germany.

At this moment the General Assembly of the United Nations was meeting in London for the first time. Before leaving London, Hillman presented himself to the UN Assembly and petitioned once more for the right of the World Federation of Trade Unions to be represented in the UN in some advisory capacity. The head of the American delegation, Senator Tom Connally of Texas, raised strenuous objections to this, remarking that if labor bodies were to be invited in, then representatives of industrial corporations also should be included. This time, however, over the resistance of the American delegation, the UN General Assembly authorized the WFTU, in behalf of international labor, to "sit in" in a consultative capacity in its Economic and Social Council—a recently established auxiliary body of the UN. This was a forward step, victory of a sort. Hillman, an old Fabian, was nothing if not patient in his tactics. He had, in truth, large ambitions for the WFTU, and declared that it would avail itself as fully as possible of its advisory position with the UN.

The WFTU was considered at first to be little more than another international labor "congress," with power to do nothing more than pass resolutions. Yet by virtue of Hillman's strategy—not unlike Sidney and Beatrice Webb's tactics of "permeation"—the WFTU had won, after a six-month campaign, semi-official recognition from the UN General Assembly.

On January 31, 1946, Hillman left with his party for Germany, to visit the notorious Nazi concentration camps, observe conditions of military occupation in the four zones, and also attend sessions of the Nuremberg trials of war criminals.

Germany was going to be the key problem of the post-war settlement, as everyone realized. Hillman said that he was bent on finding out if Hitlerism was "the end product" of Germany, or if the German people could show the capacity to live as citizens of a democracy in the American style. On his tour of Western Germany he was taken aback at discovering how far the German working classes had actually gone in supporting Hitler by accepting wages "which, to an American, approached the coolie standard." As for terms of peace with them, he said he was for neither a "hard peace" (as some charged) nor a "soft peace," but for one "that will make it possible for all the rest of us to live in peace." This required, to his mind, a thorough-going denazification of German industry.[24] He also inspected factory conditions in the Russian zone. Russian officers, to be sure, accompanied the WFTU delegation and kept it under surveillance, but Germans who spoke with them seemed to feel free to make their complaints to Hillman's party against the Russians.

At the end of February, he was received by General Lucius D. Clay and entertained by him and other U. S. Army big "brass" in very friendly style. Hillman had disliked what he had seen of the British Zone, where the occupation officers seemed to be doing business, as a matter of preference, with former Nazi officials and managers of large industrial cartels who were known "collaborators." The AMG, in its own zone, seemed to him to be doing a better job, at the start, than the British. (This was, of course, about two years before the Truman Administration and the Russians reached a complete deadlock in the UN, and Truman felt obliged to turn away from the policy of seeking an accommodation with Russia toward that of waging cold war against Communism everywhere.) Hillman, therefore, on March 21, 1946, wrote Truman, as he had been asked to do, a letter reporting somewhat favorably on what he had seen of General Clay's administration. President Truman acknowledged the letter with expressions of mingled gratitude and relief.[25]

The visits to the Nazi concentration camps for political and "racial" prisoners and the sight of their relics of horror made an unforgettable impression on Hillman, of which he spoke movingly on his return to New York. Moreover, he had the experience of attending part of the Nuremberg trials and seeing before him as prisoners in the dock the Nazi war lords who had launched a world war they had not known how to finish. He told his union members later:

Everyone should have had the opportunity to go to Germany and visit the damnable concentration camps, see the torture chambers, see where they have annihilated human beings by the millions, and see the instructions in crematoriums that the bodies are to be put in at two minutes to ten, and they are to stay there until five minutes to eleven. . . .

Yes, it was a pleasure to go to Nuremberg and see the top leadership of world gangsterism on trial. There sat the . . . filthy Goering. But there also was that smooth world swindler, Hjalmar Schacht. Let us not fool ourselves that men of their evil stripe are confined to Germany or to Italy alone. We must uproot Fascism everywhere.

In Germany one might conceive how the Nazis had actually murdered fully six million Jews in their gas chambers or by other means. At the time, Hillman expressed great indignation that the few surviving Jews in Germany should still be obliged to live in concentration camps. He said on his return home:

These people want to get out of Germany and there is only one place they want to go to, and that is Palestine. . . . And I say that none has the moral right to stop them! [26]

The World Federation of Trade Unions, at its October 1945 convention in Paris had voted a resolution urging that a Jewish state be established in Palestine and immigration bans be lifted there. The labor federations of France, Britain, and, in the United States, the CIO and almost all other labor groups passed similar resolutions. Hillman now gave vigorous support to the campaign to open Palestine to unlimited Jewish immigration. The crusade for the new Israel was now fully launched. It was as one who had lost virtually half of his own kin to the Nazis that Hillman, in several conferences with President Truman, made most earnest appeals to him for American assistance in the relief of the displaced Jews. Truman's positive response to these and other petitions coming from notable American Jews was, in the end, to be one of the decisive factors in the founding of an independent Israel in 1948.

IV

At the time when Harry S. Truman succeeded to the presidency in April 1945, there had been intense speculation in political circles on whether the New Deal policies would be continued and on what the future relations of the powerful CIO leaders, Hillman and Murray, would be with the White House. At the outset of his Administration Mr. Truman, in phrases of a touching humility, expressed his sense of embarrassment at finding himself in the shoes of one who had been a master among politicians. Franklin Roosevelt, as party leader, for twelve years had directed a sort of Grand Alliance among the Northern city bosses, the liberal middle classes, the laborites, and the Southern Democrats. Few other men could be expected to maintain such an uneasy marriage and yet give the effect of an administration at once "realistic" on the political plane and progressive, or sympathetic to labor and the common man.

To be sure, Mr. Truman had vowed to continue the Roosevelt program, which, however, he now redefined as the Fair Deal, a term suggesting dilution. But after the passing of Roosevelt, the "gay reformer," with his light touch, his cape, and his agile cigarette holder, there was a decided relaxation in the political standards maintained under the New Deal. It was a change, as one of Mr. Truman's personal aides, the irrepressible General Harry Vaughan, remarked, from a diet of caviar to plain corned beef and cabbage.

Sidney Hillman knew that Harry Truman was a man of much good will and of honest and likable character. But under Truman there was a relapse to the rather casual pre-Rooseveltian type of presidential leadership that switched unpredictably and jaggedly from efforts to feed the politicians, ever hungry for "patronage," to spells of plumping for reform legislation, ineffectually enough, before a Congress that seemed ripe for reaction.

For the post of Secretary of Labor, Truman appointed former Senator Lewis Schwellenbach of Washington in place of Miss Perkins, who, with other New Dealers, had resigned on Roosevelt's death. The President's chief assistant in the work of labor mediation was now Dr. John Steelman. This last appointment presaged the altered climate of relations with labor.

However, so far as Hillman was concerned, the new President, though discreetly, continued to show him much deference as the man who had been labor's victorious political general in 1944. In May 1945, only a few weeks after assuming office, Mr. Truman called Hillman to the White House and had a long talk with him, after which he communicated with Hillman regularly, though not as frequently as F.D.R. had done. At this time, with no little subtlety, Hillman made the public statement that the PAC intended to be extremely active in the 1948 contest, which, it was observed, "could give Harry Truman the presidency for a second term." [27]

On several occasions the new President hinted that he would like to have Hillman stay in Washington, where he might be more avail-' able to advise the Administration. The suggestion of a public office or appointment of some sort was placed before Hillman, but he seemed now strongly determined to avoid such presidential favors.

On October 20, 1945, Truman wrote Hillman, inviting him to attend another of those labor-management conferences at Washington (often seen under Roosevelt), which he had set for November 5. A week later the President's secretary called Hillman to the White House for an off-the-record appointment. By then the post-war labor situation had begun to boil over.

The coming of peace and the partial abandonment of price controls, which meant inflation, led to a wave of strikes such as had not been seen in almost a decade. By the end of 1945 and the winter of 1946, masses of steel and auto workers and railway men were out on the picket lines. Organized labor had emerged stronger than ever from World War II, with an army of some 15,000,000 union members. Truman strove to moderate the angry spirits of the trade unionists and also keep the employing class in good humor. But in January 1946, there were big walkouts of the steel workers; Truman's attempts at mediation at first brought down upon him the vehement attacks of Philip Murray, who declared that his compromise proposals were unsatisfactory and "tended to weaken and ultimately to destroy labor organization." [28] Yet after the angry words and challenges had blown over, Truman eventually helped to bring about a settlement of the steel workers' demands by a grant of a substantial wage increase. Hillman thereupon sent Truman a congratulatory telegram on January 22, declaring that his intervention had served to protect the workers from a drastic decline in their standard of living.

- Hillman was by no means bent on forcing a breach with the new President, but showed rather the desire to "play close" to him, it was noticed, while Philip Murray's part (at least some of the time) was to pound away at Truman.

On the other hand, when reports were heard that the State Department contemplated a "softer" or friendlier approach to the government of Generalissimo Franco, Hillman, from the PAC headquarters, this time dispatched a very heated message to the President by telegram, reminding him that

WORLD WAR II STARTED IN SPAIN WHEN NAZI GERMANY AND FASCIST ITALY REPLACED THE LEGAL GOVERNMENT WITH ILLEGAL NAZI REGIME LED BY FRANCO. FRANCO'S STATUS AS ENEMY POWER AND SATELLITE OF MUSSOLINI AND HITLER WAS RECOGNIZED BY HIS EXCLUSION FROM THE UN AT SAN FRANCISCO AND POTSDAM. . . . URGE YOU REQUEST THAT BYRNES MAKE THIS SUBJECT OF MOSCOW DISCUSSIONS AND THAT ALLIED NATIONS COMPLETE ERADICATION OF NAZIS BY WITHDRAWING RECOGNITION FROM FRANCO AND ALLOWING SPAIN TO REINSTATE ITS OWN LEGAL DEMOCRATIC GOVERNMENT.

Truman replied mildly enough on December 21, thanking Hillman for his message and saying he would like to see him soon on the question of Spain and other matters as well.[29] When Hillman left in January, on his second German tour for the WFTU, he was armed with a letter from President Truman and every courtesy was extended him by the American Army command.

Nevertheless, the swing of the pendulum toward reaction after the war had begun, and it needed only a few slight pushes now and then from Mr. Truman, or his political aides, or Congress to give it great momentum. The broad liberal movement constituted by the two Political Action Committees suffered the disadvantage of no longer having a Roosevelt at their front. And Sidney Hillman was in failing health, especially after his return from that depressing voyage to Germany in March 1946.

When Mr. Truman, tacking before the wind, went to Congress during the railway strike of May 1946 and called for legislation enabling the government to take over essential industries or plants and draft workingmen in cases of disputes affecting the nation's safety, he brought down upon himself the odium of all union men. Hillman, from his sickbed in New York, sent telegrams to all members of the Senate condemning this ill-considered anti-strike legislation. Such proposals, he said, "were put forward in a moment of national hysteria deliberately provoked by the reactionary forces of big business" and threatened to impose "the most extreme controls over the rights and liberties of American workers."[30]

The crisis passed; the proposed "draft" of labor was forgotten;

Truman, by letter, assured Sidney Hillman that he was a much misunderstood man, but still union labor's staunch friend.

That spring of 1946 there was considerable debate over the future of the PAC: some of the CIO's radicals urged that it be adapted as the instrument of a third-party movement. Hillman, however, strongly opposed such a course as merely serving to ensure the victory of reactionary Republicans. He laid great stress on what he called the proven vitality of the two-party system in our country. The PAC, for the present, was to be limited to "riding on the back" of one or the other of the two major parties, according to the merit of the local candidates (though these were, in all but a few cases, Democrats); the other alternative, which he rejected, was that of becoming the organ of a protesting minority group without any office or bargaining power. (This second alternative was to be chosen two years later, in 1948, by Hillman's successors in charge of the reorganized National Citizens' PAC, with results as disappointing as Hillman had prophesied.)

Hillman would have liked to have a *permanent* instead of a temporary grass-roots organization built up for the PAC through the CIO's local union offices all over the country. Powerful influences in the CIO Executive Board, however, discouraged such advances. Fears were persistently expressed by certain CIO executives that the PAC would overshadow the CIO itself. It was they who urged that the National Citizens' PAC should be wound up after the 1944 elections, or turned over to some liberal group outside the labor movement. On May 11, 1945, Hillman, under pressure, resigned as chairman of the National Citizens' PAC (while retaining his post as chairman of the CIO-PAC), and ex-Governor Elmer Benson of Minnesota was elected in his place, C. B. Baldwin, vice-chairman, remaining the executive director. As for the professional politicos in the Democratic Party, from President Truman down to the old ward captains, they heartily wished that the two Political Action Committees might be buried and forgotten.

Nevertheless, plans for the PAC's intervention in local and congressional elections in 1946 were laid out by Hillman and his aides in the spring of that year on an ambitious scale. During the latter part of 1945 a nationwide survey of voters' sentiment was made by C. B. Baldwin, and the strategy of the campaign was to be based on his report. Attention was to be focused at various points in the country on the defeat and replacement of approximately 100 congressmen and 26 senators singled out as unrepentant allies of the "economic royalists." Hillman's own notes show how carefully he studied the lists of those marked by the PAC for attack or support; in each case he wrote down his estimate of what it would cost to do the job.

Despite much thunder on the left against President Truman's domestic and foreign policy, Hillman indicated clearly that the CIO-PAC would endorse the Truman Administration in 1946. But in May the primary elections in Ohio and New Jersey proved disappointing, several candidates espoused by the PAC being defeated— in one instance by Representative Fred A. Hartley of New Jersey, who was to be co-author of the Taft-Hartley Act, which severely amended labor's "Magna Charta," the Wagner Act. These were bad omens for November. Hillman felt deep misgivings about the political trend at this time, but continued to exhort his friends to work in the "mainstream" of our political life.

Yet whatever might happen to the CIO-PAC after he had passed away, the blueprint of it would always be there, a boldly original design for political action which others who came after him might use again when the need or occasion arose.*

---

*The PAC was to suffer serious setbacks in the November 1946 congressional elections, when its guiding genius was gone.

At about this period there was much debate in high CIO circles over the future disposition of the PAC, and it was reported that certain of the CIO leaders would like to "let the PAC run down like an unwound clock." They did not like the possibility of its being used as a national political machine and hoped that it would be absorbed by some liberal organization, while the CIO stopped being a political party. (Victor Riesel in New York *Post,* July 24, 1946.)

This was more or less what happened in 1948 when the Independent Citizens' Committee of the Arts, Sciences and Professions, an auxiliary organization that had sprung up in 1944, was merged with the NC-PAC and renamed the Progressive Citizens of America. This group became the nucleus of the Progressive Party, which campaigned as a third party for Henry Wallace as President that year.

In the summer of 1946, Vice-President Jack Kroll, head of the Amalgamated's Cincinnati Joint Board, was named by the CIO Executive Board to succeed Hillman as chairman of the CIO-PAC. Close ties between the political organization and the CIO were continued. In the presidential elections of 1948, the CIO-PAC gave very effective support to Truman and the Democratic ticket generally, with good results in strategic areas. However, the organization has been much reduced in scale of late years.

V

Hillman's family and friends had seriously warned him against taking that last trip to Germany in February and March 1946. One of his assistants at the PAC, Thomas F. Burns, wrote later:

We who had worked closely with Sidney Hillman knew he was overexerting himself—what's more, he knew it; but he was in relentless pursuit of a vision he wanted to see materialize, one that he knew was in the grasp of the American people, a vision of plenty for all in this land of plenty, a vision of peace and security.[31]

Shortly after he returned home in the second week of March, terribly fatigued and depressed, he had a second heart attack and was confined to his New York apartment under medical care during all the month that followed. At this time preparations were being made for the Fifteenth Biennial Convention of the Amalgamated Clothing Workers, which was to open at Atlantic City on May 6.

The great needle-trades union had for a decade or more become accustomed to "lending" Sidney to the country's labor movement, to the wartime government, and even to the international trade-union movement. Under the veteran triumvirate of General Secretary Potofsky and Vice-Presidents Rosenblum and Blumberg, with the help of a strong Executive Board of twenty, the union had managed its affairs quite well during Sidney's absences. Its membership had risen by 1946 to the neighborhood of 350,000, organized around 496 locals in 36 states and four provinces of Canada. Only recently, in December 1945, a nationwide trade agreement for an average wage increase of 15 cents an hour had been negotiated, helping the clothing workers to keep pace with the cost of living. The union's various "fringe benefits," moreover, in the form of retirement pensions, life insurance, and health or hospitalization plans, had also been widely extended lately to cover more than two thirds (then about 250,000) of its members. Meanwhile the retirement age had been lowered from 70 to 65, and the annuities added, through the union's funds, to state and Federal pension payments greatly increased.

As delegates arrived for the convention from all over the country there were gloomy reports that their president might not be well enough to preside over this gathering as he had done for thirty-two years. But for Hillman the thought of absence from an Amalgamated convention was well-nigh unbearable. At the beginning of May he had recovered enough to pick himself up out of bed and go to his office for a few days. When the convention opened on May 6, he was on hand as usual.

He was but fifty-nine. Up to this stage he had always looked young for his age. But now the union delegates were appalled to see how pale he was, how deeply lined his face, and how weak and slow were his movements.

Despite his evident weakness, he insisted upon holding the chair a great deal of the time, opening each session himself. When reports or resolutions were being read he would turn the gavel over to one of his old lieutenants and retire to his hotel room for a while, after which he would wander back and inject himself into the discussion. As always, the convention was a forum where national and international issues were debated as often as questions of "pork chops" for the union members.

In his opening speech Hillman was discursive; he rambled over the subjects of political action at home and the country's foreign policy. At moments also he reminisced with less reserve than usual and gave expression to his hopes and fears for the future, as if he sensed that there was little time left and these might be among his last thoughts and last words. It is traditional for a union president to "view with pride" the administration term just ended; and this he did too, though on a note of idealism and almost, one might have said, of reverie, quite unusual with him. He said of the newly introduced old-age pension plan, then based on a payment by the employers of 3 per cent of payroll:

It was our dream to give security to our members, security within the framework of liberty, of individual freedom. . . . Today, our membership enjoys paid vacations, health and life insurance and maternity benefits. Once again we are using the clothing industry as an experiment before bringing it to the rest of the membership.

All this had been won, he pointed out, without strikes or the threat of them, an illustration of the union's maturity. Yet men had been called "dreamers" and "utopians" when they voiced the hope of winning such conditions thirty-two years before. It was always his thought that the enactment of real social security for wage workers would bring about a tremendous lift in their whole outlook on life and in their spirit.

For a few moments Hillman evoked the picture of their situation three decades ago, when most tailors labored over their bundles in malodorous sweatshops from ten to eleven hours a day, or up to seventy hours a week, for a dollar to two dollars a day. How often the old-timers at this convention, and Sidney Hillman himself and his wife Bessie, who sat beside him, had suffered from actual hunger.

And now, he went on proudly:

I say it is given to very few people to see their dreams realized and in their own lifetime. Yet there are many now in this hall who attended our first constitutional convention. We have come a long way since then. . . .

Yes, many of the dreams of the men and women who met in Webster Hall in New York in 1914 have become realities. . . .

He reverted then to the subject of the great war just ended:

Today we meet in a world that, for the first time in fifteen years, is free from the ever-present threat or the terrible reality of Fascist aggression. . . . If, two years ago, our primary concern was the winning of the war, today our first concern is the winning of the peace. This can be our only compensation for the terrible price paid by humanity. . . .

I do not want to be misunderstood. I am not critical of what is being done. At least for the record, I am not critical. I do not know enough to understand it all or to be critical. Of course you have to have diplomats. You have to have Secretaries of State to conduct the negotiations just as your officers do for your industry.

But labor, in its organized strength, must play its part in all decisions that affected the nation and the world at large:

We propose to have something to say, and a great deal to say, before the world is thrown into another catastrophe. I am sure that when the voice of America is heard, it will be to the effect that *there must not be another war in our lifetime.*

We in our organization . . . will strive for an ever-higher standard of living. But, my friends, *we must be permitted to live, to enjoy it.* And unless we take an interest in our national and international policies, there may not be an opportunity to enjoy a decent life.

He recalled the time of Roosevelt's leadership in the world crisis and, with his intimate knowledge of the man, interpreted the "creative vision" underlying Roosevelt's plan for the United Nations. The hard fact was that, with Germany and Japan defeated, only three nations today had the power to wage modern warfare: the United States, Russia, and Great Britain. So long as they worked together, so long would the United Nations be an effective instrument for peace:

But if the unity of the Big Three fails, then I am afraid . . . the UN will become no more than an arena for the play of power politics, another League of Nations, as futile and ineffective as the League.

Recognition of this basic fact was the cornerstone of the Roosevelt foreign policy. . . . I was close enough to him to know that this was the cornerstone of his policy—an independent American policy, neither pro-British nor pro-Russian. With all of his great skill, Roosevelt preserved the sometimes delicate balance, blunting the sharp edges of conflict between our two allies, and maintaining the Big Three as an effective working team.

If today, a short year after the defeat of Hitler, it is possible for us even to contemplate war, it is because cracks have begun to appear in the war-born unity of the Big Three. And now is the time to stop those cracks from widening. We cannot afford to drift to a point where we have to take sides, because that would mean disaster. . . .

Hillman's own actions in the international labor scene, he made clear, had closely paralleled Roosevelt's foreign policy. By working out a unanimous agreement among the Russian, British, and American delegations at the World Trade Union Conference in London, as later at the Paris founding convention, labor had shown the way to peace.

Of course we have basic disagreements with our friends from Russia. That did not stop us from mutual agreement on policies. We did not sacrifice any of our ideals, nor did they. We agreed that in Russia it is their business to build the kind of government they feel they want. We expect them to have the same respect for us. If nations deal with each other on the same basis, I see nothing in the way of agreement between Russia, Great Britain, the United States, France, and all the rest of us.

Turning to domestic affairs, Hillman observed that while labor had grown tremendously strong, reactionary elements in both political parties seemed to have combined since V-J Day to make the dismal legislative record shown by the then existing Congress. Thus a country which could build incredible quantities of war material found itself "suddenly" incapable of providing homes even for its returned war heroes. The reactionary bloc in Congress, instead of moving toward the Economic Bill of Rights which the majority of the people desired, now centered its attention upon

an undemocratic and un-American campaign of harassing progressive men and organizations and violating their civil rights and liberties under the Hitler-like guise of a holy crusade against "Communism." Not really Communism; they just use the word to describe anything progressive.

The only answer was to speed the political action of labor and its liberal allies. He recalled the impressive achievements of the PAC in 1944, accomplished with small funds. Good-humoredly he observed:

We are no match for the Republicans when it comes to raising or spending money. And they are no match for us when it comes to making friends and influencing people!

Hillman ended this speech with a moving peroration:

My friends, we have accomplished much. But we cannot rest on our laurels. *This is a time when everything is at stake. There is no middle way. This is either going to be a free world or a world where only slaves will live.* [Italics added]

Though obviously very tired, Hillman remained in Atlantic City until May 10 to preside over the formal adjournment of the convention. More than one of the delegates present, noticing how weak he looked, wondered whether they would ever see him again at an ACWA gathering. It was with this thought in mind that one newspaperman, who was an admirer of Hillman, sent up a message to the chair, urging that he make some general statement that might be a summation of his own philosophy of labor and political action.

Hillman smiled, then rose to the occasion like an old battlehorse. For about a quarter of an hour, though in weak voice, speaking quietly, he reviewed the business completed at the convention and then ended with a few general reflections, in phrases simple indeed, yet filled with his own special inward glow. Everyone listened with intense interest, sensing that those words were perhaps his valedictory:

It is within the power of America to provide for our people conditions beyond the dreams of generations past.

Not only do we have a tremendous productivity, but now is the time when we can open the door to the atomic age.

This earth can be made a place where men and women can walk together in peace and friendship and enjoy all that this world can provide for; but we must see to it that the power of government is placed at the service of the people instead of in the control of the privileged few, selfish, greedy people who do not accept the right of the common man and do not understand what democracy means. . . . Our program is not a class program. Ours is not a selfish program. Ours is a program for all America.

We want a better America, an America that will give its citizens, first of all, a higher and higher standard of living, so that no child will cry for food in the midst of plenty. We want to have an America where the inventions of science will be at the disposal of every American family, not merely for the few who can afford them. An America that will have no sense of insecurity and which will make it possible for all the groups to live in friendship, and to be real neighbors; an America that will carry on its great mission of helping other countries to help themselves, thinking not in terms of exploitation, but of creating plenty abroad so we can all enjoy it here.[32]

VI

A short time after his appearance at the union convention Hillman was stricken again, in early June, by a third attack of coronary thrombosis. Now more dead than alive, he was brought to the cottage at Point Lookout, Long Island, where he remained in seclusion for several weeks, under a doctor's care. His wife and younger daughter Selma, and the child of Selma, his infant granddaughter, Dorothy Lerner, were with him constantly; and his old union comrades came faithfully to see him in the evening. At frequent intervals also "Beanie" Baldwin and Raymond Walsh of PAC called to bring up-to-the-minute news of developments in current primary and election campaigns.

After having so often missed the compensations of family life, through long absences from home, he now was happy to spend his days in the company of his wife, his daughter Selma, and his granddaughter. His mood was gentle and relaxed. He said calmly to Selma one day: "Now I know I won't have very much longer to live." He knew that all sorts of difficult human problems faced Selma and her daughter, as well as Philoine, and he said regretfully that he would have liked to plan everything and foresee everything for them. "I wish I could have arranged things better. I should have tried to spare myself and live a few years longer. Now there is little time. You must follow my advice—listen to me carefully——" and he would begin laying plans for all of them, as in the days when he charted his union's campaigns years ahead.

After about three weeks at the beach, feeling somewhat recovered, he returned to his office in New York on Monday, July 8. This was in spite of his doctors' warnings that he must henceforth live in retirement. He enjoyed a day of the old routine; but on the next day, feeling poorly again, he remarked to his secretary: "I think I will go home to Point Lookout early this afternoon." Hyman Blumberg arranged to drive home with him early in the afternoon, together with Mrs. Blumberg. They were accompanied also by Mrs. Tecia Davidson, Hillman's secretary for the past twenty years, who had a summer place at Long Beach, a few miles from Point Lookout.

He had been told that the Amalgamated Bank, in the same building as the union's executive offices, had been freshly painted and redecorated, and before getting into the car he went to see how it looked. This high, ornate counting room, with its slender iron columns, once the home of Tiffany's elegant jewelry emporium in the days of President Grant, was thronged by its worker-depositors and hummed with the trade of the garment district's small business. The bank had always meant a great deal to Sidney Hillman, symbolizing as it did his union's varied administrative and social welfare services. He stood at the doorway a moment and looked about him, smiling. "The tailors have come a long way!" he said to Blumberg.

His secretary related afterward:

We got into the car and started for Point Lookout. Mr. Hillman sat next to the driver in the front seat with the inevitable batch of afternoon papers. Hyman and Bess Blumberg and I sat in back. Before very long Hymie dozed off. Bess and I talked quietly. It was the usual relaxed, pleasant trip away from the cruel heat of the city, to coolness and relief.

At the toll bridge leading to Point Lookout, the "boss" mischievously awakened Blumberg, ordering him to "pay up." But the toll fee had already been paid; Hillman laughed heartily at the surprised, drowsy man. It was just the sort of horseplay that Blumberg would have indulged in. In any case, they were but a few minutes now from the end of the journey.

Suddenly the car stopped; the driver said they had a flat tire. Blumberg got out and helped him change the tire, while Hillman and Mrs. Blumberg sat down in the grass beside the road. It was a sunny afternoon, very quiet and peaceful here along the bay shore, with only the tall green reeds rustling in the wind and an occasional cry of a sea gull. Hillman sat in the sun, opening his collar, looking very pleased with everything, and humming a tune from *Oklahoma!* A few moments later they were at his home, and his granddaughter Dorothy, whom he adored, came running out, weeping. She had hurt her arm while playing and showed it to him. He sat down on the step, gathered her into his arms, and kissed the bruised spot, whispering to her tenderly. The others drove off.

It was their last sight of him alive.

That night he went to bed at his usual hour, toward midnight, but awoke very early, before seven. After stirring about for a few minutes and trying to dress, he returned to bed, saying to Mrs. Hillman: "I feel like hell. I'm going to lie down again." Then suddenly he sank back in a dead faint. Mrs. Hillman called a local physician, Dr. John Cahill, at once, and also telephoned his New York physicians, Dr. Frank Boas and Dr. Mack Lipkin. Within a few minutes the Nassau County police arrived with oxygen tanks and a respirator, while Dr. Cahill worked over him. The two New York heart specialists came an hour later.

There was a vigil of three hours. This was his fourth heart attack. His wife and daughter, joined by their neighbors, the Blumbergs, waited in terrible suspense. But as the minutes passed he did not revive from his state of coma and his pulse grew ever weaker.

He had been saying of late to his friends that we were now faced with the greatest dangers, and also very great opportunities, and that unfortunately there was so little time. By now he fairly embodied the public conscience of millions of liberal and humane Americans. And so he had never really halted to catch his breath or renew his waning strength, continuing in full career to the very end—all anxiety and zeal and hope. But at 10 A.M. on July 10, 1946, the restless heart of Sidney Hillman at last came to a stop.

SOURCE
REFERENCE
NOTES

Primary source materials used in this work have been drawn in great part from documentary records such as Hillman's correspondence and speeches and the correspondence of his union associates as well; also from the stenotyped proceedings of labor-union conventions, as in *ACWA Documentary History, 1914–52,* published biennially at New York and now totaling eighteen volumes; and from contemporary newspaper or periodical articles and labor-union publications. For the period of Hillman's service under the Federal Government, memoranda and reports by Hillman and members of his staff, official government agency releases, and the minutes of various government commissions have been drawn upon, as well as the papers of President Franklin D. Roosevelt (at the Roosevelt Memorial Library, Hyde Park, New York). This material has necessarily been supplemented by use of a large amount of oral testimony gathered by interviewing many participants or eyewitnesses of the events described in this book, for much recent political and labor history remains as yet unpublished. The names of persons who accorded such interviews, as well as citations from newspaper and documentary records, are indicated in the Notes following.

In this field the range of published books, as secondary sources, has been found quite limited as yet. One contemporary biography, *Sidney Hillman, Labor Statesman,* by George Soule (1939), appeared prior to the present work, but treats mainly the first half of Hillman's career. A series of interesting studies of its industry has been issued by the ACWA during the past thirty years, notably *The Chicago Clothing Workers,* edited by Leo H. Wolman (1924), and the publications edited later by J. B. S. Hardman. Reference to these and other pamphlets and books touching on the history of the Amalgamated Clothing Workers, the contemporary labor movement in America, and recent political history has been given in the Notes, at the point where such published sources are first cited in the text.

Quotations from *John L. Lewis,* by Saul Alinsky, have been made by permission of the author.

CHAPTER ONE: Pages 17 to 37.

1. S. Hillman to Charles Paiken, Oct. 28, 1908. **2.** Leah Hillman Suckow to M. J. **3.** Ibid. **4.** Memorandum of Dr. Matis to J. S. Potofsky, dated 1924. **5.** J. S. Potofsky: *Notes on Hillman* (Ms. 1924–38). **6.** M. Zacharias to M. J.

CHAPTER TWO: Pages 38 to 58.

1. Hillman to C. Paiken, Nov. 1908. **2.** Hillman to J. S. Potofsky, Aug. 23, 1914. **3.** Hillman's testimony before the U. S. Commission on Industrial Relations, Washington, D.C., 1914, 64th Congress, 1st Session, Sen. Doc. 415, Vol. 1, pp. 566–71. **4.** C. W. Ervin to M. J. **5.** L. Wolman *et al.: The Chicago Clothing Workers* (publication of the Chicago Joint Board, ACWA), Chicago, 1924, pp. 19–20. **6.** Jane Addams: *Twenty Years at Hull House* (N.Y.: The Macmillan Company, 1929), pp. 98–99. **7.** Statement of Annie Schapiro, Illinois State Senate Committee Hearings, Feb. 2–10, 1911, pp. 1178 ff. **8.** E. D. Howard to M. J. **9.** Hillman's testimony before the U. S. Commission on Industrial Relations, Washington, D.C., 1914. **10.** Mrs. Bessie Hillman to M. J. **11.** Hillman, speech at Montreal, Jan. 29, 1918. **12.** A. D. Marimpietri: *From These Beginnings* (publication of the Chicago Joint Board, ACWA), Chicago, 1928, p. 15. **13.** S. Rissman, article in *The Tailor Retailored* (publication of the Chicago Joint Board, ACWA), Chicago, 1928, p. 55. **14.** Ibid., p. 56. **15.** Hillman's testimony before the U. S. Commission on Industrial Relations, Washington, D.C., 1914. **16.** A. D. Marimpietri, op. cit., p. 16. **17.** Hillman's testimony before the U. S. Commission on Industrial Relations, Washington, D.C., 1914. **18.** Proceedings of the UGWA convention, 1912, p. 24. **19.** Chicago *Daily Socialist,* Nov. 7, 1910. **20.** Wolman *et al.,* op. cit., pp. 38 ff. **21.** Chicago *Daily Socialist,* Dec. 8, 1910. **22.** Wolman *et al.,* op. cit., pp. 38 ff.

23. E. D. Howard to M. J.   24. A. D. Marimpietri, op. cit., pp. 13–14.   25. J. S. Potofsky, op. cit.   26. Mrs. Bessie Hillman to M. J.   27. Professor Graham Taylor in *The Survey*, Mar. 7, 1914.   28. Hillman, article in *The Tailor Retailored*, pp. 26–27.   29. A. D. Marimpietri, op. cit., p. 15.   30. Wolman *et al.*, op. cit., pp. 47–48.

CHAPTER THREE: Pages 59 to 85.

1. Karl Braun, *Union-Management Cooperation* (Brookings Institution, Washington, D.C., 1947), pp. 22–23.   2. E. D. Howard, article in *The Annals of the American Academy of Political and Social Science*, Jan., 1922.   3. E. D. Howard to M. J.   4. Ibid.   5. A. D. Marimpietri, op. cit., pp. 20–21.   6. Wolman *et al.*, op. cit., p. 52.   7. Hillman's testimony before the U. S. Commission on Industrial Relations, Washington, D.C., 1914.   8. Ibid.   9. *John E. Williams, an Appreciation, with Selections from His Writings;* ed. by J. S. Potofsky (ACWA publication, Chicago, 1930), pp. i-vi.   10. Meyer Kestnbaum (President of Hart, Schaffner and Marx), "Thirty Years of Labor Peace," *Harvard Business Review*, Autumn, 1940.   11. E. D. Howard to M. J.   12. John Fitzpatrick, article in *The Tailor Retailored*, p. 31.   13. Mrs. Bessie Hillman to M. J.   14. J. S. Potofsky to M. J.   15. Fitzpatrick, op. cit., p. 47.   16. J. S. Potofsky, *Notes on Hillman.*   17. Ibid.   18. Ibid.   19. *John E. Williams*, p. 20.   20. J. E. Williams' testimony before the U. S. Commission on Industrial Relations, Washington, D.C., pp. 697 ff.   21. *John E. Williams*, p. 22.   22. John E. Williams in Streator (Ill.) *Independent-Times*, Mar. 7, 1914.   23. *The Tailor Retailored*, p. 27.   24. E. D. Howard to M. J.   25. John E. Williams, op. cit.   26. F. G. Taylor, article in *The Survey*, Mar. 14, 1914.   27. Hillman's testimony before the U. S. Commission on Industrial Relations, Washington, D.C., 1914.   28. *John E. Williams*, pp. 24–25.   29. E. D. Howard to M. J.   30. J. S. Potofsky, op. cit.   31. E. D. Howard to M. J.   32. Hillman to J. S. Potofsky, May 28, 1914.   33. *Life and Labor* (pamphlet), Chicago, May 1913.   34. J. E. Williams in Streator (Ill.) *Independent-Times*, June 28, 1913.   35. Hillman to J. E. Williams, Jan. 28, 1914.   36. *John E. Williams*, p. 51.   37. A. D. Marimpietri to M. J.

CHAPTER FOUR: Pages 86 to 110.

1. J. E. Williams, in Streator (Ill.) *Independent-Times*, May 22, 1915.   2. Ibid., May 29, 1915.   3. Joseph Seidman: *The Needle Trades* (N.Y.; Farrar and Rinehart, 1942), pp. 108–9.   4. J. S. Potofsky, op. cit.   5. Hillman to J. S. Potofsky, Aug. 23, 1914.   6. Wolman *et al.*, op. cit., pp. 80–81.   7. August Bellanca to M. J.   8. Sam Levin to M. J.   9. A. D. Marimpietri to J. S. Potofsky, Oct. 11, 1914.   10. Sam Levin to M. J.   11. Judge Jacob H. Panken to Mrs. Bessie Hillman, July 14, 1946.   12. *Sidney Hillman, Labor Statesman*, ed. by J. B. S. Hardman (ACWA publication); N.Y., 1946.   13. ACWA Files, 1914.   14. Letter of Apr. 12, 1915, in ACWA Files.   15. ACWA Files, 1914.   16. Hillman to Sam Levin, Nov. 12, 1914.   17. Ibid.   18. J. S. Potofsky,

op. cit.   **19.** Letter of E. G. Starr in *The New Republic,* Jan. 8, 1915.   **20.** Letter of Samuel Gompers to *The New Republic,* Jan. 22, 1915.   **21.** Selig Perlman, *A Theory of the Labor Movement,* Madison, Wis., 1928, pp. 163–64. **22.** Samuel Gompers, op. cit., Jan. 20, 1915.   **23.** Lewis Lorwin: *The American Federation of Labor,* pp. 220–21.   **24.** *ACWA Doc. Hist.,* 1914–16, pp. 43–46. **25.** J. B. S. Hardman, article in *American Labor Year Book,* N.Y., 1916, p. 33. **26.** N.Y. *Times,* Nov. 1, 1914.

CHAPTER FIVE: Pages 111 to 132.

1. Hillman to S. Levin, Nov. 26, 1914.   **2.** H. Blumberg to M. J.   **3.** J. Schlossberg letters of Nov. 25 and Dec. 2, 1914.   **4.** H. Blumberg to M. J.   **5.** David Drechsler to M. J.   **6.** Hillman to F. Rosenblum, Feb. 9, 1915.   **7.** F. Rosenblum to M. J.   **8.** Hillman to J. Schlossberg, Mar. 15, 1915.   **9.** F. Rosenblum to Hillman, Apr. 15 and May 3, 1915.   **10.** *ACWA Doc. Hist.,* 1916, p. 133. **11.** Hillman to F. Rosenblum, Apr. 13, 1915.   **12.** Ibid.   **13.** Letter of Feb. 19, 1915.   **14.** *ACWA Doc. Hist.,* 1916, pp. 135–37.   **15.** Hillman to J. Schlossberg, Sept. 15, 1915.   **16.** Ibid.   **17.** *John E. Williams,* pp. 58–59.   **18.** Chicago *Tribune,* Sept. 30, 1915.   **19.** ACWA Files, 1915.   **20.** Chicago *Examiner,* Oct. 4, 1915.   **21.** Chicago *Herald,* Oct. 16, 1915.   **22.** Hillman to J. Schlossberg, Oct. 21, 1915 and Nov. 6, 1915.   **23.** Article by J. S. Potofsky in *The Tailor Retailored,* p. 55.   **24.** Chicago *Tribune,* Oct. 14, 1915.   **25.** Chicago *Herald* (interview), Dec. 13, 1915.   **26.** Telegram of October 27, 1915, in ACWA Files, 1915.   **27.** Hillman to J. Schlossberg, Nov. 6, 1915.   **28.** *J. E. Williams,* pp. 58–59.   **29.** Hillman to J. Schlossberg, Nov. 8, 1915.   **30.** *J. E. Williams,* p. 59.   **31.** Mrs. Bessie Hillman to M. J.

CHAPTER SIX: Pages 133 to 159.

1. J. Schlossberg, letter of Dec. 28, 1915.   **2.** Ibid.   **3.** Hillman to J. S. Potofsky, Jan. 14, 1916.   **4.** J. Schlossberg, letter of Jan. 5, 1916.   **5.** C. W. Ervin to M. J.   **6.** Adapted from U.S. Census of Manufactures, 1919, Vol. IX. **7.** J. Seidman, op. cit., p. 87.   **8.** Earl D. Strong, *The Amalgamated Clothing Workers;* Herald-Register Publishing Company, Grinnell, Ia., 1940, p. 74. **9.** *ACWA Doc. Hist.,* 1918, p. 19.   **10.** Elias Rabkin to M. J.   **11.** J. Schlossberg to E. Rabkin, Oct. 27, 1916.   **12.** Letter of Leo Krzycki, Aug. 7, 1916; letter of August Bellanca, June 30, 1916.   **13.** N.Y. *Daily News-Record,* May 16, 1916.   **14.** Letter of Hillman, Mar. 15, 1916.   **15.** *ACWA Doc. Hist.,* 1918, pp. 89–90.   **16.** Mrs. Bessie Hillman to M. J.   **17.** Hillman, letter of May 1, 1917.   **18.** Hillman, letter of Jan. 29, 1918.   **19.** C. W. Ervin to M. J. **20.** Hillman to F. Rosenblum, May 18, 1916.   **21.** Hillman to F. Rosenblum, June 8, 1916.   **22.** *ACWA Doc. Hist.,* 1918, p. 83.   **23.** A. Bellanca to Hillman, July 3, 1916.   **24.** Letter of July 17, 1916.   **25.** ACWA Files, 1916.   **26.** *The Weekly People,* Baltimore, Aug. 31, 1916.   **27.** N.Y. *Daily News-Record,* Apr. 22, 1916.   **28.** Kestnbaum, op. cit.   **29.** Chicago *Tribune,* Apr. 14, 1916. **30.** Wolman *et al.,* op. cit., pp. 132–33.   **31.** Letter of Apr. 17, 1916.

32. Mrs. Bessie Hillman to M. J. **33.** Letter of Feb. 3, 1917. **34.** Chicago *Herald,* May 2, 1916; Chicago *Tribune,* May 1, 1916. **35.** J. S. Potofsky, op. cit. **36.** Ibid. **37.** Mrs. Bessie Hillman to M. J. **38.** *ACWA Doc. Hist.,* 1914–16, pp. 141–42. **39.** Ibid., p. 113.

CHAPTER SEVEN: Pages 160 to 193.

1. Frank Rosenblum, letter of June 2, 1917. **2.** *The New Republic,* July 7, 1917. **3.** *ACWA Doc. Hist.,* 1918; Baltimore speech of May 13, 1918; p. 10. **4.** Letter of Aug. 17, 1917. **5.** Florence Kelley to Walter Lippmann, June 26, 1917; ACWA Files, 1917. **6.** Hillman to J. E. Williams, July 3, 1917. **7.** Hillman speech, May 13, 1918; *ACWA Doc. Hist.,* 1918, pp. 9–11. **8.** Hillman to J. E. Williams, July 3, 1917. **9.** Hillman to Hyman Blumberg, July 11, 1917. **10.** Hillman to Secretary of War Newton D. Baker, Oct. 16, 1917. **11.** Report to members of the General Executive Board, Aug. 31, 1917. **12.** *The Advance,* Aug. 31, 1917. **13.** *ACWA Doc. Hist.,* 1918, p. 140. **14.** George Kirstein to M. J. **15.** Hillman to J. E. Williams, Jan. 2, 1918. **16.** *The Advance,* Aug. 24, 1917. **17.** N.Y. *Times,* Dec. 28, 1917. **18.** *ACWA Doc. Hist.,* 1918, p. 190. **19.** W. Z. Ripley to Louis Kirstein (memorandum), July 2, 1918 (ACWA File). **20.** J. S. Potofsky to L. Marcovitz, May 25, 1917. **21.** J. B. S. Hardman (ed.): *Labor Dynamics* (N.Y.: Harcourt, Brace, 1928), p. 294. **22.** W. Z. Ripley, telegram to Hillman, June 14, 1918. **23.** Hillman to L. Hollander, July 9, 1918. **24.** Bertram Kahn to M. J. **25.** Hillman to Alex Cohen, Nov. 10, 1918; J. S. Potofsky to H. Brenner, Oct. 11, 1918. **26.** D. B. Straus: *Hickey-Freeman and the ACWA, A Case Study;* Twentieth Century Fund, N.Y., 1947, pp. 8–9. **27.** J. S. Potofsky to M. J. **28.** D. B. Straus, op. cit., pp. 37–39. **29.** Dr. W. M. Leiserson to M. J. **30.** J. S. Potofsky to M. J. **31.** Dr. W. M. Leiserson to M. J. **32.** Telegram of J. S. Potofsky, Jan. 8, 1919. **33.** Report of the Advisory Board for Men's Clothing, N.Y., Jan.–Feb. 1919, pp. 135; 294–95; 299. ACWA Files, 1919. **34.** W. Z. Ripley, "Bones of Contention," *The Survey,* Apr. 29, 1922, pp. 169–73. **35.** Dr. W. M. Leiserson to M. J. **36.** Sam Levin, letter of Nov. 2, 1918. **37.** Wolman *et al.,* op. cit., pp. 112 ff. **38.** Sam Levin to M. J. **39.** Wolman *et al.,* op. cit., p. 113. **40.** Ibid., p. 119; Jack Kroll to M. J. **41.** Sidney Rissman to M. J. **42.** Ibid. **43.** Hillman to Mrs. J. E. Williams, Jan. 31, 1919. **44.** J. B. S. Hardman, "Fifty Years of American Labor," *The New Republic,* Oct. 28, 1931. **45.** Mary Heaton Vorse, article in *The Nation,* May 22, 1920. **46.** J. S. Potofsky, letter of Jan. 10, 1920. **47.** *ACWA Doc. Hist.,* 1920 (speech of Alderman B. C. Vladeck), p. 21. **48.** *The New Republic,* editorial, Feb. 1, 1919. **49.** *ACWA Doc. Hist.,* 1918, pp. 15 ff. **50.** Montreal *Star* and Montreal *Herald,* Jan. 29, 1918. **51.** Montreal *Gazette,* Jan. 30, 1918.

CHAPTER EIGHT: Pages 194 to 212.

1. N.Y. *World,* July 27, 1919, article by James Henle. **2.** Paul Blanshard, "The Class Struggle in a Ballroom," *The New Republic,* June 5, 1921. **3.** D. B.

Straus, op. cit., p. 25. **4.** J. S. Potofsky to M. J. **5.** N.Y. *World,* July 11, 1920, article by Louis Levine. **6.** Alex Cohen (interview), Oct. 3, 1951. **7.** A. J. Muste to M. J. **8.** Benjamin Schlesinger to Hillman, June 30, 1920. **9.** Dr. Leo Wolman to M. J. **10.** *ACWA Doc. Hist.,* 1920, p. 221. **11.** Earl Strong, op. cit., pp. 176 ff. **12.** *ACWA Doc. Hist.,* 1918, pp. 122 ff. **13.** William E. Chenery in *The Survey,* May 22, 1920. **14.** *ACWA Doc. Hist.,* 1920, p. 236. **15.** Baltimore *Sun,* May 10, 1920. **16.** *ACWA Doc. Hist.,* 1920, p. 321. **17.** Mary Heaton Vorse, op. cit. **18.** N.Y. *World* (interview), July 27, 1919. **19.** D. B. Straus, op. cit., pp. 26–27. **20.** J. S. Potofsky to M. J. **21.** *ACWA Doc. Hist.,* 1920, pp. 348–50. **22.** William Hard in *The New Republic,* May 22, 1920.

CHAPTER NINE: Pages 213 to 241.

1. Hillman's report to the General Executive Board, July 7, 1920. **2.** S. Perlman and P. Taft, *History of Labor in the U. S.* (N.Y.: Macmillan, 1935), Vol. IV, pp. 489 ff. **3.** J. Schlossberg to Representative F. H. La Guardia, Aug. 16, 1919. **4.** Letter of Joseph Schlossberg, Aug. 21, 1919, *ACWA Doc. Hist.,* 1920, pp. 37–39. **5.** Chicago *Daily News,* Apr. 28, 1920; *ACWA Doc. Hist.,* 1920, pp. 125 ff. **6.** Letter of J. S. Potofsky to Sam Levin, cited in N.Y. *Times,* Nov. 10, 1919. **7.** *ACWA Doc. Hist.,* 1920, p. 129. **8.** Ibid., pp. 120–29. **9.** Michaels, Stern *vs.* Sidney Hillman, pp. 1159–62. **10.** N.Y. *Times,* Jan. 3, 1920. **11.** Mr. Justice Felix Frankfurter to M. J. **12.** Michaels, Stern *vs.* Sidney Hillman *et al.* (*Record on Appeal,* Vol. III, pp. 1097–1529); N.Y. State Supreme Court, Appellate Division. **13.** Minutes of the General Executive Board, ACWA, July 8, 1920. **14.** *ACWA Doc. Hist.,* 1922, pp. 7–10. **15.** *The Advance,* Oct. 22, 1920. **16.** *ACWA Doc. Hist.,* 1922, pp. 15 ff. **17.** N.Y. *Times,* Jan. 24, 1921. **18.** N.Y. *Times,* Dec. 8, 1920; H. Blankenhorn and C. W. Ervin to M. J. **19.** W. M. Leiserson to M. J. **20.** *ACWA Doc. Hist.,* 1922, pp. 44–45; N.Y. *Post,* Mar. 30, 1921. **21.** Max Lowenthal to M. J. **22.** *The Freeman,* Apr. 13, 1921. **23.** *ACWA Doc. Hist.,* 1924, pp. 40–42. **24.** *ACWA Doc. Hist.,* 1922, p. 62. **25.** Ibid., pp. 143–45. **26.** *The Advance,* Jan. 8, 1921. **27.** Hillman speech of Dec. 29, 1920; ACWA Files, 1920. **28.** Mrs. Bessie Hillman to M. J. **29.** N.Y. *Times,* Apr. 29, 1921, May. 2, 1921. **30.** George Soule, *Sidney Hillman* (N.Y.: The Macmillan Co., 1938), pp. 116–17.

CHAPTER TEN: Pages 242 to 267.

1. *ACWA Doc. Hist.,* 1924, p. 181. **2.** Leo Wolman, "Economic Conditions and Union Policy," *Labor Dynamics,* pp. 37 ff. **3.** Speech before the United Cloth Hat and Cap Workers, 1927, ACWA Files, 1927. **4.** Clarence Darrow, speech at ACWA convention, 1922, *ACWA Doc. Hist.,* 1922, pp. 306–8. **5.** J. M. Budish and George Soule, *The New Unionism* (N.Y.: Harcourt, Brace and Howe, 1920), p. 172. **6.** George Soule, *Sidney Hillman,* p. 144. **7.** Leo Wolman, "Labor Banking," *The New Republic,* Aug. 21, 1929. **8.** Harry A.

Millis and Royal E. Montgomery, *Organized Labor* (N.Y.: McGraw-Hill, 1945), pp. 451–52. **9.** Earl Strong, op. cit., p. 250. **10.** Speech before the United Cloth Hat and Cap Workers' Convention, 1927 (copy in Hillman Papers). **11.** Soule, op. cit., pp. 136–37. **12.** Ibid., pp. 135–36. **13.** *ACWA Doc. Hist.*, 1930, p. 163. **14.** *ACWA Doc. Hist.*, 1924, pp. 84–89; 1922, pp. 138–42. **15.** N.Y. *Times,* Oct. 8, 1923. **16.** *The Advance,* July 22, 1921. **17.** Ibid., Nov. 13, 1921. **18.** Mrs. Bea Bisno Oppenheimer to M. J. **19.** Speech of Nov. 13, 1921; *The Advance,* Nov. 25, 1921; N.Y. *Daily News-Record,* Nov. 18, 1921. **20.** Ibid. **21.** Ibid. **22.** Benjamin Stolberg in *The Survey,* May 22, 1922.

CHAPTER ELEVEN: Pages 268 to 281.

1. *ACWA Doc. Hist.*, 1924, p. 308. **2.** J. S. Potofsky, *Notes on Hillman.* **3.** *ACWA Doc. Hist.*, 1924, pp. 308–10. **4.** Ibid. **5.** Earl Strong, op. cit., p. 81. **6.** Hillman, speech of Dec. 9, 1924. **7.** Hardman (ed.), *Labor Dynamics,* p. 295. **8.** David Drechsler to M. J. **9.** *ACWA Doc. Hist.*, 1926, pp. 37–45. **10.** *ACWA Doc. Hist.*, 1926, p. 43. **11.** C. Zaretz, *The Amalgamated Clothing Workers of America* (N.Y.: Ancon, 1934), pp. 250–51, citing *Die Freiheit,* July 8, 1924; Nov. 10, 1923. **12.** *ACWA Doc. Hist.*, 1924, pp. 16–19. **13.** Ibid., p. 188. **14.** *The Advance,* Feb. 20, 1925. **15.** Statement of Hillman to the General Executive Board, ACWA, July 1924 and Dec. 1924, cited in *ACWA Doc. Hist.*, 1926, pp. 47–48, 66–67. **16.** Zaretz, op. cit., p. 254. **17.** N.Y. *Times,* Apr. 26, 1925. **18.** *The Advance,* Apr. 3, 1925. **19.** Sam Levin to M. J. **20.** *The Advance,* Oct. 28, 1927. **21.** *ACWA Doc. Hist.*, 1928, p. 54. **22.** Dr. W. M. Leiserson to M. J., also interview with Alex Cohen. **23.** A. Chatman to M. J.

CHAPTER TWELVE: Pages 282 to 310.

1. F. Rosenblum (speech), *The Advance,* Mar. 14, 1930. **2.** N.Y. *Times,* Mar. 19, 1926; *ACWA Doc. Hist.*, 1926, pp. 102–3. **3.** Hillman speech, May 12, 1924; *ACWA Doc. Hist.*, 1924, p. 181. **4.** Hardman, op. cit., p. 133. **5.** Ibid., p. 135. **6.** Ibid., p. 138. **7.** Arthur Nash, *The Golden Rule in Business* (N.Y.: F. H. Revell Co., 1923), pp. 52–53. **8.** Ann W. Craton to M. J. **9.** Ann W. Craton in *The Advance,* Dec. 23, 1921. **10.** *ACWA Doc. Hist.*, 1926, p. 211 (speech of Nash, Apr. 8, 1925). **11.** Jack Kroll to S. Hillman, June 11, 1925. **12.** E. D. Howard to M. J. **13.** A. Nash to L. Wolman (telegram), Nov. 23, 1925. **14.** *ACWA Doc. Hist.*, 1926, p. 211 (speech of Nash). **15.** Ibid., p. 207. **16.** Jack Kroll to M. J. **17.** Ibid. **18.** *The Advance,* Dec. 11, 1925. **19.** *ACWA Doc. Hist.*, 1926, pp. 211 ff. **20.** Henry Bruère in *The Survey,* Dec. 23, 1925. **21.** *ACWA Doc. Hist.*, 1926, pp. 225–26. **22.** Ibid., 1928, pp. 250–51. **23.** *The Advance,* July 5, 1928. **24.** *ACWA Doc. Hist.*, 1930, p. 21. **25.** J. S. Potofsky in *The Advance,* Aug. 30, 1929. **26.** *ACWA Doc. Hist.*, 1930, pp. 177–85. **27.** *The Advance,* Aug. 9, 1929. **28.** Ibid., Aug. 16, 1929. **29.** Ibid., Aug. 30, 1929. **30.** N.Y. *Daily News-Record,* Sept. 13, 1929. **31.** *ACWA Doc. Hist.*, 1930, p. 3. **32.** *The Advance,* Aug. 16, 1929.

CHAPTER THIRTEEN: Pages 311 to 326.

1. St. Louis *Post-Dispatch,* Dec. 9, 1928. 2. Bea Bisno Oppenheimer in *The Advance,* Sept. 5, 1924. 3. Agnes Hamilton, "The New Force in American Labor: Sidney Hillman," *The Contemporary Review,* London, Feb. 1927. 4. A. E. Kazan, "Houses and Gardens, Too," *Labor and Nation,* Sept. 1949. 5. N.Y. *Times,* Jan. 14, 1929 (speech by Hillman). 6. Clinton W. Gilbert in N.Y. *Evening Post,* Dec. 23, 1924. 7. Harold Callender in N.Y. *Times,* June 21, 1925. 8. National City Bank Bulletin, July 1925; Hartford *Times,* Feb. 20, 1929; *Catholic Charities Review,* Jan. 1928; *Argus,* Melbourne, July 13, 1929. 9. *The New Leader,* London, Feb. 17, 1928. 10. Tecia Davidson to M. J. 11. Agnes Hamilton, op. cit. 12. Ibid. 13. Hardman, op. cit., p. 161. 14. J. S. Potofsky to Hillman, Mar. 1, 1922. 15. Hardman, op. cit., p. 160.

CHAPTER FOURTEEN: Pages 327 to 339.

1. *ACWA Doc. Hist.,* 1930, pp. 110–13. 2. Sidney Rissman to M. J. 3. David Drechsler to M. J. 4. Sidney Hillman to M. J. (interview of Sept. 1932). 5. Malcolm Johnson, *Crime on the Labor Front* (N.Y.: McGraw-Hill, 1950), pp. 240–41. 6. J. S. Potofsky to M. J. 7. *The Advance,* June 26, 1931. 8. N.Y. *Daily News-Record,* June 22, 1931. 9. David Drechsler to M. J. 10. N.Y. *Times,* June 26, 1931. 11. N.Y. *Times,* July 1, 1931. 12. J. S. Potofsky to M. J. 13. *The Advance,* Sept. 4, 1931.

CHAPTER FIFTEEN: Pages 340 to 358.

1. Mr. Justice Felix Frankfurter to M. J. 2. *ACWA Doc. Hist.,* 1928, p. 133. 3. *ACWA Doc. Hist.,* 1930, pp. 110–13. 4. C. W. Ervin to M. J. 5. Sidney Hillman to M. J. (interview of Sept. 1932). 6. N.Y. *Times,* Aug. 9, 1932. 7. J. S. Potofsky, *Notes on Hillman.* 8. N.Y. *Times,* Dec. 5, 1930. 9. C. W. Ervin in *The Advance,* Dec. 12, 1930. 10. U.S. Senate Sub-Committee on Manufactures, Jan. 8, 1932, 72nd Congress, S. 172 and S. 174. 11. *ACWA Doc. Hist.,* 1934, p. 132. 12. Ibid. 13. George Soule, *Sidney Hillman,* pp. 158–59. 14. U.S. Senate Sub-Committee on Manufactures, Jan. 8, 1932, 72nd Congress, S. 172 and S. 174. 15. C. W. Ervin in *The National Guardian,* Nov. 13, 1931. 16. Mr. Justice Hugo Black to M. J. 17. Hallgren, Mauritz, *Seeds of Revolt* (N.Y.: Knopf, 1933), pp. 44–45. 18. U.S. Senate Sub-Committee on Manufactures, Jan. 8, 1932, 72nd Congress, S. 172 and S. 174. 19. J. S. Potofsky to M. J. 20. Memorandum (for Frances Perkins), dated Dec. 1932, Hillman Papers.

CHAPTER SIXTEEN: Pages 359 to 380.

1. Matthew Josephson, "Jurist: A Profile of Felix Frankfurter," *The New Yorker,* Nov. 30, 1941. 2. Mrs. Bessie Hillman to M. J. 3. Frances Perkins,

The Roosevelt I Knew (N.Y.: Viking, 1946), pp. 197 ff. **4.** *Newsweek,* Apr. 29, 1933. **5.** N.Y. *Daily News-Record,* May 6, 1933. **6.** Ibid., May 22, 1933. **7.** *The Advance,* June 1933. **8.** N.Y. *Times,* May 23, 1933. **9.** Charles A. Madison, *American Labor Leaders* (N.Y.: Harper & Bros., 1950), p. 182. **10.** *ACWA Doc. Hist.,* 1934, pp. 378–80. **11.** N.Y. *World-Telegram,* Aug. 19, 1934. **12.** *ACWA Doc. Hist.,* 1934, p. 148. **13.** *The New Yorker,* Aug. 25, 1934. **14.** R. Dutcher in the N.Y. *World-Telegram,* Aug. 30, 1933. **15.** N.Y. *Times,* Aug. 19, 1933; N.Y. *World-Telegram,* Aug. 30, 1933. **16.** The American Academy of Political and Social Science, *Annals,* Mar. 1934; Lewis, pp. 58–63; Hillman, pp. 70–75. **17.** *The New Republic,* Aug. 16, 1934. **18.** N.Y. *Times,* Sept. 14, 1934. **19.** Leon Henderson to M. J. **20.** Pearson and Allen in the Washington *Post,* Oct. 22, 1934. **21.** N.Y. *Times,* Sept. 22, 1934; R. Dutcher in the *World-Telegram,* Nov. 9, 1934. **22.** N.Y. *Times,* Dec. 8, 1934. **23.** Tecia Davidson to M. J. **24.** Letter of T. Davidson, May 20, 1934. **25.** Drew Pearson in the Washington *Post,* Dec. 12, 1934. **26.** U.S. Senate Committee on Finance, 74th Congress, 1st Session, Hearings on S.R. Investigation of NRA, Vol. I, pp. 319–55. **27.** Paul Ward in the Baltimore *Sun,* Mar. 22, 1935. **28.** J. S. Potofsky, *Notes on Hillman,* Mar. 22, 1935. **29.** Leon Henderson to M. J.

CHAPTER SEVENTEEN: Pages 381 to 415.

1. Speech before New York Joint Board, ACWA, June 13, 1935. **2.** *ACWA Doc. Hist.,* 1936, p. 36, citing telegram dated May 28, 1935. **3.** E Levinson, *Labor on the March* (N.Y.: Harper's, 1938), p. 52. **4.** *ACWA Doc. Hist.,* 1934, p. 161. **5.** Speech before the United Textile Workers' convention, Sept. 15, 1936 (Hillman Papers). **6.** AFL Convention Proceedings, 1935, pp. 574–75. **7.** Ibid., pp. 534–42. **8.** James Wechsler, *Labor Baron* (N.Y.: William Morrow & Co., 1944), p. 54. **9.** Millis and Montgomery, op. cit., Vol. IV, pp. 209–11. **10.** J. S. Potofsky, op. cit., Mar. 3, 1936. **11.** Ibid. **12.** J. L. Lewis to Hillman, Dec. 7, 1937 (Hillman Papers). **13.** A. Bellanca to M. J. **14.** N.Y. *Times,* Nov. 24, 1935. **15.** *ACWA Doc. Hist.,* 1936, p. 139 (speech of May 25, 1936). **16.** Ibid. **16a.** N.Y. *Times,* Feb. 1, 1936. **17.** Statement of George Berry, *ACWA Doc. Hist.,* 1936, p. 283. **18.** Minutes of the ACWA General Executive Board, Apr. 20, 1936. **19.** Ibid. **20.** Hillman to F.D.R. (telegram), May 29, 1936; F.D.R. to Hillman (letter), June 8, 1936, F.D.R. Papers, Hillman Papers. **21.** N.Y. *Times,* Aug. 3, 1936. **22.** Statement of E. P. Oliver, cited by Philip Taft in *American Journal of Political Economy,* Vol. 47, 1937, pp. 634 ff. **23.** N.Y. *Times,* Sept. 24, 1936. **24.** George Berry to F.D.R., Nov. 11, 1936, F.D.R. Papers, CIO File. **25.** R. Dutcher in N.Y. *World-Telegram,* Apr. 2, 1935. **26.** Raymond Gram Swing in *The Nation,* Mar. 24, 1935. **27.** Hillman to Philoine Hillman, Nov. 9, 1936. **28.** J. S. Potofsky, op. cit., Dec. 22, 1936. **29.** Letter to Philoine Hillman, dated Dec. **30.** N.Y. *Times,* Dec. 22, 1936. **31.** J. S. Potofsky, op. cit., Feb. 8, 1937. **32.** Perkins, op. cit., p. 321. **33.** Hillman to Philoine Hillman, Oct. 25, 1936. **34.** R. McKenney, *Industrial Valley* (N.Y.: Harcourt, Brace, 1937), pp. 249–50. **35.** N.Y. *Times,*

Jan. 31, 1937. **36.** Perkins, op. cit., p. 325. **37.** Letter of Tecia Davidson, Jan. 25, 1937. **38.** Perkins, op. cit., p. 324. **39.** *ACWA Doc. Hist.*, 1938, p. 241. **40.** R. Dutcher in N.Y. *World-Telegram,* Feb. 5, 1937. **41.** Saul Alinsky, *John L. Lewis* (N.Y.: G. P. Putnam's Sons, 1949), pp. 133–34. **42.** Lee Pressman to M. J. **43.** J. S. Potofsky, op. cit., Mar. 3, 1937. **44.** Levinson, op. cit., p. 236. **45.** *Newsweek,* Apr. 3, 1937. **46.** Interview, St. Louis *Post-Dispatch,* May 5, 1935. **47.** Frank Kent in Baltimore *Sun,* Aug. 15, 1937.

CHAPTER EIGHTEEN: Pages 416 to 430.

1. Soule, op. cit., p. 90. **2.** *ACWA Doc. Hist.*, 1938, p. 56. **3.** *ACWA Doc. Hist.*, 1938, pp. 58–60. **4.** Ibid., pp., 60–63. **5.** Washington *Daily News,* June 18, 1937. **6.** Providence *Journal,* Mar. 19, 1937 (interview.) **7.** Reuben Block to M. J. **8.** Joseph Salerno to M. J. **9.** George M. Harrison to M. J. **10.** AFL Convention Proceedings, 1937, pp. 383, 416–17. **11.** Drew Pearson, in the Washington *Post,* Oct. 14, 1937. **12.** AFL Convention Proceedings, 1937, p. 417. **13.** N.Y. *Times,* Oct. 13, 1937. **14.** George M. Harrison to M. J.; J. S. Potofsky to M. J. **15.** Matthew Woll, speech before United Cloth Hat Workers, June 15, 1939; *The Position of the International Ladies' Garment Workers' Union in Relation to the CIO and AFL, 1934–38* (pamphlet), pp. 38–63. **16.** *ACWA Doc. Hist.*, 1938, p. 347.

CHAPTER NINETEEN: Pages 431 to 460.

1. F.D.R. Papers, Hillman File, No. 3585, Nov. 15, 1937. **2.** F.D.R. Papers, Hillman File, No. 3585. **3.** Undated letter from Miami, Fla., 1938, Hillman Papers. **4.** Hillman to Philoine Hillman, Jan. 30, 1937. **5.** Hillman Papers, letters from Miami, 1938. **6.** Joseph Gollomb, "The Mystery of Sidney Hillman," *Jewish Digest,* Feb. 1941. **7.** Hillman Papers, letters from Miami, 1938. **8.** *ACWA Doc. Hist.*, 1938, p. 425. **9.** Ibid., pp. 163, 291–92. **10.** Hearings before Committee on Education and Labor, U.S. Senate, and Committee on Labor, House of Representatives, 75th Congress, 1st Session, S. 2475 and H.R. 7200, pp. 943 ff. **11.** Ibid. **12.** N.Y. *Times,* Aug. 22, 1937. **13.** *ACWA Doc. Hist.*, 1938, pp. 240–41. **14.** J. S. Potofsky, op. cit., June 13, 1938. **15.** Ibid., June 13, 1938. **16.** F.D.R. Papers, June 13, 1938, memo of T. Corcoran to F.D.R., No. 3585. **17.** *CIO Daily News,* Sept. 15, 1939. **18.** Washington *Post,* July 28, 1939. **19.** Statements of John L. Lewis and Lee Pressman to M. J. **20.** *ACWA Doc. Hist.*, 1938, p. 164. **21.** N.Y. *Times,* June 13, 1938; Charles Ervin to M. J. **22.** *ACWA Doc. Hist.*, 1938, p. 19. **23.** E. P. Oliver to M. J. **24.** Abraham Miller to M. J. **25.** J. S. Potofsky, op. cit. **26.** N.Y. *Times,* July 3, 1938. **27.** Ibid., June 29, 1938. **28.** N.Y. *Times,* Sept. 29, 1938. **29.** Philip Murray to M. J. **30.** *ACWA Doc. Hist.*, 1940, p. 219; N.Y. *Times,* Jan. 27, 1939. **31.** N.Y. *Times,* Jan. 26, 27, 1939. **32.** *Business Week,* Dec. 24, 1938. **33.** CIO Convention Proceedings, 1938 (Nov. 15, 1938).

CHAPTER TWENTY: Pages 461 to 502.

1. McGeorge Bundy and Henry L. Stimson: *On Active Service in Peace and War* (N.Y.: Harper and Bros., 1947), p. 314. **2.** *ACWA Doc. Hist.*, 1938, pp. 448–49. **3.** Ibid., 1940, p. 203. **4.** N.Y. *Times*, Mar. 15, 1937. **5.** Wechsler, op. cit., p. 110; Saul Alinsky, *John L. Lewis* (N.Y.: G. P. Putnam's Sons, 1949), p. 200. **6.** N.Y. *Times,* May 5, 1939. **7.** W.H. Davis to M.J. **8.** Alinsky, op. cit., p. 171. **9.** Ibid., pp. 194–95; C. Sulzberger, *Sit Down with Lewis* (N.Y.: Random House, 1938), p. 134. **10.** Alinsky, op. cit., p. 201. **11.** Wechsler, op. cit., pp. 111–12. **12.** Alinsky, op. cit., p. 202. **13.** Washington *Post,* Mar. 16, 1939. **14.** H. Blankenhorn to M. J. **15.** F.D.R. Papers, CIO File, No. 2546, Oct. 30, 1939. **16.** Wechsler, op. cit., p. 103. **17.** Washington *Post,* Oct. 25, 1939. **18.** Wechsler, op. cit., p. 103. **19.** Letter of Tecia Davidson, Oct. 25, 1939. **20.** F.D.R. Papers, No. 2546, memo of General Watson to F.D.R., Oct. 31, 1939. **21.** San Francisco *Chronicle,* Oct. 11, 1939. **22.** N.Y. *Times,* Jan. 7, 1940. **23.** Perkins, op. cit., pp. 126–27. **24.** UMW Convention Proceedings, 1940, p. 103. **25.** C. W. Ervin to M. J.; L. Stark to M. J. **26.** Jan. 25, 1940, UMW Proceedings, p. 293. **27.** N.Y. *Times,* Jan. 26, 1940; Jan. 28, 1940; Jan. 30, 1940. **28.** Minutes of the ACWA General Executive Board, May 7, 1940. **29.** *ACWA Doc. Hist.,* 1940, p. 194. **30.** D. Pearson in Washington *Post,* May 9, 1940. **31.** E. J. Flynn: *You're the Boss* (N.Y.: Viking, 1947), pp. 154–55. **32.** R. Sherwood, *Roosevelt and Hopkins* (N.Y.: Harper & Bros., 1948), p. 172. **33.** Maxwell Brandwen to M. J. **34.** Sherwood, op. cit., p. 192. **35.** Washington *Post,* July 7, 1940. **36.** Detroit *Free Press,* Aug. 1, 1940. **37.** N.Y. *Times,* Sept. 22, 1940. **38.** N.Y. *Times,* Oct. 20, 1940. **39.** M. Brandwen to M. J. **40.** N.Y. *Times,* Oct. 27, 1940. **41.** Interview with Jack Kroll, Cincinnati *Inquirer,* Oct. 20, 1940. **42.** Sherwood, op. cit., p. 192. **43.** ACWA, Minutes of the General Executive Board, Nov. 14, 1940. **44.** CIO Convention Proceedings, 1940, pp. 49 ff. **45.** N.Y. *Times,* Nov. 20, 1940. **46.** J. Wechsler, op. cit., pp. 126–27. **47.** CIO Convention Proceedings, 1940, pp. 123–24. **48.** Ibid., pp. 158–63. **49.** N.Y. *Times,* Oct. 20, 1946. **50.** Mrs. Bessie Hillman to M. J. **51.** Drew Pearson in Washington *Post,* Nov. 30, 1940. **52.** C.I.O. Convention Proceedings, 1940, p. 192. **53.** L. Stark in N.Y. *Times,* Nov. 22, 1940. **54.** J. S. Potofsky to M. J.

CHAPTER TWENTY-ONE: Pages 503 to 528.

1. Sherwood, op. cit., p. 127. **2.** F.D.R. Papers, Aug. 22, 1940, File 813, Box 1. **3.** Minutes of New York Joint Board, May 5, 1941. **4.** Perkins, op. cit., p. 360. **5.** N.Y. *Times,* May 29, 1940. **6.** Minutes of New York Joint Board, May 7, 1941. **7.** Richard J. Purcell, *Labor Policies of the NDAC & OPM* (Washington: Historical Reports on the War Administration, War Production Board, Special Study No. 23, 1951), p. 11. **8.** F.D.R. Papers, memorandum to Hillman, June 18, 1940. **9.** A. Krock in N.Y. *Times,* Dec. 1, 1940. **10.** Herbert J. Emmerich, "The War Contributions of Sidney Hillman" (manuscript, May

1949). **11.** Minutes of the OPM, May 6, 1941, p. 20, citing F.D.R.'s letter of Apr. 30, 1941. **12.** F.D.R. Papers, memorandum of June 3, 1940. **13.** Ibid., Aug. 13, 1940. **14.** Hillman, memorandum to F.D.R., June 26, 1940, Hillman Papers. **15.** Lewis to Hillman, July 29, 1940. **16.** Hillman to Lewis, July 31, 1940. **17.** L. Stark in N.Y. *Times,* July 12, 1940. **18.** Purcell, op. cit., p. 5. **19.** NDAC release, Oct. 25, 1940. **20.** Hillman to Secretary Frank Knox, July 19, 1941, Hillman Papers. **21.** NDAC Minutes, July 10, 1940, p. 26. **22.** Emmerich, op. cit. **23.** Ibid. **24.** Leon Henderson to M. J.; Emmerich to M. J. **25.** Emmerich, op. cit. **26.** Hillman to Lewis, July 23, 1940, Hillman Papers. **27.** Philip Murray to Hillman, Aug. 7, 1940, Hillman Papers. **28.** NDAC Minutes, July 2, Aug. 7, Aug. 23, 1940; J. D. Biggers, memorandum to Hillman, Aug. 23, 1940. **29.** Purcell, op. cit., p. 19. **30.** NDAC Minutes, Sept. 6, 1940, pp. 82–83. **31.** F.D.R. Papers, NDAC File, 813A; memo of W. McReynolds, Sept. 9, 1940. **32.** Hillman to Lewis, Sept. 13, 1940; Lewis to Hillman, Sept. 16, 1940. **33.** N.Y. *Times,* Oct. 2, 1940. **34.** Lewis to Hillman, Oct. 7, 1940; Hillman to Lewis, Oct. 11, 1940. **35.** M. Brandwen to M. J. **36.** N.Y. *Times,* Oct. 9, 1940. **37.** N.Y. *Times,* Oct. 19, 1940. **38.** CIO Convention Proceedings, 1940, pp. 186–87. **39.** NDAC Minutes, Sept. 11, 1940, p. 85. **40.** Robert P. Patterson to M. J. **41.** NDAC Minutes, Dec. 19, 1940. **42.** Hillman to Dr. J. R. Walsh, Nov. 13, 1940. **43.** Purcell, op. cit., p. 52. **44.** Washington *Post,* Dec. 17, 1940. **45.** *PM,* Jan. 30, 1941. **46.** Dr. Isador Lubin to M. J.; Robert P. Patterson to M. J. **47.** I. F. Stone in *PM,* Jan. 31, 1941. **48.** N.Y. *Times,* Feb. 26, 1941. **49.** F.D.R. Papers, File 4245, OPM, Feb. 20, 1941. **50.** Dr. Isador Lubin to M. J. **51.** Minutes of New York Joint Board, ACWA, May 5, 1941.

CHAPTER TWENTY-TWO: Pages 529 to 565.

1. McGeorge Bundy and Henry L. Stimson, op. cit., p. 360. **2.** F.D.R. Papers, memo of Leon Henderson to Roosevelt, Oct. 22, 1940, No. 813A, Box 2. **3.** Dr. Isador Lubin to M. J. **4.** Perkins, op. cit., p. 355. **5.** Harold Laski, *Trade Unionism in the United States* (N.Y.: Viking Press, 1949), p. 45. **6.** N.Y. *Times,* Dec. 21, 1940. **7.** *Wall Street Journal,* Dec. 31, 1940. **8.** F.D.R. Papers, Grace Tully to General Watson, Jan. 3, 1941, File 4245, Box 1, OPM File. **9.** F.D.R. Papers, transcript of press conference, Jan. 7, 1941. **10.** J. L. O'Brian to M. J. **11.** H. J. Emmerich, op. cit. **12.** H. J. Emmerich to M. J. **13.** J. L. O'Brian to M. J. **14.** Perkins, op. cit., p. 359. **15.** Washington *Post,* Feb. 16, 1941. **16.** Washington *Post,* Apr. 6, 1941; Purcell, op. cit., pp. 48 ff. **17.** Washington *Post,* Feb. 20, 1941; Purcell, op. cit., pp. 48 ff; U.S. House of Representatives, Judiciary Committee, 77th Congress, 1st Session. Delays in National Defense Preparations, Hearings, pp. 73–133. **18.** F.D.R. Papers, OPM File, Mar. 14, 1941. **19.** W. H. Davis to M. J. **20.** Ibid. **21.** *The Nation,* Apr. 5, 1941. **22.** Washington *Post,* Apr. 9, 1941. **23.** George Kirstein (former secretary of NDMB) to M. J. **24.** John Ohly, memorandum for the War Department on the NAA strike. **25.** Ibid. **26.** CIO Convention Proceedings, 1940, p. 274. **27.** J. Wechsler, op. cit., pp. 138–39.

28. N.Y. *Times,* July 8, 1941. 29. Hillman, memorandum to Roosevelt, F.D.R. Papers, OPM File, July 23, 1941. 30. N.Y. *Times,* Oct. 1, 1941. 31. Seattle *Times,* Oct. 2, 1941. 32. San Francisco *Chronicle,* Oct. 9, 1941. 33. N.Y. *Times,* Oct. 23, Oct. 24, 1941. 34. J. L. O'Brian to M. J. 35. Hillman memorandum, Oct. 10, 1941, Hillman Papers. 36. Donald Nelson, *Arsenal of Democracy,* p. 309. 37. House of Representatives, Committee on Ways and Means, 77th Congress, 2nd Session, Feb. 11, 1942, Hearings, pp. 4–9, 19–56. 38. F.D.R. Papers, OPM File, May 28, 1941. 39. Ibid., Roosevelt to Hillman, July 9, 1941. 40. Bundy, op. cit., p. 380. 41. F.D.R. Papers, Roosevelt to Hillman, May 7, 1941, Hillman File. 42. Ibid., La Guardia to F.D.R., July 7, 1941; OPM Minutes, p. 38, July 1, 1941. 43. OPM press release, Jan. 9, 1942. 44. L. Henderson to M. J. 45. Dr. Isador Lubin to M. J. 46. F.D.R. Papers, OPM File, memo to Hillman, Nov. 25, 1941. 47. Ibid., May 26, 1941; F.D.R. to Knudsen and Hillman. 48. J. L. O'Brian to M. J. 49. Bundy and Stimson, op. cit., p. 381, citing Stimson's diary. 50. Alinsky, op. cit., pp. 231 ff.; Wechsler, op. cit., p. 152. 51. Alinsky, op. cit., p. 237. 52. George Kirstein to M. J. 53. Washington *Post,* Nov. 20, 1941. 54. Wechsler, op. cit., p. 168.

CHAPTER TWENTY-THREE: Pages 566 to 586.

1. OPM press release, Jan. 4, 1942. 2. Transcript of proceedings of Joint Meeting of Labor and Industry Subcommittee on Automotive Problems, January 6, 1942, Hillman Papers. 3. Hillman Papers, copy of memorandum to Roosevelt, Dec. 12, 1941. 4. Ibid. 5. Perkins, op. cit., p. 308. 6. A. H. Raskin in N.Y. *Times,* Jan. 19, 1942. 7. Sherwood, op. cit., pp. 474–75. 8. Purcell, op. cit., p. 30. 9. Hillman Papers, 1941. 10. Ibid. (copy). 11. F.D.R. Papers, File 4245, Box 1, Jan. 27, 1942. 12. Ibid., Feb. 11, 1942. 13. H. J. Emmerich, op. cit. 14. Hillman Papers, draft of a proposed executive order and accompanying memorandum. 15. N.Y. *Daily News,* Mar. 26, 1942. 16. Minutes, WPB, Mar. 3, 1942, p. 21. 17. Ibid., Mar. 10, 1942, p. 27. 18. N.Y. *Times,* Mar. 3, 1942; Congressional Record, Vol. 88, Pt. 2, pp. 1867–70. 19. WPB, release of Mar. 8, 1942, with statements of Donald Nelson and Sidney Hillman, answering Rep. Engels. 20. Josef Israels II, "Mrs. Fix-It," *Saturday Evening Post,* Oct. 16, 1943. 21. Memorandum, dated Feb. 28, cited in Purcell, op. cit., p. 32. 22. Hillman Papers (copy), Mar. 22, 1942. 23. D. Pearson in Washington *Post,* Apr. 26, 1942. 24. F.D.R. Papers, OF 4910, Hillman File. 25. J. L. O'Brian to M. J. 26. Purcell, op. cit., p. 33. 27. Hillman Papers.

CHAPTER TWENTY-FOUR: Pages 587 to 612.

1. *ACWA Doc. Hist.,* 1944, pp. 92–137. 2. Philip Murray to M. J. 3. Perkins, op. cit., pp. 364–65. 4. Mrs. Eleanor Roosevelt to M. J., Sept. 9, 1951. 5. F.D.R. Papers, No. 8172, Sept. 16, 1942, Hillman File. 6. Ibid., Oct. 9, 1942, Hillman File. 7. N.Y. *Times,* July 10, 1942; PM, Aug. 6, 1942. 8. Louis Stark in N.Y. *Times,* July 12, 1942. 9. Philip Murray to M. J., May

18, 1950.   **10.** N.Y. *Times,* July 12, 1943.   **11.** Mrs. Philoine Hillman Fried to M. J.   **12.** Interview in Detroit *Free Press,* Sept. 14, 1943.   **13.** CIO Convention Proceedings, 1943, p. 249.   **14.** N.Y. *Times,* Aug. 18, 1943.   **15.** *New Leader,* Sept. 4, 1943.   **16.** N.Y. *Times,* Jan. 27, 1944.   **17.** Ibid., Jan. 21, 1944.   **18.** Ibid., Feb. 9, 1944.   **19.** F.D.R. Papers, D. Niles to F.D.R., Feb. 7, 1944, File 8172; General Watson to F.D.R., Mar. 22, 1944, File 4910.   **20.** H. Fuller in *The New Republic,* Jan. 24, 1944.   **21.** N.Y. *Times,* Feb. 14, 1944. **22.** After extracts from Report of the House Un-American Activities Committee on the PAC, in N.Y. *Journal-American,* Mar. 29, 1944.   **23.** N.Y. *Times,* May 19, 1944.   **24.** N.Y. *Times,* July 31, 1944.

CHAPTER TWENTY-FIVE: Pages 613 to 635.

1. E. J. Flynn, op. cit., pp. 178–79.   **2.** George Allen's account, Washington *Times-Herald,* Jan. 22, 1945.   **3.** F.D.R. Papers, No. 4910, memo of David Niles, May 31, 1944.   **4.** J. Daniels, *The Man from Independence* (N.Y.: Harper & Bros., 1950), p. 231.   **5.** M. Brandwen to M. J.   **6.** Daniels, op. cit., p. 240.   **7.** George Allen, op. cit.   **8.** Philadelphia *Inquirer,* July 14, 1944. **9.** N.Y. *Times,* July 25, 1944.   **10.** Chicago *Daily News,* July 17, 1944. **11.** A. Krock in N.Y. *Times,* July 17, 1944.   **12.** Chicago *Tribune,* July 20, 1947.   **13.** N.Y. *Journal-American,* July 20, 1944.   **14.** N.Y. *Daily News,* Jan. 20, 1944.   **15.** Daniels, op. cit., p. 245.   **16.** George Allen in Washington *Times-Herald,* Jan. 22, 1945.   **17.** N.Y. *Daily Mirror,* July 20, 1944. **18.** Daniels, op. cit., pp. 248–49.   **19.** A. Krock in New York *Times,* July 25, 1944.   **20.** Mrs. Philoine Hillman Fried to M. J.   **21.** Joseph Gaer, *The First Round* (N.Y.: Duell Sloan & Pearce, 1944), pp. 212 ff.   **22.** Hearings, House Campaign Expenditures Committee, 78th Congress; 2nd Session, Pt. 1, pp. 91–94. **23.** N.Y. *Post,* July 26, 1944.   **24.** N.Y. *Times,* Oct. 23, 1944.   **25.** Sherwood, op. cit., p. 820.   **26.** *Time Magazine,* July 24, 1944.   **27.** Baltimore *Sun,* July 12, 1944.   **28.** N.Y. *Times,* Aug. 30 and Aug. 31, 1944.   **29.** CIO Convention Proceedings, 1944, p. 204.   **30.** N.Y. *Herald-Tribune,* Sept. 29, 1944. **31.** N.Y. *Post,* Aug. 29, 1944.   **32.** N.Y. *World-Telegram,* Nov. 8, 1944; *Newsweek,* Nov. 18, 1944.   **33.** F.D.R. Papers, No. 4910, Nov. 8, 1944.   **34.** Ibid., memorandum to Hillman, Nov. 25, 1944; Hillman to Roosevelt, Nov. 29, 1944.

CHAPTER TWENTY-SIX: Pages 636 to 670.

1. CIO Convention Proceedings, 1944, pp. 203–9.   **2.** *ACWA Doc. Hist.,* 1944, p. 155.   **3.** Chicago *Daily News,* Nov. 2, 1944.   **4.** London *Times,* Dec. 6, 1944; *Manchester Guardian,* Dec. 6, 1944.   **5.** Report of the WFTU, London, 1945, pp. 46–49.   **6.** Ibid., pp. 67 ff.   **7.** London *Times,* Feb. 17, 1945. **8.** N.Y. *Times,* Mar. 13, 1945.   **9.** Statement of George Meany, N.Y. *World-Telegram,* Apr. 6, 1945.   **10.** N.Y. *World-Telegram,* Apr. 13, 1945.   **11.** M. Brandwen to M. J.   **12.** *ACWA Doc. Hist.,* 1946, p. ix.   **13.** N.Y. *Post,* Apr. 16, 1945.   **14.** Hillman Papers, 1945.   **15.** San Francisco *Chronicle,* Apr. 25, 1945.   **16.** Sidney Hillman, "One Voice for 60,000,000," *Collier's,* Sept. 29,

1945. **17.** Ibid. **18.** *ACWA Doc. Hist.,* 1946, p. 95. **19.** N.Y. *Herald-Tribune* (Paris Edition), Sept. 23, 1945. **20.** *Time Magazine,* Oct. 15, 1945. **21.** *ACWA Doc. Hist.,* 1946, p. 96. **22.** *The Nation,* Oct. 27, 1945. **23.** Hillman Papers, letter to H. S. Truman, Mar. 21, 1946. **24.** New York *Herald-Tribune,* Feb. 6, Feb. 13, 1946. **25.** H. S. Truman to Sidney Hillman, Mar. 26, 1946, Hillman Papers. **26.** ACWA Proceedings, 1946, pp. 97–98. **27.** *Time Magazine,* May 28, 1945. **28.** N.Y. *Herald-Tribune,* Jan. 22, 1946. **29.** Hillman Papers, Telegram of Dec. 19, 1945; H. S. Truman to Hillman, letter, Dec. 21, 1945. **30.** N.Y. *Times,* May 20, 1946. **31.** PAC News Service, July 22, 1946. **32.** *ACWA Doc. Hist.,* 1946, speech of May 6, 1946, pp. 92–101.

INDEX

Abbot, Grace, 51
Abramowitz, Bessie (*See* Mrs. Sidney Hillman)
Abt, Jacob, 122, 186
Abt, John, 597
Academy of Political Science (Columbia University), 317
Acton, Lord, quoted, 587, 632
ACW Corp., 315–17
ACWA (Amalgamated Clothing Workers of America): admitted into AFL, 369–70; attack of New York manufacturers against, in 1920, 213–41; Baltimore campaign, 143–48; Chicago campaign, 117–18, 121–33, 142–43, 184–86; Communist effort to take over, 274–81; constitution of, 107–9, 231–32; cooperative enterprises of, 244–51; during depression, 341–49; development of, 111–59; dues of, 118; executive organization of, 201; financial strength by end of World War II, 588–89; first big strike of, 111–15; formation of, 97–110; indictment of Chicago officers, 218–19; Montreal campaign, 141–42; under New Deal, 365–66, 382–83; 1916 convention, 156–59; 1920 convention, 201–12; during 1920's, 242–44; 1922 convention, 262–66; 1926 convention, 280–81; 1938 convention, 440–41; 1946 convention, 663–68; Philadelphia campaign, 301–10; racketeer effort to take over, 327–39; Rochester campaign, 140, 172–76, 182–83; unemployment insurance initiated by, 252–55; World War I, 160–78

Adamic, Louis, 464
Addams, Jane, 51, 53–54, 127, 153; Hillman influenced by, 70; quoted, 42–43
Addes, George, 407, 456, 567
Adler and Sons, 250
Administration of Control and Labor Standards for Army Clothing, World War I, 168–71
Advance, The, ACWA newspaper, 160, 178, 216, 351 *n.*; quoted, 251
AFL (American Federation of Labor), 105–6; ACWA admitted into, 369–70; attempt to have New UGWA accepted by, 101–5; campaign for closed shop, 183; CIO formed within, 383–93; CIO unions expelled from, 425–30; in 1920's, 243; under NRA, 382 *n.*; organization of steel workers, 189, 199–200; original clothing workers' union in, 45–58; program at close of World War I, 177; and wages-and-hours bill, 443, 446
Aldermanic Committee, Chicago strike (1915), 126
Aleichem, Sholem, quoted, 24
Alexander II, Czar, 24
Alfange, Dean, 590–91
Alfred, Decker and Cohn, organizing, 117, 184–86
Alinsky, Saul, *John L. Lewis,* cited, 402 *n.*, 483 *n.*
All-American Farmer Labor Co-operative Congress, 245
All-Canadian Labor Union Congress, 279
Allen, George, 616, 621–22
Allis-Chalmers Co., 538–44

Amalgamated Bank of New York, 246–50, 267, 348–49, 358
Amalgamated Clothing Workers of America. See ACWA
Amalgamated Dwellings, Inc., 316–17
Amalgamated Life Insurance Assn. of Chicago, 588
Amalgamated Textile Workers, 198
Amalgamated Trust and Savings Bank, Chicago, 246–50, 267, 348–49
America First Committee, 463
American Academy of Political Science (Philadelphia), 346, 371
American Federation of Hosiery Workers, 417
American Federation of Labor. See AFL
American Institute of Architecture, citation, 317
American Labor Party, 400–1, 454–55, 473, 486, 590, 600–6, 633
American Legion anti-strike actions, 215
American Liberal Party, 606, 633
American Men's and Boys' Clothing Manufacturers' Assn., 178–82, 183
American Men's Clothing Manufacturers' Assn., 368–70, 451–52
"American Plan" unions, 214, 243, 289–90, 382 n.
American Woolen Co., 422, 424
Anacostia Flats, Bonus Marchers at, 355–56
Anti-Red panic (1919–20), 214–15
Anti-strike legislation, 560, 563, 567–68, 660
Anti-union discrimination, prohibition of, World War I, 167
Anti-union drive, post-World War I period, 213–40
Anti-war resolution of CIO, 470
Antin, Mary, The Promised Land, 82
Arbitration plan: established at Hart, Schaffner and Marx, 59–67; government, in World War I, 173–76; for New York men's clothing trade, 183–84; in Rochester agreement, 183; in women's garment industry, 88–90
Army uniforms, manufacture of, World War I, 161–70
Arnold, Thurman, 548
Arnone, Paul, 137, 140
Attlee, Clement, 642
Automobile industry: code, 375–76; conversion to war production, 566–67; in 1920's, 243
Automobile Labor Board, 374–76

Babb, Max D., 539–43
Baker, Newton D., 163, 165–66
Baker, Ray Stannard, 81
Baldanzi, George, 494
Baldwin, Calvin B., 608, 623, 628, 661, 668
Baltimore: ACWA campaign in, 143–48; lockout of clothing workers (1920), 228, 234; strike of clothing workers (1914), 111–15
Bandler, William, 227–39
Bank Holiday, 349, 358
Bank of United States, 348
Bankhead, J. H., 620–24
Banks, co-operative, establishment of, 206–7, 245–50
Barkley, Alben, 378, 615
Barnett, George E., 113
Baruch, Bernard M., 357, 361, 504, 530, 532, 559, 571, 614
Bates, Harry, 468
Batt, W. L., 524, 526
"Battle of the Scissors," Baltimore (1916), 147–48
Beaverbrook, Lord, 571
Beckerman, Abraham, 300, 327–28, 336–39
Bédaux, Charles, 243
Bell, George H., 183
Bellanca, August, 93, 112–14, 138–39, 145, 147, 272, 587; quoted, 392
Bellanca, Mrs. August, 112, 139, 370, 589
Bellanca, Frank, 93, 112–14
Bennett, Harry, 375, 458
Bennett, John J., 590–91
Benson, Elmer A., 626, 661
Berle, A. A., 400, 602
Berry, George L., 374, 394–95, 401
Bethlehem Steel Corp., 372, 486, 518–19, 527–28, 562
Bevin, Ernest, 462 n., 482, 530, 573, 642–43
Biddle, Francis, 603 n., 623
Biggers, John D., 517, 519, 526
Bijur, Justice Nathan, 232
Bisno, Abraham, 89
Bisno, Beatrice, 312–13
Bittner, Van, 523, 527–28, 596
Black, Hugo, 354–55, 378, 404, 442
Black-Connery Bill, 354–57, 360, 441–42
Blaine, Mrs. Emmons, 626
Blankenhorn, Heber, 229
Blumberg, Hyman, 112–15, 138, 280, 285–89, 328, 419, 494, 582, 663, 669–70; organizing in Baltimore, 144–48, 272; Philadelphia campaign, 301–8

Board of Arbitration: under Hart, Schaffner and Marx Plan, 62–66; in women's garment industry, 88–89
Board of Control and Labor Standards for Army Clothing, World War I, 165–68
Bolshevism, American Socialist reaction to, 262–66
Bonus Marchers, 355–56
Borah, William E., 239, 309
Boston: lockout of clothing workers (1920), 228, 234; strike of clothing workers (1915), 118–19
Brailsford, H. N., 318
Brais, Eugene, 104
Brandeis, Louis D., 62, 75, 86–87, 89, 377
Brandwen, Maxwell, 309, 336, 489, 507–8, 517, 532–33, 535
Branshaw, Col. C. E., 546
Bransome, Edwin D., 509, 538
Brewster, Owen, 549
Bricker, John, 630
Bridges, Harry, 432
British Labor Party, 189, 271, 462
British Trade Union Congress, 638
Bromfield, Louis, 620
Brookhart, Smith W., 350
Brookwood Labor College, 198
Brophy, John, 321 n., 364, 387, 392
Brotherhood of Locomotive Engineers, 245–46
Brotherhood of Railroad Trainmen, 77 n.
Brotherhood of Tailors, 90–91
Broun, Heywood, 463
Brown, Clarence, 633
Brown, J. Douglas, 556
Brownlow, Louis, 531, 533
Buchalter, Louis "Lepke," 329, 333, 339, 603
Buckner, Emory, 222–23
Budd, Ralph, 504
Budish, Joseph, 197 n.; quoted, 204 n.
Bugniazet, G. M., 428
Bund, trade-union organization of Russian Jews, 28–35
Burleson, A. S., 161
Burns, Thomas F., 391, 417, 663
Byrnes, James F., 592, 614–21

Cahan, Abraham, 87, 89, 92, 262 n., 265
Carey, James, 562, 622–23
Catalanotti, Joseph, 383
CCC (Civilian Conservation Corps), 511
Chatman, Abraham, 279–80, 368, 369, 419, 589

Chenery, William L., 203
Cherry Mine disaster, 65
Chicago: campaign to organize for ACWA, 117–18, 121–33, 142–43, 184–86; garment-industry strike (1910–11), 47–57; garment industry at time of Hillman's arrival, 38–47; state's attorney's attack on ACWA, 217–19; unemployment insurance plan initiated in, 252–55
Chicago Federation of Labor, 50, 269
Chicago Socialist, 49
Chicago Wholesale Clothiers' Assn., 44, 45–46, 52, 121–30, 186, 282–83
Child labor, in World War I, 162–68, 447
Children's clothing locals of ACWA, 215–16
Children's Clothing Workers Joint Board, ACWA, 273
Ching, Cyrus, 542, 569
Christian Century, 295
Christoffel, Harold, 539–40
Chrysler Corp., 375, 527
Church League for Industrial Democracy, 294–95
Churches of Christ, Federal Council of, 295
Churchill, Winston, 482, 529, 571, 639
Cincinnati: organization of Nash Co., 290–300
CIO (Congress of Industrial Organization): formation of, 387–93; Lewis' withdrawal from, 570–71, 593; organizing drives of, 405–25; political activity of, 394–401, 474–90, 594–637; reverses of, in late 1930's, 466–67; separated from AFL, 425–30; split following 1940 elections averted, 490–502; turbulence of early years, 456–60
CIO Daily News, 471, 491, 494
Citrine, Sir Walter, 638–39, 543–45, 650–53, 655
"City Hall agreement" in Chicago clothing strike (1910–11), 54
Civic Federation, 215 n.
Clark, Bennett C., 629
Clark, John M., 351
Class collaboration, 66–67
Class-struggle theme in ACWA, 107–9, 135–38, 198, 231–32, 324
Clay, Gen. Lucius T., 655, 656
Clayton, E. T., 298–99
Cloakmakers' Protocol, 62, 87–90
Closed shop: AFL campaign for, 182–83; garment union efforts toward, 48–49, 56, 73–78
Clothing Code Authority, 365

Clothing factories: co-operative, 250–51; at turn of century, 41–47. *See also* Garment industry

Cluett-Peabody Co., 589

Coal mines, "captive," campaign to organize, 372, 562–65

Coatmakers' union, Local 39, of UGWA, Hillman as first business agent of, 57–59, 67

Cohen, Alex, 280

Cohen and Goldman, 134, 225

Collaboration, class, 66–67

Collective bargaining: ACWA pattern, 120–21; World War I, 167

Commercial loans made by ACWA and Amalgamated Banks, 248–50

Commissary stores during 1920–21 lockout, 235

Commissioner of Industrial Relations, creation of post of, 81

Committee for Industrial Organization. *See* CIO

Committee for United Labor Party, 602

Commons, John R., 253–54

Communism, terror of (1919–20), 214–15

Communist Party, American, 267–70, 355; in CIO, 472–73, 544–46, 561; effort to take over ACWA, 274–81; during World War II, 598

Company unions, 214, 243, 289–90, 382 *n.*

Conference for Progressive Political Action, 269–70

Congress of Industrial Organizations. *See* CIO

Connally, Tom, 655

Connery, William, 442

Consumers' co-operatives, 245

Control Administrator for Army clothing, World War I, 168–71

Control Board for Army Clothing, World War I, 165–68

Cook County Circuit Court, injunction against ACWA issued by, 143

Cooke, Morris Llewellyn, 350, 509, 554, 555

Coolidge, Calvin, 269

Co-operative enterprises undertaken by ACWA, 204–8. 244–51. 314–17

Copeland, Royal, 350

Corcoran, Thomas G., 447, 454

Corwin, Norman, 630

Costello, John, 611

Costigan, Edward, 350, 378

Cotton-garment code, 371, 372–73

Coughlin, Father, 462

Counts, George, 604

Court injunctions against unions, 221, 224, 233–34, 286–87, 308–9

Court-packing bill, 404, 412

Cox, Edward, 444–45, 482

Coyne, J. P., 550

Craft-union principles of AFL, 45, 103, 105, 383–93

Crain, Thomas C. T., 331

Craton, Ann Washington, 291–92

Creel, George, 81

Cresap, Mark, 367

Croly, Herbert, 189 *n.*

Crump, Edward H., 615

Cunnea, William, 217

Curlee, Francis, 368–69

Curlee Clothing Co., 284

Curran, Joseph, 508, 600

Currier Corp., 549–51

Cursi, Aldo, 172

Cutters' local (No. 4), ACWA, 273, 328–39

Cutters' union of UGWA, 46–57, 67

Daily Forward Assn., 315–16

Dalrymple, Sherman, 441, 484, 596

Damage suits against ACWA: by Michaels, Stern and Co., 220–24; during New York lockout (1920), 231–32

Daniel, Franz, 419, 423

Daniel Boone Woolen Mills, 288

Daniels, Jonathan, 615, 621

Daroff and Sons, 305–6

Darrow, Clarence, 52, 60, 63, 71, 107, 244, 377

Davidson, Tecia, 583, 669–70

Davis, Chester C., 504

Davis, John W., 269

Davis, William Hammatt, 465, 542–43, 567–68, 592, 662–64

Davis, William Rhodes, 467

Debs, Eugene, 93, 161

Defense, World War II: budget, 555; program, 461–70, 480–84, 503–86

Democratic National Convention (1944) 613–25

Depression, great, 341–80; post-World War I, 213–40; Senate inquiry on, 351–54; *see also* recession of 1937–38

Dewey, John, 255, 411

Dewey, Thomas, 484, 592, 603 *n.*, 627–34

Dickason, Dr. Gladys, 588, 589

Dies, Martin, 603–4. 608–11

Dietz, J. W., 510

Di Novi, Michael, 303

Discrimination in employment. 558–59

Dodge, T. Witherspoon, 419–20
Dooley, Channing R., 510
Dorfman, J., *Thorstein Veblen and His America,* quoted, 215 *n.*
Doughton bill, 556–57
Douglas, William O., 575, 579, 615–22
Drechsler, David, 272–73, 328, 331–32, 368
Dubinsky, David, 325–26, 365, 387, 400, 426–28, 455, 472, 570, 578, 600–6; quoted on AFL-CIO split, 430
Duffield, Eugene, 532
Dunbar, Dr. Flanders, 583 *n.*
Duplan Co., 421
Dvorak, Robert, 49
Dykstra, Clarence, 542

Eaton, Fredrick, 517, 532–33
Economic Council Bill, La Follette, 351–54
Economic Stabilization Board, 592
Educational Department, ACWA, during 1920–21 lockout, 235–36
Efficiency movement of 1920's, 243
Eisenhower, Dwight, 654
Elliott, Harriet, 504
Emergency labor controls proposed by Hillman, 567–68
Emmerich, Herbert J., 536; quoted, 542, 580–81
Employment exchange bureaus, 252, 314
Emspak, Julius, 569
Engel, Albert J., 578–79
England: in 1921, 257; stay of Hillman in, 35–36
Epstein, Abraham, 321 *n.*
Ervin, Charles W., 203, 303–9, 319, 320, 350–51, 444–45
Ethridge, Mark, 559

Factory inspection, 86, 127
Fair Employment Practices Committee (FEPC), 558–59
Fair Labor Standards Bill, 404, 442–49
Farley, James, 394, 438, 455
Farm bloc, and wages-and-hours bill, 443
Farmer Labor Party, 269, 396
Fashion Park Co., 173
Federal Council of Churches, 229
Federal relief, Hillman's efforts on behalf of, 347, 350–55
Federal Surplus Commodity Corp., 450
Federal Works Administration, 549
FEPC (Fair Employment Practices Committee), 558–59

Ferguson, John W., 144–46
Ferry, Wilbur, 629
52-hour week won by men's clothing workers, 92
Fisher Body Plant No. One, 407–12
Fitch, John A., 232, 350
Fitzpatrick, John, 50–51, 54, 199–200, 269; quoted, 67
Flint, auto workers' strike (1936–37), 407–12
Flynn, Edward J., 480–81, 591, 614–22
Ford, Edsel, 566
Ford, Henry, 248, 340, 372, 374, 515–16, 526
Ford Motor Co., 267, 375, 524, 526–27; campaign to organize, 456–58
Foreman, Clark, 626
Forrestal, James, 520–21, 530, 543, 566–67
40-hour week under NRA, 367
44-hour week, campaign for, 176, 179
48-hour week, won by Rochester clothing workers, 176
49-hour week at Hart, Schaffner and Marx, 150
Foster, William Z., 199–200, 262 *n.*, 274–75
Franco, Gen. Francisco, 463–64
Frankensteen, Richard T., 407, 456, 484, 545
Frankfurter, Felix, 163, 165, 167, 180–82, 203, 221–23, 356; quoted, 194
Franklin, Joseph, 364
Frey, John P., 364, 374, 384, 426
Friedman and Co., J., 231–32
Fur workers' union, 199

Gaer, Joseph, 629; *The First Round,* quoted, 607 *n.*
Garment industry, early: in Chicago, 38–47; in New York, 20–21; strike at Hart, Schaffner and Marx, 47–57. *See also* Unionism in clothing industry
Garner, John, 446–48
Gaulle, Gen. Charles de, 653
General Electric Co., 267
General Executive Board of ACWA, 200–1
General Motors Corp., 375; strike (1936–37), 403–4, 407–12
Genis, Sander, 279
Germany: in 1921, 257; post-World War II visit to, 655–57
Gitchell, Maj. B. H., 183, 226–27
Gitlow, Ben, 275, 277
Goddard, Celestine, 294–95
"Golden Rule" Nash Co., organization of, 290–300

Goldfarb, Dr. Max, 138
Goldstein, Isaac, 91, 93, 112
Gollomb, Joseph, 438–39; quoted, 439–40
Gompers, Samuel, 45, 87, 101–5, 164
Goodimate Co., 304
Gordon, Harry A., 227–39
Gorman, Francis J., 417, 458–59
Government mediation: in World War I, 168–76; in World War II, 538–43
Grace, Eugene, 523, 527–28
Grading of workers, 197
Graham, Frank P., 542
Grandinetti, Emilio, 172
Grant, Dr. Percy Stickney, 229
Green, William F., 317–38, 360–61, 368–69, 379, 383–84, 392, 425, 506, 511, 513, 569–70, 592
Greif and Co., L., 144–47, 368, 589

Haas, Father Francis J., 318
Hague, Frank, 614–19
Hall, Ed, 456
Hamilton, Agnes, quoted, 319–20
Hamilton, Walton, 374
Hannegan, Robert, 614–23
Hapgood, Powers, 364
Harbison, Fred H., 556
Hardman, J. B. S., 93, 99, 203, 235, 314, 321 n.
Harmon Foundation award, 318
Harrison, George M., 426, 428, 542
Hart, Harry, 46
Hart, Schaffner and Marx, 250–51; adoption of preferential shop, 75–78; arbitration plan established at, 59–67; contract of 1916 with ACWA, 149–51; contract of 1919 with ACWA, 179; in depression, 348; Hillman employed at, 41–47; strike of 1910, 47–57
Hart, Schaffner and Marx Plan, 59–67
Hartley, Fred A., 662
Heil, Julius, 543
Henderson, Gerard, 222
Henderson, Leon, 371–72, 374, 376, 380, 438, 504, 517–19, 530, 559
Herrick, Mrs. Elinore, 440
Hershey, Gen. Lewis, 546
Hickey, Jeremiah, 173–74, 182–83, 368
Hickey-Freeman Co., 173
Hill, A. C. C., 576
Hill, Lister, 445
Hillman, Harry (brother), 35–36
Hillman, Joseph (brother), 35
Hillman, Judith Paiken (mother),22–26, 257–58, 641, 649–50
Hillman, Leah (sister), 641

Hillman, Mordecai (brother), 641, 649
Hillman, Mordecai (grandfather), 22–23
Hillman, Philoine (daughter), 155, 192–93, 437–38, 582, 597
Hillman, Samuel (father), 22–25, 28–29, 257–58, 641
Hillman, Samuel Isaac (cousin), 22
Hillman, Selma (daughter), 156, 437, 650, 668–70
Hillman, Sidney: as associate director-general of OPM, 526–73; Chicago years, 38–85; in CIO split, threatened by Lewis, 490–502; early life, 22–37; first years as union officer, 57–82; in formation of ACWA, 93–110; in formation of CIO, 383–93, 405–30; in formation of WFTU, 637–47, 650–57; home life of, 435–38; as ILGWU officer, 83–100; immigration to America, 18–21, 36; marriage, 152–56; as member of National Defense Advisory Commission, 481–84, 490–92, 503–26; as member of National Industrial Recovery Board, 374–80; as member of National Labor Advisory Board, 363–74, 382; political activities of, 394–405, 441–48, 454–55, 474–90, 594–637; post-World War II activities, 658–70; as president of ACWA during crusading years, 111–59; retirement from government service, 571–86; trade-union activity in Russia, 30–35; during World War I, 160–78
Hillman, Sidney, quoted: on Chicago strike of 1915, 131; on CIO, 381; on craft and industrial organization, 387, 392–93; on depression, 345, 346; on early arbitration plan, 63; on early conditions at Hart, Schaffner and Marx, 44; on efficiency methods, 196–97; on Federal Government, 167; on Federal relief, 347, 355; on functions of labor in industry, 320; on independent political party, 270–71; on internal dissension, 275–76, 281; in "Labor Attitudes," 311, 321–23; on labor legislation, 357; on labor-management struggle, 180; on labor power, 69; on labor situation in 1918, 192–93; on minimum-wage bill, 443–44; on national economic planning, 353–54; on New Deal, 397–98; on 1910 strike, 48, 57; on open shop, 238; on post-World War I attack against labor, 213; on Russian visit of 1921,

Hillman, Sidney, quoted (*Cont.*) 260; on strikes, 284; on Trade. Board, 64; on unemployment problem, 252; on union shop, 79; on West Coast OPM trip, 552–53; on World War I, 161, 162. *See also* Speeches of Sidney Hillman

Hillman, Mrs. Sidney, 44, 47, 55, 67, 73, 96–100, 106–07, 434–37, 668, 670; romance with Sidney Hillman, 83, 85, 152–56

Hillman Housing, 317

Hillquit, Morris, 87, 89

Hoffman, Clare, 540

Hoffman, Paul, 567

Holderman, Carl, 419

Hollander, Louis, 112, 169; union revival in New York (1933), 363, 383

Holt, Hamilton, 89

Holtz, Max, 173, 182, 368

Hoover, Herbert, 340–41, 345

Hopkins, Harry, 450, 453–55, 466, 481–82, 486–90, 507, 530, 532–33, 385

Housing, co-operative, of ACWA, 314–17

Howard, Charles, 385, 387, 389, 392, 409, 428

Howard, Earl Dean, 53–54, 266, 295, 367; as manager of Hart, Schaffner and Marx labor department, 60–67, 74–79, 149–50

Hutcheson, William, 384, 387, 426, 550, 570

Ickes, Harold, 52, 623

ILGWU (International Ladies' Garment Workers Union), 365, 455; arbitration of 1910 strike, 62; Hillman as chief clerk of, 83–100; in 1914, 89–90; proposed merger with ACWA, 325–26; relations with ACWA, 198–99; return to AFL, 600–1; unemployment-insurance plan, 253 *n.*

Illinois State Legislature, investigation of Chicago clothing-industry strike, 52–53

Impartial Chairmanship: establishment of, 64–65; for New York men's clothing trade, 183–84; for Rochester clothing trade, 183

Independent Citizens' Committee of the Arts, Sciences and Professions, 662 *n.*

Industrial Advisory Board, under NRA, 363–70

Industrial arbitration, development of, 62–67

Industrial Recovery Assn. of Clothing Manufacturers, 368–70

Industrial recovery measures under New Deal, 360–80, 393–94, 449–50

Industrial unionism: ACWA founded on principle of, 107–9; collective bargaining under, 120–21; vs. craft unionism, 103

Industrial Workers of the World. *See* IWW

Injunctions, labor, 221, 224, 233–34, 286–87, 308–9

Inside-shop system in clothing manufacture, 41, 135

International Federation of Trade Unions (IFTU), 638–47, 653

International Labor Organization (ILO), 638

International Ladies' Garment Workers Union. *See* ILGWU

International Tailoring Co., 283–89

Israel, crusade for, 657. *See also* Zionist movement

IWW (Industrial Workers of the World), 56, 81, 106, 145–46

Jackson, Gardner, 395, 467 *n.*

Jackson, Robert, 521–22, 532

Jacobs, Dorothy, *see* Mrs. August Bellanca

Jaffee, Charles O., 331

Jenkins, T. A., 557

Jewish Daily Forward, 83, 92, 262

Jewish immigration to America, 17–21

Johnson, Hugh S., 361, 363–67, 371, 373, 374

Johnson, Tom L., 163

Joint Board, definition of, 144 *n.*

Joint Boards, ACWA, 201; reorganization of, 216, 300

Jones, Jesse, 577

Jouhaux, Léon, 655

Journeymen Tailors' Union, AFL, 103–4, 383

Kallen, Dr. Horace, 319

Kapper, Samuel, 128–29

Kaufman and Baer Co., 147

Kazan, A. E., 235, 315–17

Keenan, Joseph, 509, 538; quoted, 580

Keller, Heumann, Thompson Co., 369–70

Kelley, Mrs. Florence, 162–63, 166, 232

Kellog, Paul, 93

Kelly, Edward, 614–19

Kennedy, Joseph P., 454

Kennedy, Thomas J., 417, 421, 484, 542, 563

Kent, Frank R., 630
Keynes, J. M., 345
King, Mackenzie, 142
King, William H., 378
Kirchwey, Freda, 626
Kirkpatrick, W. H., 308–9
Kirstein, Louis, 162–67, 174
Knights of Labor, 105
Knox, Frank, 486, 515, 521–23, 530, 543
Knudsen, William S., 407, 410, 481, 504–43, 566–72
Knutson, H., 557
Kovno: revolutionary activity in, 30–33; school days in, 25–29; visit of Hillman in 1920's, 258
Kreusi, Capt. Walter, 166
Krock, Arthur, 506, 617–18
Kroll, Jack, 290–98, 496, 628; quoted, 184, 185
Krug, Julius, 560–61
Krzycki, Leo, 137
Ku Klux Klan, 423
Kuppenheimer Co., organizing, 117, 142–43, 184–86
Kusnetzov, V. V., 643, 650, 655

Labor Advisory Board, NRA, 363–70, 382
Labor Advisory Committee, Defense Commission, World War II, 490
"Labor Attitudes," article by Sidney Hillman, 320–24
Labor: banks, 245–50; and industry conference (1942), 568–69; injunctions, 221, 224, 233–34, 286–87, 308–9; legislation under New Deal, 354–57, 360, 381–82, 393–94, 397, 404, 412, 421, 442–49
Labor movement in America: craft vs. industrial unionism in, 103–5; industrial arbitration initiated, 59–67; around 1910, 45–58; in 1920's, 242–44; political activities of, 268–71, 394–401, 454–55, 474–90, 594–637; post-World War I, 188–93; Socialist inclinations of, 89, 108–9, 135–38, 160–61, 189, 201–12
Labor movements: in England, 36, 190; in Russia, 28–35, 190
Labor Party. See ALP; British Labor Party
Labor Priorities Branch, OPM, 556
Labor-training program, World War II, 510–11, 556 n.
Labor's Non-Partisan League (LNPL), 395–401, 441, 594
La Follette, Robert M., 269–70

La Follette, Robert M., Jr., 309, 350–53, 375
La Guardia, Fiorello, 93, 145, 247, 350, 400, 432, 479, 559, 605
Lamm and Co., 130
Lamont, Thomas W., 454
Lapham, Roger, 542
Larger, B. A., 48, 91, 94–95, 101
Larkin, Joseph, 527–28
Laski, Harold J., 189 n., 462 n., 531
Lasswell, Harold, 321 n.
Lauck, W. Jett, 197
Lazinskas, Charles, 52
Lehman, Herbert, 315–17, 400, 455
Leiserson, Dr. William M., 183, 221, 225–27, 280, 542
Lemke, William, 399–400
Lend-Lease, 490, 529–30
Lenin, Nikolai, 256, 259–60
"Lepke," Louis, see Buchalter
Lerner, Dorothy, 668, 670
Lerner, Max, 466 n.
Levin, Sam, 57, 67, 73, 84; as Chicago leader of the ACWA, 93–100, 150, 278
Levinson, Edward, Labor Marches, quoted, 417 n.
Levy, Julius H., 331
Lewis, Dennie, 548, 564
Lewis, Fulton, Jr., 578–79
Lewis, John L., 189, 243, 323, 362–65, 369, 379; in defense program, 506, 413, 518, 521, 523, 546–49, 561–65, 569–71; in formation of CIO, 383–93, 405–30; as head of CIO, 432, 456–91; political activities of, 394–405, 474–90; quoted, 431; retirement from CIO presidency, 491–502; and wages-and-hours legislation, 443, 448; withdrawal from CIO, 570–71, 593
Liberty League, 399
Lippmann, Walter, 163–65
Lipzin, Sam, 275, 277
Lithuania: early life of Hillman in, 22–35; 1921 trip to, 256–58; in World War II, 641, 649–50
Little Steel Formula, 559, 592
LNPL (Labor's Non-Partisan League), 395–401, 441, 594
Lockout of clothing workers, New York (1920–21), 224–40
Loeb intrigue to discredit ACWA, 215–19
Long, Huey, 414
Lonker and Stevens, 171
Lovestone, Jay, 458 n.
Lovett, Robert A., 580

Lowenthal, Max, 222–23, 231–32, 247, 348–49, 615
Lubin, Isador, 351–52, 438, 507–9, 559–60
Luce, Clare Boothe, 631
Lusk Committee, 215, 221

MacArthur, Gen. Douglas, 355
Macaulay, Fred R., 247
McCloy, John, 545
McCormick, Mrs. Medill, 125
MacDonald, David, 596
MacDonald, Ramsay, 462 n.
McGill, James H., 626
McGrady, Edward F., 36, 364, 410
McKeough, Raymond, 628–29
McMahon, Thomas, 387
McNutt, Paul V., 575–83, 585, 620–24
McReynolds, William, 505, 520, 531
McSherry, Gen, Frank J., 577
Manhattan Shirt Co., 589
Marcantonio, Vito, 473, 600
Margus, S. S., ACWA relief ship to Russia, 257
Marimpietri, A. D., 54–55, 57, 67, 84–85, 95–97; quoted, 48, 61–62, 68
Marshall, Gen. George C., 537
Marshall, Leon C., 374
Marshall, Louis, 62, 318
Martin, Homer, 407, 412, 456–58
Martin, Mederic, 142
Marx, Karl, 30
Marxists, Daniel De Leon, 105
Mason, Lucy Randolph, 420
Matis, Dr. and Mrs., 28–32
Maurer, James, 321 n.
May, Andrew, 579
May, Stacy, 512
May Day parade, Chicago, 1915, 118; 1916, 152
Mead, James, 455
Meany, George, 400, 542, 569, 570
Mediation machinery: in World War I, 168–76; in World War II, 538–43
Meigs, Merrill, 551–52 n.
Men's clothing code under NRA, 367–70
Men's clothing industry: early years of, 41–47; trade agreements, efforts to establish, 195–97; unemployment insurance, 205–6, 341; unionization of, 135–59
Merriam, Charles E., 52
Metropolitan Life Insurance Co., 316
Meyer, Carl, 60, 64
Meyer, Eugene, 352–53, 542
Michaels, Stern and Co., 140, 219–24, 368–70
Middishade Co., 307–8

Mill, John Stuart, 30, 70
Miller, Abraham, 116, 300; quoted, 138 n.
Miller, Dr. Alexander, 431
Millis, Harry A., 186
Millis and Montgomery, Organized Labor in the United States, quoted, 382 n.
Milwaukee, co-operative clothing factory in, 250–51
Mines, "captive," campaign to organize, 372, 562–65
Minimum-wage law, 355, 382, 397, 404, 442–49
Mitchell, Charles E., 352
Mitchell, John P., 87, 162
Montreal: garment-trade strikes (1915, 1917), 140–42; Hillman speeches in (1918), 189–93
Morgan, T. H., 30
Morse Co., Leopold, strike at (1915), 118–19
Mortimer, Wyndham, 456
Moses, George H., 239
Mullenbach, Dr. James, 51, 63–64
Mulrooney, Edward P., 331, 334, 336
Murphy, Frank, 407–12
Murray, Philip, 387, 413, 428–29, 433, 441, 449; the UAW dissensions, 456–58, 474 n, 484; CIO 1940 convention, 490–502, 523, 527–28; in defense program, 542, 592; as president of CIO, 541, 547–48; rupture with Lewis, 562–64, 569–71, 580, 590; launching of CIO-PAC, 593–95, 599–600, 613, 637–39, 647
Muste, A. J., 198, 321 n.

Nagrekis, Frank, 55–56
Nance, A. Steve, 419, 423
Nash, Arthur ("Golden Rule"), 290–300
National Assn. of Manufacturers, 214, 569, 592
National Bank Holiday, 349, 358
National Citizens' Political Action Committee (NC-PAC), 626–29, 661
National Consumers' League, 162
National Defense Advisory Commission. See NDAC
National Defense Mediation Board. See NDMB
National Economic Council, Senate inquiry on, 351–54
National Industrial Recovery Bill, 360–62. See also NRA
National Industrial Recovery Board. See NIRB

National Labor Board, 373, 374
National Labor Relations Board. *See* NLRB
National Maritime Union (CIO), 508
National Recovery Administration. *See* NRA
Navytone Co., 304
NDAC (National Defense Advisory Commission), 481–84, 490–92, 503–26, 529–31
NDMB (National Defense Mediation Board), 542–44, 562–63
Needle trades: alliance proposed, 199, 325; immigrant labor in, 20–21, 42–43
Negro movement, 598
Nelson, Donald, 519, 525, 553–54, 558, 560, 571–78; quoted, 556 *n.*
New Deal, 359–80, 393–94, 449–50
"New" UGWA, 97–108
New Unionism, The, Joseph Budish and George Soule, quoted, 204 *n.*
New York: arrival of Hillman in, 19–21, 36; clothing workers' strike (1918), 178–82; Hillman engaged as union official in, 83–86; lockout of clothing workers (1920–21), 224–40; reorganization of ACWA in (1924–26), 271–74, 300; strike of men's clothing workers (1912–13), 91–92; walkout of ACWA members (1915), 120
New York Clothing Manufacturers' Assn., 134, 225–27, 239–40
New York Clothing Manufacturers' Exchange, 273, 284, 301
New York Industrial Union Council (CIO), 485–86
New York Joint Board of ILGWU, 89–90
New York State American Labor Party, formation of, 400
Newlands Act, 77 *n.*
Nicoll, Eric, 576
NIRA. *See* NRA
NIRB (National Industrial Recovery Board), 374, 377, 378–79. *See also* NRA
NLRB (National Labor Relations Board), 394, 421, 518–21
Nockels, Edward, 50
Non-discrimination policy in employment, 558–59
Non-Partisan League, 269
Norris, George W., 354–55, 626
Norris-La Guardia Anti-Injunction Act, 224
North American Aviation Co., 544–46

North American Rayon Co., 420
Norton, Mary, 442, 445–46
NRA (National Recovery Administration, 360–79, 382 *n.*
NYA (National Youth Administration), 511

O'Brian, John Lord, 535–36, 552, 553, 560, 584; quoted, 503
O'Brien and Powell, 222
O'Connor, Basil, 534
O'Connor, John J., 454
Office of Production Management. *See* OPM
Ohly, John, 579 *n.*
Oldenbroek, J. H., 650
Oliver, Eli P., 292, 395, 444, 465, 555
"One Big Union," 204
OPA (Office of Price Administration), 559
Open shop: industry drive for, post-World War I, 214–41, 289; Hillman on, 238
OPM (Office of Production Management), 526, 529–73
Orlofsky, Philip, 328–39
Out-of-town contract shops: ACWA campaign against, 327–39, 343–44; movement toward, 225, 301
Outside-shop system in clothing manufacture, 41–43, 135
Owens, John, 509, 538

PAC (Political Action Committee, CIO), 594–637, 659–62
Packing House strike, Chicago, 181
Paiken, Charles, 35–36
Palestine, Zionist plan for, 27–28, 641–42
Panken, Jacob, 97–99
Pares, Sir Bernard, *History of Russia,* cited, 33 *n.*
Patterson, Robert P., 486, 520–23, 530, 578–79
Patton, James G., 626
Pearson, Drew, 583 *n.*
Peel, John A., 419
Pegler, Westbrook, 603, 620
People's Councils, World War I, 168
Perkins, Frances, 353, 357, 402, 404; in defense preparations, 506, 508, 530, 541–42; in labor disturbances after 1936 elections, 408–10; quoted, 405, 474; and recovery legislation, 360–64
Perlman, Selig, 306 *n.*; *A Theory of the Labor Movement,* cited, 108 *n.*
Person, Harlow, 350, 351

Peth, H. R., 43–44, 60–61, 75
Philadelphia, campaign to organize, 301–10
Piece rates: adjustment of, under early arbitration plan, 63; early system of setting, 43; price-adjusting machinery for establishing, 72–73
Piecework system, vs. week work with production standards, 209–12, 224–25, 240–41, 300
Pinchot, Gifford, 350, 626
Police: Chicago, in 1915 strike, 125–26, 128–29; New York, in campaign against racketeers, 331–38, in 1925 clothing strike, 285–88
Political Action Committee, CIO. See PAC
Political activities of organized labor: in 1920's, 268–71; in 1936, 394–401; 1940 campaign, 474–90; 1944 campaign, 594–635
Porter, Paul R., "Labor in the Shipbuilding Industry," quoted, 554
Post, Louis F., 81
Potofsky, Jacob, 67–68, 80, 152, 429, 436, 453, 548, 587–88, 663; clean-up campaign against racketeers, 331–38; organization of shirtworkers, 363; quoted, 129, 172–73, 188
Preferential union shop, 75; adopted by Hart, Schaffner and Marx, 76–78; in Rochester agreement, 182–83
Prentis, H. W., 522
Presidential campaigns: 1936, 394–401; 1940, 474–90; 1944, 594–635
Pressman, Lee, 561–62
Price-adjusting machinery for piece rates, 72–73
Price control, 559
Production standards urged by Hillman, 209–12, 225, 240–41
Progressive Citizens of America, 662 n.
Progressive Party, 106, 269–70, 274, 350, 396, 662 n.
"Protection" of non-union shops by racketeers, 328–30
"Protocol of Peace" in New York cloakmakers' industrial arbitration, 62, 87–90
Public works program, proposal for, 356
Publications of ACWA, 314

Quartermaster Corps, World War I, 161–67
Quill, Michael, 441, 494, 600
Quittance pay for workers permanently displaced by machines, 282–83

Rabinowitz, Aaron, 317
Rabkin, Elias, 138, 279
Racketeers in clothing industry, struggle with, 327–39
Railway Brotherhoods, 77 n., 189, 245–46; third-party movement of, 269; and wages-and-hours bill, 443
Recession of 1937–38, 424–25, 433, 449–50
Recovery measures under New Deal, 360–80, 393–94, 449–50
"Red Terror" of 1919–20, 214–15
Reed, James, 368
Reeves, Floyd W., 510
Reiss, J. L., 283–89
Reiss, Raymond, 289
Relief measures for depression advised by Hillman, 345–36
Reston, James, 624
Reuther, Walter, 407, 547, 567, 580
Revolutionary movement in Russia at turn of century, 18, 28, 30–35
Richberg, Donald R., 374, 377, 379
Rickert, Thomas, 48–57, 90–92, 94–97, 101, 368
Rieve, Emil, 417, 441, 459, 473, 484, 639
Riis, Jacob, How the Other Half Lives, quoted, 20–21
Ripley, William Z., 167–71, 173–76, 179–82, 203
Rissman, Sidney, 48, 186, 328
Robins, Margaret D. (Mrs. Raymond), 50–51, 70, 84 n., 153
Rochester: damage suit by Michaels, Stern and Co. against ACWA, 219–24; disturbances of 1920's, 279–80; organization of, 140, 172–76, 182–83
Rochester Clothiers' Exchange, 140, 173, 182–83, 219, 234
Rodenbeck, A. J., 220–24
Rogers Peet Co., 231
Roosevelt, Eleanor, 404, 468–69, 590
Roosevelt, Franklin D., 354, 356–59; death of, 647–49; defense preparations of, 461–70, 480–84, 503–34; and labor movement, after 1936 elections, 401–5, 407–12, 414–15, 432, 443–47; 1936 campaign, 394–401; 1940 campaign, 474–90; 1944 campaign, 605, 611–35; recovery measures under, 359–80, 393–94, 449–50; wartime measures, 557–86; wartime relations with Hillman, 590–92
Root, Clark, Buckner and Holland, 222–23
Rose, Alex, 400, 600–1, 604

Rosenberg, Mrs. Anna, 575, 579, 583
Rosenblum, Frank, 250–51, 419, 494, 663; Chicago years, 46–47, 57, 67, 96–98; organizing of Chicago men's clothing trade, 117–18, 121–32
Rosenman, Samuel, 575, 579
Rosenwald, Lessing, 333
Royal Tailoring Co., organizing, 117
Russia: Hillman's 1921 trip to, 256–61; Jewish life in, 22–28; revolutionary movement at turn of century, 18, 28, 30–35; seizure of government by Bolsheviks, 189; trade-union movement in, 28, 30–35
Russian-American Industrial Corp., 261–67, 285
"Russian Jew in American Industry, The," by J. E. Williams, quoted, 82
Russian relief (1921), 257
Russo-Japanese War, 31, 32
Ryan, Msgr. John A., 353
Ryan, Joseph P., 400

Saillant, Louis, 644, 650, 653
Salerno, Joseph, 419, 421–22, 494
Saposs, Dr. David, 236
Schaffner, Joseph, 47, 53–56, 59–61, 64, 71, 74, 78, 83, 149–50
Schechter Case decision of Supreme Court, 379
Schevenels, Walter, 650
Schlesinger, Benjamin, 89–90, 102, 199, 325
Schlossberg, Joseph, 93, 98–101, 105, 127, 138, 161, 201 n., 231, 398, 453
Schneid, H., 94
Schneiderman, Rose, 360
Schwab, Charles M., 191
Schwellenbach, Lewis, 658
Scotch Woolen Mills, 169–70, 184
Seabury, Samuel, 231–32
Sears, Roebuck and Co., Hillman employed at, 38–41
Seasonal employment in clothing trades, efforts to control, 205–6, 252–55
Security League, 215 n.
Selective Service Act, 485, 529
Seligman, Edwin R. A., 232
Shahn, Ben, 630
Sherman Anti-Trust Act, 244
Shirt industry, 194
Shirtwaist girls' union, 45
Sigman, Morris, 89
Silva, Joseph, 458
Silver Shirts, 462
Silverman, Sam, 115
Silverman and Turner, 332
Sinclair, Upton, 69

Sit-down strikes, 405, 407–12, 414
Skala, Stephen, 118
Sloan, Alfred P., 353, 376, 408, 409
Smith, Clyde H., 443–44
Smith, F. A., 143
Smith, Harold D., 531–33, 575, 579
Smith, Howard, 522, 560, 567, 609
Smith-Connally bill, 593
Smolenskin, Peretz, quoted, 26
Social Democratic Party, Russian, 32
Social security, 205–6, 252–55
Social Security Act of 1935, 254, 442
Socialism in America, 93, 105–9, 135–38; post-World War I, 189, 203–5; World War I, 160–61
Socialist Labor Party, American, 105
Socialist Party, American, 89, 106, 138 n., 161, 262 n., 268, 274, 396, 598; in 1920, 203–5; in 1936 campaign, 398–400
Somervell, Gen. Brehon, 553
Sonneborn and Co., Henry L., 144–48; strike at, 111–15
Soule, George, 66, 197 n.; quoted, 204 n., 240, 351, 471
Soviet Clothing Trust, 266
Soviet Union. See U.S.S.R.
Spanish Loyalists, American sympathy for, 463–64
Speeches of Sidney Hillman: Boston (1920), 236–38; at Church of Ascension (1920), 229–30; on co-operative enterprises, 207–8; at last ACWA convention, 664–68; at 1916 ACWA convention, 58; at 1922 ACWA convention, 263–66; at 1940 CIO convention, 498–502; on social security, 205–6
Spencer, Herbert, 30
Spofford, Rev. William B., 294–95
Starnes, Joe, 611
Starr, Ellen Gates, 51, 70, 104, 125–26
Steel industry, in 1920's, 243
Steel workers, organization of by AFL, 189, 199–200
Steel Workers' Organizing Committee, CIO, 413
Steelman, John, 538–39, 563–64, 658
Stettinius, Edward, 504, 518, 650
Steuer, Max D., 231–32
Stevenson, Archibald, 227
Stewart, Bryce M., 252–53
Stimson, Henry L., 463, 529–30, 535–37, 560–61, 571
Stock-market crash, 341
Stollberg, Benjamin, quoted, 265–66
Stone, Dr. N. I., 169, 173–74
Stone, Warren S., 245–46
Straus, Jesse I., 333

Strikes: Allis-Chalmers, 538–44; coal, World War II, 562–64; in 1919, 189; after 1936 elections, 403–14; North American Aviation, 544–46; post-World War II, 659–60; in Russia, 32; steel workers' (1919), 199–200; World War I, 167, 170–71

Strikes in clothing industry: early, 43; Baltimore (1914), 111–15, (1916), 144–48; Boston (1915), 118–19; Chicago (1910), 47–57, (1915), 123–32; Chicago and New York (1925), 284–89; "against gangdom" (1931), 332–36; New York (1912–13), 91–92 (1918), 178–82; Rochester (1919), 220–24

Strouse and Bros., 144–47

Sumners, Hatton, 536, 541

Supply, Priorities and Allocations Board, 558

Surplus clothing, government purchase and distribution of, 450

Sutherland, Robert, 220, 222

Sweatshop system in needle trades, 20–21, 42–43, 86; revival of, in World War I, 162–68

Swing, Raymond Gram, 402

Swope, Gerard P., 346, 353, 357, 361

Szold, Robert, 222, 231, 233, 315

Taft, Robert, 484

Taft, William Howard, 167

Tailors' Council, 274

Tailors' union of UGWA, 90–92; formation of ACWA, 97–110

Tarassov, D. M., 650, 653

Tawney, R. H., 462 n.

Taylor, Frederick, 243

Taylor, Myron C., 413, 465

Taylor and Co., J. L., 283, 287

Taylor Society, 350

Taylor System, 111–13

Teagle, W. C., 452, 569

Technocracy, 345

Temporary National Economic Committee, 517

Textile industry, 416–17

Textile Workers' Organizing Committee (TWOC), 417–25, 458–59

Textile Workers' Union of America, CIO, 459, 560. See also United Textile Workers

Third-party movement, 1920's, 269–71

30-hour bill, 354–57, 360

35-hour week in women's garment code, 367

36-hour week in men's clothing code, 367

Thomas, Elbert, 569

Thomas, Norman, 398, 399–400

Thomas, R. J., 457–58, 473, 484, 540, 575–76, 596, 639, 644

Thompson, Dorothy, 464

Thompson, William H. ("Big Bill"), 126, 128

Thompson, William O., 63–64, 71, 81, 87, 165, 266

Time-and-motion studies, 243

Tobin, Daniel, 369, 384, 394, 426

Toledano, Lombardo, 644, 650

Tracy, Daniel, 506

Trade agreements, efforts of Hillman to establish, 195–97

Trade Board, establishment of, in early arbitration plan, 63–64

Trade Union Educational League. See T.U.E.L.

Trade-union movement. See Labor movement.

Training-within-industry system, World War II, 510–11, 556 n.

Travis, Robert, 407

Triangle Waist Co. fire, 86

Truman, Harry S., 551, 615–23, 648, 655, 657–62

Truman Committee, U.S. Senate, 550

T.U.E.L. (Trade Union Educational League), 274–81

Tugwell, Rexford, 356, 449

Tully, Grace, 532–33, 617

TWOC (Textile Workers' Organizing Committee), 417–25, 458–59

Typographers' union, 47, 62, 385, 389

UAW (United Auto Workers), 375, 406–12, 527, 544–46; internal troubles, 1938, 456–58; withdrawal from CIO, 571, 593

UGWA (United Garment Workers of America), 45–47; Chicago strike of 1910–11, 47–57; convention of 1914, 95–97; demand for closed shop, 74–78; growth of, 67–81; Hillman elected officer of, 57–59; internal conflict, 90–95; secession of progressive faction, 92–93; struggle with ACWA, 111–22, 143–48, 220, 368–70

UMW (United Mine Workers), 71, 189, 243, 323, 363–65, 387–89

UN (United Nations), 638–39, 650–51, 655

Unemployed Councils, during depression, 355, 472

Unemployment insurance, 205–6, 252–55, 300, 341–42

Union Party, 399–400

Unionism in clothing industry: early, 43, 45–58; expansion of, by ACWA, 111–59; formation of ACWA, 97–110; formation of CIO, 387–93, 405–30; impetus of World War I on, 167–71, 187; under New Deal, 362–70, 382 n., 383–89; during 1920's, 242–44; organization activity after 1910 strike in Chicago, 58–81; post-World War I attack against, 213–40
United Auto Workers. See UAW
United Cloth Hat and Cap Workers, 199
United Construction Workers (CIO), 548–49
United Garment Workers of America. See UGWA
United Mine Workers. See UMW
United Rubber Workers, 384–85, 405–6
United Steel Workers, 528
United Textile Workers' Union, 198, 387, 416–24, 458
Untermeyer, Irwin, 339
U.S. Army seizure of defense plants, 545–46
U.S. Chamber of Commerce, 214, 569
U.S. Department of Justice, 214
U.S. Employment Services, 511
U.S. House of Representatives: Military Affairs Committee, 579; Rules Committee, and wages-and-hours bill, 444–46; Un-American Activities Committee, 603, 608–10
U.S. Industrial Commission, testimony of Hillman before, 63–64
U.S. Senate: Campaign Expenditures Committee, 625–26; Committee on Education and Labor, 204, 408 n., 568–69; Committee on Manufactures, statement of Hillman to, 347; Finance Committee, hearings on NRA, 377–79; inquiry on causes of depression, 351–54
U.S. Steel Corp., 372, 413, 562–63
U.S. Supreme Court: decisions favorable to labor, 442, 527; membership "packing" move, 404, 412; Schechter Case decision, 379
U.S.S.R.: Hillman visit of 1921, 258–61; visit of 1922, 266. See also Russia

Vandenberg, Arthur, 651
Vaughan, Gen. Harry, 658
Vayo, J. Alvarez del, 464; quoted, 654
Veblen, Thorstein, 189 n., 204, 206 n., 215 n.

Vertical unionism, opposition of Gompers to, 103
Vineland sweatshops, World War I, 168
Viscose Co., 420
Vladeck, B. Charney, 137–38
Vorse, Mary Heaton, 203, 236
Vultee Aircraft Co., 509, 524

Wage increase, apportionment system in Hart, Schaffner and Marx contract (1916), 150–51
Wage standards, World War I, 167
Wages, weekly, vs. piecework system, 209–12, 224–25, 240–41, 300
Wages-and-hours legislation under New Deal, 382, 393–94, 397, 404, 441–49
Wagner, Robert, 350, 373, 404, 442, 455
Wagner-Connery labor-disputes bill, 381
Wagner Labor Relations Act, 393–94, 404, 412, 421, 442, 447
Wald, Lillian, 92–93
Walker, Frank, 616, 622
Walker, James, 330, 333–34
Walkout of ACWA members, N.Y. (1915), 120
Wall Street crash (1929), 341
Wallace, Henry, 558, 614–24
Walsh, Frank P., 167
Walsh, Dr. J. Raymond, 525, 597, 628, 668
Walsh-Healey Act, 520
Wanamaker and Brown, 169
War Labor Board, World War I, 167–69
War Labor Board, World War II. See WLB
War Labor Disputes Act, 593–94
War Labor Policies Board, World War I, 167
War Manpower Commission, 573–84
War Production Board. See WPB
Warbasse, James P., 203
Warren, Earl, 631
Watson, Gen. Edwin, 575
Weaver, Dr. Robert C., 626
Weber, Dr. Frederick Palmer, 630
Week work with production standards vs. piecework system, 209–12, 224–25, 240–41, 300
Weill, Samuel, 173–74, 182, 219
Weinstein, Charles, in Philadelphia organizing campaign, 303–9, 310; 417, 419

Weinstein, Murray, 339
Welfare system used by Rochester manufacturers, 172
Wells, Walter N., 456
Wharton, Arthur O., 384
Wheeler, Burton K., 269–70
Whiteside, Arthur D., 374, 377
Whitney, A. F., 360, 627
Wiggin, Albert H., 346, 353
Willard, Daniel, 352
Williams, John E., 99, 122–31, 155, 186–87; on Chicago strike of 1915, 124, 129–30; as Impartial Chairman in women's garment industry, 87–90; as Impartial Chairman of Board of Arbitration, 66, 71–85; quoted, 149, 151; on Russian Jews, 81
Williams, S. Clay, 374, 376, 377
Willkie, Wendell, 484–90, 633
Wilson, C. E., 566
Wilson, Woodrow, 81, 86, 106, 160, 162–64, 189
WLB (War Labor Board), 542, 568–69, 592, 606
Wobblies. See IWW
Woll, Matthew, 403, 426, 428, 506, 569, 570
Wolman, Dr. Leo, 197, 222, 232, 246–47, 252–53, 277–78, 293–95, 321, 323, 348–49, 363–64, 372, 374–76

Women's garment industry: arbitration in, 62; conditions in (1914), 86–90
Women's Trade Union League, 50, 53
Woolen industry code, 371–72
Workers' Party, American, 262 n., 274–78
World Federation of Trade Unions, formation of, 600, 637–47, 650–57
World War I, 160–78; condition of labor following, 188–93
World War II, 461, 470, 481, 566–86; preparations for, 461–70, 480–84, 503–65
WPA, purchase of surplus clothing by, 450
WPB (War Production Board), 571–76
Wright, R. R., Jr., 626

"Yellow-dog" contracts, 307–8
Yeshiva at Kovno, 26–29
Young, Owen D., 510

Zacharias, Michael, 27–34, 38–39
Zagare, Lithuania: birthplace of Hillman, 22–25, 33–35; 1921 visit to, 257–58
Zangwill, Israel, The Melting Pot, 82
Zimmerman, Charles, 417
Zionist movement, 27–28, 642

Sidney
Hillman

Fred Hes

Homework

The March of the Forty
Thousand Clothing
Strikers in 1910

Our Employers
Are Powerful
We shall be
More Powerful
when we get on Job

we shall
FIGHT
until
WE WIN

Our Employers
HAVE WEALTH
We Have the Power
of Production

Chicago Clothing Workers
on Strike in 1915